Abhidharmakośabhāṣyam

Volume I

Abhidharmakośabhāṣyam

by
Louis de La Vallée Poussin

Volume I

English Translation by
Leo M. Pruden

ASIAN HUMANITIES PRESS
Berkeley, California
1988

ASIAN HUMANITIES PRESS

Asian Humanities Press offers to the specialist and the general reader alike the best in new translations of major works and significant original contributions to our understanding of Asian religions, cultures and thought.

1988

Asian Humanities Press
Berkeley, California

ISBN 0-89581-908-2
Library of Congress Catalog Number 87-71231

CONTENTS

A Brief Biography of Louis de La Vallée Poussin xv

Translator's Preface xxi

The Abhidharma:
The Origins, Growth and Development
of a Literary Tradition
by Leo M. Pruden

1. Origin and Growth of *Abhidharma* xxx
2. *Abhidhamma* as "higher *dhamma*" xxxi
3. *Abhidhamma* alone xxxiii
4. *Abhidhamma-kathā* xxxv
5. Traditional Explanations of *Abhidhamma* xxxvi
6. Abhidharma in the *Mahāvibhāṣā* xxxvi
7. The *Abhidhamma Piṭaka* xxxvii
8. The *Mātikā* xxxviii
9. *Mātikā* and *Abhidharma* xxxix
10. *Abhidharma* in the *Āgamas*: the Religion of the *Āgamas* xl
11. The *Āgamas* and the *Nikāyas* xli
12. *Abhidharmic* Tendencies in Extant *Āgamas*: Numerical Categories, *Saṁyuktas*, and *Vibhaṅgas* xlii
13. Sarvāstivādin *Āgamas* xliii
14. Śamathadeva's Commentary xlv
15. Sarvāstivādin *Abhidharma* Literature xlvi
16. Origin of the *Abhidharma* xlvi
17. The Second Period of Early Sarvāstivādin Literature xlix
18. The *Jñānaprasthāna* li
19. The *Vibhāṣās* lii
20. Development of the Literature After the *Vibhāṣās* liii
21. The *Abhidharma-hṛdaya* liii
22. The *Abhidharmakośabhāṣyam* liv
23. Sanskrit Remains of the *Abhidharma* lv

24. The Sanskrit *Kośabhāṣyam* lvi
25. Translations of the *Abhidharmakośabhāṣyam* lvii
26. Commentaries on the *Abhidharmakośabhāṣyam* lvii
27. The Tibetan *Kośabhāṣyam* lviii
28. Translations of the *Kośabhāṣyam* and the *Vyākhyā* lix
29. Indexes to the *Kośabhāṣyam* lix
Footnotes lxii

Abhidharmakośabhāṣyam of Vasubandhu
by Louis de La Vallée Poussin

Introduction 1
I. Bibliography of the *Kośa* 7
A. Additions to the Bibliography, by Hurbert Durt 12
II. The Date of *Vasubandhu*. The Former *Vasubandhu* 13
III. The Seven Canonical Treatises of the *Abhidharma* 17
A. The *Jñānaprasthāna* 17
B. The *Prakaraṇa* of *Vasumitra* 20
C. The *Vijñākāya* 21
D. The *Dharmaskandha* 23
E. The *Prajñāptiśāstra* 24
F. The *Dhātukāya* 27
G. The *Saṁgītiparyāya* 28
IV. Some Masters of the *Vibhāṣā* 28
A. *Vasumitra* 28
B. *Ghoṣaka* and the *Abhidharmāmṛtaśāstra* 31
C. *Buddhadeva* 32
D. *Dharmatrāta* 32
E. The *Bhadanta Dharmatrāta* 33
V. Some Schools of the *Vibhāṣā* 35
A. *Dāaṣṭānitkas* and *Sautrāntikas* 35
B. *Vibhajyavadins* 38
C. *Yogācārins* 41
VI. The *Śariputrābhidharma* 42
VIII. The *Abhidharmasāra* 44
Footnotes 49

Chapter One: The *Dhātus*

General Introduction 55
- A. Homage to the Buddha 55
  - 1. The Three Qualities of a Buddha 55
- B. Definition of *Abhidharma* 56
  - 1. Absolute Sense of the Word 56
  - 2. Conventional Sense of the Word 56
- C. Definition of *Abhidharmakośa* 57
- D. Purpose of the *Abhidharma* 57
- E. Authors of the *Abhidharma* 58

I. The Division of the *Dharmas* 58
- A. The Defiled *Dharmas* 59
- B. The Undefiled *Dharmas* 59
- C. The Unconditioned *Dharmas* 59
  - 1. Discussion of the Two Types of Disjunction 59
  - 2. Is Disjunction Single or Multiple? 59
- D. Conditioned *Dharmas* 61
  - 1. Synonyms of "Conditioned" 61
  - 2. Synonyms of "Defiled" 62

II. The Five *Skandhas*, the Twelve *Āyatanas*, and the Eighteen *Dhātus* 63
- A. *Rūpa Skandha* 63
  - 1. Visible Matter 64
  - 2. Sound 65
  - 3. Taste 66
  - 4. Odor 66
  - 5. Tangible Things 66
- B. The Relationship between the Five Consciousnesses and the Five *Viṣayas* 66
- C. *Avijnaptirūpa* 67
- D. The Four Primary Elements 68
- E. The Definition of "*Rūpa*" 70
- F. The Ten *Āyatanas* and the Ten *Dhātus* 72
- G. The *Vedanā, Saṃjñā*, and *Saṁskāra Skandhas* 72

H. The *Vijñāna Skandha* and the *Mana Āyatana* 74
I. The Seven *Dhātus* 74
J. The *Manodhātu* and the Eighteen *Dhātus* 75

III. The Threefold Classification of the *Dharmas* 76
A. The Threefold Classification of the *Dharmas* 76
B. The Nature of the Eighteen *Dhātus* 76
C. The Definition of "*Skandha*," "*Āyatana*," and "*Dhātu*" 77
D. Their Provisional Existence 79
E. The Reason for the Threefold Classification 80
F. Distinctions between *Vedanā* and *Saṁjñā* 81
G. The Five *Skandhas* and the Unconditioned Dharmas 81
H. The Order of the Five *Skandhas* 82
I. The Order of the *Āyatanas* and *Dhātus*, with Reference to the Six *Indriyas* 83

IV. Some Problems Raised by the Threefold Classification 85
A. The *Rūpa Āyatana* and the *Dharma Āyatana* 85
B. Inclusion in Other *Skandhas*, *Āyatanas*, and *Dhātus* 86
C. The Eighty-four Thousand *Dharmaskandhas* 86
D. The Dimension of a *Dharmaskandha* 86
E. The Characteristics of the *Skandhas* and the Threefold Classification 87
F. *Vijñānadhātu* and *Ākāśadhātu* 88

V. Classification of the *Dharmas* in the Eighteen *Dhātus* 90
A. Visible and Invisible *Dharmas* 90
B. Resistant and Non-Resistant *Dharmas* 90
C. Good, Bad, and Morally Neutral *Dharmas* 90
D. The Eighteen *Dhātus* and the Three Realms ??
E. Pure and Impure *Dhātus* 95
F. *Vitarka* and *Vicāra* 96
G. *Vitarka*, *Vicāra*, and the Five Sense Consciousnesses 97
H. Discussions
1. How many *Dhātus* Serve as an Object? 98
2. How many are Non-Appropriated to Living Beings? 98

I. Primary and Derived Elements 99
J. Discussion
1. Can the Atoms be Accumulated? 101
2. How many of the *Dhātus* Cut or are Cut? Burn or are Burned? Weight or are Weight? 102
3. How many of the *Dhātus* are *vipāka*? Accumulations? Outflowings? 103
4. How many of the *Dhātus* are Real Substances? 105
5. How many of the *Dhātus* are Momentary? 105
K. Possession of a *Dhātu* versus a *Vijñānadhātu* 106
L. Internal and External Elements 107
M. *Sabhāga* and *Tatsabhāga* 108
N. How are the *Dhātus* Abandoned? 111
O. How many of the *Dhātus* are "View?" 113

VI. Subsidiary Discussions 118
A. Are Visible Things Seen by One or Two Eyes? 118
B. Do the *Indriyas* and the *Viṣayas* Touch? 119
C. The Dimension of the Organs and their *Viṣayas* 122
D. Atoms within the Organs 123
E. Are Atoms *Sabhāga* or *Tatsabhāga*? 123
F. Time and the Support of the Consciousnesses 124
G. Why are the Organs, and not the Object, the Support of the Consciousness? 125
H. How are the Different Consciousnesses Named? 125
I. The Body, the Organ of Sight, Visible Things, and the Consciousness, and their Relationship to the Different *Bhūmis* 126
J. Which *Dhātu* is Discerned by Which Consciousness? 129
K. How many of the *Dhātus* are Eternal? 130
L. How many of the *Dhātus* are *Indriyas*? 130
Footnotes 131

Chapter Two: The *Indriyas*

I. The *Indriyas* 153
  A. Definition 153
    1. Objection 155
  B. General Explanation 155

II. The Twenty-two *Indriyas* 158
  A. A Different Definition 159
  B. The Organs of Sensation 160
    1. The Saint 162
  C. Pure and Impure *Indriyas* 163
  D. *Vipāka* and Non-*Vipāka Indriyas* 165
    Discussion: Prolonging and Shortening Life 166
    Discussion: *Jīvita* and *Āyus* 167
  E. How Many *Indriyas* have Retribution 171
  F. Their Moral Nature 171
  G. The *Indriyas* in the Three Dhātus 172
  H. Abandoning the *Indriyas* 173
  I. How Many *Indriyas* are initially possessed in each Dhātu? 174
  J. How Many *Indriyas* perish at Death 176
  K. *Indriyas* and the Stages of the Religious Life 177
    1. The Quality of Arhat 179
  L. Possessing the *Indriyas* 180
  M. The Smallest Number of *Indriyas* 183
  N. The Largest Number of *Indriyas* 183
    Discussion: The Atom 184

III. The Mental States 188
  A. Definition 189
  B. The *Mahābhūmikas* 189
  C. The *Kuśalamahābhūmikadharmas* 190
    Discussion: *Praśrabdhi* 191
    Discussion: Equanimity 192
  D. The *Kleśamahābhūmikadharmas* 193
    1. A Different List 194

2. Is a *Mahābhūmika* also *Kleśamahābhūmika?* 194
E. The *Akuśalamahābhūmikadharmas* 195
F. The *Parīttakleśikadharmas* 196
G. The Number of Mental States that can Arise Together 196
H. Differences between Mental States 200
1. Disrespect versus Absence of Fear 200
2. Affection versus Respect 201
3. *Vitarka* versus *Vicāra* 202
4. Pride versus Pride-Intoxication 204
I. Synonyms 205

IV. *Dharmas* not Associated with the Mind 206
A. Definition 206
B. *Prāpti* and *Aprāpti* 206
C. The Time Periods 212
D. How is *Prāpti* Abandoned? 213
E. Types of *Aprāpti* 215
F. How does *Aprāpti* Perish? 217
Discussion: *Prāpti* and *Anuprāpti* 217
G. Genre (*Sabhāgatā*) 219
H. The *Dharma* of Non-Consciousness 221
1. The Absorption of Non-Consciousness 223
I. The Absoption of Extinction 225
J. The Differences between the Two Absorptions 229
Discussion: How is a Mind produced after Absorption? 230
Discussion: Do the Two Absorptions exist as Real Substantial Entities? 232
K. The Vital Organ 233
Discussion: Warmth, Consciousness, and Life 233
Discussion: How does Death take place? 235
Discussion: Premature Death 235
L. Characteristics of Conditioned *Dharmas* 238
1. Primary and Secondary Characteristics 239
2. Arising 247
M. Words, Phrases, and and Phonemes 250
1. Voice 251

N. Other *Dharmas* not Associated with the Mind 254

V. The Six Causes 254
A. General Comments 255
B. Reason for Existence 255
C. Coexistent Cause 257
Discussion: The Sautrāntikas Criticize the Doctrine of Coexistent Causes 260
D. Similar Casuses 262
1. Definition 262
2. Objections 264
3. Similar Causes and the Path 267
E. Causes through Association 272
F. Universal Causes 273
G. Retributive Causes 274
1. Definition 275
2. *Skandhas* as Results 275
3. *Āyatanas* as Results 276
H. The Time Periods 277
I. Causes and their Results 278
Discussion: Disconnection 280
Discussion: Are Unconditional Things Real Entities? 280
Discussion: Is Extinction or Nirvāṇa Real? 281
J. The Five Results 286
1. Their Characteristics 288
2. The Time Periods 291
K. A Different List of Results 295
L. How Many Causes produce the Different *Dharmas*? 295

VI. The Four Conditions 296
A. General Comments 296
B. Equal and Immediately Antecedent Conditions 297
C. Objects as Conditions 302
D. Predominating Conditions 303
E. The Time Periods 304
F. How Many Conditions Cause the Different *Dharmas*? 305

Discussion: The Impossibility of a Single Cause 306
G. The Relationship between the Primary Elements and Derived Matter 308
H. The Arising of Mind and Mental States 310
1. The Twelve Minds and the Three Dhātus 310
2. The Twenty Minds and the Three Dhātus 314
3. Acts of Attention 323
I. The Number of Mental States Acquired in the Twelve Minds 323
Footnotes 326

A Brief Biography of Louis de La Vallée Poussin

Louis de La Vallée Poussin, born in Liége on the lst of January, 1869, was of French origin through his father's side of the family. His grandfather, Étienne-Pierre-Rémy de La Vallée Poussin, took part in the last Napoleonic campaigns and in 1832 was one of a group of French officers charged, under the direction of Marshall Girard, with the organization of the Belgian army at the request of King Leopold I. He married Marie-Thérèse de Cauwer in Namur, with whom he had four sons. The second, Gustave, was born in La Rochelle in 1829 and died in Paris in 1910; he married Pauline de Monge de Franeau, who was born in Liége in 1845. The eldest of the four children born of this marriage was Louis de La Vallée Poussin.

Orphaned from his mother at the age of 7, Louis, as well as his two brothers and his sister, were raised in Liége by his maternal grandparents. He was an outstanding student at the College Saint-Servain, in Liége, and in 1884 he entered the University of Liége where, four years later, he received the *docteur en philosophie et lettres*. His reading of Charles Lyall's *Asiatic Studies* awakened in him a desire to pursue Oriental studies, and it was at Louvain, under the direction of Charles de Harlez and Philippe Colinet, that he learned the elements of Sanskrit, Pali, and Avestan. He then went to Paris where he enrolled, from 1890 to 1893, at the Sorbonne and in the courses of Sylvain Lévi at the École pratique des Hautes-Études.

In 1892 he published a timid essay, a translation of Buddhist tales, in collaboration with Godefroy de Blonay. But as early as this same year there appeared in *Muséon* an academic study, *Le Bodhicaryāvatāra de Çāntideva*, a first indication of his tendency to research "the Saint and Sanctity in Buddhism" which marks all of his work; a first stage in this enormous task of investigating this theme pursued throughout the various Buddhist schools and the canons of scriptures.

In 1893–1894, he studied Buddhist Sanskrit and Sanskrit poetical meter "at the feet" of the great Orientalist H. Kern.

At the beginning of his activities as a Sanskrist, Louis de La Vallée Poussin was attracted by the curious and still unexplored doctrines of Tantrism. His *Note sur le Pañcakrama* (1894) as well as his edition of this text (1896), "an authoritative summary of the nihilistic doctrines of Nāgārjuna" and *Une pratique des Tantras* (1897) prepared the way for his first great work which is already the work of a master: *Bouddhisme, Études et Matériaux*, published by the Royal Academy of

Belgium (1898). This is a capital work which studies, with the method of an accomplished scholar, the relationship between Indian asceticism and the left-handed rituals. In spite of the tact and finesse with which he treated this topic, the subject let loose the righteous indignation of the great Rapson who, in a long review article, protested with severity against this exposure of "the Tantric infection". This English scholar, imbued with the theories current in his period—theories which have not yet completely disappeared—would consider that Buddhism is only a pure philosophic system, whose only true literature are the words of the Buddha, and he openly manifested his dislike for such a subject of study as Tantrism. His criticism must have been cruelly felt by the young scholar since he did not hesitate to justify himself publically. He showed in fact, in his *Tantras*, that for Rapson Buddhism is only the doctrine preached by Śākyamuni, whereas for him Buddhism is the general state of beliefs which have condensed around the name of the Buddha. The Tantras are the inheritors of all the forms of Indian religions and their study is necessary to that which de La Vallée Poussin called Buddhism.

One would have thought that after this lively reaction against formalism, his works on the manifestations of popular Buddhism would have continued to occupy a large place in the activity of the young master, but he did nothing more with respect to Tantrism, with the exception of a study published in 1901, *The Four Classes of Buddhist Tantras*, the documents of this type, a new and living sphere of study, no longer formed the object of his publications. Following upon this excursion into the Indian jungle if badly viewed by traditionalist scholars, Louis de La Vallée Poussin returned to monastic Buddhism, never to leave it.

It was then, in full possession of Tibetan, he did not hesitate—at more than forty years of age—to also learn Chinese. He continued the editing of enormous scholastic texts: *Prajñākāramati*, Śāntideva's commentary on the *Bodhicaryāvatāra* (1901–1905, 605 pages) of which he published the annotated translation; an edition of the Tibetan translation of the *Mādhyamakāvatāra* of Candrakīrti (1907–1912, 427 pages); and the *Mūlamādhyamakakārikā* of Nāgārjuna with the commentary of Candrakīrti (1903–1913, 658 pages). Taking refuge in Cambridge during the war of 1914, he edited the *Mahāniddesa* (in collaboration with E. J. Thomas) and the third chapter of the *Abhidharmakośa* of Vasubandhu (1914–1918, 368 pages).

In mentioning these voluminous editions which come to a total of hundreds of pages, we do not pretend to evaluate his work in terms of its weight. But these figures are eloquent for anyone who has edited with the same scruples as has Louis de La Vallée Poussin, if not with the same mastery, only several pages of

Sanskrit text for which one must always have recourse to the Tibetan and Chinese versions. These enormous works would suffise to fill several lives and yet how much research has sprung out of his work, and how much has been enriched by it! Such are the over fifty articles in Hastings' *Dictionary of Religion and Ethics*, his studies on the doctrine of Karman (*La négation de l'âme et la doctrine de l'Acte*, 1902), on the concatenation of the Twelve Causes (*La theorie des Douze Causes*, 1913), on the Three Bodies (*The three bodies of a Buddha*, 1906; *Note sur les Corps du Buddha*, 1913); and his constructions of the theory of Nirvāṇa. All of the presentations of dogma that he developed, and by the approval that they received as well as by the reactions that they generated, have brought about the progress of Buddhist exegetical and philosophical studies up to the point where we find it today, that is, based on texts scrupulously established and patiently collated.

In the course of his long career filled with immense labor, the curiosity of Louis de La Vallée Pousin was brought to bear on all of the forms of Buddhism and on the principal aspects of Indian civilization, but the subject to which he returned most spontaneously in conversation and in his writings was Buddhist philosophy, or more precisely Buddhist scholasticism. Whereas Western philosophy is always more or less systematic, Indian scholasticism strives less to combine and to construct, than to set up an evaluation of the mind and of the universe by defining, enumerating, and classifying concepts. Louis de La Vallée Poussin found in this a field of study conforming to his spontaneous and to his well considered aspirations, for never was there a mind less systematic. This characteristic manifested itself not only in his choice of subjects but in his research and in the manner in which he presented the results of this research. One of his most important works, *Bouddhisme*, has the subtitle *Opinions sur l'histoire de la dogmatique* ("*Opinions on the History of Dogma*"). He recalls in the Introduction (p. xii) that, according to the Buddha, the ignorant "recognize only a part of things and imprudently judge the whole". He always applied all of his efforts in seeing the different aspects of doctrines. For him, Buddhist ethics is not a collection of principles which direct the conduct of humans, but adapts them to the social milieu and evolve in parallel fashion to this milieu. He presents it rather as a jurisprudence, as a selection of prohibitions.

One of the most useful books that he wrote, *L'Inde au temps des Mauryas*, is above all a presentation of contradictory thesis in which modern erudition appears to be swallowed up: he however always maintains an equilibrium, a lucidity, an admirable patience, and facts which in another author would appear fastidious, taking under his pen taking on color, relief, and the intensity of life. "A book to be written" one has said of this work. In fact, no literary anxiety if not that of clarity appeared in this work; precise facts, indisputable documents and their interpretation are also extricated from any artificial bonds that the author judged detrimental to the pure instruments of his work.

The desire to see the opposite aspects of problems never left him. One day he said to one of us who complimented him on one of his books, "There are some footnotes at the bottom of the pages which contradict the text . . ." He had us understand by this willfully paradoxical remark that he had chosen to place in this work opposing points of view, one after the other. From this we can see that he had a sometimes surprising method of expressing his ideas: he would advance in zigzags. He proceeded often through juxtaposed remarks. His style never brought about a change in the cohesion or in the unity of his thought. He did not seek to create any illusion either for the reader or for himself. Probity and sincerity were his masterful qualities, and he had a small bit of affectation to his sincerity.

But no one was less dogmatic than this specialist in dogmas. Very frequently at our pleasure, he would avoid anything that in a conversation, be it broached and directed by the speaker in a scientific direction, would appear to be tinged with pedantry, anything that would lead one to believe that he took himself seriously. The same worry is found in the numerous letters addressed to one of us where the serious answer solicited is bracketed with sudden changes having an irresistible comic effect. This attitude on several occasions led one to suppose that his religious convictions led him to mistake the various thesis that he presented. Was it not rather, himself whom he judged unworthy of attention? Better than elsewhere his character appeared in the numerous and valuable review articles which marked his work on Buddhism that appeared during almost a half century. Reviews, criticisms, controversies, are proposed and maintained in a fine, perceptive, and infinitely courteous manner. The well-chosen word takes the place of a long phrase; it is often unforeseen if not unforeseeable, but always precise.

One might ask if his aversion with respect to a systematic spirit did not come from that which, being ultimately impassioned, he mistrusted himself more than any other of the bonds of this passion. In politics and in religion, as in his relationship with his friends and those close to him, he was also so distant that one could say that he was the very soul of indifference and of lukewarmness. His sensibility explains the role that the criticism of his peers played in his academic career. And those that were acquainted with him know that the clash of ideas which followed the war of 1914 echoed sadly in his conscious and doubtlessly contributed to the ruin of his health by causing him to lose any peace he may have enjoyed.

After many years we saw him decline physically at a slow but unchanging pace; he became more and more thin and frail. And yet up to his last moments he maintained a fine and lucid mind and his scientific activity. He concluded the publication of two monumental works of scholarship: the *Siddhi* of Hsüan-tsang, and the *Abhidharmakośa* of Vasubandhu; he supervised the editing of the *Mélanges chinois et bouddhiques* to which he abundantly contributed; our *Bibliographie bouddhique* which he supported and sustained from its beginnings was always the object of his attentions. In the summer of 1936, he explained to one of us, in order to gain us over to his project, his last academic project the enormity of which did not alarm him: to establish an index of Buddhism which would be at one and the same time both literary and archaeological. One year later, in Switzerland, he pointed out with serenity to this same visitor that he had no more than a few weeks to live. Six months later, he would have reached the age of 69.

At the present, our duty is to contribute to the better knowledge and to the utilization of his work. As soon as circumstances permit, we shall publish in the *Bibliographie bouddhique* his analytic bibliography which is now finally ready. Our Master himself had the aid of one of us in completing it, but on the condition that he not see it published.

Marcelle Lalou
Jean Przyluski

TRANSLATOR'S PREFACE

The Sanskrit word "Abhidharma" means the systematic philosophy of Buddhism. From the time of the Buddha onward, the Buddha's disciples, and many later generations of his followers studied, analyzed, and re-classified the teachings of the Buddha, and in the process created a unique field of study which has come to be known as the Abhidharma. The development of Buddhist philosophy,—the Abhidharma—has continued to be developed up to the present day, especially within the field of Tibetan Buddhism.

The early part of this Abhidharma literature,—dating from the death of the Buddha to approximately the 5th century A.D.—is today preserved in Chinese translations, translations carried out largely by Hsuan-tsang in the mid-7th century; and the bulk of the later Abhidharma literature—dating from the 5th to the 12th century—is largely preserved in Tibetan translation. Only a small but important portion of this literature has been preserved in its original Sanskrit: Vasubandhu's *Abhidharmakośabhāṣyam*, and its commentary, Yaśomitra's *Vyākhyā*. The student of the Abhidharma is therefore obliged to develop a reading ability in Buddhist Chinese, Tibetan, and of course, Sanskrit and Pali.

A significant Abhidhamma literature exists in the Pali language, a very close dialect of Sanskrit (the word "Abhidharma" is Sanskrit, the word "Abhidhamma" is Pali). In this Pali tradition of Theravada Buddhism (the predominant form of Buddhism in Ceylon, Burma, Thailand, Laos, and Cambodia), the Abhidhamma forms one of the Baskets (Pali: Pitaka) of canonical Buddhist scriptures, and so assumes the role of canonical authority. Even though the Pali Canon, the *Tipiṭaka*, was closed at the Third Council of the Theravadins held in approximately 237 B.C., Abhidhamma works continued to be composed after this date, although with less frequency. Theravadin scholar-monks continued to study the Abhidhamma, and this tradition gave rise to a subcommentarial literature composed in both Pali and the regional languages of South and Southeast Asia (Singhalese, Burmese, Thai, etc.). Much of this later, post-canonical Pali Abhidhamma literature remains unpublished, and almost all of it remains untranslated into any Western language.[1]

So too only a small portion of the Sanskrit language Abhidharma literature exists in English translation, although at the present time slightly more exists in French.

Although English language materials for the study of the Abhidharma literature are quite limited,—especially when viewed in comparison with the bulk of the extant literature of this tradition,—there are some excellent books which may be read with profit by the beginning student of Buddhist philosophy.

The student would do well to read the excellent essay by Chogyam Trungpa Rimpoche, *Glimpses of the Abhidharma* (Boulder, Prajna Press, 1978) which distills the essential message of Buddhist scholasticism and demonstrates the importance of the Abhidharma to the *sādhaka* of the still vital Tibetan Buddhist tradition.

Another excellent work of great benefit to the student of Abhidharma is Prof. Herbert V. Guenther's *Psychology and Philosophy in the Abhidharma* (New Delhi, Motilal Banarsidass, lst edition, 1970, and many subsequent editions) which gives the author's presentation and analysis of the content of both the Northern or Sanskrit Abhidharma tradition with that of its Southern or Pali cousin.

***

It may not be out of place here to say a few words, by way of a *nidāna*, concerning my involvement with the *Abhidharmakośabhāṣyam*.

In the years 1964 to 1966 I was enrolled in Tokyo University, in the Department of Indian and Buddhist Studies, where I studied the text of Gyōnen's *Risshū-kōyō*[2] under the direction of Prof. Akira Hirakawa. After I had finished my studies on this text, I asked Prof. Hirakawa what he would recommend I study next. He asked me if I wanted to continue with *Vinaya* studies,—Prof. Hirakawa's specialty,—but I replied that I should like to study another field of Buddhism. Prof. Hirakawa then recommended that I begin the study of Buddhist philosophy in the traditional manner, that is, with the study of Vasubandhu's *Abhidharmakośabhāṣyam* (in Japanese, the *Kusharon*).[3] I replied that this would be a fine idea, and so in token of my new direction in study, Prof. Hirakawa gave me a set of books dealing with the philosophy of the *Kusharon*, the ten volume set, *Kusharon-kōgi* ("Lectures on the *Kusharon*"), a work which is the compilation of a series of 238 lectures given on the *Kusharon* by one Rev. Hōrei Sakurai (1861–1923). Rev. Sakurai was a cleric of the Higashi Honganji Tradition of Jōdo Shin Buddhism, and was the incumbent (*jūshoku*) of the Hakutōji temple, Fukuoka Prefecture, Kyushu.[4] Rev. Sakurai gave these lectures in Kyushu in the last decade of the 19th century, and they were published in 1898 (Meiji 31) by the Shisōkan, Kyoto: the set of Sakurai's lectures that Prof. Hirakawa gave me had in turn been given to him by his teacher, Prof. Shōson Miyamoto (1893–1984) and so contained the annotation of both of these scholars.

Sakurai's book is a very useful scholarly tool, since his lectures were based on the text of the *Kusharon* (in Hsuan-tsang's Chinese translation) and the Chinese commentaries on this work by Fa-pao and P'u-kuang, two masters who had worked directly with Hsüan-tsang.[5] I began reading Sakurai's work in June of 1966 and completed it several months later. My reading of Sakurai's work taught me two things: 1) the commentaries of Fa-pao and P'u-kuang are both valuable sources of information about the contents of the *Kusharon* as seen through the eyes of two eminent Chinese scholar-monks, since they record the oral teaching of Hsüan-tsang concerning many of the philosophical positions presented in the *Kusharon*; but 2) for a thorough understanding of the *Kusharon*, it would be desirable, and in many places necessary to read the text of this work in its original language, Sanskrit.

At approximately this same time (the middle of 1966) a xerox copy of the Romanized Sanskrit text of the First Chapter (the *Dhātunirdeśa*) of the *Abhidharmakośabhāṣyam* began to circulate privately among the students in the Department of Indian and Buddhist Studies at Tokyo University. I was told that this copy was typed out from photographs secretely taken of a manuscript copy of the *Abhidharmakośabhāṣyam* discovered by Rahūla Saṁkṛtyāyana at the Śa-lu Monastery in Tibet in May of 1934. The photographs were taken of the manuscript which was then kept at the K. P. Jayaswal Research Institute, Patna; the desire of the Japanese to see the original text of the *Abhidharmakośabhāṣyam* was so great, and the publication of this text had been delayed so long, that "drastic means" were called for, and, I was later told, a Japanese nun had secretely taken pictures of the manuscript and brought them back to Japan. In any case, I now had the First Chapter of the Sanskrit text of the *Abhidharmakośabhāṣyam* in my hands, and, upon my return to the United States, I began to study the text in earnest.

To aid my study and my subsequent teaching, I translated portions of Louis de La Vallée Poussin's French translation of the *Abhidharmakośabhāṣyam* (Brussels, Institute Belge des Hautes Études Chinoises, 1923 - 1931; reprint edition, 1971) into English. I began with the Ninth Chapter (the *Pudgala-pratiṣedha*) and not with the First Chapter, holding to the Asian superstition that one will never finish a work if one begins on its first page; I also Romanized the Sanskrit text of the Ninth Chapter, by now available in Prof. P. Prahdhan's first edition (Patna, K. P. Jayaswal Research Institute, 1967), and for two years I taught this Chapter as part of a Seminar in Reading Buddhist Texts at Brown University (Providence, Rhode Island).[6] Reading and teaching this Chapter reinforced my earlier thought, namely that the *Abhidharmakośabhāṣyam* can best be understood from its Sanskrit original.

I then translated the First Chapter from the French of de La Vallée Poussin, and compared it with the original Sanskrit of Pradhan, and so began my work on a full translation from the French of de La Vallée Poussin, collated with the Sanskrit original of the text.

De La Vallée Poussin's annotation is based on three major sources. First, the greater part of his commentary, both in his footnotes and frequently in the body of the text itself, is based on the commentaries of Fa-pao and P'u-kuang: these Chinese masters are responsible for determining the filiation of many of the philosophical positions, objections, and.replies ("The Vaibhāṣikas maintain", "The Sautrāntikas object", etc) in the text. Likewise Fa-pao and P'u-kuang were responsible for supplying most of the references to passages quoted from the *Āgamas*, the *Jñānaprasthāna* (and its related *pādaśāstras*, the *Prakaraṇapāda*, the *Vijñānakāya*, etc.), the *Vibhāṣā*, and the works of Samghabhadra. In their commentaries, Fa-pao and P'u-kuang also traced the development of many of the *Abhidharmakośabhāṣyam's* ideas into later Chinese Mahāyāna thought.

In 1869 (Meiji 2), the eminent Japanese scholar-monk, Kyokuga Saeki (1828–1891) published his edition of the *Kusharon*, the so-called *Kandō* edition of the *Kusharon*, or simply, the *Kandō-bon Kusharon.*[7] Saeki's edition is rich with annotation placed at the top (or "crown", *kan-*) of the page of text. In his *Kandō-bon* edition of the *Kusharon*, Saeki gives all of the various references first found by Fa-pao and P'u-kuang: he gives the name of the source, its volume and page number, and in the marginal notes to the text, Saeki also gives the filiation of thought ("The Vaibhāṣikas maintain", etc., as above) first traced out by Fa-pao and P'u-kuang.

Louis de La Vallée Poussin translated the *Abhidharmakośabhāṣyam* from the Sanskrit as preserved by Yaśomitra, and from the Chinese of the *Kandō-bon* edition of the *Kusharon*. In fact, almost all of de La Vallée Poussin's references to the *Vibhāṣā* and his marking of the filiation of the thought in the body of the text, are taken directly from the work of Saeki. In those instances where the attribution of a philosophical position is not in the body of the Sanskrit text, but is based on de La Vallée Poussin's reading of Saeki, I have kept the attribution, but have enclosed it in [square brackets] in the body of the translation. And when in his footnotes de La Vallée Poussin refers to "the Japanese editor", he is refering to Kyokuga Saeki.

In all instances, I have kept de La Vallée Poussin's footnotes, since they are a valuable guide to the philosophy of the *Abhidharmakośabhāṣyam*, and to its roots in earlier literature; my only addition to his work is that I have searched out the Taishō Canon references to these works, since de La Vallée Poussin did not have the Taishō Canon at his disposal when he was working on the *Abhidharma-kośabhāṣyam*. (He did however have the Taishō Canon at his disposal when he was working on the *Vijñapti-mātratā-siddhi* of Hsuan-tsang, cf. his *Le Siddhi de Hiuan-tsang*). In the few instances where I was unable to find the Taishō Canon references, I have kept the annotation as given by de La Vallée Poussin.

Also in many places in the text de La Vallée Poussin added a great deal of explanatory material: this I have also kept, since without it many important passages in the *Abhidharmakośabhāṣyam* would remain unintelligible. Also, since de La Vallée Poussin did not have a Sanskrit copy of the *Abhidharmakośabhāṣyam* as an integral text, but only as it was quoted in the body of Yaśomitra's *Vyākhyā*, he grouped many of the *padas* of the Kārikās into single Kārikās (as did Hsüan-tsang). The Sanskrit manuscript of the *Abhidharmakośabhāṣyam* however divides various Kārikās into five or six different *padas*: I have divided these Kārikās into their various *padas* to match the structure of the Sanskrit original.

In fact, it was my original intention to publish this work with the English translation on the right facing page, and the Romanized Sanskrit on the left facing page, and much work by me and my assistant, the Bangladeshi Bhikkhu, Ven. Lokananda, went into preparing the text in this manner. Unfortunately due to the high cost of publishing this work, this format had to be abandoned, but I hope that some day the *Abhidharmakośabhāṣyam* may be reissued in this format.

A second concern of de La Vallée Poussin was to give the original Sanskrit of the Kārikās and to reconstruct those passages in the *Bhāṣyam* which were of special importance or difficulty: since the Sanskrit of the *Abhidharmakośa-bhāṣyam* is now widely available, I have omitted all of these footnotes with the mention that in almost all cases, de La Vallée Poussin was correct in his reconstructions!

A third source for de La Vallee Poussin's references was this great Belgian scholar's encyclopediac knowledge of Indian Buddhist literature: these footnotes have of course also been kept, and it is they that stand as perhaps our greatest legacy from Louis de La Vallée Poussin.

***

Back in the United States, one day I happened to meet an old friend, the Rev. Hōryū Itō (1911–1985), who was at that time and for many years previous the Rimban of the Higashi Honganji Betsuin in Los Angeles. He asked me what I was studying, and I told him of my work on the *Kusharon*. He asked me what commentaries I was using, and I told him about the work of Hōrei Sakurai. Rimban Itō asked me how this work was regarded in Japan, and I told him of the praise that it had received from both Prof. Miyamoto and Prof. Hirakawa, and that a copy of this work was used by them as a symbol of the traditional study of the *Kusharon.* Rimban Itō's eyes clouded over, and he said softly, "Hōrei Sakurai was my father." From that time on Rimban Itō maintained a close interest in my work on the *Kusharon*, and it is sad that he did not live to see the completion of this work, a work which owes its very inception to the work of Hōrei Sakurai.

At this point I should like to thank a number of persons who contributed much to the completion of this work: first, Mrs Sara Webb, who has helped me much in translating the finer points of de La Vallée Poussin's French; her aid has been and remains invaluable. I should also like to thank Mr Jean-Louis d'Heilly, who typed much of the translation of the *Abhidharmakośabhāṣyam* into the computer of the University of Oriental Studies, who rendered me great assistence in making sure that the text was understandable, and who successfully urged me to translate into English the vast bulk of the technical Sanskrit terms kept by de La Vallée Poussin in the body of his text.

I should also like to express my gratitude to my parents, Olivia Maude (Arwedson) and Dr. L. Leo Pruden for their continued support of my studies both in America and in Japan: it is a source of regret that neither of them lived to see the completion of this work.

This work must be dedicated however to the small but eminent band of Japanese scholars whose work on the *Abhidharmakośabhāṣyam* has kept alive the flame of traditional Buddhist scholarship in the 20th century, scholars such as Prof. Akira Hirakawa and Prof. Ken Sakurabe. May the merit of this publication accrue to their health and long life.

Los Angeles
June 1986

Leo M. Pruden

1. For example, Prof. Kōgen Mizuno lists some four major and sixteen minor Pali language commentaries to the *Abhidhammatthasaṅgaha*, a work composed in tenth century Ceylon by the Elder Anuruddha; eighteen of these commentaries were composed in Burma. See Kōgen Mizuno, general editor, and U. Vepunla and Tadashi Toda, translators, *Abidammattasangaha: Nampō-bukkyō tetsugaku kyōgi gaisetsu*, p. 16, published by the Abidammattasangahakankōkai, 1980, privately printed. See also Mrs. Mabel Bode (=Mabel Haynes Bode), *The Pali Literature of Burma*, London, Royal Asiatic Society, 1909.

2. Our work on the *Risshū-kōyō* was published in the *Kokuyaku-issaikyō: Wakan-senjutsu-bu*, vol. 97, p. 1–72, Tokyo, Daitō-shuppan-sha, 1970.

3. According to an account preserved in the 1321 work, the *Genkō-shakusho* (compiled by Kōkan Shiren, 1298–1346), the Far Eastern student of Buddhist philosophy is traditionally supposed to study the *Kusharon* (=the *Abhidharmakośabhāṣyam*) for eight years, and then follow this with a three years' study of the *Jō-Yuishikiron* (=the *Vijñapti-matrata-siddhi*). In the words of the adage, *yuishiki sannen, kusha hachinen*; (the sequence is reversed for reasons of syllable count).

4. Much information concerning the life and career of Rev. Hōrei Sakurai was given to me by Mrs. Kazuko Itō, the widow of Rimban Hōryū Itō, and their son, the Rev. Noriaki Itō. I wish to express my appreciation for their aid.

5. Fa-pao, whose dates are unknown, worked with Hsuan-tsang on the translation of the *Abhidharmakośabhāṣyam* in 654; he also worked with Hsuan-tsang on his translation of the *Vibhāṣā* in 659, and in this latter instance he is reported to have objected to Hsuan-tsang's addition of sixteen additional characters to the text for purposes of elucidating an obscure point. Fa-pao is counted, together with P'u-kuang, as one of Hsuan-tsang's major disciples. After Hsuan-tsang's death in 664, Fa-pao is recorded to have worked with I-ching from 700 to 703; under I-ching, Fa-pao served as the proof-reader (ch'eng-i) for some twenty works. See Mochizuki, *Bukkyō-daijiten*, V.4661.

P'u-kuang, also an early disciple of Hsuan-tsang, worked on the translation of the *Abhidharmakośabhāṣyam*, and in addition is reported to have worked with Hsuan-tsang on his translation of the *Mahā-Prajñāpāramitā Sūtra* in the period 656 to 663. His dates are also unknown. See Mochizuki, *op. cit.*, V.4408.

6. I began my teaching of the Abhidharma—more specifically readings from the text of the *Abhidharmakośabhāṣyam*—in the academic year 1970 - 1971 at Brown University, and I have continued this teaching at both the Nyingma Institute (Berkeley, California), and at the University of Oriental Studies (Los Angeles). When I first taught at the Nyingma Institute in the summer of 1971, I prepared a draft translation of my *Introduction* ("The Abhidharma: The Origins, Growth and Development of a Literary Tradition") for the benefit of the students, to serve as an introduction to the historical process that led to the growth of the Sanskrit tradition of Abhidharma literature. The first part of the essay is a free translation of the introductory section (pages 13 to 61) of Prof. Ken Sakurabe's outstanding Japanese translation of the first two chapters of the *Abhidharmakośabhāṣyam*, his *Kusharon no kenkyū* ("A Study of the *Abhidharmakośabhāṣyam*"), Kyoto, Hōzōkan, 1969 (first edition). The second part of this *Introduction* is a translation of pages 110 to 114 of Prof. Ryūjō Yamada's *Bongo Butten no shobunken* ("The Manuscript Sources of Sanskrit Buddhism", Kyoto, Heirakuji-shoten, 1959 [first edition]) which deals with the Sanskrit fragments of the Abhidharma literature. This part of the *Introduction* has also been augmented by the bibliographical material given in volume one of Prof. Akira Hirakawa's *Kusharon-sakuin* ("Index to the *Abhidharmakośabhāṣyam*", Tokyo, Daizō -shuppan kabushiki-kaisha, 1973).

7. Kyokuga Saeki appears to have been the first to term his works the "*kandō*" editions. His first *Kandō-bon* was his edition of the *Kusharon*, the *Kandō Abidatsuma Kusharon*, published by the Hōzōkan, Kyoto, in 1869. He followed this by *Kandō* editions of the *Sankoku-buppō-denzū-engi* (1888), and the *Yuishiki-sanruikyō-sen'yō* and the *Jō-Yuishikiron* (both in 1890). *Kandō* editions were continued after his death (cf. the *Immyō-sanjūsanka-honsa-hōsange* in 1895) by his disciples and students, Shundō Sugihara and Etō Senabe.

For the life of Kyokuga Saeki, see Mochizuki, *op. cit.*, I.624.

The Abhidharma: The Origins, Growth and Development of a Literary Tradition

Leo M. Pruden

1. *Origin and Growth of abhidharma.*

Today the word *abhidharma* signifies the third of the Three Pitakas (Skt: *Tripiṭaka*) or collections of scriptures that go to make up the full Buddhist Canon. These three Piṭakas, or collections, are: 1) the *Sūtras* or *Āgamas*, the words of the Buddha, directed to both laymen and clerics, dealing with a host of different topics: ethics, philosophical questions, legends and tales, etc.; 2) the *Vinaya*, directed to the monks and nuns of the Buddhist Sangha, spelling out the prohibitions to be followed by the clerics and injunctions on the carrying out of various seasonal events, adjudicating disputes, the distribution of property, etc.; and 3) the *Abhidharma Piṭaka*, a number of texts[1] later in compilation than either the *Sūtra Piṭaka* or the *Vinaya Piṭaka*.

If the word *abhidharma* does not signify the Third Piṭaka in its totality, then the word signifies the contents of this Third Piṭaka, its style of thinking and writing, and thus a certain type of commentarial literature, the *Śāstras* or commentaries on the *Sūtras* of the Buddha.

Since the *Sūtras* and *Vinaya*, it is believed, took their essential form before the Third Piṭaka was given its final form, the word *abhidharma* as used in the *Sūtras* and in the *Vinaya*, was a word that did not signify the Third Piṭaka. What then did the word *abhidharma* signify when it was first used in the *Sūtras* and *Vinaya*, in the reputed words of the Buddha?

There are two meanings to the word *abhidharma*: 1) referring to the Dharma; and 2) the higher, or superior Dharma.

The first person interested in the etymology of the term *abhi-dharma* was N.W. Geiger, in his work, *Pali Dhamma* (1921), where he states, "abhidhamma originally mean the highest Dhamma; such is the interpretation of later commentators, that is, abhidhamma as uttaradhamma." The earliest meaning of the word *abhidhamma*, he held, is "concerning the dhamma, or referring to the dhamma." In the *Sūtras*, indeed,this word always appears in the locative case, as *abhidhamme*, ("with respect to Dhamma") and in this manner parallels the form *abhivinaye* ("concerning the *Vinaya*").

This definition ("concerning the dhamma") was adopted by the *Critical Pali Dictionary* (1935, lst edition) where this form was termed (p. 350) a prepositional compound, and the word itself defined as: "as regards the dhamma."

described. Horner feels that two *dhammas* are spoken of: 1) *dhamma-kāmo*, and 2) *abhidhamma* and that *abhidhamma* is used to distinguish it from the first and lower type of dhamma. According to Sakurabe, this is a forced meaning, an interpretation not necessary for an understanding of the passage.

3. *Majjhima Nikāya*, I, p. 472:

> āraññaken'āvuso bhikkhunā abhidhamme abhivinaya yogo karaṇīyo. Sant'āvuso āraññakaṁ bhikkhuṁ *abhidhamme* abhivinaye pañhaṁ pucchitāro. Sace āvuso āraññako bhikkhu *abhidhamme abhivinaye* pañhaṁ puṭṭho na sampāyati tassa bhavanti vattāro:
> . . . āraññaken'āvuso bhikkhunā ye te santā vimokhā atikkamma rūpe arūppā tattha yogo karaṇīyo . . . ārannaken'āvuso bhikkhunā uttarimanussdhamme yogo karanīyo.
>
> "Your reverences, earnest study in Further-Dhamma, in Further-Discipline should be made by a monk who is forest-gone. Your reverences, there are those who will question a monk who is forest-gone on *Further-Dhamma* and *Further-Discipline.* If, your reverences, a monk who is forest-gone, on being asked a question on *Further-Dhamma*, on *Further-Discipline*, does not succeed in answering it, there will be those who speak about him and say . . .
>
> "Your reverences, earnest study should be made by a monk who is forest-gone concerning those that are the peaceful deliverances and are incorporeal having transcended material shapes . . .
>
> "Your reverences, earnest study in states of further-men would be made by a monk who is forest-gone . . ." (English translation by I.B. Horner, *Middle Length Sayings*, II, p.145).

Here Horner maintains that since the three accomplishments of the forest-dwelling monk are all put in the locative case (*abhidhamme, abhivinaye, yogo* . . .), *abhidharma* and *abhivinaya* refer to superior states of attainment. According to Sakurabe, however, this passage is like the *Dīgha* passage (no. 2 above). This occurrence of the terms *abhidhamma-abhivinaya* is the only place in the *Sūtras* where *abhidharma* and *abhivinaya* are ranked together with supernormal states of attainment, but such an explanation as Horner's is not necessary for understanding the sense of this passage.

3. *Abhidhamma alone.*

There are, to be sure, a number of passages where the word *abhidhamma* occurs apart from the word *abhivinaya*.

1. *Majjhima Nikāya*, I, p. 214 gives:

idh'āvuso sāriputta dve bhikkhū *abhidhammakathaṁ* kathenti, te aññamaññaṁ pañhaṁ pucchanti, aññamaññassa pañhaṁ putthā vissajjenti no ca saṁcādenti, dhammī ca nesam kathā pavattanī hoti.

"In this connection, reverend Sāriputta, two monks *are talking on further dhamma*; they ask one another questions; in answering one another's questions they respond and do not fall, and their talk on dhamma goes forward."

2. *Majjhima Nikāya*, II, p. 239:

tasmātiha, bhikkhave, ye vo maya dhammā abhiñña desotā, seyyathīdaṁ: cattāro satipaṭṭhānā, cattāro sammappadhānā, cattāro iddhipādā, pañc'indriyāna, pānce balāni, satta bojjhaṅgā, ariyo aṭṭhaṅgiko maggo,—tattha sabbeh'va samaggehi sammodamānehi avivadamānehi sikkhitabbaṁ; tesañ ca vo, bhikkhave, samaggānaṁ sammodamānānaṁ avivadamānānam sikkhataṁ, siyaṁsu dve bhikkhū *abhidhamme* nānāvādā.

"Wherefore, monks, those things taught to you by me out of super-knowledge, that is to say the four applications of mindfulness, the four right efforts, the four bases of psychic power, the five controlling faculties, the five powers, the seven links in awakening, the ariyan eightfold Way—all together, in harmony and without contention you should train yourselves in each and all of these. But when you, monks, all together, in harmony and without contention have trained yourselves in these, there might be two monks speaking differently about *Further-Dhamma*." (English translation by I.B. Horner, *Middle Length Sayings*, III, p. 25.)

After the Buddha has taught, through his *dhammā-abhiññā* (his higher or superior knowledge of the dharma), the thirty-seven factors of enlightenment, two monks are now depicted as having *abhidhamme nānāvādā*, "differing views on abhidhamma," and the other monks should try to settle the contentions of these two. The 37 dhammas so taught are by definition *dhammā abhiñña*, or *abhidhamma*. Thus the two monks' contentions are regarding these itemized, 37 superior dharmas. This is the opinion of I.B. Horner.

Sakurabe points out that the word *dhammā* is given in the plural whereas *abhidhamma* is given in the singular locative case, so this connection between *dhammā-abhiññā* and *abhidhamma* is unnatural. Geiger translates this passage as "zwei Bhikkhu, die uber den dhamma verschiedenes aussagen," and so translates *abhidhamme* as "concerning the teaching."

4. *Abhidhamma-kathā.*

The phrase *abhidhamma-kathā* occurs some three times in the Pali Canon.

1. *Majjhima Nikāya*, I, p. 214:

idh'āvuso sāriputta dve bhikkhū *abhidhammakathaṁ kathenti*, te aññamaññaṁ panham pucchanti, aññamaññassa pañhaṁ putthā vissajjenti no ca saṁsādenti, *dharmmī* ca nesaṁ *kathā* pavattani hoti.

"In this connection, reverend Sāriputta, two monks are talking on further *dhamma*; they ask one another questions; in answering one another's questions they respond and do not fall, and their talk on *dhamma* goes forward."

In this passage the phrase *abhidhamma-kathā* is followed by the words *dhammī . . . kathā . . .* So too the following passages from *Majjhima Nikāya*, I, p. 218:

sādhu sādhu sariputta, yathā taṁ Moggallāno va sammā byākaramāno byākareyya. Moggallāno hi Sāriputta *dhammakathiko* ti.

"It is good, Sāriputta, it is good. It is so that Moggallāna, in answering you properly, should answer. For, Sāriputta, Moggallāna is a talker on *dhamma*." (I.B. Horner, *Middle Length Sayings*, I, p. 270; see also her note on this passage.)

Here we see that anyone who gives a correct, clear account of dhamma is a *dhamma-kathiko*, a "speaker on dhamma." But later commentators (namely, Buddhaghosa, in his *Asl.* p. 29) terms a *dhamma-kathiko* to be an *abhidhamma-bhikkhu*, a monk who specializes in the study (and teaching) of the abhidhamma.

In another passage (*Aṅguttara*, III, p. 392), a monk who can do *abhidhamma-kathā* well is to be respected and honored. According to Sakurabe, this refers to one who can preach correctly and well, and the term *abhidhamma* in this passage as yet has no specific sense of a superior doctrine, but rather just the superior talent of being able to present the dharma well.

In another passage (*Aṅguttara*, III, p. 107) an ignorant monk confuses abhidharma-talk, and becomes verbose and long-winded (*vedalla-kathā*) and, by doing so, pollutes the Dharma and the *Vinaya.*

5. *Traditional Explanations of Abhidhamma.*

In the Pāḷi commentarial literature, the word *abhidhamma* clearly means "a special, superior dharma." This is seen in some of the words and phrases used by the later Pāḷi commentators in describing the abhidhamma.

In commentaries on the *Sūtras*, the abhidharma is termed *uttara-dhamma*, "the highest dharma," and *abhi-visittha dhamma*, "the very distinguished dhamma."

In commentaries on the *Abhidhamma*, the words *dhamma-atireka* (unique dhamma) and *abhamma-visesa* (distinguished) are used. Abhidhamma is called in the plural *vuddhimanto dhammā* (the expanded, augmented dhammas), *salakkhanā dhammā* (unique dharmas), *pūjitā dhammā* (dharmas to be honored, worshipped), *parichinnā dharmā* (special dharmas), and *adhikā dhammā* (excellent dharmas). Such traditional Pali commentators have influenced the Western translators of the *Suttas* to see in the word *abhidhamma* more than it probably originally intended (as Rhys-Davids, Woodward, Hare, Chalmers, et al.)

This understanding was roughly the same in the case of the Sanskrit tradition of Northern Buddhism. In the Chinese translation of the *Majjhima Nikāya*, (termed the *Madhyama Āgama* in Sanskrit and traditionally held, in Far Eastern Buddhism, to be a Sarvāstivādin compilation), we see such phrases as "He discusses the very deep abhidharma," or "He speaks the very profound abhidharma . . ." (T. 1, p. 450a, p. 634c, p. 688c, and p. 727b which corresponds to *Majjhima*, I, p. 214). The translation of the phrase *abhidharma-katham kathenti* ("he speaks abhidharma-talk," as above *Majjhima*, I, p. 214) is, in the Chinese translation, prefaced by the word "deep" or"profound" (Skt. *gambhiram*), added by the translator, based on his idea of the Abhidharma as a unique and superior teaching.

6. *Abhidhamma in the Mahāvibhāṣā*

The major Sarvāstivādin compendium of thought, the *Mahāvibhāṣā (The Great Commentary)* gives a full list of synonyms and definitions of the word *abhidharma* (T. 27, p. 4) recognized by various Sarvāstivādin masters, as well as by masters of various other traditions (the Mahīśāsakas, the Dharmottaras, the Grammarians, etc.), which reflect by and large the prevailing traditional definition of abhidharma as "a superior teaching"; but in the *Mahāvibhāṣā's* list of definitions, covering some 20 pages in its Chinese translation, the definition "concerning the dharma" appears a large number of times also.

The *Abhidharmakośabhāṣyam* reflects this approach when, in its analysis of the word *abhidharma*, it says that *abhi* means *abhimukha*, "facing," "with reference to," "in the direction of," "taking something as the object of study or analysis."

7. *The Abhidhamma Piṭaka.*

From whence then did the third collection of writings, the Third Pitaka, the *Abhidhamma Piṭaka*, arise?

There are two major scholarly opinions concerning how the *Abhidhamma Piṭaka* came into existence.

The first opinion was initially propounded by Taiken Kimura in his book *Abidatsuma-ron no kenkyū (A Study of the Abhidharma Śāstras*, now vol. VI of the *Kimura Taiken Zenshū.*) According to Kimura, *abhidharma* signified "concerning the dharma," and soon referred to discussions centered on the dharmas, their various classifications, itemizations, etc. This discussion was termed *abhidhamma-kathā* (*kathā* = discussion, debate), and such discussions came to be collected together to form the *Abhidhamma Piṭaka.* This view is the generally accepted view among Japanese scholars. (For this view in recent Japanese publications, see *Bukkyōgaku-jiten*, edited by Taya, Ōchō, and Funabashi, 1955 edition, under the entry *abidatsuma*, p. 6; and the article "Bukkyō tetsugaku no saishō no tenkai" by Tetsuro Watsuji, in the *Watsuji Tetsuro Zenshū*, vol. 5, p. 311, 344).

The second view was introduced by Geiger (in his *Pali Dhamma*, p. 118 ff.) and has been adopted by most Europeans (as A. Bareau, *Dhammasaṅgiṇi*, traduction annotee, 1951, p. 8 ff.; Étienne Lamotte, *Histoire*, p. 197; E. Frauwallner, *WZKSO* (1964), p. 59; see also Pāḷi Text Society, *Pali-English Dictionary*, under *mātikā*). This opinion holds that the earliest form of what we now call the *Abhidhamma Piṭaka* is seen in what is termed in Pali the *mātikā* (Skt: *mātṛkā*). In the Pali Canon there very frequently occurs (some 18 times) the set phrase: *dhammadharo vinayadharo mātikādharo* ("holding, grasping," i.e. "study and recitation of *Dhamma*, of *Vinaya*, of *Mātikā*"). Here there are three distinct objects of study, the *Dhamma* (the *Sūtras*), the *Vinaya*, and the *Mātikās*, or "summaries".

8. *The Mātikā.*

The word *mātikā* is used in a variety of contexts. It is used to signify: 1. commentarial literature on the sūtras (*Pat.* I.1); 2. the books that go to make up the *Abhidhamma Piṭaka* (*Asl.*, p. 3); and 3. commentaries not included within the *Abhidhamma Piṭaka* (*Vism.* p. 536, 546, 626, etc.).

Generally then, the meaning of *mātikā* is: a list of items or words that serve as the object of debate or discussion, the technical terms of the commentarial literature.

Within the *Vinaya Piṭaka*, the word *mātikā* is used in the order: *Vibhaṅga*, *Khanddhaka*, *Parivāra*, and *Mātikā*, so that here the word means the Patimokkha list of rules, that is, the essential items or rules of the *Vinaya*, devoid of illustration and elaboration.

So *mātikā* with reference to the *Suttas* and *Vinaya* has points of similarity:the usage in both contexts signifies a bare, skeletal itemization of words or terms apart from their explanations or elaborations.

In the commentarial literature, then, *mātikā* signifies an (earlier) bare-bones list of dharmas, which underwent later elaboration, and the eventual codification of this elaboration developed into the various books of the Pali *Abhidhamma Piṭaka*. In the *Vinaya*, then, the *mātikā* referred to the Pratimokkha list of rules, which *mātikā* then led to the elaboration of these rules, the circumstances surrounding their promulgation by the Buddha, the exceptions to the rules, their penalties, etc.

The earliest meaning of the word *mātikā*, then, was merely a list. It was only later that the word *mātikā* came to mean the Patimokkha rules themselves (the present-day meaning of the word), a change in meaning from "a list" to "the List," a change likewise seen in its further meaning as a list of technical terms, of dharmas, used in abhidharma discussions.

Thus the word *mātikā*, as used in *Vinaya Piṭaka*, means a list of essential items (here the *Vinaya* rules) within the *Vinaya Piṭaka*; when the word is used in the *Suttas*, it refers to a list of items (a list of dharmas) within the *Suttas*.

Within the *Suttas*, the word *mātikā* occurs, according to Sakurabe, in only those passages in a later stratum of the Canon, texts which themselves are already close to being abhidharmic texts. Likewise this is the case with the *Vinaya Piṭaka*: the word occurs in its later passages, or in passages that have already assumed a commentarial status. So the list: *dhamma-vinaya-mātikā* could conceivably be translated "the teaching, its monastic rules, and the itemized lists of their contents or essentials."

One Japanese scholar even goes to far as to say that the phrase *bahussuto āgatāgamo dhammadharo vinayadharo mātikādharo* be interpreted by *āgata-āgamo* equalling *dhamma dharo*, and *vinaya* equalling *mātikā* (Egaku Mayeda, in his *Genshi Bukkyō Seiten no Seiritsu-shi kenkyū*, p. 194), that is, "the learned *āgata-āgamo* (understander of the tradition) who is a *dhamma-dharo*, (and the learned) upholder of the *Vinaya* who is an upholder of *mātikā*."

9. *Mātikā and Abhidharma.*

There are several passages in the scriptures that do show that the term *mātṛkā* was seen as synonymous with the word *abhidharma.*

A. In one text preserved in Chinese translation (T. 24, p. 408b), vol. 40 of the *Kṣudrakavastu* of the Mūla-Sarvāstivādin *Vinaya*, it states that after the First Council had finished reciting the *Sūtras* and the *Vinaya*, Kātyāyana said, "Persons of later generations will be of little wisdom and of dull faculties; their understanding will be based on the text [of scriptures], and they will not penetrate to its deeper meaning. Now I shall myself recite the *Mātṛka*, in order that the meanings of the *Sūtras* and the *Vinaya* will not be lost." He then recited the 37 components of enlightenment (the *bodhyaṅgas*, see above, *Majj*. II. 239), and he then said "Know therefore, this is the *Sūtra*, this is the *Vinaya*, this is the *Abhidharma*." Here then *Mātṛkā* means the itemized dharmas in the *Sūtras* and the *Vinaya*,and the identification is made between it and the *Abhidharma.*

B. The identification is also made in the *Kathāvatthu*, reputedly the latest work in the Pali *Abhidhamma Piṭaka*, where in the "Journal of the Pali Text Society," 1898, p. 7, Geiger regards this identification as being the original word of the Buddha.

C. This identification is also made in the *Aśoka-avadāna*, the biography of the Emperor Aśoka; see its Chinese translation, the *O-yü-wang ch'uan*, T. 50, p. 113c.

D. In the Yogācāra's huge encyclopaedic work, the *Yogācarabhūmi*, vol. 81 (T. 30, p. 753b), one of the twelve classes of literature into which all Buddhist literature is divided is *upadeśa*, discussions or debates wherein all the dharmas are correctly analyzed. Here *upadeśa* is otherwise termed *mātṛkā* or *abhidharma.* Further, this *mātṛkā* is an exhaustive and thorough-going analysis (of the dharmas).

From the above, then, we can see that the *Mātikās* (or *Mātṛkās*) performed an important function in the development of the corpus of Buddhist literature, as admitted in traditional Buddhist literature itself.

By itemizing the component parts of the *Dharma* and the *Vinaya*, the

Mātṛkā did play an important part in the later elaboration which is Abhidharma literature. However, the Abhidharmikas worked on these lists, minutely analyzed the items on these lists, and then proceeded to give long, exhaustive treatises on each item. So the *Mātṛkā* represents but one aspect of the whole picture of the growth of the *Abhidharma*.

If the Abhidhamma was merely speaking on the dhamma as some scholars maintain, and if the *Mātikā* served as the nucleus of later Abhidhamma elaborations, why, when the literature was codified into a *Piṭaka*, was it named the *Abhidhamma Piṭaka*, and not the *Mātikā Pitaka*? It appears then that the *Mātikās* did not *directly* develop into the Abhidharma literature as we now have it.

As Kimura has shown, in the earliest Buddhist Sangha, *abhidhamma-kathā*—discussion on the dharma—had a direct relationship with the later development of the commentarial literature on the *Dhamma*, the *Abhidhamma* commentaries. In the process, there were two tendencies; one: to summarize and to itemize, and two: to analyze and elaborate. This latter tendency came to predominate, and the name for this—*abhidhamma*—came to be attached permanently to this new corpus of literature.

10. *Abhidharma in the Āgamas: the Religion of the Āgamas.*

There are abhidharmic tendencies in the extant sutras, in Pāḷi as well as in those preserved in Chinese translation. Let us say a few words first, however, about the religion of the early Buddhist canon, the religion of the *Āgamas*.

According to de La Vallée Poussin, all the teachings of the Buddha were not publically given out. Instead, much of the philosophy and the more subtle forms of the teaching were embodied in texts which were reserved for the study of monks in their monasteries; and the *Āgamas* (or *Nikāyas*), the earliest form of the Buddhist sermons which have been preserved for us, are such philosophical texts as were transmitted from one generation of monks to those of a subsequent generation. Such texts are then the "clericalized" texts, and in these texts we see only a small bit of the popular side of early Buddhism.

Such is the case, to be sure, in any religion, and this is especially so in the case of Indian religions. Any Indian religion has two sides to it: a clerical, well worked-over doctrine, and a popular aspect of the religion, which includes many elements brought over in the mind of the new converts to the religion. But the important point to remember is that the extant literature of any religion is the technical literature used in the monasteries. The real face of early Buddhism in all of its aspects cannot be gotten at only through its literature, but must also be obtained through archaeology, art and chronology (*Le dogme et la philosophie du Bouddhisme*, 1930, Chap. VII). Such a mass Buddhism was the Buddhism that preceeded the canon, "precanonical Buddhism" (*Bouddhisme precanonique*). Its contents were not only a *darśana*—a systematic school of Indian philosophy, a consistent world-view—but a faith concerned with spirits and the release of these spirits from the round of birth and death, having, according to scholars, little in common with the doctrines of *anitya, anātman*, and *duḥkha* so often stressed in the *Āgamas* (see de La Vallée Poussin's *Nirvāṇa*, 1925, p. 85, 115, 131). The spread of Buddhism was dependent upon its moral teaching, the personality of its founder, its wisdom embodied in memorable sentences and couplets (the *Dhammapada* or *Udānavarga*), coupled with popular animal tales (the *Jātakas*) (see *The Way to Nirvāṇa*, 1917, Chap. V). Buddhism was also closely related to ancient Indian nature worship, the worship of certain trees, and the veneration of snakes.

Buddhism also came to be changed, especially on its popular level, by virtue of the influence of non-Buddhist religions, through the conversion to Buddhism of many non-Buddhists who brought their own ideas into the company of older believers. Popular Buddhist religion absorbed much of the pan-Indian pantheon of deities. However formal and set its doctrines might have been, most of the believers of Buddhism were but "*demi-civilize*" or semi-civilized (*Bouddhisme*, 1909, p. 349 ff.). Such is also the view of A.B. Keith (*Buddhist Philosophy in India and Ceylon*, 1923) and C.A.F. Rhys-Davids (*Śākya or Buddhist Origins*, 1931, p. 431 ff.).

11. *The Āgamas and the Nikāyas.*

This above view was strongly opposed by Stcherbatsky (*The Conception of Buddhist Nirvāṇa*, 1927). De La Vallée Poussin would appear to oppose the popular elements of early Buddhism to the scholarly works of later Buddhism: such would imply that there is something essentially different between early Buddhism and Abhidharma Buddhism. Stcherbatsky held that the Buddha was a product of the philosophical environment of his time, and that he obviously had a well-defined philosophy with its attendant metaphysic.

But even if the set passages and formulas were removed from the *Āamas*, de La Vallée Poussin and Rhys-Davids cannot say that Buddhism is merely a faith concerned with spirits and immortality. So-called popular Buddhism and "pure" clerical Buddhism cannot be so clearly distinguished one from the other. Yet the *Āgamas* do not give a clear picture of early Buddhism, especially in its popular aspects: the Āgamas are the traditions (*āgama*) of a scholarly elite, as de La Vallée Poussin maintains.

The *Āgamas*, literally the "transmitted" (doctrines) were in a sense also *Nikāyas* (compilations): the transmitted doctrines were collected together, formalized, and their vocabulary became technical terms; these terms came to be analyzed through *vibhaṅgas* (long, explanatory definitions) and *niruktas* (etymologies); these same terms were also organized on the basis of numerical categories or on the basis of similarities (*saṁyukta*) into *mātṛkās*. So the tendencies that led ultimately to a systematic Abhidharma literature led in this same process to the systematization of the *Āgamas* (the traditions) into *Nikāyas* (formal literary compilations).

In summary, the *Āgamas* are doctrinal compilations from an early stage of Buddhism, and their recensions (*Nikāyas*) are in a sense Abhidharmic compilations and, being largely abhidharmic in tendency, they led ultimately to the growth of the *Abhidharma* as a separate literary genre.

12. *Abhidharmic Tendencies in Extant Āgamas: Numerical Categories, Saṁyuktas, and Vibhaṅgas.*

Abhidharmic tendencies, tendencies that led eventually to the growth of a separate literature, can be seen early in some scriptures. The use of numerical categories is one such tendency.

A. The *Saṅgīti-suttanta* (the "recited" sūtra, *Dīgha Nikāya* no. 33, vol. III, pp. 207-271) lists a variety of items in a list from one to ten (one item, two items, three items . . .) *Dīgha Nikāya* no. 34, the *Dasuttara-suttanta*, lists items in a list from one to ten, but now analyzes them according to various other categories, marking then a further development along abhidharmic lines.

This same tendency is seen in the case of the *Aṅguttara Nikāya* (*aṅguttara*, "increasing by an item"), which classifies all of the *suttas* in its collection on the basis of numerical categories: thus all *suttas* dealing with any group of "four" items are collected together, followed by all *suttas* dealing with "five" of anything (up to eleven items). This scheme then forms the basis for this one collection of texts, or *nikāya*.

B. Many other *suttas* or *āgamas* were joined to one another on the basis of their affinity in subject matter. To be sure, this is not sharply distinguishable from the above numerical classification, but now the items are more meaningfully arranged. Such texts are called *saṁyuktas* (Pali: *samyuttas*) or "conjoined" texts.

Examples of this tendency are the *Ṣaḷ-āyātana vagga* (*vagga* = section or chapter) in the *Majjhima Nikāya*, and the *Kamma-samyutta vagga* in the *Majjhima*: i.e., all those texts dealing with the *āyatanas* were grouped together, as were all those texts dealing with *karma*.

This too became the guiding principle in the compilation and editing of the *Saṁyutta Nikāya* and parts of the *Khuddaka Nikāya*.

C. The concept of an expanded commentary (a *vibhaṅga*) is best seen in individual *suttas* in the *Saṁyutta Nikāya* and in the *Majjhima Nikāya*. Many such texts have the word *vibhaṅga* in their titles:

Samyutta Nikāya XII.2: the *Vibhaṅgam* (II, pp. 2-4), which is an expansion of XII.1 (*deśanā*); XLV.8, the *Vibhaṅgo* (V. pp. 8–10), which is a commentary on the Noble Eightfold Path; and LI.20, the *Vibhaṅga* (V, pp. 276–281), which is a commentary on the *siddhi*, or supernormal powers, of a Buddha.

The *Majjhima Nikāya* has *Majj.* 135, the *Cūḷa-kamma-vibhaṅga sutta* (*cuḷa* = smaller, lesser) (III, pp. 202–206), which treats of Karma, and is followed by the *Mahā-kamma vibhaṅga-sutta*, *Majj.* 136 (pp. 207–215) which is an elaboration of certain of the former *sutta's* sections; *Majj.* 137, the *Ṣaḷāyatana-vibhanga-sutta* on the six *āyatanas* (p. 215–222) and all of its following *suttas* are *vibhangas*: *Majj.* 138, 139, 140 (on the *dhātus*), 141, 142. Synonymous with the *vibhaṅga* is the word *vedalla*, which also means "expanded": as the *Cūḷa-vedalla-sutta*, and the *Mahā-vedalla-sutta*. The Buddha would give a short sermon, and one of his disciples, such as Kātyāyana, or the Buddha himself, would elaborate on it; or the disciples would discuss it among themselves, and in this way it would reach its present form.

The *āgamas* (in their Chinese translations) which have the characteristics of *vibhangas* can be rather closely identified with these same *Suttas* extant in Pali: they are largely the same text (especially *Majj.* 131 to 142, as above), a fact which does not hold for the other *āgamas*.

Thus abhidharmic tendencies are clearly seen in many texts in both Pāḷi and Chinese, so far advanced in many cases that it is merely a short step to real Abhidhamma literature, as the *Saṁgīti-sutta* has led to the *Saṁgīti-paryāya*. There is in fact very little internal change from abhidharmic *āgamas* to Abhidhamma works; indeed, greater internal changes have come about in later Abhidharma works at a susequent period, as we shall see below.

13. *Sarvāstivādin Āgamas*.

There are sectarian, Sarvāstivādin *āgamas*, but there must have been some chronological distance between the Sarvāstivādin *āgamas* and those *āgamas* in their final shape (in the form that we have them today) before the split of the Sarvāstivādins from the rest of the Sangha.[2]

Thus early *āgamas*, non-sectarian in content, led to the growth of sectarian, i.e., Sarvāstivādin *āgamas*, which in turn led to the growth of Sarvāstivādin *Abhidharma*. So to know the Sarvastivadin *Abhidharma*, it is important to know the Sarvāstivādin *āgamas*. This however is almost impossible.

In the Abhidharma literature, when for instance the four types of *pratyayas* (conditions) are mentioned (as in *Kośa* T. 29, p. 36b, and the *Nyāya-anusāra*, T. 29 p. 440a) the reference "as given in the Sūtra" is given, and since this particular sūtra can be fully reconstructed (as explained below), this one text can be claimed for the Sarvāstivādins. However this specific sūtra is today not found in any of the extant Pāḷi Canon or in the Chinese translation of the *Āgamas*.

Since the publication, in the latter half of the 18th century, of the scholar-monk Hōdō's work, the *Kusha-ron Keikō*, it has come to be generally agreed upon by scholars that the *Madhyama Āgama* and the *Kṣudraka Āgama*, as they presently exist in Chinese translation, are, if not Sarvāstivādin in affiliation and editorship, at least very close to it. But as we know from the *āgamas* quoted in Sarvāstivādin *Abhidharma* works, there was a difference between the Sarvāstivādin *āgamas* that exist in Chinese and those *āgamas* that are directly quoted by the Sarvastivadin *Abhidharma* literature. How great a distance there was, we have no idea.

It is clear further that the Sarvāstivādin authors of their *Abhidharma* literature were clearly aware that there were sutras which claimed various sectarian affiliations and that there were differences among them. In the *Kośa*, phrases like "sūtras of the Mahīśāsakas" (p. 11.12a; 12.16a), "sūtras of the Kāśyapīyas" (p. 23.17a), "sūtras of the Sthaviravādins" (p. 19.19b), and sūtras of other groups (4.48a, 5a) occur very often. In one passage in the *Kośabhāṣyam* where the question whether *sukha* (pleasure) is experienced by the mind, or by the mind *and* by the body (the former is a Sautrāntika position, the latter, Sarvāstivādin), the Sarvāstivādins quote as proof of their position a sūtra which the Sautrāntikas criticize by saying that "all sūtras hold that pleasure is experienced by the mind, whereas the sūtras of the Sarvāstivādins add the word 'body' in this passage."

In another passage, the *Nyāya-anusāra* (T. 29, p. 330a-b) says, "This is not the teaching of the Buddha, but of the sūtras. We see differences in words and meanings in the scriptures of the different sectarian groups. Because the sūtras have different meanings, the sectarian teachings are different. That is, the

Sautrāntikas recite *The Sūtra of the Seven States of Existence*, and (on the basis of this) posit, in their *Abhidharma*, the existence of an *antara-bhava* (an intermediary existence), and so too posit a gradual manifestation of insight. There is also a text, *The Basic Teachings of All the Schools* (*Sarva-darśana mūla-paryāya?*) which is not read by the Sarvāstivādins. The work *The Simile of Grasping with the Fist* (the *Hasta-dvala?*) collects together many scriptural quotations, but there are those groups, among all groups, who do not read this work. For although it collects together a number of scriptures which are unanimously read by all the sects, yet there are differences in their phraseology."

So it would thus be worthwhile to attempt a reconstruction of the sectarian *sūtras* of the Sarvāstivādins.

14. *Śamathadeva's Commentary.*

How can we know the Sarvāstivādin *āgamas*, and especially those *āgamas* quoted by Vasubandhu in the *Kośabhāṣyam*? One source is a commentary on the *Kośabhāṣyam* by one Śamathadeva, an Indian scholar-monk about whom nothing is known. Only one work bearing his name remains, preserved in the Tibetan *Tanjur* (Tohoku no. 4094; Peking no. 5595), entitled the *Upāyika-nāmā Abhidharmakośa-Ṭīkā*. Although entitled a *ṭīkā* (sub-commentary), the *Upāyika* is not a commentary in the usual sense of that word; in fact, the *Upāyika* is only about half the length of the *Kośabhāṣyam*.

Rather, wherever there is a passage in the *Kośabhāṣyam* that quotes from an *āgama*, that passage is given by Śamathadeva by the full quotation of the passage from out of the *sūtra* text. Often the whole paragraph is given, or if not, he gives the title of the *āgama* and the chapter or section title where the passage is to be found. Occasionally, if there is no passage to be found in relevant *āgamas*, related passages are given from *āgamas* which illustrate examples of usage. The *Upāyika* is valuable, not so much for understanding the *Kośabhāṣyam*, but for the reconstruction of sectarian, Sarvāstivādin *āgamas*.

It is premature to suppose that the *āgamas* quoted in the *Upāyika* are the same as those seen by Vasubandhu. Still they are close enough to get a good idea of the influences of the Sarvāstivādin *āgamas* on Sarvāstivādin Abhidharma. Yet the difficulties inherent in the *Upāyika* are still great.

For example, the *Kośabhāṣyam* gives "in the ninth sūtra of the *Dīrgha Āgama* . . ." (19.17b), or "in the third sūtra, included in the thirteenth śloka of the *Śrāvaka-vyākhyāna* . . ." (2.7b), or "in the second sūtra in the *Vibhaṅga-saṁgraha* . . ." (10.10b), or sometimes simply "*śrāvastyam nidānam* . . ." ("in the episode at Śrāvasti"), or "*Evam mayā śrutam* . . ." ("Thus have I heard"). But since many of these works cannot be found in the extant Chinese or Pāḷi editions of the Canon, comparison is impossible.

Sakurabe (in an article on pp. 155–161 of the *Yamaguchi Hakase Kanreki-kinen Indogaku Bukkyōgaku Ronsō*) traces a number of Sarvāstivādin *āgamas*, and found a remarkably close correlation between the *āgamas* quoted in the *Kośabhāṣyam* (and the *Upāyika*) and those texts traditionally held to be Sarvāstivādin *āgamas* in the Chinese Canon.

Several of Sakurabe's findings are: 1. that the Sarvāstivādins had a fifth *āgama* (as does the Pāḷi Canon today), for the *Upāyika* gives the sentence "in the *Artha-vargīya sūtra* of the *Kṣudraka*" (see *Kośabhāṣyam* 1.10a), which *Kṣudraka* (miscellany) is the same name given the fifth *nikāya* (the *Khuddaka Nikāya*) of the Pāḷi Canon; 2. that the Sarvāstivādin *Kṣudraka Āgama* has texts that a) are in the Chinese *Tso O-han Ching* (the Chinese translation of the *Kṣudraka Āgama*), b) which circulated separately, and c) which do not exist in the Pāḷi Canon; and 3. that the *Dīrgha Āgama* of the *Kośabhāṣyam* and *Upāyika* is totally different from the Chinese edition of the *Dīrgha Āgama*, the *Ch'ang O-han Ching*. His studies have shown that whereas the arrangement within the texts is often very close, texts not in the Pāḷi can exist in both the *Kośabhāṣyam* (and *Upāyika*) and in the Chinese Canon.

15. *Sarvāstivādin Abhidharma Literature.*

We can thus see that the early period of this literary genre went through three major states of development, as given above: 1. the early usage of the word *abhidharma*, 2. Abhidharmic elements in the *Āgamas* and *Nikāyas*, which in turn formed the basis for 3. an independent, elaborated literature, a literature the vast bulk of which (with the exception of the *Kośabhāṣyam* and its commentary, the *Vyākhyā*) exists today only in Chinese and Tibetan translation.

16. *Origin of the Abhidhamma*

According to the Pāḷi tradition, at night the Buddha would ascend to Tāvatiṁśa Heaven, and there he preached the Abhidhamma to his mother, Māyā, and to the Devas residing in that Heaven. In the daytime he would return to the earth, where he preached this same Abhidhamma to his disciple Sāriputta. Sāriputta, through his supernormal powers of memory, memorized the totality of this teaching, and in turn recited it to Bhaddaji; Bhaddaji in turn recited it, *in toto* and without any error whatsoever, to his disciple, and in this way it was finally recited to Revata who, in turn, recited it publicly at the Third Council, held in Pāṭaliputra in 251 B.C. some 235 years after the death of the Buddha.

In the Theravāda tradition of Pāḷi Buddhism there are some seven long books that go to make up the third *Piṭaka,*the *Abhidhamma Piṭaka.* These books are, in the traditional order in which they are listed:

1. *Dhamma-saṅgaṇi*, "Enumeration of the Dhammas"
2. *Vibhaṅga*, "The Book of Treatises"
3. *Patthāna*, "The Book of Origination"
4. *Dhātu-kathā*, "Discussion of the Dhatus"
5. *Puggala-paññatti*, "Description of Individuals"
6. *Yamaka*, "The Book of Pairs"
7. *Kathā-vatthu*, "The Book of Controversy."

Historians, however, place the *Dhamma-saṅgaṇi* and the *Vibhaṇga* as the earliest of these works, followed by the *Dhātu-kathā*, the *Puggala-paññatti*, the *Kathā-vatthu*, the *Yamaka* and the *Paṭṭhāna*. With the end of the composition of the *Paṭṭhāna*, the *Abhidhamma Piṭaka* is closed, and no subsequent Abhidhamma work in Pāḷi is included within the Canon.

The Sarvāstivādins claimed some six treatises (see below); these six works went to make up the *Jñāprasthāna*, the *Jñāprasthāna* gave rise to the *Mahāvibhāṣā*, and this work in turn gave rise to later compilations of doctrine.

There was no closed canon for the Sarvāstivādins as far as the *Abhidharma Piṭaka* was concerned, and the numerous references to "the seven Abhidharma books of the Sarvāstivādins" must be understood in this context.

In the traditional view of the six smaller works that stand in relation to the *Jñānaprasthāna*, it is held that the *Jñānaprasthāna* is an earlier, more important work (the body), and that the other six works—shorter in length and dealing with only one or two topics—are its legs (Skt., *pāda*), implying by this that they were written subsequent to the *Jñānaprasthāna* in order to comment in greater detail on topics raised first in the *Jñānaprasthāna*. The contemporary scholarly opinion, however, is that these six works were the precursors of the larger *Jñānaprasthāna*.

These six, the *padaśāstras*, are:

la. *Saṅgīti-paryāya*, by Śāriputra (var. by Mahākauṣṭhila) composed approximately 200 years after the Nirvāṇa of the Buddha. The contents of this work closely resemble the *Dasuttara-suttanta* of the *Dīgha Nikāya*; exists in Chinese translation, T. vol. 26, no. 1536.

lb. *Dharma-skandha*, by Maudgalyāyana (var. by Śāriputra). This work also exists in Chinese translation, T. vol. 26, no. 1537.

2a. *Vijñānakāya*, by Devaśarman, composed approximately one hundred years after the death of the Buddha. Exists in Chinese translation, T. vol. 26, no. 1539.

2b. *Dhātukāya*, by Vasumitra (var. by Pūrṇa). Composed approximately three hundred years after the death of the Buddha. Preserved in the Chinese Canon, T. vol. 26, no. 1540.

2c. *Prakaraṇa-pāda*, by Vasumitra, composed some three hundred years after the death of the Buddha. This work, which closely resembles the Pali *Vibhaṅga-prakaraṇa*, exists in two Chinese translations, T. vol. 26, no. 1541 and no. 1542.

2d. *Prajñapti-śāstra*, composed by Maudgalyāyana. This work exists in one late, incomplete Chinese translation (T. vol. 26, no. 1538), and in a Tibetan translation.

According to Sakurabe, the bulk of Sarvāstivādin Abhidharma literature is divided into three major periods: 1. the early period, the period of the six *padaśāstras*, before the composition of the *Jñanaprasthāna*; 2. the period of the *Jñanaprasthāna*, its commentaries (the *vibhāṣās*), to the composition of the *Amṛta-rasa*; and 3. all works subsequent to the *Amṛta-rasa*.

Abhidharmic tendencies found within the *Sūtras* were extended and developed into such texts as the *Saṅgīti-paryāya* (la) and the *Dharma-skandha* (lb).

There is a *Saṅgīti-suttanta* in the *Dīgha Nikāya*; the Sarvāstivādin text entitled the *Saṅgīti-puryāya* is an extension of this *sūtra*.

The *Dharma-skandha* is not an extension or commentary on a sūtra, but it takes a topic from the sūtra literature and reclassifies it. The topic is taken from one sūtra preached by the Buddha at the Jetavana-vihāra, and quotations are taken from other texts to serve as a commentary to its subject matter.

The *Dharma-skandha* is made up of 21 chapters, and all but two of them are taken verbatim from sūtras. Of these two, one is a miscellaneous chapter, and one is on the *indriyas*.

The miscellaneous chapter in the *Dharma-skandha* lists some 78 different types of defilements, a list found verbatim nowhere in the sūtras. What the editor of this text obviously did was to bring together any and all descriptions of the defilements found scattered throughout the Canon, and collect them in this one work where they now form a total of some 78 defilements.

The chapter on the *indriyas* in the *Dharma-skandha* gives 22 different types of *indriyas*; again nowhere in the sūtras are the number of *indriyas* given as 22, but the editor collected all sutra references to the *indriyas,* and these came to 22.

According to Kimura, these *śāstras* were composed as a type of commentary to the *Sūtras*, and in the words of Lamotte, these works are "tres proches des sūtra cathechetiques," "close to those sūtras which are catechetical in form."

According to Kimura, these two works have already left the *sūtra* form (that is, they are not attributed to the Buddha) and are now in the form of an independent Abhidharma śāstra. Nevertheless they are not totally outside of sūtra influence, and so they still have the appearance of being an edition (Lamotte: *recension*) of a sūtra.

Further, these works are not fully abhidharmic in their treatment of their subject matter; that is, there is no attempt to be inclusive in their range of topics; rather they are devoted to only one topic. Their sectarian tendencies are still quite small, and there is no attempt at polemics or defense of their specific doctrines. In this last respect, the Pāḷi *Vibhaṅga*, the *Dharma-skandha*, and the *Śāriputra-Abhidharma* are very close to one another. And too, both the *Saṅgīti-paryāya* and the *Dharma-skandha* are attributed to direct disciples of the Buddha, to Śāriputra and to Maudgalyayana respectively (with the variants, to Mahākausthila and to Sariputra, respectively).

The *Prajñapti-śāstra* (2d) is included by Lamotte (*Histoire*, p. 206), Frauwallner and Ryūjō Yamada in the earliest period of this Abhidharma literature. Indeed, the fact that it is not fully abhidharmic in its treatment of subject matter, that its sectarian or polemical tendency is small, and that it is attributed to a direct disciple of the Buddha (here Maudgalyāyana) does apply to this text as well as to the *Saṅgīti-paryāya* and the *Dharma-skandha*. Nevertheless this work is not as close as these other two works to their origins, that of the *sūtra* form, but appears to mark a further step away from, or a development from its *sūtra* prototype, and so is placed by Sakurabe in the second stage of the development of early Abhidharma literature.

Both Frauwallner and Sakurabe place the *Saṅgīti-paryāya* as the earliest Abhidharma text, and the *Dharma-skandha* as being slightly later in time than the *Saṅgīti-paryāya*. De La Vallée Poussin and Lamotte place these texts however at approximately the same period of composition.

17. *The Second Period of Early Sarvāstivādin Literature.*

A slightly later period in the development of this Abhidharma literature saw an advance in terms of the texts' internal organization and their doctrinal development. Characteristics of the literature of this period are a) the numerical classification of items, b) the detailed commentary given to each item of the series, and c) a greater elaboration in the contents of these works than was seen in the earlier period of the literature. In this period of literature we have the growth of Sarvāstivādin sectarian concepts and vocabulary, and by now the vocabulary comes to be set.

The Sarvāstivādin sectarian influence can be seen primarily in their method of dividing, or classifying the *dharmas*: the *dharmas* are divided into defiled (*aśrava*) and undefiled (*anaśrava*) *dharmas*, or into the mind (*citta*) and its mental events (*cetasika, caitasika*). In this period too we have an elaboration of cause and effect relationships.

The *Prakaraṇa-pāda* (2c), a work from this period, is noteworthy in three respects: a) in form it is the first purely śāstra work of this literature; b) in doctrine it is the first purely Sarvāstivādin sectarian work; and c) it is the first work to divide the *dharmas* into five major divisions: uncompounded *dharmas* (*asaṁskṛtā dharmā*) and compounded (*saṁskṛtā*) *dharmas*. The compounded *dharmas* are made up of four groups: physical matter (*rūpa*), the mind (*citta*), mental states (*caitasikā dharmā*) and *dharmas* or elements that are neither mind nor matter. (Sakurabe, however, finds evidences of the fivefold division of the *dharmas* in both the *Saṅgīti-paryāya* and the *Dharma-skandha*.)

The *Prakaraṇa-pādā* is made up of eight chapters. Several chapters (nos. I, IV, and V) have had an independent translation into Chinese, which might point to the fact that they had an independent circulation in India itself.

According to the *Prajñā-pāramitā Upadeśa* (the *Ta-chih-tu lun*, traditionally attributed to Nāgārjuna), the *Prakaraṇa-pādā* comes from two different sources, Vasumitra and the Kaśmīrian Arhats, each writing four chapters apiece. Each of the eight chapter deals with a different subject: even though the chapter divisions in this work are meaningful divisions, each chapter is almost totally unrelated to the other chapters. The *Prakaraṇa-pādā* is thus perhaps a collection of eight independent works, brought together by one or two persons who were the final editors of this work. Frauwallner terms the *Prakaraṇa-pādā* "ein Sammelwerk."

Chapter Four of the *Prakaraṇa-pādā* is an elaboration of the mental states as first raised in the *Dhātukāya*; however, they are revised and augmented here by the editor of the *Prakaraṇa-pādā*.

Chapters Six and Eight have traceable origins in the *Saṅgīti-paryāya*, but the *Prakaraṇa-pādā* has added considerable new material to them. Chapter Seven is one chapter from the *Dharma-skandha*; here, however, the contents undergo a reclassification.

The remaining chapters, I, II, III, and V, are the *Prakaraṇa-pādā's* independent contribution to the development of Sarvāstivādin thought, for it is in these chapters that we find the fivefold division of the *dharmas*, the tenfold wisdoms, a new classification of the *āyatanas*, and an elaboration of some 98 types of mental laziness.

18. *The Jñānaprasthāna.*

The *Jñānaprasthāna* is a major compendium of Sarvāstivādin thought, and its bulk is considerably larger than all of the previous works. Its 44 chapters occupy (in Chinese translation) some 120 pages of the Taishō edition of the Canon.

The *Jñānaprasthāna (The Foundation of Knowledge)* also presents original contributions to Sarvāstivādin doctrinal development: it applies dependent origination (*pratītyasamut-pāda*) to biological life, and it elucidates some six different types of material causes (*hetu*).

Because of its central position in the development of Sarvāstivādin Abhidharma thought, it is termed the *mūla-śāstra* (Ch. *pen-lun*) and "the basic Abhidharma treatise" (*gen-pen o-pi ta-mo*).

Both the *Vibhāṣā* and the *Abhidharmakośa* state that Kātyāyaniputra collected the teachings of the Buddha which had hithertofore been scattered throughout the Scriptures, and brought them together in one work, the *Jñānaprasthāna.*

The internal organization of the work leaves much to be desired: within each topic, all information relevant to this topic is indeed collected together in one spot, but the overall organization of the text is haphazard.

The *Jñānaprasthāna* exists in two very different Chinese translations. Traditionally this was thought to be simply two rather differing editions of the same work, the one work (now termed the *Aṣṭa-grantha*, T. no. 1544) being the basic text, and the other translation (now termed the *Abhidharma-śāstra*, T. no. 1543) being a variant of it. Modern Japanese scholars now hold, however, that these two works represent two different traditions of Sarvāstivādin Abhidharma learning, one tradition being centered in Kásmīr (the *Aṣṭa-grantha*), another being centered in Gandhāra (the *Abhidharma-śāstra*). This is also seen in the fact that the *Mahāvibhāṣā* (ostensibly a commentary on the *Jñānaprasthāna*) is also preserved in two very different Chinese translations.

	(Kásmīr)		(Gandhāra)
3a	*Aṣṭa-grantha* trans. 383 (in 30 *chüan*) by Sanghadeva and Chu Fo-nien	3a	*Abhidharma-śāstra* trans. 657–660 (in 20 *chüan*) by Hsüan-tsang

4a *Mahā-Vibhāṣā*
by Vasumitra and the
500 arhats, compiled
400 years after the
Parinirvāṇa of the Buddha.
trans. 656–659 (in 200 *chüan*)
by Hsüan-tsang

4b *Vibhāṣā*
by Katyayaniputra
trans. 437–439 (in 14 *chüan*)
by Buddhavarman

19. *The Vibhāṣās*

The *Jñānaprasthāna* was commented upon (in both Kaśmīr and Gandhara?) and its commentaries (*vibhāṣā*) were termed simply "The Commentary," or *Vibhāṣā*. Since these works exist in two Chinese translations, the commentary from Kásmīr is termed the *Mahāvibhāṣā* (*The Great Commentary*, T. 1545), and the commentary from Gandhāra is termed simply the *Vibhāṣā* (T. 1546).

The *Mahāvibhāṣā* is a voluminous commentary upon the *Aṣṭa-grantha*. It is made up of some 43 long chapters and the whole work occupies some 200 fascicules (volumes) in its Chinese translation, or one whole volume, vol. 27, of the *Taishō Tripiṭaka*. Volume 27 is 1,004 pages in length, each page having at most some 1,392 Chinese characters!

The Gandhāran *Vibhāṣā*, however, is much shorter in length, occupying only 14 fascicules in its Chinese translation: it has only 16 chapters to its text.

Such a voluminous commentary demonstrates to us the importance of the *Jñānaprasthāna* to the Sarvāstivādins, and secures for the *Jñānaprasthāna* a position as the authoritative text of the Sarvāstivādins.

The *Mahāvibhāṣā* is a detailed analysis of everything in the *Jñānaprasthāna*; in one place, the *Mahāvibhāṣā* devotes some 76½ pages to commenting on one passage in the *Jñānaprasthāna* of only 100 characters. The work also raises new issues, issues not raised previously in the *Jñānaprasthāna*. Much new doctrine is introduced, and in addition, the *Mahāvibhāṣā* quotes differing opinions on topics from outside orthodox Sarvāstivādin ranks. Also many non-Buddhist theories are quoted at length.

By way of illustration, at the start of the work the *Jñānaprasthāna* asks the question, "What is the highest worldly dharma (*laukika dharma*)?" The answer in the *Aṣṭa-grantha* version of the *Jñānaprasthāna* is in some 70 Chinese characters, while the *Mahāvibhāṣā's* answer to this same question is in more than 8,000 Chinese characters, and takes up some two Chinese fascicules.

In the *Mahāvibhāṣā*, in answer to the question, "Why, in the Scriptures, did the Blessed One first teach the highest worldly *dharma*?", some 33 different answers are given, from this question's doctrinal implications for the concept of adherence (*prāpti*), to the various types of mindfulness (*smṛtyupasthāna*), to the four different types of conditions (*pratyaya*), and gives, in all, the names of eight different masters and schools.

The *Mahāvibhāṣā* spends many pages on important points and problems but, in the main, it follows the *Jñānaprasthāna's (the Aṣṭa-grantha's)* internal organization.

20. *Development of the Literature After the Vibhāṣās.*

Sakurabe places the *Abhidharma-amṛta-rasa (The Abhidharma Taste of the Deathless)* between the *Jñānaprasthāna* and the *Mahāvibhāṣā* on the basis of its doctrines, for it introduces points not found in the *Jñānaprasthāna*, points which, however, are found in the *Mahāvibhāṣā*: the doctrine of the five types of results (*phala*), the theory of atoms (*paramaṇu*), etc.

This work is a simple summary of all Sarvāstivādin doctrine. It is made up of 16 chapters, and so, according to Sakurabe, constitutes the first work in the third period of Sarvastivadin Abhidharma literature, the period after the composition of the *Jñānaprasthāna*. In its internal organization it appears to be a precursor to Dharmajina's *Abhidharmahṛdaya*, which was in turn the direct precursor to the *Abhidharmakośabhāṣam.*

21. *The Abhidharmahṛdaya.*

The *Abhidharmahṛdaya (Heart of the Abhidharma)* is a work in seven integral chapters, the order of which almost perfectly parallels the later order of the chapters in the *Abhidharmakośabhāṣyam.*

The chapters of the *Abhidharmahṛdaya* are:

	(*Kośa* chapters)
I. *Dhātu-nirdeśa*	I. *Dhātu-nirdeśa*
II. *Saṁskāra-nirdeśa*	II. *Indriya-nirdeśa*
	III. *Loka-nirdeśa*
III. *Karma-nirdeśa*	IV. *Karma-nirdeśa*
IV. *Anuśaya-nirdeśa*	V. *Anuśaya-nirdeśa*
V. *Pudgala-mārga-nirdeśa*	VI. *Pudgala-mārga-nirdeśa*

VI.	*Jñāna-nirdeśa*	VII.	*Jñāna-nirdeśa*
VII.	*Samāpatti-nirdeśa*	VIII.	*Samāpatti-nirdeśa*
		IX.	*Pudgala-pratiṣedha*

The *Abhidharmahṛdaya* concludes with a supplement (a *Miscellanea*) and an appendix (a *Discussion*), for a total of nine chapters.

The *Abhidharmahṛdaya* was the first work to use *kārikās*, or verses, followed by their prose commentary (*bhāṣyam*). This was the first real innovation in the internal organization of an Abhidharmic text. The work is internally coherent from beginning to end, and it is not merely a summary or an elaboration of a previous text: it is a well thought-out presentation of doctrine. The author of this work, Dharmajina (or Dharmaśreṣṭhi) clearly had a self-conscious awareness of this work as a whole, complete text.

This sevenfold chapter division of the *Abhidharmahṛdaya* was adopted by later works, by the *Abhidharmahṛdaya* of Upaśānta (Taishō no. 1551), the *Kṣudraka-Abhidharmahṛdaya* (also called the *Saṁyukta-Abhidharmahṛdaya*, Taishō no. 1552) of Dharmatrāta, and, with some modifications, by Vasubandhu, in his *Abhidharmakośabhāṣyam*.

22. The *Abhidharmakośabhāṣyam*.

Even though Vasubandhu's *Abhidharmakośabhāṣyam* is the outstanding Abhidharma text of Far Eastern Buddhism, it is not the purpose of this article to discuss the question of the authorship of the *Kośabhāṣyam*, nor the circumstances surrounding its composition: these topics will be discussed in a later article. I should like rather to merely say a few words on the place of the *Kośabhāṣyam* in the general course of development of the Sarvāstivādin Abhidharma literature.

Vasubandhu changed the name of the second chapter (from *Saṁskāra-nirdeśa*) to *Indriya-nirdeśa*, and added another chapter, the third chapter, *Loka-nirdeśa*, for a total of nine chapters. The former supplement and appendix material was incorporated into the body of the work, and Vasubandhu added a new appendix chapter, the *Pudgala-pratiṣedha (Refutation of the Soul)*, to the end of the work as a ninth chapter.

Later post-*Kośa* works, and indeed even anti-Ko*śa* works like Sanghabhadra's *Nyāya-anusāra* and his *Samaya-pradīpika*, not only kept the *kārikā-bhāṣyam* style of composition, but Saṁghabhadra even adopted the *Kośa's* (Vasubandhu's) *kārikās* verbatim, adding his own prose commentary, or *Bhāṣyam*. Saṁghabhadra changed the chapter names, and he took the ninth chapter, the *Pudgala-*

pratiṣedha, from the end of the work and put it at the beginning as a first chapter, there to serve as an introduction to what is the most essential feature of Buddhist thought, its doctrine of *anātman*.

Another work, the *Abhidharma-dīpa* (*Lamp on the Abhidharma*, or the *Abhidharma-vṛtti Marmadīpa-nāma*) was composed somewhat later than these above works. The author of this work (known only in Tibetan as Phyogs-kyi-glan-po) renamed the first chapter (the *Dhātu-nirdeśa*) the *Skandha-āyatana-dhātu-nirdeśa*, and the sixth chapter (the *Pudgala-mārga-nirdeśa*) became simply the *Māraga-nirdeśa*. The author kept the *kārikā-bhāṣyam* format, which was by now a distinctive feature of Sarvāstivādin Abhidharma literature.

The *kārikā-bhāṣyam* format has only one exception to it: the *Abhidharma-avatāra*. This work, whose full name is the *Sārasamuccaya-nāma Abhidharma-avatāra-ṭikā* (*Entry into the Abhidharma, being a Compendium of its Essentials*) is a work roughly contemporary with the composition of the *Kośa*. Tradition names the author as one Parśva (or Skandati). This work does not have the *kārikābhāṣyam* format but is, rather, a short treatise completely in prose; moreover the work lacks chapter divisions. It classifies all Sarvāstivādin doctrine on the basis of the five *skandhas* and the three uncompounded *dharmas*, an original departure from the division based on uncompounded and compounded *dharmas* (see above).

23. *Sanskrit Remains of the Abhidharma.*

Very little remains of the bulk of Abhidharma literature in its original Sanskrit or Indic languages, especially when compared with the remains of the various *vinayas* and *sūtras* which have been uncovered. Thus the Abhidharma literature of the schools of Kaśmīr and Gandhara—the Sarvāstivādins and the Sautrāntikas—exist primarily in their Chinese and Tibetan translations, and almost not at all in their original Sanskrit.

A fragment thought to be of the *Saṅgīti-paryāya* was found on 31 July 1930 in Bamiyan. In the village of Akkan, in the foothills of the Himalayas, there is a 35-meter-high image of the Buddha, and to the east of this image is a cave. It was from the collapsed roof of this cave that one page of text, written in Guptan script, was found. This fragment was studied by Professor Sylvain Lévi, and he discovered that it corresponded to a part of the *Saṅgīti-paryāya*. The results of his study were published in the *Journal Asiatique* (1932), and were translated and reprinted in two Japanese journals within that same year.

The passages in question were from that part of the *Saṅgīti-paryāya* which is in close agreement with a *Dīgha Nikāya* passage and, indeed, the rediscovered passage was so fragmentary that it could also be from the *Vinaya* or from the *Aṅguttara Nikāya*! But if it is indeed a section of the *Saṅgīti-paryāya*, there is then but one page from the early period of Sarvāstivādin Abhidharma literature which has been preserved for us in its original language.

Furthermore, Bamiyan is 150 kilometers to the west of the city of Kabul, the present-day capital of Afghanistan. This area was the center—as Gandhāra—of Sarvāstivādin studies, a fact perhaps relevant to the identification of this fragment with the text of the *Saṅgīti-paryaāya*.

24. *The Sanskrit Kośabhāṣyam.*

Another piece of Sanskrit Abhidharma literature that has been found is the full text of the *Abhidharmakośabhāṣyam*.

The *Abhidharmakośabhāṣyam* is made up of two parts, the *kārikā* or verse sections (the *Kośa*), and the auto-commentary to these verses (the *bhāṣya*) by Vasubandhu.

The *kārikā* section has traditionally been known. It has in fact a separate translation into Chinese, which points to its having had an independent circulation in India.

The prose or commentarial section, the *bhāṣyam*, had long been lost, but in 1935 Rahula Saṁkṛtyāyana discovered a palm-leaf manuscript of both the *kārikā* and the *bhāṣyam* of the *Abhidharmakośa*, that is, the full text of this work, in the Tibetan monastery of Ngor, a Sakyapa institution located some two days' ride south of Shigatse.

This palm-leaf manuscript dates from the 12th or the 13th century. It is an incomplete text: in the sixth chapter, *kārikās* nos. 53 to 68 are missing. Nevertheless, the manuscript has some 600 *kārikās*, plus 13 from the last chapter.

The *kārīkā* section of this manuscript find was published in the *Journal of the Bombay Branch of the Royal Asiatic Society*, by V.V. Gokhale; but it was only recently (1967) that the prose section, the *bhāṣyam*, was published together with these *kārikās* (see below).

Preceeding the find by Saṁkṛtyāyana, however, much scholarly work had already been done on the text of the *Abhidharmakośabhāṣyam*.

25. *Translations of the Abhidharmakośabhāṣyam.*

A team of Japanese and French scholars had worked on the *Kośa*, based on the *kārikās* as they had been preserved in the *Sphuta-arthā Abhidharmakośa Vyākhyā*, a Sanskrit commentary on the *Kośabhaṣyam* by Yaśomitra. In this *Vyākhyā* the *kārikās* are quoted, as well as large parts of the prose text (the *bhāṣyam*). Working with a Cambridge manuscript of Yaśomitra's *Vyākhyā* and with the Tibetan translation of the *Vyākhyā*, Louis de La Vallée Poussin published a complete French translation of the Chinese text of the *Abhidharmakośabhāṣyam* (i.e., the Chinese text of Hsuan-tsang's translation) in six volumes in Brussels (1923–1931). In chapter six of his translation, de La Vallée Poussin published the complete text of all the *kārikās* as then recently discovered by Sylvain Lévi in Nepal, a total of some 210 *ślokas*.

Based on de La Vallée Poussin's work, Saṁkṛtyāyana published the *kārikās* with his own Sanskrit commentary (1933).

In 1935 the Japanese scholar Yoshio Nishi published the *Kusharon* (the *Abhidharmakośabhāṣyam* in Hsüan-tsang's Chinese translation) in the *Kokuyaku-issaikyō* series, and in this work he included the Sanskrit text of the *kārikās*. (The *Kokuyaku-issaikyō* series was an edition of important works from the Far Eastern Buddhist Canon, translated into Japanese with often valuable introductions and annotations to the texts). In 1936 Ryūjō Yamada published the *kārikās* of the first chapter of the *Kośabhāṣyam*, the *Dhātu-nirdeśa*, with their Chinese and Tibetan Tibetan versions (in Japanese translation) in a leading Japanese cultural journal, *Bunka (Culture)*.

More recently, Narendra Nath Law's edition of Yaśomitra's commentary served as the basis for Aiyaswami Sastri's publishing all the *kārikās* to the third chapter, the *Loka-nirdeśa*, and his translation of them into English in the *Indian Historical Quarterly*, vol. XXIV (1953).

26. *Commentaries on the Abhidharmakośabhāṣyam.*

There are altogether some seven Indian commentaries to the *Abhidharmakośabhāṣyam* preserved in Tibetan, Chinese, and Uighur translations. The only one whose complete Sanskrit text has been preserved is Yaśomitra's *Vyākhyā* (which also exists in Tibetan translation). Manuscripts of the *Vyākhayā* exist in libraries in Paris, Cambridge, Leningrad, and Calcutta, and partial editions of this text are preserved in the libraries of Tokyo University and Kyoto University, Japan. The Paris manuscript, the best edition of this *Vyākhyā*, is preserved in the collection of the Societe Asiatique; this text was reproduced by the Japanese scholars Bun'yu Nanjō and Kenjū Sasahara, and deposited in the Ōtani

University Library, Kyoto.

In 1912, international efforts were begun to publish this work under the leadership of Sylvain Lévi. Lévi, Stcherbatsky, and Unrai Ogiwara began the publication of this work in *Bibliographie Bouddhique*, getting as far as the middle of the second chapter (1918, 1931). De La Vallée Poussin independently published the text and French translation of the third chapter, the *Loka-nirdeśa* (1914–1918).

In Japan an association was formed to aid in the publication of the *Vyākhyā*, an association headed by Ogiwara. This edition of the *Vyākhyā* was to be based primarily on the Calcutta manuscript, with reference to the Paris manuscript. It was then that the whole text of the *Vyākhyā* was finally published in Roman script in Tokyo (1932–1936). This work was recently reprinted (1971) in Tokyo, and is still readily available. In this work Ogiwara compared the text of the *Abhidharmakośabhāṣyam* with its Chinese and Tibetan translations. The text of the *Kośabhāṣyam* is italicized in the body of Yaśomitra's work, and all of the works quoted in both Vasubandhu and Yaśomitra are checked out in the footnotes.

More recently, Narendra Nath Law has published Yaśomitra's *Vyākhyā* as far as the fourth chapter, *Karma-nirdeśa*, in Devanagari script, based on the Cambridge manuscript edition of this text. Law's work was published in the *Calcutta Oriental Series*, no. 31 (1949–1955).

27. *The Tibetan Kośabhāṣyam.*

All of the work described above is based almost exclusively on the Sanskrit editions of the *Kośabhāṣyam* and the *Vyākhyā*, and on its Chinese translations. Nevertheless, the Tibetan translation of the *Kośabhāṣyam* has also received some attention from Western and Japanese scholars.

Stcherbatsky published the Tibetan text of the first chapter, the *Dhātu-nirdeśa*, in *Bibliographie Bouddhique*, XX, Part I (1918), and, in Part II (1930) of this same series, continued the publication of the text up to the 46th *kārikā* of the second chapter.

In Japan, Shunga Teramoto published the Tibetan text of the first chapter in Kyoto (1936), and the Department of Buddhist Studies (Bukkyōgaku kenkyū-shitsu) of Kyoto University published the Tibetan text of the first chapter of the *Kośabhāṣyam* along with the *Vyākhyā* of Yaśomitra: they have now gotten as far as the sixth chapter of the work.

28. *Translations of the Kośabhāṣyam and the Vyākhyā.*

At the present time there exists a number of translations of the *Kośabhāṣyam* and of the *Vyākhyā.*

A complete French translation of the *Kośabhāṣyam* was carried out by de La Vallée Poussin. This translation is primarily based on the Chinese translation of Hsuan-tsang, but frequent reference is made to the Sanskrit text of Vasubandhu (as preserved in Yaśomitra), the Chinese translation of Paramārtha, and the Tibetan. This work was published from 1921 to 1931 (see above).

Stcherbatsky "translated" the ninth chapter, the *Pudgala-pratiṣedha,* from the Tibetan into English, under the title "The Soul Theory of the Buddhists" (1920). This translation was first published in the *Bulletin de l'Academie des Russie,* but it has been recently reprinted in India. This work is actually a very loose paraphrase of the ninth chapter.

Yasomitra's *Vyākhyā* has also undergone a number of partial translations. De La Vallee Poussin translated the Vy*ākhyā's* commentary on the third chapter of the *Kośabhāṣyam* into French (1914-1919), and the combined efforts of Ogiwara, Susumu Yamaguchi, Gadjin Nagao, and Issai Funabashi have translated the *Vyākhyā* into modern Japanese up to the second chapter of the *Kośabhāṣyam.* In addition, Yamaguchi and Funabashi have published a Japanese translation of the *Vyākhyā* commentary on the third chapter, the *Loka-nirdeś*a (1955). In this work, each sentence of the Sanskrit is compared with its Tibetan translation, Yaśomitra's commentary is added, and illustrative material from Sthiramati and other Indian masters is added. Working in this same format, Funabashi translated parts of the fourth chapter, *Karma-nirdeśa,* in 1956.

More recently, Sakurabe has translated the first and the second chapters of the *Kośabhāṣyam* into Japanese (1969), based on the full Sanskrit text edition of Pradhan (Patna, 1967).

29. *Indexes to the Kośabhāṣyam*

The first index to the *Abhidharmakośabhāṣyam* was an index based on the Chinese translation of this work. This index was called the *Kandō-Kusharon-sakuin.* This index lists all of the Chinese words of the *Kusharon* (the *Kośabhāṣyam*) in the order of their Japanese reading. The text used as the basis for this index was the *Kandō-bon,* or *Kandō* edition of this text. The word *kando* literally means that the annotation or commentary (*-dō*) to the text was placed at the top or crown (*kan-*) of the page. When a text is termed the *Kandō* edition, this means that the editing of the work was done by one eminent scholar monk of the late 19th and the early 20th century, Kyokuga Saeki. Saeki's edition (i.e:, the *Kandō* edition) of the *Kusharon* was the edition of this text used by de La Vallée Poussin in his French translation, and most of de La Vallée Poussin's annotation is taken directly from the work of Saeki.

With the publication in 1946 of the Sanskrit *kārikas* by V.V. Gokhale (see above), and especially with the publication, in Devanagari script, of the full text of the *Abhidharmakośa-bhāṣyam* (Saṁkṛtyāyana's manuscript find) by P. Pradhan in 1967, it now became possible to compile an index to the Sanskrit text of the *Kośabhāṣyam*. This was done in the *Kusharon-sakuin*, compiled by Professor Akira Hirakawa of Tokyo University. The English title of this index is "Index to the *Abhidharmakośa-bhāṣyam*, Part One", and it was published in Tokyo in 1973. The lead words in this index are given in Sanskrit, with their Tibetan and Chinese translations. The Chinese words are given as they appear in Hsüan-tsang's translation of the *Kośabhāṣyam*, with the variants of Paramārtha given when needed. In this index, the first and all subsequent occurrences of the Sanskrit lead words are given (as found in Pradhan's edition of the text), followed by the use of each word in a compound, then by its Tibetan and Chinese translation. Part One of the *Kusharon-sakuin* is prefaced by a long English essay by Professor Hirakawa dealing with a number of topics raised by the *Kośabhāṣyam*: the date of Vasubandhu, the relation of the *Kośabhāṣyam* to the Yogācāra tradition of Indian Mahāyāna Buddhism, the relation of the Sautrāntikas and Mahāyāna Buddhism, and a review of the internal structure and the contents of the *Kośabhāṣyam*.

Part Two of this Index was published in 1977 and in this index the lead entries are given in Chinese, with their Sanskrit equivalents; the occurrence of the Chinese words in both the translations of Hsüan-tsang and Paramārtha are shown, as well as the location of their Sanskrit originals in Pradhan's edition of the text.

Part Three was published in 1978 and is a Tibetan-Sanskrit index to the *Kośabhāṣyam*. The references to the Tibetan *Kośabhāṣyam* are taken from the Peking edition (vol. 115) of the Tibetan Canon, with occasional readings adopted from the Derge edition of the Canon. Part Three also includes a complete page concordance from the Pradhan edition of the *Kośabhāṣyam* (published in the *Bauddha Bharati Series*, vols. V, VI, VII, IX), to the Taishō editions of the text (the translations of Hsüan-tsang and Paramārtha), to the *Kandō* edition of Kyokuga Saeki (see above), and to both the Peking and the Derge edition of the Tibetan *Kośabhāṣyam*.

Part Three also contains an Addenda section with a supplement to the Sanskrit of Part One, and a valuable supplement to the corrigenda of Pradhan's text; and a 53-page corrigenda to Parts One and Two of this index concludes this work.

1. The Theravadin Tradition of Hināyāna Buddhism—the religion of Ceylon, Burma, Thailand, Laos, and Cambodia—recognizes some seven works as comprising the totality of their *Abhidharma Piṭaka*: the Sarvāstivādins of Kaśmīr and Gandhara also have an *Abhidharma Piṭaka*, but the contents of this corpus are not limited to seven and include a larger number of works: nor it appears, was it ever a closed system like the Theravadins'.

2. On the split, see the Prefatory Notes of C.A.F. Rhys-Davids, in her *Points of Controversy*. According to Vasumitra, the original Sangha split into two, the Mahāsānghikas and the Sthaviravādins (Pāḷi: Theravadins), and the Sthaviravādins then split into two: the Haimavata (the "snow dwellers", the present-day Theravādins) and the Sarvāstivādins. This last split occurred around 250 B.C.

Abhidharmakośabhāṣyam
of Vasubandhu

Louis de La Vallée Poussin

INTRODUCTION[1]

The earliest literature of Buddhism is divided into two parts or "baskets": The *Vinaya*, the rules and regulations of the monastic discipline, including a history and commentary on this discipline; and the Dharma,[2] later termed *Sūtra*, a collection of discourses which explain the Dharma, that is to say, everything that directly or indirectly concerns the path to salvation—a little moral law (powerless though it is to definitively deliver one from suffering), and above all the Eightfold Path, the methods of contemplation and of meditation which lead to the definitive deliverance from suffering, that is to Nirvāṇa. This is the essential thing, for "the sole taste of the Good Law is the taste of deliverance."

The *Sūtra* or Dharma cannot be practiced exclusively. One effectively combats desire and hatred (*lobha, dveṣa*) only by destroying ignorance (*moha*); the moral law presupposes *samyagdṛṣṭi* or correct view with respect to the existence and retribution of action. Even more so, the elimination of the defilements and their most minute traces, indispensable to liberation from the round of rebirth, presupposes penetrating illumination into the nature of things, their accidental and transitory character. The sūtras always contained, we can believe, much psychology and ontology.[3] When catechesis developed, numerous discourses of the Buddha were edited, which contained enumerations, filled with glosses, of technical terms. These are what the early tradition calls *mātṛkās* or indices.[4] The *Aṅguttara*[5] and *Dīgha* 33–4, where these categories are arranged according to the increasing number of their terms, have preserved for us an early type of this literature. [One of the most notable *mātṛkās* is the *Saṅgītisuttanta*. The Pāḷi Canon has made a sūtra of this text and places it in the *Dīgha*. Under the name of *Saṅgītiparyāya*, this *mātṛkā* takes its place among the seven canonical Abhidharma texts of the Sarvāstivāda.][6]

One school, more famous than the others, and which was perhaps the first to constitute standardized baskets of *Vinaya* and of *Sūtra*, was the school of the Pāḷi language, also the first to compile a third basket. The first catechism had been incorporated into the *Sūtra*. The name *Abhidharma* was given to the new, more systematic, catechisms. It was a name which designated a special manner of presenting the Dharma and the authenticity (if not historical, at least doctrinal) of these texts came to be affirmed and they were grouped into a "basket" placed on the same level as the baskets of *Vinaya* and *Sūtra*. [For a discussion of the authenticity of the *Abbidhammapiṭaka*, see for example *Atthasālinī*, p. 35.] "Let it, then, be clearly understood," says Mrs. Rhys Davids, "that our present knowledge of such philosophy as is revealed in the Buddhist Pāḷi canon would be practically undiminished if the whole of the *Abbidhammapitaka* were non-existent . . . The burden, then, of Abhidhamma is not any positive contribution to the philosophy of early Buddhism (?), but analytic and logical and methodological elaboration of what is already given . . . The chief methods of that (=Abhidhamma) training were: first, the definition and determination of all names or terms entering into the Buddhist scheme of culture; secondly, the enunciation of all doctrines, theoretical and practical, as formulas, with coordination of all such as were logically interrelated; and finally, practice in reducing all possible heterodox positions to an absurdity . . ."[7] Nevertheless, the word Abhidhamma takes on a higher scope, which we can understand by example. The prohibition against drinking alcohol is a precept of the *Vinaya*; but to examine the transgression of alcohol as a transgression of nature or a transgression of disobedience is to bring pure theory to play upon the *Vinaya*, to "refined the *Vinaya*, and this is what is called Abhivinaya. In the same way, the Abhidharma did not remain a stranger to scientific research and philosophy; it concerns itself with questions whose relationship with the Dharma properly so-called are quite loose. This tendency is very much accentuated in the latest of the Pāḷi Abhidhamma treatises, the *Kathāvatthu*, which tradition dates from the Council of Aśoka.[8] This work is an account of heresies, and fixes their positions very clearly with respect to a mass of purely speculative points: in this work one can verify the long work of exegesis of which the *Sūtra* had been the object.

The Pāḷi Abhidhamma does not form part of the ancient patrimony common to all the sects—which is not to say that it is Singhalese! Whereas all the soundings carried out in the canonical literature of purely Indian Buddhism reveals to us some *Vinayas* and sūtras that have developed out of the Pāḷi literature, or which have a close connection with this literature, no one has yet discovered the presence of any "prototypes" of the Pāḷi *Abhidhammas*.[9]

In any case, according to the tradition itself, the *Kathāvatthu* belongs in its own right to a certain philosophic school, the Vibhajjavādins, "the followers of distinction."[10] To the old question, discussed in the sūtras, "Does all exist?",[11] these philosophers answered by distinguishing (*vibhajya*): "The present, and the past which has not yet brought forth its result exist; the future and the past which have brought forth their result do not exist.[12]

To this school there is opposed—from ancient times, we may believe—the school of "all exists," Sarvāstivāda, (Sarvāstivādinas, Sabbatthivādino). This school—which also formed a sect, which had a special *Vinaya* and its own canon, and which was Sanskritized[13]—"carved out" the Dharma. In addition to "casuists," *vinayadharas*, they had "philosophers," *ābhidhārmikas*. [Their Devasarman, the proponent of the existence of the past and the future, was opposed to Mu-lien or Moggaliputta.] A long work, with regard to which we are little informed,[14] led to the redaction of numerous works among which are the seven books of the *Abhidharma, Treatises* (*śāstra*) or *Works* (*prakaraṇa*), the *Jñānaprasthāna* and its six "feet" (*pāda*), the *Dharmaskandha*, etc. There were philosophies which came out of this first level of wisdom literature.[15] But the speculative work continued and, towards the end of the first century of our era (Council of Kaniṣka),[16] a commentary was written on the *Jñānaprasthāna*: the *Vibhāṣā*, a collective work which gives its name to all the masters who adopted it. The Vaibhāṣikas are the philosophers who refer to the *Vibhāṣā* (Watters, i.276). The center of the school appears to have been Kaśmīr, even though there were Sarvāstivādins outside of Kaśmīr,—Bahirdeśakas, "masters from foreign lands"; Pascattyas, "Westerners [relative to Kaśmīr]"; Aparāntakas, "masters from the western borders"—and some Kaśmīris who were not Vaibhāṣikas.

The Sarvāstivādins and the Vaibhāṣikas believed that the Abhidharmas were the word of the Buddha. But there were masters who did not recognize the authenticity of these books. When they were obliged to observe that there is no "basket of the *Abhidharma*" outside of the Abhidharmas of the Sarvāstivādins but that each one of them knew that the word of the Buddha was embraced within three "baskets," they answered that the Buddha taught the *Abhidharma* in the *Sūtra* itself—which is quite true. They recognized only the authority of the *Sūtra*, and took the name of Sautrāntikas.[17]

But we should not be mistaken with respect to their attitude. Even though formally opposed to some of the theses of the *Vibhāṣā* and of the Vaibhāṣikas, the Sautrāntikas had a modern enough speculation and perhaps a Buddhology. They did not systematically combat their opponents, who were, without doubt, their predecessors. They admitted everything from the system of the Vaibhāṣikas which they had no formal reason to deny.

Such is, at least—to speak with greater prudence,—the attitude of our author, Vasubandhu.[18]

His work, the *Abhidharmakośa*, a collection of approximately six hundred verses, describes itself as "a presentation of the *Abhidharma* as taught by the Vaibhāṣikas of Kaśmīr." This is not to say that Vasubandhu is a Vaibhāsika; neither is he a Sarvāstivādin. He has evident sympathies for the Sautrāntikas, and utilizes the opinions of the "early masters"—namely "the Yogācārins, the chief among them being Asaṅga"—but without doubt, in his own mind, the system of the Vaibhāṣikas is indispensable: the Vaibhāṣikas are "the School." One does not find anywhere else a body of doctrine as organized or as complete as theirs. Nevertheless they are sometimes in error, and on important points too. Vasubandhu completes his collection of technical verses, an impartial presentation of the Vaibhāṣika system, with a prose commentary, the *Abhidharmakośa-bhāṣyam*, wherein his personal opinions, objections, and the opinions of diverse schools and masters are found presented among numerous theses rejected by the School.[19] We know that Vasubandhu was, in his turn, combated and refuted by orthodox Vaibhāṣikas.

But it matters little to us whether he is always right! The essential thing, for us as for the masters who followed him, is that his book and his *bhāṣyam* are truly a treasure (*kośa*).

***

From the point of view of dogmatics the *Abhidharmakośa*, with the *Bhāṣyam*, is perhaps the most instructive book of early Buddhism (the Hīnayāna). It renders a great service in the study of canonical philosophy and in the study of scholasticism properly so-called.

It would be very wrong to say that we do not know the philosophy of canonical Buddhism: we know its essentials, its principle teachings, its major affiliations, and many of its details. But the history of this philosophy, its origins and development, is less clear: even though we can imagine that Buddhism, like the Buddha himself, took many steps at its birth, and these in all directions. But it is fair to say (and encouraging to repeat) that if the history of the canonical philosophy has not yet been done, the image that scholars such as Rhys Davids and Oldenberg have given of this philosophy either remains definitive or calls for but light retouching. We may believe, however, that we do not fully know any part, because we so imperfectly know the scholasticism which certainly enriched it and perhaps deformed it, but which certainly unfolded within it; which moreover should be, by its methods and its tendencies, completely parallel to the early speculation from whence the canonical philosophy itself arose. This philosophy is made up of the earlier strata of a speculation which continues within scholasticism proper, Pāḷi as well as Sanskrit.

The impression of ignorance is very strong when we attempt to read early works such as the *Dhammasaṅgaṇi* or the *Kathāvatthu*; or when, with some rigor, we attempt to determine the sense of the sūtras themselves, word for word (*avayavārtha*). How many terms the exact significance of which escape us! It is easy and often correct to observe that these terms originally did not have a precise meaning; that the general orientation of Buddhist thought alone merits our interest; that, if we were to ignore precisely the four *dhyānas* and the four *ārūpyasamāpattisā, vitarka* and *vicāra, rūpa*, the "fruits" and the "candidates for these fruits," we nevertheless have a sufficient idea of the major purport of and the methods leading to holiness within Buddhism; and that it is the candidates for these fruits who should preoccupy themselves with the details of the Eightfold Path rather than Western historians. Some think that scholasticism is not interesting; that, throughout Buddhist history, it remains alien to religion proper, as with the early doctrine. This is wrong: *iti cen na sūtravirodhataḥ*, "If you think thus, no, for this is in contradiction with the *Sūtra*!" Buddhism was born complicated and verbose; its scholastic classifications are often pre-Buddhist; it is our good fortune to be able to examine them up close, in sources more ancient than Buddhaghosa; and the *Abhidharmakośa* bestows this good fortune upon us in the measure in which we have the courage to be worthy of it.

An example of this is given by the Buddhists themselves. The *Abhidharmakośa* has had a great destiny: "This work . . . had an enormous influence. From the time of its appearance, it became indespensable to all, friend and foe, we are told; and there is reason to believe this, for the same fortune followed it everywhere, first in China with Paramārtha, and Hsüan-tsang and his disciples, and then in Japan, where to this day specialized Buddhist studies begin with the *Kośaśāstra*."[20]

The author assures us that we will find in his book a correct summary of the doctrine of the Vaibhāṣikas; but, however close may be his dependence on earlier Abhidharma masters, we may believe that he improves upon what they have said. When the *Kośa* has been read, the earlier works of the Sarvāstivādins, the *Abhidharmas* and the *Vibhāṣā*, undoubtedly lose part of their practical interest. Though the Chinese have translated these works, the Tibetan Lotsavas did not think it proper to put these works into Tibetan (with the sole exception of the *Prajñapti*[21]), doubtless because the *Abhidharmakośa*, in accord with the resolution of Vasubandhu, constitutes a veritable *summa*, embracing all problems—ontology, psychology, cosmology, discipline and the doctrine of action, the theory of results, mysticism and sanctity—and treating them with sobriety and in clear language, with all the method of which the Indians are capable. After Vasubandhu, the Northern Buddhists—whichever school they belonged to, and whether or not they adhered to the Mahāyāna—learned the elements of Buddhism from the *Kośa*. All schools, in fact, are in agreement with respect to a great number of fundamental items, the same admitted by Pāḷi orthodoxy, and the same, we may add, which are often subjacent to the sūtras themselves. These items, which the Vaibhāṣikas have elucidated, are nowhere so wisely presented as in the *Abhidharmakośa*. This sufficiently explains the reputation of the author and the popularity of the book.

If Vasubandhu is an excellent professor of Buddhism, of Buddhism without epithet of sect or school, he furthermore renders us a precious service by initiating us into the systematic philosophy of these schools. He constructs before us the spacious edifice of Vaibhāṣika dogma; he shows us its flaws; he explains what the Sautrāntika says, what the Vaibhāṣika answers, and what he himself thinks. Like many philosophical treatises, and like the best of them, the *Abhidharmakośa* is a creature of circumstances, written *sub specie aeternitatis*. We find in it many proper names, and many allusions to contemporary debates.[22] This is not a dull book.

We also find in it a great number of quotations which are shortened elsewhere. Because of this, the *Kośabhāṣyam* is a precious testament for the study of the earlier literature.[23] Its quotations add to the numerous fragments of the Sanskrit canon which the sands of Turkestan have given us or which have been discovered under the modernist prose of the *Divyāvadāna* and the sūtras of the Great Vehicle. These bear most often on texts of a doctrinal order, and we become clear with respect to the doctrinal, if not the historical, relationships of the canons.

***

For a long time the importance of the Abhidharma has been recognized by European scholars, initially by Burnouf. Let us see why the study of this work has been deferred for such a long period of time.

The work of Vasubandhu is made up of two distinct parts: the *Abhidharmakośa* or the *kārikās*, a collection of approximately six hundred verses; and their commentary or *bhāṣyam*.

And of the vast exegetical literature that fills eight volumes of the Tibetan canon, the Nepalese scribes have preserved only a single document for us, a commentary on the *Bhaṣya* by Yasomitra, the *Abhidharmakośavyākhyā*, which bears the name of *Sphuṭārthā*, "of clear meaning."

This commentary by Yaśomitra is not a complete commentary. It occasionally quotes the stanzas of Vasubandhu, and it elucidates such and such a passage of the *Bhāṣyam*, indicating the passage in question by the first words of that passage, following the general usage of commentators. "The subject itself," says Burnouf, "is difficult to follow because of the form of the commentary, which detaches each word from the text, and develops it or argues with it in a gloss which ordinarily is very long. It is only very rarely possible to distinguish the text from among those commentaries in the midst of which it is lost." Let us add that Yaśomitra passes over in silence everything that appears easy to him or without interest, and he plunges the reader *ex abrupto* into discussions of items and "positions" which are not indicated. In the First Chapter, he explains nearly every word of the text. Elsewhere he applies himself only to the points with respect to which there is something important to say.

The commentary of Yaśomitra is thus, as Burnouf says, "an inexhaustible mine of precious teachings" (*Introduction*, p. 447); we read thousands of interesting things in it; but it is, by itself, a very ineffective instrument for the study of the *Abhidharmakośa.*

This is why this work has been neglected for such a long time. Or, better, why, even though it solicited the attention of many seekers, no one has yet set his hand to work on it. A knowledge of Sanskrit is insufficient; one must join a knowledge of Tibetan and Chinese to this, for until recently it was solely in its Tibetan and Chinese versions that there existed, integrally, the book of Vasubandhu, *Kārikā* and *Bhāṣyam.*

ii. Bibliography of the *Kośa.*

1. Burnouf, *Introduction*, 34, 46, 447 (its importance), 563; Wassiliew, *Buddhismus*, 77, 78, 108, 130, 220; S. Lévi, *La science des religions et les religions de l'Inde* (École des Hautes-Études, Syllabus 1892), Hastings' *Encyclopedia*, I.20 (1908); Minayew, *Recherches et Matériaux*, 1887, trans. 1894.

J. Takakusu, "On the Abhidharma Literature," *JPTS*, 1905.

Noël Péri, "A propos de la date de Vasubandhu," *BEFEO*, 1911.

De La Vallée Poussin, *Cosmologie Bouddhique, Troisiéme chapitre de l'Abhidharmakoca, kārikā, bhāṣya et vyākhyā, avec [uneintroduction et] une analyse de la Lokaprajñāpti et de la Kāraṇaprajñāpti de Maudgalyāyana*, 1914–1919; Paul Demiéville, "Review of the Kosa i–ii," *Bulletin*, 1924, 463; 0. Rosenberg, *Probleme der buddhistischen philosophie*, 1924, trans. of the work published in Russian in 1918 (the appendix contains a rich bibliography of Abhidharma literature, Chinese sources and Japanese works); Th. Stcherbatsky, 1. *The Central Conception of Buddhism and the Meaning of the Word "Dharma,"* 1923 (the first appendix is a translation of *Kośa*, v, p. 48–65 of the French translation; the second is a list of the 75 *dharmas* with substantial notes); 2. an English translation of the *Pudgalapratiṣedhaprakaraṇa* or the ninth chapter of the *Kośa*, Ac. de Petrograd, 1918.

Sōgen Yamakami, *Systems of Buddhistic Thought*, Calcutta, 1912, Chap. iii, "Sarvāstivādins." Bibliography of contemporary Japanese articles and works in Péri, Demiéville, Rosenberg, and notably in Suisai Funabashi, *Kusha Tetsugaku*, Tokyo, 1906.

2. The *Kośa* and its commentaries, Sanskrit, Tibetan, and Chinese sources.

a. *Abhidharmakośavyākhyā, Bibliotheca Buddhica, Sphuṭārtha Abhidharmakoçavyākhyā*, the work of Yaçomitra, first *Koçasthāna*, edited by Prof. S. Lévi and Prof. Th. Stcherbatsky, lst fasc., Petrograd, 1918; 2nd fasc. by Wogihara, Stcherbatsky and Obermiller, (part of the second chapter), Leningrad, 1931.

Text of the third chapter, *kārikās* and *vyākhyā*, in *Bouddhisme, Cosmologie* . . . L. de La Vallée Poussin [with the collaboration of Dr. P. Cordier], Brussels, 1914–1919.

b. Tibetan translation of the *Abhidharmakoçakārikāḥ* and of the *Abhidharmakoçabhāṣya* of Vasubandhu, edited by Th. I. Stcherbatsky, lst fasc. 1917, 2nd fasc. 1930.

3. Tibetan sources, Palmyr Cordier, *Catalogue de fonds tibetain de la Biblioteque Nationale*, third part, Paris 1914, p. 394 and 499:

a. *Abhidharmakośakaārikā* and *Bhāsya* of Vasubandhu, Mdo 63, fol. 1-27, and fol. 28—Mdo 64, fol. 109.

b. *Sūtrānurūpā nāma abhidharmakośavṛttiḥ* of Vinītabhadra, 64, fol. 109–304.

c. *Sphuṭārthā nāma abhidharmakośavyākhyā* of Yaśomitra, 65 and 66. This is the commentary preserved in Sanskrit.

d. *Lakṣaṇānusārinī nāma abhidharmakośaṭīkā* of Pūrṇavardhana, a student of Sthiramati and master of Jinamitra and Śīlendrabodhi, 67 and 68.

e. *Upāyikā nāma abhidharmakośaṭīkā* of Śamathadeva, 69 and 60, fol. 1–144.

f. *Marmapradīpo nāma abhidharmakośavṛttiḥ* of Dignaga, 70, fol. 144–286.

g. *Lakṣaṇānusāriṇi nāma abhidharmakośaṭīkā*, an abridged recension of the "Brhattika," above item d, 70, fol. 286–316.

h. *Sārasamuccayo nāma abhidharmāvatāraṭīkā*, anonymous, 70, fol. 315–393.

i. *Abhidharmāvatāraprakaraṇa*, anonymous, 70, fol. 393–417.

j. *Tattvārtho nāma abhidharmakośabhāṣyaṭīkā* of Sthiramati, 129 and 130.

4. *Abhidharmakośaśāstra*, of Vasubandhu, trans. by Paramārtha in the period 564–567, Taishō volume 29, number 1559, p. 161–309; trans, by Hsüan-tsang, 651–654, Taishō volume 29, number 1558, p. 1–160.

The references in our translation are to the edition of Kyokuga Saeki, the

Kandō Abidatsuma Kusharon (Kyoto, 1891), the pages of which correspond to those of the Ming edition, a remarkable work which notably contains, in addition to interesting notes of the editor, copious extracts 1. from the two major Chinese commentators, 2. from the *Vibhāṣā*, 3. from the commentary of Saṃghabhadra, and 4. from the work of K'uei-chi on the *Triṁśikā*.

5. Among the Chinese commentaries on the *Kośa*:

a. Shen-t'ai, the author of a *Shu*: the *Chü-she lun shu*, originally in twenty Chinese volumes, today only volumes 1, 2, 4, 5, 6, 7, and 17 are extant; *Manji Zoku-zōkyō*- I.83.3–4.

b. P'u-kuang, the author of the thirty-volume *Chü-she lun Chi*; *TD* 41, number 1821.

c. Fa-pao, the author of a thirty-volume *Chü-she lun Shu*; *TD* 41, number 1822.

Two other disciples of Hsüan-tsang, Huai-su and K'uei-chi, have written commentaries on the *Kośa* which are lost. P'u-kuang has also written a short treatise on the teachings of the *Kośa.*

d. Yuan-hui wrote a thirty-volume *Shu* on the *Kārikās* of the *Kośa*, a work with a preface written by Chia-ts'eng and dated before 727; this work, the *Chü-she lun sung Shu* (var. *Chü-she lun sung shih)*, is preserved in *TD* volume 41, number 1823. This *Shu* "was commented upon many times in China and very widely disseminated in Japan; it is from this intermediary text that Mahāyānists in general draw their knowledge of the *Kośa.* But from the point of view of Indology, it does not offer the same interest as the three preceding commentaries."

Hsüan-tsang dictated his version of Saṁghabhadra to Yuan-yu. There are some fragments of a commentary written by him.

6. Guṇamati and the *Lakṣaṇānsāra.*

Guṇamati is known through his commentary on the *Vyākhyāyukti*; many fragments of this commentary are quoted in the *Chos-'byuṅ* of Bu-ston, trans. Obermiller, 1931. It is mentioned four times by Yaśomitra in his *Abhidharmakośavyākhyā.*

a. Introductory stanzas: Guṇamati comments on the *Kośa*, as has Vasumitra; Yaśomitra follows this commentary when it is correct.

b. "Guṇamati and his disciple Vasumitra say that the word *namas* is declined in the fourth case. But when the word *namas* is not independent, we have the accusative. This is why this master (Vasubandhu), in the *Vyākhyāyukti*, says, 'Saluting the Muni with my head' . . ." (*Kośa, Vyākhyā*, i p.7).

c. Guṇamati holds that the *Kośa* wrongly teaches that "Conditioned things, with the exception of the Path, are *sāsrava (Kośa,* i. 4b)," for all of the *dharmas,* without exception, can be taken as an object by the *āsravas(Vyākhyā* i, p. 13).

d. On the subject of the continuity of the mental series, "the master Guṇamati, with his disciple the master Vasumitra, through affection for the doctrine of his own *nikāya,* instead of confining themselves to explaining the *Kośa,* refute it" (*Kośa,*iii. lla–b, note).

N. Péri (*Date,* 41) recalls that Burnouf mentioned (*Introduction,* 566), according to Yaśomitra, the commentary of Guṇamati. He adds: "An author very rarely quoted. His *Lakṣaṇānusāraśāstra* (Taisho 1641) forms part of the Canon, where it is classified among the Hīnayāna works. It summarizes the ideas of the *Kośa,* and then presents his own opinions on several points. The *Hsi-yü-chi,* after having listed him among the celebrated monks of Nālandā (*TD* 51, p. 924a2), tells us that he left the monastery where he had been living in order to move to Valabhī (p. 936c2)."

Taishō 1641 is only an extract of the treatise of Guṇamati, the chapter which examines the sixteen aspects of the truths (*Kośa,* vii. 13): "Do we have sixteen things or sixteen names? The masters of the *Vibhāṣā* say that sixteen names are posited because there are sixteen things. But the *sūtra-upadeśa* masters say that there are sixteen names, but only seven things; four things for the first Truth, one thing for each of the three others. In the beginning the Buddha promulgated the *Upadeśasūtra.* After the disappearance of the Buddha, Ānanda, Kātyāyana, etc., recited that which they had heard. In order to explain the meaning of the *Sūtra,* as disciples do, they composed a śāstra explaining the *Sūtra,* which is thus called a *sūtra-upadeśa.* Then the *Vibhāṣā* extracted an *upadeśa* from that which was to be found [in this *upadeśa*]; since it only indirectly comes from the *Sūtra,* it is not called a *sūtra-upadeśa.*"

Guṇamati continues as in the *Kośa,* vii.13a, "According to the first explanation, *anitya,* impermanent, because it arises dependent on causes (*pratyayādhinatvāt*)." And he comments, "Conditioned things, without force, do not arise in and of themselves . . ."

The first volume ends, "The thesis of Vasubandhu is similar to the meaning of the *sūtra-upadeśa* masters."

The second begins, "The author says, 'I am now going to give the explanation of what I believe. ***Anitya,*** impermanent, because, having arising, it has extinction. Conditioned things, having arising, and extinction, are not permanent. Arising is existence . . ."

The treatise touches on diverse points of philosophy, the absence of *ātman,* etc. In this work we encounter some very interesting notes, for example (Taishō, page 168b9), "In the Hīnayāna, the *pretas* are superior to animals; in the Mahāyāna, the opposite. In fact, the *pretas* are enveloped in flames . . ."

It is curious that the title of the work of Guṇamati, literally *Laksanānusāraśāstra*, is exactly identical to that of the book attributed to Pūrṇavardhana in the Tanjur. We have Guṇamati, a teacher of Sthiramati, and Purṇavarudhana, a student of Sthiramati.[25]

7. Sthiramati, a student of Guṇamati, defended the *Kośa* against Samghabhadra. "His commentary on the *Kośa* is mentioned many times by Shen-t'ai, P'u-kuang, and Fa-pao in their work on the same text. The precise manner in which they quote it, in which they note and discuss its opinions, causes us to believe that Hsüan-tsang may have brought it to China, and perhaps they themselves had also read it" (N. Péri, *Date*, 41). Sthiramati, the author of the *Tsa-chi*, is one of the great masters of the Vijñaptimātratā system.

There exists (Taishō 1561) a small treatise by Sthiramati (transcription and translation) entitled *Kośatattvārthaṭīkā* or *Abhidharmakośaśāstratattvārathaṭīkā*, which is doubtless an extract of a voluminous work of the same name and by the same author preserved in Tibetan (Cordier, 499).

We observed, at the beginning, the commentary on the seven points indicated in the introductory stanza of the *Kośa*.

On the wisdom of the Buddha, superior to that of the saints, the author quotes the *Kalpanāmaṇḍitikā* stanza (Huber, *Sūtrālaṁkara*), *Kośa*, i.1, vii.30; and recalls the ignorance that Mauḍgalyāyana had of the place where his mother had been reborn, *Kośa*, i.1.

In order to demonstrate the thesis of the *Kośa* that *śraddhendriya* can be impure, ii.9, the author quotes at length the sūtra on the request of Brahmā to the Buddha (setting into motion the Wheel of the Law), a sūtra briefly indicated by Vasubhandu.

The work ends with some remarks on the duration of life: The stanza says: "Among the Kurus life is always 1,000 years in length; half of this to the west and the east. In this continent, it is not set: at its end, some ten years; in the beginning, without measure" (*Kośa*, iii. 75–77), "There are, in fact, in this world, some beings who have extra meritorious actions and who make the resolution, 'May I have a long life!, without desiring more precisely, 'May I live one hundred years, ninety years, eighty years!' Or rather some venerable persons, parents and friends, say, 'May you live long!' without saying more precisely how long a time. If one makes similar vows, it is because the actions done by persons of this continent are associated with thoughts of desire. The Sūtra says, 'Know, oh Bhikṣus that the length of life was over 80,000 years under Vipaśyin, 20,000 years under Kāśyapa;

the length of life is now 100 years; few will go beyond this, and many will have less.' If the length of life is not set, why does the Blessed One express himself in this way? . . ." The treatise concludes with the well-known stanza: *sucīrṇa-brahmacarye'smin . . . (Kośa*, vi.60a).

8. Saṁghabhadra has written two works.

The first (*TD* 29, number 1562), the title of which is transcribed into Chinese as *Abhidharmanyāyanusāraśāstra*—or perhaps better as *Nyāyānusāro nāma Abhidharmaśāstram*—is a commentary which reproduces without any changes the *Kārikās* of the *Abhidharmakośa*. But this eighty-volume commentary criticizes the *Kārikās*, which present the Vaibhāṣika doctrine by noting them with the word *kila*, which means "in the words of the School"; it refutes the *Bhāṣyam*, the auto-commentary of Vasubandhu, when this work presents views opposed to those of the Vaibhāṣikas,and it corrects them when it attributes to the Vaibhāṣikas views which are not theirs.

The title of the second treatise (*TD* 29, number 1563) is not completely transcribed: *Abhidharmasamaya-hsien-śāstra or Abhidharmasamaya-kuang-śāstra*. J. Takakusu proposes *Abhidharmasamayapradīpikāśāstra*, which is not bad; however *pradīpa*, "lamp," is always *teng*, and we have for *hsien* the equivalents *prakāśa* and *dyotana*.

This is a forty-volume extract from the *Nyāyānusāra*, from which all polemic is excluded and which is thus a simple presentation of the system (*samaya*) of the *Abhidharma*. It differs from the *Nyāyānusāra* by the presence of a rather long introduction, in seven stanzas and prose, and also by the manner in which it treats the *Kārikās* of Vasubandhu: these *Kārikās* are either omitted (ii.2–3) or corrected (i.11, 14) when they express false doctrines or when they cast suspicion on true doctrines by the addition of the word *kila*.[26]

Saṁghabhadra is an innovator, and K'uei-chi distinguishes the earlier and the later Sarvāstivādins, *Siddhi*, 45 (theory of atoms), 65 (*lakṣaṇas* of "conditioned things"), 71 (the *viprayukta* called *ho-ho*), 147 (*vedanā*?), and 311 (divergent Sarvastivadins, on *adhimokṣa*).

***

(Additions to the Bibliography, by Hubert Durt.)

The following titles are editions of texts and works related to the *Abhidharmakośabhāṣyam*, which have appeared in print since the first appearance of de La Vallée Poussin's French translation (1923–1931).

Sanskrit:

Gokhale, V.V., *The Text of the Abhidharmakośakārikā of Vasubandhu, Journal of the Bombay Branch, Royal Asiatic Society*, n.s., vol. 22, 1946, p. 73–102.

Pradhan, P., *Abhidharm-Koshabhaśya of Vasubandhu*, Tibetan Sanskrit Works Series, vol. viii, K.P. Jayaswal Research Institute, Patna, 1967; 2nd edition, revised with introduction and indices, by Dr. Aruna Haldar, 1975.

Shastri, Swami Dwarikadas, *Abhidharmakośa & Bhāṣya of Acharya Vasubandhu with Sphutārthā Commentary of Ācārya Yaśomitra*, Part I (I and II *Kośasthāna*), critically edited, Bauddha Bharati, Varanasi, 1970.

Wogihara, Unrai, *Sphuṭārthā Abhidharmakośavyakhya*, 2 vols., Tokyo 1933–1936; photomechanical reprint edition, Tokyo, 1971.

Tibetan:

Otani University, *The Tibetan Tripiṭaka*, Peking Edition, vol. 115 (number 5590), to Vol. 119 (number 5597), Suzuki Research Foundation, Tokyo, 1962.

Chinese:

Takakusu, J.K. Watanabe, *The Tripiṭaka in Chinese*, vol. 29 (numbers 1558 to 1563), The Taishō Issai-kyō kankō kwai, Tokyo 1926.

Otani University, *Index to the Taishō Tripiṭaka*, no. 16, Bidon-bu III (vol. 29), Research Association for the Terminology of the Taishō Tripitaka, Tokyo, 1962.

Funabashi, Suisai and Issai Funabashi, *Kandō Abidatsuma Kusharon Sakuin*, Kyoto, 1956. This index is based on the Chinese version of Kyokuga Saeki—the Chinese version used by de La Vallée Poussin—, the *Kandō-bon Kusharon*, in thirty volumes,Kyoto, 1887.

iii. The Date of Vasubandhu. The Former Vasubandhu.

We shall not undertake here a bibliography of Vasubandhu. But his treatise, the *Pratītyasamutpādavyākhyā* (Cordier, iii. 365), calls for the attention of the reader of the *Kośa*. G. Tucci has published some fragments of this work (*JRAS*. 1930, 611–623) where the twelve links in the chain are explained in detail, with numerous quotations from scriptures. G. Tucci also proposes to publish the *Trisvabhāvakārika*[27] and some parts of the commentary to the *Madhyāntavibhāga*.

Concerning the "definition of *pratyakṣa* by Vasubandhu," *vāsubāndhava pratyakṣalakṣaṇa*, known through the *Tātaparyaṭikā, 99,* and the *Vādavidhi* attributed to Vasubandhu, see the articles by G. Tucci, A.B. Keith, R. Iyengar, JRAS. 1929, 473; *Ind. Hist. Quarterly*, 1928, 221; 1929, 81; Stcherbatski, *Logic*, ii.161,382; G. Tucci, *Maitreya [nātha] et Asanga,* 70–71, and finally *Pramāna-*

samuccaya, chap. i, by R. Iyengar, pp. 31–35. It appears that Dignāga denies the authorship of the *Vādavidhi* to Vasubandhu,in spite of universal opinion, and the *Ṭīkā* quotes *Kośa* ii.64, which contradicts the above-mentioned definition of *pratyakṣa*. There are also numerous passages of the *Vyākhyayukti* in the *Chos-'byuṅ* of Bu-ston (above p.16).

Wassiliew, Buddhismus, 235 (1860): "Life of Vasubandhu."

Kern, Geschiedenis, trans. Huet, ii.450.

S. Lévi, *JA.*, 1890, 2.252; *Theatre indien*, 1890, i.165, ii.35; "Donations religieuses des rois de Valabhī" (*Htes Etudes*, vii, p. 97); "Date de Candragomin," *BEFEO.*, 1903, 47; *Sūtrālaṁkāra*, trans. preface, 2–3, 1911.

Bühler, *Alter der indischen Kunst-Poesie*, p. 97, 1890.

J. Takakusu, "Life of Vasubandhu," *T'oung-pao*, 1904; "A Study of Paramārtha's Life of Vasubandhu and the date of Vasubandhu," *JRAS.*, 1905; "*Sāṁkhyakārikā*," *BEFEO*, 1904.

Wogihara, *Asaṅga's Bodhisattvabhūmi*, 14, Strasbourg thesis, Leipzig, 1908.

Noël Péri, "A propos de la date of Vasubandhu," *BEFEO.*, 1911, 339–392.

Pathak, Bhandarkar, *Indian Antiquare*, 1911 - 1912 (V. Smith, *History*, 3rd edition 328, 4th edition, 346).

B. Shiiwo [Benkyō Shiio], Dr. Takakusu and Mr. Péri on the date of Vasubandhu (270-350), *Tetsugaku Zasshi*, Nov.-Dec. 1912.

Winternitz, *Jeshichte*, ii.256 (1913), iii.693 (1922).

H. Ui, "On the Author of the *Mahāyānasūtrālaṃkāra*," *Z. für Ind. und Iranistik*, vi.1928, 216–225.

A group of articles, many of which are summaries of articles written in Japanese, in *Mélanges Lanman* (Indian Studies in Honor of Charles Rockwell Lanman), 1929; J. Takakusu, *Date of Vasubandhu, the Great Buddhist Philosopher*; T. Kimura, *Date of Vasubandhu Seen from the Abhidharmakośa*; G. Ono, *Date of Vasubandhu Seen from the History of Buddhistic Philosophy*; H. Ui, *Maitreya as an Historical Personage*. Further, mention of the opinions of B. Shiiwo, S. Funabashi, E. Mayeda, S. Mochizuki.

"H.P. Sastri pointed out the historicity of Maitreyanātha from the colophon of the *Abhisamayālaṁkārakārikā*, which is a commentary, from the Yogācāra point of view, on the *Pañcaviṁśatisāhasrikā-prajñā-pāramitā-sūtra* by Maitreyanātha" Kimura, *Origin of Mahāyāna Buddhism*, Calcutta, 1927, p. 170).

The date of Vasubandhu is bound to that of Asaṅga, his brother. Now some parts of the *Yogaśāstra*, the work of Asaṅga, were translated into Chinese in 413–421, and in 431. However, the opinion is accepted among Japanese scholars that the works attributed to Asaṅga, writing under the inspiration of the future

Buddha Maitreya, are in reality the works of a master Maitreya, an *ācārya,* "an historical personage." This thesis permits us to strip Asaṅga of one part of the library of which we thought he was the pious redactor, and to place him, along with his brother Vasubandhu, toward the middle or end of the 5th century, or—why not?—towards the 6th century. "If a scholar named Maitreya is found to be the author of those works hitherto attributed to Asaṅga, then the date of the latter ought to be shifted later, at least by one generation, if not more. The ground for an earlier date for Vasubandhu should give way altogether" (Takakusu, *Mélanges Lanman*, 85).

H. Ui, in *Philosophical Journal of the Imperial University, Tokyo,* number 411, 1921, takes into account the arguments, developed afterwards in his *Studies of Indian Philosophy*, i.359, summarized in *Mélanges Lanman.* These arguments appear to be weak and, to my mind, non-existent (*Note bouddhique*, xvi, *Maitreya et Asaṅga*, Ac. Royale de Belgique, January 1930). I do not think that they gain any force from the observations of G. Tucci ("On some aspects of the doctrines of Maitreya-[nātha] and Asaṅga," *Calcutta Lectures*, 1930). The tradition of the Vijñaptimātrāta school establishes, as Tucci observes, the lineage Maitreya-nātha-Asaṅga-Vasubandhu, but Maitreyanātha is not the name of a man, but rather "He who is protected by Maitreya"; *nātha* is a synonym of *buddha*, or more precisely of *bhagavat.*[28] The commentary of the *Abhisamayālaṁkāra* (p. 73 of the Tucci edition) gives to Maitreya the title of *bhagavat* in one place where he explains how "Asaṅga, in spite of his scriptural erudition and his insight (*labdhādhigamo'pi, Kośa*, viii.39), did not understand the *Prajñāpāramitā* and lost heart. Then the Bhagavat Maitreya, for his sake (*tam uddiśya*) explained the *Prajñāpāramitā* and composed the treatise which is called the *Abhisamayālaṁkārakārikā.*" It is with the title of the Maitreyanātha that Śāntideva designates the saint who, in the *Gaṇḍavyūha*, explains to the pilgrim Sudhana the virtues of "the Bodhi mind" (*Bodhicaryāvatāra*, i.14, Rajendralal Mitra, *Buddhist Nepalese Literature*, 92). If the School holds as sacred, as *āryā deśanā*, the treatises of Asaṅga, it is because the Bhagavat Maitreya has revealed them. That the Tibeto-Chinese tradition varies in its attributions, sometimes naming as author a revealing deity, sometimes an inspired master, does not pose any difficulty.

***

The biography of Vasubandhu (by Paramārtha) is not without its difficulties. The *Kośa* excited the criticism of Saṁghabhadra who, in his large *Nyāyānusāra*, brings up innumerable heresies of a Sautrāntika character which mar the work of

Vasubandhu. We are told that Vasubandhu refused to enter into controversy: "I am now already old. You may do as you please" (Takakusu's version). But we are also assured that Vasubandhu was then converted to the Mahāyāna by his brother Asaṅga, that he decided to cut out his tongue in order to punish it for not confessing the Mahāyāna earlier, and, more wisely, that he wrote numerous treatises wherein the doctrines of the Mahāyāna were brilliantly elaborated.

Yaśomitra, the commentator on the *Kośa*, says that the expression *pūrvācāryās*, "former masters," of the *Kośa*, designates "Asaṅga, etc." (*āsangaprabhṛtayas*). N. Péri thinks that Yaśomitra means to designate the school of the Pūrvācāryas by their most illustrious name, and that the text does not imply that Asaṅga is in fact *pūrva* relative to Vasubandhu (see my *Cosmologie bouddhique*, p. ix).

The *Kośa* was only translated in 563, whereas the work of Dharmatrāta, an imperfect draft of the *Kośa*, was translated in 397–418, 426–431, and 433–442. Takakusu observes, "If the *Kośa* had existed, why did so many translators linger over the book of Dharmatrāta? (*Mélanges Lanman*). And it is difficult to give a pertinent answer to this question.[29]

But it appears almost impossible to believe that Paramārtha the biographer of Vasubandhu and first translator of the *Kośa*, arriving in China in 548, erred when he made the author of the *Kośa* the contemporary and the brother of Asaṅga. It is a hopeless hypothesis to identify the brother and the convert of Asaṅga with the former, or earlier, Vasubandhu.

One should admit the existence and the "Abhidharmic" activity of an earlier Vasubandhu. The problem, which I have taken up in the preface to *Cosmologie bouddhique* (above, p.6), has been taken up again by Taiken Kimura, "Examen lumineau de l'Abhidharma" (contents in *Eastern Buddhism*, iii, p.85), fifth part: "On the sources of the *Kośa*." We can see a summary of his conclusions in *Mélanges Lanman*. Subsequently, see *Note Bouddhique* xvii, Acad. de Belgique: "Vasubandhu l'ancien."

Yaśomitra, in three places (*Kośa*, i.13, iii.27, iv.2–3), recognizes in a master refuted by Vasubandhu the author of the *Kośa* (and a disciple of Manoratha according to Hsuan-tsang), a "Sthavira Vasubandhu, the teacher of Manoratha,"[30] an "earlier master Vasubandhu," *vṛddhācāryavasubandhu*. P'u-kuang (Kimura, *Mélanges Lanman*, 91) confirms Yaśomitra, and designates the master in question under the name of "the earlier Vasubandhu, a dissident Sarvāstivādin master."

On the other hand, the gloss of the initial five stanzas of the treatise of Dharmatrāta, the re-edition of the *Abhidharmasāra* of Dharmaśrī,[31] attributes an edition of the same book in 6,000 verses to Vasubandhu. These stanzas and this gloss are not very clear. Kimura has studied them (*Mélanges Lanman*); I have amended his interpretation (*Note bouddhique* xvii).

iv. The Seven Canonical Treatises of the Abhidharma.

The Sarvāstivādins recognize the authority of seven Abhidharma treatises, "the word of the Buddha." Among them, the Ābhidhārmikas, "who only read the *Abhidharma* with its six feet,"[32] are distinct from the Vaibhasikas "who read the *Abhidharma*."

The *Abhidharma* "with its six feet"[33] is the great treatise of Kātyāyaniputra, entitled the *Jñānaprasthāna*, upon which the *Vibhāṣā* is a long commentary, and six treatises the order and authorship of which vary somewhat according to our sources. Following the order of *Abhidharmakośavyākhya*, there are: the *Prakaraṇapāda* of Vasumitra, *Vijñānakāya* of Devaśarman, *Dharmaskandha* of Śāriputra (or of Maudgalyāyana, according to Chinese sources), *Prajñaptiśāstra* of Maudgalyāyana, *Dhātukāya* of Pūrṇa (or of Vasumitra, Chinese sources), and *Saṅgītiparyāya* of Mahākauṣṭhila (or of Śāriputra, Chinese sources).

One should note that the Tibetans list the *Dharmaskandha* first, and the *Jñānaprasthāna* only as sixth: "The Tibetans seem to regard the *Dharmaskandha* as the most important of all." This is also the opinion of Ching-mai (664 A.D.), the author of the Chinese colophon (Takakusu, 75, 115).

Takakusu, in "On the *Abhidharma* Literature" (*JPTS*, 1905), brings together a number of details on these seven books which Burnouf was the first to list; he gives the contents of the chapters of each of them. The remarks which follow are an addition to this fine work.

a. *Jñānaprasthāna.*[34]

1. According to Hsüan-tsang, Kātyāyanīputra composed this śāstra in the monastery of Tāmasavana 300 years after the Parinirvāṇa (the fourth century).[35]

However, the *Vibhāṣā* (*TD* 26, p. 21c29), commenting on the *Jñānaprasthāna* (*TD* 26, p. 918) says, "When the Bhadanta composed the *Jñānaprasthāna*, he lived in the East, and this is why he cites as an example the five rivers that are known in the East." (*Kośa*, iii.57).

2. We know through the quotations of Yaśomitra that the chapters bore the name of *skandhaka* (*Indriyaskandhaka*, *Samādhiskandhaka*), and that the work which he is referring to was written in Sanskrit.

However, the first translation has for its title "Śāstra in eight *chien-tu*"; Paramārtha has "Śāstra in eight *ch'ien-tu*." We reminded of *khaṇḍa*, but

Paramārtha explains that *ch'ien-tu* is equivalent to *ka-lan-ta*, which is evidently *grantha*. S. Lévi thinks that *ch'ien-tu* is the Prakrit *gantho*. Takakusu concludes, "All we can say is that the text brought by Saṁghadeva seems to have been in a dialect akin to Pali . . . But this supposition rests solely on the phonetic value of Chinese ideographs."[36]

3. The *Jñānaprasthāna*, a very poorly composed work, begins with the study of the *laukikāgradharmas*.[37]

"What are the *laukikāgradharmas*? The mind and mental states which are immediately followed by entry into *samyaktvanyāma* (see *Kośa*, vi.26). There are those who say the five moral faculties (*indriyas*, faith, etc.) which are immediately followed by entry into *samyaktvanyāma* are called the *laukikāgradharmas*." The text continues, "Why are this mind and these mental states so called . . . ?"

The *Vibhāṣā*, TD 27, p. 7c1,[38] reproduces the two definitions of the *Jñānaprasthāna* and explains: "Who are the persons who say that the *laukikāgradharmas* are the five faculties? The former Ābhidhārmikas. Why do they express themselves in this way? In order to refute another school: they do not intend to say that the *laukikāgradharmas* consist solely of the five faculties. But the Vibhajyavādins hold that the five faculties are exclusively pure (*anāsrava*) (see *Kośa*, ii.9) . . . In order to refute this doctrine, the former Ābhidhārmikas say that the *lokottaradharmas* consist of the five faculties. Now these *dharmas* are produced in the person of a *pṛthagjana*: thus it is proven that the five faculties can be impure."

The interest of this commentary lies in the fact that it distinguishes the "former Ābhidhārmikas" from Kātyāyanīputra and from the *Jñānaprasthāna*.

4. One of the last stanzas of the last chapter is the *śloka* on the meaning of which, according to Vasumitra (*Sectes*, Masuda, p.57), the Vātsīputrīyas disputed among themselves: whence the separation of the four schools, Dharmottarīyas, etc.

5. But if the *Jñānaprasthāna* is the work of Kātyāyanīputra, how can the Sarvāstivādins consider this treatise as the word of the Buddha?

The *Vibhāṣā* answers this question:[39]

"Question: Who has composed this treatise, that is, the *Jñānaprasthāna*?

"Answer: The Buddha Bhagavat. For the nature of the *dharmas* to be known is very profound and very subtle: apart from the omniscient Buddha Bhagavat, who would be able to understand them and to teach them?

"[Question]: If this is the case, who in this treatise, asks the questions, and who answers?

"[Answer]: There are many opinions on this: 1. the Sthavira Śāriputra asks the questions and the Bhagavat answers; 2. the five hundred arhats ask the questions and the Bhagavat answers; 3. the gods ask the questions and the Bhagavat answers; 4. some fictive (*nirmita*) bhikṣus ask the questions and the Bhagavat answers. This is the law (*dharmatā, fa-erh*) of the Buddhas, that they should teach to the world the nature of the *dharmas* to be known. But is there no one who asks the questions? Then the Bhagavat creates some bhikṣus of correct appearance and aspect, agreeable to behold, shaven headed, dressed in robes; he causes these beings to ask the questions and he answers them . . .

"Question: If this is the case, why does tradition attribute the writing down of this treatise to the Āryan Kātyāyanīputra?

"Answer: Because this Aryan has upheld, and published this treatise in such a manner that it became widely propagated; this is why it is said to be his. But the treatise was spoken by the Bhagavat. Nevertheless, according to another opinion, this treatise is the work of the Āryan Kātyāyanīputra.

"Question: Have you not said above that no one, with the exception of the Buddha, is capable of understanding and of teaching the nature of the *dharmas*? How was the Āryan able to compose this treatise?

"Answer: Because the Āryan himself also possesses a subtle, profound, ardent, and skillful intelligence; knows well the unique and the common characteristics of the *dharmas*; penetrates the meaning of texts from the beginning to the end (*pūrvāparakoṭi*); knows well the Three Baskets; has abandoned the defilements of the Three Dhātus; is in possession of the three *vidyās*; is endowed with the six *abhijñās* and the eight *vimokṣas*; has obtained the *pratisaṁvids*; has obtained *praṇidhijñāna*; formerly, under five hundred Buddhas of the past, he practiced the religious life; he made the resolution: (In the future, after the Nirvāṇa of Śākyamuni, I shall compose the Abhidharma.) This is why it is said that this Treatise is his work. In the mass of disciples of all the Tathāgatas Samyaksaṁbuddhas, it is the law (*dharmatā*) that there shall be two great masters (*Śāstrācāryas*) who uphold (*dhātar, Kośa*, viii.38,39) the Saddharma: in the lifetime of the Tathāgata as the Āryan Śāriputra, and after his Nirvāṇa as the Āryan Kātyāyanīputra. Consequently this Āryan, by the power of his resolution, has seen what was useful to the Dharma and composed this Treatise.

"Question: If this is the case, how do you say that it is the Buddha who spoke the Abhidharma?

"Answer: The Bhagavat, when he was in this world, explained and taught the Abhidharma in different places by means of diverse theoretical presentations (lit. *vāda-patha*). Either after his Nirvāṇa or when the Bhagavat was still in this world, the Āryan disciples, by means of their *praṇidhijñāna*, compiled and brought together [these teachings], arranging them into sections. Thus Kātyāyanīputra also, after the departure of the Bhagavat, by means of his *pranidhajñāna* compiled, brought together, and composed the *Jñānaprasthāna*. Among the theoretical teachings of the Bhagavat, he established the gates of a book (*vākyadvāra*); he arranged stanza summaries, and he composed diverse chapters to which he gave the name of *Skandhaka*. He brought together the diverse teachings dealing with disparate subjects and composed a *Miscellaneous Skandhaka* out of them; the teachings relative to the *saṁyojanas*, to the *jñānas*, to *karman*, to the *mahābhūtas*, to the *indriyas*, to *samādhi* and to the *dṛṣṭis* constitute the *Saṁyojanaskandhaka*, etc. In this same way all the *Udānagāthās* were spoken by the Buddha: the Buddha Bhagavat spoke them, in diverse places for the benefit of different persons, in accord with circumstances. After the Buddha left the world the Bhadanta Dharmatrāta, who knew them from tradition, compiled them together and gave [to the groups] the name of *varga*. He brought together the *gāthās* relative to impermanence and made the *Anitya-varga* out of them, and so forth.

"The Abhidharma was originally the word of the Buddha; it is also a compilation of the Āryan Kātyāyanīputra.

"Whether the Buddha spoke [the Abhidharma], or whether the disciple spoke it does not contradict Dharmatā, for all the Buddhas want the bhikṣus to uphold the Abhidharma. Thus this Āryan, whether he knew the Abhidharma from tradition, or whether he sees and examines it by the light of his *praṇidhijñāna*, composed this treatise in order that the Good Law should remain a long time in the world . . ."

b. The *Prakaraṇa* of Vasumitra.

This is also called the *Prakaraṇagrantha*, or the *Prakaraṇapādaśāstra*: it is an important work, but little systematized (for many things have been brought together in the chapter of "The One Thousand Questions"); frequently quoted in the *Kośa* (for example, i.7, 9, ii.41, 51, 54 . . .).

On one important point it differs from classical Vaibhāṣikavāda: it ignores the *akuśalamahābhūmikas* (iii.32). Sometimes it expresses itself in terms which one must interpret with some violence to make them correct (ii.46, 52, ii.4, 41). It differs from the *Jñānaprasthāna*, v.10.

Ignorance of the *akuśalamahābhūmika* category seems to prove that the *Prakaraṇa* is earlier than the *Jñānaprasthāna*.

Sometimes the authors of the *Vibhāṣā* (p. 231c3) are unsure:

"Why does this treatise (the *Jñānaprasthāna*) say *pṛthagjanatva* and not *pṛthagjanadharma*, whereas the *Prakaranapada* says *pṛthagjanadharma* and not *pṛthagjanatva*? . . . This Treatise having said *pṛthagjanatva*, the *Prakaraṇapāda* does not repeat it; this Treatise not having said *pṛthagjanadharma*, the *Prakaranapada* says *pṛthagjanadharma*. This indicates that this treatise was composed after that one. There are some persons who say: that Treatise having said *pṛthagjanadharma*, this Treatise does not repeat it . . . ; this indicates that that Treatise has been composed after this one."

The *Prakaraṇa* does not enumerate the *indriyas* in the same order as the *Sūtra*, the *Jñānaprasthāna*, or early Pāḷi scholasticism (*Kośa*, i.48).

c. The *Vijñānakāya*.

This is a work that some Chinese sources (quoted in Takakusu) place one hundred years after the Parinirvāṇa; attributed to Devaśarman or to *lha-skyid* (Devakṣema?). Concerning its author, who has the title of arhat in Hsüan-tsang, see Wassiliew in Tāranātha, 296, Hiouen-thsang [=Hsuan-tsang], *Vie*, 123, Watters, i.373.

The interest of this book, though small from the point of view of doctrine, is notable from the point of view of history. The first chapter, *Maudgalyāyanaskandhaka*, and the second, *Pudgalaskandhaka*, are related to two great controversies, the existence of the past and the future, and the existence of the *pudgala*.[40]

Devaśarman refutes the doctrine of Mu-lien or Maudgalyāyana: this latter denies the existence of the past and future, exactly as does Tissa Moggaliputta in the Pāḷi language ecclesiastical histories.

Here we have, from the Sarvāstivādin side, the controversy which gave rise to the council of Aśoka. According to the legend that Buddhaghosa has spread to Ceylon and to London, the king was assured that the Buddha was "a follower of distinction" (*vibhajyavādin*)—that is to say, probably, not totally accepting "the existence of all" (*sarvāstivāda*); he then charges Tissa Moggaliputta, that is to say, I believe, our Mu-lien, to preside over a council where only the opponents of the existence of the past and the future were admitted.[41]

There is not a very close relationship between the *Maudgalyāyanaskandhaka* and the work of Tissa (*Kathāvatthu*, i.6 and following). We should not be surprised at this, since the two works represent and bring about the triumph of two opposing doctrines.

On the contrary, the *Pudgalaskandhaka* presents, together with *Kathāvatthu*, i.1, some close analogies to this text even down to an identity of phrases.

Devaśarman speaks of two masters—a follower of *pudgala* (*pudgalavādin*),[42] who admits a vital principle, a type of soul or self (*pudgala*), and a follower of emptiness (*śūnyatavādin*), that is to say a negator of the soul (*ātman*), an orthodox Buddhist who does not recognize any permanent principle.

1. The thesis of the *pudgalavādin* is formulated in terms which are partially identical to those that the *puggalavādin* of the *Kathāvatthu* employs.[43]

2. The arguments are in part the same:

a) Argument taken from the passing from one realm of rebirth to another (compare *Kathāvatthu*, i.1, 158–161).

b) Argument taken from the passing from one degree of holiness into another (*ibid.*, i.1, 221).

c) Connection between the doer of the action and the "partaker of its results" (*ibid.*, i.1, 200).

d) Is suffering "done by oneself" or "done by another"? (*ibid.*, i.1, 212).

e) Is the *pudgala* conditioned (*saṁskṛta*) or unconditioned? (*ibid.*, i.1, 127).

f) The *pudgala* is not perceived by any of the six consciousnesses; the consciousnesses arise from well-known causes, without the intervention of a *pudgala* (*Kathāvatthu, passim*).

3. The method of argumentation is the same in the Sanskrit source and in the Pāḷi source. The negator of the *pudgala* puts the follower of the *pudgala* in contradiction to the sūtras, that is to say in contradiction with himself—for the follower of *pudgala* recognizes that the Buddha has well said all that he has said.

"The *pudgalavādin* says: There is a self (*ātman*), a living being (*sattva*), a living principle (*jīva*), a being that arises (*jantu*), a being that nourishes itself (*poṣa*), a person (*puruṣa*), a *pudgala.*[44] Because there is a *pudgala*, he does actions which should bear an agreeable result (*sukhavedanīya*), a disagreeable result, or a result neither disagreeable nor agreeable. Having done these three types of actions, he experiences, accordingly, sensations which are agreeable, disagreeable, neither disagreeable nor agreeable.

"The *śūnyatavādin* asks him: Yes or no, it is the same person who does the action and who experiences the sensation?

"The *pudgalavādin* answers: No.

"Recognize the contradiction into which you fall![45] If there is a *pudgala*, and if, because there is a *pudgala*, he does actions and experiences their proper retribution, then one should say that it is the same person who does the action and who experiences the sensation: hence your answer is illogical. If you now deny that it is the same person who does the action and who experiences the sensation, then one should not say that there is a self, a living being *et cetera*. To say this is illogical.

"If the *pudgalavādin* answers: 'It is the same person who does the action and who experiences the sensation', then he should be asked: Yes or no, is what the Bhagavat says in the *Sūtra* well said, well defined, well declared, namely, 'Oh Brahmin, to say that it is the same person who does the action and who experiences the sensation, is to fall into the extreme opinion of permanence'?"[46]

"The *pudgalavādin* answers: Yes, this is well said.

"Recognize the contradiction into which you fall . . ."

The relation between the Pāḷi and the Sanskrit *Abhidharma* treatises is close. The comparison between the *Prakaraṇa* and the *Dhātukāya* with the *Dhammasaṅgaṇi* brings out, as does that of the *Vijñānakāya* with the *Kathāvatthu*, numerous evidences of the unity of this scholasticism. The controversy of the *pudgala* is, without doubt, one of the *kathāvatthus*, one of the oldest subjects of discussion. Presented in Pāḷi and in Sanskrit according to the same principles, with, often, the same arguments and striking coincidences of phraseology—clearer in Devaśarman, but more archaic, it appears to me, in Tissa—it cannot fail to clarify to a certain degree the history of the gravest conflict to agitate early Buddhism. We may be surprised that Devaśarman's *pudgalavādin* does not make anything of the sūtra on the bearer of the burden, a sūtra which is one of the principal authorities of Vasubandhu's *pudgalavādin* (*Kośa*, ix).

As for the *Kathāvatthu*, it is not imprudent to think that this book is made up of bits and pieces. Certain parts are old, other parts are suspect.

d. The *Dharmaskandha.*

Takakusa asks if the compilation of this name is the work of Śāriputra (Yaśomitra) or of Maudgalyāyana (Chinese title); but this is quite a useless concern.

This is a collection of sūtras, promulgated in Jetavana, addressed to the bhikṣus, preceded by two stanzas: "Homage to the Buddha . . . The Abhidharma is like the ocean, a great mountain, the great earth, the great sky. I wish to make an effort to present in summary the riches of Dharma which are found in it."

The author, in fact, comments most frequently on the sūtras which he quotes by quoting other sūtras: "Among these four, what is stealing? The Bhagavat says . . ."

Without any doubt, the author was a scholarly man and well informed concerning the most subtle doctrines of the Sarvāstivāda: "The Bhagavat, in Jetavana, said to the bhikṣus: 'There are four *śrāmanyaphalas*, results of the religious life. What are these four? The result of *srotaāpanna* . . . What is the result of *srotaāpanna*? It is twofold, conditioned and unconditioned (*saṁskṛta*, *asaṁskṛta*). Conditioned, that is to say the acquisition of this result and that which is acquired through this acquisition, the precepts of the Śaikṣa . . . all the *dharmas* of the Śaikṣa. Unconditioned, that is to say the cutting off of the three bonds . . ." (compare *Kośa*, vi. 51, 76).

e. The *Prajñāptiśāstra.*

a. The Tibetan *Prajñāptiśāstra* is made up of three parts: *Lokaprajñāpti*, *Karaṇaprajñāpti*, and *Karmaprajñāpti.*

The first two are described and analyzed in *Cosmologie bouddhique*, pp. 295–350.

The third is in the same style. The text is divided into chapters preceded by a summary. Here is the beginning:

"Summary: Intention, volition, past, good, object, sphere of desire, stanza, resume of actions.

"1. Thus have I heard. The Bhagavat resided in Jetavana in the park of Anāthapiṇḍada; he said to the bhikṣus, "I teach the retribution of intentional actions, done and certain, retribution in this life . . ." Thus spoke the Bhagavat.

"2. There are two actions: volition action (*cetanā karman*), and action after having willed (*cetayitvā karman*). What is the first? It is called: *cetanā, abhisaṁcetanā, cintanā, cetayitatva, cittābhisaṁskāra, mānasa karman*; this is called volitional action . . .

"3. Volitional action is past, future, present. What is past volitional action? That which is *jāta, utpanna, abhinirvṛtta . . . abhyatīta, kṣīṇa, niruddha, vipariṇata, atītasaṁgṛhīta, atītādhvasaṁgṛhīta* . . .

"4. Volitional action is good, bad, or neutral . . .

"5. Is the object of volitional action good?

"6. Volitional action is of the three Dhātus. What is of the sphere of desire and of *kāma?*

"7. A stanza in honor of the Buddha who teaches the different types of action.

"8. One action: all actions done (literally: *ekahetunā karmaṇāṁ saṁgrahaḥ karmeti*). Two actions; volition and action after having been willed. Three actions: bodily, vocal, mental. Four actions: of Kāmadhātu, of Rūpadhātu, of Ārūpyadhātu, and not belonging to the Dhātus. Five Actions: definite (=either good or bad) and neutral actions which are abandoned through Meditation, those not to be abandoned (*aheya*) . . . And so forth up to twelve."

Almost all of the theories presented in *Kośa*, iv, are treated, with long quotations from the sūtras.

Many details deserve to be mentioned. For example, "Lying arisen from ignorance (*Kośa*, iv. 68)." Asked by a hunter if he had seen the deer, one thinks,

"It is not fitting that the hunter should kill the deer," and he answers that he has not seen it (compare the story of Kṣāntivādin, Chavannes, *Cing cents contes*, i. 161). Asked by the king's army if he has seen the bandits . . . Asked by the bandits if he has seen the king's troops . . . And, above all, in the case of frivolous speech arisen from desire, "or further, through attachment to examining the word of the Buddha."

Chapter xi is interesting from another point of view. In relation to the definition of death from exhaustion of life or merit (paragraph copied by Vasubandhu, ii. 107), the story of Kāśyapa the Nude (*Saṁyutta*, ii. 19-22) is cited, with some long developments: "A short time after he left the Bhagavat, he was killed by a bull. At the moment of his death, his organs became very clear; the color of his face became very pure; the color of his skin became very brilliant." Of note also is the fact that Kāśyapa was received as an *upāsaka*: "Master, I go to the Bhagavat: Master; I go to the Sugata; Master, I take refuge in the Bhagavat, I take refuge in the Dharma and in the Saṅgha. May the Bhagavat recognize (*dhāretu*) me as an *upāsaka* having renounced killing . . ." (compare *Saṁyutta*, ii.22 and *Dīgha*, i.178).

Then: "The acquisition of *karman* is of four types. They are enumerated as in the *Saṅgītiparyāya*" Then follow three paragraphs on giving: "Four gifts: it happens that the giver is pure and the recipient is impure . . . and so forth as in the *Saṅgītiparyāya*. Eight gifts: the *āsadya* gift (*Kośa*, iv.117), and so forth as in *Saṅgītiparyāya*. Eight gifts: it happens that a person of little faith gives little, to immoral persons, for a short period of time . . ."

b. The Chinese *Prajñāptiśāstra* is incomplete. This edition, from its first part, gives only the title, "In the great *Abhidharmaśāstra*, the *Lokaprajñāpti*, or first part." And a gloss says that the Indian original is missing. There follows immediately the title of the second part: *Karaṇaprajñāpti*.

The text begins as follows: "In the *śāstra*, the question is posed: For what reason does the Cakravartin have the jewel of a woman . . . ?" In comparing the Tibetan *Kāraṇaprajñāpti*, we see that the Chinese text omits the First Chapter on the *lakṣaṇas* and on the Bodhisattva; and that the Second Chapter omits the enumeration of the jewels and discussions on the wheel, the elephant, the horse and the jewel.

The third chapter, in Chinese as in Tibetan, is made up of stanzas on the Buddha, a king like the Cakravartin, and the jewel of the Buddha: the Dharma is a wheel; the *ṛddhipādas* are an elephant. The Tibetan tells us that these stanzas are the *Śailagāthās*. This refers to an edition that departs from the *Suttanipāta*, where the single stanza 554 has two *pādas* corresponding to the Tibetan: "Śaila, I am king, sublime king of the Dharma. In the circle of the earth, I set in motion the Wheel of the Dharma; like a Cakravartin king, consider the Tathāgata as compassionate, full of pity, a Muni beneficial to the world."

The Chinese text has fourteen chapters; the last, which is meteorological (rain, etc.), corresponds closely, like the others, to the Tibetan text. This latter has four supplementary chapters: the four *gatis*, the five *yonis*, to which womb do beings of the different realms of rebirth belong, etc. It is likely that Vasubandhu had read this chapter, for his version has, like the Tibetan *Prajñāpti*, the story of the *pretī* who eats her ten children every day, the story of Śaila, of Kapotamālinī, etc. (*Kośa*, iii.9; *Vibhāṣā*, *TD* 27, p626c).

Takakusu has ingeniously supposed that the *Lokaprajñāpti*, omitted either by mistake or on purpose in the Chinese *Prajñāptiśāstra*, of which it should be the first "gate," is found in fact in the *śāstra* (Taishō 1644) entitled *Li-shih*: "Nanjio translates *Lokasthiti* (?)*-abhidharmaśāstra*. But *li* signifies constructing, establishing, and is practically equivalent to *shih-she* or *prajñapti*." Thus Takakusu translates *Lokaprajñāpty-abhidharmaśāstra*.

Taishō 1644 exhibits the characteristics of a sūtra. Some editions precede the title with the words, "Spoken by the Buddha."

The text begins: "As the Buddha Bhagavat, the Arhat, said, 'Thus have I heard.' The Buddha resided in Śrāvastī, in the monastery of the upāsikā Mṛgāramātar Visākhā, with many bhikṣus, all arhats . . . with the exception of Ānanda. Then the earth shook. And Pūrṇa Maitrāyaṇīputra asks . . ." The chapters begin normally, "Then the Buddha said," "The Buddha said to the bhikṣu Pūrṇa," "The Buddha said to the bhikṣus," and end, "This is what the Buddha said; thus have I heard."

The contents of the chapters, established by Takakusu, show that, even though it treats of subjects that the Tibetan *Lokaprajñāpti* treats, Taishō 1644 has nothing in common with this *Lokaprajñāpti*. In this latter there is nothing that corresponds to the chapter on the *yakṣas* and notably to the conversion of "Sātāgira" and "Hemavata" (the stanzas of the *Hemavatasutta* of the *Suttanipāta, Uragavagga*, Taishō, p. 177). The *Lokaprajñāpti* has only a summary indication of the heavenly gardens, concerning which Taishō 1644 has some long developments. But in both works there is the battle of the *suras* and the *asuras*, the movements of the sun and the moon, the length of life, the hells, the three small and the three great calamities. Their order, however, differs.

The title of the chapters of Taishō 1644 do not give, sometimes, a precise idea of the contents of the book.

For example, in the First Chapter, we have 1. the two causes of the shaking of the earth (movement of wind, water; and the magical power of the saint who "considers the earth as small, the water as great"). 2. After two stanzas on the shaking of the earth, the Buddha says to Pūrṇa, "There are some winds named Vairambhas . . ." (*Kośa*, vi.12). In this circle of wind, there is the water and the earth whose thickness and height are fixed as in the *Kośa* (iii.45). 3. The Buddha explains the great hell called "Black Obscurity" which is found between the universes (and which is not mentioned in the *Kośa*), and the ten cold hells (*Kośa*, iii.59a-c, second note) . . . A little later, Ānanda manifests his admiration for the Buddha and his power. Udāyin reprimands him and is, in his turn, reprimanded by the Master. This is an edition of the celebrated Suttanta (*Aṅguttara*, i.228), which differs from the Pāḷi by the prophesy, "Aquatic beings are many, terrestial beings are few . . . *Samayavimukta* arhats (*Kośa*, vi.56), are many, *asamayavimukta* arhats are few, and are difficult to encounter in this world: and I declare that Ānanda will become an *asamayavimukta* Arhat."

f. The *Dhātukāya*.

1. At the beginning of this work, one finds the enumeration and the definition of the *dharmas* of the Sarvāstivādins: 10 *mahābhūmikas*, 10 *kleśamahābhūmikas*, 10 *parittakleśas*, 5 *kleśas*, 5 *dṛṣṭis*, 5 *dharmas* . . .

The *kuśalamahābhūmikas* are missing, as are the *akuśalas*.

The five *kleśas* make a strange list: *kāmarāga, rūparāga, ārūpyarāga, pratigha* and *vicikitsā*.

More curious is the list of the five *dharmas: vitarka, vicāra, vijñāna* (understood as the six consciousnesses, eye, etc.), *āhrīkya* and *anapatrāpya*.

We can imagine that this book is from the early Sarvāstivāda. 2. The second part treats of *saṁprayoga*, association, and *saṁgraha*, inclusion.

"*Vedanā*, which forms part of the *mahābhūmikas*, is associated with how many of the six *vedanendriyas* (pleasure, etc.)? With how many is it not associated? . . ." and so forth until: "Affection arisen from mental contact is associated with how many of the *vedanendriyas*? With how many is it not associated?

"That which is associated with *vedanā* is included (*saṁgṛhīta*) in what? In the mind and mental states, eight *dhātus*, two *āyatanas*, three *skandhas*. What is it that is left over? *Vedanā, rūpa, asaṁskṛta*, the *viprayuktasaṁskāras*; that is to say, eleven *dhātus* . . ."

These are precisely the type of questions that the *Dhātukathāpakaraṇa* examines: *sukhindriyam . . . kehici saṁpayuttaṁ katīhi vippayuttam* . . .? These are the same questions: *Vedanākkahandhena ye dhammā saṁpayuttā te dhammā katīhi khandhehi katīhāyatanehi katīhi dhātūhi saṁgahītā? te dhammā tīhi khandhehi dvīhāyatanehi aṭṭhahi dhātūhi saṁgahītā* (Section xii).

3. We can thus affirm the close relationship between the *Dhātukāya* and the *Dhātukathāpakaraṇa*. The first, in its second part, is only a Sarvāstivādin recension (theory of the *mahābhūmikas*, of the *viprayuktasaṁskāras* . . .) of an earlier volume of scholastic exercises on the *dharmas*.

g. The *Saṅgītiparyāya*

The *Saṅgītiparyāya* is a recension of the *Saṅgītisuttanta* which forms part of the *Dīghanikāya*.

Same *nidāna*: The Buddha at Pāvā; the death of the Nirgrantha; Śāriputra invites the monks to chant together the Dharma and the Vinaya so that, after the Nirvāṇa of the Tathāgata, his sons will not dispute them. Then follow chapters on the single *dharmas*, the pairs of *dharmas* . . . the tenfold *dharmas*. Finally the eulogy of Śāriputra: *sādhu sādhu*, by the Bhagavat, "You have well collected and recited with the bhikṣus the *Ekottaradharmaparyāya* taught by the Tathāgata . . ."

The close relationship of the Pāḷi and the Sanskrit texts do not exclude some variants. It is thus that, among the eight-fold *dharmas*, the *Abhidharma* omits the eight *mithyātvas* (number one of the Pāḷi list) and adds the eight *vimokṣas* (omitted in the Pāḷi list, but which figure in the *Dasa-uttara*). The order also differs. On the one hand *mārgāṅga, pudgala, dāna, kausīdyavastu, ārabhayavastu, puṇyotpatti, parṣad, lokadharma, vimokṣa, abhibhvāyatana*; and on the other hand *micchatta, sammatta, puggala, kusītavatthu, ārabbhavatthu, dāna, dānuppatti, parisā, lokadhamma, abhibhāyatana*. Note that *puṇyotpatti* is better than *dānuppatti*.[47]

Yasómitra and Bu-ston attribute the *Saṅgītiparyāya* to Mahākauṣṭhila; the Chinese sources attribute it to Śāriputra. Should we believe that in one recension, that known by Yaśomitra, Mahākauṣṭhila had the role that fit the Pāḷi and the Chinese texts assigned to Śāriputra?

Takakusu says that the *Saṅgītiparyāya*, in volumes 15 and 18, quotes the *Dharmaskandhaśāstra*. I have not encountered these quotations. The *Prajñāptiśastra* refers its reader to the *Saṅgītiparyāya*.

v. Some Masters of the *Vibhāṣā*.

The *Vibhāṣā* frequently quotes the divergent opinions of masters and different schools. This presentation is often followed by the opinion of P'ing or of the P'ing-chia: "The P'ing-chia says that the first opinion is the best one."

Elsewhere, as the commentators remark, "there is no P'ing-chia" (*Kośa*, iii. 14, 20, 41, *Siddhi*, 552, 690).

A good specimen of the methods of the *Vibhāṣā*: "If there is a pure *prajñā* outside of the sixteen *ākāras*" (*Kośa*, vii. 12, *Vibhāṣā*, p. 529), why does the *Vijñānakāya* not say this . . .? If not, why do the *Prakaraṇa* and the *Saṁgītiparyāya*, and even this treatise, the *Vibhāṣā*, say that . . .? And how does one explain such a sūtra? One should say that there is no pure *prajñā* outside of the sixteen *ākāras*. In this case, one understands the *Vijñānakāya*, but how does one explain the *Prakaraṇa* . . .? There are five reasons which justify this text . . ."

Among the masters of the *Vibhāṣā*, of special note are Parśva, frequently quoted, and who, along with many anonymous commentators, comments on the *Brahmajāla* (*Vibh.* 98, p. 508, but see also *Vibh.* 175, p. 881, on the Śuddhāvāsikas and 177, p. 889, on the number of the *lakṣaṇas*); Pūrṇāśa (*Kośa* iii. 28, *Vibh.* 23, p. 118b: *Śamadatta* (?), iii. 45, *Vibh.* 118c); Samghavasu (*Vibh.* 19, p. 97a, 106, p. 547a; 142, p. 732a) who recognizes only six *indriyas* in the absolute sense, the *jīvita* and the eight, eye, etc., because these six are the root of being, *sattvamūla* (*Kośa*, ii. 5); and, with respect to this, Kuśavarman, who only admits one *indriya*, the *manas*, a doctrine which leans towards the Vijñānavāda.

a. Vasumitra.[48]

1. Vasumitra is one of the great masters of the *Vibhāṣā*, and one of the leaders of the Sarvāstivādin school. His theory on "the existence of all" is, Vasubandhu says, preferable to that of the three other masters, Dharmatrāta, Ghoṣaka, and Buddhadeva (*Kośa*, v. 26).

One searches in vain in the two *Abhidharmas* (of the collection of seven) attributed to Vasumitra, the *Prakaraṇapāda* and the *Dhātukāya*, for an allusion to this theory. Tāranātha says, moreover, that the author of the *Prakaraṇa* has nothing in common with the Vasumitra of the *Vibhāṣā* (p. 68).

2. The Āryan Vasumitra Bodhisattva gives his name to a treatise (Taishō 1549). According to the preface, this was the Vasumitra who, after Maitreya, will be the Siṁhatathāgata; the Vasumitra to whom the fathers refused entrance to the Council because he was not an arhat, and who later became the president of the Council (*Hiuan-tsang*, Watters, i.271). Watters does not think that he is the great master of the *Vibhāṣā*; indeed, the thirteenth chapter of Taishō 1549, entitled "*Sarvāsti-akhaṇḍa*," does not contain any references to the system of *avasthānyathātva* of the Bhadanta Vasumitra. This is all that I dare say about this very complicated chapter.

The theory of the time periods is encountered in the second volume (p. 780b), where the following text is discussed: "The past and the future are impermanent, and even more so, the present." Why does the Bhagavat say "And even more so, the present"? Six explanations follow (among which the fifth: "In former times the length of life was 80,000 years; it will again become 80,000 years"); then: "The Bhadanta says, 'The present appears for a short period of time; the past and the future do not remain permanently, but they come and go reciprocally. This is what conforms to the sūtra.'"

The paragraph devoted to *avidyā* (p. 722) does not formulate the opinion of the author. There is only "It is said," notably the opinion of the Mahīśāsakas. Is this *ajñāna*, the five *nīvaraṇas, ayoniśomanaskāra, viparyāsa*, etc.? (See *Kośa*, iii.28). It appears, from the silence of Kyokuga Saeki, the editor of the *Kośa*, that the *Vibhāṣā* does not treat this point.

The problem of alcohol is treated on p. 786 (*Kośa*, iv.34, *Vibhāṣā*, jp. 645).

The discussion on *lābha* and *bhāvanā (Kośa*, vii.63), in which Vasumitra takes part (according to the *Vyākhyā*,) should be referred to Taishō 1549, for Vasumitra is not named in *Vibhāṣā*, p. 554b. The same remark applies to the erroneous opinion of Vasumitra on the falling away from the *nirvedhabhāgīyas, Kośa*, vi.21.

The *śloka* on the eight *aniyatas (Kośa*, ii.27) is not found in Taishō 1549.

For the discussion, "Does it happen that the *dharma* which is *hetupratyaya* of a *dharma* is not *hetupratyaya* of this *dharma*?", see Taishō 1549, p. 791a, and compare the *Jñānaprasthāna* in *Kośa*, ii.52.

On living longer than a *kalpa,* see p. 782b; *manodaṇḍa*, schism, p. 785, classical doctrines.

3. Vasubandhu (ii.44) quotes the *Paripṛcchā*,[49] and has also written a *Pañcavastuka (Vyākhyā).* The *Paripṛcchā* teaches a doctrine which is clearly Sautrāntika (that *nirodhasamāpatti* is accompanied by a subtle mind). Also, K'uei-chi (*Siddhi*, 211) says that this Vasumitra is a divergent Sautrāntika master.

As for the *Pañcavastuka*,[50] we possess a commentary, the *Pañcavastukavibhāṣā*, from the hand of Dharmatrāta (Taishō 1555). The five *vastus* are the *vastus* explained in *Kośa*, ii.55-56 (*svabhāvavastu, ālambanavastu* . . .).

This work does not appear to contain Sautrāntika opinions;[51] it is divided into three chapters, *Rūpavibhāga, Cittavibhāga,* and *Caittavibhāga.*

Vasubandhu adopts the demonstration of "seeing by the two eyes" through the argument of seeing the two moons (*Kośa*, i.43, *Pañcavastukavibhāṣā*, p. 991c), and he probably adopts the theory (i.38) that the five *vijñānas* are both of retribution and out-flowing and that the sixth is also *kṣaṇika (Pañcavastuka*, p. 933c).

The demonstration of the existence of *sukha* (*Kośa*, vi.3) is very similar to the demonstration established in the *Pañcavastuka*, p. 994c.

K'uei-chi, in his treatise on the sects (Sarvāstivādin thesis, 28), mentions the opinion of the *Pañcavastuka* on the nature of the *svalakṣaṇa* which is the object of the *vijñānas (Kośa*, i.10).

b. Ghoṣaka and the *Abhidharmāmṛtaśāstra.*

After the Council and the death of Kaniṣka, a Tho-gar or Tukhāra was invited with Vasumitra to the country of Aśmaparānta—to the west of Kaśmīr and close to Tukhāra (Tāranātha, 61)—by its ruler; he was the proponent of a theory that "all exists," and is frequently quoted in the *Vibhāṣā*; he was also the author of the *Abhidharmamāmṛtaśāstra* (Taishō 1553).

This treatise is a truly exquisite, small book, very readable (in spite of the early date of its translation, 220–265), very complete (for example, Chap. vi, on the doctrine of the *lakṣaṇas* and sub-*lakṣaṇas*, *Kośa*, ii. 45), but concise; however, we find some well-chosen details (for example, the enumeration of the fields of merit: father, mother, an old person, a sick person . . .).

The list of the *viprayuktas*, p. 970, is related to that of the *Prakaraṇa (Kośa*, ii. 35–36a): *prāpti, jāti, sthiti, anityatā, asaṁjñisamāpatti, nirodhasamāpatti, asaṁjñi-āyatana, nānādeśaprāpti* (?), *vastuprāpti* (?), *āyatanaprāpti* (?), the three *kāyas, pṛthagjanatva.*

The *Kośa* (ii.44) reproduces the essentials of a discussion between Ghosaka and the Sautrantika Vasumitra, the author of the *Paripṛcchā* (see above p. 30), on the existence of the mind in the absorption of *nirodha*. The *Vibhāṣā*, it appears, ignores the author of the *Paripṛcchā.*

Among the opinions of Ghoṣaka mentioned in the *Vibhāṣā* and mentioned again in the *Kośa*, the most notable is that "visibles are seen by *prajñā* associated with the visual consciousness," an opinion that departs from orthodoxy (*Vibhāṣā*, p. 61c, *Kośa*, i.42).

Elsewhere Ghoṣaka is very orthodox,[52] or his divergences, which are minimal, indicate a progress; for example, *Kośa*, vi. 19, 20, 78. The references iv.4, 79 and v.66 merit examination.

Vibhāṣā, p. 397b, is interesting: "Ghoṣaka says: The five *skandhas* which form part of one's own series, of the series of another, which belong to living beings and which do not belong to living beings, are "Suffering" and the Truth of Suffering. The ascetic, upon understanding (*abhisamaya*), sees only that the five *skandhas* of his own series are suffering; he does not see that the others are suffering. Why is this? Because one understands suffering under the aspect of torment : now the *skandhas* of another's series . . . do not torment his own series."

c. Buddhadeva.

S. Lévi asks (*JA.* 1896, 2, 450, compare Barnett, *JRAS.* 1913, 945) if the Buddhadeva of the *Vibhāṣā* should be identified with the Āryan Buddhadeva, a Sarvāstivādin, the Lion of Mathurā. The Sarvāstivādin Budhila mentions this same Lion who appears to be related to the Mahāsāṁghikas and who is perhaps the Fo-t'i-lo of Hsüan-tsang,[53] the author of the *Chi-chin-lun* (*Tattvasamuccayaśāstra*) used by the Mahāsāṁghikas (?) (Lévi, *ibid.*; Watters, i.82).

We will find in Konow (*Kharoshṭhī Inscriptions*, 44–49) the most recent remarks on these difficult inscriptions. There is nothing wrong with Buddhadeva being very much earlier than the *Vibhāṣā.* The Sarvāstivādins owe their name to the theory that "all exists," which Buddhadeva was probably one of the first to have explained.

In addition to his theory that "all exists" (*Kośa*, v.26), Buddhadeva is unique in maintaining that derived matter (*bhautika*) is only a mode (*avasthā*) of primary matter (*mahābhūtas*) (i.64), and that the mental states (*caittas*, sensation, ideas, volition) are only modes of the mind (*citta, vijñāna*) (ii.23, ix; *Siddhi*, 395, *Vibhāṣā*, p. 661c, p. 730b), a doctrine which connects Buddhadeva to Dharmatrāta and to the Dārṣṭāntikas-Sautrāntikas.[54]

d. Dharmatrāta.

There are at least two Dharmatrātas:

1. The Bodhisattva who compiled the *Udānavarga.* The *Vibhāṣā*, followed by the *Kośa*, quotes it to show that a work can be the "word of the Buddha" even though edited by a master. According to the preface to Taishō 212 (A.D. 399), this Dharmatrāta was the maternal uncle of Vasumitra (Chavannes, *Cinq cents contes*, iii. 297).

2. The master quoted in the *Vibhāṣā*, the proponent of a theory of "all exists" (*Kośa*, v.26) which appeared to the Vaibhasikas to be too close to the systems of the heterodox.

3. This master of the *Vibhāṣā* is also the author of an *Abhidharmasāra* which bears his name (Taishō 1552), a commentary and a new edition of the *Abhidharmasāra* of Dharmaśrī (Taishō 1550). In fact, the Dharmatrāta of the *Vibhāṣā* (p. 383b) denies the *rūpa* which forms part of the *dharmāyatana*, that is

to say, *avijñatirūpa*; the same negation, somewhat more involved, but clear nevertheless, appears in the *Sāra* (chapter on action, p. 888, see below).

4. There is nothing to prevent this same Dharmatrata from being the commentator on the *Pañcavastuka* of Vasumitra, Taishō 1555, the *Pañcavastukavibhāṣā*.[55]

e. The Bhadanta Dharmatrāta.

The *Vibhāṣā*, it appears, ignores Kumāralāta and Śrīlāta, who were the heads of the Sautrāntika school (*Siddhi*, 221, told to us by K'uei-chi). The Sautrāntika school, or, more exactly, the school which should take the name of Sautrāntika, is represented in the *Vibhāṣā* by the Dārṣṭāntikas and by two masters: Dharmatrāta, a divergent Sarvāstivādin, and the master whom the *Vibhāṣā* simply calls "Bhadanta," whom the *Vyākhyā* of the *Kośa* calls "the Sautrāntika Bhadanta" (*Kośa*, viii.9), who is at the "head of the list of Sautrāntikas" (viii.40), and who adheres to or leans toward the Sautrāntika system (i.20).[56]

Hsüan-tsang, P'u-kuang, and Bhagavadviśeṣa recognize on occasion, in the "Bhadanta" of the *Vibhāṣā*, the Sthavira or Bhadanta Dharmatrāta (*Kośa*, i.20, iv.4). Yaśomitra declares that Bhagavadviśeṣa is wrong: "Bhadanta is the philosopher that the *Vibhāṣā* calls simply by the name of Bhadanta, a philosopher who adheres to the Sautrāntika system or leans toward this system; whereas Dharmatrāta, whom the *Vibhāṣā* calls by his name, is a Sarvāstivādin, the author of one of the four theories of the Sarvāstivāda (*Kośa*, i.20)." On the other hand, "the first version of the *Vibhāṣā* gives the name of this master [Bhadanta] in transcription and precedes this, like those of the other masters, with the title of venerable" (note of N. Péri, in *Cosmologie bouddhique*, 276).

Dharmatrāta expresses some opinions on important points which clearly depart from the system of the *Vibhāṣā* and from the orthodox Sarvāstivādin system; the same may be said of Buddhadeva.

1. The Bhadanta does not admit that the eye sees: it is the visual consciousness that sees (i.42); he has a particular theory on the non-contact of atoms (Wassiliew, 279), which Vasubandhu accepts and which Saṁghabhadra discusses (i.43);[57] he admits three *caittas* (ii.23, Add.), a position which distinguishes him from the Dārṣṭāntikas; like the Sarvāstivādins, he denies that *rūpa* is *samanantarapratyaya* (ii.62); he admits the prolonged existence of *antarābhava*, against the Sarvāstivādins (iii.14); he has a particular opinion on *pratītyasamutpāda* and *samutpanna* (iii.28); he denies *avijñapti*, which is clearly anti-Sarvāstivādin (iv.4); on the four modes of *kuśala*, he has a very orthodox doctrine (iv.8); he holds to the "mortal" sin of intelligent animals (iv.97): he gives an explanation of the word *vimokṣa*

(viii.33); he mixes the *dhyānas* and the *śuddhāvāsikas (Vibhāṣā*, p. 881c); he treats the last thought of the arhat (p. 954a); on *uccheda* and *śāśvata* (p. 1003c); on the meaning of *alpa, sulabha, anavadya*, and on the praise of his disciples by the Buddha (p. 909a, and p. 900b, where he differs from Vasumitra).[58]

The Bhadanta is very clear on *vicāra-vitarka*[59] (*Vibhāṣā*, p. 744b, and p. 269, *Kośa*, ii.33 and viii.23): the author of the *Jñānaprasthāna* wants to refute what the Dārṣṭāntika says. The latter says: "There is *vitarka-vicāra* from Kāmadhātu up to Bhavāgra. Why is this? Because the Sūtra says that grossness of mind is *vitarka* and that subtlety of mind is *vicāra*: now grossness and subtlety of mind exist up to Bhavāgra." The Bhadanta says: "The masters of the *Abhidharma* say that *vitarka-vicāra* are grossness and subtlety of mind. Now grossness and subtlety are relative things and exist up to Bhavāgra. However, these masters only admit *vitarka* and *vicāra* in Kāmadhātu and in Brahmaloka. This is poorly said, this is not well said." The masters of the *Abhidharma* say, "What we say is well said, not poorly said. In fact . . ."

2. Vasubandhu (*Kośa*, vii.31) attributes to the Bhadanta Dharmatrāta (see the correction *ad* vii.31) an opinion on the power of the Bhagavat which is an opinion of the Bhadanta according to *Vibhāṣā*, p. 155c.

In the *Vibhāṣā* (p. 61c) Dharmatrāta says that visible matter is seen by the visual consciousness (*cakṣurvijñāna*): an opinion that the *Kośa* attributes to a Vijñānavādin (i.42), and which differs from that of the Bhadanta (*Vibhāṣā*, p. 62b) who says that the eye sees by reason of light and the *manas* knows by reason of the act of attention.

3. *Vibhāṣā*, p. 661c16: the *Jñānaprasthāna* wants to refute what the other masters say. In this school there are two masters, the first Buddhadeva and the second Dharmatrāta.

Buddhadeva says that *rūpa* is only the four *mahābhūtas*, that the *caittas* are *citta*. Derived *rūpa (upādāyarūpa)* is only *mahābhūtaviśeṣa*; the *caittas* are only *cittaviśeṣa*. Sūtras quoted in support of this theory: 1. "What is in the eye is solid . . ." (*Kośa*, i.35); 2. "Sam*ādhi* is *cittaikāgrya* . . ." (viii.2). How does Buddhadeva prove the existence of *dhātus, āyatanas, skandhas*? . . . The Abhidharmācāryas say, "The quoted sūtras do not have this meaning . . ."

Dharmatrāta admits the existence of derived *rūpa* apart from primary *rūpa*, and of the *caittas* apart from *citta*. But he holds that derived tangibles and the *rūpa* which forms part of the *dharmāyatana* do not exist. He thus attempts to prove the existence of the *dhātus, āyatanas, skandhas*, as does the Abhidharma system. But the derived tangibles exist separately, as do the other derived *rūpas*; but if the *rūpa* of the *dharmāyatana* does not exist, *avijñapti* does not exist (*Kośa*, i.35, iv.3).

4. *Vibhāṣā*, p. 383b: The *Abhidharma* says, "What is *rūpaskandha*? Ten *rūpāyatanas* and the *rūpa* included in the *dharmāyatana* (that is to say the *avijñapti*)." What system does it want to refute? It wants to refute the Dārṣṭāntikas, for they deny any *rūpa* in the *dharmāyatana*. And Dharmatrāta also says, "Everything that is *rūpa* is either support or the object of *vijñāna*. How could there be *rūpa* which is neither one or the other?" It is in order to refute these opinions that the above-mentioned definition of *rūpaskandha* is given. But if the *rūpa* which is included within the *dharmāyatana* is real, how can one explain what Dharmatrāta says? It is not necessary to explain it, for this is not in the *Tripiṭaka*. Or, if one should explain it, one can say . . . that the *rūpa* included within the *dharmāyatana*, arising from the *mahābhūtas* which are the object of touch, can be considered as the object of touch consciousness. Thus the declaration of Dharmatrāta is without error.

5. *Vibhāṣā*, p. 730b: Among the twenty-two *indriyas* or "organs" (*Kośa*, i.48), how many are separate things, and how many are only names? The Ābhidhārmikas say that for twenty-two names there are seventeen things, for the two sexual *indriyas* (parts of the organ of touch) and the three pure *indriyas* (combinations of faith, etc.) are not separate things (*Kośa*,ii.2, 9).

Dharmatrāta only admits fourteen things: the first five *indriyas*, the *jīvitendriya*, the *upekṣendriya*, and the *samādhīndriya* are not things. In fact the *jīvitendriya*, the vital organ, is one of the *viprayuktasaṁskāras* (*Kośa*, ii.45) and these are not real.[60] There are no sensations apart from the agreeable and the disagreeable: thus the sensation of indifference (*upekṣendriya*) is not a thing. There is no *samādhi*, concentration, apart from the mind.

Buddhadeva says that only a single *indriya* is real, namely the *mana-indriya*, the mental organ: "The *saṁskṛtas*, he says, are of two types: *mahābhūtas* and *cittas* . . ."

The index of proper names contains information, nearly complete, on the references to the Bhadanta in the *Vibhāṣā*.

vi. Some Schools of the *Vibhāṣā*.[61]

a. Dārṣṭāntikas and Sautrāntikas.

The history of this school, though long, is not yet clear. The notes of K'uei-chi (*Siddhi*, 221–224; Masuda, "Sects," *Asia Major*, ii.67; Lévi, *Dṛṣṭāntapaṅkti*, p. 97) show that Hsüan-tsang was not well informed with respect to them. Takakusu (*Abhidharma Literature*, 131) says that the *Vibhāṣā* speaks of the Sautrāntikas: rarely, in any case, for I have only found a single reference to the Sautrāntikas; we can say that the *Vibhāṣā* only knows the Dārṣṭāntikas.

We have reason to establish a relationship between this name and the book of Kumāralāta, the *Dṛṣṭāntapaṅkti.* We may ask if the Dārṣṭāntikas are characterized by the use of "comparisons," as the Tibetans say (Wassiliew, 274, according to whom Sautrāntika = Dārṣṭāntika); however, the sense of the word *dṛṣṭānta* is not proven with certainty. J. Przyluski thinks the *Dṛṣṭānta* is opposed to scripture. This way of looking at it is confirmed, I believe, by the *Vibhāṣā* (p. 782b18). It is said in traditional *Dṛṣṭānta*:[61] "He who gives alms to a person who has left *nirodhasamapātti* is endowed with an action which bears a result in this life. Why is this? There is no reason to explain this text. Why is this? Because this is neither in the *Sūtra*, the *Vinaya*, nor the *Abhidharma*, but only in the traditional *Dṛṣṭānta.* That which is said in the traditional *Dṛṣṭānta* may be true or not true. If, however, one desires an explanation of this, one should say that this alms-giver obtains a result in this life or obtains great results. The text mentions only the first alternative, because it is pleasing to people of the world."[62]

We can speak of a Dārṣṭāntika-Sautrāntika school: in looking at it more closely, the *Vibhāṣā* assigns to its Dārṣṭāntikas almost all of the theses that the *Kośa* assigns to the Sautrāntikas.

Here are the more important disagreements between the Sarvāstivādins and the Dārṣṭāntikas-Sautrāntikas.

1. The *Abhidharmas* of the Sarvāstivādins are not authoritative (*Kośa*, i.2, ii.1, vii.11).

2. The *asaṁskṛtas* do not have any real existence (ii.55).

3. The *viprayuktas* (ii.35–36) do not have any real existence: negation of the *prāptis*, of the *jīvitendriya*, etc.

4. The past and the future do not have any real existence (v.25–26).

5. The existence of the past permits the Sarvāstivādins to explain the play of causality; the *prāptis* serve the same function. Negating the past, the *prāptis*, etc., the Dārṣṭāntika-Sautrāntika school admits a subtle mind, either of the *bījas* or of *vāsanā* (perfuming), and thus takes into account the changes of the series (ii.36, 50, iv.79, ix. . . .).

6. Extinction does not have a cause; things do not have any duration (*sthiti*): the *kṣaṇa* or moment, is of a size that tends to zero (iv.2–3) (See *Rocznik*, vol. viii).

7. Notable divergence with respect to action: negation of the *avijñapti* (iv.3), of bodily action (iv.3), of the necessary character of retribution of an *ānantarya* transgression (*Vibhāṣā*, p. 359b20).

8. On the *caittas* and the *bhautikas*: opinions which depart from the Sarvāstivādin system (ii.23).

9. Explanation of the three *rāśis (Kośa*, iii.44), which exist from hell to Bhavāgra; beings having the *dharmas* of Nirvāṇa; beings not having them; indeterminate beings (*Vibhāṣā*, p. 930b15; compare the *Siddhi* and its *gotras*).

10. The body of the Arhats is pure, being produced through "wisdom" (i.4, Saṁghabhadra, p. 331b).

11. Simultaneity of the Buddha (iii.95–96).

The references which follow, complete in the index of proper names (Dārṣṭāntika-Sautrāntika), are classified according to the material in the *Kośa*.

1. The Dārṣṭāntika rejects certain sūtras: how does he pretend to the name of Sautrāntika? (Saṁghabhadra, p. 332a).

The *vijñānas*, including the *manovijñāna*, have a special object (*Kośa*, ix, *Vibhāṣā*, p. 449a16).

If the eye sees the visible (*Kośa*, i.42, *Vibhāṣā*, p. 61b19).

2. The Sthavira (=Śrīlāta) and all the other Dārṣṭāntika masters deny *ākāśa* (Saṃghabhadra, p. 347b).

Negation of *prāpti*, of *apratisaṁkhyānirodha* (*Vibhāṣā*, p. 479a19, p. 796b6, p. 931b23).

The *lakṣaṇas* of "conditioned things"—Dārṣṭāntikas, Vibhajyavādins, Saṁtānasābhāgikas (*Vibhāṣā*, p. 198a15 and foll.).

Pratyayatā is not real (*Vibhāṣā*, p. 680b27).

There is no *vipākahetu* outside of the *cetanā*, no *vipākaphala* outside of the *vedanā (Vibhāṣā*, p. 96a26).

Rūpa is not "a similar cause" of *rūpa*—the opinion of the Dārṣṭāntika according to the gloss of Kyokuga Saeki (*Kośa*, ii.52), but, according to the *Vibhāṣā* (p. 87c20), the opinion of the Bahirdeśakas.

"Among the Sautrāntikas, the Bhadanta Dārṣṭāntika holds to the separate existence of *vedanā-saṁjñā-cetanā*; Buddhadeva adds *sparśa* and *manasikāra*: the other *caittas* are only *citta*; the master Śrīlāta holds that the *asaṁskṛtas* and the *viprayuktas* have nominal existence" (Wassiliew, 281, 309, corrected).

Subtle mind in *nirodhasamāpatti* and in *asaṁjñisamāpatti* (so too the Vibhajyavādins) (*Kośa*, ii.44, viii.33, *Vibhāṣā*, p. 774a14, p. 772c21).

Negation of the reality of dreams (*Vibhāṣā*, p. 193b5).

The *caittas* arise in succession, according to the Dārṣṭāntikas and the same Bhadanta (*Vibhāṣā*, p. 493c26, p. 745a7); the mind cannot be accompanied by *jñāna* or *ajñāna* (p. 547).

Vitarka and *vicāra* in the Three Dhātus (*Kośa*, ii.33, viii.23, *Vhibāṣā*, p. 269b9, p. 744b9).

3. *Antarābhava* and *nirmita (Vibhāṣā*, p. 700a15).

Sparśa is not a thing in itself (*Vibhāṣā*, p. 149a25).

4. Arising depends on *hetupratyaya* but not extinction; the Dārṣṭāntikas as against the Ābhidhārmakas (*Kośa*, iv.2–3; *Vibhāṣā*,p. 105a27).

Negation of the *dharmāyatanarūpa* (=*avijñapti*); Dharmatrāta and the Darṣṭāntikas (*Vibhāṣā*, p. 383b16).

On the four and eight types of actions from the point of view of their determination, Dārstāntikas, or Sautrāntikas according to *Vyākhyā* (*Kośa*, iv.50–51; *Vibhāṣā*, p. 593b10): all actions can be "reversed," action in *antarābhava* (*Kośa*, iii.14), *ānantaraya*, action in Bhavāgra, action in *asaṁjñisamāpatti* (*Vibhāṣā*, p. 359b20, p. 773c29).

Whether *abhidhyā*, *vyāpāda*, and *mithyādṛṣṭi* are actions (opinion of the Dārṣṭāntikas, *Kośa*, iv.65, 78; of the Vibhajyavādinikāya, *Vibhāṣā*, p. 587a9).

5. All the *kleśas* are "bad" (Dārṣṭāntikas, *Vibhāṣā*, p. 259cll); contra, *Kośa*, v.20–21).

Anuśayana (*Vibhāṣā*, p. 110a21; *Kośa*, v.16).

In *saṁvṛtijñāna*, the *pṛthagjana* does not cut off the *kleśas* (Dārṣṭāntikas and the Bhadanta, *Vibhāṣā*, p. 264b19, p. 741c20).

The object of attachment and the *pudgala* are unreal, Dārṣṭāntikas (compare the *cittamātravāda*); the object of attachment and the *pudgala* are real, Vātsīputriyās (*Vibhāṣā*, p. 288b15 and following).

Reincarnation solely by reason of desire and hatred (*Vibhāṣā*, p. 309all)—in fact, by reason of any *kleśa*.

On the time periods (*Vibhāṣā*, p. 919b12).

6–7. Definition of the Truths (*Kośa*, vi.2; opinion of the Ābhidhārmikas, Dārṣṭāntikas, Vibhajyavādins, Ghoṣaka, Pārśva . . . *Vibhāṣā*, p. 397b4).

On *kṣānti* and *jñāna* (*Kośa*, vii.1, 20, 22; Dārṣṭāntikas, the Bhadanta, *Vibhāṣā*, p. 489b16).

Purity of the body of the Arhat (*Kośa*, i.4, iv.4; Dārṣṭāntikas, according to Saṁghabhadra, p. 331b25).

8. Doctrine of *dhyāna* (the Bhadanta, Dārṣṭāntika-Sautrāntika, *Kośa*, viii.9).

The *sāmantakas* are "good" (Dārṣṭāntikas, *Kośa*, viii.22, *Vibhāṣā*, p 832a).

Mixed *dhyāna* (*Kośa*, vi.42, 58, vii.23) explained by perfuming (Dārṣṭāntikas and Yogācārins, *Vibhāṣā*, p. 879c26; compare *Siddhi*).

Falling away from *asaṁjñisamāpatti* (Dārṣṭāntikas, *Vibhāṣā*, p. 773c29.

Nirmita is not real (Dārṣṭāntikas and the Bhadanta, *Vibhāṣā*, p. 700a15).

b. Vibhajyavādins.

They are clearly defined as "those who distinguish" and admit the existence of a certain kind of past and a certain kind of future (*Kośa*, v.22, P'u-kuang quotes *Kośa*, v.9, and Vinitadeva, *Traité sur les Sectes*).

However, the information that we possess on the Vibhajyavādins is confused: the Vibhajyavādins are the Mahāsāṁghikas, the Ekavyavahārikas, the Lokottaravādins, or the Kaukkuṭikas (K'uei-chi, *Siddhi*, 109).

1. Vasumitra, in his *Treatise on the Sects*, does not mention them. Vinītadeva, presenting his theories concerning the history of the Sarvāstivādins, makes them the seventh Sarvāstivādin school. Bhavya (the Sthavira theory) makes them a division of the Sarvāstivādins, and (the Mahāsāṁghika theory) the third original school. According to Bhikṣvagra, they are the fourth Mahāsāṁghika school.

2. The note by Kyokuga Saeki (edition of the *Kośa*, xix, fol. 14a-b).[64]

K'uei-chi, commentating on the *Siddhi* [iv.1, 35, p. 179 of the French translation], says, "Those who were called Vibhajyavādins are now called Prajñaptivādins." [This should be understood: Paramārtha, in his version of the *Treatise of Vasumitra*, has written "Vibhajyavādin," whereas] Vasumitra [in the version of Hsüan-tsang] says, "In the second century, a school called the Prajñaptivāda came out of the Mahāsāṁghikas." In connection with this, the commentator Fa-pao says, "According to these two translations, the Vibhajyavādins make up only one school [with the Prajñaptivādins"].[65] In the *Vibhāṣā*, p. 116c5, the Mahāsāṁghikas, etc., are called Vibhajyavādins [that is to say: the *Vibhāṣā* attributes to the Vibhajyavādins an opinion that we know to be the opinion of the Mahāsāṁghikas, see *Kośa*, iii.28]. Consequently the *Arthapradīpa*, p. 48, says, "The Vibhajyavādins are either some divergent Mahāyāna masters, or all the schools of the Hīnayāna are called Vibhajyavādins: they are not a definite school. Consequently, in the *Mahāyānasaṁgraha* (Taishō 1593), the Vibhajyavādins are explained as Mahīśāsakas; in the *Vibhāṣā*, as Sāṁmītiyas."[66]

3. In many texts, the meaning of the word Vibhajyavādin is clearly defined.

a. Bhavya: We call [the Sarvāstivādins] by the name of Vibhajyavādin when they distinguish (*vibhaj*) by saying, "Among these things, some exist, namely the former action whose result has not occurred; some do not exist, namely the former action whose result has been consumed, and future things."

b. *Kośa*, v. 25-26: Those who admit the existence of the present and a part of the past (namely the action which has not produced its result) and the non-existence of the future and a part of the past (namely the action which has produced its result), are held to be Vibhajyavādins; they do not belong to the Sarvāstivādin school.

c. P'u-kuang, p. 310b23 (on *Kośa*, v.25-26): They say that there is no opinion which is completely correct; that some part exists, and some part does not exist [or: in part true, in part false]: one should thus distinguish. Thus they are called Vibhajyavādins.

d. The Kāśyapīyas (Vasumitra, thesis 1 and 2) hold a clearly Vibhajyavādin position: "The action whose result has matured does not exist; the action whose result has not matured exists." Now Buddhaghosa (*Kathāvatthu*, i.8) attributes to the Kassapikas, a branch of the Sarvāstivādins, the opinion that one part of the past and future exists: this is the second Vibhajyavādin thesis of the summary of Vinītadeva. Now the Theravādin, which should be Vibhajyavādin like the Buddha, denies and refutes this.

4. Elsewhere: One calls Vibhajyavādins those who, distinguishing, admit that the *skandhas* are real, and that the *āyatanas* and the *dhātus* have nominal existence.

5. *Vibhāṣā*, p. 571c24 and elsewhere, opposes the Vibhajyavādin and the Yuktavādin.

6. Vinītadeva attributes to the Vibhajyavādins the following thesis:

a. The *pudgala* exists "absolutely"; b. the past does not exist, with the exception of the cause the result of which has not ripened; the future does not exist, with the exception of the result; the present *rigs mi mthun pa* (?) does not exist; c. *dharma* does not become an "immediate cause"; d. *rūpa* does not have a "parallel cause," as the Dārṣṭāntikas claim (*Kośa*, ii.52).

7. More notable is the note of Hsüan-tsang (*Siddhi*, 179) which associates the Vibhajyavādins and the Sthaviras with belief in *bhavāngavijñāna*.

And also: pure mind, *Siddhi*, 109–111; persistence of a subtle mind in *nirodhasamāpatti* (with the Dārṣṭāntikas), 207; see also 770.

8. References to *Kośa-Vibhāṣā*:

a. Sound is of retribution (with the Vātsīputrīyas) (*Kośa*, i.37–38a, *Vibhāṣā* p. 612c13, *Siddhi*, 190).

The body of arising (*janmakāya*) of the Buddha is "pure" (with the Mahāsāṁghikas) (*Vibhāṣā*, p. 871c2, *Siddhi*, 769–770).

b. Śraddhā, etc., are pure (*Kośa*, ii.9, *Vibhāṣā*, p. 7c3).

Life is *cittānuvartin* (*Kośa*, ii.50, *Vibhāṣā*, p. 770c6—refuted by Vasumitra).

Consequently, there is a subtle mind in *asaṁjñisamāpatti*, and in *nirodhasamāpatti* (*Kośa*, viii.33, *Vibhāṣā*, p. 772c21, p. 774a14).

c. Negation of *antarābhava* (*Kośa*, iii.10, *Vibhāṣā*, p. 356c15, p. 700a15. From whence the complicated explanation of the *antarāparinirvāyin*, *Kośa*, iii.12, *Vibhāṣā*, p. 357b9).

Pratītyasamutpāda is *asaṁskṛta*, like the Path (*Kośa*, iii.28, *Vibhāṣā*, p. 116c5, p. 479—like the Mahāsāṁghikas and the Mahīśāsakas).

d. Greed, anger, false views are "action" (*Vibhāṣā*, p. 587a9, *Kośa*, iv.65: Dārṣṭāntikas).

Definition of "good by nature" (as *jñāna*), "through association" (as *vijñāna*), "in origin" (as action of the body . . .) (*Kośa*, iv.8, ix, *Vibhāṣā*, p. 741a15).

The mind of the Bhagavat is always absorbed (*Kośa*, iv.12, *Vibhāṣā*, p. 410b26).

e. The thirst for non-existence is abandoned through *bhāvanā* (*Kośa*, v.10–11, *Vibhāṣā*, p. 138c3).

On the *viparyāsas* (*Kośa* v.9, *Vibhāṣā*, p. 536c9).

f. Definition of the Truths (*Kośa*, vi.2, *Vibhāṣā*, p. 397b4).

Comprehension of the Truths at once (*Kośa*, vi.27, *Vibhāṣā*, p. 532a).

The Arhat does not fall (*Kośa*, vi.58, *Vibhāṣā*, p. 312b9).

Forty one *bodhipākṣikas* (*Kośa*, vi.66, *Vibhāṣā*, p. 499a.4).

g. Rūpa in Ārūpyadhāto (*Kośa*, viii.3, *Vibhāsā*, p. 432a22).

Only the First Dhyāna has *aṅgas* (*Vibhāsā*, p. 813c28).

The Āryan of the fourth *ārūpya* obtains the quality of an Arhat without the aid of the Path (*Vibhāṣā*, p. 929b14). (This is thesis 12 of the Mahīśāsakas in the treatise of Vasumitra).

c. Yogācārins

Or *yoga-ācāryas*, as the Chinese reads; we also have *yogācāracitta* (*Vyākhyā* ii.49, *ad Kośa*, ii.23).

1. People who practice *yoga* or the contemplation of *yogins*;[67] (see *Kośa*, iv.4, note, and the *Vibhāṣā, passim*) they seek *nirodhasatya* (p. 534a19), practice *śūnyatāsamādhi*, p. 540cll), are disgusted with *vedanā* (Rūpadhātu) and *saṁjñā* (Ārūpyadhātu) (p. 775b3; also p. 35b25; p. 529b4; p. 832a22). The *Ratnarāśisūtra* (*Śikṣāsamuccaya*, 55) examines the obligations of the *vaiyāvṛtyakara bhikṣu*,[68] the intendent and the minister of the monastery, with respect to the *āraṇyaka*, to the *piṇḍacārika*, to the contemplative or *yogācārin bhikṣu*, to the student or *bāhuśrutye'bhiyukta*, to the preacher, *dharmakathika*.

2. Devoted to *yoga*, to breathing exercises, to *dhyāna*, etc., the *yogācārin* becomes, as the Chinese say, a "master of *yoga*," a *yogācārya*: they had theories on *prāṇāyama*, on *śūnyatāsamādhi* . . . The *Kośa*, iv.18-19, mentions a thesis of this school of meditators on *rūpa* which arises through the power of absorption.

3. [This school of meditators became a philosophical school, the Yogācāra school, when, under the influence of Maitreya-Asaṅga, it became attached to the older formula of the *Daśabhūmaka*: "The threefold world is only mind." One can indeed see the relationship between the theories of ecstasy and idealism, and we

can see how the practice of the "mindless absorption" can lead to the affirmation of a subtle mind . . . Asaṅga utilizes Dārṣṭāntika-Sautrāntika speculations.]

Below are the references in the *Kośa* to the Yogācārins:

Explaining mixed *dhyāna* (*Kośśa*, vi.42) by perfuming, (*Vibhāṣā*, p. 879c26, as do the Dārṣṭāntikas).

Related to the Sautrāntikas (*Kośa*, ii.34, *Vyākhyā*: "the opinion of the Sautrāntikas or the Yogācārins.").

The Yogācāracitta admits that an agglomeration can be formed from a single *mahābhūta*, as a piece of dry earth; from two, the same, but wet . . . (*Kośa*, ii.22, *Vyākhyā*, ii.49).

In the *yogācāradarśana*, there is a *manodhātu* which is distinct from the six *vijñānas* (*Vyākhyā*, i.40, ad i.17; compare the Tāmraparṇīyas).

(The Vijñānavādin denies that the eye sees, *Kośa*, i.42).

The Yogācāracitta defines *adhimukti* (*Kośa*, ii.24, *Vyākhyā*, ii.51).

According to the Yogācārins, the mindless absorptions are endowed with mind from the fact of the *ālayavijñāna* (*Vyākhyā* ad ii.44). Yaśomitra speaks here of the school of Asanga; the same in *Kośa*, iii.2; *Vyākhyā*, *ad* v.8 (the 128 *kleśas* of the *Yogācārins*).

(The "ancient masters" of the *Kośa*, ii.44, should be the Dārṣṭāntikas).

Elsewhere, the *Vyākhyā* explains the "ancient masters" of the *Bhāsya* as being "the Yogācārins" or "the Yogācārins, Asaṅga, etc." (*Vyākhyā* ad iii.15, iv.75, vi.4).

vii. The *Śariputrābhidharma*.

This book, Taishō 1548, is divided into four parts: *sapraśnaka, apraśnaka, saṁprayukta-saṁgraha* (three titles which correspond to the first four sections of the *Abhidharma* according to the Dharmaguptas-Haimavata [J. Przyluski, *Concile*, 179, 353–4] and reminds us of the *Dhātukāya-Vibhaṅga-Dhātukathā*, above p. 27; and "succession" (*karma* or *nidāna*?).

This is, properly speaking, a śāstra, without any appearance of a sūtra, with its beginning phrase, "Thus have I heard . . ." It was compiled by Śāriputra, either during the lifetime of the master (according to the *Ta-chih-tu-lun*) or after his Nirvāṇa, to put an end to heresy, for some have "counterfeited the Dharma" (*dharmapratirūpaka*).

However this may be, it is a very extensive and old treatise, much in the style of the Pāḷi *Vibhaṅga*.

The *Ta-chih-tu lun* establishes some relations between the *Abhidharma* of Śāriputra and the Vātsīputrīyas.[69] But I have not encountered, in the work of Śāriputra, any mention of the *pudgala* in the Vātsīputrīya sense of the word.

Kyokuga Saeki (*Kośa*, viii.3) mentions the fact that the *Śāriputrābhidharma* admits the existence of *rūpa* and Ārūpyadhātu. See in fact p. 552a, at the end of the chapter on the *skandhas*. This *rūpa* is *avijñapti*. The book admits the *avijñapti*, which is a Sarvāstivādin invention.

But it is not orthodox Sarvāstivādin. It believes that *anuśaya* is disassociated from the mind (p. 690; *Kośa*, v.2). It does not contain anything on the existence of the past and the future,[70] nor on "unconditioned" space. It explains *prahāṇadhātu*, "which should be abandoned" (576c; *Kośa*, vi.78). Its system of *pratyayas*, very developed (p. 679b), and its list of the *dhātus* (p. 575) have nothing Sarvāstivādin about them.

We can get an idea of the style of the *Śāriputrābhidharma* by comparing its description of *rūpaskandha* (p. 543) with the *Kośa*, i. 20 and *Vibhaṅga*, 1 and following; its definition of *dharmadhātu* (p. 535) with *Vibhaṅga*, 89; and its definition of *nirodhasaṭva* (p. 553) with *Vibhaṅya*, 103.

1. *Dharmadhātu.*

The *dharmadhātu* is first defined as identical to the *dharmāyatana*; then, as made up of *vedanāskandha, saṁjñāskandha, saṁskāraskandha*, invisible and impalpable *(anidarśana, apratigha) rūpa*, and the *asaṁskṛtas* (compare *Vibhaṅga*, 86). A third definition enumerates, after *vedanā* and *saṁjñā*, the series of *saṁskāras* associated with the mind (beginning with *cetanā* and ending with *kleśānuśaya*); the series of the *saṁskāras* disassociated from the mind (*viprayukta*, see p. 547b): *jati, jarā, maraṇa . . . nirodhasamāpatti*; finally: *pratisaṁkhyānirodha, apratisaṁkhyānirodha, niyamadharmasthiti[tā], ākāśāyatana, vijñānāyatana, ākiṁcanyāyatana, naivasaṁjñānāsaṁjñāyatana*,[71] that is to say the list of the *asaṁskṛtas*: "this is what is called the *dharmadhātu*."

On the one hand, the *viprayuktas* are not those of the Sarvāstivādins; although there is some doubt with respect to the equivalents of the translators (Dharmagupta and Dharmayaśas, 414 A.D.), the *nāmakāya* . . . are missing.

On the other hand, the *asaṁskṛtas* of Śāriputra recall those of the Mahāsāṁghikas and the Mahīśāsakas (*Siddhi*, p. 78).

2. *Nirodhasatya.*

To the question: "What is *duḥkhanirodha āryasatya?*", our text answers in canonical terms: *yo tassā yeva taṅhāya asesavirāganirodho cāgo patinissagqo mutti anālayo (Vibhaṅga* 103), and adds: "already cut off, not to arise anew: this is what is called *duḥkhanirodha āryasatya*."

The question is repeated: "What is *duḥkhanirodha āryasatya? Pratisaṁkhyānirodha* is called *duḥkhanirodha āryasatya*. This *duḥkhanirodha āryasatya* is in truth like that, not like that, no different, not a different thing. As the Tathāgata has well spoken the truths of the Āryans, it is *āryasatya*."

But, "what is *pratisaṁkhyānirodha*?" The question is repeated three times: "If a *dharma* is destroyed when one obtains the Āryan Path, the destruction of this *dharma* is called *pratisaṁkhyānirodha*" . . . "The four *śrāmaṇyaphalas* are called *pratisaṁkhyānirodha*."

"What is *srotaāpannaphala*? If the three *kleśas* to be cut off by Seeing are cut off; if *satkāyadṛṣṭi, vicikitsā* and *śīlavrata* are exhausted, this is called *srotaāpanna-phala*."[72] Śāriputra takes up the question again, "What is *srotaāpannaphala*? The three *kleśas* to be cut off by Seeing being cut off, *satkāyadṛṣṭi-vicikitsā-śīlavrata* being exhausted: if one obtains *amṛta*, this is what is called *srotaāpannaphala*."

It appears that what we are encountering here is a terminology alien to the *Abhidharma* and to the Sarvāstivāda.

viii. The *Abhidharmasāra*.[73]

1. Before Vasubandhu, many masters undertook to summarize the doctrines of the Abhidharma. We possess notably three works: 1. The *Abhidharmasāra* of Dharmaśrī in ten chapters, made up of *kārikās* (probably in *āryan* stroph)[74] and a commentary; 2. a second edition of this same *Sāra* by Upaśānta, to which the Chinese give the name of *Abhidharmasāra-ching* [=sūtra]: the same *kārikās* with a more developed commentary; and 3. a third edition of the *Sāra*, the *Tsa* [=Miscellaneous] *Abhidharma-ching*, by Dharmatrāta, which is in fact a new work, containing a new chapter and many new *kārikās*.[75]

2. The preface to the *Vibhāṣā* (Taishō 1546)[76] by Tao-yen places the work of Dharmaśrī before the *Jñānaprasthāna*: "After the *nirodha* of the Buddha, the bhikṣu Dharmaśrī composed the four volumes of the *Abhidharmasāra*. Then Kātyāyanīputra composed the *Abhidharma* in eight books . . ."

3. The work of Dharmaśrī contains ten chapters: *Dhātu, Saṁskāra, Anuśaya, Ārya, Jñāna, Samādhi, Sūtra, Tsa* and *Śāstravarga* or *Vādavarga.*

Between the ninth and the tenth chapters of Dharmaśrī, Dharmatrāta places a new chapter, the *Pravicayavarga*, which indeed appears to constitute an independent work.

There is a stanza of introduction: "even though many *dharmas* have been spoken of, their meaning remains confused . . ." and four concluding stanzas: "The author has composed this book based on the book of Dharmaśrī, not through pride or in order to acquire a reputation . . .".

It begins with the *dharmacakra*, the Wheel of the Dharma: "The Muni said that the *darśanamārga* is called *dharmacakra*, either because it goes into the mind of others . . . (*Kośa*, vi.54).

There then comes the *brahmacakra* (vi.54, vii.31), the *upāsaka* (iv.69), the four parts of *śīla* (iv.29), the *prātimokṣa* . . . Later (p. 959b), cosmology: the periods of loss, etc. (iii.99), destruction by fire, etc. (iii.102); and then there follows the theory of the three "fallings away" (p. 960c; *Kośa*, vi.59) and the definition of the Bodhisattva (iv.108).

Suddenly (p. 961c): "How many types of Sarvāstivāda are there?" Presentation of the four doctrines (*Kośa*, v.25–26) without mentioning the name of the four masters. The second and the fourth are bad because they confuse the time periods. The first (difference in *bhāva*, translated *fen*): "One should know that this is the *pariṇāma-sarvāstivāda*."[77]

There is a diversity of opinion as to whether the Truths are seen at the same time (*Kośa*, vi.27), Sarvāstivādins and Vātsīputrīyas on the one hand, Dharmagupta on the other; *antarābhava* (iii.34); then the Sarvāstivādin proof. And at the end of the paragraph, the discussion "whether the Buddha is part of the Samgha." Finally, the concluding stanzas.

4. The *Saṁskāravarga* treats of the simultaneous arising of the *citta-caittas* and of atoms (*Kośa*, ii.22), of the four *lakṣaṇas* of "conditioned things" (ii.45), of the *hetus* and the *pratyayas* (ii.48, 61).

The *Sūtravarga* is a collection of notes on the three Dhātus and a calculation of the places that they contain: sixteen in Rūpadhātu, but, according to some, seventeen (*Kośa*, iii.2): the *sattvāvāsas* (iii.6), the *vijñānasthitis* (iii.5–6); the three *vartman* of *pratītyasamutpāda* (iii.20, 25), the twelve limbs; the *mahābhūtas*, the Truths, the fruits of the Āryans, etc.

The *Tsa-varga* defines the mind-mental states as *saṁprayukta, sāśraya*, etc. (ii.34); it enumerates the *viprayuktas: āsaṁjñika*, two non-conscious absorptions, *sabhāgatā, nāmakāyādayas, jīvitendriya, dharmaprāpti, pṛthagjanatva*, four *lakṣaṇas* (compare ii.35-36); it concludes with half a kārikā on the four bhavas (iii.13) and a kārikā on "disgust" amd "detachment" (vi.79).

The *Śāstravaraga* (or *Vādavarga*) is made up of ten questions in verse, followed by answers in prose, relative to *saṁvara* (iv.13), to the results, etc. Dharmatrāta adds sixteen questions.

5. In order to appreciate the character of the treatises of Dharmaśrī, Upaśānta, and Dharmatrāta, and Vasubandhu's debt with respect to Dharmatrāta, which appears to be notable, we may see how two *dharmaparyāyas*, the chapter of the three obstacles (*āvaraṇas*) and that of *avijñapti*, are treated by the different masters.

a. Obstacles, *Kośa*, iv.95–102, *Vibhāṣā*, p. 599.

Dharmaśrī, p. 815: "The Bhagavat says that there are three *āvaraṇas: karman, kleśa*, and *vipāka*. What is their definition?

"*Ānantarya* actions which are without remedy, developed defilements, bad action experienced in the painful realms of rebirth, are the *āvaraṇas*.

"These three form an obstacle to the Dharma; they hinder the grasping of the Āryan *dharmas*; they are thus called 'obstacles.' Which is the worst action?

"The action which divides the Saṁgha is said to be the worst.

"This action is the worst. One guilty of this remains a *kalpa* in Avīci hell. Which is the best action?

"The *cetanā* or 'volition' of Bhavāgra is the greatest.

"*Naivasaṁjñānāsaṁjñāyatana* is Bhavāgra. The volition which belongs to the realms of this sphere is the greatest and finest: its result is a life of some 80,000 *kalpas* in length."

Upaśānta, p. 843b–c, has the same two stanzas, but a less meager commentary:

"That which hinders the Path of the Āryans and the means (*upāya*) to this path is said to be an obstacle. The obstacles to action are the five *ānantaryas*, namely, the killing of one's father, etc . . . He who commits such an action is immediately and necessarily reborn in Avīci: thus the action is *ānatarya*. The killing of one's father and mother destroys goodness, hence it is Avīci hell. Those guilty of the other three are led to injure a field of merit. The obstacles of the defilements are 'agitated' and 'sharp' defilements: the first is habitual defilement; the second is the overriding defilement. This refers to the 'present' defilements, not to the defilements that one 'possesses' (that one has as potential), for all beings 'possess' all the defilements . . ."

There is a variant to the second stanza: "Lying which divides the Samgha . . . ; volition in Bhavāgra, among good actions, has the greatest result," which is better. The commentary notes the differences in the two schisms (*cakrabheda, karmabheda*).

Dharmatrāta is longer (p. 898b–899c) and very close to Vasubandhu:

According to the first stanza of Dharmaśrī: 1. the *āvaraṇa* of *kleśa* is the worst; the *āvaraṇa* of action, mediocre; and the *āvaraṇa* of retribution, the least; 2. the division of the Saṁgha, by nature, is non-concord; this is a *viprayukta saṁskāra* of the *anivṛta-avyākṛta* class; 3. the division is a thing of the Saṁgha; the transgression is of him who divides the Samgha; he experiences, in Avīci, a retribution of *kalpa*; 4. the bhikṣus are divided in their opinion of who is the Master, of what is the Path: this is the division of the Saṁgha which was united, and he who breaks it is 'one who possesses views' (*dṛṣṭicarita*); 5. in three continents, a minimum of eight persons is required for *karmabheda*; in

Jambudvīpa, a minimum of nine persons is required for *cakrabheda*; 6. *cakrabheda* is impossible in six time periods: when a boundary is not delimited; at first; following; when the Muni has passed into Nirvāṇa; when the running sore has not been produced; when the pair of chief disciples has not been established (six *pādas*); 7. lying which divides the Saṁgha is the worst of actions; the volition of Bhavāgra is said to bear the greatest result.

b. *Avijñapti, Kośa*, iv.2, 3.

Dharmaśrī (p. 812c):

"Bodily action is *vijñapti* and *avijñapti*. The *vijñapti* of the body is the movement of the body, good, bad, or neutral: good when it arises from a good mind . . . For *avijñapti*: when one does an action in a firm manner, the mind can change, but the seed remains. If, for example, a person undertakes the precepts, his mind can then be bad or neutral: nevertheless the precepts continue . . . Action of the *manas* is solely *avijñapti* . . . because this action is not visible . . . *vijñapti* is good, bad, or neutral; the same for the *avijñapti* which belongs to the *manas*. The other *vijñaptis* are never neutral."

Upaśānta (p. 840) adds a bit. The hunter is regarded as free from bodily *avijñapti*. Mental action is called *avijñapti* because it does not inform others. Some say that it is called *vijñapti* because it is discourse (*jalpa*?).

Dharmatrāta (p. 888b) replaces the terms *vijñapti* and *avijñapti* with "doing" and "not doing" (*karaṇa, akaraṇa*) (*Kośa*,iv.14):

"Bodily action is of two types: *karaṇasvabhāva*, or *akaraṇasvabhāva*. 'Doing' (*karaṇa*): movement of the body, exercise[78] of the body is the 'doing of the body.' 'Not doing' (*akaraṇa, wu-tso*): when the movement of the body has ended, the nature (good or bad) of this movement, of this action which is the movement, continues to arise, simultaneous with minds of a different nature, even as the good precepts produced by their undertaking (*kuśalasamādānaśīla*) continue to arise even when bad or neutral minds are present. Like the immoral person (*dauḥśīlya-puruṣa*): even when good or neutral minds are present, his immorality continues to arise."

". . . Action of the *manas* is *cetanā*, volition, by nature . . .

"'Not doing' (*akaraṇa*) is also called *nirati* (? *Vyut*. 21, 114), *virati; upekṣā, akriyā (pu-tso)*. Because it does not do, it is called 'not doing.' If one says that this is not an action (*karman*), this is wrong, because it does. Good does not do evil, evil does not do good: this is also an action. As the *upekṣā* part of Bodhi is not *upekṣā* by reason of what is called *upekṣā*; but the practice of the Path, the arresting of things, is called *upekṣā*. The same here. Furthermore, in doing the cause one does the result: . . .'not doing' is not *rūpa*, but the doing of it (which is the cause of the 'not doing' or *avijñapti*) is *rūpa*; 'not doing' is thus called *rūpa*. In this same way then, 'not doing' is action.[79]

1. Originally printed as a Foreword to de La Vallée Poussin's *Cosmologie bouddhique*: 1913, and published 1919 in the four-part *Memoires* of l'Acadmie royale de Belgique (Luzac, London). This contained the restoration of the *kārikās* of the third chapter of the *Kośa*, the Tibetan *kārikās*, the *Bhāṣya*, and the text of the *Vyākhyā*; in the appendix, a summary of the *Lokaprajñapti* and the *Karaṇaprajñapti*.

2. *Cullavagga*, xi.1.8. [For a more exact presentation, J. Przyluski, *Concile de Rājagṛha*, p. 311, 345, 349].

3. Oldenberg, *Buddha* . . ., 6th edition, p. 202; Fr. trans. Foucher, 2nd edition, p. 177. [Psychology, yes; but ontology is doubtful].

4. In the *Divya*, a Sarvāstivādin work, where we encounter the expressions *sūtrasya vinayasya mātṛkāyāh*: "The monks ask with respect to the *Sūtra*, the *Vinaya*, and the *Mātṛkā*" (p. 18, 15), and *sūtram mātṛkā ca*, equivalent to *āgamacatuṣṭayam* (p. 333, 7), Kern (*Manual*, p. 3) thinks that the term *mātṛkā* is employed "as synonymous with *abhidharma*." It cannot in any case designate the *Abhidharmas* of the Sarvastivadins of which we are speaking below (p. 3) which are treatises; it fits the *Abhidhammas* a little less poorly, but without being satisfying. Does it designate some lists "omitting all the explanations and other details" (Childers, 243), lists of items which form part of the *āgama* and which are not specifically *Abhidharma*? The Sautrāntikas, who deny the existence of an *Abhidharma Piṭaka* distinct from the *Sūtra*, certainly had such an "index," exactly like the Sarvāstivādins of that period, and earlier than the *Abhidharmas* to which the expressions of the *Divya* refer. Does it designate some presentations, in the manner of the sūtras, like those that constituted the *mātikās* of the *Vibhaṅga*? In this book, which is the property of the *Abhidharma*, it is often a type of commentary in the form of glosses.

5. See the article of Rhys Davids in Hastings' *Encyclopedia of Religion and Ethics*.

6. *Developpement de l'Abhidharma, Dogme et philosophie*,p. 122; J. Przyluski, *Concile*, third chapter and 179, 353; *Açoka*, 322; *Funérailles*, 49; Lévi, *Seize Arhats*, 20, 39.

7. In Hastings' *Encyclopedia*, I.19–20; Winternitz, *Geschichte*, 134. Scholastic definitions of the *Abhidharma: Attasālini*, 48–50 and following; *Sūtrālaṁkāra*, XI.3.

8. It knows, however, that the author of the *Kathāvatthu* foresaw and refuted in advance the heresies to come; see *Atthakathā*, pp. 6–7. The remark is by Minayeff, and the observations by H. Oldenberg (*Buddh. Studien*, p. 633, 676) do not demonstrate that the *Kathāvatthu* has not been amplified in the course of time.

9. This is incorrect. The *Saṁgītiparyāya* is only the *Saṁgītisuttanta*. The second part of the *Dhātukāya* has a close relationship with the *Dhātukathāprakaraṇa*. A careful study will show other points of contact, and one can see that the Sarvāstivādins simply enriched by their inventions (theory of the *viprayuktas*, of the *mahābhāmikas*, etc.) the earlier material of the *Abhidhamma*.

10. The account of Buddhaghosa, *Kathāvatthu-Atthakāthā*, p. 6, holds that because of this, at least the Vibhajjavādins are the orthodox party.

11. This is one of the aspects of the problem of *kiriyāvāda*.

12. This definition of the two schools is borrowed from the *Abhidharmakośa*, v.9; see *Kathāvatthu*, I.8 (which does not entirely confirm our interpretation). The controversy of time and the *pudgala* in the *Vijñānakāya*, *Etudes Asiatiques*, 1925.

13. Geography of the Sarvāstivādin sect, J. Przyluski, *Açoka*. I know that Sinologists, notably Takakusu, are not settled on the language in which the first of the *Abhidharmas* of the

Sarvāstivādins, the *Jñānaprathāna*, was written: "In what language, however, the original text was composed we have no means of ascertaining. All we can say is that the text brought by Saṁghadeva and Dhammapiya [Dharmapriya] from Kaçmīra [383 A.D.] seems to have been in a dialect akin to Pali, whereas the text used by Hiuen-tsang [657 A.D.], as in other cases, seems to have been in Sanskrit. But this supposition rests solely on the phonetic value of Chinese ideographs employed in these translations, and is not corroborated by any other evidence . . . It seems to me more than probable that the *Jñānaprasthāna* at least was written in some dialect: one thinks naturally of the dialect of Kaçmīra, but we really have no certainty that the *Jñānaprasthāna* was not composed in Kosala (*JPTS*; 1905, p. 84, 86)."

We possess a fragmentary quotation from the Sarvāstivādin Prātimokṣa which proves that some earlier forms, Pāḷi or dialect, remained in use: "When, in the Poṣadha ceremony, the Vinayadhara asks, 'Are you pure?' (*bhikṣupoṣadhe hi kacci ttha pariśuddhā iti vinayadhareṇānuśrāvite*), if any bhikṣu does not confess his transgression . . ." (*Abhidharmakośavyākhyā* ad iv. 72; compare the introduction of the *Pātimokkha* and the remarks of Rhys Davids, *Dialogues*, II, p. 257). (See L. Finot, "Prātimokṣasūtra des Sarvāstivādins," *JA*, 1913, 2.177–9).

But we possess a fragment of the *Jñānaprasthāna*, quoted in the *Abhidharmakośavyākhyā* (ad i.49): *katamad buddhavacanaṁ tathāgatasya yā vāg vacanaṁ vyavahāro gīr niruktir vākpatho vāgghoṣo vākkarma vāgvijñaptiḥ // buddhavacanaṁ kuśalaṁ vaktavyam athāvyākṛtaṁ vaktavyam / syāt kuśalaṁ syād avyākṛtam // katarat kuśalam / kuśalacittasya tathāgatasya vācaṁ bhāṣamāṇasya yā [vāg]vijñaptiḥ // katarad avyākṛtam / . . . pūrvavat // punas tatraivānantaram uktam / buddhavacanaṁ ka eṣa dharmaḥ / nāmakāyapadakāyavyañjanakāyānāṁ yānupūrvavacanā anupūrvasthāpanā anupūrvasamayoga iti /*

14. Invention of the *prāptis*, of *sabhāgatā*, of the existence of the past and the future, of diverse types of cause, of *apratisaṁkhyanirodha*, not to mention the *nirvedhabhagiyas, etc.*

15. The *Abhidharmakośavyākhyā* speaks of *ṣaṭpādābhidharma-mātrapāṭhina* Ābhidhārmikas, Ābhidhārmikas "who read only the six-legged *Abhidharma*," which we understand to mean "who do not read the *Vibhāṣā*." These are Sarvāstivādins; but all Sarvāstivādins are not "followers of the *Vibhāṣā*" (Vaibhāṣikas). We know, for example, that there were four ways of understanding "all exists," those of the Sarvāstivādins Dharmatrāta, Ghoṣaka, Vasumitra, and Buddhadeva: the Vaibhāṣikas of Kaśmīr condemn the first, the second and the fourth; and the first for the serious reason that it is confused with the non-Buddhist teaching of the Sāṁkhyas.

16. Better, "after the reign of Kaniṣka," *Inde sous les Mauryas* . . ., p. 328.

17. See this Introduction, Dārṣṭāntikas, and Index, Sautrāntikas.

18. I omit here the rather long note where the bibliography on the "dating" of Vasubandhu is summarized, and where the texts proving the existence of an "earlier Vasubandhu" were brought together; see below.

19. All the opinions, or almost all the opinions, marked in the *Kośa* or in the *Bhāṣyam* by the adverb *kila* ("certain," "it is said," *grags so*), are erroneous opinions of the Vaibhāṣikas. A correct translation would be: "The School says, wrongly, that . . ."

20. N. Péri, "A propos de la date de Vasubandhu," *BEFEO*, 1911, p. 374. The Tibetan Siddhāntas also take a great deal from the *Kośa*. Note that it was translated into Chinese only in 563, and the Tibetan version, by Jinamitra and Śrīkūṭarakṣita, during the period of Ral-pa-can (816–838).

21. This does not exist *in extenso* in Chinese (*JPTS*, 1905, p. 77). This is the treatise the first two parts of which are analyzed in the Appendix of *Cosmologie bouddhique*.

22. The *Vyākhyā*, the commentary on the *Bhāṣyam* by Yaśomitra, adds many details.

23. It is from this point of view that Oldenberg recommends the study of the *Abhidharmakośa*, in *Buddhistische Studien*, ZDMG; LII; p. 644 (1898).

24. According to P. Demiéville, *BEFEO*, 1924, p. 463.

25. With reference to Guṇamati, see H. Ui, *Studies in Indian Philosophy* [=*Indo-tetsugaku Kenkyū*], 5th volume, pp. 136–140.

26. Missing in the two treatises of Saṁghabhadra, the Āryan quoted in *Vyākhyā* i.31, which is a criticism of *Kośa* i, *kārika* 11.

In the two treatises of Saṁghabhadra, the first chapter is entitled *Mūlavastunirdeśa*, the second *Viśeṣanirdeśa*, the third *Pratītyasamutpādanirdeśa*. As is proper, the *Pudgalapratiṣedha-prakaraṇa*, an appendix to the *Kośa*, is ignored.

27. It has been preceded by Susumu Yamaguchi [September 1931].

28. See *Kośa* i.1. Obermiller, in the preface to his translation of the *Uttaratantra* (*Asia Major*, 1931), digresses from the thesis of Ui.

29. Perhaps because the work of Dharmatrāta enjoyed, for a long time, a great reputation; because, in the eyes of the Sarvāstivādins, the *Kośa* passed, with good reason, for heretical and tendentious.

30. Quoted iii.59, on the explanation of the word *utsada*.

31. See below.

32. *Ṣaṭpādābhidharmamātrapāṭhinas*, a good reading for the *Kośa*, v.22, note 80.

33. An account of the council in *Ta-chih-tu-lun*. Przyluski, *Concile de Rājagṛha*, p. 72.

34. Translated in 383 by Gotama Saṁghadeva of Kaśmīr, and by Hsüan-tsang.

35. Watters, i.294; S. Lévi, *Catalogue geographique des Yakṣas*, 55; J. Przyluski, *Açoka*, 263.

36. On the language in which the *Jñānaprasthāna* was written, see Takakusu, p. 82, 84, 86. See above p. 3.

37. On the *laukikāgradharmas*, *Kośa*, vi. 19c, and "Pārāyaṇa quoted in the *Jñānaprasthāna*," *Mélanges Linossier* (where we see that the *Jñānaprasthāna* poorly presents the problem of the *nirvedhabhāgīyas*).

38. Same text, *Small Vibhāṣā*, p. 5b.

39. Compare *Kośa*. i.3, and *Documents d'Abhidharma; Vibhāṣā*, p. 236b.

40. The controversy of time and of the *pudgala* in the *Vijñānakāya*, in *Etudes Asiatiques*, 1925, i.343–376; *Inde sous les Mauryas*, 1930, 138; Note in *Bouddhique*, ii. *AC. Belgique*, Nov. 1922.

The fourth volume of the Japanese translation reached me in September, 1931. It contains the *Vijñānakāya*. The translator, Bun'yu Watanabe, in a short preface, treats of the philosophic import of the book, of its compilation, and its relation with the *Abhidhammas*.

41. One must be more precise with respect to the remarks made by Barth (ii.355): in truth the editors of the *Dīpavaṁsa* are alone in knowing a Tissa Moggaliputta "who must have presided over the council of Ashoka and composed the *Kathāvatthu*." But the Sarvāstivādin tradition knows of a Mu-lien to whom it attributes, in the controversy of the past and the future, the position that the *Dīpavaṁsa* assigns to Tissa. There is certainly much legend in Singhalese hagiography.

42. The enigmatic Gopāla of Hsüan-tsang? Our sources are in agreement in attributing to the

Sammitīyas, and to the Vātsīputrīyas, the doctrine of the *pudgala*. See *Madhyamakavṛtti*, pp. 275–276.

43. *Kathāvatthu: saccikaṭṭhaparamaṭṭhena puggalo upalabbhati.* The Sanskrit formula is not restored with any certainty. We have *tattvārthataḥ (satyārthataḥ?) paramārthataḥ pudgala upalabhyate sākṣīkriyate saṁpratividyate* (?) *saṁvidyate*. The edition of Devaśarman, more developed than that of Tissa, appears to be later.

44. Sanskrit sources like the expression *puruṣapudgala*; for example, the Sanskrit edition of *Majjhima*, iii.239 (*chadhāturo ayam puriso*) has *ṣaḍdhātur ayaṁ puruṣapudgalaḥ*. See *Madhyamakavṛtti*, pp. 129, 180, etc

45. The expression that I translate as "Recognize the contradiction into which you fall!", *ju t'ing tuo fu*, corresponds to a Sanskrit original *ājānīhi nigraham*. *Tuo fu* is in fact translated by *nigraha sthāna* in a word list (*Tetsugaku Daijisho*, Tokyo, 1912) abstracted by Rosenberg ("Introduction to the study of Buddhism," i, *Vocabulary*, Tokyo, 1916). Thus we have here the exact equivalent of the formula *ājānāhi niggaham* of the *Kathāvatthu* and the *Milinda*.

46. The doctrine of the Bhagavat is a path between two extremes. It avoids the extreme theory of permanence by saying that he who eats the fruits of the action is not the same person who carried out the action (*sa karoti so'nubhavati?*): it avoids the theory of annihilation by denying that he who eats the fruit is anyone other than he who carried out the action. Compare *Samyutta*, ii. p. 23.

47. The edition of the *Dīrgha* has only four octades: *vimokṣa, abhibhū, lokadharma* and *samyagmārga* (which recalls the Pali *samattas*).

48. On the different Vasumitras, see Watters, i.274–5; the Introduction to the *Traite sur les Sectes*, Masuda, *Asia Major*, ii. p. 7; Tāranātha, 174.

49. Who (*Vibhāṣā*, p. 152a) declares that all *citta-caitta* disappears in *nirodhasamāpatti*?

50. Perhaps Taishō 1556, anonymous: *Sarvāstivādasamaya-pañcavastuka*, notable for its enumeration of the *viprayuktas*; 997c: *prāpti, asaṁjñisamāpatti, nirodhasamāpatti, āsaṁjñika, jīvitendriya, sabhāgatā, deśaprāpti (?), āyatanaprāpti, jāti jarā, sthiti, anityatā, nāma-pāda-vyañjanakāyas*.

51. It quotes the Abhidharma-ācāryas. It admits the *mahābhūmikas*, p. 994b3, and also *avijñapti*, p. 992c, which it explains, along with the *saṁvaras*, exactly as the *Kośa* does. But the formula, "There are two gates to *amṛta*, the contemplation of the loathsome and the regulation of the breath," is to be noted, p. 989b.

52. On the *anāgāmin*, *Vibhāṣā*, p. 879b; on the meaning of *bhava*, p. 960b; on the absorptions which follow a good mind of Kāmadhātu, p. 961c.

53. One gloss says that the word signifies "Bodhi-taking," which would give Bodhilāta.

54. The Dārṣṭāntikas deny the *caittas*; the Sautrāntikas admit the *caittas*, but differ on their number.

55. See above, p. 30.

56. *Sautrāntikā Bhadantādayaḥ; sautrāntikadarśanavalambin.*

57. According to Wassiliew, 279, Saṁgharaksita differs a little. We do not know this master, nor the Bhūmisena of p. 280.

58. The opinion on seeing through the visual consciousness, on the number of the *caittas*, on the non-existence of *avijñapti*, are clearly non-Vaibhāṣika. Moreover, the *Vibhāṣā* carefully notes the opinions of the Bhadanta.

59. See also *Vibhāṣā*, p. 219.

60. However Dharmatrāta, in *Abhidharmasāra*, p. 885, explains the causes of the *viprayuktas*.

61. See the references to the Mahāsāṁghikas, the Vātsīputrīyas, the Mahīśāsakas, and the Dharmaguptas in the index.

62. *Ch'uan-yü*; *Ch'uan* translates *āgama* or *avavāda*.

63. Vasubandhu, *Kośa*, iv. 56, as well as Saṁghabhadra, p. 572 (which is surprising enough), do not take into account the second alternative and follow the doctrine of the *ch'uan-yü*.

64. A note translated imprecisely in *Kośa*, v. 9d, note.

65. The truth is that Paramārtha wrote one word for another.

66. This is obscure; the *Saṁgraha* quotes the *Āgama* of the Mahīśāsakas and ignores the Vibhajyavādins; the *Vibhāṣā*, it appears, ignores the Sāṁmitīyas.

67. This is the meaning of *yogācāra* in the *Saundarananda*, and in the *Mahāvastu*.

68. Or *vaiyāpṛtya*, *Avadānaśataka*, ii.235.

69. "Some say: 'When the Buddha was in this world, Śāriputra, with an end to explaining the words of the Buddha, compiled the *Abhidharma*. Later, the monk Vātsīputrīya recited [this work]. Up to the present day, this is what is called the *Abhidharma* of Śāriputra,'" J. Przyluski, *Concile*, p. 73.

The only book of the *Abhidharma* which teaches the doctrine of the *pudgala* appears to be Taishō vol. 32, no. 1649, the *Sāṁmitīya-nikāya-śāstra*, *Kośa*, ix.

70. "The past is that which has arisen and is destroyed; the future is that which has not arisen, not appeared," p. 543b.

71. For the last terms, compare the variant p. 526c: the Sanskrit reading is doubtful: *ākāśāyatanajñāna* . . . and *ākāśāyatanapratyaya[jñāna]*.

72. Compare the doctrine of the *Dhammasaṅgaṇi*, *Kośa* v.4, note.

73. Taishō volume 28, numbers 1550, 1551, 1552, *Abhidharmahṛdaya*; see above p. 16.

74. We have the Sanskrit text of one of the *kārikās*, *Kośa*, v, note 14.

75. For example, the ninth chapter: Dharmatrāta takes up twenty *kārikās* of Dharmaśrī and interpolates six new *kārikās*; he continues with twenty-two new *kārikās*.

76. Taishō 1546; mentioned by Takakusu, p. 128.

77. The third doctrine, difference in *avasthā*, (trans. *fen-fen*).

78. We have *fang-pien*, which should translate *vyāyāna* (see Demieville, *Milinda*) more often than *upāya*.

79. See above p. 33.

CHAPTER ONE

The Dhātus

Oṁ. Homage to the Buddha.

1. He has, in an absolute manner, destroyed all blindness; He has drawn out the world from the mire of transmigration: I render homage to Him, to this teacher of truth, before composing the treatise called the *Abhidharmakośa.*

Desiring to compose a treatise, with the intention of making known the greatness of his master, the author undertakes to render him homage and to first present his qualities.

"He" refers to the Buddha, the Blessed One.

"He has destroyed all blindness," that is to say, by him or through him blindness with respect to all things is destroyed.

"Blindness" is ignorance, for ignorance hinders the seeing of things as they truly are.

By this, the Buddha, the Blessed One[1] is sufficiently designated, for he alone, through the possession of the antidote to ignorance (v. 60), has definitely destroyed all ignorance with respect to all knowable things, so that it cannot rearise.

But the Pratyekabuddhas and the Śrāvakas have also destroyed all blindness, for they are freed from all ignorance defiled by the defilements.

But they do not know the qualities proper to the Buddha (vii.28),[2] objects very distant in space or time (vii.55),[3] nor the infinite complex of things;[4] therefore, they have not destroyed blindness in an absolute manner, for the ignorance freed from the defilements is active in them.[5]

Having thus praised the Blessed One from the point of view of qualities useful to himself, the author praises him from the point of view of qualities useful to others: "He has drawn out the world from the mire of transmigration." Transmigration is a mire, because the world is bound up in it, and because it is difficult to traverse. The Blessed One, having pity on the world which finds itself drowned without recourse in this mire, has pulled it out, as much as possible,[6] by extending to each one the hands of the teaching of the Good Law.[7]

"I render homage," by prostrating myself even to my head "to this teacher of truth:"[8] teacher of truth," because he teaches in conformity with that which is, without error. By thus qualifying the Blessed One, the author indicates the manner in which the Blessed One is useful to others. It is by the true teaching that the Blessed One, the teacher, has pulled the world out of the mire of transmigration, not by his supernatural powers, nor by the granting of favors.[9]

After having rendered homage to this teacher of truth, what will the author do? "I shall compose a treatise." A treatise is that which instructs disciples. Which treatise?

The *Abhidharmakośa.*

***

What is *Abhidharma*?

> 2a. *Abhidharma* is pure *prajñā* with its following.

Prajñā which will be defined below (ii.24, vii.1) is the discernment of the *dharmas.*[10]

Pure *prajñā* is undefiled *prajñā.*[11]

The "following" of *prajñā* is its escort, namely the five pure *skandhas* (i.7a) which coexists with *prajñā.*[12]

Such is the absolute meaning[13] of *Abhidharma.*

> 2b. It is also *prajñā*, and the Treatise which brings about the obtaining of pure *prajñā.*

In common usage, the word Abhidharma also designates all *prajñā* which brings about the obtaining of Abhidharma in the absolute sense of the word; defiled *prajñā* whether it is innate or natural, or whether the result of an effort, the result of hearing, reflection, absorption (*śrutacintābhāvanā-mayī*, ii.71c), receives, along with its following, by convention, the name of Abhidharma.

One also gives the name of Abhidharma to the Treatise,[14] for the Treatise also brings about the obtaining of pure *prajñā*: it is thus a factor in Abhidharma in the absolute sense of the word.

Dharma is that which bears (*dhāraṇa*) self-(or unique) characteristics.

The Abhidharma is called *abhi-dharma* because it envisions (*abhimukha*) the *dharma* which is the object of supreme knowledge, or the supreme *dharma*, Nirvāṇa; or rather it is so-called because it envisions the characteristics of the *dharmas*, both their self-characteristics and their common (or general) characteristics.

***

Why is the present work called the *Abhidharmakośa*?

> 2c-d. The present work is called the *Abhidharmakośa* because the Abhidharma enters into it through its meaning; or because the Abhidharma constitutes its foundation.

The Treatise that bears the name of Abhidharma enters by its meaning into this work, which is thus the *Abhidharmakośa*, "the sheath of the Abhidharma." Or rather as the Abhidharma is the point of support of this work, one can say that this work is drawn from out of the Abhidharma, as from a sheath; it is thus called the *Abhidharmakośa*, "the work which has the Abhidharma for a sheath."

Why was the Abhidharma taught? By whom was the Abhidharma originally taught? The answer to these two questions will tell us why the author piously undertakes the writing of the *Abhidharmakośa*.

> 3. Apart from the discernment of the *dharmas*, there is no means to extinguish the defilments, and it is by reason of the defilements that the world wanders in the ocean of existence. So it is with a view to this discernment that the Abhidharma has been, they say, spoken [by the Master].[15]

Apart from the discernment of *dharmas*, there does not exist any means for the extinguishing of the defilements (v.1), and these are the defilements which cause the world to wander in the great ocean of transmigration. This is why, say the Vaibhāṣikas,[16] with a view to the discernment of the *dharmas*, the master, the Buddha, the Blessed One, spoke the Abhidharma. For, without the teaching of the Abhidharma, a disciple would be incapable of discerning the *dharmas*.

However, the Vaibhasikas explain, the Blessed One spoke the Abhidharma in fragments. And in the same way that the Sthavira Dharmatrāta made a collection of the Udānas scattered throughout the Scriptures,—the *Udānavarga*,[17]—in this same way the Āryan Kātyāyāniputra and the other Saints established the Àbhidharma [by collecting it into the seven Abhidharmas].[18]

***

What are the *dharmas* of which the Abhidharma teaches the discerning?

> 4a. The *dharmas* are impure, "in a relationship with the defilements," or pure,"with no relationship to the defilements."

This is the complete teachings of all the *dharmas*.

What are the impure *dharmas*?

> 4b-c. Conditioned *dharmas*, with the exception of the Path, are impure.

With the exception of the Path, all conditioned *dharmas* are defiled. Why is this?

> 4d. They are impure because the defilements adhere to them.[19]

(For the *saṁkṛtadharmas* see i.7a, ii.45c-d. For the defilements, the *āsravas*, see v.40.)

Without doubt certain defilements, for example false views, can have the Path or the unconditioned *dharmas*, for their object. This does not make the Path or these *dharmas* impure, or in a (necessary) relationship with the defilements, because the defilements do not adhere to them. This point will be explained later in the Fifth Chapter.

What are the pure *dharmas*?

5a-b. The undefiled truth of the Path and the three unconditioned things are pure.[20]

What are the three unconditioned things?[21]

5c. Space and the two types of extinctions.[22]

The two extinctions are *pratisaṁkhyānirodha*, extinction due to knowledge, and *apratisaṁkhyānirodha*, extinction not due to knowledge.

The three unconditioned things and the truth of the Path are pure *dharmas* because the defilements do not adhere to them.

5c. Space is "that which does not hinder."

Space has for its nature not hindering matter which, in fact, takes place freely in space; and also of not being hindered by matter, for space is not displaced by matter.[23]

6a. *Pratisaṁkhyānirodha* is disjunction.[24]

(Conscious) disjunction (*visaṃyoga*, ii.57d) from the impure *dharmas* is *pratisaṃkhyānirodha* (ii.55) [or Nirvana]. *Pratisaṃkhyāna* or *pratisaṃkhya* signifies a certain pure *prajñā*, the comprehension of the Truths. The "extinction" of which one takes possession by this *prajñā* is called *pratisaṁkhyānirodha*; we could say *pratisaṃkhya-[prāpya]-nirodha*, "the extinction obtained through *pratisaṃkhyā*," but the middle word (i.e., *prāpya*) is elided, as in the expression "ox-cart," and not "cart hitched to oxen" (*goratha* = *go-[yukta]-ratha*).

***

Is there but one single *pratisaṁkhyānirodha* from all of the impure *dharmas*?

No.
Why is this?

6b. Each [disjunction occurs] separately.

Each disjunction taken seperately is *pratisaṁkhyānirodha.* The objects of "disjunction" are as numerous as the objects of "junction."[25] If it were otherwise, if *pratisaṁkhyānirodha* were single, then a person who has experienced the extinction of the defilement which is abandoned by seeing the Truth of Suffering, would have obtained at the same time the extinction of the defilements which are abandoned by the Seeing of the other Truths, and by Meditation. It would be useless for him to cultivate the part of the Path which is opposed to these defilements. (*Vibhāṣā, TD* 27, p. 164c16).

This does not mean that all extinction is alike, that there is not an extinction corresponding to another extinction. This means that extinction does not have a "cause corresponding to its effect (*sabhāgahetu*)," and that it is not a "cause corresponding to its effect" (ii.52).[26]

6c-d. A different type of extinction, which consists of the absolute hindering of arising, is called *apratisaṁkhyānirodha.*

Apratisaṃkhyānirodha is an extinction which is different from "disjunction;" it consists of the absolute hindering of the arising of future *dharmas*. It is so called because it is obtained, not by the comprehension of the Truths, but by the insufficiency of the causes of arising.[27]

For example, when the organ of sight and the mental organ are occupied with a certain visible matter, other visible things, sounds, odors, tastes and tangibles pass from the present into the past. It follows that the five sense consciousness, the visual consciousness, etc., which have had for their object other visible matter, sounds, odors, tastes and tangibles, cannot arise, for the sense consciousnesses are not capable of grasping their object when the object is past. There is thus an absolute hindering of the arising of the said consciousnesses, by reason of the insufficiency of the cause of arising.

Here we have a four-fold alternative (*Vibhāṣā*, *TD* 27,p. 164c16):

1. solely *pratisaṁkhyānirodha* of the impure *dharmas*, past, present, and destined to arise;

2. solely *apratisaṁkhyānirodha* of pure, conditioned *dharmas*, not destined to arise;

3. *pratisaṁkhyānirodha* and *apratisaṃkhyānirodha* of impure *dharmas*, not destined to arise; and

4. neither *pratisaṃkhyānirodha* nor *apratisaṁkhyanirodha* of pure dharmas, past, present or destined to arise.[28]

***

We have said that the impure *dharmas* are the conditioned *dharmas*, minus the Path. What are the conditioned *dharmas*?

> 7a-b. Conditioned things are the fivefold *skandhas*, matter, etc.[29]

These are the aggregate of matter, the aggregate of the sensations, the aggregate of ideas, the aggregate of mental formations, and the aggregate of consciousness.

Saṃkṛta, conditioned, is explained etymologically as "that which has been created (*kṛta*) by causes in union and combination." There is no *dharma* which is engendered by a single cause (ii.64).

Even though the expression *saṁskṛta* signifies "that which has been created . . ," it also applies to future *dharmas* and to present *dharmas*, as well as to past *dharmas*; in fact, a *dharma* does not change its nature by changing its time period. In the same way, one calls milk in the udder *dugdha*, "that which has been drawn," and kindling *indhana*, or "wood to be burned."

> 7c-d. Conditioned things are the paths; they are the foundations of discourse; they are "possessed of leaving;" they are "possessed of causes."

1. Conditioned things are paths—that is to say, the time periods, the past, present and future—because they have for their nature

having gone, of going, of shall be going. In the same way, one says that a path led somewhere, that it goes, or that it will go to the town.

Or rather conditioned things are called paths (*adhvan*) because they are devoured (*adyante*) by impermanence (ii.45c).

2. Discourse (*kathā*), means words, or speech (*vākya*); discourse has names or words (*nāman*, ii.36)[30] for its foundation.

Should one take literally the definition given by the stanza, and say that conditioned things are words?

No. By "foundations of discourse" one should understand "the foundations of discourse, that is, words, together with that which the words signify." If we understand "foundations of discourse" to be only words, we would be at variance with the *Prakaraṇapāda*[31] which says; "The *kathāvastus*, the foundations of discourse, are embraced within the eighteen *dhātus*." (*Vibhāṣā*, *TD* 27, p. 74a20).[32]

3. *Niḥsāra* signifies "leaving" (*sāra* = *niḥsaraṇa*) which is the Nirvāṇa of all conditioned things. As one should depart from conditioned things, one qualifies them as "endowed with leaving."[33]

4. Conditioned things are dependent on causes; they are thus qualified as *savastuka*, that is, "having causes."[34]

The Vaibhāṣikas believe that, in the expression *savastuka*, *vastu* signifies cause (*hetu*).[35]

Such are the diverse synonyms of "conditioned things."

8a-b. When they are impure, they are *upādānaskandhas*.[36]

Impure conditioned things constitute the five *upādānaskandhas*. Everything that is *upādānaskandha* is *skandha*; pure conditioned things are included within the *skandhas*, but are not included within the *upādānaskandhas* (*Vibhāṣā*, *TD* 27, p. 387a9).

The *upādānas* are defilements (*kleśas*, v.38).

The *upādānaskandhas* are so called (1) because they proceed from the defilements, as one says "grass fire" or "straw fire;" (2) or rather because they are governed by the defilements, as one says "the king's man;" (3) or rather because they give rise to the defilements, as one says "flower-bearing tree" or "fruit-bearing tree."

8c. They are called "of battle."[37]

The defilements are of battle because they injure oneself and others. Impure conditioned things are qualified "of battle," "in a relationship with battle," because the defilements of battle adhere to them; equally, as we have seen, they are qualified as "impure," "possessing impurity,"because the defilements adhere to them.

> 8c-d. They are also suffering, arising, the world, the locus of false opinions, existence.

1. Suffering, because they are odious to the Saints (vi.2).
2. Arising, because suffering arises from them (vi.2).
3. World, because they are in the process of decomposition.[38]
4. Locus of opinions, because the five opinions abide in them and adhere to them (v.7) (*Prakaraṇa*, p. 33b7).
5. Existence, because it exists.[39]

***

We have seen that there are five *skandhas* (i.7, 20). Let us first study *rūpaskandha* (i.9-14b).

> 9a-b. *Rūpa*, or matter, is the five sense organs, five objects, and *avijñapti*.[40]

The five organs are the organs of sight, hearing, smell, taste and touch.

The five objects of the five organs are visible matter, sounds, odors, tastes and tangibles.

And *avijñapti* (i.11); such is *rūpaskandha*.

***

We have enumerated five things, visible matter, sound, etc.

> 9c-d. The points of support of the consciousnesses of these things, namely the subtle material elements, are the five organs, the organ of sight, etc.[41]

The five which are the point of support of the consciousnesses of visible matter, sounds, odor, taste and tangibles, and which consist of the suprasensible subtle material elements, are, in this order, the organs of sight, hearing, smell, taste, and touch.

The Blessed One said in fact, "The eye, Oh Bhikṣus, an internal *āyatana*, a subtle matter derived from the primary elements . . ."[42]

Or rather, (the point of support of the consciousnesses of these organs, are) the points of support of the visual consciousness, or eye consciousness, etc.[43] This interpretation is in conformity with the *Prakaraṇa* (p. 692c12) which says: "What is the organ of sight? It is the subtle matter which is the support of the consciousness of sight."

***

Let us now examine the five objects beginning with visible matter, *rūpāyatana*.

10a. Visible matter is twofold.[44]

1. Visible matter is color and shape. Color is fourfold: blue, red, yellow, white; other colors proceed from out of these four colors. Shape (*saṁsthāna*, iv.3c) is eightfold: long, short, square, round, high, low, even, uneven.[45]

10a. Or twentyfold.

2. Or there are some twenty types: the four primary colors, the eight shapes, and eight more colors: cloud, smoke, dust, mist, shade, hot light, light, darkness. Some make a color of the firmament [which appears like a wall of lapiz-lazuli]; this would give us the number twenty-one.

"Even" signifies "of even shape;" "uneven" is the opposite; mist is the vapor which rises from the ground and from water; "hot light" is the light of the sun; "light" is the light of the moon, the stars, fire, grasses and gems; "shade"—arisen from an obstacle to light—is where forms still remain visible; "darkness" is the opposite.

The other terms do not call for any explanation.

3. Visible matter can be color without being shape:[46] blue, red, yellow, white, shade, hot light, light, darkness.

There can be shapes without there being color: that part of the long, of the short, etc., which constitutes bodily action (*kāyavijñapti*,[47] iv.2).

There can be color and shape at one and the same time: all the other categories of visible matter.

Some other Masters maintain that only hot light and light are exclusively color; for blue, red, etc., present themselves to the sight under the aspect of long, short, etc.

4. But, say the Sautrāntikas, how could a single thing be (*vidyate*) twofold, [color and shape together? For, in the system of the Vaibhāṣikas, color and shape are distinct things, *dravya*, iv.3.]

Because color and shape are perceived in a single substance. The root *vid* has here the sense of "to know," and not the sense of "to exist."

But, reply the Sautrāntikas, you should admit that bodily action is at one and the same time color and shape.

> 10b. Sound is eightfold.[48]

1. It is fourfold: having for its cause present primary elements forming part of the organs, having for its cause other primary elements (*upāttānupāttāmahābhūtahetuka*, i.34c-d), belonging to living beings, and not belonging to living beings.[49] Each of these four categories is agreeable or disagreeable.

First category: sound caused by the hand or by the voice.

Second category: sound of the wind, of the trees, of water.

Third category: sound of vocal action (iv.3d). Fourth category: every other sound.

2. According to other masters, one sound can belong to the first two categories at one and the same time, for example, a sound produced by the coming together of a hand and a drum. But the School (*Vibhāṣā*, *TD* 27, p. 663c12) does not admit that one atom [of matter] has for its cause only two tetrades of the primary elements; thus one cannot admit that one atom [of sound] is produced by the four primary

elements of a hand and the four primary elements of a drum.

10b-c. Taste is of six types.[50]

Sweet, sour, salty, pungent, bitter, and astringent.

10c. Odor is fourfold.[51]

For good odors and bad odors are either excessive or non-excessive. But, according to the *Prakaraṇa* (p. 692c22), odor is threefold: good, bad, and equal or indifferent.

10d. The tangible is of eleven types.[52]

1. Eleven things are tangible things: the four primary elements, softness, hardness, weight, lightness, cold, hunger, and thirst.

2. The elements will be explained below (i.12). "Softness" is smoothness; "hardness" is roughness; "weight" is that by which bodies are susceptible of being weighed (i.36); "lightness" is the opposite; "cold" is what produces a desire for heat; "hunger" is what produces a desire for food; "thirst" is what produces a desire for drinking. In fact the tangible which produces hunger and thirst is designated by the word hunger: the cause is designated by the name of the effect. In the same way that it is said "The appearance of the Buddha is (the cause of) happiness; the teaching of the religion is happiness; happiness, the harmony of the community; happiness, the austerities of monks who are in agreement."[53]

3. Both hunger and thirst are lacking in Rūpadhātu,[54] but the other tangibles are found there.

It is true that the clothes of the gods of Rūpadhātu, individually, have no weight; but, brought all together, they have weight.

It is true that bothersome cold is lacking in Rūpadhātu but beneficent or pleasing cold is found there: such is the opinion of the Vaibhāṣikas. [It is the absorption that the gods enjoy, not the cold.]

It is possible[55] for one visual consciousness to arise from a single thing, from a single category of visible matter: when a characteristic of this thing (blue, etc.) is separately distinguished. In other cases, one consciousness is produced by many things: when such a distinction is lacking; for example, when one sees the multiple colors and shapes that an army or a pile of jewels present at a distance and bunched together. The same remark is applicable to the auditory consciousness, the olfactory consciousnesses, etc.

But one touch consciousness arises from only five things at most, namely the four primary elements and one another of the other tangibles, soft, hard, etc. Such is the opinion of certain masters.

But, according to another opinion, one touch consciousness can arise from eleven tangibles at one and the same time.

[Objection]. According to what you say, each of the five sense consciousnesses bears on a totality, for example the visual consciousness bears on blue, red, etc.; consequently the sense consciousnesses have "general characteristics for their object" and not, as Scripture teaches us, "specific characteristic" (*svalakṣaṇa*).

[The Vaibhāṣikas (*Vibhāṣā*, *TD* 27, p. 65c12) answer that the Scripture] means by specific characteristic not the specific characteristic of things, but the specific characteristic of an *āyatana* (ii.62c).[56]

When the organs of touch and of taste attain their object at the same time (i.43c-d), which consciousness is the first to arise?

The one whose object is the strongest. But if the strength of the two objects is equal, the consciousness of taste arise first, because the desire for food dominates.

***

We have explained the objects of the five organs of sense consciousness, and how these objects are preceived. Let us now examine the *avijñapti*, which is the eleventh category of *rūpaskandha*.

> 11. There is a serial continuity also in a person whose mind is distracted, or who is without mind, pure or impure, in dependence on the primary elements: this is called the *avijñapti*.[57]

"One whose mind is distracted" is one who has a mind different from the mind that provoked the *avijñapti*,—for example, a bad mind when the *avijñapti* has been provoked by a good mind.

"One without mind" is one who has entered into one of the absorptions of non-consciousness called *asaṁjñisamāpatti* [and *nirodhasamāpatti*] (ii.42).

"Also in a person . . :" the word "also" indicates that *avijñapti* also exists in a person with a non-distracted mind, and in a person whose mind is not in the two absorptions.

"A serial continuity" is a flux.

"Pure or impure" means good or bad.

"In dependence on the primary elements:" this in order to distinguish the *avijñapti* series from the *prāpti* series (ii.36). *Avijñapti* depends on the primary elements, because they are its generating cause, etc. (ii.65; *Vibhāṣā, TD* 27, p. 663a26).

"This is called the *avijñapti*" in order to indicate the reason for the name *avijñapti*.

This serial continuity, while being by its nature matter and action,—like *vijñapti*, bodily and vocal action,—nevertheless does nothing by way of informing another as *vijñapti* does.

"Is called," in order to show that the author here expresses the opinion of the Vaibhāṣikas, and not his own.

In short, *avijñapti* is a *rūpa*, good or bad, arisen from *vijñapti* or from absorption.

***

What are the primary elements?

> 12a-b. The primary elements are the elementary substance "earth," and the elementary substances "water," "fire" and "wind."[58]

These four are the four *dhātus*, so called because they bear their own unique characteristics, as well as derived or secondary matter.

They are called "great" (=primary) because they are the point of support for all derived matter. Or it is because they assemble on a large scale in the mass of the earth, the water, the fire and the wind, where their modes of activity are manifested together (*Vibhāṣā*, *TD* 27, p. 681a17, p. 663all).[59]

What activity establishes the existence of these *dhātus*, and what is their nature?

12c. They are proven to exist by the actions of support, etc.

The elements of earth, water, fire, wind, are, in this order, proven to exist by the actions of support, cohesion, ripening and expansion. Expansion signifies growth and deplacement. These are their actions.

12d. They are solidity, humidity, heat and motion.[60]

As for their natures, the earth element is solidity, the water element is humidity, the fire element is heat, and the wind element is motion.[61] Motion is what causes the series of states which constitutes a thing to reproduce itself in different places;[62] in the same way that one speaks of the motion of a flame (iv.2c-d).

The *Prakaraṇa*[63] and the *Sūtra*[64] say: "What is the wind element? It is lightness;" the *Prakaraṇa* also says: "Lightness is a derived *rūpa*." Consequently, the *dharma* which has motion for its nature is the wind element:[65] its nature (lightness) is manifested by its act of motion.

What is the difference between the earth element, and earth, etc?

13a. In common usage, what is designated by the word "earth" is color and shape.

That is, when one sees earth, one sees its color and its shape. As is the case for the earth,

13b. The same for water and fire.

In common usage, that which one designates (by the word water or fire) is color and shape.

13c. Wind is either the wind element,

But the wind element is simply called "wind" in the world.

13d. Or else [color and shape].[66]

What is called "wind" in the world is also the wind element; in fact, one speaks of "black wind," or "circular wind."

***

Why do all these *dharmas*, from visibles to *avijñapti*, receive the name *rūpa*? Why do they together constitute the *rūpaskandha*?

i. The Blessed One said: "Because it is incessantly broken, Oh Bhiksus, one terms it *rūpa upādānaskandha*. By what it is broken? It is broken by contact with the hand."[67]

"To be broken" signifies "to be damaged," as stated in the *Arthavargīya* stanza of the *Kṣudrakāgama* (=*Aṭṭhakavagga*, i.2):[68] "If the pleasures are lacking in a person who ardently searches out these pleasures, such a person is broken, as a person pierced by an arrow is broken." (Compare *Mbh* xiii.193, 48).

But how is *rūpa* damaged?

By deteriorating, by being transformed.

ii. According to other masters, the quality that makes physical matter *rūpa*, namely *rūpaṇa*, is not cutting off, deterioration, but rather impenetrability, impact or resistance,[69] the obstacle thaṭ a *rūpa* opposes to its place being occupied by another *rūpa* (see i.43c-d).[70]

[iii. Objections.]

1. If this is so, the *rūpa* that constitutes an atom, a "monad," will not be *rūpa*, for a monad, not susceptible to deterioration or resistance, is free from *rūpaṇa*.

Without doubt, a monad is devoid of *rūpaṇa*; but a monad never exists in an isolated state;[71] in the state of agglomeration, being an agglomerate, it is liable to deterioration and to resistance (*Vibhāṣā*, *TD* 27, p. 390al).

2. *Rūpas* of the past and the future are not *rūpa*, for one cannot say that they are now in a state of resistance.

Without doubt, but they have been, and they shall be in this state. Whether past or future, they are of the same nature as the *dharma* which is now in a state of resistance. In the same way *indhana* is not only (presently) kindled wood, but also (future) fuel.

3. *Avijñapti* is not *rūpa*, for it is devoid of resistance.

Without doubt, but one can justify the quality of *rūpa* attributed to *avijñapti*:

a. *Vijñapti*, bodily or vocal action, from whence proceeds *avijñapti*, is *rūpa*; thus *avijñapti* is *rūpa*, as the shadow moves when the tree moves.

No. For *avijñapti* is not subject to modifications; further, in order that the comparison be exact, the *avijñapti* should perish when the *vijñapti* perishes, as is the case for the shadow and the tree.

b. Second explanation. *Avijñapti* is *rūpa*, for the primary elements, which constitute its point of support, are *rūpa*.[72]

[Objection.] According to this principle, the five sense consciousnesses would be *rūpa*, for their point of support (the organ of sight, etc.) is *rūpa*.

This response is not valid. *Avijñapti* exists dependent upon the primary elements, as a shadow exists dependent on a tree, as the brilliance of a jewel exists dependent upon the jewel. The visual consciousness is not dependent upon an organ which is solely the cause of its arising.

[Answer.] That the shadow, or the brilliance of a jewel exists dependent upon the tree, or on the jewel, is a hypothesis that does not conform to the principles of the Vaibhāṣikas (*Vibhāṣā*, TD 27, p. 63c22). The Vaibhāṣikas hold that each one of the atoms of color which constitute shade and brilliance, exists dependent upon a tetrad of primary elements. And even supposing that: "The shadow is dependent upon the tree, since the shadow is dependent on the primary elements which are proper to it, and these are dependent upon the tree,"—the comparison to the shadow and *avijñapti* is inadmissible. The Vaibhāṣikas admit that *avijñapti* does not perish when the primary elements which serve as its point of support perish (iv. 4c-d). Consequently your refutation ("This response is not valid. *Avijñapti* . . .") is worthless.

But, we would say, one can refute the objection: "According to this principle, the five sense consciousnesses would be *rūpa*."

In fact, the support of visual consciousness is twofold: 1. the organ of sight, which is in a state of "impact" (i.29b), which is *rūpa*; and 2. the mental organ (*manas*, i.44c-d) which is not *rūpa*.

Now the same does not hold for *avijñapti* whose point of support is exclusively *rūpa*. Thus, from the fact that *avijñapti* is called *rūpa* because its point of support is *rūpa*, one cannot conclude that visual consciousness should be called *rūpa*. Therefore, the second explanation is the right one.

***

The organs and objects which have been defined as *rūpaskandha*,

> 14a-b. These same organs and objects are regarded as ten *āyatanas*, ten *dhātus*.[73]

Considered as *āyatana*, origin of the mind and of the mental states (i.20), they are ten *āyatanas*: *cakṣurāyatana*, *rūpāyatana*, . . . *kāyāyatana*, *spraṣṭavyāyatana*.

Considered as *dhātu*, a mine (i.20), they are ten *dhātus*: *cakṣurdhātu*, *rūpadhātu* . . . *kāyādhatu*, *spraṣṭavyadhātu*.

***

We have explained *rūpaskandha* and how it is distributed into *āyatanas* and *dhātus*. We must now explain the *skandhas*.

> 14c. Sensation is painful impression, etc.[74]

Vedanāskandha is the threefold mode of feeling or experiencing sensation which is painful, pleasant, neither-painful-nor-pleasant. One should distinguish six classes of sensations: those which arise from the contact of the five material organs, the organ of sight, etc., with their object; and those which arise from contact with the mental organ (ii.7 and following).

> 14c-d. Ideas consist of the grasping of characteristics.[75]

The grasping of the diverse natures—perceiving that this is blue, yellow, long, short, male, female, friend, enemy, agreeable, disagreeable, etc.—is *saṁjñāskandha* (see i.16a). One can distinguish six types of *saṁjñā*, according to organ, as for sensation.

> 15a-b. *Saṁkāraskandha* are the *saṁskāras* different from the other four *skandhas*.[76]

The *saṁskāras* are everything that is conditioned (*saṁskṛta*,i.7a); but the name is reserved for those conditioned things which are not included in either the *skandhas* of *rūpa*, *vedanā*, or *saṁjñā*, explained above, or in the *skandha* of *vijñāna* explained below (i.16).

It is true that the Blessed One said in a Sūtra, "The *saṁskāraskandha* is the six classes of volition;"[77] but this definition excludes from *saṁskāraskandha* 1.) all the *viprayuktasaṁskāras* (ii.35), and 2.) the *saṁprayuktasaṁskāras* (ii.23b, 34), with the exception of volition itself. But the Sūtra expresses itself thus by reason of the capital importance of volition, which, being action by its nature,[78] is by definition the factor which creates future existence. Also the Blessed One said, "The *upādānaskandha* called *saṁskāra* is so called because it conditions conditioned things,"[79] that is to say, because it creates and determines the five *skandhas* of future existence.[80]

If we take the definition of the Sūtra literally, we would then arrive at the conclusion that the mental *dharmas*, with the exception of volition, and all of the *dharmas* of the *viprayukta* class (ii.35), do not form part of any *skandha*. They would thus not form part of the Truths of Suffering and Arising: one would not either know them, nor abandon them. Now the Blessed One said, "If there is a single *dharma* which is not known and penetrated, I declare that one cannot put an end to suffering" (vi.33). And again "If there is a single *dharma* which is not abandoned . . . " (*Saṁyukta TD* 2, p. 55b7, b23). Thus the collection of mental states and *viprayuktas* is included within the *saṁskāraskandha*.

> 15b-d. These three *skandhas*, with *avijñapti* and unconditioned things, are the *dharmāyatana*, the *dharmadhātu*.

Vedanāskandha, saṁjñāskandha, saṁskāraskandha, plus *avijñapti* (i.11) and the three unconditioned things (i.5b), are seven things which are called *dharmāyatana* or *dharmadhātu*.

16a. Consciousness is the impression relative to each object.[81]

Vijñānaskandha is the impression relative to each object, the "raw grasping"[82] of each object.[83] *Vijñānaskandha* is six classes of consciousness, visual, auditory, olfactory, taste, touch, and mental consciousness.

Considered as *āyatana* (i.20a),

16b. It is the mental organ.

Considered as *dhātu* (i.20a),

16c. It is seven *dhātus*.

What are the seven?

16d. The six consciousnesses and the *manas*.

That is to say: the *dhātu* of the eye or visual consciousness (*cakṣurvijñānadhātu*), the *dhātu* of the ear or auditory consciousness (*srotravijñānadhātu*), the *dhātu* of the nose or olfactory consciousness (*ghrāṇavijñānadhātu*), the *dhātu* of tongue or taste consciousness (*jihvāvijñānadhātu*), the *dhātu* of body or touch consciousness (*kāyavijñānadhātu*), the *dhātu* of mind or mental consciousness (*manovijñānadhātu*), and the *dhātu* of the mind (*manodhātu*).

We have seen that there are five *skandhas*, twelve *āyatanas*, and eighteen *dhātus*.

1. *Rūpaskandha* is ten *āyatanas*, ten *dhātus*, and *avijñapti*.

2. The *dharmāyatana*, or *dharmadhātu* is *vedanā, saṁjñā and saṁskārāskandha*; *avijñapti*; and the unconditioned things.

3. *Vijñānaskandha* is the *mana-āyatana*; it is seven *dhātus*, namely the six classes of consciousness (*vijñānakāya* = *vijñānadhātu*) and the mental organ.

Could a *manas* or *manodhātu* be distinct from the six classes of consciousness, distinct from the sense consciousness and from the mental consciousness?

There is no *manas* distinct from the consciousness.[84]

17a-b. Of these six consciousness, the one which continually passes away, is the *manas*.[85]

All consciousness which has just perished receives the name of *manodhātu*; in the same way, a man is both son and father, the same vegetable element is both fruit and seed.

[Objection.] If the six consciousnesses which make up six *dhātus* constitute the *manas*, and if the *manas* is not a thing other than the six consciousnesses, then there would be either seventeen *dhātus*,—by excluding the *manas* which is co-functional with the six consciousnesses,—or else twelve *dhātus*, by excluding the six consciousnesses which are co-functional with the *manas*,—supposing of course that you want to enumerate distinct things and not mere designations.

This is true; but

17c-d. One counts eighteen *dhātus* with a view to assigning a point of support to the sixth consciousness.

The first five consciousnesses have for their point of support the five material organs, organ of sight, etc. (see i.44c-d); but the sixth consciousness, the mental consciousness, does not have such a point of support. Consequently, with a view to attributing a point of support to this consciousness, one calls *manas* or *manodhātu*, or again *mana-āyatana* and *mana-indriya*, that which serves it as its point of support, that is to say, any one of the six consciousnesses which depend on these six points of support, and six objects.

[Objection.] If the consciousness or mind is called *manas* when, having perished, it is the point of support of another consciousness, the last mind of an Arhat will not be a *manas*, for it is not followed by a mind of which it would be the immediately antecedent cause and point of support (i.44c-d).

This last mind has indeed the nature of *manas*, the nature of being a point of support. If it is not followed by a new mind, namely the consciousness-of-conception of a new existence (*punarbhava*), this is not related to its nature; rather, this results from the absence of other causes, actions and defilements, necessary to the production of a new thought.

***

All conditioned *dharmas* are included within the totality of the *skandhas* (i.7); all of the impure *dharmas* are included within the totality of the *upādānaskandhas* (i.8); and all the *dharmas* are included within the totality of the *āyatanas* and the *dhatus* (i.14). But, more briefly,

> 18a-b. All the *dharmas* are included in one *skandha*, one *āyatana*, and one *dhātu*.[86]

In *rūpaskandha, mana-āyatana* and *dharmadhātu.*

> 18c. A *dharma* is included in its own nature.[87]

Not in another nature. Why is this?

> 18d. For it is distinct from the nature of others.

A *dharma* is not included (*saṁgraha*) in that from which it is distinct. For example, the organ of sight is included within the *rūpaskandha*, being *rūpa* by its nature; within the *cakṣurāyatana* and within the *cakṣurdhātu*, for it is the *cakṣurāyatana* and *cakṣurdhātu*; within the Truth of Suffering and Arising, for it is suffering and arising; but it is not included within the other *skandhas, āyatanas*, etc., for it is distinct by its nature from that which is not itself.

Without doubt the assemblies are won over by alms-giving and other *saṁgrahavastus*:[88] there is therefore *saṁgraha* of one thing by a thing different from it.

But the *saṁgraha* is occasional and as a consequence, not real, but conventional.

But, there are two organs of sight, of hearing, and of smell; consequently one should count twenty-one *dhātus*.

> 19a-c. The organs of sight, of hearing, and of smell, although twofold, form only, in pairs, one *dhātu*, for their nature, their sphere of activity, and their consciousnesses are common.

The two organs of sight have a community of nature, for they are—both of them—the organ of sight; community of sphere, for they both have visible matter for their sphere; and community of consciousness, for they are both the point of support of the visual consciousness. Consequently the two organs of sight form a single *dhātu*.

The same holds for the organs of hearing and smell.

> 19d. It is for beauty's sake that they are twofold.

Although they form only one *dhātu*, these organs are produced in pairs, with a view to the beauty of the body. With but a single eye, a single ear, or a single nostril, one would be very ugly (ii.1a; i.43, 30).[89]

***

What is the meaning of the terms *skandha, āyatana*, and *dhātu*?

> 20a-b. *Skandha* signifies "heap," *āyatana* signifies "gate of entry," "gate of arising," and *dhātu* signifies "lineage."

i. In the Sūtra, *skandha* signifies "heap:" "Whatever *rūpa* there is, past, present, or future, internal or external, gross or subtle, inferior or excellent, far or near, if one puts together all this *rūpa*, that which is past, etc., one has that which is called *rūpaskandha*."[90]

[According to the Vaibhāṣikas,] (1) past *rūpa* is *rūpa* destroyed by impermanence,[91] future *rūpa* is *rūpa* which has not arisen, and present *rūpa* is *rūpa* which has arisen and which has not been destroyed; (2) *rūpa* is internal when it forms part of the series called "me" (i.39); all other *rūpa* is external; or rather the terms internal and external are understood from the point of view of *āyatana*: the organ of sight is internal because it forms part of my series or of the series of another; (3) *rūpa* is gross when it offers resistance; or rather these two designations are relative and not absolute.

Should one say that, in this second hypothesis, the gross and the subtle are not proven, since the same *rūpa* is gross or subtle according to whether one compares it to a *rūpa* more subtle or gross?

This objection is invalid, for terms of comparison do not vary:

when a *rūpa* is gross in relation to another *rūpa*, it is not subtle in relation to this same other *rūpa*: like father and son.

(4) Inferior *rūpa* is defiled *rūpa*; excellent *rūpa* is non-defiled *rūpa*; (5) past and future *rūpa* are distant; present *rūpa* is near.[92]

The same for the other *skandhas*, with this difference: gross consciousness is that which has for its point of support the five organs; subtle consciousness is the mental consciousness; or rather consciousness is gross or subtle according to whether it belongs to a stage which is inferior or superior.

According to the Bhadanta,[93] (1) gross *rūpa* is that which is perceived by the five organs; all other *rūpa* is subtle; (2) "inferior" signifies "unpleasant," "excellent" signifies "pleasant;" (3) distant *rūpa* is that which is found in an invisible place; near *rūpa* is that which is found in a visible place.

[The explanation of the Vaibhāṣikas is bad, for] past *rūpa*, etc., has already been designated by its name. The same for sensation; it is far or near according to whether its point of support is visible or invisible; it is gross or subtle according to whether it is corporeal or mental (ii.7).

ii. *āyatana* signifies "gate of entry or of arising of the mind and of the mental states" (*cittacaitta*, ii.23). Etymologically, *āyatana* is that which extends (*tanvanti*) the entry (*āya*) of the mind and of the mental states.[94]

iii. *Dhātu* signifies *gotra*, race, lineage.[95] In the same way that the place, the mountain, where there are many "families" of gems,—iron, copper, silver, gold,—is said "to have numerous *dhātus*," in this same way in the human complex or series, there are eighteen types of "families" which are called the eighteen *dhātus*.

Gotra is thus a mine.[96] Of what is the organ of the eye the mine? Of what are the other *dhātus* the mine?

The *dhātus* are the mine of their own species: the eye, being a "cause similar to its effect" (*sabhāgahetu*, ii.52) of the later moments of the existence of the eye, is the mine, the *dhātu* of the eye.

But then unconditioned things, which are eternal, cannot be considered as *dhātu*?

Let us say that they are the mine of the mind and mental states.

According to another opinion, *dhātu* signifies species. The specific nature of the eighteen *dhātus* is what is understood by the eighteen *dhātus*.

iv. [Objections.[97]] 1. If *skandha* signifies "heap," the *skandhas* have only a nominal existence, not a real existence, for collections are not a thing: for example a pile of wheat, or the *pudgala*.[98]

[99]No, [reply the Vaibhāṣikas,] for an atom is a *skandha*.

As an atom in this hypothesis cannot have the quality of being a heap, do not say that *skandha* signifies "heap."

2. According to another opinion (*Vibhāṣā TD* 27, p. 407c9), *skandha* signifies "that which bears the burden, namely its effect."[100] Or else *skandha* signifies "part, section,"[101] as one says in the world, "I will lend you three *skandhas*, if you promise to return them to me."[102]

These two explanations are not in conformity with the Sūtra.[103] The Sūtra, in fact, attributes the sense of heap to *skandha* and no other sense: "Whatever *rūpa* there is, past, present, or future, . . . if one puts together all this *rūpa* . . ."

3. [The Vaibhāṣikas say: The Sūtra teaches that] all *rūpa*,—past *rūpa*, future *rūpa*, etc.,—is, individually, called *skandha*, the same way that it teaches that hair, etc., is earth-element (below, note 120); thus each "real" (atomic) element of past *rūpa*, future *rūpa*, etc., receives the name of *skandha*. Thus the *skandhas* have real existence and not merely nominal existence.

This interpretation is inadmissible, for the Sūtra says ". . . if one puts together all this *rūpa*, . . . one has that which is called *rūpaskandha*."

4. [The Sautrāntikas:] If this is the case, then the material *āyatanas*,—the organs and objects of the five sense consciousnesses,—have only a nominal existence, for the quality of being a "gate of arising of the mind or mental states" does not belong to atoms taken one by one, which are solely real, but to collections of atoms which constitute an organ of sight, a visible object, etc.

[Answer:] No, since each of these atoms individually possesses the quality of being "a gate of the arising of the mind," of being the cause of consciousness (compare i.44a-b.iii). If you do not accept this doctrine, you will refuse to the organ, in its totality, the quality of being a cause of consciousness, for it does not produce a consciousness by itself, without the cooperation of an object.

5. On the other hand, the *Vibhāṣā* (*TD* 27, p. 384a18) expresses itself thus: "When the Ābhidhārmikas[104] take into consideration the fact that the term *skandha* is only the denomination of a heap, they say that an atom is part of a *dhātu*, an *āyatana*, and a *skandha*; when they do not take this fact into consideration, they say that an atom is a *dhātu*, an *āyatana*, a *skandha*."[105] In fact, one metaphorically designates the part by the whole; for example, "The robe is burned," for "One part of the robe is burned."

***

Why did the Blessed One give *skandhas*, *āyatanas* and *dhātus* as the triple designation of the *dharmas*?

> 20c-d. The teachings of the *skandhas*, etc., because error, faculty, joy are threefold.[106]

1. Error is threefold: the first catagory of persons go astray by considering mental phenomena as together constituting a self; the second are similarly mistaken with respect to the material elements; and the third similarly err with respect to both the mental and the material elements.

2. The moral faculties (ii.3c-d), the faculty of speculative consciousness (*prajñendriya*, ii.24d), are of three catagories, sharp, mediocre, dull.

3. Joy is threefold: the first category of persons apply themselves to that which is said in brief; the second to that which is said normally; the third to that which is said at great length.

The teaching of the *skandhas* addresses itself to the first category of hearers, to those who are mistaken with respect to mental phenomena, who are of sharp faculties, and who are fond of a brief teaching; the teaching of the *āyatanas* addresses itself to the second category, and the teaching of the *dhātus* addresses itself to the third category.[107]

***

Sensation and ideas each constitute a seperate *skandha*: all the other mental *dharmas* (ii.24) are placed within the *saṁskāraskandha* (i.15). Why is this?

> 21. The two mental states, sensation and ideas, are defined as distinct *skandhas* because they are the causes of the roots of dispute, because they are the causes of transmigration, and also by reason of the causes which justify the order of *skandhas*. (i.22b)[108]

1. There are two roots of dispute:[109] attachment to pleasure, and attachment to opinions. Sensation and ideas are, respectfully, the principal causes of these two roots. In fact, if one becomes attached to pleasures, it is because one relishes the sensation; if one becomes attached to opinions, it is by reason of erroneous or false ideas (*viparītasaṁjñā*, v.9)

2. Sensation and ideas are the causes of transmigration: those who are greedy for sensation and whose ideas are erroneous transmigrate.

3. The reasons which justify the order of the *skandhas* will be explained below (i.22b-d).

***

Why do unconditioned things, which form part of the *dharmāyatana* and the *dharmadhātu* (i.15d), not form part of the *skandhas*?

> 22a-b Unconditioned things are not named with respect to the *skandhas*, because they do not correspond to the concept.[110]

1. Unconditioned things cannot be placed within any of the five *skandhas*, for they are not matter, nor sensation . . .

2. One cannot make a sixth *skandha* of the unconditioned: it does not correspond to the concept of *skandha*, since *skandha* signifies "heap," "capable of being put together." One cannot say of the unconditioned what the Sūtra says of matter: "If one puts together all this unconditioned, that which is past . . . , one has that which one calls the a *asaṁskṛtaskandha*," for the distinctions of past, etc., do not exist with respect to unconditioned things.

3. Furthermore, the expression *upādānaskandha* (i.8a) designates the totality of that which is the cause of defilements; the expression *skandha* designates the totality of that which is the cause of defilement (impure conditioned things) as well as the cause of purification (pure conditioned things: the Path). Thus unconditioned things, which are neither the cause of defilement, nor the cause of purification, cannot be placed either among the *upādānaskandhas* nor among the *skandhas*.

4. According to one opinion, the same way that the end of a jug is not a jug, in this same way unconditioned things, which are the end or cessation of the *skandhas*, are not *skandhas* (*Vibhāṣā*, *TD* 27, p. 385b18). And so according to this reasoning unconditioned things will be neither *āyatanas* nor *dhātus*.

***

We have defined the *skandhas*. We should now explain the order in which the *skandhas* are enumerated.

> 22b-d. The order of the *skandhas* is justified by their grossness, their defilement, the characteristic of the jug, etc., and also from the point of view of their spheres of influence.[111]

1. Matter, being subject to resistance (i.29b), is the grossest of the *skandhas*. Among the non-material *skandhas*, sensation is the grossest, by reason of the grossness of its functioning: in fact, one localizes sensation in the hand, in the foot, etc. Ideas are grosser than the last two *skandhas*. The *saṁskāraskandha* is grosser that the *skandha* of consciousness. The *skandhas* are thus arranged in order of their diminishing grossness.

2. In the course of external transmigration, men and women are mutually infatuated by their bodies (*rūpas*) because they are attached to the pleasures of sensation (*vedanā*). This attachment proceeds from erroneous ideas (*saṁjñviparyāsa*), which are due to the defilements which are *saṁskāras*. And it is the mind (*citta*) which is defiled by the defilements. The *skandhas* are thus arranged according to the process of their defilement.

3. Matter is the pot, sensation is the food, ideas are the seasoning, the *saṁskāras* are the cook, and the mind is the consumer. We have a third reason for the order of the *skandhas*.

4. Finally, in considering the *skandhas* on the one hand, and the *dhātus* or spheres of existence (ii.14) on the other, one sees that Kāmadhātu is characterized by matter, namely by the five objects of sense enjoyment (*kāmaguṇa*: *Dharmaskandha*, 5.15, *Vibhāṣā*, *TD* 27, p. 376all: compare *Kathāvatthu*, viii.3). Rūpadhātu, that is to say the Four Dhyānas, is characterized by sensation (organs of pleasure, satisfaction, and indifference, viii.12). The first three stages of Ārūpyadhātu are characterized by ideas: ideas of infinite space, etc. (viii.4). The fourth stage of Ārūpyadhātu, or the summit of existence, is characterized by volition, the *saṁskāra* par excellence, which there creates an existence of twenty-four thousand cosmic ages (iii.81c). Finally, these diverse stages are the "abodes of consciousness" (*vijñānasathiti*, iii.6): it is in these places that the mind resides. The first four *skandhas* constitute the field; the fifth constitutes the seed.

There are thus five *skandhas*, no more, no less. One sees how the reasons which justify the order of the *skandhas* also justify the doctrine that makes sensation and ideas seperate *skandhas*: they are grosser than the other *saṁskāras*; they are the cause of the process of defilement; they are the food and the seasoning; and they reign over the two spheres of existence.

***

One should now explain the order in which the six *āyatanas* or *dhātus* which are the six organs of consciousness, the organ of sight, etc., are enumerated: an order the function of which is to arrange the objects (*viṣaya*) and the consciousnesses which correspond to these organs (*rūpadhātu, cakṣurvijñānadhātu* . . .)

> 23a. The first five are the first because their object is present.

Five, beginning with the organ of sight, are called the first, because they bear only on present, simultaneous objects. Conversely, the object of the mental organ can be either (1) simultaneous to this organ; (2) earlier or past; (3) later or future; (4) tritemporal, that is to say simultaneous, earlier and later; or (5) beyond time.

> 23b. The first four are the first because their object is solely derived or secondary matter.

The organs of sight, of hearing, of smell and of taste do not attain to the primary elements (i.12), but solely to matter which derives from the primary elements (*bhautika*, ii.50a, 65).

The object of touch is not constant (i.35a-b, 10d): sometimes primary elements, sometimes derived matter, sometimes both at the same time.

> 23c. These four are arranged according to the range and speed of their activity.

Their activity is at a distance, at a greater distance, very rapid.

The organ of sight and the organ of hearing bear on a distant object (i.43c-d). They are thus named first.

The organ of sight bears on objects at a greater distance than does the organ of hearing: for one can see a river of which one cannot make out the sound. The organ of sight is thus named before the organ of hearing.

Neither odor nor taste are perceived at a distance. But the activity of smell is more rapid than that of taste. The organ of smell perceives the odor of food before the organ of taste perceives its taste.

> 23d. Or rather the organs are arranged according to their position.

The point of support or the place of the organ of sight, that is to say, the eye, is the highest; below that, the place of the organ of hearing; below that, the place of the organ of smell; below that, the place of the organ of taste. As for the place of the organ of touch, that is to say the body, it is, for the most part, lower than the tongue. As for the mental organ, it is not matter (i.44a-b).

***

Among the ten *āyatanas* included within *rūpaskandha*, only one receives the name of *rūpa-āyatana*. And although all the *āyatanas* are *dharmas*, only one is called *dharma-āyatana*. Why?

> 24. A single *āyatana* is called *rūpa-āyatana* with a view to distinguishing it from the others, and by reason of its excellence. A single *āyatana* is called *dharma-āyatana* with a view to distinguishing it from the others, and because it includes many of the *dharmas* as well as the best *dharma*.[112]

The ten material *āyatanas* (i.14a-b) are, each one separately, *āyatana*: five are subjects, and five are the objects of a specific consciousness. They are not, in their totality, a single *āyatana*, a single source of consciousness, so that they could be called a *rūpa-āyatana*. Nine are individualized by specific names: *cakṣurayātana*, *śrotrāyatana*, *śabdāyatana* . . . The *āyatana* which does not bear any of these nine names, and which is matter, is sufficiently designated by the expression *rūpa-āyatana*, without there being any need to give it another name. name.

But the nine other *āyatanas* are also both *āyatana* and *rūpa*: why is the name of *rūpa-āyatana* given in preference to the object of the organ of sight?

By reason of its excellence. It is *rūpa*, in fact, (1) by reason of *pratigha*: being subject to resistance, it is "deteriorated" through contact with the hand, etc.; (2) by reason of *deśanidarśana* (i.13, p. 70): one can indicate it as being here, as being there; and (3) by reason of common usage: that which one understands in the world by *rūpa*, is visible matter, color and shape.

The *dharmāyatana* (i.15b-d) is sufficiently distinguished from the other *āyatanas* by the name of *dharmāyatana.* Same explanation as above. It includes numerous *dharmas*, sensations, ideas, etc.; it includes the best *dharma*, that is to say, Nirvāṇa. This is why the general name, *dharmāyatana*, is attributed to it *par excellence.*

According to another opinion,[113] visible matter is called *rūpāyatana* because it includes twenty varieties (blue, etc.), and because it is the sphere of three types of eyes, a fleshy eye, the divine eye, and the wisdom eye (*māṁsa-*, *divya-*, and *prajñācakṣus*; *Itivuttaka*, 61).

***

The Sūtras name other *skandhas*, other *āyatanas*, and other *dhātus*. Are these included within the *skandhas*, *āyatanas*, and *dhatus* described above?

> 25. The eighty thousand *dharmaskandhas* that the Muni promulgated, depending on whether one regards them as "voice" or as "name," are included within the *rūpaskandha* or the *saṁskāraskandha.*[114]

For the teachers who say "The word of the Buddha is, by its nature, voice," these *skandhas* are included within the *rūpaskandha*; for those who consider the word of the Buddha as "name," these *skandhas* are included within the *saṁskāraskandha* (ii.36, 47a-b).

***

What is the dimension of a *dharmaskandha*?

> 26a. According to some, a *dharmaskandha* is of the dimension of the Treatise.[115]

That is to say, of the dimension of an Abhidharma Treatise known by the name of *Dharmaskandha*, which is six thousand stanzas long.[116]

> 26b. The exposition of the *skandhas*, etc., constitutes so many *dharmaskandhas*.[117]

According to another opinion, the exposition of the *skandhas*, *āyatanas*, *dhātus*, *pratītyasamutpāda*, the Truths, the foods, the *dhyānas*, the *apramāṇas*, the *ārūpyas*, the *vimokṣas*, the *abhibhvāyatanas*, the *kṛtsnāyatanas*, the *bodhipakṣikas*, the *abhijñās*, the *pratisaṁvids*, *praṇidhijñāna*, or *araṇā*, etc., are each one of them separately so many *dharmaskandhas*.

> 26c-d. In fact, each *dharmaskandha* has been preached in order to heal a certain category of believer.

Beings, with respect to their dispositions (ii.26), number eighty thousand: some are dominated by affection, others by hatred, others by error, others by pride, etc. Eighty thousand *dharmaskandhas* have been preached by the Blessed One in order to cure them.

***

In the same way that the *dharmaskandhas* are included within *rūpaskandha* or *saṁskāraskandha*,

> 27. In this same way the other *skandhas*, *āyatanas* and *dhātus* should be suitably arranged within the *skandhas*, *āyatanas* and *dhātus* as described above, by taking into account the characteristics that have been attributed to them.

The other *skandhas*, *āyatanas* and *dhātus* which are mentioned in other Sūtras should be arranged within the five *skandhas*, twelve *āyatanas* and eighteen *dhātus*, by taking into consideration the unique characteristics which have been attributed to them in these works.

There are five pure *skandhas*, *śīla* (iv.13), *samādhi* (vi.68), *prajñā* (ii.25), *vimukti* (vi.76c), and *vimuktijñānadarśana*: the first forms part of the *rūpaskandha*, the others of the *saṁskāraskandha* (*Saṁyutta*, i.99, *Dīgha*, iii.279, *Dharmasaṁgraha*, 23).

The first eight *kṛtsnāyatanas* (viii.35), being by their nature absence of desire, form part of the *dharmāyatana.* If one considers them along with their following, they are by their nature five *skandhas*, and they are included within the *mana-āyatana* and the *dharmāyatana.*

The same holds for the *abhibhvāyatanas* (viii.34).

The last two *kṛtsnāyatanas* and the four *ārūpyāyatanas* (viii.2c) are, by their nature, four *skandhas*, with the exclusion of *rūpa.* They are included within the *mana-āyatana* and the *dharmāyatana.*

The five "gates of entry into deliverance" (*vimuktyāyatana*) [118] are, by their nature, speculative knowledge (*prajñā*); they are thus included within the *dharmāyatana.* If one considers their following, they are included within the *śabdāyatana*, the *mana-āyatana*, and the *dharmāyatana.*

Two other *āyatanas* are left: 1. the Asaṁjñisattvas (ii.41b-d), which are included within the ten *āyatanas*, with the exception of smell and taste; and 2. the Naivasaṁjñānāsaṁjñayatanopagas, which are included within the *mana-āyatana* and the *dharmāyatana.*

In this same way the sixty-two *dhātus* enumerated in the *Bahudhātuka* should be arranged within the eighteen *dhātus* by taking their nature into consideration. [119]

***

Among the six *dhātus* or elements mentioned in the Sūtra, [120]—earth element, water element, fire element, wind element, space element, and consciousness element—the last two have not been defined. Is the space element the same thing as all space, the first of the unconditioned things (i.5c)? Is all consciousness (*vijñāna*, i.16) the consciousness element?

> 28a-b. Cavities are called the space element; it is, one says, light and darkness.

[The cavity of the door, the window, etc., is the external space element; the cavity of the mouth, the nose, etc., is the internal space element.] [121]

According to the School (*kila*), the void of the space element is light or darkness—that is to say, a certain type of color, of matter (i..9b), for that which one perceives in a cavity is light or darkness. Being by its nature light or darkness, the void will be day or night.[122]

The void is called *aghasāmantaka rūpa* (*Vibhāṣā*, *TD* 27, p. 388b5).

Agha, some say, is etymologically explained as *atyartham̐ ghātāt*: "because it is extremely capable of striking or of being struck."[123] One should thus understand *agha* as solid, agglomerated matter. The void is thus a type of matter close (*sāmantaka*) to *agha*.

According to another opinion, [our own], *agha* signifies "free from striking" (*a-pratighātāt*). A void is *agha* because other matter does not strike it; it is at the same time close to other matter; it is thus both *agha* and *samāntaka*.

28c. The consciousness element is an impure consciousness.

[Impure consciousness, that is to say, the mind which does not form part of the Path.] Why is it not called pure?

Because these six *dhātus* are

28d. The support of arising.

The six *dhātus* are given in the Sūtra (note 120) as support, as the *raison d'etre* of arising, that is to say, of the "mind at conception", and of all existence until the "mind at death".

The pure *dharmas* are opposed to arising, to existence. Thus the five sense consciousnesses, which are always impure, and the mental consciousness when it is impure, give us the consciousness element (*Vibhāṣā*, *TD* 27, p. 389a8).

***

Of these six *dhātus*, the first four are included within the tangible, the fifth is included within visible matter, and the sixth within the seven *dhātus* enumerated above i.16c.

***

Among the eighteen *dhātus*, how many are visible, "capable of being pointed out?"

29a-b. Only *rūpadhātu* is visible.

One can indicate its place, here, there. The other *dhātus* are invisible.

29b-c. The ten *dhātus* which are exclusively material are capable of being struck.[124]

The ten *dhātus* which are included within the *rūpaskandha* are capable of being struck.[125]

1. Striking, or collision, is of three types: *āvaraṇapratighāta*, *viṣayapratighāta*, and *ālambanapratighāta* (*Vibhāṣā, TD* 27, p. 391c6).

a. *Āvaraṇapratighāta*, being struck by reason of resistance: the quality that belongs to a body of making an obstacle to the arising of another body in the place where it itself is found; impenetrability. When a hand strikes a hand or a rock, when a rock strikes a rock or a hand, it is counterstruck or repelled.

b. *Viṣayapratighāta*, the striking of the organ with that which is its sphere of action. According to the *Prajñapti*:[126] "There is an eye, an organ of sight, which is struck by water and not by dryness, namely the eye of a fish; there is an eye which is struck by dryness and not by water, namely, the eyes of humans in general, (with the exception of fishermen); there is an eye which is struck by water and by dryness, namely, the eye of a crocodile, a crab, a frog, or fishermen; there is an eye which is neither struck by water nor by dryness, namely the eyes which are not of the preceeding categories (for example, the eyes of beings who perish in the womb). There is an eye struck by night, namely the eye of a bat, an owl, etc.; there is an eye which is struck by daylight, namely the eye of humans in general, (with the exception of thieves, etc.); there is an eye which is struck by the night and by daylight, namely the eye of a dog, a jackal, a horse, a leopard, a cat, etc.; there is an eye which is not struck by either night or daylight, namely the eyes which are not of the preceeding categories."[127]

c. *Ālambanapratighāta*, the striking of the mind and mental states with their object. (ii.62c).

What is the difference between a sphere, *viṣaya*, and an object, *ālambana*?

Viṣaya is the place where the organ exercises its activity, seeing, hearing, etc.; *ālambana* is what is grasped by the mind and the mental states. Thus, whereas the mind and mental states have both *viṣaya* and *ālambana*, the eye, the ear, etc., have only *viṣaya*.

Why term "striking" or "evolving" the activity of the organ or the mind with respects to its *viṣaya* or *ālambana?*

Because the organ does not proceed, is not active, beyond the *viṣaya*: thus it is struck by the *viṣaya* (for one says in common usage that one is struck by a wall beyond which one cannot "proceed"). Or rather, "to strike" signifies "to encounter:" this is the process or activity of the organ with respect to its own sphere.

2. When we say that ten *dhātus* are capable of being struck, or *sapratigha*, "characterized by *pratighāta*," we are speaking of *āvaraṇa-pratighāta*: these bodies are mutually impenetrable, capable of collision.

3. Are the *dharmas* which are *sapratigha* through "striking the sphere of action," also *sapratigha* through "impenetrability?"

Four alternatives: 1. the seven *cittadhātus* (i.16c) and one part of the *dharmadhātu*, namely the *saṁprayuktas* (ii.23), are *sapratigha* solely through "striking the sphere of action;" 2. the five spheres, visible matter, etc. (i.9) are *sapratigha* solely through "impenetrability;" 3. the five organs, eye, etc. (i.9) are *sapratigha* from the above two points of view; 4. one part of the *dharmadhātu*, namely the *viprayuktas* (ii.35), are not *sapratigha* through "striking the sphere of action," but are *sapratigha* through "striking the object."

Let us now answer the second term of the question: the *dharmas* which are *sapratigha* through "striking the object"are also *sapratigha* through "striking the sphere of action": but there are *dharmas* which are *sapratigha* through "striking the sphere of action" without being at the same time *sapratigha* through "striking the object," namely the five organs.

4. The Bhadanta Kumāralābha says: "*Sapratigha* is that in which and with regard to which the consciousness can be hindered from

arising by a foreign body; *apratigha* is the opposite."[128]

***

Among the eighteen *dhātus*, how many are good, how many are bad, and how many are morally neutral (*avyākṛta*, iv.8, 9, 45)?

29c. Eight *dhātus* are morally neutral.

What are the eight? These are the ten *dhātus* which are characterized as *sapratigha* (i.29b-c),

29d. Minus visible matter and sound.[129]

"Minus visible matter and sound," that is to say, eight *dhātus*: the five material organs, odor, taste and the tangible, are neutral, not being defined as good or bad; or rather, according to another opinion, not being defined from the point of view of retribution (*vipāka*).

30a. The others are of three types.

The other *dhātus* can be, according to the case, good, bad, or neutral.

1. The seven *dhātus* (*cittadhātavaḥ*, i.16c). are good when they are associated with the three good roots (iv.8), bad when they are associated with bad roots, and neutral in all other cases.[130]

2. The *dharmadhātu* (i.15c-d) includes (1) the good roots, the *dharmas* associated with these roots, the *dharmas* that issue from these roots, and *pratisaṁkhyānirodha* or Nirvāṇa; (2) the bad roots, the *dharmas* associated with these roots, the *dharmas* that issue from these roots; and (3) neutral *dharmas*, for example space.

3. *Rūpadhātu* and *śabdadhātu*, the visible matter and the audible, are good or bad when they constitute a bodily or vocal action (iv.26, 3d) that issued from a good or bad mind. They are neutral in all other cases.

***

Among the eighteen *dhātus*, how many exist in each sphere of existence, Kāmadhātu, Rūpadhātu, and Ārūpyadhātu (iii.1-3)?

> 30a-b. All exist in Kāmadhātu.[131]

All the *dhātus* are associated with, or bound to Kāmadhātu, not disassociated from Kāmadhātu (*Vibhāṣā*, *TD* 27, p. 746cl).

> 30b. Fourteen exist in Rūpadhātu.

There are fourteen *dhātus* in Rūpadhātu.

> 30c-d. With the exception of odor, taste, the consciousness of odor, and the consciousness of taste.[132]

1. Odor and taste are lacking there, for they are "morsel-food" (iii.39) and no one is born into Rūpadhātu who is not detached from this food. Since odor and taste are lacking, the consciousness of odor and taste are lacking also.

Objection: Tangible things should be lacking also, for it is also tangible food by the "mouthful."

No, for tangible things are not exclusively food. Tangibles which are not food do exist in Rūpadhātu.

Objection: One can reason in the same way with respect to odor and taste.

No. The tangible has a useful function apart from food: it serves as the point of support of the organs; it serves as a support in general; and it serves as clothing. Odor and taste have no function outside of eating: they are of no use to beings detached from food.

ii. Śrīlābha gives a different explanation: When a person in Kāmadhātu enters into absorption or *dhyāna*, he sees visible matter; he hears sounds; his body is comforted by a certain tangible which accompanies physical well-being produced by the *dhyāna* (vii.9b). One can conclude from this fact that, in the celestial abodes of Rūpadhātu which bear the name of *dhyāna* (*upapattidhyāna*, iii.2, viii.1), there are visible, audible and tangible things, but not taste and odor.

iii. We think that, if odor and taste are lacking in Rūpadhātu, the organs of smell and taste should also be lacking, for they do not serve any purpose. (Thus there are only twelve *dhātus* in Rūpadhātu.)

1. [Answer of a master who speaks for the Vaibhāṣikas, *vaibhāṣikadeśīya.*] The organs of smell and taste are useful in Rūpadhātu, for, without them, beauty and elocution would be missing.

The nose, support of the subtle matter that constitutes the organ of smell, suffices for beauty (i.44); the tongue, the place of the organ of taste, suffices for elocution.

[The Vaibhāsikadeśīya.] The members,—nose and tongue,—which support the organ, cannot be deprived of this organ. There is no nose or tongue where the subtle matter that constitutes the organ of smell or the organ of taste is missing, in the same way that the sexual member is always endowed with a special organ of touch which is called the sexual organ (i.44a, ii.2c-d).

One can well conceive that the sexual member is lacking when the sexual organ is lacking, for, stripped of this organ, it serves no function; but the nose and the tongue are useful independent of the organs of smell and taste. Thus the nose and tongue exist in Rūpadhātu, although the organs which correspond to them are lacking. Thus there are only twelve *dhātus* in Rūpadhātu.

2. [Answer of the Vaibhāṣikas:] But an organ can arise without having any use, for example the organs of beings destined to perish in the womb.

Agreed! The arising of an organ can be without usefulness: but it is never without a cause. What is the cause of the arising of an organ, if not a certain act commanded by a desire relative to this organ? Now whoever is without attachment to the object, odor, is also without attachment to the organ, the organ of smell. Thus there is no reason for the organs of smell and taste to appear among beings who are reborn in Rūpadhātu, since these beings are detached from odors and tastes. Otherwise, why is the sexual organ lacking in Rūpadhātu?

Reply of the Vaibhāṣikas. The sexual organ is a cause of ugliness (ii.12).

Is it not beautiful among beings who possess the marks of the Mahāpuruṣas? Moreover, it is not by reason of its utility that the sexual organ arises, but rather by reason of its cause. Given its cause, it will arise, even if it is ugly.

3. [Argument from authority.] According to the Vaibhāṣikas, to maintain that the organs of smell and taste are lacking in Rūpadhatū is to contradict the Sūtra. The Sūtra[133] teaches that beings of Rūpadhātu possess, complete, all the organs: they are never one-eyed, or only one-eared (iii.98a).

This text teaches that beings of Rūpadhātu possess, complete, the organs that exist in Rūpadhātu. If the Vaibhāṣikas do not understand it thus, they must then attribute the sexual organ to those beings.

[4. Reply and conclusion of the Vaibhāṣikas.]

Although odor and taste are lacking there, the organs of smell and taste exist in Rūpadhātu.

In fact, a person who is detached from odors keeps his attachement with respect to the organ of smell which is part of his person. Thirst (=desire) enters into action with regard to these six organs of consciousness, not by reason of the object of these six organs, but by reason of the person himself. Thus the arising of the organs of smell and taste has a cause, even if one were detached from odors and tastes. But the same does not hold for the sexual organ. Attachment relative to this organ has for its principle attachment to the tactile consciousness of sexual union. Now beings who will be reborn in Rūpadhātu are detached from this consciousness; thus they have not accomplished actions commanded by a desire relative to the sexual organ; thus this organ is lacking in Rūpadhātu.[134]

31a-b. In Ārūpyādhatu, there is a mental organ, an object of the mental consciousness, and the mental consciousness.

Beings detached from matter arise in Ārūpyādhatu, thus the ten *dhātus* which are material, namely the five organs and their objects, and the five consciousnesses which have for their point of support and for their objects a material *dhātu* (viii.3c), are lacking in Ārūpyādhatu.

***

How many *dhātus* are impure? How many are pure?

31c-d. The three *dhātus* which have just been named can be

pure or impure.

They are pure when they form part of the Truth of the Path or of unconditioned things; in the opposite case they are impure (i.4).

31d. The others are impure.

The other *dhātus*, fifteen in number, are solely impure.[135]

***

How many *dhātus* are associated with *vitarka* and with *vicāra*, free from *vitarka* and associated with *vicāra*, or free from both *vitarka* and *vicāra?*[136]

32a-b. Five consciousnesses always include *vitarka* and *vicara.*

They are always associated with *vitarka* and with *vicāra*, for they are gross, being turned towards externals. The word *hi*, "always," indicates restriction; they are exclusively *dharmas* which include *vitarka* and *vicāra.*

32c. The last three *dhātus* are of three types.

These *dhātus* are the mental organ, the object of mental consciousness, and the mental consciousness.

1. In Kāmadhātu and in the First Dhyāna (viii.7, 11), (1) the *manodhātu*, (2) *manovijñānadhātu*, and (3) that part of the *dharmadhāytu* which is associated with the mind (ii.23), with the exception of *vitarka* and *vicāra* themselves, are associated with *vitarka* and *vicāra.*

2. In the intermediary *dhyāna* (*dhyānāntara*, viii.22d), these same are free from *vitarka*, but associated with *vicāra.*

3. In the higher stages up to and including the last stage, these same are free from both *vitarka* and *vicāra* (viii.23c-d).

4. The part of the *dharmadhātu* which is disassociated from the mind (ii.35) and the *vicāra* of the intermediary *dhyāna* are free from both *vitarka* and *vicāra.*

5. As for *vitarka*, it is always accompanied by *vicāra*; it is always free from *vitarka*, since two simultaneous *vitarkas* are impossible. But

the *vicāra* of Kāmadhātu and the First Dhyāna are not placed within any of the three categories: in fact, it is always associated with *vitarka*, and it is never accompanied by *vicāra*, two simultaneous *vicāras* being impossible.

We therefore say that, in the stages which include *vitarka* and *vicāra* (viii.7), there are four categories: 1. The *dharmas* associated with the mind, with the exception of *vitarka* and *vicāra*, are accompanied by *vitarka* and *vicāra*. 2. *Vitarka* is free from *vitarka*, but accompanied by *vicāra*. 3. The *dharmas* disassociated from the mind are free from *vitarka* and *vicāra*. 4. *Vicāra* is free from *vicāra*, and is accompanied by *vitarka*.

> 32d. The other *dhātus* are free from the one and the other.

The other *dhātus* are the ten material *dhātus*. Not being associated with the mind, they are free from both *vitarka* and *vicāra*.

***

But, if the five sense consciousnesses are always accompanied by *vitarka* and *vicāra*, how are they defined as free from *vikalpa*?

> 33a-b. They are free from *vikalpa* to the extent that they are free from *nirūpaṇāvikalpa* and from *anusmaraṇavikalpa*.[137]

According to the Vaibhāṣikas,[138] *vikalpa* is of three types: *vikalpa* in and of itself or by definition, *vikalpa* consisting of examination, and *vikalpa* consisting of remembering.[139] The five sense consciousnesses include the first type of *vikalpa* but not the other two.[140] This is why one says that they are free from *vikalpa*, in the same way that when a horse has only one foot, one says that it does not have any feet. "*Vikalpa* by definition" is *vitarka*, which we shall study in the chapter on the mental states (ii.33). As for the other two *vikalpas*:

> 33c-d. They are dispersed mental *prajñā*, mental memory whatever it may be.

Mental *prajñā*, that is, the discernment of the *dharmas* associated with the mental consciousness, but dispersed, that is to say, not concentrated, not in the state of absorption (viii.1), is either *vikalpa* of examination or by definition. All mental memory, concentrated or not concentrated, is *vikalpa* of remembering.[141]

***

How many *dhātus* "have an object," that is to say, are the subject of consciousness?

34a-b. The seven *dhātus* which are mind have an object.[142]

Only the *dhātus* of visual, auditory, olfactory, taste, touch, and mental consciousness have an object, because they always grasp their spheres.

34b. And also one part of the *dharmadhātu.*

That part which consists of the *dharmas* associated with the mind (ii.23). The other *dhātus*, namely the ten material *dhātus* and the part of the *dharmadhātu* which is not associated with the mind (ii.35), do not have an object.

***

How many *dhātus* are non-appropriated? How many are appropriated?

34c. Nine are non-appropriated.

What are these nine? The seven that have been mentioned which have an object, together with one-half of the eighth.

34c. The eight that have been mentioned, and sound.

These nine are never appropriated: the seven *dhātus* of mind (i.16c), the *dharmadhātu* (i.15c), and sound are never appropriated.

34d. The other nine are of two types.

They are sometimes appropriated, sometimes non-appropriated.

1. The five organs of sense consciousness (*cakṣurdhātu*, etc.), of the present time, are appropriated. They are not appropriated in the future and in the past.

Four objects,—visible matter, odor, taste, and tangible things,—are appropriated when they are present, when they are an integral part of the organs. Every other visible matter, every other odor, every other taste, and every other tangible is not appropriated: for example, the physical matter,—color and shape—, of hair, body hair, nails and teeth,—with the exception of their roots, which are bound to the body or to the organ of touch; color and shape of excrement, urine, saliva, mucus, blood, etc.; the color and shape of earth, water, fire, etc.

2. What is the meaning of the expression "appropriated?" That which the mind and the mental states grasp and appropriate to themselves in the quality of a support is called "appropriated." Organic matter, that is to say matter which constitutes the five organs of consciousness, as well as matter not separable from organic matter, is "appropriated," is "made one's own," by the mind: this results from the fact that, in the case of well-being or illness, there is a reciprocal reaction between the mind and this matter. Matter that the Abhidharma calls "appropriated," is called in common language, *sacetanā* or sensitive matter.[143]

***

How many *dhātus* are primary matter, or the great, primary elements? How many are secondary matter, matter derived from the primary elements?[144]

35a. The tangible is of two types.

Tangibles are (1) the four primary elements, solidity, fluidity, heat, and motion (i.12); and (2) sevenfold secondary matter, the soft, the hard, etc. (i.10d).

35b. The other nine material *dhātus* are solely secondary matter.

The other material *dhātus*, the five organs and the objects of the first four organs, are solely secondary matter.

35c. As is the part of the *dharmadhātu* which is material.[145]

The same for *avijñapti* (i.11), which forms part of the *dharmadhātu* (i.15c-d).

The *dhātus* of mind (i.16c) are neither primary matter nor secondary matter; the same for the *dharmadhātu*, with the exception of *avijñapti*.

i. According to the Bhadanta Buddhadeva, the ten *āyatanas*, that is, the five organs of consciousness and their objects, are solely primary matter.[146]

An inadmissible opinion. The Sutra teaches, in a limited manner, that there are four primary elements, and it defines them in a limited manner as being solidity, fludity, etc., (i.12d). Now solidity, fluidity, etc., are tangibles and solely tangibles: solidity is not preceived by the organ of sight. Furthermore, each organ attains to the secondary matter which is appropriate to it: color is not preceived by the organ of touch.[147]

Further, that the tangible is primary matter and secondary matter, and that the nine other materials *āyatanas* are solely secondary matter, results from the same words of the Sūtra: "Oh Bhikṣus, the eye, the internal source of consciousness (i.39), a subtle matter derived from the primary elements, material sources, invisible, capable of being struck," and so on with respect to the four other material organs which are described in the same terms. With respect to the first four objects: "The visible matter is an external sources of consciousness, deriving from the primary elements, material, visible, capable of being struck." The same with respect to odor and taste. But, with respect to the tangible: "Tangibles are an external source of consciousness, the four primary elements and matter deriving from the four primary elements . . ."

ii. One can maintain that the five organs are primary matter, for the Sūtra (*Saṁyukta*, 11.1) says: "Everything that is in the eye, a ball of flesh, is solid, resistant . . ."

Reply. Here the Sūtra refers to the ball of flesh which is not separable from the organ of sight, and not to the organ itself.

So be it. But, according to the *Garbhāvakrāntisūtra* (note 120) "a person is the six *dhātus*," the primary element of earth, the primary element of water, the primary element of fire, the primary element of wind, the space element and the *vijñāna* element. Thus, in the embryonic state, the body is made up of primary matter, not secondary matter.

No. For in this first phrase, "a person is the six *dhātus*," the Sūtra means to describe the essence of a person,[148] and it does not pretend to give an exhaustive definition. In fact, the Sūtra then says that a person is the six points of support of the mental *dharma* called contact (ii.24), that is to say, the six organs.[149] Further, to take this definition literally: "a person is the six *dhātus*," one would infer the non-existence of the mental states (*caitta*, ii.24, 34), for the mental states are not included within *vijñānadhātu*, which is the mind.

Would one maintain that the mental states are the mind, and as a consequence are included within *vijñānadhātu*?

One cannot, for the Sutra says "Sensation and ideas are *dharmas* which are mental states, *dharmas* associated with the mind, having the mind for their point of support;" and the Sūtra speaks of a "mind possessing desire;" thus desire, which is a mental state, is not the mind (vii.lld).

It is thus proven that our definition (i.35a-c) is correct.[150]

***

How many *dhātus* are agglomerations? How many are not agglomerations?

> 35d. The ten material *dhātus* are agglomerations.[151]

The five organs of sense consciousness, and their objects, are agglomerations of atoms (ii.22).

***

Among the eighteen *dhātus*, how many cut, and how many are cut; how many burn, and how many are burned; and how many weigh, and how many are weighed?

36e. Four external *dhātus* cut, are cut;

Visible matter, smell, taste and tangible cut, when they bear the name of axe, etc.; they are cut, when they bear the name of wood, etc.

What is the *dharma* that is called "to cut?"

To cut is to produce the sectioning of the procress of an agglomeration the nature of which is to continue itself in an uninterrupted series. The axe cuts a piece of wood which is a series, and makes of it two series which exist and which develop separately.

The organs cannot be cut off. For example, when all of the parts of the organ of touch or the body are cut off, they are not, for all this, multiple: the members which have been cut, that is to say, seperated from the trunk, do not possess touch.

The organs themselves do not cut, by reason of their translucidity, like the sparkle of a jewel.

36b. The same are burned and weighed.

The same holds for being burned and weigh as for cutting off and being cut off. Four external *dhātus* alone are burned. They weigh, for example, when they constitute a scales. Not the organs, by reason of their translucidity, like the sparkle of a jewel.

Sound does not cut off, is not cut off, is not burned, and does not weigh, for it does not exist in a series.

36c-d. There is no agreement with respect to that which is burned and weighed.[152]

There is no agreement with respect to what burns and what is weighed. According to some, the same four external *dhātus* burn and are weighed. According to others, only the primary element of fire burns, when it manifests its own manner of being in the flame; only weight, which is one type of secondary matter (i.10d), is weighed: lightweight things, light, etc., where nevertheless *rūpa* manifests its own manner of being, are not weighed.

***

Among the eighteen *dhātus*, how many are fruition, accumulation, or outflowing? How many are conjoined with material substances? And how many are momentary?

37a. Five internal *dhātus* are of fruition and accumulation.

i. Definitions.

1. *Vipākaja*, "of fruition," or literally, "arisen from fruition" instead of "arisen from the cause of fruition" (*vipākahetuja*, ii.54), by ommission of the middle word, the same way that one says "ox-cart" for "ox-drawn cart."

Or else, in the expression *vipākaja*, "arisen from *vipāka*," the word *vipāka* designates not the fruition, but the ripened action, the action arriving at the time period when it gives forth its fruit.[153] That which arises from ripened action, namely the fruit of retribution, is called "arisen from *vipāka*." The fruit is furthermore also called *vipāka*, because it is cooked (=done).[154]

Or else the expression *vipākaja*, "arisen from fruition," signifies "arisen from the causes of fruition," but one should not say that the word "cause" is omitted. In fact, a cause is often designated by the name of its effect, the same way that an effect is often designated by the name of its cause: "The present six organs are past action" (*Ekottara*, p. 9a7; *Saṁyutta*, ii.65, iv.132; below ii.28).

2. *Aupacayika*, "of accumulation," that is to say "that which is accumulated nearby" through certain foods (iii.39), certain actions (bathing, etc.), certain sleep, or certain absorptions (iv.6c). According to one opinion,[155] chastity is also a cause of accumulation; but in reality, chastity causes there to be no diminution; it is not a cause of accumulation.

Matter "of accumulation" protects the matter "of retribution" as a wall does, by surrounding it.

3. *Naiṣyandika*, "of outflowing," that is to say, *niṣyandaphala*

(ii.57), "that which is produced by a cause similar to its effect."

ii. Five organs or internal *dhātus*, with the exclusion of the mental organ, are of fruition and accumulation. They are not outflowing, for they are outflowing only when they are fruition and accumulation.[156]

iii. Sound is accumulation, for the voice is in a weak state when the body is emaciated.[157] It is also outflowing. It is not a cause of fruition, for the voice proceeds from a desire for action (*chanda*, ii.24).[158]

> 37b. Sound is not of retribution.

Objection. The *Prajñaptiśāstra* says, "This mark of the Mahāpuruṣa (iii.98) which is called 'the voice of Brahmā' results from the perfect practice of abstaining from harmful language (iv.76c)."[159] Thus sound is fruition.

Etiology of sound. First opinion. One should distinguish three moments: (1) action; (2) primary elements arising from this action which are of retribution; and (3) sound, which arises from the primary elements.

Second opinion. One should distinguish five moments: (1) action; (2) primary elements of retribution; (3) primary elements of accumulation; (4) primary elements of outflowing; and (5) sound. Thus sound is not retribution, because it does not immediately proceed from action.

Objection. To reason thus, bodily sensation (ii.7), not being produced immediately through action but being immediately produced through the primary elements arisen from action (iii.32), will not be retribution.

Reply. But sensation is not provoked by a desire to experience such a sensation, whereas sound is provoked by a desire to speak. If it were provoked by desire, it would not be retribution.

> 37c-d. The eight *dhātus* free from resistance are of outflowing and also of fruition.

iv. The eight *dhātus* not capable of resistance (i.29b), namely the seven *dhātus* of mind and the *dharmadhātu*, are outflowing and retribution; they are outflowing when they are produced by similar causes (*sabhāgahetu*, ii.52) or universal causes (*sarvatragahetu*, ii.54), retribution when they are produced by retributive causes (*vipākahetu*, ii.54c). They are not accumulation, because the non-material *dhātus* have nothing in common with agglomeration.

38a. The others are of three types.

v. The other *dhātus*, that is, the four not mentioned above,—visible matter, smell, taste, and tangibles,—are of three types: retribution, when they are not separable from organic matter (i.34); accumulation and outflowing.

***

38a. A single *dhātu* "is real."

The unconditioned, being permanent, is a "real thing." The unconditioned forms part of the *dharmadhātu* (i.15); the *dharmadhātu* is thus the single *dhātu* which "contains a real thing."

***

38b. The last three *dhātus* are momentary.

The last three *dhātus* are the mental organ, the object of mental consciousness, and the mental consciousness.

In the *dharmas* of the moment called *duḥkhe dharmajñānakṣānti*, which is the first moment in the Path of Seeing the Truths (vi.25) and as a consequence the first moment which is pure, these three *dhātus* are "not produced by a cause similar to its effect" (*sabhāgahetu*, ii.52), for, in the series which constitutes the person under consideration, a pure *dharma* has not yet appeared which would be a "cause similar to its effect" of *duḥkhe dharmajñānakṣānti*. This is why these three *dhātus* are called momentary, because, for a moment, they do not proceed from this type of cause.

In the group under consideration, the mind to which the *kṣānti* is associated is *manodhātu* and *manovijñānadhātu*; the *dharmas* which coexist with this mind are *dharmadhātu*: pure discipline (iv.13c);

sensations, ideas, volition and other mental states; plus the *prāptis* (ii.36) and the *saṁskṛtalakṣaṇas* (ii.46).

***

There is a problem to be examined. Does he who obtains possession of the organ of sight where he had previously been lacking it, also obtain possession of the visual consciousness? And does he who obtains possession of the visual consciousness where he was previously lacking it, also obtain possession of the organ of sight?

> 38c-d. He can obtain the organ of sight and the visual consciousness either separately or together.[160]

1. A person lacking the organ of sight takes possession of it without at the same time taking possession of the visual consciousness: (a) a being of Kāmadhātu whose organs progressively appear (ii.14), for, before the organ of sight appears within him, he is already in possession of his past and future visual consciousness (in the intermediary state, iii.14; on "possession," ii.36b); and (b) a being who dies in Ārūpyadhātu and who is reborn in the heavens of the three higher Dhyānas, where the visual consciousness is lacking although the organ of sight exists there (viii.13a-c).

2. A person devoid of the visual consciousness takes possession of it without at the same time taking possession of the organ of sight: (a) a being born in a heaven of the three higher Dhyānas can manifest a visual consciousness of the sphere of the First Dhyāna (viii.13): he does not take possession of the organ of sight which he possesses already; and (b) a being who falls from one of the three higher Dhyānas and who is reborn in a lower sphere.

3. A person devoid of the two takes possession of the two: a being who falls from Ārūpyadhātu and who is reborn either in Kāmadhātu or in the First Dhyāna (world of Brahmā).

We have up to now understood the term that the stanza employs, "to obtain" (*lābha*) in the sense of *pratilambha*, taking possession; but one can also understand it in the sense of *prāpti*, possession (ii.36b).

The question is thus posed: Is one who is endowed with the visual organ also endowed with visual consciousness? Four cases are possible:

(a) a being born in a heaven of the three higher Dhyānas necessarily possesses the visual organ, but possesses only the visual consciousness if he manifests a visual consciousness of the sphere of the First Dhyāna;

(b) a being in Kāmadhātu who has not taken possession of the visual organ in the course of his embryonic life or who becomes blind: he remains in possession of the visual consciousness acquired in the course of his intermediary existence (iii.14) or at conception;

(c) a being in Kāmadhātu who has taken possession of the organ of sight and who has not lost it, a being born in the heaven of the First Dhyāna, a being born in a heaven of the three higher Dhyāna who manifests a visual consciousness of the sphere of the First Dhyānas: these three categories of beings are endowed with both the organ and the consciousness;

(d) all other beings,—beings of Ārūpyadhātu,—are devoid of both the organ of sight and visual consciousness.

The taking possession of and possession, simultaneous or not, of the organ of sight and visible matter, of the visual consciousness and visible matter, of the organ of hearing and sound, etc., shall be defined, as fitting, in each case.

***

How many are external?

39a. Twelve are personal

What are these twelve?

39b. With the exception of visible matter, etc.[161]

Twelve *dhātus* are personal, the six organs and the six consciousnesses; six *dhātus* are external, the six objects of consciousness, visible matter, etc.

But how can one speak of personal *dhātus*, or of external *dhātus*, since there is no *ātman*?

The mind is the object of the idea of self, the mind is what persons falsely grasp for their self. This mind receives, metaphorically, the name of *ātman*. Compare, for example, these two line of Scripture: "The sage obtains heaven, by means of a well subdued *ātman*," and "It is good to subdue the mind; the subdued mind brings happiness."[162] Now the organs and the consciousnesses are close to the mind to which one gives the name of *ātman*: they are in fact the point of support of them; then one qualifies them as "internal," or "personal," whereas the visible and the other objects of the consciousness are held to be "external."

But can one say that the six consciousnesses are the point of support of the mind?

They are the point of support of the mind only when, having perished, they acquire the quality of mental organ (i.17). Thus they are not personal.

This objection is worthless. When the consciousnesses, having perished, becomes the point of support of the mind, it is indeed these consciousnesses themselves which become the point of support; thus, before becoming a point of support, they are not foreign to the quality of point of support. They are thus personal by reason of their future quality of point of support. If it were otherwise, the mental organ would be solely past; it would be neither present nor future. Now it is well understood that the eighteen *dhātus* belong to the three time periods. Moreover, if the present or future consciousness does not have the characteristic of *manodhātu*, it is absurd to attribute this characteristic to it once it is past. For a *dharma* does not change its characterstics in the course of time (v.25; *Vibhāṣā*, *TD* 27, p. 109a18, p. 200b2).

***

Among the eighteen *dhātus*, how many are *sabhāga*, "active" or "in mutual assistance?" How many are *tatsabhāga*, "analogous to *sabhāga*?"

39b-c. The *dhātu* called *dharmas* is *sabhāga.*[163]

An object of consciousness is qualified as *sabhāga* when the consciousness which constitutes its proper sphere arises or is destined to arise with respect to it.

Now there is no *dharma* with respect to which an unlimited mental consciousness has not arisen or is destined to arise. All the Saints in fact necessarily produce the thought "All *dharma* are impersonal" (vii.13a). It is true that this thought bears neither on itself, nor on the *dharmas* which are coexistent with it (*sahabhū*, ii.50b); but this thought and the *dharmas* which are coexistent with it are the object of a second moment of a thought of universal impersonality; all the *dharmas* are thus included within the object of these two moments of thought (vii.18c-d). Therefore the *dharma-dhātu*, the proper object of the mental consciousness, is, in its totality, *sabhāga*, active as an object.

39c-d. The other *dhātus* are also *tatsabhāga.*

The word "also" shows that they are both *sabhāga* and *tatsabhāga.* When are they *tatsabhāga?*

39d. When they do not do their proper work.

This implies the definition: they are *sabhāga* when they do their proper work.

1. The organ of sight which has seen, does now see or shall see visible matter, is termed *sabhāga.* The same with respect to the other organs, by indicating for each its own object and its own operation (*karitra*, ii.58).

2. According to the Vaibhāṣikas of Kaśmīr, the organ of sight is *tatsabhāga* in four cases: the organ of sight which has perished, which is now perishing, which will perish without having seen, and the organ of sight destined to arise (*anutpattidharman*, v.24). According to the Westerners, the organ of sight not destined to arise constitutes two categories depending on whether it is accompanied by visual consciousness or not.

The same with respect to the other organs of sense consciousness.

The mental organ is *tatsabhāga* only when it is not destined to arise; in fact, when it arises, it always has an object.[164]

3. Visible matter, which has been seen, which is now seen, or which will be seen by the organ of sight, is *sabhāga*.

It is *tatsabhāga* when it has perished, is now perishing or shall perish without having seen, or when it is not destined to arise.

The same with respect to the other objects of sense consciousness by indicating for each organ the function which corresponds to it.

4. The organ of sight which is *sabhāga* or *tatsabhāga* is such for everyone, for the person to whom this organ belongs, and for other persons. The same for the other organs. But a certain visible thing is *sabhāga* for the person who sees it. In fact, the visible matter that a person sees can be seen by many, for example, the moon, a stage performance, or a contest, whereas two persons do not see by means of the same organ. Consequently, since one organ of sight is not general, it is though relationship with one person that it will be qualified as *sabhāga* or *tatsabhāga*; the organ of sight is *sabhāga* when he sees a visible thing, even though he has not seen, does not now see, or will not see another visible thing. On the contrary, the visible thing is general: one would qualify it as *sabhāga* and *tatsabhāga* by putting oneself in the point of view of numerous persons: it is *sabhāga* in relation to those who see it, *tatsabhāga* in relation to those who do not see it.

The same holds for sounds, smells, tastes, and the tangible things as for visible matter.[165]

Granted, one would say, with respect to sound which, like visible matter, is perceived at a distance and can be perceived by many persons (i.43c-d). But smells, tastes and tangibles are not perceived at a distance, and are perceived only when they enter into a close relationship with the organ: thus the smell that one person perceives is not perceived by another. Thus these objects are not general, and we should compare them to the organs with respect to the qualification of *sabhāga*, or *tatsabhāga*: when they are *sabhāga* to one person, they are *sabhāga* to everyone.

We would answer: We regard these objects as general, because they can be so. It can be the case that smell—the same atomic group of a smell—which produces a consciousness of smell in one person, is also perceived by another. Now this does not hold for the organs. Consequently smells, tastes and tangibles should be compared to visible matter and sounds.

5. The six consciousnesses are *sabhāga* or *tatsabhāga* depending on whether they are destined to arise, or are not destined to arise, like the mental organ.

6. What is the meaning of the expressions *sabhāga* and *tatsabhāga*?

Bhāga signifies the mutual services that the organs, their objects and their consciousnesses, render one another in their quality of point of support of the consciousness, of objects of consciousness, of consciousness supporting itself on the organ. Or else *bhāga* signifies possession of the activity or function; the function of the organ is to see, etc.; the function of the object is to be the subject of the consciousness (*viṣaya* or *ālambana*), of being seen, etc.; the function of consciousness is to be the subject of consciousness, to be "the discerner."

The *dharmas* which possess (*sa-*) *bhāga* are termed *sabhāga*, that is to say, the organs, objects and consciousnesses which are endowed with their proper function, or else the organs, objects and consciousness which render one another mutual service. Or else the *dharmas* which have "contact" for their effect, that is, the encounter of the eye, visible matter, the visual consciousness, etc., (iii.22), are *sabhāga*.[167]

That which is not *sabhāga*, but is nevertheless analogous to *sabhāga*, is called *tatsabhāga*, that is to say "analogous (*sabhāga*) to that (*tat*)," that is, "analogous to *sabhāga*."[167]

***

How many *dhātus* can be abandoned (*hā*, v.28, vi.1) by Seeing the Truths, in other words, by the Path of Seeing or through Seeing (*darśana*, vi.25b)? How many can be abandoned by Meditation or repeated consideration of the Truths, in other words, by the Path of Meditation or by Meditation? How many *dhātus* are not to be abandoned, or cannot be abandoned?

40a. Ten and five are abandoned through Meditation.

i. The ten material *dhātus*, organs and objects, and the five sense consciousnesses, are abandoned through Meditation.

40b. The last three are of three types.[168]

From the point of view of abandoning them, the last three *dhātus*,—the mental organ, the mental object, and the mental consciousness,—include three types of *dharmas*:

(a) Eighty-eight *anuśayas* (v.4), with their coexistent *dharmas*—whether these coexistents be of the *saṁprayukta* class (ii.24) or of the *viprayukta* class (ii.46, i.e., *lakṣaṇas* and *anulakṣaṇas*)—are abandoned by Seeing, with the *prāptis* (ii.36) of the said *anuśayas* and the said coexistents, with their following (*anuprāptis* and *lakṣaṇas*) of the said *prāptis*.

(b) The other impure *dharmas* are abandoned by Meditation: 1. ten *anuśayas* (v.5) with the coexistents, *prāptis*, etc.; 2. the good-impure (*kuśalasāsrava*) and undefiled-neutral (*anivṛtāvyākṛta*, ii.66) *saṁskāras*; 3. the impure *avijñapti* with its following (iv.13).

(c) The pure *dharmas*, that is, unconditioned things and the *dharmas* which form part of the Path, are not to be abandoned.

ii. Objection. [The Vātsīputrīyas believe that,] not only the eighty-eight *anuśayas*, but also some other *dharmas* are abandoned by Seeing. (1)The quality of Pṛthagjana[169] is a *dharma* which is undefiled-neutral, and yet you place it among the *dharmas* abandoned by Meditation; (2) bad bodily or vocal action, retributed by a bad realm of rebirth, is "visible matter," and yet you also place it within the second category. Now the quality of Pṛthagjana and the action which causes a bad realm of rebirth are in contradiction with the Path of Seeing the Truths. Thus, according to us, both are abandoned through Seeing.

In order to refute the thesis [of the Vātsīputrīyas,] the author says in summary:

40c. Neither the "undefiled," nor matter, are abandoned by Seeing the Truths.[170]

1. Nothing that is defiled, that is bad, nor defiled-neutral (*nivṛtāvyākṛta*, ii.66), and nothing that is material, can be abandoned by the Seeing of the Truths.

Now the quality of Prthagjana is not defiled: it can belong to a person who has cut off the good roots (iv.79), but it can also belong to a person who is "detached."

Bodily action and vocal action are *rūpa*.

The quality of Pṛthagjana and bodily or vocal action are not contradictory to the Truths,—for the former 1. is not defiled by the defilements, and 2. is not a consciousness, a *dharma* which has an object. Thus neither are abandoned by the Seeing of the Truths.

Further, if the quality of Pṛthagjana were abandoned by Seeing, it would follow that it would exist in the first state of the Path of Seeing—which is incorrect.[171]

40d. Nor that which has arisen from the non-sixth.

2. "Sixth" signifies the mental organ. "Arisen from the non-sixth" is what has arisen from an organ different from the sixth organ, that is to say, what has arisen from the five organs, the organ of sight, etc. This then referes to the visual consciousness, etc. These are also not abandoned by Seeing.

***

Among the eighteen *dhātus*, how many are "view," how many are not "view?"

41a. The organ of sight and part of the *dharmadhātu* are view.

How many [parts are there to the *dharmadhātu*]?

41b. Eight parts.

What are these eight parts of the *dharmadhātu*?

(1-5) The five false views, of which the first is belief in a self and mine; they will be defined in the Chapter on the Defilements (v.7). (6)

Worldly correct views, that is to say, *prajñā* (ii.24) associated with the mental consciousness, good but impure. (7-8) And the view of the Śaikṣas and the Aśaikṣas, that is to say, pure view which is proper to the Arhat (vi.50).

These eight *dharmas*, which form part of the *dharmadhātu*, are "views."

Comparison. In the manner in which visible matter is seen at night and in the daytime, on a cloudy day and on a clear day, in this same way the *dharmas* are seen (1) by defiled worldly views,—five false opinions; (2) by non-defiled worldly view or worldly correct views; (3) by Śaikṣī views; and (4) by non-Aśaikṣī views.

***

Why are correct worldly views understood solely as *prajñā* associated with the mental consciousness?

> 41c-d. The *prajñā* which arises with the five sense consciousnesses, is not "view" because it is not judgment after deliberation.[172]

"View" is judgment that preceeds from the consideration of an object (*upadhyāna*, viii.1). Now the *prajñā* which arises with the five sense consciousnesses does not present this characteristic. Thus it is not "view." For the same reason, it happens that *prajñā*, even though mental, defiled or non-defiled, is not "view" when it is purely intuitive (vii.1).

***

But, one would say, the organ of sight does not possess "judgment which proceeds from a consideration of the object." How do you then say that it is "view?"

"View" is understood here as the seeing of visible matter.

> 42a. It is the organ of sight which sees visible matter.

i. A Vijñānavādin is a master who attributes sight, not to the organ of sight, but to visual consciousness. He says: If an organ sees, then the organ of a person occupied with hearing or touch consciousness, would see (i.6c-d).

42b. When it is *sabhāga*.

We do not say that all organs of sight see. The organ of sight sees when it is *sabhāga* (i.39), that is to say, when it is conjoined with visual consciousness.

42c. It is not the consciousness of which this organ is the point of support.

But then, that which sees is indeed the consciousness which is supported by the organ of sight.

42d. For obscured visible matter is not seen. Such is the opinion of the Vaibhāṣikas.[173]

No, for visible matter, obscured by a wall or any other screen, is not seen. Now the consciousness is non-material, not capable of being repulsed (*apratigha*, i.29b). Thus, if the visual consciousness were to see, it would see even the visible matter obscured by a screen.

[The Vijñānavādin replies.] The visual consciousness does not arise with respect to obscured visible matter; not arising with respect to them, it does not see them.

But why does it not arise with respect to these visible things? For us, the Vaibhāṣikas, who attribute seeing to the organ and who admit that the organ, being *sapratigha* or capable of being arrested, does not exercise its activity with respect to obscured visible matter, we could easily explain how the visual consciousness does not arise with respect to obscured visible matter: the consciousness, in fact, exercises its activity on the same object that its point of support does. But if you believe that the consciousness sees, how would you explain the fact that it does not arise with respect to obscured visible matter?

2. The author takes into consideration the opinion of the Vijñānavādin and responds to the last reply of the Vaibhāṣika.

Do you maintain that an organ of sight sees its object by entering into a close relationship with its object, in the manner in which the organ of touch feels a tangible object (i.43c-d)? In this hypothesis I would understand that the organ of sight, being capable of being arrested, does not see obscured visible matter. But you maintain that the organ of sight sees at a distance: you do not then have the right to say that, being capable of being arrested, it does not see obscured visible matter. Moreover, one sees obscured visible matter through a glass, a cloud, a crystal and water: how would you explain this fact? I would say then that the visual consciousness sees, it arises with respect to obscured visible matter when the screen does not form an obstacle to light; it does not arise in the contrary case.[174]

3. The Vaibhāṣikas make an appeal to Scripture. The Sūtra says, "Having seen visible matter through the organ of sight."[175] Thus the organ sees, not the visual consciousness.

We would reply that the Sūtra intends to say, "Having seen visible matter by means of the organ of sight as point of support." In fact, the same Sūtra says, "Having discerned the *dharmas* through the mental organ": now this organ, being past (i.17), does not discern; it is through the mental consciousness that one discerns; therefore, if the text says "through the mental organ," it means "by supporting itself on the mental organ, the point of support of mental consciousness." The same for sight and the organ of sight.

One can also admit that the Sūtra attributes to the point of support, to the organ, the action which belongs to that which grasps this point of support, that is to say, to the consciousness. It is said in the world "the benches cry out," whereas the benches are actually the persons seated on the benches.

This way of speaking is common to Scripture. We read that "agreeable and disagreeable visible matter is discerned by the organ of sight." Now you do not maintain that the organ of sight discerns. You attribute discernment to the consciousness of which organ of sight is the point of support.

The Sūtra (*Saṁyukta*, *TD* 2, p. 64a10) also says "The organ of sight, Oh Brahmin, is the gate of the sight of visible matter." This text proves that the visual consciousness sees by this gate which is the organ of sight. You would not maintain that "gate" signifies "sight," for it would be absurd to say "The organ of sight is the sight of the sight of visible matter."

4. [Objection of the Vaibhāṣikas.] If the visual consciousness sees, what it is that discerns (i.48a)?

What is the difference between the two functions of seeing and discerning which would account for a single *dharma* not seeing and discerning at one and the same time? Is it not admitted that a certain type of *prajñā* (*darśanātmika*, vii.1) sees and comprehends?[176] In this same way a certain consciousness, the visual consciousness, sees and discerns. There is here only a single function designated by two names.

5. [Certain followers of the thesis "The visual consciousness sees," namely the Vātsīputrīyas, object:] If the organ of sight sees, what is then the separately existing action of seeing that you attribute to this organ, the agent of this action?

The objection cannot be made. In the same way that you would have it that the consciousness discerns, without admitting any difference between the agent and the action, in that same way we hold that an organ sees.

6. According to another opinion, [that of the Dharmaguptakas,] it is the visual consciousness which sees; but, as the organ of sight is the point of support of this consciousness, one says that it sees, the same way one says that the bell rings, because it is the point of support of the sound.

But, according to this principle, one should also say that the organ of sight discerns, for it is the point of support of the visual consciousness.

No. For in the world one agrees to give the name of "seeing" to the visual consciousness; in fact, when this consciousness is produced, one says "The color is seen;" one does not say that the color is discerned. And the *Vibhāṣā* (*TD* 27, p. 489c19) confirms: "One terms 'seen' that which is attained by the organ of sight, that which falls within its line of vision and is perceived by the visual consciousness." One says then in the world that the organ of sight sees, because it is the point of support of the visual consciousness which sees; one does not say that it discerns, because the function attributed to the visual consciousness is seeing and not discernment. On the other hand, when one says that consciousness discerns, one does not mean that it discerns to the extent that it would be the point of support of a certain discernment, as one understands that the organ of sight sees because it is the point of support of the visual consciousness. One means that the consciousness discerns by itself, that it is in and of itself discernment, in the same way that one says that the sun creates the day.[177]

7. Opinion of the Sautrāntikas. What an empty discussion! The Sūtra teaches: "By reason of the organ of sight and of visible matter there arises the visual consciousness": there is not there either an organ that sees, or visible matter that is seen; there is not there any action of seeing, nor any agent that sees; this is only a play of cause and effect. In the light of practice, one speaks, metaphorically, of this process: "The eye sees, and the consciousness discerns." But one should not cling to these metaphors. The Blessed One has said that one should not take them in the manner of popular speech, that one should not seriously grasp an expression in use in the world.[178]

8. According to the system of the Vaibhāṣikas of Kaśmīr, the organ of sight sees, the organ of hearing hears, the organ of smell smells, the organ of taste tastes, the organ of touch touches, and the mental organ discerns.

***

Is visible matter seen by one eye or by both eyes?

> 43a-b. Visible matter is seen by the two eyes also, as the clarity of sight demonstrates.[179]

[There is no fixed rule: one sees by one eye; one also sees by two eyes.]

The Ābhidhārmikas say: "Seen also by the two eyes; the two eyes being open, sight is clearer." Furthermore,[180] when one eye is covered and the other half closed, one perceives two moons; but not when one completely closes or half closes that which was open, or when one opens or completely closes that which has been half closed.

One should not conclude that the visual consciousness is twofold from the fact that its point of support is twofold, for the consciousness is not material like *rūpa*; not having a mass it is not situated in a place.

***

We have said that the organ of sight sees, that the organs of hearing, smell, taste, and touch each perceive their objects; and that the mental organ discerns. Do these organs attain their object, [do they enter into a close physical relationship with their object]?

> 43c. The organ of sight, the organ of hearing, and the mental organ know their object without attaining it.[181]

i.1. The organ of sight sees visible matter at a distance: it does not see the eye-salve placed on the eye; the organ of hearing hears distant sounds.

The mental organ, being non-material, does not enter into a close physical relationship with its object.

2. If the organs of sight and hearing must necessarily enter into a close relationship with their object, then ascetics in *dhyāna* would not attain divine sight or divine hearing, in the same way that they do not attain a divine sense of smell (vii.42).

[Objection.] If the organ of sight sees an object with which it is not in a close relationship, why does it not see visible matter which is too distant or obscured?[182]

[Reply.] Why does a magnet not attract all iron? Moreover, the same difficulty remains even if you suppose that the organ enters into a close relationship with the object: why does the organ of sight not see the eye salve, the brush, and all the objects with which it is in close relationship? Or else, let us say that the same rule applies to the organ of sight and to the organs of smell and taste: the organ of smell senses only the smell with which it is in close relationship, but it does not sense the odor which constitutes the organ itself; in the same way, the organ of sight sees only certain distant visible matter, but it does not see all distant visible matter.

According to certain masters, from the fact that one hears noise from the interior of the ear, one can conclude that the organ of hearing hears the sound with which it is in close relationship, as it also hears distant sound.[183]

3. The other three organs, smell, taste, touch, perceive an object with which they are in close relationship. For smell, this results from the fact that in-breathing is necessary to the perception of the smell.[184]

43d. For the other three organs, the opposite.

ii. What should one understand by the expression "to attain" (to enter into a close relationship)? What does one mean when one says that the nose "attains" its object, knows its object "after having attained it?"

To attain is "to arise in *nirantaratva*," in a state of non-separation.[185] The object, which renews itself from moment to moment (iv.2c-d), is found to be arisen in *nirantaratva* with the organ and vice versa.

[What does *nirantaratva* mean? According to the Bhadanta, immediate juxtaposition, absence of interval; according to the Vaibhāṣikas, immediate vicinity, absence of an interposed body].[186]

iii. The question is therefore posed whether the atoms do or do not touch one another.

1. The Vaibhāṣikas of Kaśmīr (*Vibhāṣā* TD 27, p. 683a24) say that atoms do not touch one another; (1) if atoms touch one another in their totality, things, that is to say, the different atoms, would "mix with one another," that is, they would only occupy one place; and (2) if atoms touched each other in one spot, they would thus have parts: and atoms do not have any parts.[187]

But, if there is no contact among the atoms, how is sound produced?

For the very reason that there is no contact, sound is possible: if atoms were to touch one another, a hand in collision with a hand would dissolve into it, a rock in collision with another rock would dissolve into it, as gum dissolves into gum. And sound would not be produced.

But if atoms do not touch one another, why does an agglomeration of atoms not fall to pieces when it is struck?

Because the wind element holds it together. A certain wind element has dispersion for its function, for example the wind of the period of the destruction of the world; a certain wind element has concentration for its function, for example the wind at the period of creation (iii.91, 100).[189]

2. [The Vaibhāṣikas continue the presentation of their doctrine].

One says that three organs attain their object, because their object is in a state of non-seperation from them. What does non-seperation consist of?

It consists of the fact that there is nothing which is in the interval between the two. This is also what is meant by "to attain."

Furthermore, as agglomerations have parts, there is no difficulty in agglomerations touching one another. And, from this point of view the definitions of the *Vibhāṣā* (*TD* 27, p. 684all; see also p. 380a19) are justified: "Does a thing-in-contact arise having for its cause a thing-in-contact, or does it arise having for its cause a thing-outside-of-contact?" Same question with respect to a thing-outside-of-contact.

"One cannot reply in an absolute manner. Sometimes a thing-outside-of-contact arises from a thing-in-contact, as when a thing-in-contact falls to pieces. Sometimes a thing-in-contact arises from a thing-outside-of-contact, as when a thing-outside-of-contact comes together. Sometimes a thing-in-contact arises from a thing-outside-of-contact, as when agglomerations come together. And sometimes a thing-outside-of-contact arises from a thing-outside-of-contact, for example the particles of dust suspended in the void of a window."

The Bhadanta Vasumitra says: "If atoms touched one another, they would therefore endure two moments."[189]

iv. Opinions of Vasubandhu. 1. The Bhadanta says: "There is not, in reality, any contact. One says, metaphorically, that atoms touch one another when they are juxtaposed without interval." (Quoted in *Vibhāṣā*, *TD* 27, p. 684a2; see note 189, end).

This opinion is the correct one.[190] In fact, if atoms were to allow an interval between themselves, since this interval would be empty, what would hinder the progress of atoms into this interval? For it is admitted that atoms are impenetrable.[191]

2. Agglomerations are not anything other than atoms. They are the same atoms which, in a state of aggregation, are a "thing-in-contact," in the same way that they are *rūpa* (i.13). It is thus absurd to deny that atoms touch one another, and yet to admit that agglomerations touch one another.

3. If you admit spatial division to the atom, then an atom certainly has parts, whether it enters into contact or not. If you deny it, why would the atom, even if it enters into contact, have parts?[192]

***

Should we think that the organs solely grasp an object of their dimension,—if one believes that one sees suddenly extended objects, a mountain for example, it is through illusion, it is because one rapidly sees parts of a mountain: it is evidently thus when one sees the circle of fire delineated by an ember;—or else do the organs indifferently grasp an object of their dimension and of a different dimension?

> 44a-b. The three organs of which the organ of smell is the first, grasp an object of their dimension.[193]

A given number of atoms of an organ, attaining the same number of atoms of an object, produce consciousness. This also holds for smell, taste, and touch.

But there is no rule for seeing and hearing. Sometimes the object is smaller than the organ, as when one sees the end of a hair; sometimes equal to the organ, as when one sees a grape; and sometimes larger than the organ, when, the eye being hardly open, one sees a mountain. The same for sound; one hears the buzzing of a mosquito, the noise of thunder, etc.

The question does not arise for the mental organ which is non-material.

***

(Here are some problems relating to the organs.)

i. How are atoms of the different organs arranged?

The atoms of the organ of sight are arranged on the pupil like the flower of the cumin, that is to say, on the surface; they are covered again by a membrane, of translucent color, which prevents them from dispersing. According to another opinion, they are arranged in depth, like a pill; being translucent, like crystal, they do not obscure one another.[194]

The atoms of the organ of hearing are arranged in the interior of the *bhūrja*, that type of birch leaf which is found within the ear.

The atoms of the organ of smell are arranged within the interior of the nostril.

These first three organs from a garland.[195]

The atoms of the organ of taste are arranged on the upper surface of the tongue in the form of a half-moon. In the middle of the tongue a space the dimension of the end of a hair is not occupied by the atoms of the organ. Such is the opinion expressed in Scripture.[196]

The atoms of the organ of touch have the shape of the body.

The atoms of the female organ are like a drum. The atoms of the male organ are like a thumb.

***

ii. The atoms of the organ of sight can be *sabhāga* (i.39) in their totality; *tatsabhāga* in their totality; some *sabhāga*, others *tatsabhāga*. The same for the organs of hearing, smell and taste. But, it does not occur that the atoms of the organ of touch are all *sabhāga*; even when the body is enveloped in the flames of Pratapana hell (iii.59), an infinite number of atoms are *tatsabhāga*; for, says the School, the body would fall to pieces if all the atoms of touch were to work at the same time.

iii. It does not occur that consciousness is produced by one atom of organ, or by one atom of object. In fact the five categories of consciousness have agglomerations for their support and their object.

It results from this that atoms are not perceived; they are thus "imperceptible". (Compare i.20a-b, iv.4).

***

The object of the first five consciousnesses is simultaneous with them; the object of the sixth consciousness is either earlier than it, simultaneous with it, or later than it; in other words, it is past, present, or future (i.23). Does the same hold for the point of support of the consciousness?

No, it does not.

Why is this?

> 44c. Relative to consciousness, the point of support of the sixth consciousness is past.

The sole point of support of the mental consciousness is the mental organ, this is, the consciousness which has just perished (i.17).

> 44d. The point of support of the first five is also simultaneous.

The point of support of the five consciousnesses is also simultaneous with them: that is, it is both earlier than, and simultaneous to the consciousness. In fact, the point of support of these consciousnesses is twofold: 1. the sense organ, organ of sight, etc., which is simultaneous with consciousness; and 2. the mental organ, which is past at the moment when the consciousness arises.

The five consciousnesses thus have two points of support.

One poses the question: Is that which is the point of support of the visual consciousness at the same time the "immediately antecedent and parallel cause" (*samanantarapratyaya*, ii.62) of this consciousness? Four cases: 1. the organ of sight, which is solely a point of support; 2. the totality of mental states, sensation, etc. (ii.24) which have just perished: they are solely the immediately antecedent cause; 3. the consciousness which has just perished, or mental organ, which is at one and the same time a point of support and an immediately antecedent cause; and 4. the other *dharmas* are neither one nor the other.

The same for the consciousness of hearing, smell, taste and touch.

With respect to mental consciousness, one replies by speaking of the first term of the question: that which is the point of support of mental consciousness is always the parallel and immediately antecedent cause of this consciousness, but items that have perished are not its point of support.

***

Visual consciousness depends on the organ of sight and on visible matter. Why is the organ considered as the point of support of consciousness, to the exclusion of the object?

> 45a-b. The point of support of a consciousness is its organ, for consciousness changes according to the modality of the organ.[197]

When the organ of sight is the object of attention (employment of eye salve, etc.); when it is injured by dust, etc.; when it is alert; when it is sluggish and weak, consciousness reproduces modality: it is accompanied by pleasure or by pain, it is alert or weak. The object, on the contrary, has no influence on the modality of consciousness. Consequently, it is the organ, and not the object, which is the point of support of consciousness (ii.2a-b).

***

Consciousness knows the object. Why is it designated by the name of its organ "eye consciousness" . . . "*manas* consciousness" . . . "*dharma* consciousness?"

> 45c-d. For this reason, and also because it is "its own," it is the organ which gives its name to the consciousness.

The consciousness takes the name of an organ because the organ is its point of support.

Because the organ is "its own:" the organ of a certain person is the point of support of the visual consciousness of this person alone. Visible matter, on the contrary, is general, for a certain visible thing is perceived by both the visual consciousness and the mental consciousness, by one person and by another person. The same observation holds for the organs of hearing, smell, taste, and touch, and for their objects, sounds, smells, tastes, and tangibles.

We conclude that the consciousness is named according to its organ because the organ is its point of support, and because the organ is its own thing. But the same does not hold for its object. One says in the world "sound of the drum," and not "sound of the stick;" "sprout of the wheat," and not "sprout of the field."

***

A being is born in a certain stage of the world, in Kāmadhātu, in the First Dhyāna, etc.; he is of this stage, and his body is also of this stage, and he sees, by the organ of sight, visible matter. Do the body, the organ of sight, visible matter and consciousness belong to the same stage or to different stages?

All can belong to different stages.

i. When a being born in Kāmadhātu sees, by means of an organ of sight of his stage, visible matter of his stage, then body, organ, visible matter and consciousness are in the same stage.

When this being sees visible matter of his stage, by means of an organ of sight of the First Dhyāna, then the body and visible matter are of Kāmadhātu, but his organ and consciousness are of the First Dhyāna; if he sees visible matter of the First Dhyāna by means of the same organ, then only the body is in Kāmadhātu; the other three are of the First Dhyāna.

When this being sees visible matter of Kāmadhātu by means of an organ of sight of the Second Dhyāna, then the body and visible matter are in Kāmadhātu, the organ is in the Second Dhyāna, and consciousness is in the First Dhyāna; if he sees, by the same organ, visible matter of the Second Dhyāna, then the body is in Kāmadhātu, the organ and visible matter are in the Second Dhyāna, and consciousness is in the First Dhyāna. (viii.13a-c).

One would explain in the same way these cases where a being born in Kāmadhātu sees, by the organ of sight of the Third or Fourth Dhyāna, visible matter of these same stages or of a lower stage.

ii. When a being in the First Dhyāna sees visible matter of his stage by means of an organ of sight of his stage, then body, organ, visible matter and consciousness are of the same stage; if he sees visible matter of a lower stage by the same organ, then the body, organ, and consciousness are of his stage, the First Dhyāna.

When this being sees visible matter of his stage by means of an organ of sight of the Second Dhyāna, then three are of his stage (First Dhyāna), but the organ is in the Second Dhyāna; if he sees, by the same organ, visible matter of Kāmadhātu, then the body and consciousness are of his stage (First Dhyāna), visible matter is in a lower stage, and the organ is in the Second Dhyāna; if he sees visible matter of the Second Dhyāna by the same organ, then the body and consciousness are of his stage (First Dhyāna), but the organ and the visible matter are in the Second Dhyāna.

One would explain in the same way these cases where a being in the First Dhyāna sees, by means of an organ of sight of the Third or the Fourth Dhyāna, visible matter of these stages or of a lower stage.

iii. According to these same principles, we can explain those cases where a being in the Second, Third or Fourth Dhyāna, sees, by means of an organ of sight of his stage or of a different stage, visible matter of his stage or of a different stage.

The rule is the following:

> 46a. The organ of sight is not inferior to the body.

The body, the organ of sight, and visible matter can belong to five stages: Kāmadhātu, and the Four Dhyānas.

The consciousness of sight is of two stages only: Kāmadhātu and the First Dhyāna (viii.13a-c).

Thus stated, the organs of sight which a certain being uses can be of the stage to which the body of this being belongs, that is, of the stage where this being has arisen; it can be of a higher stage; but it can never be lower.

Visible matter and consciousness, through relationship to the organ, is either of the same stage or lower, but never of a higher stage.

> 46b. Visible matter is not higher than the organ.

Visible matter of a higher stage cannot be seen by an organ of sight of a lower stage.

> 46c. Nor consciousness.

A visual consciousness of a higher stage cannot arise from an organ of a lower stage.

> 46d. Visible matter, in relation to consciousness, and visible matter as well as consciousness, through relation to the body, is of all types.

Visible matter, through relationship with the visual consciousness, is either equal, or higher, or lower.

Visible matter and the visual consciousness, through relationship to the body, are as visible matter is through relationship to the consciousness, this is to say, equal, higher, or lower.

> 47a. The same holds for the organ of hearing.

The organ of hearing is not lower than the body, sound is not higher than the organ of hearing, nor is auditory consciousness; sound, through relationship to this latter, and sound and consciousness through relationship to the body, can be of all types.

> 47a-b. Three organs belong to their own stage.

With respect to the organs of smell, taste, and touch, the body, organ, object and consciousness belong exclusively to the stage where the being is born.

After having formulated this general rule, the author mentions one exception.

> 47c-d. The consciousness of touch is of its own stage or of a lower stage.

The body, the organ of touch and tangibles are always of the stage where the being is born. But the consciousness of touch (1) is of this stage, in the case of a being born in Kāmadhātu or in the First Dhyāna; or (2) is of a lower stage (First Dhyāna) in the case of a being born in the Second Dhyāna or above.

> 47d. There is no restriction with respect to the mental organ.

Sometimes the mental organ is of the same stage as the body, the *dharmadhātu* and the mental consciousness; sometimes it is lower or higher. If a body belongs to the first five stages—Kāmadhātu and the Four Dhyānas—, then the mental organ, the *dharmadhātu,* and the mental consciousness can be, in absorption or at conception, of any stage, all the stages not being moreover the same in each case. This will be explained in the Eighth Chapter which treats of the absorptions (viii.19c-d). We shall not speak here of this for the sake of brevity, the profit being small and the pains great.

***

There are eighteen *dhātus* and six consciousness. Which *dhātu* is discerned by which consciousness?

> 48a. Five external *dhātus* are discerned by two types of consciousness.

Visible matter, sounds, odors, tastes and tangibles are known respectively, by the consciousness of sight, hearing, smell, taste, and touch. They are all discerned by the mental consciousness. Each of these external *dhātus* is thus discerned by two consciousness.

The thirteen other *dhātus*, not being of the sphere of the sense consciousness, are discerned by a single mental consciousness.

***

How many of the *dhātus* are eternal?
No *dhātu* is totally eternal. But

> 48b. Unconditioned things are eternal.[198]

Unconditioned things (i.5b) form part of the *dharmadhātu* (i.15c). Thus one part of the *dharmadhātu* is eternal.

***

How many of the *dhātus* are *indriyas*, that is to say, predominate (ii.1)?

> 48c-d. The twelve internal *dhātus* and one part of the *dharmadhātu* are *indriyas*.[199]

A Sūtra[200] enumerates twenty-two *indriyas*: 1. organ of sight, 2. organ of hearing, 3. organ of smell, 4. organ of taste, 5. organ of touch, 6. mental organ, 7. male organ, 8. female organ, 9. vital organ, 10. faculty of sensation of pleasure, or sensation of pleasure, 11. faculty of sensation of displeasure, or sensation of displeasure, 12. faculty of sensation of satisfaction, or sensation of satisfaction (*saumanasyendriya*), 13. faculty of sensation of dissatisfaction, or sensation of dissatisfaction, 14. faculty of sensation of indifference, or sensation of indifference, 15. faculty of faith, 18. faculty of energy, 17. faculty of memory, 18. faculty of absorption, 19. faculty of discernment of *dharmas*, or faculty of *prajñā*, 20. *anājñātamājñāsyāmīndriya*, 21. *ājñendriya*, and 22. *ājñātāvindriya*.

The Ābhidhārmikas (*Prakaraṇapāda*, fol. 31b) do not count the group that forms the six organs of consciousness (the *āyatanas*), i.e., the organs of sight, hearing, smell, taste, touch, and the mental organ. They do not place the mental organ after the organ of touch, but after the vital organ, for the reason that the mental organ, the same as the organs of sensation (10-14), also have an *ālambana* (i.29b-d) and not solely a *viṣaya* as do the organs of sense consciousness (1-5).[201]

Among the twenty-two *indriyas*, eleven—namely the vital organ (9), the five faculties of sensation (10-14), the five moral faculties

(15-19)—and one part of the last three, form part of the *dharmadhātu.*[202]

The twelve internal *dhātus* are (1) the five organs of sense consciousness which form five *dhātus* and five *indriyas* (1-5); (2) the mental organ (i.16c), that is to say, the sixth *indriya,* which make up seven *dhātus*; and (3) one part of the last three *indriyas.*

The five remaining *dhātus* and one part of the *dharmadhātu* are not *indriyas.*

1. The authors of the *Vinayavibhāṣā* say: (1) there is a Buddha who is not a Bhagavat, namely the Pratyekabuddha, because he is *svayambhū*, that is because he has obtained Bodhi by himself, because he has not fulfilled the task of *dānapāramitā*, etc. (vii.34); (2) there is a Bhagavat who is not a Buddha, namely the Bodhisattva in his last existence; (3) there is a Buddha Bhagavat; and (4) there are persons who are neither Buddha, nor Bhagavat (*Vyākhyā*, 3.12). One can also say that the Śrāvakas, or Disciples, are Buddhas (Āryadeva, *Śataka*, 270), for they have acquired Bodhi (vi.67).

2. Śāriputra did not know the five pure *skandhas* (the precepts, etc.) of the Tathāgata.

3. Maudgalyāyana did not see that his mother was reborn in Marīcilokadhātu.

Śāriputra did not discover the roots-of-good of a candidate for the state of Bhikṣu (see vii.30); but the Buddha declares:

mokṣabījam aham hy asya susūkṣmam upakṣaye /
dhātupāṣāṇavivare nilīnam iva kāñcanaṁ //

Compare Huber, *Sūtrālaṁkāra*, p. 286.

4. As the stanza says:

sarvākāraṁ kāraṇam ekasya mayūracandrakasyāpi nāsarvajñair jñeyaṁ sarvajñajñāna-balaṁ hi tat.

5. The Pratyekabuddhas and the Śrāvakas have also abandoned (*prahīṇa*) non-defiled ignorance (*akliṣṭam ajñānam*), in exactly the same way as they have abandoned the organ of sight, etc., that is, by abandoning all desire (*chandarāga*) with respect to it. But this non-defiled ignorance remains active within them (*samudācarati*) even though it is abandoned, exactly like the organ of sight.

Such is not the case for the Buddha: this is why the author says that he has destroyed (*hata*) obscurity in such a manner that it will not arise again.

6. "As much as possible," *yathābhavyam*. This holds for oneself, as when one says, "He gives food for the Brahmins to eat."

7. We have the plural because the persons to be saved are numerous.

8. Expression of Āryadeva, *Śataka*, 265.

9. First explanation: through the power of *ṛddhi* (vii.48), like Viṣṇu; through the power of giving, like Maheśvara. Second explanation: through *ṛddhi*, through giving, and through its *prabhāva* (vii.34).

It is true that the Buddhas perform miracles (*ṛddhiprātihārya*) in order to draw believers to themselves (*āvarjanamātra*); but it is through the miracle of the teaching (*anuśāsanī*) that they save the world by destroying its defilements (vii.47a-b).

10. The *dharmas* are mixed, like flowers; one discerns them and places them in bouquets: these are pure, those are impure, etc.

In this operation, a certain *dharma* associated with the mind (*caitta, caitasika*, ii.23), which is called *prajñā*, plays a primary role. As a consequence *prajñā* is defined as "discernment of the *dharmas*."

11. *mala*, stain, is a synonym for *āsrava*, vice. We translate *anāsrava* by "pure." The *āsravas* are defined v.35. See below i.4.

12. The name "Abhidharma" signifies not only the pure consciousness which discerns the nature of things, but also all of the pure elements of the psychological moment in which this consciousness is produced: sensation, etc. (i.14c). One of these elements is material (*rūpa*) and is called "pure discipline" (*anāsrava saṁvara*, iv.13c).

13. *Vyākhyā: paramārtha eva pāramārthikah / paramārthe vā bhavaḥ pāramārthikaḥ / paramārthena vā dīvyati caratīti pāramārthikaḥ*

14. The Treatise is (1) an *Abhidharma Śāstra* or an *Abhidharma Piṭaka*. In either case, some think that it should not be understood as "The Treatise, with its attendant works, receives the name of Abhidharma," for a book does not have any attendants; some believe that its attendants are made up of the *lakṣaṇas* (ii. 45c-d); (2) or the *Jñānaprasthāna*, considered as the body of the Abhidharma and having for its feet (and "attendants") the six books, *Prakaraṇapāda, Vijñānakāya, Dharmakāya, Prajñāptiśāstra, Dhātukāya*, and *Saṁgītiparyāya* (Burnouf, *Introduction*, p. 448).

15. The first two lines are quoted, with the reading *yad upaśāntaye*, in a commentary (the *Amṛtakaṇikā*) on the *Nāmasaṁgīti*, 130; the third is quoted in the *Vyākhyā*.

16. The word *kila* shows that Vasubandhu presents here an opinion, the opinion of the Vaibhāṣikas, that he does not accept. The Abhidharma treatises are not the word of the Master for the Sautrāntikas and for Vasubandhu. The problem of the authenticity of the Abhidharma treatises is studied in the *Introduction*.

17. The Tibetan version of the *Udānavarga* (Mdo XXVI) has been translated by W. Rockhill (London, 1883) and published by H. Beck (Berlin, 1911). A good part of the original has been discovered in Turkestan, *JRAS*, 1912, pp. 355–377; *J. As.* 1912, I.311, showing the correspondence with the Pali sources). S. Lévi, *J. As.* 1912, II.215–222.

18. J. Takakusu, "On the Abhidharma Literature of the Sarvāstivādins," *JPTS*, 1905, p. 75.

19. The conditioned *dharmas*, with the exception of those which form part of the Path, are termed *sāsrava*, "in a relationship with the defilements."

How and why are they "in a relationship with the defilements?"

1. One cannot say that they are "associated" (*saṁprayukta*) with the defilements, for only the mind andmental states which are defiled (*kliṣṭa*) are associated with the defilements (i.23).

2. One cannot say that they coexist (*sahotpāda*) with the defilements. In this hypothesis (1) neither the external (*bāhya*,i.39a) *dharmas*, (2) nor the five *upādānaskandhas* (i.8) of a person within whom the defilements are not presently active would be "in a relationship with the defilements."

3. One cannot say that they are the support (*āśraya*) of the defilements, for only the six organs of consciousness are the support of the defilements.

4. One cannot say that they are the object (*ālambana*) of the defilements: in this hypothesis, Nirvāṇa (=*nirodhasatya*) would be "in a relationship with the defilements," for one can have false views with respect to Nirvāṇa; in this hypothesis too, a higher sphere would be "in a relationship with the defilements" through the fact of the defilements of a lower sphere which grasps them as its object (opinions condemned v.18).

The author thus explains that a *dharma* is termed "in a relationship with the defilements" because the defilements adhere to it (*anuśerate*), that is, grow in them (*puṣṭiṁ labhante*) or take their dwelling and support in them (*pratiṣṭhā*), as a foot can stand on the earth but not on red hot fire. The defilements (*anuśaya*) develop (*saṁtāyante*) taking their growth in or support from the *dharmas* which are "in a relationship with the defilements."

According to another opinion, in the same way that one says "This food suits me" (*mama anuśete*), meaning "This food is convenient to me, is favorable to me (*anuguṇībhavati*)," in this same way the defilements "come to these *dharmas*," "are favorable to these *dharmas*." One thus terms the *dharmas* to which the defilements are favorable, namely conditioned things with the exception of the Path, to be "in a relationship with the defilements," in fact, conditioned things are created by action aroused by the defilements; the defilements are thus favorable to them.

(*Vyākhyā*)See v.1, 18, 29, 39, 40.

The various schools are not in agreement on the question: Is the body of the Buddha "in a relationship with the defilements?" See i.31d.

20. The Truth of the Path is the totality of the *dharmas* which constitute Seeing and Meditation on the Truths (vi.25d., vii3b).

On the *asaṁskṛtas*, i.48b, ii.55c-d, and the *Introduction*.

21. Certain philosophers, namely the Vātsīputrīyas, say that there is only one *asaṁskṛta*, namely Nirvāṇa. The Vaiśeṣikas admit many *asaṁskṛtas*: the *paramāṇus*, etc. (*Vyākhyā*). Some admit three *asaṁskṛtas*; others consider the *śūnyatā* which is *tathatālakṣaṇā* as an *asaṁskṛta* (*Madhyamaka*, vii.33, p. 176). Wassilief, p. 282. *Kathāvatthu*, ii.9, vi.3.

22. On the two *nirodhas*, i.6, ii.55c; on the five *nirodhas*, i.20a-b.

23. On the difference between space (*ākāśa*) and a void (*ākāśadhātu*), see i.28; on the non-existence of an *asaṁskṛta* called "space" (a Sautrāntika theory), see ii.55c-d. *Kathāvatthu*, vi.6-7.

The opinion of the Mādhyamikas on space and other unconditioned things, an opinion identical to that of the Sautrāntikas, is presented by Āryadeva, *Śataka*, ix.3 (*Madhyamaka-vṛtti*, 505; *Catuḥśatikā*, 202, *As. Soc. of Bengal*, iii, p. 483, 1914): "Where there is no matter (*rūpa*), there is nothing which opposes the arising of material *dharmas*: the absence of matter receives the name *ākāśa*, because things shine brightly there (*bhṛśam asyāntaḥ kāśante bhāvāḥ*). The Vaibhasikas suppose, in the *Abhidharmaśāstra*, that *ākāśa* is a reality (*vastu*), not seeing that Scripture must give a name to an unreal thing, to a pure negative (*avastusato'kiṁcanasya*) . . ."

24. Compare the discussion *Kathāvatthu*, xix.3.

The Sarvāstivādins consider that "disjunction from a defilement," "the suppression of future defilement or suffering" (*visaṁyoga* or *nirodha*) is a thing in and of itself, a real *dharma*, an entity (*dravya*). "Disjunction" is not produced by causes, and so is eternal. Through *pratisaṁkhya* (comprehension of the Truths) one obtains the acquisition (*prāpti*, ii.36b) of disjunction.

25. The Blessed One compared an impure (*sāsrava*) object to a post, that is to say, an object which the defilements, desire, hatred, etc. can adhere to; the defilements of bonds, *saṁyojana*, are a rope; the *pudgala* is the animal. (Compare *Saṁyutta*, iv.282). A *sāsrava* object is a *saṁyogavastu*, the *saññojaniya*.

26. Dharmadinna was questioned by her former spouse the householder Viśākha: *kiṁsabhāga ārya nirodhaḥ*? She answered: *asabhāga āyuṣman viśākha*. (*Madhyamāgama*, *TD* 1, p. 788c16, *Vibhāṣā*, TD 27, p. 162bll). Compare *Majjhima*, i.304: *nibbānassa pan'ayye kiṁ paṭighāgo* . . .

27. *Vibhāṣā*, *TD* 27, p. 164b13. The *Kathāvatthu*, ii.9, attributes to the Mahiṁsāsakas (Wassilief, p. 282) and the Andhakas the distinction between *paṭisaṁkhā-* and *appaṭisaṁkhānirodha*. Śaṁkara discusses the two *nirodhas* *ad* ii.2, 22 (see Kern *Album*, iii) but he confuses *apratisaṁkhyānirodha* and *anityatānirodha* (i.20a-b).

28. This classification rests on two principles: 1. There can be *pratisaṁkhyānirodha*, (disjunction, detachment) from impure *dharmas*, of any time period whether they have been, are now or are not now destined to arise. 2. There is *apratisaṁkhyānirodha* of all *dharmas*, pure or impure, which are not destined to arise: future *dharmas* exist: they will arise if the causes of arising cause them to pass from the future into the present; they will not arise if one obtains their *apratisaṁkhyānirodha*. For example, at a certain moment, a Saint obtains not being able to arise in an animal womb: he obtains *apratisaṁkhyānirodha* of the animal womb, which for him is henceforth "not destined to arise" (*anutpattidharman*).

The Blessed One said of the Srotaāpanna, "He has surpressed (*niruddha*) the hells, the animal wombs, existences as a preta" (Comp. *Saṁyutta*, v.356, *khīṇanirayo khīṇatiracchānayoniko* . . .)

Apratisaṁkhyānirodha is a *dharma* in and of itself which makes absolutely impossible, in one who possesses (*prāpti*) it, the arising of a certain *dharma*. This absolute non-arising does not result from an insufficiency of causes, for, if the causes should present themselves someday, the *dharma* would arise: thus it is the possession of *apratisaṁṁkhyānirodha* which makes the sufficient coming together of causes, and arising, definitely impossible.

See ii.55c-d and v.24.

29. The term *skandha* is explained i.20.

30. According to the Sūtra: *trīṇīmāni bhikṣavaḥ kathāvastūny acaturthāny apañcamāni yāny āśrityāryāh kathāṁ kathayantaḥ kathayanti / katamāni trīṇi / atītaṃ kathāvastu anāgataṁ kathāvastu pratyupannam kathāvastu.*

Compare *Aṅguttara*, i.197.

31. *TD* 26, p. 728a24: "The three paths, the three *kathāvastus* are embraced within eighteen *dhātus*, twelve *āyatanas*, and five *skandhas*; they are known by the nine knowledges, with the exception of *nirodhajñāna*; they are discerned by six consciousnesses; and they are affected by all the *anuśayas*."

32. Why is not the unconditioned a "foundation of discourse?" Because it is not the cause of discourse (ii.55); because there is no history of an unconditioned thing, in the same way that one can say "Dipamkara was such . . . ; Maitreya will be . . . ; King Kapphina (?) is such." (*Vyākhyā*)

33. According to the *Prakaraṇa, TD* 26, p. 716b23, which can be reconstructed: *saniḥsārā dharmāḥ katame? sarve saṁskṛtā dharmāḥ*, one should "leave," not only the impure *dharmas*, but also the Path. The *Vyākhyā* quotes the text on abandoning the raft, *Majjhima*, i.135, *Vajracchedikā*, para. 6: *kolopamaṁ dharmaparyāyam ājānadbhir dharmā api prahātavyāh prāg evādharma iti* (Compare *Bodhicaryāvatāra*, ix.33; *Kaṭha*, ii.14).

34. According to the *Prakaraṇa, TD* 26, p. 716a3: *savastukāḥ sapratyayā dharmāḥ katame? saṁskṛtā dharmāḥ*. See ii.55 end.

35. *Vastu* signifies *hetu* according to the etymology: *vasanty asmin prāk kāryāṇi paścāt tata utpatteḥ.*

The *Vyākhyā* quotes here a fragment of the *Bhāṣyam ad* ii.55 on the five meanings of the word *vastu* in Scripture (*Vibhāṣā TD* 27, p. 980b12) For Vasubandhu *savastuka* signifies "real": conditioned things are real; unconditioned things are unreal.

36. The *Vibhāṣā*, TD 27, p. 386c12 and foll., presents fourteen explanations of the term *upādānaskandha*. Vasubandhu quotes the first three.

On *khandha* and *upādānakkhandha*, *Visuddhimagga*, xiv, *apud* Warren, p. 155.

37. On *raṇa, saraṇa, araṇā* (vii.35c), see *Muséon*, 1914, p. 35; Walleser, *Die Streitlosigkeit des Subhūti* (Heidelberg, 1917).

38. *asmin eva rohita vyāyāmamātre kalevare lokaṁ prajñapayāmi lokasamudayaṁ ca* (*Aṅguttara* ii.48: *rohitassadevaputta*). The Blessed One further said: *luhyate praluhyate tasmāl lokaḥ* (*Saṁyutta*, iv.52). *Aṣṭasāhasrikā-*, p. 256; *Mahāvyutpatti*, 154.16 (Wogihara, *Bodhisattvabhūmi*, Leipzig 1908, p. 38). The root is *luji*, not *loki*.

39. *Vyākhyā*: According to the text: *bhavaḥ katamaḥ / pañcopādānaskandhāḥ*.

Hsüan-tsang translates, "They are the threefold existence."

Vasubandhu's source appears to be the *Prakaraṇa, TD* 26, p. 715a9: "Which *dharmas* are *bhava*? Impure *dharmas*. Which *dharmas* are not *bhava*? Pure *dharmas*."

40. Compare the *Prakaraṇapāda*, Chapter I, translated in the *Introduction*.

41. The five organs (*indriya*) are suprasensible (*atīndriya*), transparent (*accha*), distinct from the object of the organs, distinct from visible things, from tangible things, etc. It is through reasoning or deduction that we cognize their existence. They have for their support (*adhiṣṭhāna*) what popular language calls the eye, etc. (i.44a-b).

On *pasādacakkhu, cakkhupasāda*, see *Dhammasaṅgaṇi*, 616, 628.

42. See the Sūtra quoted i.35. Compare *Vibhaṅga*, 122, *Psychology*, 173.

43. The first interpretation according to the *Vibhāṣā, TD* 27, p. 369b21.

44. *Vibhāṣā, TD* 27, p. 64a5: *Mahāvyutpatti*, 101; compare *Dhammasaṅgaṇi*, 617.

45. The Sautrāntikas deny that shape is anything other than color.

46. *Vijñānakāya, TD* 26, p. 583a14, *Vibhāṣā, TD* 27, p. 390b24.

47. *Dhammasaṅgaṇi*, 636.

48. *Dhammasaṅgaṇi*, 624.

49. *Sattvākhya* = *sattvam ācaṣṭe*, any *dharma* which denotes a living being is called *sattvākhya*. When one understands the sound which constitute vocal action (*vāgvijñapti*, iv.3d), one knows "This is a living being." Any sound different from speech is *asattvākhya*.

50. According to the *Dharmaskandha, TD* 26, p. 500b24, it is of fourteen types. Compare *Dhammasaṅgaṇi*, 629.

51. *Dhammasaṅgaṇi*, 625.

52. *Vibhāṣā, TD* 27, p. 661c14 and foll., *Dhammasaṅgaṇi*, 648. See i.35.

53. *Dhammapada*, 194; *Udānavarga*, xxx.23. The appearance of the Buddhas is a cause of happiness, not happiness itself.

54. See i.30b.

55. According to *Vibhāṣā, TD* 27, p. 64all.

56. The *manovijñāna*, or mental consciousness, grasps the totality of the objects of the sense consciousnesses, visual consciousness (*cakṣurvijñāna*), etc.; this is why one considers that it has *samānyalakṣaṇa* for its sphere; in other words, it is not specialized with respect to its object.

If, in the same way, one says that the visual consciousnesses bears on blue, yellow, red and white, we should say that it has the *samānyalakṣaṇa* for its sphere, because the characteristics of the "visible" *rūpāyatana* are its object; the same for the auditory consciousness, the olfactory consciousness, etc. Now this is in opposition to Scripture.

Answer: When Scripture teaches that each one of the five sense consciousnesses has a *svalakṣaṇa* for its sphere, this refers to the unique or self (*sva*) characteristics (*lakṣaṇa*) of the *āyatanas*, namely the quality of being *rūpāyatana*, that is, the quality of being visible, the "quality of being cognizable by the visual consciousness," or the quality of being *śabdāyatana*, the "quality of being cognizable by the auditory consciousness," etc. Scripture does not refer to the unique characteristic of things, namely the "quality of having a blue aspect" or the "quality of being cognizable by a visual consciousness having a blue aspect," etc. It is not from the point of view of the unique characteristics of these objects that the five consciousnesses are said "to have *svalakṣaṇa* for their sphere," or in other words, are called "specialized with respect to their object."

57. *Avijñapti* will be described in detail iv.3d etc. This can be translated as "non-information" or "non-informative." This is an action which does not cause anything to be known to another, and

in this it resembles mental action; but it is matter (*rūpa*), in that it resembles bodily and vocal action. We shall see that the Sautrāntikas and Vasubandhu do not admit the existence of a specific *dharma* called the *avijñapti*.

Saṁghabhadra thinks that the definition of *avijñapti*, as formulated by Vasubandhu, does not conform to the Vaibhāṣika doctrine. His objections (in the *Nyāyānusāra*) are reproduced, and refuted, by Yaśomitra (*Vyākhyā*, 31.16 -34.5). In the *Samayapradīpikā*, he substitutes a new *kārikā* for one by Vasubandhu, which Yaśomitra quotes:

> *kṛte'pi visabhāge'pi citte cittātyaye ca yat / vyākṛtāpratighaṁ rūpaṁ sā hy avijñaptir iṣyate //*

58. Saṁghabhadra explains: Why are the *mahābhūtas* termed *dhātu*? Because they are the place of origin of all the *rūpadharmas*; the *mahābhūtas* themselves have their origins in the *mahābhūtas*. Now, in the world, a place of origin receive the name of *dhātu*: it is thus that gold mines, etc., are called *dhātus* of gold, etc. Or rather they are called *dhātu* because they are the place of origin of the variety of sufferings. Example as above. Some say that they are called *dhātu* because they bear the unique characteristics of both the *mahābhūtas* and derived *rūpa* (*TD* 29, p. 335c13-17).

The *dhātus* also bear the name of *mahābhūta*. Why *bhūta*? Why *mahābhūta*?

At the moment when the diverse types of derived *rūpa* (blue, etc.) arise, each one of them comes forth under different aspects: this is why they are called *bhūta*.

According to other masters it is by reason of the predominating (*adhipati*) power of the action of living beings, in the course of eternal *saṁsāra*, that they always exist: this is why they are called *bhūta*. Or rather, the appearance (*utpāda*) of the *dharmas* is what is called *bhava* . . .

59. The etymological explanation of *bhūtāni* is *bhūtaṁ tanvanti*.

60. Water (in the popular sense of the word) supports vessels: thus the earth element manifests its own, proper activity; it is warm, it moves, etc.

See ii.22; *Dhammasaṅgaṇi*, 962–966; *Compendium*, Appendix, p. 268.

61. *Prakaraṇa*, *TD* 26, p. 757a23. The *Mahāvyutpatti* (101) has *khakkhaṭatva, dravatva, uṣṇatva*, and *laghusamudīraṇatva*.

62. *deśāntarotpādanasvabhāvā . . . īraṇā*, compare the source quoted in the *Compendium: desantaruppattihetubhāvena*.

63. The Sanskrit and the Tibetan have the plural. Hsüan-tsang: the *Prakaraṇapāda*; Paramartha: the *Fen-pieh tao-li lun*. *Prakaraṇa*, *TD* 26, p. 699c5, *vāyudhātuḥ katamah? laghusamudīraṇatvam*.

64. The Sūtra in question (*Samyuktāgama*, *TD* 2, p. 72c, *Vibhāṣā*, *TD* 27, p. 388a18) is perhaps the *Garbhāvakrāntisūtra* (*Majjhima*, III.239, below note 120). In the redaction known through the *Śikṣāsamuccaya* (p. 244), there is (1) for earth *kakkhaṭatva kharagata* (compare *Mahāvastu*, i.339, *Divyāvadāna*, 518.2; *Dhammasaṅgaṇi*, 648; *Harṣacarita*, *JRAS*. 1899, p. 494); (2) for water: *āpas abgata aptva sneha snehagata snehatva dravatva*; (3) for fire: *tejas tejogata uṣmagata*; (4) for wind: *vāyu vāyugata laghutva samudīraṇatva*.

65. This is to say: light (*laghu*) is derived *rūpa*; lightness (*laghutva*), which by its nature is movement (*īraṇa*) is the wind element; the wind element is thus *laghusamudīraṇatva*: that which produces lightness and motion.

66. Quoted in *Vyākhyā*, viii.35.

See viii.36b (*vāyukṛtsnāyatana*). Two opinions in *Vibhāṣā*, *TD* 27, p. 441a, p. 689b3 as to whether the wind is visible or not.

67. It appears that the Tibetan and Chinese sources call for the translation: "What is it that is broken? By contact with the hand . . ."

Saṁyutta, iii.86: *ruppatīti kho bhikkhave tasmā rūpaṁ ti vuccati / kena ruppati / sītena . . . siriṁsapasampassena ruppati.* (See the interpretation of Shwe Zan Aung in the *Compendium*: "*rūpa* means that which changes its form under the physical conditions of cold . . .").

The *Mahāvyutpatti* has: *rūpaṇād rūpam.* (111.3, 245.1137, 1153, 1154).

There are two roots: (1) *rūp*, which gives *rūpa*, form, color, beauty, *rūpya*, gold, etc.; and (2) *rup, rumpere*, in Vedic Sanskrit: *rupyati, ropana*, etc.; in Pāḷi: *ruppati* (=*kuppata ghaṭṭiyati pīliyati domanassito hoti*); in Classical Sanskrit *lup, lumpati.*

68. The Sarvāstivādins understand: "Useful Chapters;" the Pāḷi signifies "The Octades." (S. Lévi, *J. As.* 1915, i.412, 1916, ii.34).

Mahāniddesa, p. 5. Kern, *Verspreide Geschriften*, ii.261 (La Haye 1913) illustrates the meaning of *rup* by *Jātaka* iii, 368, *Cariyapiṭaka*, 3.6, etc.

69. *Pratighāta* signifies *svadeśe parasyotpatti pratibandha.* See above p. 90.

Elsewhere, the thing which is *sapratigha*, "impenetrable," is defined: *yad deśam āvṛṇoti*, that which "covers" a place, that which is extended.

One shall see (i.43) the type of *pratighāta* refered to in the *Dhammasaṅgaṇi*, 618-619.

70. There is a third definition of *rūpaṇa, Madhyamakavṛtti*, 456.9: *tatredam ihāmutreti nirūpaṇād rūpam* = "This is called *rūpa* because one can indicate it as being here or there," and *Vyākhyā ad* i.24 *pāṇyādisaṁsparśair bādhanālakṣaṇād rūpaṇāt / idam ihāmutreti deśanidarśanarūpaṇac ca.* Compare *Mahāvyutpatti*, 245.1139, *deśanirūpaṇa.*

We have thus: *rūpa*, that which is impenetrable, that which occupies a place; thus "physical matter."

Saṁghabhadra also has another explanation: *rūpa* is so called because it indicates previous action as "This man has cultivated an action, anger, which has produced his bad appearance."

71. See i.43c-d and ii.22.

72. This formula has passed into the *Mahāvyutpatti*, 109.2. The Japanese editor refers to *Vibhāṣā*, *TD* 27, p. 390al.

The *Vyākhyā* mentions that this second explanation is due to the Vṛddhācārya, or "former master," Vasubandhu.

On the Vasubandhu the teacher of Manoratha, in turn the teacher of Vasubandhu the author of the *Kośa*, see *Bhāṣyam* iii.27 and iv.3a, and the sources discussed in the *Avant Propos* to *Cosmologie Bouddhique*, p. viii (London,1918).

73. Saṁghabhadra, in the *Samayapradīpikā*, reads: *ta evoktā.* Vasubandhu employs the expression *iṣṭa*, "is regarded by the Vaibhāṣikas," because, for him, the *skandhas* do not really exist (i.20).

74. *Vedanānubhava*, ii.7, 8, 24; iii.32; *Saṁyutta*, iii.96; *Dhammasaṅgaṇi*, 3; *Theorie des douze causes*, p. 23.

75. *Nimitta*, characteristic, is understood as *vastuno'vasthāviśeṣa*, the diverse conditions or manners of being of the thing. *Udgrahaṇa* signifies *paricheda*, determination or discernment.

The *Vijñānakāya*, *TD* 26, p. 559b27, quoted in the *Nyayabindupūrvapakṣasaṁkṣepa* (Mdo, 111, fol. 108b) and in the *Madhyamakavṛtti* (p. 74), says that the visual consciousness knows blue (*nīlam jānāti*), but does not know "This is blue" (*no tu nīlam iti*). See the note *ad* i.33a-b. It is through *saṁjñā* that one gives a name to the visual impression, and to the external cause of the visual impression.

Objection: The consciousness (*vijñāna*) and ideas (*saṁjñā*) are always associated (ii.24); thus the visual consciousness will know the characteristics (*nimitta*) of the object. Answer: The *saṁjñā* which accompanies sense consciousness is weak and indistinct. Only the mental consciousness is

accompanied by an efficacious *saṁjñā*, and only it is *savikalpaka* (i.32-33).
Compare *Saṁyutta* iii.86; *Atthasālinī*, 291; *Milinda*, 61.

76. On the *saṁskāras*, *Theorie des douze causes*, p. 9-12.

77. Compare *Saṁyutta*, iii.60: *katame ca bhikkhave saṁkhārā / chayime cetanākāyā / rūpasaṁcetanā . . . dhammasaṁcetanā; Vibhaṅga*, p. 144; *Sumaṅgalavilāsinī*, p. 64.

78. Volition is action (iv.1), the cause of *upapatti*, and by opposition to thirst, the cause of *abhinirvṛtti* (vi.3).

79. This is to say: "because it conditions that which should be conditioned," as one says: "Cook the porridge that should be cooked."

80. a. *Saṁyutta* iii.67: *saṁkhatam abhisaṁkharontīti bhikkhave tasmā saṁkhārāti vuccanti / kiñ ca saṁkhatam abhisaṁkharonti / rūpaṁ rūpattāya saṁkhatam abhisaṁkharonti / vedanaṁ vedanattāya* . . .
b. *Saṁyutta* v.449: *jātisaṁvattanike'pi saṁkhāre abhisaṁkharonti / jarāsaṁvattanike'pi . . . / maraṇasaṁvattanike'pi . . . / te jātisaṁvattanike'pi samkhāre abhisaṁkharitvā . . . jātipapātam pi papatanti* / . . .
c. *abhisaṁskaraṇalakṣaṇāḥ saṁskārāḥ* (*Madhyamakavṛtti* 343.9); *cittābhisaṁskāramanaskārakṣaṇā cetanā* (ibid. 137.7, *Mahāvastu*, i. 26 and 391).

81. See ii.34.

82. The *Vyākhyā* explains *upalabdhi* by the gloss *vastumātragrahaṇa*, and adds *vedanādayas tu caitasikā viśeṣagrahaṇarūpāḥ* (The text of the *Biblotheca Buddhica* has wrongly: *caitasikaviśeṣa-*): "The consciousness (*vijñāna*) or mind (*citta*) apprehends (*grahaṇa*) only the thing itself (*vastumātra*); the 'mental states' (*caitasika*) or *dharmas* associated with the consciousness (ii.24), that is to say, sensation, etc. (*vedanā samjñā* . . .), apprehend particular characteristics, special conditions." For example, the consciousness of touch (*kāyavijñāna*) apprehends unevenness, softness, etc. (i.10d); it is associated with an agreeable sensation (*vedanā*) which apprehends a certain characteristic of unevenness or softness, the characteristic of being the cause of an agreeable sensation (*sukhavedanīyatā*). The visual consciousness apprehends color (blue, etc.) and shape; it is associated with a certain "mental state" called *saṁjñā*, an idea, which apprehends a certain characteristic of color and shape under consideration: "This is a man, this is a woman, etc." (i.14c-d).
This doctrine has been adopted by the School of Nāgārjuna. *Madhyamakavṛtti*, p. 65 *cittam arthamātragrāhi caitta viśesāvasthāgrāhiṇaḥ sukhādayaḥ*; and by the School of Dignāga, *Nyāyabinduṭīkā*, p. 12, Tibetan version, p. 25.
The Japanese editor of the *Kośa* here quotes the *Kōki* (=the *Chi* of P'u-kuang, *TD* 41, p. 26a14) and the *Vibhāṣā* which mentions four opinions on this problem.
See ii.34b-d.

83. According to Saṁghabhadra: "Even though numerous material objects are present, visual consciousness solely grasps visible matter, not sound; it grasps the blue, etc., but does not say that it is blue, etc., or that it is agreeable, disagreeable, male, female, etc., a stump, etc. . . . " (*TD* 29, p. 342a15).

84. The consciousnesses (*vijñāna*) succeed one another; they can be visual . . . mental. The consciousness which disappears is the immediately antecedent cause (ii.62a), the support (*āśraya*) of the consciousness which immediately follows. Under this aspect it receives the name of *manas, mana-āyatana, manodhātu*, and *mana-indriya* (ii.1). It is to the consciousness which follows what the organ of sight is to the visual consciousness.

85. See i.39a-b.

According to the *Vyākhyā*, the Yogācārins admit a *manodhātu*, a *manas* or mental organ, distinct from the six consciousnesses. The Tāmraparṇīyas, the masters of Taprobanė, imagine (*kalpayanti*) a material organ, the heart (*hṛdayavastu*), a support of the mental consciousness. This heart also exists in Ārūpyadhātu, the non-material sphere: these masters admit in fact the existence of matter in this sphere (viii.3c); they explain the prefix *a* in the sense of "a little," as in *āpiṅgala*, "a little red."

The *Paṭṭhāna* (quoted in *Compendium of Philosophy*, p. 276) assigns a material (*rūpa*) support to the mental consciousness, without giving the name of "heart" to this support, whereas it terms "eye" the support of the visual consciousness. But the later Abhidhamma (*Visuddhimagga, Abhidhammasaṅgaha*) considers the heart as the organ of thought.

The teaching of the *Vibhaṅga*, p. 88, is less clear: "From the visual, auditory consciousness . . . tactile consciousness which has just perished there arises the mind, the *manas*, the mental organ (*mānasa* = *manas*), the heart (=the mind), the *manas*, the *manas* organ . . ." (*Atthasalinī*, 343).

86. *Avijñapti* forms part of *rūpaskandha* and *dharmadhātu*.

87. The problem of inclusion (*saṁgraha*) is examined in the *Dhātukathāpakaraṇa, Kathāvatthu*, vii.1, *Dhātukāya*, and *Prakaraṇa* (see below i.20, note 105).

88. *Digha*, iii.232; *Dharmasaṁgraha*, 19; *Mahāvyutpatti*, 35, etc.

89. Great ugliness results from the fact of having only one eye, one ear, or one nostril. But many animals, camels, cats, owls, etc., are not beautiful for having two eyes! They are not beautiful in comparison with other species, but, among their species, individuals having only one eye, etc., are ugly.

Saṁghabhadra explains *śobhārtham* in the sense of *ādhipatyārtham*, "with a view to its predominating factor" (see ii.1). He who possesses predominance is beautiful, and shines in the world. Individuals who only possess one eye do not possess "predominance," the capacity for clear vision; for sight is not as clear with one eye as with two eyes . . . (i.43).

90. *Saṁyukta, TD* 2, p. 14c4: *yat kiṁcid rūpam atītānāgatapratyutpannam ādhyātmikam vā bāhyaṁ vā audārikaṁ vā sūkṣmaṁ vā hīnaṁ vā praṇītaṁ vā dūraṁ vā antikaṁ vā tad ekadhyam abhisaṁkṣipya ayam ucyate rūpaskandhaḥ.*

Compare *Vibhaṅga*, p. 1.

The edition of the *Vyākhyā* has *aikadhyam*, but the *Mahāvyutpatti* 245, 243 has *ekadhyam abhisaṁkṣipya*. Wogihara mentions *ekadhye* in *Divya*, 35.24, 40.22.

91. *Anityatāniruddha*: destroyed by impermanence which is one of the characteristics of conditioned things (ii.45c-d).

There are five types of *nirodha*: (1) *lakṣaṇanirodha* (ii.45c-d) which is posed here, (2) *samāpattinirodha* (ii.41c), (3) *upapattinirodha* (=*āsaṁjñika*, ii.41b), (4) *pratisaṁkhyānirodha* (i.6a-b), and (5) *apratisaṁkhyānirodha* (i.6c-d).

If the texts were to say, "In the past, *rūpa* is destroyed," one could understand that this refers to *nirodhas* two to five. Now *nirodhas* two and three are the destruction of future mind and mental states; *nirodha* four is the destruction of an impure mind and mental states; and *nirodha* five is the destruction of future *dharmas* not destined to arise (*anutpattidharman*).

92. Āryadeva, *Śataka*, 258, shows that this definition contradicts the thesis of the existence of the future.

93. Hsüan-tsang translates: The Bhadanta Dharmatrāta. But the *Vyākhyā* says: The Bhadanta is a Sautrāntika Sthavira, or a Sautrāntika Sthavira of this name. Bhagavadviśeṣa thinks that this refers to the Sthavira Dharmatrāta.

We object to this: Dharmatrāta is a follower of the teaching of the existence of the past and future, thus a Sarvāstivādin, and we are concerned here with a Sautrāntika, this is, a Dārṣṭāntika. But the Bhandanta Dharmatrāta has a Sarvāstivādin theory presented later (v.25). The "Bhadanta" is a philosopher that the *Vibhāṣā* quotes under the simple name of Bhadanta, a philosopher who adhers to the Sautrāntika system (*sautrāntika-darśanāvalambin*), whereas the *Vibhāṣā* calls the Bhadanta Dharmatrāta by his name. Thus we have here a certain Sautrāntika Sthavira Bhikṣu, who differs from Dharmatrāta.

The Japanese editor refers to *Vibhāṣā TD* 27, p. 383b16, where it is said that Dharmatrāta does not admit that the *dharmāyatana* is *rūpa* (see iv.4a-b).

94. *Vibhāṣā, TD* 27, p. 379a12, presents twenty opinions on the meaning of the term *āyatana*. The definition of the *Kośa* is reproduced in the *Mahāvyutpatti*, p. 552.

95. *Vibhāṣā, TD* p. 367c21, has eleven etymologies. We have here the first one.

96. *Dhātu* signifies "mine" in the expression *suvarṇagotra*, Asaṅga, *Sūtrālaṁkāra*, iii.9 and note of the translater.

97. The Vaibhāṣikas believe that the *skandhas*, the *āyatanas* and the *dhātus* really exist; the Sautrāntikas hold that the *dhātus* are real, the *skandhas* and the *āyatanas* only "nominally" so; Vasubandhu holds the *skandhas* to be "nominal," whereas the *āyatanas* and the *dhātus* are real.

98. The doctrine of the *pudgala* is discussed in a supplement, Chapter IX, of the *Kośa*, translated by Stcherbatsky, Académie de Petrograd, 1920.

99. Saṁghabhadra: "This objection does not hold. *Skandha* does not signify 'mass,' but 'that which is susceptible of being collected together in a mass' . . ." (*TD* 29, p. 343c25).

100. In the way that, in the world, *skandha* signifies shoulder, *nāmarūpa* are the two shoulders which bear the *ṣaḍāyatana* (iii.21).

101. That part which is *rūpa*, that part which is sensation . . .

102. Paramārtha: "I shall return to you three *skandhas*." Tibetan: *dbul bar bya ba'i phuṅ po gsum dag tu dbul bar bya'o.*

103. *Utsūtra: Mahābhāṣya*, i. p. 12; Kielhorn, *JRAS*, 1908, p. 501.

104. The Ābhidhārmikas are not always clearly distinguished from the Vaibhāṣikas. See *Introduction.*

105. Compare *Prakaraṇapāda*, Chapter VI (TD 26, p. 731c19): The *cakṣurdhātu* is embraced within one *dhātu*, one *āyatana*, and one *skandha*; it is known (*jñeya*) by seven *jñānas* (see *Kośa*, vii) with the exception of *paracittajñāna, nirodhajñāna*, and *mārgajñāna*: it is discerned by one *vijñāna*; it exists in Kāmadhātu and Rūpadhātu; it is affected by the *anuśayas* to be abandoned through Meditation (see *Kośa*, v.).

Dhātukathāpakaraṇa (PTS ed. 1892) p. 6: *cakkhudhātu ekena khandhena ekāyatanena ekāya dhātuya saṁgahitā.*

106. According to *Vibhāṣā, TD* 27, p. 366c26.

107. Teaching of the *skandhas* to persons of sharp faculties (*prajñendriya*). Example: *yad bhikṣo na tvaṁ sa te dharmaḥ prahātavyaḥ / ājñātaṁ bhagavan / katham asya bhikṣo saṁkṣiptenoktārtham ājānāsi / rūpaṁ bhadanta nāhaṁ sa me dharmaḥ prahātavyaḥ /*

The three types of hearers—*udghaṭitajña, avipañcitajña*, and *padaṁparama*—correspond to the three types of faculties (*Puggalapaññatti*, p. 41; *Sūtrālaṁkāra*, trans. p. 145).

108. *Dharmaskandha, TD* 26, p. 501a7; *Vibhāṣā, TD* 27, p. 385a29.

109. Six *vivādamūlas* in *Dīgha*, iii.246, etc.

110. *Vibhāṣā, TD* 27, p. 385b15.

111. According to *Vibhāṣā, TD* 27, p. 384bl-6.

112. The *Vibhāṣā, TD* 27, p. 399c4-7, enumerates eleven reason which justify the terms *rūpāyatana* and *dharmāyatana*.

113. This is the opinion of Dharmatrāta (see his *Saṁyukta Abhidharmahṛdaya, TD* 28, p. 873a28-b2). i.17.

114. (1) According to the Sautrāntikas, the word of the Buddha (*buddhavacana*) is *vāgvijñapti* (iv.3d); according to another school (*nikāyāntarīya*) it is *nāman*. The *Vyākhyā* quotes, on this point, the *Jñānaprasthāna* (See *Cosmologie bouddhique*, p. vii, note).

(2) In another canon, the Sūtra says that there are eighty-four thousand *dharmaskandhas*. The Sūtra has Ānanda saying, "I have learned from the Buddha more than eighty-four thousand *dharmaskandhas: sātirekāṇi me'śītir dharmaskandhasahasrāṇi bhagavato'ntikāt saṁmukham udgṛhītāni* (See Burnouf, *Introduction*, p. 34; *Sumaṅgalavilāsinī*, p. 24; *Theragāthā*, 1024; *Prajñāpāramitā* in the *Akutobhaya* of Nāgārjuna, i.8; *Avadānaśataka*, ii.155).

115. *Vibhāṣā, TD* 27, p. 385c18: the *Dharmaskandhaśāstra* contains six thousand *gaāthās*.
See Takakusu's analysis, *JPTS*, 1905, p. 112.

116. Eighty thousand *dharmaskandhas* have perished; a single *dharmaskandha* has been preserved (*Vyākhyā*).

117. This is the explanation of Buddhaghosa, *Sumaṅgalavilāsini*, i.24.

118. The *Vyākhyā* quotes a Sūtra, a more developed form of *Dīgha*, iii.241 and *Aṅguttara*, iii.21.
Vimuktyāyatana = *vimukter āyadvāram*.

119. These are opposed to the sixty-two *dṛṣṭis* (*Vibhāṣā, TD* 27, p. 376c6 and foll.). The *Bahudhātuka* (*Madhyama, TD* 1, p. 723c13 , *Dharmaskandha*, Chapter XX) is closely related to *Majjhima*, iii.61 (41 *dhātus*). Compare Asaṅga, *Sūtrālaṁkāra*, iii.2.

120. This refers to the Sūtra which explains the constituent elements of a person: *ṣaḍdhātur ayaṁ bhikṣo puruṣaḥ*. Vasubandhu quotes it (i.35) under the name of *Garbhāvakrāntisūtra* (*Vinayasaṁyuktakavastu*, Sec. 11, *TD* 24, p. 253a21; and in the *Ratnakūṭa*, Chap. 14, *TD* 11, p. 326b). In the *Majjhima*, this Sūtra is called the *Dhātuvibhaṅgasutta* (iii.239); it constitutes one of the sources of the *Pitāputrasamāgama* extracts of which are preserved in the *Śikṣaāsamuccaya*, p. 244, *Bodhicaryāvatāra*, ix.88, *Madhyamakāvatāra*, p. 269.

See note 62, and note 143 and *Prakaraṇapada* quoted in the note *ad* ii.23c-d.

On the six *dhātus, Aṅguttara*, i.176, *Vibhaṅga*, p. 82-85, *Abhidharmahṛdaya*, viii.7.

121. *Dharmaskandha*, Chapter XX, *Vibhāṣā, TD* 27, p. 388a29. Same definition in *Vibhaṅga*, p. 84: *katamā ajjhattikā ākāsadhātu? yaṁ ajjhattaṁ paccattam ākāso ākāsagataṁ aghaṁ aghagatam vivaro vivaragatam . . . kaṇṇacchiddaṁ nāsacchiddaṁ . . .*

122. P'u-kuang says (*TD* 41, p. 32c28): "One says that *ākāśadhātu* is light and darkness in order to show that it is a type of color (*varṇa*) and a real thing. The author does not believe that *ākāśadhātu* is a real thing, and this is why he adds the word *kila*." For Vasubandhu and the Sautrāntikas, *ākāśadhātu* is solely the absence of a resistent body (*sapratighadravyābhāvamātra*). See ii.55c-d.

Vibhāṣā, TD 27, p. 388b19: What difference is there between *ākāśa* and *ākāśadhātu*? The first is non-material (*arūpin*), invisible (*anidarśana*), non-resistent (*apratigha*), pure (*anāsrava*), unconditioned (*asaṁskṛta*); the second is material . . .

123. One edition of the *Vyākhyā* reads *āgha*: *āghaṁ kila citasthaṁ rūpam iti citasthaṁ saṁghātastham / atyarthaṁ hanti hanyate cety āgham / . . . atyarthaśabdasya ākārādeśaḥ kṛto hanteś ca ghādeśah*. But the Burnouf MSS reads *agham . . . akārādeśaḥ*; we have, *ad* iii.72, *agha* = *citastharūpa; Mahāvyutpatti*, 245.162.

124. See above p. 70 and following.

125. The *dharmadhātu* is apart from cause: it includes *avijñapti* which is material and non-susceptible to being struck.

126. See *Kāraṇaprajñaptiśāstra*, analyzed in *Cosmologie bouddhique*, p. 339.

127. Compare *Saṁyutta*, iv.201: *puthujjano cakkhusmiṁ haññati manāpāmanāpehi rūpehi.*

128. This means that the consciousness which arises having blue for its object (*viṣaya*) and the eye for its support (*āśraya*), can be hindered from arising through the interposition of a foreign body between the eye and the blue object: the eye and the blue are thus *sapratigha*. But neither the *manodhātu*, which functions as the organ of the mental consciousness (*manovijñāna*), nor the *dharmadhātu*, which is the object proper of the mental consciousness (for example sensation), are not *sapratigha*: nothing can hinder, by making an "obstacle" or a "screen" (*āvaraṇa*), the mental consciousness from arising from the mental organ (*manodhātu*) with respect to the *dharmadhātu*.

129. See ii.9a; *Vibhāṣā, TD* 27, p. 263c12, p. 740b8.

130. The Mahīśāsakas believe that the first four consciousnesses are always neutral; the consciousness of touch and the mental consciousness are of the three types.

131. The *dharmas* which do not belong to any sphere of existence, which are transcendent to existence (*adhātupatita, adhātvāpta, apariyāpanna*) are unconditioned things.

132. The examination of this problem is taken up again ii.12.
Compare *Kathāvatthu*, viii.7.

133. Compare *Dīgha*, i.34, 186.

134. *Vibhāṣā, TD* 27, p. 746a4: "Do the male and female organs exist in Rūpadhātu? Neither of the sexual organs exist there. First opinion: it is because one desires to abandon these organs that one cultivates the *dhyānas* and is reborn in Rūpādhatu. If beings in Rūpadhātu were to possess these organs, they would not desire to be reborn in this sphere. Second opinion: these organs are created by gross food (iii.39); the Sūtra (iii.98c) says in fact that human beings at the beginning of the cosmic age do not possess these organs, that they all have the same form; later, when they eat of the juice of the earth, the two organs arise, and the difference of male and female appear; in the absence of gross food, the two organs will be missing. Third opinion: the two organs have a use in Kāmadhātu, but they do not have a use in Rūpadhātu: thus they are missing in Rūpadhātu . . .
On the gods of Kāmadhātu, see iii.70.

135. The Mahāsāṁghikas and the Sautrāntikas maintain that the body of the Buddha is pure (*anāsrava*) (see iv.4a-b, discussion of *avijñapti*) (Compare *Kathāvatthu*, iv.3, xiv.4). *Vibhāṣā, TD* 27, p. 229a17, p. 391c27: "Certain masters, the Mahāsāṁghikas, maintain that the body of the Buddha is pure. They say, 'Scripture says that the Tathāgata remains above the world, that he is not mundane, that he is not defiled; thus we know that the body of the Buddha is pure.' In order to refute this opinion, we show that the body of the Buddha is impure. To say that it is pure is to contradict the Sūtra."

The body of the Buddha is not pure (*anāsrava*), because it can be the occasion of the defilement of another. *Vibhāṣā, TD* 27, p. 871cll: The body of the Buddha is the result of ignorance and thirst; it is thus not pure. The Sūtra says that ten complete *āyatanas* (organ of sight . . . ,visibles . . .), and two partial *āyatanas* (*manaāyatana dharmas*) are impure . . . If the body of the Buddha were pure, women would not have affection for him; he would not produce, among others, any desire, hatred, confusion, or pride . . .

Compare *Vyākhyā*, p. 14; above p. 58.

136. Same question in *Vibhaga*, 97, 435. *Vitarka* and *vicāra* are defined ii.28, 33.

137. These are called *avikalapaka* by reason of the text: *caksurvijñānasamaṅgī nīlaṁ vijānāti no tu nīlam iti* (See above note 75).

138. *Kila*: this is an opinion of the Vaibhāṣikas without support in the Sūtras.

The opinion of Vasubandhu is explained later, ii.33. For him as for the Sautrantikas, *vitarka* and *vicāra* are *citta, manovijñāna*.

139. *Vibhāṣā, TD* 27, p. 219b7: *svabhāvavikalpa* is *vitarka-vicāra; anusmaraṇavikalpa* is the memory associated with mental consciousness; *nirūpaṇāvikalpa* is non-absorbed *prajñā* of the sphere of the mental consciousness. In Kāmadhātu, the five consciousnesses have only the first type of *vikalpa*: they include memory, but not *anusmaraṇavikalpa*, for they are not capable of recognition; they include *prajñā*, but not *nirūpaṇāvikalpa*, for they are not capable of examination.

Nyāyānusāra (*TD* 29, p. 350bll): The nature of *svabhāvavikalpa* is *vitarka*.

140. Saṁghabhadra: *Prajñā* and memory are associated with the five sense consciousnesses, but their functions are reduced therein (*TD* 29, p. 350b17).

141. *Prajñā* which is mental (*mānasī*), that is to say *manasi bhavā*, proceeds either from the hearing of Scripture or from reflection (*śrutacintāmayī*), or is innate (*upapattipratilambhikā*); is dispersed (*vyagrā*), that is, non-concentrated *prajñā*, having different objects (*agra*), or "dis-crowned" (*vigatapradhānā*) by the fact that it successively grasps after different object.

Why give the name of *abhinirūpaṇāvikalpa* to this *prajñā*?

Because it applies to a certain object in respect to its name (*nāmāpekṣayā*) and examines (*abhinirūpaṇā*): "this is *rūpa, vedanā, anitya, duḥkha*," etc. However, concentrated (*samāhitā*) *prajñā*, proceeding from absorption (*bhāvanāmayī*), is applied to an object without taking into consideration its name. Thus it is not *abhinirūpaṇāvikalpa*.

All mental memory (*smṛti*), that is to say, the mental memory, is or is not concentrated. For, according to the School, the mental memory uniquely has for its object the thing previously experienced and does not take into consideration its name, according to the definition: "What is memory? Expression of the mind (*cetaso'bhilāpaḥ*)." The mode of existence of memory connected to the five consciousnesses is not an expression (*abhilāpa*) of a thing previously experienced. It is thus not *anusmaraṇavikalpa* (*Vyākhyā*). See ii.24.

142. On the meaning of *ālambana*, i.29b.

Compare *Vibhaṅga*, p. 95.

143. The Abhidhamma (*Vibhaṅga*, p. 96, *Dhammasaṅgaṇni*, 653, 1211, 1534) understands *upādinna* in the same sense. The modern commentators of the Abhidhamma translate *upādinna* as "issue of grasping;" they do not see the *upādā* = *upādāyarūpa, bhautika*, and so create a great confusion.

Moreover the *Vibhaṅga* does not classify the *dhātus* as does the Abhidharma. (See also *Suttavibhaṅga*, p. 113; *Mahāvyutpatti*, 101.56; *Divyāvadana*, p. 54; *Bodhicaryāvatāra*, viii.97, 101). And there is some fluctuation even in Sanskrit sources. For example, *Majjhima* iii.240, reproduced in the *Pitāputrasamāgama* (see above p. 54, n. 1), gives the hair . . . excrements as *ajjhattaṁ paccattam kakkhalam upādinnam*. Now hair is not *upādinna*. A description of corporeal matter (*ādhyātmikā*, see *Majjhima*, iii.90) has been confused with a description of organic matter (*upātta*)

Upātta matter, plus the *manas*, is called *āśraya* (see ii.5). This is the subtle bodies of the non-Buddhists.

144. *Bhūta, mahābhūta; upādāya rūpa, bhautika*; see i.22, 23-24, ii.12, 50a, 65. *bhautika* = *bhūta bhava* = derived from the *bhūtas*.

145. Compare *Vibhaṅga*, p. 96.

146. *Vibhāṣā, TD* 27, p. 661c14. There are two masters in this school, Buddhadeva and Dharmatrāta. Buddhadeva says: "*Rūpa* is solely the primary elements; the mental states (*caitta*) are solely mind (*citta*)." He says that *upādāyarūpa*, secondary matter, is a species of the primary elements (*mahābhūtaviśeṣa*), and that the mental states are a species of mind . . ." (Compare *Kathāvatthu*, vii.3). *Vibhāṣā, TD* 27, p. 383c24. The Sūtra says: "*Rūpa* is the four primary elements and that which derives from the four primary elements." Which opinion does the Sūtra intend to refute? It intends to refute the opinion of Buddhadeva. The Buddha sees that, in the future, there will be a master, Buddhadeva, who will say: "There is no derived, distinct *rūpa* apart from the primary elements." In order to refute this opinion, the Buddha says: "*Rūpa* is the four primary elements . . ." *Vibhāṣā, TD* 27, p. 730b26: "All conditioned things are either *mahābhūta* or *citta*; there is no *upādāyarūpa* apart from the *mahābhūtas*; and there is no *caitta* (mental states) apart from the *citta* (the mind).

On the mind and mental states, see below p. 101 and ii.23c.

Buddhadeva is perhaps the master named on the lion inscription of Mathura.

147. Thus (1) the organs are not primary matter, not being "solid," etc.; (2) tangible things include primary matter, since a solid is perceived by touch; and (3) secondary matter perceived by the other organs is not perceived by touch.

148. See ii.5. The first four *dhātus* (earth . . . wind) are "radical substances," because the organs arise from these *dhātus*; the *vijñānadhātu* or *manodhātu* is a "root," because it gives rise to *manaḥsparśāyatana*. Or rather the first four *dhātus* are roots because they give rise to secondary matter; the *vijñānadhātu* is a root because it gives rise to mental states (*caitta, caitasika*).

149. Thus the first five "supports of contact," the five organs of sense consciousness, are "secondary matter:" otherwise, they would be included in the definition: "A person is made up of the six *dhātus*."

150. According to the Abhidhamma (*Dhammasaṅgaṇi*, 647), derived *rūpa* is not tangible. Saṁghabhadra (*TD* 29, p. 352cl) refutes this opinion which he attributes to the Sthavira. On this subject see the *Introduction* for a discussion of the authenticity of the Sūtras.

151. *Vibhāṣā, TD* 27, p. 391c6.

151. *Vibhāṣā, TD* 27, p. 689c5 and foll.

153. This is the etymology *vipacyata iti vipākaḥ*; the *vipāka* is what has become ripe.

154. This is the etymology *vipāka* = *vipakti*.

155. It appears that this is the opinion of Dharmatrāta i.45 (*TD* 28, number 1552).

156. Let us consider one moment or state of existence of this subtle matter which is the organ of sight. One part of this matter is retribution of a former action; another part proceeds from food: all this matter is the outflowing result of a previous moment or state in the existence of the eye. But this previous moment or state is not, in and of itself, capable of generating the present moment: in fact, at death, the organ of sight ceases producing itself through outflowing. Thus by

definition the organ of sight is not an outflowing. But consider, on the contrary, the flesh that constitutes the body: it persists after death; it is thus an outflowing, the result, in each of the moments of its existence, of the previous moment.

The *Kathāvatthu*, xii,4, xvi.8, does not hold that matter is retribution.

157. Nine reason are enumerated in *Vibhāṣā, TD* 27, p. 612c. Vasubandhu quotes the third.

158. The Vātsīputrīyas and the Vibhajyavādins maintain that sound is retribution.

159. Compare *Dīgha*, iii.173, quoted by the Mahāsāṁghikas in the *Kathāvatthu*, xii.3: *saddo vipāko*.

160. See *Vibhāṣā, TD* 27, p. 823a20, p. 449a16, and Dharmatrāta, *TD* 29, p. 396c20. These passages are discussed by Fa-pao in his *Shu, TD* 41, p. 502a18 and following.

161. *Vibhāṣā, TD* 27, p. 714a7 and foll. The difference between internal (*ādhyātmika*) *dharmas* and external (*bāhya*) *dharmas* is threefold: 1. difference from the point of view of the series (*saṁtāna*): the *dharmas* that are to be found in the person himself (*svātmabhāva*) are internal; those that are to be found within another, and also those which are not integral to living beings (*asattvākhya*, i.10b), are external; 2. difference from the point of view of the *āyatanas*: the *āyatanas* which are the support (*āśraya*) of the mind and mental states are internal; those which are objects (*ālambana*) are external; 3. difference from the point of view of living beings: the *dharmas* integral to living beings are internal; the others are external.

162. See *Udānavarga*, xxiii; *Madhyamakavṛtti*, p. 354; *Dhammapada*, 160.

163. *Prakaraṇa, TD* 26, p. 699a3-28.

164. *Vibhāṣā* (*TD* 27, p. 368a21): The organ that has seen, now sees or shall see *rūpa*, and its *tatsabhāga* (that is to say the organ which resembles this organ) is the *cakṣurdhātu*. The organ which has seen is past *cakṣurdhātu*; the organ which now sees is present *cakṣurdhātu*; and the organ that shall see is future *cakṣurdhātu*. As for *tatsabhāga*, the masters of this land say that it is of four types: the past, present, and future *tatsabhāga* eye is the *cakṣurdhātu* which has perished, is now perishing, or shall perish without having seen the *rūpa*; one should add, as a fourth, the *cakṣurdhātu* which absolutely will not arise.

Foreign (*bahirdeśaka*) masters say that it is of five types: past, present, future, as above. Further, future *cakṣurdhātu* which absolutely will not arise, is of two types, accordingly as it is, or is not, associated with the consciousness.

165. *Vibhāṣā, TD* 27, p. 368b13. Three opinions. Can one see *rūpa* by means of the eye of another? Who maintains such an opinion? If one cannot see by means of the eye of another, how can the eye of a certain being be called *sabhāga* through relationship with other beings? Because the activity of the eye is definite: this activity consists of seeing. When the eye, after having been active, has perished, it is called *sabhāga*: neither for the person himself, nor for another, does this name *sabhāga* change. In this same way . . .

166. By explaning *bhāga* in the passive, *bhajyata iti bhāgaḥ*.

167. The eye that perishes without having seen is similar to the eye that sees, etc.

The Mādhyamikas (*Vṛtti*, p. 32 and the note that should be corrected) make the best of this theory: "In reality, the *sabhāga* eye does not see visible things, because it is an organ, exactly like *tatsabhāga*:" *na paramārthataḥ sabhāgaṁ cakṣuḥ paśyati rūpāṇi, cakṣurinidriyatvāt, tadyathātatsabhāgam*.

168. *Vibhāṣā, TD* 27, p. 265cb. The same problem is examined in the *Vibhaṅga*, pp. 12, 16, 97, and the *Dhammasaṅgani*, 1002, 1007, 1008.

169. On the quality of *pṛthagjana*, ii.40c, vi.26a, 28c-d. In *Vibhāṣā, TD* 27, p. 231c13-23, divergent explanations of Vasumitra, the Bhadanta, and Ghoṣaka.

170. See ii.13, iv.lla-b.

171. We shall see that the first stage is *ānantaryamārga*, "the path which destroys the defilements;" the second stage is *vimuktimārga*, "the path of deliverence," the path in which the defilements are destroyed (vi.28).

172. *Dhī* in place of *prajñā*, for prosodical reasons (ii.57d).

173. See *Nyāyabinduṭīkāṭippaṇī*, p. 26; *Bodhicaryāvatārapañjikā*, p. 520; *Atthasālinī*, p. 400; Warren (*Visuddhimagga*), p. 207; *Buddhist Psychology*, p. 351, note; Spence Hardy, *Manual*, p. 419. *Kathāvatthu*, sviii.9, where the thesis "the eye sees" is attributed to the Mahāsāṁghikas. Compare *Samayabheda*, Wassilief, p. 262. Wassilief summarizes the discussion of the *Kośa*, p. 308 (Read: "das Auge nicht das Mass des Sichtbaren *sieht*," and not "*ist*").

Vibhāṣā, TD 27, p. 489b14: According to another opinion, all the *saṁskṛtas* are, by their nature, view (*dṛṣṭi*). View means the manifested characteristic of its manner of being (*paṭupracāra*). All the *saṁskṛtas* possess this characteristic. Some others say that the consciousness of the supression of the defilements and of non-production (*kṣayānutpādajñāna*, vii.1) is view. *Vibhāṣā, TD* 27. p. 61c and foll.: Dharmatrāta says that the visual consciousness (*cakṣurvijñāna*) sees visible things. Ghoṣaka says that the *prajñā* associated with visual consciousness sees visible things. The Dārṣṭāntikas say that the "complex" (*sāmagrī*) sees visible things. The Vātsīputrīyas say that one eye alone sees visible things . . . If the visual consciousness sees visible things, then consciousness would have view for its characteristic; now this is not the case: thus this opinion is false. If the *prajñā* associated with visual consciousness sees visible things, then the *prajñā* associated with the consciousness of hearing would understand sounds; now *prajñā* does not have hearing for its characteristic: thus this opinion is false. If the "complex" sees visible things, then one would always see visible things, for the "complex" is always present. If one eye, not the two eyes, sees visible things, then parts of the body would not feel tangibles at one and the same time: in the same way that the two arms, however distant they may be from each other, can simultaneously feel tangible things and produce a single tactile consciousness, in this way what obstacle is there to the two eyes, however distant they may be from each other, simultaneously seeing and producing a single visual consciousness?

174. This is the thesis of the Bhadanta (*Vibhāṣā, TD* 27, p. 63b23, c12).

175. *cakṣuṣā rūpāṇi dṛṣṭvā* . . . quoted iii.32d. *Saṁyukta, TD* 1, p. 87c26, p. 88a; *Vibhaṅga*, p. 381; *Madhyamakavṛtti*, p. 137; *Dhammasaṅgaṇi*, 597. This is the argument of the Māhāsaṁghikas, *Kathāvatthu*, xviii.9.

176. Compare the formula: *tasyaivaṁ jānata evaṁ paśyataḥ*.

177. *Vyākhyā: vijñānaṁ tu sāṁnidhyamātreṇti nāśrayabhāvayogeneti darśayati / yathā sūryo divasakara iti/yathā sāṁnidhyamātreṇa sūryo divasaṁ karotīty ucyate tathā vijñānaṁ vijānatīty ucyate / kasmāt /loke tathā siddhatvāt.*

178. Or rather: "One should not reject expressions in worldly use for the reason that they do not correspond to realities." *janapadaniruktiṁ nābhiniveśeta saṁjñāṁ, ca lokasya nātidhavet.* (*Madhyama TD* 1, p. 703a2, *Saṁyukta*, 13.12). Compare *Majjhima*, iii.230: *janapadaniruttiṁ nābhiniveseyya samaññaṁ nātidhāveyya; Saṁyutta*, iv.230: *yaṁ ca sāmaṁ ñātaṁ ca atidhāvanti, yaṁ ca loke saccasaṁmataṁ taṁ ca atidhāvanti. Itivuttaka*, 49.

179. According to the *Jñānaprasthāna, TD* 26, p. 919c27; *Vibhāṣā, TD* 27, p. 62bl.
Against the Vātsīputrīyas. See above note 173, at the end.

180. Argument of Vasubandhu, *Pañcavastuka*, i.10.

181. Compare *Atthasālinī*, 629.

Vibhāṣā, *TD* 27, p. 63b14 and foll: One says that the object is attained (*prāpta*) in a twofold sense: either because it is "grasped as object" or "perceived;" or because there is a juxtaposition (*nirantaratva*) of the object and the organ. In the first sense, the six organs attain the object. In the second sense, only three organs—the organs of smell, taste and touch,—attain the object; but on the contrary, three organs, the organs of sight and hearing and the mental organ, perceive without attaining.

The organ of sight preceives visible things by reason of light; when a visible thing is close to the organ, it hinders the light: the organ does not see. The organ of hearing perceives sound by reason of space or the void; when a sound is close to the organ, it does not hinder the void: the organ hears . . . The organ of smell perceives by reason of the wind; the organ of taste, by reason of water; the organ of touch, by reason of the earth; and the mental organ, by reason of the act of attention (*manaskāra*).

Fa-pao (see *TD* 41, p. 508a19 and foll.) observes that the *rūpa* of the moon does not leave the moon in order to juxtapose itself on the eye.

Compare Āryadeva, *Śataka*, 288.

182. An objection of the Vaiśeṣikas.

183. This doctrine is refuted by Saṁghabhadra (*TD* 29, p. 370b12 and foll.); Shen-t'ai attributes it to the Sāṁmitīyas; Fa-pao, to certain masters of the *Vibhāṣā* (*TD* 41, p. 508b17).

184. Saṁghabhadra discusses this thesis (*TD* 29, p. 370b23 and foll.).

185. Here and below (the definition of Bhadanta, p. 106), our Tibetan version translates *nirantara* by *'dab chags pa*. But the Tibetan Siddhantas analyzed by Wassilief (p. 307) oppose the *nirantara* of the Bhadanta (*bar med pa*) to the *nirantara* of the other masters (*'dab chags pa*).

According to the *Bodhicaryāvatāra*, p. 516, the organ and its object cannot be either separated (*savyavadhāna, sāntara*) or contiguous (*nirantara*).

186. Saṁghabhadra (*TD* 29, p. 371c7): What is the meaning of "to attain?" When an object arises in proximity to an organ, this latter grasps it. Thus one can say that smell, taste, and touch grasp the objects that they attain; in the same way one says that the organ of sight does not see eyelids, eye-lashes and the other visible matter that it attains. The eyelid does not touch the organ of sight: one says nevertheless that the organ attains it. From the fact that the eyelid arises in proximity to the organ, one says that this latter attains it. As the organ of sight does not see the visible matter thus attained, one says that the organ of sight grasps without attaining, not by attaining; moreover it does not grasp a very distant object. In this same way, even though smell grasps the object that it attains, it does not grasp what is very close.

187. Compare the *Viṁśaka* of Vasubandhu, 12-14; *Bodhicaryāvatāra*, p. 503; *Praśastapāda*, p. 43, etc.

188. According to *Vibhāṣā*, *TD* 27, p. 683c24: Do the atoms touch one another? They do not touch one another; if they touch one another, they touch one another in either their totality or partially. If they touch one another in their totality, they form but one single thing; if they partially touch one another they would thus have parts. And atoms do not have parts.

How is it that agglomerations, striking against one another, do not fall to pieces? They do not fall to pieces because *vāyudhātu* holds them together.

But does not *vāyudhātu* fall to pieces? Sometimes it falls to pieces, for example at the end of the cosmic period. Sometimes it holds together, for example at the beginning of the cosmic period.

If atoms do not touch one another, how can striking produce sound? Sound is produced for this very reason. For, if the atoms were to touch one another, how could there be the production of sound? If atoms touch one another, the hand and the body that it strikes would mix with one another, and there would be not free space, and how could sound arise? Vasumitra says: "Atoms do not touch one another: if they touch one another, they would thus last for a second moment." The Bhadanta says: There is no real contact; it is through acquiescense to popular truth that one say that there is contact when atoms arise in a union without interval (*nirantara*).

Does the thing in contact arise having for its case a thing in contact . . .

189. They should have arisen (first moment) in order to touch one another (second moment).

190. Vasubandhu believes that the Bhadanta understands "juxtaposition without interval" in the sense that atoms do not allow any intermediate space bewteen them. Saṁghabhadra is of a different opinion.

191. For Vasubandhu, atoms are immediately juxtaposed; nevertheless they do not mix one with another, for being impenetrable, they remain distinct in spite of their contiguity. See p. 70.

Here are the essentials of Saṁghadra's explanations.

Nyāyānusāra, (TD 29, p. 372b12): The Bhadanta nevertheless says: "Atoms do not touch one another; but one says, by metaphor, that they touch one another, because they are juxtaposed without interval" (*nirantara*). The Sautrāntika (that is, Vasubandhu), indicating that that is the best theory, says: "This doctrine is the best; otherwise, the atoms would present some intermediate space (*sāntara*) between them; since these intermediate spaces are empty, what would hinder the atoms from going (one towards the other)? One admits that they are impenetrable (*sapratigha*)." This theory of the Bhadanta can neither be approved nor criticized; one should solely examine how there can be any absence of an intermediate space without there being contact: since this is not explicit, this theory is difficult to understand. If one says that atoms absolutely are without any intermediate space between them, and yet are not mixed one with another, they must have parts: a false opinion. Otherwise, if *nirantara* signifies "without interval" (*anantara*), how is it that the atoms do not touch one another? Consequently, the word *nirantara* signifies "close." The prefix *nis* signifies "certitude." As there is certainly an interval, the atoms are *nirantara*, "possessing intervals:" the same way as *nirdahati*, "he burns." Or rather the prefix *nis* signifies "absence." The atoms are called "without interposition" (*nirantara*), because there is not any *rūpa* of contact (*spṛṣṭa*) of the dimension of a atom between them. When the atoms of the primary elements arise close to one another, without "interposition," they are said, by metaphor, to touch one another. We approve the understanding of the Bhadanta thusly . . .

192. Saṁghabhadra (*TD* 29, p. 372c5) reproduces this paragraph (The Sautrāntika says: 'If you admit . . .), and following: "This is not correct. 'To have parts' and 'to be spatially divided' are two expressions of the same idea. When one says that 'an atom does not have any parts,' one says in fact that it is foreign to all spatial division. How can you be in doubt with respect to this point and still say: 'If you admit spatial division . . . ?' Since the atoms are foreign to this division, how can they touch one another? We have explained that contact can only be total or partial; thus the atom, foreign to any spatial division, cannot enter into contact. How can you thus say 'If you deny spatial division, there will be no difficulty in the atoms touching one another.' Thus the atoms are called *nirantara*, 'not separated,' because there is not any *rūpa* of contact of the dimension of an atom between them."

See ii.22 and the *Introduction*.

193. According to *Vibhāṣā TD* 27, p. 63c12.

194. The first opinion is that of the Sarvāstivādins.

195. *mālāvad avasthita* = *maṇḍalena samapanktyāvasthita*.

196. The text has *kila*. As a general rule, Vasubandhu uses the word *kila* when the opinion in question is a wrong opinion of the Vaibhāṣikas; but here the *Vyākhyā* says: *āgamasūcanārthaḥ kilaśabdaḥ*.

197. According to *Vibhāṣā TD* p. 369c10 and foll.

198. Unconditioned things are eternal because they do not go from one time period to another time period (*advasaṁcārābhāvāta*, v.25). *Asaṁskṛta, nitya, dhruva*, (iv.9) and *dravya* (i.38) are synonyms.

199. According to another reading (*kecit paṭhanti*): *dharmārdham* . . .
See *Dhammasaṅgaṇi*, 661.

200. The *Vyākhyā* quotes the conversation of the Brahmin Jātiśrona with the Blessed One: *indriyāṇīndriyāṇi bho Gautama ucyante /kati bho Gautama indriyāṇi /kiyatā cendriyāṇāṁ saṁgraho bhavati* . . .

201. The order of the *indriyas* is justified ii.6. We have the order of our Sūtra in *Vibhaṅga*, p. 122, *Kathāvatthu*, trans. p. 16, *Visuddhimagga*, xvi; and also in the *Indriyaskandhaka* (*TD* 26, p. 991b24), sixth book of the *Jñānaprasthāna* (Takakusu, "Abhidharma Literature," *JPTS*, 1905, p. 93).

The small treatise of Anuruddha (*Compendium*, p. 175) follows the same order as the *Prakaraṇapāda*.

The *Mahāvyutpatti* (108) places the vital organ at the end.

202. The last three *indriyas* are made up of (1-3) three sense faculties; (4-8) the five moral faculties; and (9) the mental organ (ii.4); 1-8 are *dharmadhātu*.

CHAPTER TWO

The Indriyas

Oṁ. Homage to the Buddha.

We have enumerated the organs or *indriyas* with regard to the *dhātus* (i.48). What is the meaning of the word *indriya*?

The root *idi* signifies *paramaiśvarya* or supreme authority (*Dhātupāṭha*, i.64). Whatever exercises supreme power or authority is called an *indriya*. Thus, in general, *indriya* signifies *adhipati* or ruler.[1]

What is the object of the predominating influence of each *indriya*?

> la. According to the School, five are predominate with regard to things;[2]

i. Each of the five *indriyas* of which the organ of sight is the first—the five organs of sense consciousness—is a predominating influence (1) with regard to the beauty of the person; (2) with regard to the protection of the person; (3) with regard to the production of a consciousness and the mental states associated with this consciousness; and (4) with regard to their special mode of activity (*Vibhāṣā*, *TD* 27, p. 730a29).

The organs of seeing and hearing are predominating influences (1) with regard to beauty, for the body in which they are missing is not beautiful (i.19); (2) with regard to protection, for by seeing and hearing, a person avoids that which would destroy him; (3) with regard to the production of the seeing and hearing consciousnesses, and of the mental states associated with them; and (4) with regard to their special activities, i.e., seeing visible things and hearing sounds.

The organs of smell, taste, and sensation are predominating influences (1) with regard to beauty, as above; (2) with regard to protection, through the consumption of solid foods (*kavaḍīkārāhāra*, iii.39); (3) with regard to the production of their three consciousnesses; and (4) with regard to their special activities, i.e., perceiving smells, tasting tastes, and touching tangibles.

lb. Four predominate with regard to two things;

ii. Four *indriyas*, namely the two sexual organs, the vital organ, and the mental organ are each a predominating influence with regard to two things (*Vibhāṣā, TD* 27, p. 731b12; see also b23, b5).

1. The sexual organs are the predominating influence (1) with regard to the distribution of living beings: it is by reason of these two that living beings form the categories of male and female; and (2) with regard to the differentiation of living beings: by reason of these two organs, there are, among the sexes, differences of physical form, voice, and manner of being.[3]

Some other masters[4] do not admit this explanation. In fact there are sexual differences among the gods of Rūpadhātu who, however, do not possess sexual organs (i.30), and their distribution into sexes results from these differences. Thus, if the sexual organs are the predominating influences from two points of view, they are the predominating influences with regard to defilement and purification: in fact, the three types of eunuchs and bisexual beings are alien (1) to the *dharmas* of defilement, lack of discipline (iv.13b), mortal transgression (iv.103), the cutting off of the roots of good (iv.80); and (2) to the *dharmas* of purification, discipline (iv.13b), acquisition of the fruits (vi.51), and detachment (*vairāgya*, vi.45c) (see ii.19c-d).

2. The vital organ is the predominating influence (1) with regard to the "joining" of the *nikāyasabhāga* (ii.41a), i.e., that which concerns the arising of an existing thing; and (2) with regard to "maintaining" this *nikayāsabhāga*, i.e., that which concerns the prolongation of an existing thing from its arising to its extinction.

3. The mental organ is predominate (1) with regard to rebirth, as the Sūtra explains, "Then there is produced among the Gandharvas, beings in the intermediate existence, one or the other of two minds, a mind of desire or a mind of hatred . . ." (iii.15); (2) with regard to domination: the world and the *dharmas* submit to the mind. As the

stanza says: "The world is lead by the mind, conducted by the mind: (all *dharmas* obey this one *dharma*, the mind.)"[5]

iii. The five *indriyas* of sensation (i.e., the five sensations of pleasure, displeasure, satisfaction, dissatisfaction, and indifference; ii.7,) and the eight *indriyas* of faith, (force, memory, absorption and discernment (ii.24) and the three pure faculties, ii.10)

> lc. Five and eight with regard to defilement and to purification.

are, respectively, predominant with regard to defilement and to purification.

The sensations are predominant with regard to defilement, for the defilements, lust, etc., attach themselves to the sensations, and take shelter therein. Faith and the seven other faculties are predominant with regard to purification, for it is by them that one obtains purity.[6]

According to other masters (*Vibhāṣā, TD* 27, p. 73b6), the sensations are also predominant with regard to purification, so that the Sūtra says: "*sukhitasya cittaṁ samādhīyate,*[7] *duḥkhopaniṣacchraddhā*[8] *ṣaṇ naiṣkramyāśritaḥ saumanasyādhayaḥ*[9] ("There are, by reason of visible things, etc., six sensations of satisfaction, six sensations of dissatisfaction, six sensations of indifference, favorable to *naiṣkramya*.") Such is the explanation of the Vaibhāṣikas.

[The Sautrāntikas[10] criticize this explanation:] (1) the sense organs, the eyes, etc., are not predominant with regard to the protection of the person. Here predominance belongs to the consciousnesses, visual consciousness, hearing consciousness, etc.; and it is after having distinguished that one has avoided anything harmful that one takes solid food. (2) That which you understand as the "proper activity of the organ," namely the seeing of visible things, etc., belongs to the consciousness (i.42) and not to the organ. The explanations relative to the predominance of the other *indriyas* are equally incorrect.

How then should one understand the predominance of the *indriyas*?

> 2a-b. By reason of their predominance (1) with regard to the perception of their special object, (2) with regard to all objects, six organs.

That is, by reason of their predominance through their affinity to the six consciousnesses. The five organs, the first of which is the organ of sight, are predominant through their affinity to the five sense consciousnesses, visual consciousness, etc., each one of which distinguishes its own object, visible things, etc. The mental organ is predominant with regard to the mental consciousness which distinguishes all objects. It is in this way that the six sense organs are predominant.

But, we might say, the sense objects, visibles, etc., are also predominant through their affinity to the consciousness, and as a consequence, should they not also be considered as *indriyas*?

They are not predominant merely by this. "Predominance" means "predominant power." The eye is predominant, for (1) it exercises this predominance with regard to the arising of the consciousness that knows visible things, being the common cause of all consciousnesses of visible things, whereas each visible thing merely aids the arising of but one consciousness; (2) the visual consciousness is clear or obscure, active or well, accordingly as the eye is active or weak: now visible things do not exercise a similar influence. The same holds for the other sense organs and their objects (i.45a-b).

> 2c-d. It is by reason of their predominance in masculinity and femininity that one must distinguish two sexual organs within the body.

There are two separate sexual organs within the *kāyendriya*, or the organ of touch. These two organs are not distinct from the *kāyendriya*: they too cognize tangible things. But there is a part of the *kāyendriya* that receives the name of male organ or female organ because this part exercises predominance over masculinity or femininity.[11] Femininity is the physical form, the voice, the hearing, and the dispositions proper to women. The same for masculinity. Since the differences of these two natures are due to these parts of the body, we know that these two parts are predominant through their two natures. Hence they constitute *indriyas*.

> 3. It is by reason of their predominance with regard to the

> duration of existence, to defilement, to purification, that one considers the vital organ, the sensations, and the five the first of which is faith, as *indriyas*.

1. The vital organ is predominant with regard to the prolongation of existence from birth to death, but not, [as the Vaibhāṣikas say,] with regard to the connection of one existence with another: this connection depends on the mind.

2. The five sensations are predominant with regard to defilement, for the Sūtra[12] says, "Lust finds its shelter in the sensation of pleasure; hatred, in the sensation of displeasure; confusion, in the sensation of indifference."[13] [On this point the Sautrāṇtikas are in agreement with the Vaibhāṣikas.]

3. The five faculties,—faith, force, memory, absorption, and discernment—are predominant with regard to purification, for, through their power, the defilements are disturbed and the Path is brought about.[14]

> 4. By reason of their predominance with regard to ascending acquisitions, with regard to Nirvāṇa, etc., the *anājñātamājñāsyāmīndriya*, the *ajñendriya*, and the *ājñātāvīndriya*, are likewise.[15]

"Likewise," that is, these three are, likewise, considered as predominating influences or *indriyas*. These are the three pure *indriyas*, which will be defined ii.10a-b.

1. The first is predominant through the acquisition of the second.

The second is predominant through the acquisition of the third.

The third is predominant through the acquisition of Nirvāṇa, or *nirupadhiśeṣanirvāṇa*. For there is no Parinirvāṇa when the mind is not delivered.[16]

2. The word "et cetera" indicates that there is another explanation:

The first is predominant with regard to the extinctions of the defilements which are abandoned through Seeing the Truths (v.4).

The second, with regard to the extinction of the defilements which are abandoned through Meditation on the Truths (v.5a).

The third, with regard to blessedness-in-this-life, that is, the experience of the satisfaction (*prīti* = *saumanasya*) and the well-being (*sukha* = *praśrabdhisukha*, viii.9b) that comes from deliverance from the defilements. (See below note 22).

***

Why are there only twenty-two *indriyas*? If you regard a "predominating influence" as an *indriya*, ignorance and the other parts of *pratītyasamutpāda* (iii.21) would be *indriyas*, for these causes (*avidyā*, etc.) are predominant with regard to their effects (the *saṁskāras*, etc.). In the same way, the voice, hands, feet, the anus, and the penis are predominant with regard to words, grasping, walking (*viharaṇa*= *caṅkramaṇa*), excretion, and pleasure.[17]

We would answer that there is no reason to add ignorance, etc., to the list proclaimed by the Blessed One.

In enumerating the *indriyas*, the Blessed One took into account the following characteristics:

> 5. The support of the mind; that which subdivides, prolongs, and defiles this support; that which prepares the purification and which does purify it: these are all the *indriyas*.[18]

1. The support of the mind consists of the six organs of consciousness, from the organ of sight to the mental organ. These are the six internal *āyatanas* (i.39, iii.22) which are the primary constituents of a living being.[19]

2. This sixfold support is differenciated by reason of the sexual organs.

3. It lasts for a time by reason of the vital organ.

4. It is defiled by reason of the five sensations.

5. Its purification is prepared by the five moral faculties, faith, etc.

6. It is purified by the three pure faculties.

The *dharmas* that possess the characteristic of being predominant with regard to the constitution, the subdivision, etc. of a living being are considered to be *indriyas*. This characteristic is missing in other *dharmas*, in voice, etc.

(Some other masters give a different definition:)

> 6. Or rather there are fourteen *indriyas*, support of transmigration, origin, duration, enjoyment of this support; the other *indriyas* have the same function with regard to Nirvāṇa.

The expression "or rather" introduces the explanation of other masters.

(1-6) The six organs (*ṣaḍāyatana*, iii.22), from the organ of sight to the mental organ, are the support, the *raison d'etre* of *saṁsāra.*[20]

(7-8) It is through the sexual organs that the *ṣaḍāyatanas* arise.[21]

(9) It is through the vital organ that the *ṣaḍāyatanas* last.

(10-14) It is through the five sensations that the *ṣaḍāyatanas* enjoy.

On the other hand:

(15-19) The five faculties,—faith, force, memory, absorption, discernment,—are the support of Nirvāṇa.

(20) Nirvāṇa is generated, appears for the first time, through the first pure faculty, *anājñātamājñāsyāmīndriya.*

(21) Nirvāṇa lasts, is developed, through the second pure faculty, *ājñendriya.*

(22) Nirvāṇa is "experienced" by the third pure faculty, *ājñātāvīndriya*, for, through this faculty, one experiences the satisfaction and well-being of deliverance (see above ii.4).

This determines the number of *indriyas*, as well as the order in which the Sūtra places them.

***

The voice, hands, feet, the anus, and the sexual parts are not *indriyas.*

1. The voice is not predominant with respect to words, for words suppose a certain instruction;[22] 2-3. Hands and feet are not predominant with regard to grasping and walking, for grasping and walking are simply the hands and feet arising a second moment in another place and with a new figure (iv.2b-d). On the other hand, we

see that hands and feet are not indispensable for grasping and walking, for example with snakes.[23] 4. The anus is not predominant with regard to the expulsion of matter, for heavy things always fall in a void; further, wind pushes this matter and makes it go out; 5. The sexual parts are not predominant with regard to pleasure for pleasure is produced by the sexual organs.[24]

If you consider the hands, the feet, etc., as *indriyas*, you must then place the throat, the teeth, the eyelids, and the joints, whose function it is to swallow, to chew, to open and close, to fold up and to extend the bones, among the *indriyas*. In this way, everything that is a cause, which exercises its action (*puruṣakāra*, ii.58) with regard to its effects, would be an *indriya*. But we must reserve the name of *indriya* to whatever possesses predominance.

***

We have defined the organs of consciousness and the sexual organs (i.9-44); the vital organ will be explained with the *cittaviprayuktas* (ii.35) among which it is placed; the five faculties,—faith, force, etc.,—being mental states, will be explained with the mental states (ii.24).

We shall examine here the organs of sensation and the pure faculties which are not found anywhere else.

7a-b. Disagreeable bodily sensation is the *indriya* of pain.[25]

("Bodily" is "that which relates to the body,"[26] that which is associated with the five sense consciousnesses, visual consciousness, etc.)"Disagreeable" is that which does harm. Sensation in relation to the five organs of sense consciousness, and which does harm, is called *duḥkhendriya*.

7b-c. Agreeable is the *indriya* of pleasure.

"Agreeable" is that which does good, which comforts, is beneficent. Agreeable bodily sensation is termed *sukhendriya*.

7c-d. In the Third Dhyāna, agreeable mental sensation is also an *indriya* of pleasure.

(Mental sensation is the sensation associated with mental consciousness.) Agreeable mental sensation of the Third Dhyāna is also called *sukhendriya*, an *indriya* of pleasure. This name, moreover, is reserved for agreeable bodily sensation; but in the Third Dhyāna, bodily sensation is absent because the five sense consciousnesses are not there. Then, when one speaks of the *sukha* or pleasure of the Third Dhyāna, one means agreeable mental sensation (see vii.9).

8a. Moreover, it is satisfaction.

"Moreover," that is, in the stages below the Third Dhyāna, in Kāmadhātu and in the first two Dhyānas, agreeable mental sensation is satisfaction or the *indriya* of satisfaction.

[Agreeable mental sensation is absent above the Third Dhyāna.]

In the Third Dhyāna, agreeable mental sensation is calm and tranquil, because the ascetic, in this Dhyāna, is detached from joy: hence it is pleasure and not satisfaction.[27]

[Below the Third Dhyāna, agreeable mental sensation is gross and agitated, because, in the stages below the Third Dhyāna, the ascetic is not detached from joy: hence it is "satisfaction."] Joy, [which has a joyous exaltation for its characteristic,] is not distinct from satisfaction.

8b-c. Disagreeable mental sensation is dissatisfaction.

(Sensation associated with mental consciousness and which harms is dissatisfaction or the *indriya* of dissatisfaction.)

8c. Intermediate bodily or mental sensation is equanimity.

Intermediate sensation, which neither comforts nor harms, is the sensation "neither-pain-nor-pleasure." This is what is termed the sensation or *indriya* of equanimity.

Is this sensation bodily or mental?

8d. It is both.

(Either bodily or mental, intermediate sensation is a sensation of equanimity.) The sensation of equanimity presents then a double characteristic; consequently it constitutes only one *indriya*, because there is no *vikalpana* here.

> 8e. For it has no *vikalpana*.

1. There is no *vikalpana*, or intellectual operation. Either bodily or mental, the sensation of equanimity is equally free from any intellectual element (*vikalpa=abhinirūpaṇāvikalpa*, i.33). As a general rule,[28] agreeable or disagreeable mental sensation proceeds from a concept, from the concept of "dear" or "hateful," etc. Contrarily, bodily sensation is produced from an external object independent of psychological states: Arhats do not have sympathies and antipathies, they do not conceive of the idea of dear or the idea of hateful, and yet they are subject nevertheless to physical pain and pleasure. Then we should distinguish *indriyas* relative to agreeable and disagreeable sensations accordingly as these sensation are bodily or mental.

But the sensation of equanimity is produced spontaneously,[29] exactly like a physical sensation; it is produced in a person who does not form any concept: hence we recognize that there is but one *indriya* for the two sensations of bodily and mental indifference.

2. There is no *vikalpana* or difference. Accordingly as the agreeable or disagreeable sensations are bodily or mental, they do good or harm according to a mode of operation that is special to them, and they are not felt in the same way. The sensation of equanimity creates neither good or harm; it is not differenciated; mental or physical, it is felt in the same way.

> 9a-b. Nine *indriyas*, in the Paths of Seeing, of Meditation and of the Aśaikṣa, constitute three *indriyas*.

The mental organ, the sensation of pleasure, the sensation of satisfaction, the sensation of equanimity, and faith, force, memory, absorption and discernment constitute the *anājñātamājñāsyāmīndriya* for the saint who is on the Path of Seeing; *ājñendriya* for the saint who is on the Path of Meditation on the Truths; and *ājñātāvīndriya* for the saint who is on the path of the Aśaikṣa (i.e., the Arhat).[30]

On the Path of Seeing,[31] the saint is engaged in knowing that which he does not know (*anājñātam ājñātuṁ pravṛtta*), namely the Four Truths: he thinks "I will know." His *indriya* is then called the *anājñātamājñāsyāmīndriya.*[32]

On the Path of Meditation on the Truths,[33] the saint does not have anything new to know, he is a wise one or *ājña*. But in order to cut off the defilements which remain in him, he newly knows and often repeats the Truths that he already knows. His *indriya* is called the *ājñendriya*, the *indriya* of the wise one, or the wise *indriya*.

On the Path of the Aśaikṣa, the ascetic becomes conscious that he knows: he obtains the knowledge (*āva=avagama*)[34] that the Truths are known (*ājñātam iti*). Possessing *ājñāta-ava*, he is an *ājñātāvin*, and his *indriya* is called the *ājñātāvīndriya*.

Or rather, the saint who is an *ājñātāvin* is one who has for his characteristics or habit knowing that the Truth is known: in fact, when the saint has obtained *kṣayajñāna* and *anutpādajñāna* (vi.70), he knows in truth, "Pain is known; I have nothing more to know" and the rest.[35]

***

We have explained the specific characteristics of the *indriyas*. We must explain their different natures: are they pure (9b-d), from retribution (10-llb), good (llc-d)? To what sphere do they belong (12)? How are they abandoned (13)?

***

How many are impure? How many are pure?

> 9b. Three are clean;

i. The last three *indriyas* are exclusively clean or pure. Stain (*mala*) and vice (*āsrava*) are synonyms.[36]

> 9c. The material organs, the vital organ and the two painful sensations are impure;

The material organs are seven in number: the five organs, of seeing, etc., plus the two sexual organs, for all these seven organs are included in *rūpaskandha.* Together with the vital organ, the sensation of pain, and the sensation of dissatisfaction, ten *indriyas* in all are exclusively impure.

9d. Nine are of two types.

The mental organ, the sensation of pleasure, the sensation of satisfaction, the sensation of equanimity, and the five moral faculties (faith, force, etc.) are nine *indriyas* that can be either pure or impure.

ii. According to other masters[37] (*Vibhāṣā, TD* 27, p. 7c3), the five moral faculties are solely pure, for the Blessed One said: "Whosoever is completely lacking, to whatever degree, any of these five *indriyas*, faith, etc., I declare him to be a person outside, one who belongs to the class of Pṛthagjanas."[38] Hence anyone who possesses them, to whatever degree, is an Āryan; hence they are pure.

This text is not proof, for the Blessed One is speaking here of a person in whom the five pure moral faculties are absent. In fact, in the passage that precedes the quotation in question, the Blessed One defines the Āryapudgalas with reference to the five moral faculties.[39] Hence he is referring to only the five moral faculties belonging to the Āryans, that is, pure. Whosoever is lacking them is evidently a Pṛthagjana.

Or rather, if this passage speaks of moral faculties in general, we would remark that there are two types of Pṛthagjana (*Vibhāṣā, TD* 27, p. 8b3): those outside, and those inside; the first have cut off the roots of good (iv.79), whereas the second have not cut them off. It is with reference to the first that the Blessed One said: "I declare him to be a person outside, one who belongs to the class of Pṛthagjanas."[40]

On the other hand, according to the Sūtra, even before setting into motion the Wheel of the Dharma (vi.54), there were in the world persons of sharp, medium, and weak faculties.[41] Hence the moral faculties of faith, etc., are not necessarily and exclusively pure.

Finally, the Blessed One said: "If I do not know truly the origin, the disappearance, the advantages, the disadvantages, the escape of the five faculties of faith, force, etc., I shall not be liberated, gone out, disassociated, delivered from the world of gods, Māras, and Brahmās, of a world wherein there are Brahmins and monks; I shall not reside with a mind free from error . . ."[42] Now a similar description does not apply to pure *dharmas*, which are free from advantages, from disadvantages, and from escape.

Hence the moral faculties of faith, force, etc., can be either pure or impure.

***

Among the *indriyas*, how many are retribution (*vipāka*, ii.57c-d), and how many are not retribution?[43]

10a. The vital organ is always retribution.[44]

(Only the vital organ (ii.45a-b) is always retribution.)

i. [Objection.] The vital energies (*ayuḥsaṁskāras*, see below) that a Bhikṣu Arhat stabilizes or increases, are evidently the vital organ. Of what action is the vital organ thus stabilized or prolonged the retribution?

The *Mūlaśāstra* (the *Jñānaprasthāna*, *TD* 26, p. 981a12) says: "How does a Bhikṣu stabilize the vital energies? An Arhat in possession of supernormal power (*ṛddhimān-prāptābhijñāḥ*, vii.42), in possession of the mastery of mind, i.e., one who is *asamayavimukta* (vi.56, 64), gives, either to the Saṅgha or to a person, things useful to life, clothing, pots, etc.: after having given these things, he applies this thought to his life;[45] he then enters into the Fourth or *prāntakoṭika* Dhyāna (vii.41); coming out of the absorption, he produces the thought and pronounces the words: 'May this action which should produce a retribution-in-joy be transformed and produce a retribution-in-life!' Then the action (the gift and the absorption) which should produce a retribution-in-joy produces a retribution-in-life."

According to other masters, the prolonged life of an Arhat is the result of the retribution of a previous action. According to them, there is a remnant of the result of retribution-in-life which should have ripened in a previous life, but which was interrupted by death before its time (ii.45). And it is the force of the absorption of the Fourth Dhyāna that attracts this remnant and makes this remnant ripen now.

[The *Mūlaśāstra* continues] "How does a Bhikṣu cast off the vital energies? An Arhat in possession of supernormal powers . . . enters into the Fourth Dhyāna . . . ; coming out of this absorption, he produces the thought and pronounces these words: 'May the action that should produce a retribution-in-life be transformed and produce a retribution-in-joy!' Then the action that should produce a retribution-in-life produces a retribution-in-joy."

The Bhadanta Ghoṣaka said: By the force of the *prāntakoṭika* Dhyāna that this Arhat produced, the primary elements of Rūpadhātu are attracted and introduced into his body. These primary elements are favorable to, or contrary to, the vital energies. It is in this manner that the Arhat prologues or casts off his life.

Along with the Sautrāntikas, we say that the Arhats, through their mastery in absorption, cause the projection of the constitutive primary elements of the organs for a certain period of duration, a projection due to previous actions, to cease; inversely, they produce a new projection, born of absorption. Thus the vital organ, in the case of the prolonged life of an Arhat, is not retribution. But in other cases, it is retribution.

ii. One question gives rise to another.

1. Why does the Arhat prologue his vital energies? For two reasons: with a view to the good of others, and with a view to the longer duration of the Dharma.[46] He sees that his life is going to end; he sees that others are incapable of assuring these two ends.

2. Why does the Arhat cast off his vital energies?

For two reasons: he sees that his dwelling in this world has only a small utility for the good of others, and so sees himself tormented by sickness, etc.[47] As the stanza says:

> "If the religious life has been well practiced, and the Way well cultivated, at the end of his life, he is happy, as at the disappearance of sickness."

3. Who, and in what place, extends or casts off his life?

In the three Dvīpas (iii.53), male or female, a *asamayavimukta* Arhat who possesses *prāntakoṭika* Dhyāna (vi.56, 64): in fact, he possesses the mastery of absorption and he is free from the defilements.[48]

4. According to the Sūtra, the Blessed One, after having extended the *jīvita saṁskāras*, casts off the *saṁskāras* of *āyus*[49]

One asks 1.) what difference is there between the *saṁskāras* of *jīvita* and of *āyus*; and 2.) what is the meaning of the plural "the *saṁskāras*?"[50]

On the first point:[51]

a. According to certain masters, there is no difference. In fact, the *Mūlaśāstra* (the *Jñānaprasthāna, TD* 26,p. 993b2; see the *Prakaraṇapāda TD* 26, p. 694a23; see also the *Vibhāṣā, TD* 27, p. 732b27) says: "What is the vital organ? It is the *āyus* in the Three Dhātus."

b. According to others[52] the expression *āyuḥ-saṁskāras* designates life which is the result of actions in a previous life; the expression *jīvita-saṁskāras* designates life which is the result of actions in this life (gifts to the Saṅgha, etc.).

c. According to other masters,[53] the *āyuḥ-saṁskāras* are that by which existence lasts; the *jīvita-saṁskāras* are that by which life is prolonged for a little while.

On the second point:

a. The Sūtra uses the plural because the Saint extends or casts off many *saṁskāras*. There is no advantage, in fact, in extending a moment, or in casting off a moment: it is only by means of a series of moments that the Saint can procure the good of others; on the other hand, a moment cannot be a cause of suffering.

b. According to another opinion, the plural condemns the teaching according to which the *jīvita* or the *āyus* is an entity susceptible of duration.[54]

c. According to another opinion,[55] the plural condemns the teaching of the Sarvāstivādins that see an entity or *dharma* in the *jīvita* and *āyus*. The terms *jīvita* and *āyus* designate a number of *saṁskāras* existing simultaneously and belonging either to four or five *skandhas* according to their sphere of existence. If it were otherwise, the Sūtra would not use the expression "the *jīvita-skandhas*;" it would say "The Blessed One extends some *jīvitas*, and casts off some *āyus*."

5. Why does the Blessed One cast off [death] and extend [life]?

With the aim of showing that he possesses mastery over death, he casts off death; with the aim of showing that he possesses mastery over life, he extends it. He extends it for a period of three months, no more, no less; after three months, there is nothing more to do for his followers, after his task is well achieved, for, short of three months, he would leave his task unachieved.[56]

Or rather,[57] with the aim of realizing this vow: "Any Bhikṣu who has well cultivated the four supernormal powers (*ṛddhipāda*, vi.69b), can live, if he so desires, a *kalpa* or more."[58]

The Vaibhāṣikas[59] say: "The Blessed One casts off or extends with the aim of showing that he triumphs over the Māra who is the *skandhas*, and over the Māra who is death. In the first watch of the night, under the Bodhi Tree, he has already triumphed over the Māra who is a demon, and, in the third watch, over the Māra who is the defilements (*Ekottarikā, TD* 2, p. 760b17 and following)."[60]

10a-b. Twelve are of two types.

Which twelve?

10b-c. With the exception of the last eight and dissatisfaction.

With the exception of the vital organ, which is always retribution, and of the nine that will be mentioned below (10b-c) which are never retribution, the remaining twelve are of two types, sometimes retribution, and sometimes non-retribution. This refers to the seven material organs, to the mental organ and to the four sensations, the sensation of dissatisfaction being excluded.

1. The seven material organs (organ of seeing, . . . male organ) are not retribution to the extent that they arise from accumulation (*aupacayika*, i.37). In other cases, they are retribution.

2. The mental organ and the four organs of sensation are not retribution 1.) when they are good or soiled, for whatever is retribution is morally neutral (*avyākṛta*,ii.57); 2.) when, still being neutral, they

are, according to their type,[61] either *airyāpathika, śailpasthānika*, or *nairmāṇika* (ii.72). In other cases, they are retribution.

3. The last eight, faith, etc., the *anājñātamājñasyāmīndriya*, etc., are good and consequently are not retribution.

4. But, we would say, how can one affirm that dissatisfaction is never retribution? In fact, the Sūtra says, "There is an action liable to result in satisfaction, there is an action liable to result in dissatisfaction, and there is an action liable to result in a sensation of equanimity."[62]

[According to the Vaibhāṣikas,] the expression *daurmanasya-vedanīya* should be understood not as "an action that should be experienced, resulting in a sensation of dissatisfaction," but rather as "an action with which a sensation of dissatisfaction is associated." In fact, the Sūtra says that contact is *sukha-vedanīya*: now pleasure (*sukha*) is not the retribution of contact.[63] From all evidence, *sukha-vendanīya* contact is contact with which a sensation of pleasure is associated. Hence *daurmanasya-vedanīya* action is action with which a sensation of dissatisfaction is associated.

[We would answer:] You should explain the expressions *saumanasya-vedanīya* and *upekṣa-vedanīya* as you explain the expression *daurmanasya-vendanīya*, since the three expressions figure in the same context in the Sūtra. It follows that a *saurmanasya-vedanīya* action is an action "with which the sensation of satisfaction is associated," not an action "liable to retribution in satisfaction;" and it follows that as a consequence, the sensation of satisfaction is not retribution.

[The Vaibhāṣikas:] We see no problem in explaining the expression *saurmanasya-vedaniya* either as "liable to retribution in satisfaction" or as "that with which satisfaction is associated." But the second explanation of *vedanīya* is only valid for the expression *daurmanasya-vedanīya*. It refers to an action with which dissatisfaction is associated.

[We answer:] One could admit your interpretation of the Sūtra if there were no other issue, that is, if it had been rationally established that dissatisfaction is not retribution.

[The Vaibhāṣikas:] Dissatisfaction is produced by the imagination, when one thinks of something that he fears; he is assuaged in the same way: when he thinks of something that he desires. Now such is not the case with retribution.

[But, we would say,] this is the case for satisfaction which will consequently not be retribution.

[The Vaibhāṣikas:] If, as you maintain, dissatisfaction is retribution, when a person has committed a serious transgression and then experiences, with regard to it, dissatisfaction and remorse (*kaukṛtya*, ii.29d), one could say that the transgression has already brought forth a ripened result—which is inadmissible (ii.56a).

But you admit that satisfaction is retribution, and we would reason as you have just done: when a person has accomplished a meritorious action and thereby experiences satisfaction, then this action immediately brings forth a result of retribution.

[The Vaibhāṣikas:] Persons detached from desire do not possess the *indriya* of dissatisfaction;[64] now, they possess the *indriyas* which are retribution, the organ of seeing, etc.; hence the *indriya* of dissatisfaction is not retribution.

[But, we would say,] how could such detached persons possess a satisfaction which would be retribution by it nature? Without doubt, they possess a satisfaction that arises from absorption, but this satisfaction is good, and it is then not retribution. They do not possess any other.[65]

The fact is that persons so detached possess the *indriya* of satisfaction, which can be the nature of this *indriya*, whether it be retribution or not, whereas dissatisfaction is never produced among them. Hence, the Vaibhāṣikas conclude, the *indriya* of dissatisfaction is not retribution.

5. Eight *indriyas*,—the five organs of sense consciousness, the vital organ, and the sexual organs,—are, in a good rebirth, the retribution of good action; in a bad rebirth, they are the retribution of bad action.

The mental organ, in a good rebirth or in a bad rebirth, is retribution for good action or for bad action.

The sensations of pleasure, of satisfaction, and of equanimity are retribution for good actions.

The sensation of dislike is the retribution for a bad action.[66]

The material organs, in a good rebirth, are, we say, retribution for good actions. To an androgyne, in a good rebirth, both organs are the retribution for good action, but the quality of being an androgyne is obtained through bad action.[67]

***

Among the twenty-two *indriyas*, how many "have retribution?" How many are "without retribution?"

10a. Only one (i.e., dissatisfaction) has retribution;[68]

1. Dissatisfaction always has retribution, for, on the one hand, it is never neutral, being the result of a concept (*vikalpaviśeṣa*: the idea of a thing liked, or of a thing hated, etc., ii.8c); but, on the other hand, it is never pure, never being produced in a state of absorption.

10b. Ten (namely, the mental organ, the four sensations—with the exception of dissatisfaction—, and faith and its following) are twofold (i.e., admit of retribution, as well as being without retribution).

2. The first eight *indriyas* (organ of sight, etc.; vital organ, sexual organs) never have retribution, because they are neutral; the last three (*anājñatamājñasyāmīndriya*, etc.) never have retribution, because they are pure (*anāsrava*, iv.80).

11a-b. The mental organ (the four sensations, with the exception of dissatisfaction), and faith and its following;

3. As for the ten remaining *indriyas*:

The mental organ, the sensations of pleasure, satisfaction, and indifference, have retribution when they are bad or good-impure; they are without retribution when they are neutral or pure.

***

Among the twenty-two *indriyas*, how many are good, how many are bad, and how many are neutral?

> 11c. Eight are good;[69]

Eight, faith, etc., the *anājñātamājñasyāmīndriya*, etc., are only good. good.

> 11d. Dissatisfaction is of two types;

Dissatisfaction is good or bad (ii.28).

> 11e. The mental organ, and the sensations,—with the exception of dissatisfaction,—are of three types.

The mental organ and the four sensations are good, bad, or neutral.

> 11f. The others, of one type.

The organ of sight, etc., the vital organ, and the sexual organs are neutral.

***

Among the twenty-two *indriyas*, how many belong to each of the three spheres of existence?

> 12. The pure *indriyas* are absent from Kāmadhātu;

1. All of the *indriyas* are in the sphere of Kāmadhātu, with the exception of the last three, the immaculate or pure *indriyas*: these are not connected with the spheres of existence, rather, they transcend the spheres of existence. Thus nineteen *indriyas*, excluding the last three, are in the sphere of Kāmadhātu.

> 12b-c. The sexual organs and the two disagreeable sensations are absent from Rūpadhātu.

2. Excluding furthermore the two sexual organs and the two disagreeable sensations, the sensation of suffering and dissatisfaction, there are fifteen *indriyas* remaining in Rūpadhātu that are common to the first two spheres of existence (viii.12a-b).

(a) The sexual organs are absent from Rūpadhātu 1.) because the beings who are born in this sphere have abandoned the desire for sexual union, and 2.) because these organs are ugly (i.30b-d).

Nevertheless the Sūtra says: "That a female being is Brahmā—such does not happen, that is impossible. That a male being is Brahmā—such happens, that is possible."[70] It appears that this Sūtra would pose difficulties.

No. Beings of Rūpadhātu are males without possessing the male organ. They possess the other aspects of masculinity that one sees among the males of Kāmadhātu, namely bodily form, sound of the voice, etc. (ii.2c-d).

(b). The sensation of suffering (*duḥkha*, physical suffering) is absent from Rūpadhātu (1) because of the "fluidity" or transparency of the body, from whence there is absence of pain produced by hurt; and (2) because of the absence of bad actions liable to retribution, from whence the absence of suffering "arisen from retribution."

(c). The sensation of dissatisfaction is absent (1) because beings in Rūpadhātu are penetrated by calm; and (2) because all causes of irritation are absent.[71]

> 12d. And all the material organs and the two agreeable sensations are absent from Ārūpyadhātu.

3. Excluding furthermore the material organs (eyes, etc, vii.3c), and the sensations of pleasure and satisfaction, there remains in Ārūpyadhātu the mental organ, the vital organ, the sensation of equanimity, and faith and its following (i.31).

***

Among the twenty-two *indriyas*, how many are abandoned through Seeing the Truths? How many through Meditation? How many are not abandoned?

> 13a. The mental organ and three sensations belong to three categories;[72]

1. The mental organ, the sensations of pleasure, satisfaction and equanimity, are of three types.

> 13b. Dissatisfaction is abandoned (through Seeing and Meditation);

2. Dissatisfaction is abandoned through Seeing and through Meditation, for, never being pure, it is always an object of abandoning.

> 13c. Nine are abandoned through Meditation alone;

3. Nine *indriyas*, namely the five sense organs and the two sexual organs, the vital organ, and the sensation of dissatisfaction, are only of the class "abandoned through Mediation," for (1) the first eight are not soiled; (2) the ninth does not arise from the mind (*aṣaṣṭhaja*, 1.40); and (3) all are always impure.

> 13d. Five are either abandoned through Meditation or are not abandoned;

4. The five *indriyas*, the first of which is faith, (1) are not soiled, and hence are not abandoned through Seeing; (2) being able to be pure, they are able to be "not the object of abandoning."

> 13e. Three are not abandoned.

5. The last three (*anājñātamājñāsyāmīndriya* etc.) are not abandoned, (1) because they are pure, and (2) *dharmas* without defects are not to be rejected.

***

How many *indriyas*, having retribution for their nature, do beings in the different spheres of existence possess from their origins?

> 14a. In the Kāmas, beings possess from their origins two *indriyas* that are from retribution,[73]

The organ of touch and the vital organ.

> 14b. With the exception of apparitional beings.

1. In Kāmadhātu, beings that are born from a womb, from eggs, and from perspiration (iii.8) possess from their origin, i.e., from their conception, two *indriyas* which are from retribution, namely the organ of touch and the vital organ. It is only gradually that the other *indriyas* appear among them.

Why is not the mental organ and the sensation of equanimity counted herein?

Because, at conception, both of these are always soiled; hence they are not from retribution, they are not retribution (iii.38).

How many do apparitional beings possess?

14c. Some possess six;

2. (Apparitional beings, iii.9, possess six, seven or eight *indriyas*.) Beings without sex, namely beings at the beginning of the cosmic age (iii.98), possess six: the five organs of sense consciousness, plus the vital organ.

14d. Or seven.

Beings with sex possess seven *indriyas*, like the gods.

14e. Or eight

Bisexual beings possess eight *indriyas*. But can apparitional beings be bisexual? Yes, in bad rebirths.

14f. In Rūpadhātu, six;

Kāmadhātu is called "the Kāmas," because of the primary role that belongs, in this sphere, to the *kāmaguṇas* or objects of desire (i.22b-d). Rūpadhātu is called "the Rūpas," because of the primary role of the *rūpas*.[74] The Sūtra employs this manner of speaking: "These calm deliverances, beyond the *rūpas* . . ."[75]

3. In Rūpadhātu, beings, from their origins, possess six *indriyas* which are from retribution, like apparitional beings without sex in Kāmadhātu.

14d. Above, one.

4. "Above" means in Ārūpyadhātu. This sphere of existence is not situated above Rūpadhātu (iii.3); but it is said to be above it because it is superior to Rūpadhātu from the point of view of absorption: the absorptions of Ārūpyadhātu are cultivated after those of Rūpadhātu; and because it outweights it from the point of view of its mode of existence, from the point of view of the duration of its existence.

In this sphere of existence, beings initially possess one *indriya* which is of retribution, the vital organ.

***

We have explained how many *indriyas*, of the nature of retribution, are obtained at conception. Now how many *indriyas* perish at death?

> 15a. In Ārūpyadhātu, dying destroys the vital organ, the mental organ, and the sensation of indifference; in Rūpadhātu, it destroys eight *indriyas*;

In Rūpadhātu one must add the five organs of sense consciousness, the organ of sight, etc. In fact, apparitional beings are born and die with all their organs.

> 15b.In Kāmadhātu, ten, nine, eight;

In Kāmadhātu, death takes place either at one stroke or gradually. In the first case, eight, nine or ten *indriyas* die, accordingly as the being is without sex, with sex, or bisexual.

> 16a. Or four when death is gradual.

In the second case four *indriyas* die lastly and together; the organ of touch, the vital organ, the mental organ and the organ of indifference. These four *indriyas* die at the same time.

The preceding concerns the case where the mind of the dying person is soiled or not-soiled-neutral.

> 16b. In the case of a good death, add all five *indriyas*.[76]

If ones mind is good, one should, in the three spheres of existence, add the five moral faculties, faith, etc.[77]

A being in Arupadhatu, at death, abandons at the last moment the three *indriyas* named in the Karika.

***

In the Teaching of the *Indriyas*[78] all of the characteristics of the *indriyas* are examined, both their natures and their operations. We ask then how many *indriyas* come into play in the acquisition of the results of the religious life (*śrāmaṇyaphala*, vi.52).

16c. One obtains the two highest results through nine *indriyas*;

The highest results are the results of Srotaāpanna and Arhat, for these two results are the first and last. The intermediary fruits are found between the the first and the last.

1. The result of Srotaāpanna (vi.35c) is obtained through nine *indriyas*: the mental organ, equanimity,[79] and the five moral faculties, faith, etc.; *anājñātamājñāsyāmīndriya* and *ājñendriya* (ii.10a-b).[80]

Anājñātamājñāsyāmīndriya constitutes *ānantaryamārga* (vi.30c), and *ājña* constitutes *vimuktimārga*:[81] it is through these two *indriyas* that one obtains the result of Srotaāpanna, for the first encourages the possession of disjunction from the defilements (*visaṁyoga*, ii.55d 1, vi.52); the second supports and makes firm this possession.[82]

2. The result of Arhat (vi.45) is obtained through nine *indriyas*: the mental organ, either satisfaction, pleasure or indifference, the five moral faculties, *ājñendriya* and *ājñātavīndriya*.

Here *ājñendriya* constitutes *ānantaryamārga*, and *ājñātavīndriya* constitutes *vimuktimārga*.[83]

16d. The two intermediary results through seven, eight or nine.

3. The result of Sakṛdāgāmin (vi.36) is obtained either by an *ānupūrvaka* (vi.33a)—an ascetic who, before pursuing the acquisition of the result of Sakṛdāgāmin, has obtained the result of Srotaāpanna; or by a *bhūyovītarāga* (vi.29c-d)—an ascetic who, before entering into the pure path, i.e., into the comprehension of the Truths, has freed

himself through the impure, worldly path, from the first six categories of defilements of Kāmadhātu: consequently, when he has achieved the Path of Seeing the Truths, he becomes a Sakṛdāgāmin without having been a Srotaāpanna first.[84]

The *ānupūrvaka*—a Srotaāpanna—obtains the result of Sakṛdāgāmin either through a worldly path, which does not admit of Meditation on the Truths, or through the Pure Path. In the first case, he possesses seven *indriyas*: the mental organ, indifference, and the five moral faculties; in the second case, eight *indriyas*: the same plus *ājñendriya*.

The *bhūyovītarāga*—who is a Pṛthagjana—obtains the result of Sakṛdāgāmin by means of nine *indriyas*. He realizes the comprehension of the Truths; he then realizes *anājñātamājñāsyāmīndriya* and *ājñendriya*, as in the acquisition of the result of Srotaāpanna.

4. The result of Anāgāmin is obtained either by an *ānupūrvaka*—the ascetic who has already obtained the previous results,—or by a *vītarāga*—the ascetic who, without having entered into the Pure Path, has freed himself from the nine categories of defilements of Kāmadhātu, or from the defilements of the higher stages, up to and including Ākiṁcanyāyatana.

The *ānupūrvaka* obtains the result of Anāgāmin through seven or eight *indriyas*, according to whether he uses the worldly path or the Pure Path, as the above *ānupūrvaka* obtains the result of Sakṛdāgāmin.

The *vītarāga* obtains the result of Anāgāmin through the comprehension of the truths, through nine *indriyas*, as the above *bhūyovītarāga* obtains the result of Sakṛdāgāmin.

These general definitions call for more precision.

1. The *vītarāga* obtains the result of Anāgāmin by "understanding the Truths." In order to understand the Truths, he places himself either in an absorption of the Third Dhyāna, an absorption of either the First or the Second Dhyāna, an absorption of *anāgamya* or *dhyānāntara*, or of the Fourth Dhyāna: according to the case, his *indriya* of sensation is the *indriya* of pleasure, satisfaction, or equanimity.

Contrarily, the *bhūyovītarāga* always obtains the result of Sakṛdāgāmin with the *indriya* of indifference.

2. The *ānupūrvaka* who seeks for the result of Anāgāmin within the absorption of *anāgamya*, can, when his moral faculties are strong, depart at the last moment (the ninth *vimuktimārga*) of the *anāgamya* and enter into the First or Second Dhyana.

When he expels the defilements through the worldly path, it is then through eight, and not seven *indriyas*, that he obtains the result: in fact, the *anāgamya* to which the next to last moment (ninth *ānantaryamārga*) belongs, admits of the sensation of equanimity, and the First or Second Dhyana, within which the last moment takes place, admits of the sensation of satisfaction. Disjunction from the defilements results then from equanimity and from satisfaction; in this same way we have seen that disjunction, in the case of the Srotaāpanna, results from *ājñāsyāmīndriya* and *ājñendriya.*

When he expels the defilements through the pure path, that is, through Meditation on the Truths, one must add the *ājñendriya* as a ninth *indriya. Ānantaryamārga* and *vimuktimārga* are both two *ājñendriyas.*[85]

***

We read in the Mūlaśāstra (*Jñānaprasthāna, TD* 26, p. 994cl): "Through how many *indriyas* is the quality of Arhat obtained? By eleven."

In fact, the quality of Arhat is obtained, as we have said, through nine *indriyas*. The Śāstra answers, "By eleven," for it does not speak with reference to the acquisition of the quality of Arhat, but with respect to the person who acquires this quality.

> 17a-b. It is said that the quality of Arhat is obtained through eleven *indriyas*, because a determined person can so obtain them.

A saint can fall many times from the quality of Arhat (vi.58) and reobtain it by means of diverse absorptions, sometimes with the *indriyas* of pleasure (Third Dhyāna), sometimes with that of satisfaction (First and Second Dhyāna), or sometimes with that of equanimity (*anāgamya*, etc.). But the three *indriyas* never coexist.

But, one would say, why does the Sūtra not speak from this same point of view when it speaks of the quality of Anāgāmin?

The case is different. It does not hold that the saint, fallen from the result of Anāgāmin, gains it again by means of the *indriya* of pleasure.[86] On the other hand, the *vītarāga*, the person detached from all the defilements of Kāmadhātu, and who has obtained the result of Anāgāmin cannot fall from this result, because his detachment is obtained through two paths: it is produced through the worldly path and confirmed through the Pure Path.

***

How many *indriyas* does the person possess who possesses such *indriyas*?

> 17c-d. He who possesses the mental organ or the vital organ or the organ of equanimity necessarily possesses three *indriyas*.

He who possesses one of these three organs necessarily possesses the other two: when one of them is absent, the other two are also absent.

The possession of the other *indriyas* is not so determined. He who possesses these three organs may or may not possess the others.

1. A being born in Ārūpyadhatu does not possess the organs of seeing, hearing, smelling, or taste. A being in Kāmadhātu does not possess these organs when he has not yet acquired them (beginning of embryonic life) or when he has lost them (through blindness, etc., or through gradual death).

2. A being born in Ārūpyadhātu does not posses the organ of touch.

3. A being born in Ārūpyadhātu or Rūpadhātu does not possess the female organ. A being born in Kāmadhātu cannot possess it when he had not acquired it or when he has lost it. The same for the male organ.

4. A Pṛthagjana[87] born in the Fourth Dhyāna, in the Second

Dhyāna,[88] or in the Ārūpyas, does not possess the organ of pleasure.

5. A Pṛthagjana born in the Fourth Dhyana, in the Third Dhyana, or in the Ārūpyas, does not possess the organ of satisfaction.

6.A being born in Rūpadhātu or in Ārūpyadhātu does not possess the organ of displeasure.

7. A detached person does not possess the organ of dissatisfaction.

8. A person who has cut off the roots of good (iv.79) does not possess the five moral faculties, faith, etc.

9. Neither a Pṛthagjana nor a Saint in possession of a result possesses *anājñātamājñāsyāmīndriya.*

10. The Pṛthagjana, the Saint who is in the Path of the Seeing the Truths (vi.31a-b) and the Arhat do not possess *ājñendriya.*

11. The Pṛthagjana and the Śaikṣas do not possess *ājñātavīndriya.*

This enumeration permits us to establish those *indriyas* possessed by those categories of non-specified beings.

> 18a. He who possesses the organ of pleasure or the organ of touch certainly possesses four organs.

He who possesses the organ of pleasure also possesses the vital organ, the mental organ, and the organ of equanimity. He who possesses the organ of tóuch does possesses these same three *indriyas.*

> 18b. He who possesses one of the organs of sense consciousness necessarily possesses five organs.

He who possesses the organ of sight also possesses the vital organ, the mental organ, the organ of indifference and the organ of touch.

The same for him who possesses the organ of hearing, etc.

> 18c. The same for him who possesses the organ of satisfaction.

He who possesses the organ of satisfaction also possesses the vital organ, the mental organ, the organ of equanimity and the organ of pleasure.

But, one would ask,[89] what sort of organ of pleasure can a being possess who is born in the heaven of the Second Dhyāna and who does not therein cultivate the absorption of the Third Dhyāna?

He possesses the organ of defiled pleasure of the Third Dhyāna.

> 18. He who possesses the organ of displeasure certainly possesses seven organs.

This being evidently belongs to Kāmadhātu since he possesses the organ of displeasure. He necessarily possesses the vital organ, the mental organ, the organ of touch and four organs of sensation: the organ of dissatisfaction is not in him when he is detached.

> 18d-19a. Whoever possesses the female organ, etc., necessarily possesses eight organs.[90]

One should understand: Whoever possesses the female organ, or the male organ, or the organ of dissatisfaction, or one of the moral faculties,—faith, force, memory, absorption, and discernment.

He who possesses a sexual organ necessarily possesses, in addition to this organ, seven organs, which have been specified in 18c-d, for this being evidently belongs to Kāmadhātu.

He who possesses the organ of dissatisfaction necessarily possesses, in addition to this organ, these same seven organs.

He who possesses one of the moral faculties can be born in any of the three spheres of existence; he necessarily possesses the five moral faculties, which are seen together, plus the vital organ, the mental organ, and the organ of indifference.

> 19b. He who possesses *ājñendriya* or *ājñatavīndriya* necessarily possesses eleven organs.

These are the vital organ, the mental organ, the organs of pleasure, satisfaction, and equanimity;[91] the five moral faculties; and the eleventh, which is either *ājñendriya* or *ājñātavīndriya.*

> 19c. He who possesses *ājñāsyāmīndriya* necessarily possesses thirteen organs.

In fact, it is only in Kāmadhātu that one cultivates the Path of Seeing the Truths (vi.55). Thus the possessor of this *indriya* is a being in Kāmadhātu. He necessarily possesses the vital organ, the mental organ, the organ of touch, the four organs of sensation, the five moral faculties and *ājñāsyāmīndriya*. He does not necessarily possess the organ of dissatisfaction, nor the organs of sight, etc.; in fact, he can be "detached," in which case dissatisfaction is not in him; he can be blind, etc.[92]

***

What is the smallest number of organs it is possible for a being to possess? (*Vibhāṣā TD* 27, p. 767b5-11).

> 20a-b. A being who is lacking any good at all possesses a minimum of eight organs, the organ of touch, sensations, the vital organ, and the mental organ.

A being who is lacking good is one who has cut off the roots of good. He necessarily belongs to Kāmadhātu (iv.79); he cannot be "detached." Thus he necessarily possesses the organs enumerated.

"Sensation" in the Kārikā is *vid*. That is, "one who feels" (*vedayate*) by understanding *kartari kvip*; or "sensation" (*vedanā*) (*bhāvasādhana: auṇādikaḥ kvip*).

> 20c. It is the same with an ignorant person who is born in Ārūpyadhātu;

The Pṛthagjana is termed ignorant (because he has not seen the Truths).

> 20d. He possesses eight organs, namely, equanimity, life, the mental organ, and the good organs.

The good organs are the moral faculties, faith, etc. Since it is a question of an ignorant person, and since the total is eight, the pure organs (*ājñāsyāmi*, etc.) are not alluded to here by the author.

***

What are the largest number of organs it is possible for a being to possess?

> 21a-b. At the maximum, nineteen: [a bisexual being,] with the exception of the immaculate organs.

A bisexual being necessarily belongs to Kāmadhātu. He is not "detached;" he can possess the moral faculties; and he can possess all the organs of sense consciousness. But he is a Pṛthagjana: thus he necessarily lacks the pure organs (*ājñāsyāmi*, etc.).

The pure organs are termed "immaculate" in the Kārikā. The *ājñāsyāmi*, the *ājñā* and the *ājñātāvin* are pure because they are not in relation with the vices either in the quality of an object, or through association (v.17).

> 21c. The Āryan, not detached, can possess all the organs,

The Āryan who is not detached, and hence a Śaikṣa and not an Arhat, possesses at most nineteen organs.

> 21d. With the exception of a sexual organ and two pure organs.

One must exclude either the male organ, or the female organ; one must exclude the *ājñātāvīndriya* in all cases; furthermore, one must exclude the *ājñendriya* when the Śaikṣa is in the path of Seeing the Truths, or the *ājñāsyāmīndriya* when the Śaikṣa is in the Path of Absorption in the Truths.[93]

***

[ii. Atoms or *paramāṇus*.]

The conditioned *dharmas* (i.7a) are, as we have seen, of different natures—physical matter, sensation, ideas, etc. One asks if, in the same way, they arise independently one from another; or rather if, in certain cases, they necessarily arise together.

Certain conditioned *dharmas* are divided into five categories: *rūpa* or physical matter; *citta* or the mind; *caittas*, mental states or *dharmas* associated with the mind (ii.23-34); *cittaviprayuktas*, i.e., *saṁskāras* not associated with the mind (ii.35-48); and the *asaṁskṛtas* or unconditioned *dharmas*. These last are unarisen (i.5, ii.58): we do not have to occupy ourselves with them here.

We shall first study the simultaneous arising of the material *dharmas*.

> 22. In Kāmadhātu, an atom into which there is no entry of sound, and into which there is no entry of any organ, is made up of eight substances;[94]

By *paramāṇu*, we do not understand here a *paramāṇu* in its proper sense, a *dravyaparamāṇu*, an atom or monad which is a thing, a substance (*dravya*, i.13), but a *saṁghātaparamāṇu*, a molecule, i.e., the most subtle among the aggregates of matter, for there is nothing, among the aggregates of matter, which is more subtle.[95]

1. In Kāmadhātu, the molecule into which sound does not enter, and into which no organ enters, is made up of eight substances, but of no less than eight: namely the four primary elements (*mahābhūtas*, i.12c), and the four derived elements,—visibles (*rūpa*, i.10a), odors, tastes, and tangibles (ii.50c-d; 65a-b).

> 22b. When the organ of touch enters into it, it is made up of nine substances;

2. The molecule into which sound does not enter, but into which the organ of touch[96] enters, admits of a ninth substance, the *dravya* which is the organ of touch.

> 22c. When any other organ enters into it, it is made up of ten substances.[97]

3. The molecule into which sound does not enter, but into which all other organs other than the organ of touch (the organ of sight, *cakṣurindriya*, etc.) enter, consists of a tenth substance, the *dravya* that is this other organ (organ of sight, etc.): for the organs of seeing, hearing, etc. do not exist independently of the organ of touch nor do they constitute distinct *āyatanas*.

4. When sound enters into the aforementioned aggregates, the

total rises to nine, ten, or eleven substances: in fact, sound which is produced by the primary elements that form part of the organism (*upātta*, i.10b) does not exist independently of the organs.[98]

5. If the four primary elements, earth element, etc., are never disassociated, but coexist in every aggregate or molecule, how is it that, in any given aggregate, one perceives either solidity, or viscosity, or heat, or movement, and not these four substances or characteristics at one given time?

One perceives in any given aggregate those substances (*dravya*, earth element, etc.) that are most active in it, and not the others. In the same way, when one touches a pile of pieces of plants and needles,[99] one perceives the needles; when one eats some salted soup, one perceives the taste of salt.

How does one know that a given aggregate consists of the primary elements when their presence in it is not perceived?

All of the primary elements manifest their presence through their own actions, namely support (*dhṛti*), cohesion (*saṁgraha*), maturing (*pakti*), and expansion (*vyūhana*) (i.12c).[100]

According to another opinion, that of the Bhadanta Śrīlābha, the aggregates are made up of the four primary elements, since, given the action of certain causes, solid things become liquid, etc.[101] The fire element exists in water, since this latter is more or less cold, a fact which is explained by the presence of the element of fire in a more or less great quantity.

But, we would say, whether cold is more or less active does not imply that there has been a mixture of a certain substance (*dravya*), the cold, with its opposite, heat. So too sound and sensation, even though homogeneous, vary in intensity.

According to another opinion, [that of the Sautrāntikas,] the primary elements which are not perceived in a given aggregate exist in the state of potentiality, and not in action, and not in and of themselves. Thus the Blessed One was able to say (*Saṁyuktāgama*, *TD* 2, p., 129a3), "There are many *dhātus* or mineral substances in this piece of wood."[102] The Blessed One meant that this piece of wood contained the seeds, the potentialities of many *dhātus*; for gold, silver, etc., do not exist in the wood at the present time.

[The Sautrāntikas again object;] How does one prove the presence of color in wind?[103]

[The Vaibhāṣikas answer:] This is an object of faith (*śraddhanīya*), and not of reasoning (*anumeya*). Or rather physical matter exists in the wind, since one perceives smell by reason of the contact of the wind with an object possessing an odor; now odor is never disassociated from physical matter.[104]

6. We know that odor and taste are missing in Rūpadhātu (i.30); one must then reduce the number of molecules in Rūpadhātu. We will have six, seven, or eight substances, and when sound intervenes, seven, eight, or nine. We shall not explain this in detail.

7. (Objection. The Vaibhāṣikas say that molecules in Kāmadhātu consist of, at a minimum, eight *dravyas*, eight things or substances.) Are we to understand *dravyas* as individual substances, as things that have their own characteristics,[105] or as *āyatanas* that one can term *dravyas*, substances, since they each possess distinctive general characteristics?[106]

In the first hypothesis the numbers proposed are too few. A molecule, you say, consists of four "derived elements," *rūpa* first: it will consist of, we would say, not only of the *rūpa* of color (*varṇa*, blue or red *dravya*, etc.) but also of the *rūpa* of figure (*saṁsthāna*, i.10, iv.3c), since many atoms are agglomerated in these. It consists of the "derived matter" called "tangible:" it will be, we should say, heavy or light, hard or soft; it could be cold or hunger, or thirst; it then consists of the *dravyas* that are either heaviness or lightness, softness or hardness, cold, hunger and thirst (i.10d). Hence the numbers proposed above are too few. But if, on the contrary, the Vaibhāṣikas mean to speak of *dravyas* as *āyatanas*, then the numbers are still too few, for the primary elements form part of the *āyatana* "tangible" (i.35a); one should then say that a molecule consists of four substances, visible, odor, taste, and touch.

[The Vaibhāṣikas answer.] Our definition of a molecule is the best one. The word *dravya* is to be understood, in this case, as substances properly so-called, and as *āyatanas*. Among the eight *dravyas* of a molecule, there are 1.) four substances properly so-called, the four primary elements, the supports and sources of derived matter; and 2.) four *āyatanas*, four types of derived matter, supported by the primary elements: visibles, odors, tastes and tangibles (abstractions created from the primary elements, and included within tangibles).

This answer is not good, for each of these four derived elements is supported by all four of the primary elements. The molecule will then consist of twenty *dravyas*.[107]

No, [answer the Vaibhāṣikas,] for we are speaking of the nature of the primary elements, solidity, etc. The nature of all four of the primary elements remains the same, in that they support the derived element of odor or the derived elements of visibles, tastes, and tangibles.

But why do you express yourself in an ambiguous manner and use the word *dravya* in two different meanings? Words are subject to caprice, but one must examine their meaning.

[iii. The mental states or *caittas*.]

> 23a. The mind and its mental states are necessarily generated together.[108]

The mind and its mental states cannot be independently generated.

> 23d. All things are necessarily generated with their characteristics.

All conditioned *dharmas*, physical matter, the mind (ii.34), its mental states, and the *saṁskāras* disassociated from the mind (ii.35), are necessarily generated with their *saṁskṛtalakṣaṇas*—arising, duration, old age, and impermanence (ii.46a).

> 23c. Sometimes with possession.

Among the conditioned *dharmas*, those that are integral to living beings (*sattvākhya*, i.10) are necessarily generated with the *prāpti* relative to each one of them (ii.37b). There is no *prāpti* for the others. That is why the Kārikā says "sometimes."

***

What are the mental states?[109]

23c-d. The mental states are of five types, *mahābhūmikas*, etc.

The mental states are the *mahābhūmikas*, those that accompany all minds; the *kuśalamahābhūmikas*, those that accompany all good minds; the *kleśamahābhūmikas*, those that accompany all defiled minds; the *akuśalamahābhūmikas*, those that accompany all bad minds; and the *parīttakleśabhūmikas*, those that have small defilements for their sphere.

Bhūmi or sphere signifies "place of origin." The place of origin of a *dharma* is the *bhūmi* of this *dharma*.

The "great sphere" or *mahābhūmi* is so called because it is the sphere, the place of origin, of great *dharmas* (that is, of *dharmas* of great extension, that are found everywhere). The *dharmas* that are inherent in the *mahābhūmi* are called *mahābhūmika*, that is, the *dharmas* that are always found in all minds.[100]

***

What are the *mahābhūmikas*, the mental states found in all minds?

24. Sensation, volition, motion, desire for action, contact, discernment, memory, the act of attention, approval, and absorption or concentration coexist in every mind.[111]

According to the School,[112] all the ten *dharmas* exist in every moment of the mind.

1. *Vedanā* is the threefold sensation, pleasant, painful, and neither-painful-nor-pleasant. (i.14).

2. *Cetanā* is that which conditions, informs, and shapes the mind (*cittābhisaṁskāra*, i.15; iv.1).

3. *Saṁjñā* is *saṁjñāna*, that which grasps the marks (male, female, etc.) of an object (*viṣayanimittodgrahaṇa*, i.14, ii.34b-d).

4. *Chanda* is the desire for action.[113]

5. *Sparśa* is the state of contact arisen out of the encounter of the organ, the object and the consciousness; in other words, the *dharma* by virtue of which the organ, the object, and the consciousness are as if they were touching one another (iii.30).

6. *Prajñā*, which the Kārikā designates under the name of *mati*, is discernment of the *dharmas* (i.2)[114]

7. *Smṛti* is non-failing with regard to the object; a *dharma* by virtue of which the mind does not forget the object, by virtue of which it cherishes it in order to so express it (*abhilaṣatīva*).[115]

8. *Manaskāra* is the modification (*ābhoga*)[116] of the mind; in other words, "to bend" or "to apply" the mind towards an object. (*Manaskāra* is explained as *manasaḥ kāraḥ* or *manaḥ karoty āvarjayati*, ii.72).

9. *Adhimukti* is approval.[117]

10. *Samādhi* is the unity of the object with the mind (*cittaikāgratā*): (*agra* = *ālambana*, i.33); this is the *dharma* by virtue of which the mind, in an uninterrupted series, remains on an object (viii.1)[118]

How do we know that these ten mental states, distinct in nature, coexist in one and the same mind?

Subtle, unquestionably, are the specific characteristics of the mind and its mental states. One discerns them only with difficulty even when one is content to consider each of the mental states as developing in a homogeneous series; how much more so when one envisions them in the (psychological) moment (*kṣaṇa*) in which they all exist. If the differences of the taste of vegetables, tastes that we know through a material organ, are difficult to distinguish, how much more so is this true with non-material *dharmas* that are perceived through the mental consciousness.

***

The "sphere" of the good *dharmas* of great extension is termed *kuśalamāhabhūmi*. The mental states that arise from this sphere are termed *kuśalamahābhūmikas*: the *dharmas* that are found in all good minds.

> 25. Faith, diligence, aptitude, indifference, respect, fear, two roots, non-violence, and energy are found only in a good mind, and are found in all good minds.[119]

These ten *dharmas* are always found in all good minds.

1. *Śraddha* or faith is clarification of the mind.[120] According to another opinion,[121] it is adherence to the doctrine of the results of actions (vi.78b), to the Three Precious Ones (vi.73c), and to the Truths.

2. *Apramāda* or diligence is *bhāvanā*, that is, the taking possession of, and the cultivation of good *dharmas*.[122]

[Objection.] The taking possession of and the cultivation of good *dharmas* is none other than the good *dharmas* being grasped and cultivated. How can you make a partial mental *dharma* of diligence?

Diligence is application to good *dharmas*. One says, by metaphor, that it is *bhāvanā* (cultivation). By this fact, it is the cause of *bhāvanā*.

According to another school,[123] diligence is the guarding of the mind.

3. *Praśrabdhi* is the *dharma* through which the mind is clever, light, and apt.[124]

But, [the Sautrantikas observe,[125]] does not the Sutra speak of the *praśrabdhi* of the body?[126]

The Sūtra speaks of the *praśrabdhi* of the body as it speaks of bodily sensation. (All sensation is, in its nature, mental; sometimes the Sūtra terms the sensation that has for its support the five organs constituted of atoms a "bodily" sensation associated with the five sense consciousnesses [ii.7a]. In the same way that *praśrabdhi* of the mind depends on the five organs, *praśrabdhi* of the five sense consciousnesses is termed "*praśrabdhi* of the body.")

[The Sautrāntikas answer:] How can the *praśrabdhi* of the body, thus understood, be counted among the parts of Bodhi (*saṁbodhyaṅga*, vi.68)? In fact, the five sense consciousnesses are of the sphere of Kāmadhātu, for they are not "absorbed," that is, they are not produced in the state of absorption, whereas the parts of Bodhi are "absorbed" (vi.71a). Thus, in our opinion, in the Sūtra alluded to, *praśrabdhi* of the body is aptitude of the body (*kāyakarmaṇyatā*, viii.9).

[The Sarvāstivādins:] How can *praśrabdhi* of the body, thus understood, be a part of Bodhi? The aptitude of the body is, in fact, impure.

[The Sautrāntikas:] But it is propitious to *praśrabdhi* of the mind, which is a part of Bodhi; for this reason it receives the name "part of Bodhi." The Sūtra often expresses itself in this manner. For example, it teaches that joy constitutes the part of Bodhi called joy (*prītisaṁbodhyaṅga*, vi.71).[127] It teaches that hostility and the causes of hostility constitute the obstacle of wickedness (*vyāpādanivarana*, v.59).[128] It teaches that insight, resolution, and effort constitute "the element of speculative consciousness" (*prajñāskandha*, vii.76): for neither resolution, which is by its nature discursive thought (*vitarka*), nor effort, which is by nature energy, are speculative consciousness; but they are favorable to this consciousness and are, consequently, considered as consciousness.[129] *Praśrabdhi* of the body, being a condition of *praśrabdhi* of the mind, is placed, as are these, with these, among the parts of Bodhi.

4. *Upekṣā* or equanimity, is mental indifference, the *dharma* by which the mind remains equal, even, free from modification.[130]

[The Sautrāntikas:] If all minds are associated with attention, which is of the nature of "inflexion" or modification, how can all good minds be associated with equanimity, which is by its nature non-inflexion?

[The Vaibhāṣikas:] We have already remarked on this: the specific characteristics of the mind and its mental states are very difficult to know and determine.

[The Sautrāntikas:] This is not the point: it is quite inadmissible that the same mind be associated with mental states which repudiate both modification and non-modification, and both pleasure and displeasure.[131]

[The Vaibhāṣikas:[132]] There is modification towards a certain object, and non-modification with regard to another object: hence, there is no contradiction to the coexistence of modification and non-modification.

[The Sautrāntikas:] If this is so, then associated mental states cannot be on the same object, which is contradictory to your definition of associated *dharmas* (ii.34d). For us, the *dharmas* that are contradictory, here *manaskāra* and *upekṣā* and otherwise *vitarka* and *vicāra* (ii.33), do not exist simultaneously, but successively.

5-6. We shall explain respect and fear later (ii.32).

7-8. The two roots of good are absence-of-desire and absence-of-hatred (*adveṣa*, iv.8). Absence-of-error, the third root of good, is "discernment," *prajñā*, by nature: hence it is already named among the *mahābhūmikas*.[133]

9. Non-violence is non-cruelty.[134]

10. Energy is endurance of the mind.[135]

Such are the mental states that are associated with all good minds.

***

The sphere of the *mahākleśadharmas* is termed *mahākleśabhūmi*. The mental states that belong to this sphere, that is, the mental states that exist in all defiled minds, are *kleśamahābhūmikas*.

What are the defiled mental states?

> 26a-c. Error, non-diligence, idleness, disbelief, torpor, and dissipation are always and exclusively in soiled minds.

1. Error, *moha* is ignorance (*avidyā*, iii.29), non-knowledge, non-clarity.[136]

2. Non-diligence, *pramāda*, the opposite of diligence, is the non-taking possession of and the non-cultivation of good *dharmas*.

3. Idleness, *kausīdya*, is the opposite of energy.

4. Disbelief, *āśraddhya*, is the opposite of faith.

5. Torpor, *styāna*, is the opposite of aptitude (vii.11d).

The Abhidharma (*Jñānaprasthāna, TD* 26, p. 925b10) says: "What is torpor? The weight of the body, the weight of the mind, inaptitude of the body, inaptitude of the mind. Torpor of the body and torpor of the mind are termed torpor."

Now torpor is a "mental state." How can one have torpor of the body?

In the same way that there is bodily sensation (as above, p. 191).
6. Dissipation, *auddhatya*, is non-calmness of the mind (vii.lld)[137]
Only these six *dharmas* are *kleśamahābhūmikas*.

***

1. But the Mūla Abhidharma[138] says, on the one hand that there are ten *kleśamahābhūmikas*, but on the other hand, it omits torpor from its enumeration. What are these ten?

They are disbelief (*aśrāddhya*), idleness (*kausīdya*), default of memory (*muṣitasmṛtitā*), distraction (*vikṣepa*), ignorance (*avidyā*), non-observation (*asaṁprajanya*), wrong judgment (*ayoniśomanaskāra*), wrong resolution (*mithyādhimokṣa*), dissipation (*auddhatya*), and diligence (*pramāda*).

How foolish you are (*devānāṁpriyaḥ*),[139] grasping the letter of the text and ignoring its intention (*prāptijño na tv iṣṭijñaḥ*)![140]

What is its intention?

Five of the *dharmas* mentioned in the Abhidharma as *kleśamahābhūmikas*, namely default of memory, distraction, non-observation, wrong judgment, and wrong resolution, have already been mentioned as *mahābhūmikas*: there is no reason to name them again as *kleśamahābhūmikas*. The same for the root of good non-error: even though it is a *kuśalamahābhūmika*, it is not catalogued as such, because, being *prajña* by nature, it is classed as a *mahābhūmika* (as above, note 114).

In fact default of memory is nothing other than defiled memory (*smṛti*). Distration (iv.58) is defiled *samādhi*. Non-observation is defiled *prajña*. Wrong judgment is defiled judgment. And wrong resolution is defiled resolution.

This is why the Mūla Abhidharma lists ten *kleśamabhābhūmikas* in admitting the state of *mahābhūmikas* to a state of defilement.

***

Is a *mahābhūmika* also a *kleśamahābhūmika*?

There are four alternatives: 1. sensation, ideas, volition, contact and desire (*chanda*) are only *mahābhūmikas*; 2. disbelief, idleness, ignorance, dissipation, and diligence are only *kleśamahābhūmikas*; 3. memory, *samādhi, prajñā*, judgment, and resolution belong to both categories; and 4. the other *dharmas (kleśamahābhūmikas*, etc.)

Certain Masters (*Vibhāṣā, TD* 27, p. 220a22) maintain that distraction is not wrong *samādhi*: the alternatives then are differently established: distraction is added to the second category, and *samādhi* is put into the third.

2. As for the statement: "the Mūla Abhidharma omits torpor from its enumeration" of the *kleśamahābhūmika*, it is admitted that torpor is associated with all defiled *dharmas*.

If torpor is omitted from the list, is this my fault or the fault of the author of the Abhidharma?

The Ābhidhārmikas[141] explain the omission: torpor should be named; but it is not named because it is favorable to *samādhi*. In fact, they claim, persons with a torpid disposition (*styānacarita*), or dull persons, realize meditation sooner than do dissipated persons.[142]

But who is dull without being dissipated? Who is dissipated without being dull? Torpor and dissipation always go together.

Yes, torpor and dissipation go together. But the term *carita* indicates excess. The person in whom torpor dominates is called "dull," even though he is also dissipated.

We know this as well as you do; but it is by reason of their nature that the *dharmas* are classified into different categories. It is then established that six *dharmas* are *kleśamahābhūmikas*, because only they are produced in all defiled minds.

***

> 26c-d. Disrespect and the absence of fear are always and exclusively found in bad minds.

These two *dharmas*, which will be defined below (ii.32) are always found in bad minds. Consequently they are called *akuśalamahābhūmikas*.[143]

***

27. Anger, enmity, dissimilation, jealousy, stubbornness, hypocrisy, greed, the spirit of deception, pride-intoxication, the spirit of violence, etc., are the *parīttakleśabhūmikas*.[144]

They are called this because they have *parīttakleśas* for their spheres. *Parīttakleśa*, "small defilement," means *avidyā* or ignorance (iii.28c-d) in an isolated state, not associated with lust, etc. (*kevalā avenikī avidyā*, v.14).

They are only associated with ignorance, with the ignorance that is cast off through the Path of Meditation, ignorance of the sphere of mental consciousness. This is why they are called *parīttakleśabhūmikas*.[145]

These will be studied in the Fifth Chapter (v.46 and following).

***

We have studied five categories of mental states. There are other mental states that are indeterminate, *aniyata*, which are sometimes associated with a good mind, and sometimes with a bad or a neutral mind: regret (*kaukṛtya*, ii.28), apathy (*middha*, v.47, vii.11d), *vitarka* (ii.33), *vicāra*, etc.[146]

***

How many mental states are necessarily produced with each mind of each class—with a good, bad, or neutral mind?

28a. The mind in Kāmadhātu, when it is good, always consists of twenty-two mental states, as it is always associated with *vitarka* and *vicāra*.

There are five classes of minds in Kāmadhātu: 1) the good mind constitutes one class; 2-3) the bad mind constitutes two classes, accordingly as it is "independent," that is, associated only with ignorance, or associated with the other defilements, lust, etc.; and 4-5) the neutral mind that is free of retribution constitutes two classes according as it is soiled, that is, associated with *satkāyadṛṣṭi* or with *antagrāhadṛṣṭi*[147] (v.3), or not defiled, that is, "possessing retribution," etc. (i.37, ii.71).

The mind in Kāmadhātu is always associated with *vitarka* and *vicāra* (ii.33a-b). This mind, when it is good, consists of twenty-two mental states: ten *mahābhūmikas*, ten *kuśalamahābhūmikas*, plus two *aniyatas*, namely *vitarka* and *vicāra*.

When the good mind includes regret (*kaukṛtya*), the total rises to twenty-three.

What does the word *kaukṛtya* (regret) mean?[148]

Kaukṛtya is, properly, the nature of that which is wrongly done, but here *kaukṛtya* means a mental state that has for its object *kaukṛtya* in its literal sense, namely regret relative to an error. In the same way, *vimokṣamukha* which has *śūnyatā* or absence of *ātman* for its object is termed *śūnyatā* (viii.24-25); non-desire which has *aśubhā* or the loathsome (vi.llc-d) for its object is called *aśubhā*. In the same way, in the world, one says that the village, the town, the country, are all brought together, designating thus the inhabitants by the name of the location. *Kaukṛtya* in its proper sense is the support, the *raison d'etre* of regret; hence regret is termed *kaukṛtya*. For the result receives the name of its cause, for example in the text: "The six *sparśāyatanas* are previous actions."[149]

But how can one designate "regret over errors," regret relative to an action not done, by the name of *kaukṛtya*?

Because one says "It is poorly done on my part not to have done this action," thus designating an omission as "done" or "poorly done."

When is regret good?

When it is relative to a good action omitted or to a bad action accomplished. It is bad when it is relative to a bad action omitted or to a good action accomplished.

These two types of regret bear on the two categories of action.

> 29a. A bad mind consists of twenty mental states when it is independent of, or associated with views (*dṛṣṭi*);

1. An independent mind is a mind associated with ignorance (*avidyā*, v.1), but not associated with other defilements, lust, etc.[150]

A bad mind associated with views is a mind associated with *mithyādṛṣṭi*, with *dṛṣṭiparāmarśa*, or with *śīlavrataparāmarśa* (v.3); a mind associated with *satkāyadṛṣṭi* and with *antagrāhadṛṣṭi* is not bad, but defiled-neutral.

In these two cases, a bad mind consists of ten *mahābhūmikas*, six *kleśamahābhūmikas*, two *akuśalamahābhūmikas*, plus two *aniyatas*, namely *vitarka* and *vicāra*.

View itself is not counted, for a view is a certain type of *prajñā*, and *prajñā* is a *mahābhūmika*.[151]

> 29b. Twenty-one, when it is associated with one of the four defilements, with anger, etc., with regret.

2. Associated with lust, hostility, pride, or doubt (*rāga, pratigha, māna, vicikitsā*, v.1), a bad mind consists of twenty-one mental states, the same as above, plus lust or hostility, etc.

Associated with anger, etc., that is, with one of the minor defilements (*upakleśas*) enumerated above, ii.27.·

> 30a. A neutral mind consists of eighteen mental states when it is defiled;

In Kāmadhātu, a neutral mind, that is, a mind free of retribution, is defiled, that is covered by defilement when it is associated with *satkāyadṛṣṭi* or *antagrāhadṛṣṭi*. This mind consists of ten *mahābhūmikas*, six *kleśamahābhūmikas*, plus *vitarka* and *vicāra*.

> 30b. In the contrary case, twelve.

Not defiled, a neutral mind consists of twelve mental states: the ten *mahābhūmikas, vitarka*, and *vicāra*.

The Foreigners believe that regret can be indefinite, for example, in a dream. An indefinite-non-defiled mind associated with indefinite regret would consist of thirteen mental states.

30c-d. Apathy is not in contradiction to any category; wherever it is found, it is added.

Apathy (*middha*, v.47, vii.lld) can be good, bad, or neutral. The mind with which it is associated would then consist of twenty-three mental states instead of twenty-two, twenty-four instead of twenty-three, etc., accordingly as it is good and free from regret, or good and accompanied by regret, etc.

31a. The bad mental states, regret and apathy, are absent from the First Dhyāna.

In the First Dhyāna there is missing 1) hostility (*pratigha*, v.1), 2) the series anger, etc. (ii.27), with the exception of hypocrisy (*sāṭhya*), deception (*māyā*), and pride-intoxication (*mada*); 3) the two *akuśala-mahābhūmikas*, disrespect and the absence of fear (ii.32); plus 4) regret, since dissatisfaction (ii.8b-c) is absent, and 5) laziness, since food through the mouth (iii.38d) is absent. The other mental states of Kāmadhātu exist in the First Dhyāna.[152]

31b. Further on, *vitarka* is also missing absent from the intermediate *dhyāna*.

Furthermore, *vitarka* is absent from the intermediate *dhyāna*.

31c. Further on, again, *vicāra*, etc.

In the Second Dhyāna and above, up to and including Ārūpya-dhātu, *vicāra*, hypocrisy, and deception are also absent.[153] Pride-intoxication exists in the three spheres of existence (v.53c-d).

According to the Sūtra,[154] hypocrisy and deception exist as far as the world of Brahmā, but not above the heavens where beings are in assembly. Mahābrahmā, sitting in his assembly, was questioned by the Bhikṣu Aśvajit: "Where do the four primary elements completely disappear?" Incapable of responding, he boasted: "I am Brahmā, great Brahmā,[155] the Lord, the Creator, the Transformer, the Generator, the Nourisher, the Father of all." Finally, when Aśvajit was leaving the assembly, Brahmā counselled him to return to the presence of the Master and ask him.[156]

***

We have seen how many mental states are associated with each type of mind of the three spheres of existence. We have to define the mental states enumerated above.

What is the difference between disrespect (*ahrī*) and absence of fear (*anapatrāpya*)?

> 32a. Disrespect is lack of veneration.[157]

Lack of respect, that is, the lack of veneration,[158] the lack of fearful submission with regard to the qualities (*maitrī, karuṇā*, etc.) of oneself and others, and with regard to persons endowed with these qualities, is *āhrīkya; ahrī* is a mental *dharma* opposed to respect.

> 32b. *Anapatrāpya* or *atrapā* is the *dharma* that causes a person not to see the unpleasant consequences of his transgressions.[159]

"Transgressions" are what are scorned by good persons.

"Unpleasant consequences" are called in the Kārikā *bhaya* or fear, because these unpleasant consequences engender fear.

The condition of the person who does not see the consequences of transgression—the *dharma* that produces this condition,—is *anapatrāpya* or *atrapā*.

[Objection:] What do you understand by the expression "does not see the unpleasant consequences" *abhayadarśitva*? Whether you interpret this phrase as *abhayasya darśitvam*, "he sees that there are no unpleasant consequences," or as *bhayasya adarśitvam*, "he does not see that there are unpleasant consequences," none of these explanations is satisfactory. In the first case, we have defiled *prajñā*, an inexact knowledge; in the second case, we simply have ignorance.

The expression *abhayadarśitvam* signifies neither "view" (defiled *prajñā*), nor "non-view" (ignorance). It describes a special *dharma* that is placed among the minor defilements (*upakleśas*, v.46), which has false views and ignorance for its cause, and which is termed *anapatrāpya* (*Vibhāṣā, TD* 27, p. 180a17).

According to other Masters,[160] *āhrīkya* is the absence of shame *vis-a-vis* oneself, in the commission of a transgression; *anapatrāpya* is the absence of shame *vis-a-vis* others.[161]

But cannot one consider oneself and others at the same time?

We do not say that the two forms of the absence of shame are simultaneous.

There is *āhrīkya*, an outflowing of lust, when the person does not experience the shame of transgression when considering oneself; there is *anapatrāpya*, an outflowing from mental confusion, when he does not experience the shame of transgression when considering others.

Hrī and *apatrāpya* are opposed to these two bad *dharma*. Their definition, according to the first theory, is "respect, veneration, fearful submission," or "fear of the consequence of transgression;" according to the second theory, "modesty," "respect for humans."

Some think that affection (*preman*) and respect (*gaurava*) are the same thing.

32c. Affection is faith.[162]

Affection is of two types, defiled and non-defiled (*Vibhāṣā, TD* 27, p. 151a8).

The first is attachment; for example, affection for wife and sons. The second is faith; for example, affection for a master or for virtuous persons.

1. All faith is not affection, namely faith with regard to the Truths of Suffering and the Arising of Suffering.

2. All affection is not faith, namely defiled affection.

3. Faith can be affection, namely faith with regard to the Truths of the Extinction of Suffering and the Path.

4. The other mental states, the *dharmas* disassociated from the mind, etc., are neither faith nor affection.

According to another opinion,—ours,—faith is a belief in qualities: affection is produced from this belief. Affection is then not faith, but the result of faith.

32c. Respect is *hrī*.[163]

As we have explained above (32a), respect is veneration, etc.

1. All *hrī* is not respect, namely *hrī* with respect to the Truths of Suffering and the Origin of Suffering.[164]

2. *Hrī* with respect to the Truths of the Extinction of Suffering and the Path is also respect.

According to another opinion, respect is veneration; shame is born from respect and this shame is called *hrī*. Hence respect, the cause of *hrī*, is not *hrī*.

There are four alternatives concerning affection and respect:

1. Affection which is not respect, namely affection with regard to wife, to children, to companions in the religious life, to pupils.

2. Respect which is not affection, namely respect with regard to someone else's master, to a person endowed with qualities, etc.

3. Respect which is affection, namely respect with regard to one's master, one's father, mother, etc.

4. Neither respect nor affection for other persons.

> 32d. Both exist in Kāmadhātu and Rūpadhātu.

Affection and respect do not exist in Ārūpyadhātu.

But you have said that affection is faith, and that respect is *hrī*: now faith and *hrī* are *kuśalamahābhūmikas* (ii.25): hence affection and respect should exist in Ārūpyadhātu.

Affection and respect are of two types: relative to *dharmas* and relative to persons. The text refers to the second type; the first type does exist in all three spheres of existence.

> 33a-b. *Vitarka* and *vicāra* are grossness and subtlety of the mind.[165]

The grossness, that is, the gross state of the mind is termed *vitarka*; the subtlety, that is, the subtle state of the mind is termed *vicāra*. How can *vitarka* and *vicāra* be associated with the mind at one and the same time? Can the mind, at one and the same time, be both gross and subtle?

According to one opinion,[166] we may compare *vicāra* to cold water, the mind to cheese which floats on the surface of this cold water, and *vitarka* to the heat of the sun which operates on this cheese. By reason of the water and sun, the cheese is not too runny nor too hard. In this same way, *vitarka* and *vicāra* are associated with the mind: it is neither too subtle, by reason of *vitarka*, nor too gross, by reason of *vicāra*.

But, we would say, it follows from this explanation that *vitarka* and *vicāra* are not grossness and subtlety of mind, but the cause of its grossness and its subtlety: the cold water and the warm light of the sun are not the hard or the runny state of the cheese, but rather the cause of these states.

Other objections present themselves. Grossness and subtlety of mind are relative things. They admit of many degrees: a mind of the First Dhyāna is subtle in comparison with a mind in Kāmadhātu, but gross in comparision with a mind in the Second Dhyāna; the qualities and the defilements can be more or less gross or subtle in one and the same stage, for they are divided into nine categories. Thus, if *vitarka* and *vicāra* are grossness and subtlety of the mind, we would have to admit that they both exist up to the highest stage of Ārūpyadhātu.[167] Now they cease at the Second Dhyāna, and adding to this the fact that no specific or generic differences can be established between grossness and subtlety, one then cannot differentiate *vitarka* and *vicāra*.

According to another opinion, [that of the Sautrāntikas,] *vitarka* and *vicāra* are the "factors of voice."[168] The Sūtra says in fact, "It is after having examined, after having judged (*vitarkya, vicārya*) that one speaks, not without having examined, not without having judged."[169] The factors of voice that are called gross are called *vitarkas*; those that are subtle are called *vicāras*. (According to this explanation, we should understand *vitarka* and *vicāra* not as two distinct *dharmas*, but rather a collection of mind and mental states which provoke speech, and which is sometimes gross, sometimes subtle.)

[The Vaibhāṣikas:] What contradiction is there in two *dharmas*, the first (*vitarka*) gross, and the second (*vicāra*) subtle, being associated with the same mind?

[The Sautrāntikas:] There would not be any contradiction if these two *dharmas* were specifically different; for example, sensations and ideas—although the first are gross and the second subtle (i.22)—can coexist. But two states of the same species, one in a strong state and the other in a weak state, one gross and one subtle, cannot coexist.

[The Vaibhāṣikas:] But there is a specific difference between *vitarka* and *vicāra*.

[The Sautrāntikas:] What is this difference?

[The Vaibhāṣikas:] This difference is inexpressible; but it is manifested through the force or the weakness of the mind.[170]

[The Sautrāntikas:] The force and the weakness of the mind do not demonstrate the presence of two specifically different *dharmas*, for the same species is sometimes strong, sometimes weak.

According to another opinion,—ours,—*vitarka* and *vicāra* are not associated with one and the same mind. They exist in turn.[171] The Vaibhāṣikas would object that the First Dhyāna has five parts (viii.7) among which are *vitarka* and *vicāra*. We would answer that the First Dhyana has five parts in the sense that five parts are possible in the First Dhyāna: but any given moment of the First Dhyāna possesses only four parts, namely *prīti, sukha*, and *samādhi*, plus *vitarka* or *vicāra*.

***

What difference is there between *māna* (pride) and *mada* (pride-intoxication) (*Vibhāṣā, TD* 27, p. 223a6)?

> 33b. *Māna*, the error of pride, is arrogance. But *mada*, pride-intoxication, is the abolition of the mind of one who is enamoured with his own qualities.

It is arrogance of mind (*cetasa unnatiḥ*) with respect to others. Measuring (*mā*) the superiority of qualities that one has, or that one believes to have over others, one becomes haughty and depreciates others.

Be reason of its attachment to its own qualities, the mind becomes puffed up, exhaults itself, and abolishes itself.[172] According to other Masters, in the same way that wine produces a certain joyous excitation that is called intoxication, so too does the attachment that a person has for his own qualities.[173]

***

We have defined the mind (*citta*, i.16) and its mental states. We have seen in what categories the mental states are placed, in what numbers they are generated together, and what their different characteristics are. The mind and its mental states receive, in the Scriptures, different names.

> 34a-b. The names mind (*citta*), spirit (*manas*), and consciousness (*vijñāna*) designate the same thing.[174]

The mind is termed *citta* because it accumulates (*cinoti*);[175] it is termed *manas* because it knows (*manute*)[176] and it is termed *vijñāna* because it distinguishes its object (*ālambanaṁ vijñānāti*).

Some say that the mind is termed *citta* because it is spotted (*citra*) by good and bad elements;[177] to the extent that it is the support (*āśrayabhūta*) of the mind that follows, it is *manas* (i.17); and to the extent that it grasps the support through the organ and its object (*āśritabhūta*), it is *vijñāna*.

Hence these three names express different meanings, but they designate the same object; in this same way

> 34b-d. The mind and its mental states "have a support," "have an object," "have an aspect," and are "associated."

These four different names, "have a support," etc., designate the same object.

The mind and its mental states "have a support" because they rely on the organs (organ of sight, etc., mental organ); "have an object" (*sālambana*, i.34) or "a subject of consciousness," because they grasp their "sphere;" "have an aspect," because they take form according to their object;[178] and are "associated," that is, similar and united, because they are similar to one another and are not separated from each other.

How are they *saṁprayukta* or associated, that is, "similar and united?"

34d. In five ways.

The mind and its mental states are associated by reason of five equalities or identities, identity of support (*āśraya*), of object (*ālambana*), of aspect (*ākāra*), of time (*kāla*), and equality in the number of *dravyas*. That is: the mental states (sensation, etc.) and the mind are associated (1-3) because they have the same support, the same object, and the same aspect; (4) because they are simultaneous; and (5) because, in this association, each type is represented by only one individual substance (*dravya*): in any given moment there can be only one mind produced; to this one, unique mind there is found associated one sensation, one idea, or one mental state of each type (see ii.53c-d).

We have explained the mind and its mental states, in full, with their characteristics.[179]

***

[iv. The *dharmas* not associated with the mind]

What are the *saṁskāras* not associated with the mind?

35-36a. The *dharmas* "not associated. with the mind" are *prāpti, aprāpti, sabhāgāta, āsaṁjñika*, and two absorptions, life, characteristics, *nāmakāya*, etc., and that which is of this type.[180]

These *dharmas* are not associated with the mind; they are not of the nature of *rūpa* or physical matter; they are included within the *saṁskāraskandha* (i.15): they are called the *cittaviprayukta saṁskāras*, (1) because they are disjoined from the mind, and (2) because, being non-material, they resemble the mind.

36b. *Prāpti* is acquisition and possession.[181]

Prāpti is of two types: (1) acquisition of that which has not been obtained (*prāpta*) or of that which had been lost; and (2) possession of that which, having been obtained, has not been lost.

Aprāpti is the opposite.

36c. There is *prāpti* and *aprāpti* of *dharmas* that belong to the person himself,[182]

1. When a conditioned *dharma* "falls into the personal series," there is *prāpti* or *aprāpti* of this *dharma*, but not if it falls into the series of another person, for no one possesses the *dharmas* of another; nor if it does not fall into any series, for no one posseses the *dharmas* "which are not of a living being" (*asattvākhya*, i.10b).[183]

2. As for unconditioned *dharmas*, there is *prāpti* of *pratisaṁkhyānirodha* and *apratisaṁkhyānirodha* (i.6, ii.55).

36d. And of the two extinctions.

a. All beings possess the *apratisṁkhyānirodha* of the *dharmas* that do not arise without a cause.

b. The Abhidharma (*Jñānaprasthāna, TD* 26, p. 1022a) expresses itself in this way: "Who possesses pure *dharmas*? All beings possess *pratisaṁkhyānirodha* with the exception of the *sakalabandhanaādikṣaṇasthas*, that is, with the exception of the Āryans bound with all the bonds and who are found in the first moment of the Path, and with the exception of the Pṛthagjanas bound by all the bonds. The others, both Āryans and Pṛthagjanas, possess *pratisaṁkhyānirodha*."[184]

c. No one possesses space (*ākāśa*). Hence there is no *prāpti* of space.

[According to the Vaibhāṣikas,] *prāpti* and *aprāpti* are in opposition: everything that is susceptible of *prāpti* is also susceptible of *aprāpti*. As shall be explained, the stanza does not speak of this in a straightforward manner.

[The Sautrāntikas] deny the existence of a *dharma* called *prāpti* or possession.

[1. How do the Sarvāstivādin-Vaibhāṣikas prove the existence of a substance (*dravyadharma*)[185] termed *prāpti*?]

[The Sarvāstivādins:] A Sūtra (*Madhyamāgama, TD* 1, p. 735b29 and following?) says, "Through the production, the acquisition, and the possession of ten *dharmas* belonging to an Arhat, the Saint becomes a person 'having abandoned five things.'"[186]

[The Sautrāntikas:] If you conclude from this text that *prāpti* exists, we would remark that one "possesses" *dharmas* "that do not belong to living beings," and also *dharmas* that do belong to another. In fact, a Sūtra (=the *Cakravartisūtra*) says, "Know, Oh Bhikṣus, that the Cakravartin King possesses seven jewels . . ."[187] Now, among the jewels, there are the jewels of a wheel, a wife, etc.

[The Sarvāstivādins:] In this text, the expression "to possess" (*samanvāgata*) signifies "master of." One says that the Cakravartin King enjoys mastery over jewels, for they go as he wishes. But in the Sūtra on the Possession of the Ten *Dharmas* of an Arhat (*Dasāśaikṣadharmasamanvāgamasūtra*), the word "possession" designates a thing in and of itself.[188]

2. [The Sautrāntikas:] If the word "possession" signifies "mastery" in the *Cakravartisūtra*, how do you ascertain that, in another Sūtra, this same word designates a supposed *prāpti*, a thing in and of itself? In fact 1.) this *prāpti* is not directly perceived, as is the case for color, sound, etc., and as is the case for lust, anger, etc.; 2.) one cannot conclude the existence of *prāpti* by reason of its effects, as is the case for the sense organs, the organ of sight, etc. (i.9): for a similar effect is not perceived.

[The Sarvāstivādins:] Error! Possession has an effect. It is the cause of the arising of the *dharmas*.[189]

[The Sautrāntikas:] This answer is unfortunate. 1. You maintain that one can posses the two extinctions; now these, being unconditioned, do not arise: only conditioned things are "caused" (i.7d). 2. As for the conditioned *dharmas*, there is not now, in any given person, possession of the *dharmas* that he has not yet acquired,[190] nor does he any longer possess the *dharmas* whose possession he has abandoned through his changing of his sphere of existence or through "detachment:"[191] the possession of the first has never existed, and the possession of the second has perished. Hence how can these *dharmas* arise if the cause of their arising is *prāpti*?

[The Sarvāstivādins:] The arising of these *dharmas* has for its cause a *prāpti* which arises at the same time as they do.

[The Sautrāntikas:] An unfortunate answer! If the *dharmas* arise by virtue of *prāpti*, 1.) arising and the arising-of-arising (ii.45c) have no use; 2.) the *dharmas* "that do not belong to living beings" do not arise; and 3.) how does one explain the difference in the degree of defilement,—weak, medium, and strong defilement,—among persons who are 'bound to all bonds'?: all in fact possess the same *prāptis* of all the defilements of Kāmadhātu. Would you say that this difference proceeds from causes distinct from *prāpti*?

We would answer that these causes are the only cause of weak, medium, or strong defilements; why would one want to assign it to *prāpti*?

3. [The Sarvāstivādins:] Who maintains that *prāpti* is the cause of the arising of *dharmas*? Such is not the role that we attribute to it. For us, *prāpti* is the cause that determines the state or condition of beings. Let us explain. Let us suppose the non-existence of *prāpti*: what difference would there be between an Āryan at the moment in which he produces a mundane thought and a Pṛthagjana? Now the difference consists solely in that the Āryan, even when he has a worldly thought, is in possession (*prāpti*) of a certain number of pure *dharmas*.

[The Sautrāntikas]: For us, there is this difference that the first has abandoned certain defilements, while the second has not yet abandoned them.

[The Sarvāstivādins:] Without doubt; but if we suppose the non-existence of *prāpti*, how can we say that a defilement is abandoned or not abandoned? There can only be the abandoning of a defilement through the disappearance of the *prāpti* of this defilement; the defilement is not abandoned as long as its *prāpti* lasts.

4. [The Doctrine of the Sautrāntikas:] To us, the abandoning or the non-abandoning of a defilement consists of a certain condition of the person (*āśraya*, ii.5 and 6, 44d). The personality of the Āryan is modified, becoming different from what it was through the power of the Path (Seeing the Truths, Meditation). The defilement, once it has been destroyed through the force of the Path, cannot be manifested again. Like seed which is burned by fire and which becomes different from what it once was, and is no longer capable of germinating, we say that the Āryan has abandoned the defilement, because his person no longer maintains the seeds capable of producing a defilement. The

worldly path does not definitively destroy the defilement; it only damages it or disturbs it: one would say that a Pṛthagjana—who is able to practice only the worldly path—has abandoned the defilement when his person no longer contains even the seeds of defilement damaged by this path. Contrarily one says that a person has not abandoned defilement when the seeds are neither burnt nor damaged. One says that a person is in possession of the defilement when he has not "abandoned" them in the manner that we have just explained; we say that he is in non-possession of the defilements when he has not abandoned it. "Possession" and "non-possession" are not things in and of themselves, but designations.

This then concerns possession and non-possession of defilement. But concerning the possession and non-possession of good *dharmas*, we must distinguish 1.) the innate good *dharmas*, which do not entail any effort, and 2.) the good *dharmas* that are obtained through effort or cultivation (*prayogika*, ii.71b).

We say that a person possesses the first when his person possesses intact the quality of being a seed of these good *dharmas*. When this quality is damaged, we say that the person does not possess the good *dharmas*. In fact, while the seeds of defilement can be destroyed completely and definitively, as is the case among the Āryans, good *dharmas* never have their roots definitively cut off, with the restriction that one says of a person who has cut off the roots of good through false views (*samucchinnakuśalamūla*, iv.79c) that he has only abandoned these roots, because the quality of being a seed of these roots, a quality that belongs to his person, has been damaged through false views.

We say that a person possesses the second—the good *dharmas* produced through effort, through hearing, reflection, and meditation—when, these *dharmas* having arisen, his capacity to produce them [anew] is not damaged.

Hence what we understand by "possession" or the "fact of being endowed with" (*samanvāgama*) is not a *dharma* constituting a separate thing in and of itself, namely the supposed *prāpti* of the Sarvāstivādins, but a certain condition of the person: 1. the seeds of defilement have not been uprooted through the Path of the Saints; 2. the seeds of defilement have not been damaged by means of the worldly path; 3. the seeds of innate good have not been damaged through false views; and 4. the seeds of good "obtained through effort" are in good condition at the moment when one wants to produce this good. When the person is in such a condition, this is what we call "possession of defilements," etc.

***

But what should we understand by "seeds" [ask the Sarvāstivādins]?

By seeds we understand *nāmarūpa* (iii.30), that is, the complex of the five *skandhas*, capable of generating a result, either immediately or mediately, by means of the *pariṇāma-viśeṣa* of its series.

The series is the *saṁskāras* of the past, the present and the future, in relation to causality, that constitutes an uninterrupted series.

The *pariṇāma*, or the evolution of the series, is the modification of this series, the fact that this series arises differently from itself at each moment.

The *viśeṣa*, or culminating point of this evolution, is the moment of this series that possesses the capacity of immediately producing a result.[192]

[The Vaibhāṣikas object:] The Sūtra says, "He who is in possession of greed is not capable of producing the foundations of mindfulness (*smṛtyupasthānas*, vi.14)."

[The Sautrāntikas:] In this text, we must understand by "possession" of greed the "consenting to greed," or "not rejecting greed." The Sūtra does not say that a person who has the seeds of greed in him is incapable of producing the foundations of mindfulness; it says rather that active greed renders this person presently incapable of producing these spiritual exercises.

In short, in whichever manner it is that we understand possession, either as "cause of the arising of the *dharmas*," or as "origin of the condition of beings," or as "special state of the person," or as "consenting to," possession appears to us, not as an entity, a thing in and of itself, but as a "*dharma* of designation." This same holds for non-possession, which is purely and simply the negation of possession.

***

The Vaibhāṣikas say that *prāpti* and *aprāpti* are things in and of themselves.

Why?

Because this is our teaching.[193]

> 37a. There is threefold *prāpti* of the *dharmas* of the three periods.

Past *dharmas* can be the object of a threefold *prāpti*, past, present, and future. The same for present and future *dharmas*.[194]

> 37b. There is good *prāpti*, etc., of good *dharmas*, etc.

The *prāpti* of good, bad, or neutral *dharmas* is, respectively, good, bad, or neutral.

> 37c. The *prāptis* of the *dharmas* belonging to the spheres of existence are of their spheres.[195]

The *dharmas* belonging to the spheres of existence are impure *dharmas*. The *prāpti* of a *dharma* in Kāmadhātu is, itself, in Kāmadhātu; and thus following.

> 37d. There is fourfold *prāpti* of the *dharmas* that do not belong to the spheres of existence.[196]

In general, the *prāpti* of these *dharmas*—the pure *dharmas*—is fourfold: it belongs to the three spheres, and it is pure. But there are distinctions:

1. The *prāpti* of *apratisaṁkhyānirodha* (see ii.36c-d) is of the sphere to which the person who obtains it belongs.

2. The *prāpti* of *pratisaṁkhyānirodha* is of Rūpadhātu, of Ārūpya-

dhātu, and pure.[197]

3. The *prāpti* of the Path (*mārgasatya*, vi.25d) is Śaikṣa; the *prāpti* of the Aśaikṣa *dharmas* is Aśaikṣa.[198]

But there is

> 38a. Threefold *prāpti* of the *dharmas* which are neither Śaikṣa nor Aśaikṣa.

These *dharmas*—the *naivaśaikṣanāśaikṣas*, vi.45b—are the impure *dharmas* and the unconditioned *dharmas*; they are called this because they differ from the *dharmas* of the Śaikṣa and from the *dharmas* of the Aśaikṣa.

In general, the *prāpti* of these *dharmas* is threefold. Their distinctions are:

1. The *prāpti* of the impure *dharmas* is neither-Śaikṣa-nor Aśaikṣa;

2. In this same way the *prāpti* of *apratisaṁkhyānirodha* and the *prāpti* of *pratisaṁkhyānirodha* are obtained by a non-Āryan;[199]

3. The *prāpti* of *pratisaṁkhyānirodha* is Śaikṣa when this *nirodha* is obtained through the path of the Śaikṣas; it is Aśaikṣa when this *nirodha* is obtained through the path of the Aśaikṣas.

***

The *prāpti* of the *dharmas* to be abandoned either through Seeing, or through Meditation, is destroyed, respectively, either through Seeing or through Meditation; it belongs then, from the point of view of abandoning them, to the category of these *dharmas* (ii.33).

As for the *dharmas* which should not be abandoned, their *prāpti* presents difficulties:

> 38b. There is twofold *prāpti* of the *dharmas* that should not be abandoned.

These *dharmas* are the pure *dharmas* (i.40b, ii.13d).

The *prāpti* of *apratisaṁkhyānirodha* is abandoned through the Path of Meditation.

The same for the *prāpti* of *pratisaṁkhyānirodha* obtained by the non-Āryan.

But the *prāpti* of *pratisaṁkhyānirodha* obtained through the Path is pure and should not be abandoned. The same for the *prāpti* of the Path.[200]

We have established the general principal that the *dharmas* of the three periods are susceptible of a threefold *prāpti* (ii.37a). We must be more precise.

38c. The *prāpti* of a neutral *dharma* is simultaneous to it.

The *prāpti* of an undefiled-neutral *dharma* is simultaneous to this *dharma*: one possesses it when it is present, not when it is past or future. When it is past, the *prāpti* is past, and when it is future, the *prāpti* is future: this by reason of the weakness[201] of this *dharma.*

38d. With the exception of the two supernormal faculties and apparition.

This rule does not apply to all undefiled-neutral *dharmas*. The supernormal faculties of seeing and hearing (*cakṣurabhijñā, śrotrabhijñā*, vii.45) and the mind capable of creating apparitional beings (*nirmāṇacitta*, ii.72) are strong, for they are realized through a special effort; consequently one possesses them in the past, the present, and the future. Certain Masters[202] maintain that the undefiled-neutral *dharmas* "of craftsmanship" and "of attitude" (*airyāpathika*, ii.72), when they have been the object of an intense practice are also possessed in the past and future.

39a. The same for the *prāpti* of defiled *rūpa.*

The *prāpti* of defiled-neutral *rūpa* is only simultaneous to this *rūpa*. This *rūpa* is bodily action and vocal action resulting from a defiled-neutral mind. This action, even through produced by a strong mind, is incapable, as is the mind itself, of creating *avijñapti* (iv.7a); hence it is weak. Thus one possesses it in the present, but not in the past or the future.

***

Is the tritemporal character of the *prāpti* of the good and the bad *dharmas* subject to any restriction, as is the case with the *prāpti* of the neutral *dharmas*?

> 39b. The *prāpti* of the *rūpa* of Kāmadhātu is not previous to this *rūpa*.

This *rūpa*, good or bad, for example the *prātimokṣa-saṁvara* (iv.19 and following), is not possessed previous to its being produced. The *prāpti* is simultaneous and later, but not earlier.

***

Can non-possession be, like *prāpti*, good, bad, or neutral?

> 39c. *Aprāpti* is undefiled-neutral.[203]

Aprāpti is always *anivṛtāvyākṛta* (ii.66).

> 39d. *Aprāpti* of the *dharmas* of the past or the future is threefold.

Aprāpti of past or future *dharmas* can be past, present, or future. But one necessarily possesses the present *dharmas*: hence the *aprāpti* of present *dharmas* can be only past or future.

> 40a. *Aprāpti* of the *dharmas* forming part of the spheres of existence, and of the immaculate *dharmas*, is threefold.

Aprāpti of the *dharmas* of the sphere of Kāmadhātu belong either to Kāmadhātu, Rūpadhātu, or Ārūpyadhātu accordingly as the person endowed with this *aprāpti* belongs to such a sphere of existence. The same for the *aprāpti* of pure *dharmas*.

In fact, *aprāpti* is never pure.

Why?

> 40b-c. According to the School, a Pṛthagjana is a person who has not acquired the Path.[204]

1. As it says in the Mūlaśāstra (*Jñānaprasthāna, TD* 26, p. 928c5;

Vibhāṣā, TD 27, p. 232b9), "What is the state of Pṛthagjana? The non-possession of the *dharmas* of the Āryans (*āryadharmāṇāṁ alābhaḥ*)." Now the state of Prthagjana is not pure; hence their non-possession (*aprāpti=alābha*) is not pure.

Let us examine this definition. When the Śāstra says that the state of Pṛthagjana is the non-possession of the *dharmas* of the Āryans, which *dharmas* of the Āryans does it mean?

The *dharmas* beginning with *duḥkhe dharmajñānakṣānti* and including the whole pure path or the Path of the Āryans (vi.25).

[The Sarvāstivādins:] The Śāstra means all these *dharmas*, since it does not specify any.

Be careful! To believe you, a person in possession of *duḥkhe kṣānti* would be a Pṛthagjana if he did not possess all of the other Āryan *dharmas*.

[The Sarvāstivādins:] The Śāstra means the non-possession that is not accompanied by possession: the person of whom you speak, although not possessing the other *dharmas* of the Āryans, is not a Pṛthagjana because the non-possession of these other *dharmas* is accompanied by the possession of the *kṣānti*. This is quite evident, for, in the contrary interpretation, the Buddha the Blessed One, not possessing the *dharmas* of the "family" of the Śrāvakas and Pratyekabuddhas (vi.23), would be a Pṛthagjana.

Very well. But then the Śāstra would say "The state of Pṛthagjana is the absolute non-possession (*alābha eva*) of the Āryan dharmas" and not ". . . the non-possession (*alābha*) . . ."

[The Sarvāstivādins:] The Śāstra expresses itself very well, for the *ekapadas* (*Nirukta*, 2.2) permit a restrictive sense and the particle *eva* is not necessary: for example *abbhakṣa* signifies "that which lives *solely* on water," and *vāyubhakṣa*, "that which lives *solely* on wind."

2. According to another opinion,[205] the state of Pṛthagjana is the non-possession of the first stage of the Path of Seeing, *duḥkhe dharmajñānakṣānti* and its concomitant *dharmas* (vi.25).

[Objection.] In this hypothesis, at the sixteenth moment (*mārge'nvayajñāna*), the saint will be a Pṛthagjana and not an Āryan, for at this moment, the initial *kṣānti* is lost.[206]

No, for the non-possession of the *kṣānti* which constitutes the state of Pṛthagjana has been absolutely destroyed in the first stage.

[Objection.] The *kṣānti* in question is threefold: of the family of the Śrāvakas, of the family of the Pratyekabuddhas, and of the family of the Buddhas (vi.23). Of which of these three types are you speaking in your definition of the state of Pṛthagjana?

We mean to speak of three types of *kṣānti*.

Be careful! The Buddha, not possessing the three types of *kṣānti*, would then be a Pṛthagjana!

We intend to speak of the non-possession of the *kṣānti* which is not accompanied by possession . . . and thus following, as above, to the example "that which lives solely on water," "that which lives solely on wind."

Hence the effort attempted in order to avoid the objection: "Be careful! To believe you, a person in possession of *duhkhe dharmajñānakṣānti* would be a Pṛthagjana . . ." is in vain. The best explanation is that of the Sautrāntikas. To them, the state of Pṛthagjana is a series in which the *dharmas* of the Āryans have not arisen.

***

How does non-possession perish?

> 40c-d. It is abandoned through acquisition (*prāpti*), and through passing to another stage.

For example, the non-possession of the Path, which constitutes the state of Pṛthagjana, is abandoned (1) when one acquires the Path,[207] and (2) when one passes to another stage.[208] The same holds for the non-possession of the other *dharmas*.[209]

[Objection:] Non-possession is abandoned (1) when one produces the non-possession of non-possession, that is to say, when, changing one's stage of existence, one ceases to possess the state of Pṛthagjana; and (2) when the possession of non-possession is cut off, that is to say, when, acquiring the Path, one cuts off the state of Pṛthagjana.

Does this mean that there is possession of possession and non-possession, and that there is non-possession of possession and non-possession?

Yes. There is possession and non-possession of possession and non-possession, which is called "secondary possession" (*anuprāpti*), or "secondary non-possession." One then distinguishes between *mūla-prāti* and *anuprāpti* or *prāptiprāpti*.

Doesn't this doctrine lead to infinite progression?

No, for one possessess possession through the fact of possession of possession and vice versa. There is possession of the one through the fact of the other. Let us explain. When a certain *dharma* is produced in a given person, three *dharmas* arise together, namely: 1) this *dharma* itself, which is called the *mūladharma*; 2) the *prāpti* of this *mūla-dharma*; and 3) the *prāpti* of this *prāpti*. The person in question possesses the *mūladharma* and the *prāpti* of the *prāpti* by the fact of the arising of the *prāpti*; he possesses this *prāpti* by the fact of the arising of the *prāpti*.[210] Hence there is no infinite progression. When a good or a defiled[211] *dharma* arises, at this very moment three *dharmas* arise together, inclusive of this good or defiled *dharma*, namely: the *mūladharma*, its *prāpti*, and the *prāpti* of this *prāpti*[212] which is the *prāpti* of the *prāptiprāpti* of the first moment, plus three *anuprāptis* through the fact that one is in possession of the three aforementioned *prāptis*. In this third moment eighteen *dharmas* arise together, namely nine *prāptis*: the *prāptis* of the three *dharmas* produced in the first moment, *prāptis* of the six *dharmas* produced in the second moment, plus nine *anuprāptis* through the fact that one in in possession of the nine aforementioned *prāptis*.

Thus the *prāptis* continue increasing in number from moment to moment.[213] The *prāptis* of present and future defilements (*kleśa* and *upakleśa*), and of innate (*upapattilābhika*, ii.71b) good *dharmas* with the *dharmas* that are associated (*saṁprayukta*, ii.53c-d) and co-existent (*sahabhū*, ii.50b) with them throughout beginningless and endless transmigration, arise, from moment to moment, in an infinite number. If one considers the series of one single being in the course of transmigration, those *prāptis* which arise at each moment are infinite in number. Considering all beings together, they (i.e., the *prāptis*) are without measure, and without limit. Happily, they possess a great quality: they are non-material, and give way one to the other. If they were material, there could not be found enough room in the universe for the *prāptis* of one single being, and even less for the *prāptis* of two beings!

***

What is "genre" or sameness of class designation?[214]

> 41a. *Sabhāgatā* is that which causes resemblance between living beings.[215]

1. There exists an entity called *sabhāgatā*, a *dharma* by virtue of which living beings, as well as the *dharmas* "that fall into the series of living beings" (*sattvasaṁkhyāta*, i.10), have resemblence between them (*Vibhāṣā, TD* 27, p. 138a9).

2. The Śāstra (*Jñānaprasthāna*, etc.) designates this entity by the name of *nikāyasabhāga*: the author uses the term *sabhāgatā* for metric reasons.

3. *Sabhāgatā* is of two types, general and particular. The first is found in all living beings: by virtue of it, there is resemblance of any living being with all other living beings. This is called *sattvasabhāgatā*.

The second has numerous subdivisions: each of these subdivisions is found only in certain beings. Living beings are differenciated according to their spheres of existence, the different stages of these spheres, their realm of rebirth (*gati*, iii.4), their wombs (iii.9), their caste (*jāti*, as Brahmins, etc.), their sex, the state of Upāsaka (iv.14), Bhikṣu, Śaikṣa, or Arhat, etc.[216] This holds as well for *sabhāgatās*, by virtue of which each living being of a certain species resembles living beings of this same species.

4. There is, furthermore, *sabhāgatā* of *dharmas* that belong to living beings, *dharmasabhāgatā*, which in turn distinguishes the *skandhas*, the *āyatanas* and the *dhātus: skandhasabhāgatā*, etc., *rūpaskandhasabhāgatā*, etc.

5. In the absence of a separate entity, namely *sabhāgatā*, how does one explain general ideas (*buddhi*) and expressions (*prajñapti*), such as "living beings," etc., applied to some beings that differ one from another? In this same way, it is solely by reason of *dharmasabhāgatā* that the ideas and expressions, "*skandha*," "*dhātus*," etc., are justified.[217]

6. Do we conclude that one transmigrates, that one dies and is born without abandoning and without taking up a certain *sattvasabhāgatā* (state of a human being, etc.)? There are four alternatives: 1. to die in a place (Kāmadhātu for example) and be reborn in the same place: the *sabhāgatā* remains the same, regardless of transmigration; 2. to enter into one's predetermined realm of rebirth (*niyāmāvakrānti*, vi.26a): without there being transmigration, there is yet the abandoning of the *sabhāgatā* of the Pṛthagjanas and the acquisition of the *sabhāgatā* of the Saints; 3. to die in one realm of rebirth, the human realm of rebirth, etc., and to be reborn in another realm of rebirth; 4. all other cases.

[The Sautrāntikas do not admit the existence of a *dharma* called *sabhāgatā* and present many objections to it.]

1. If a certain entity called "the genre of Pṛthagjana" exists, for what purpose do we imagine the state of Pṛthagjana consisting of the non-possession of the Āryadharmas (ii.40c)? Someone will be a Pṛthagjana through the genre of Pṛthagjana in the way that someone is a human through the genre "human" for the Vaibhāṣikas do not imagine a state of human different from the genre "human."

2. Ordinary people do not recoginize *sabhāgatā* through the direct preception of the senses (*pratyakṣa*); they do not infer the existence of the *sabhāgatā* through an operation of the intelligence (*prajñā*), for *sabhāgatā* does not exercise any action by which one could know it: although people do not know anything of *sattvasabhāgatā* they recognize the non-difference of the species of beings. Hence, what would be the use in supposing that a *sabhāgatā* exists?

3. Why does the School refuse *sabhāgatā* to things that are not living beings, such as rice and corn, gold and iron, mango and bread-fruit trees?

4. The different *sabhāgatās* that the School recognizes, *sabhāgatās*

of living beings, of spheres, of realms of rebirth, etc., are distinct one from another. Yet one has, for all of them, common ideas and designations: all are *sabhāgatās*.

5. [The Sarvāstivādins are the proponents of the doctrine of the Vaiśeṣikas.] The Vaiśeṣikas admit a certain entity (*padārtha*) called "sameness" (*sāmānya*), by virtue of which there is produced, with regard to things, similar ideas and designations; they believe also in another entity, called "difference" (*viśeṣa*), from whence proceeds specific ideas and designations with regard to different species.

The Vaibhāṣikas protest that their theory is not to be confused with that of the Vaiśeṣikas, who believe that genre or sameness (*sāmānya*) a unique substance (*padārtha*), exists in a multitude of individuals. Hence even if they approve of the Vaiśeṣikas admitting genre (*sāmānya*), they still condemn their interpretation of it. As for *sabhāgatā*, it exists in and of itself (as a *dravya*), for the Blessed One, speaking of a murderer who is reborn in hell, continues, saying, "If he is reborn here, if he obtains the *sabhāgatā* of humans . . ."[218]

[The Sautrāntikas answer:] By expressing itself in this way, the Sūtra does not teach the existence of a thing in and of itself called *sabhāgatā*. What then does the Sūtra designate by the word *sabhāgatā*? By the expression *sabhāgatā* of humans," etc., the Sūtra means a similarity in the manner of being: in the same way, *sabhāgatā* of rice, corn, beans, etc.

This opinion is not admitted by the Vaibhāṣikas.[219]

***

What is non-consciousness (*āsaṁjñika*)?

> 41b-c. Non-consciousness is that which, among the Non-conscious Ones, arrests the mind and its mental states.[220]

Among the beings who take birth among the Non-Conscious Ones, i.e., the non-conscious gods, there is a *dharma* that arrests the mind and its mental states, and which is called "non-consciousness." By this *dharma*, the mind and future *dharmas* are, for a certain time, hindered from being produced and do not have the power to arise. This *dharma* is similar to what arrests the water of a river, that is, to a dike.

This *dharma* is exclusively

41d. Retribution.

It is exclusively the retribution of non-conscious absorption (*asaṁjñisamāpatti*, ii.42a).[221]

Where do these non-conscious gods reside?

41d. They live in Bṛhatphala.

In the heaven of the Bṛhatphalas there is a raised place which is the dwelling of the Non-Conscious Ones, in the same way as the *dhyānāntarikā*, the dwelling of the Mahābrahmā gods, is raised within the heaven of the Brahmapurohitas (iii.2c;[222] *Vibhāṣā, TD* 27, p. 784b5).

Are the Non-Conscious Ones called this because they are always non-conscious, or are they sometimes conscious?

They are conscious at birth and at death (iii.42; *Vibhāṣā, TD* 27, p. 784c8);[223] they are called non-conscious because their consciousness is suspended for a very long time. When, after this long time, they produce a consciousness again, they die. As it says in the Sūtra "When they produce consciousness again, they die, like a person awakening after sleep."

Dying in the non-conscious heaven, they are necessarily reborn in Kāmadhātu and nowhere else. (1) In fact, the force of *asaṁjñisamāpatti* (ii.42a), by which these beings are born among the Non-Conscious Ones, is exhausted; they have not been in a position to practice *asaṁjñisamāpatti*: hence they die, as arrows fall to the ground when their impetus is spent. (2) On the other hand, beings who are reborn among the Non-Conscious Ones necessarily possess an action "retributive in Kāmadhātu" and "retributive in the second existence" (iv.50b). In this same way beings who are reborn in Uttarakuru (iii.90c-d) necessarily possesses an action retributive in a heavenly realm of rebirth immediately after their existence in Uttarakuru.

***

The Mūlaśāstra says, "What are the two *samapāttis* or absorptions?[224] They are *asaṁjñisamāpatti*, the non-conscious absorption, and *nirodhasamāpatti*, the absorption of extinction."[225]

What is the non-conscious absorption?

In the same way that *āsaṁjñika* is a *dharma* that arrests the mind and its mental states,

42a. The same for the non-conscious absorption.

The non-conscious absorption is an absorption in which the ascetic is non-conscious, or in an absorption free from consciousness.

The word "the same" shows that this absorption, like *āsaṁjñika*, arrests the mind and its mental states.

To which *bhūmi* does it belong?

42b. In the Fourth Dhyāna.

In order to cultivate this absorption, the ascetic should have entered the Fourth Dhyāna.

Why does one cultivate it?

42c. Through desire for deliverance.

The ascetic falsely imagines that *āsaṁjñika*, the non-consciousness that constitutes the result of the non-conscious absorption, is true deliverence.

Āsaṁjñika, being retribution, is necessarily morally neutral. As for the non-conscious absorption, it is

42d. Good.

It produces as its retributive result the five *skandhas* of a non-conscious god, who, as we know, is conscious at birth and at death.

To what category does it belong from the point of view of retribution?

42e. Solely retribution in the next existence.

It is not "retributive in this life" or "retributive later;" it is no longer of "unnecessary retribution" (iv.50).

Without doubt, an ascetic can fall from this absorption after having produced it; but, [according to the Vaibhāṣikas,] he will produce it again and be reborn among the Non-Conscious Ones. This is to say that the ascetic who takes possession of this absorption will certainly not enter into a "predestined" realm of rebirth (vi.26a).[226]

This absorption is cultivated only by Pṛthagjanas.

42f. Not by Āryans.

The Āryans consider this absorption as a precipice, a calamity, and do not value entering it.

On the contrary, Pṛthagjanas identify non-consciousness (*āsaṁjñika*) with true deliverance; they have no idea of "going out" with respect to it; hence they cultivate the absorption that leads to it. But Āryans know that the impure cannot be true deliverance. Hence they do not cultivate this absorption.

When Āryans enter into the Fourth Dhyāna, do they obtain the *prāpti* of this past and future absorption, the same as one obtains the *prāpti* of the Fourth Dhyāna of the past and the future as soon as one enters into the Fourth Dhyāna?[227]

Non-Āryans do not obtain the *prāpti* of the non-conscious absorption of the past and future.

Why?

Having cultivated it many time previously, this absorption can only be realized through great effort; as it is not mind,

42g. It is obtained in one time period.

One takes possession of this absorption, not in the past, not in the future, but in one time period, that is, in the present, as is also the case for the *prātimokṣa* discipline (iv.35). In the second moment of this absorption, and in all the moments that follow the obtaining of this absorption until the moment when it ends, one possesses it in the past and in the present. On the other hand, since this absorption is not mind, it is impossible for one to acquire a future *prāpti* of this absorption.[228]

***

What is *nirodhasamāpatti* or the "absorption of extinction?"[229]

43a. In the same way, the absorption that bears the name of *nirodha* or "extinction."

That is to say, the absorption of extinction is like *āsaṁjñika*, the non-conscious absorption: it is a *dharma* that arrests the mind and its mental states.

What are the differences between the non-conscious absorption and the absorption of extinction?

43b. It is viewed as tranquility;

1. Āryans cultivate this absorption because they consider it as the absorption of tranquility.[230] One cultivates the non-conscious absorption because one regards non-consciousness as being deliverance (*niḥsaraṇa-mokṣa*).

43c. Arisen from Bhavāgra;

2. It belongs to the sphere of Bhavāgra, that is, one penetrates it upon leaving *naivasaṁjñānāsamjñāyatana* absorption (viii.4), whereas the non-conscious absorption belongs to the sphere of the Fourth Dhyāna.

43d. Good;

3. It is good; it is not neutral or defiled, for its originating cause is good (iv.9b).

43e. Of two retributions and neutral;

4. It admits of two types of retribution, being either "retributive in the next existence," or "retributive later" (*aparaparyāyavedanīya*, iv.50).[231] Its retribution is also unnecessary, for the ascetic who has practiced it can obtain Nirvāṇa in the present existence.

Of what does its retribution consist?

This absorption produces the four *skandhas* of Bhavāgra, i.e., an existence in Bhavāgra (iii.3).

> 43f. Āryans

5. It is produced only by Āryans, not by Pṛthagjanas. These latter cannot produce it (1) because they fear annihilation,[232] and (2) because this absorption can only be produced through the power of the Path: in fact, it is the ascetic who has seen Nirvāṇa who is determined to obtain it.[233]

> 43g. It is obtained through effort.

6. Although obtained by the Āryans, it is not obtained merely through the fact of detachment. It is only realized through effort.

One does not possess this absorption in the past or in the future; this point has been explained in the matter of the non-conscious absorption.

> 44a. In that which concerns the Muni, it is obtained through Bodhi itself.

The Buddha obtains the absorption of extinction at the moment when he becomes a Buddha, that is, at the moment of *kṣayajñāna* (vi.67). No quality of the Buddha is obtained through effort; all of his qualities are acquired through the simple fact of detachment: as soon as he desires it, the mass of qualities arise at will.[234]

How is it that the Blessed One, without having formerly produced this absorption (i.e., *nirodhasamāpatti*), would become, at the moment of Bodhi (*kṣayajñana*), "twofold delivered," that is, delivered from the obstacles of the defilements and delivered from the obstacles to absorption (*samāpattyāvaraṇa*, vi.64)?

He becomes "twofold delivered" exactly as if he had previously produced this absorption, for he possesses the power of realizing this absorption whenever he wishes (*Vibhāṣā, TD* 27, p. 780b26).

The Masters of the West (*Pāścātya*)[235] maintain that the Bodhisattva first produced this absorption in the state of Śaikṣa, and then obtained Bodhi. Why do we not adopt this opinion?

This would be to follow the *Netrīpadaśāstra* of the Sthavira Upagupta, which says, "One who, after having produced the absorption of extinction, produces *kṣayajñāna*, should be called a Tathāgata."

44b. But not previously.

The Vaibhāṣikas of Kaśmīr deny that the Bodhisattva produces the absorption of extinction before producing *kṣayajñāna.*

44c. For the Muni conquers Bodhi in thirty-four moments.[236]

The School admits in fact (*Vibhāṣā TD* 7, p. 780b10) that the Bodhisattva obtains Bodhi in thirty-four moments, namely sixteen moments that constitute the "comprehension of the Truths" (*satyābhisamaya,* vi.27) and eighteen moments that constitute the abandoning of the defilements relative to Bhavāgra (=*naivasaṁjñānāsaṁjñāyatana*), i.e., nine *ānantaryamārgas* and nine *vimuktimārgas* (vi.44). The eighteenth moment is *kṣayajñāna.* These thirty-four moments suffice, for, before entering into the "comprehension of the Truths," the Bodhisattva, still a Pṛthagjana (iii.41), detaches himself through the worldly path from all spheres, with the exception of Bhavāgra. The eighteen moments form a path during the course of which the Saint does not produce a mind of a different nature, that is, a worldly, impure mind, for example the mind entering the absorption of extinction. Hence the Bodhisattva, in the stage of Śaikṣa, that is, before becoming an Arḥat, enters the comprehension of the Truths and the eighteenth moment of the abandoning of Bhavāgra, but he does not produce the absorption of extinction.

The Foreigners (*bahirdeśaka*)[237] say, "What harm is there in the Bodhisattva producing this impure mind?"

In this hypothesis, the Bodhisattva oversteps his resolution (*vyutthānāśayaḥ syāt*);[238] now the Bohisattva does not overstep his resolution.

This is true, he does not overstep his resolution; but this does not mean that he would not overstep the Pure Path in producing an impure mind.

How, in this hypothesis, would he not overstep his resolution?

He has taken upon himself the resolution (*Madhyamāgama, TD* 1, p. 777a12), "I shall not leave this sitting position[239] before I obtain the destruction of all the defilements." Now he does not overstep this resolution, for it is in one "sitting" (*āsana,* vi.24a-b) that he realizes his goal.[240]

Although the two absorptions, the non-conscious absorption and the absorption of extinction, present many differences, they have this in common:

> 44d. But these two absorptions take place in persons in Kāmadhātu and Rūpadhātu.[241]

To deny that the non-conscious absorption is produced in Rūpadhātu is to contradict the Mūlaśāstra,[242] which says, "There is an existence in Rūpadhātu that does not admit of the five *skandhas*,[243] namely (1) the existence of beings in Rūpadhātu who, conscious by nature, enter into the non-conscious absorption and into the absorption of extinction,[244] and (2) the existence of beings in Rūpadhātu who are in possession of *āsaṁjñika*, and who are born among the Non-Conscious Ones."

From this text it results that the two absorptions are cultivated by beings of Kāmadhātu and Rūpadhātu.

There is however this difference between the two absorptions:

> 44e. The absorption of extinction is, for the first time, among humans.

A person who has never produced the non-conscious absorption can produce this absorption either in Kāmadhātu or in Rūpadhātu; but it is necessary to be a human in order to produce the absorption of extinction for the first time. A human, an Āryan, who has produced this absorption can fall from it, and losing possession (*prāpti*) of it, can be reborn in Rūpadhātu and produce this absorption anew.

But the question is raised whether one can fall from the absorption of extinction, which is similar (*sadṛśa*) to Nirvāṇa.

Yes, [answer the Vaibhāṣikas;] to deny falling is to contradict the *Udāyi-sūtra*,[245] which says, "Brothers, a Bhikṣu is endowed with morality, with absorption, and with discernment. It is possible for him to enter many times into the absorption of extinction and leave it. If, in this life, he does not attain *ājñā*,[246] nor attain it at the moment of his death; but after the destruction of his body, going beyond the gods of gross eating, he is reborn in a heavenly mental body; and thus reborn it is possible for him to then enter many times into the absorption of extinction and leave it."

This text shows in fact that one can fall from *nirodhasamāpatti.*

On the one hand the Buddha would have us understand that the mental body that Śāriputra speaks of belongs to Rūpadhātu.[247] On the other hand, the absorption of extinction is of the realm of Bhavāgra, the highest state of Ārūpyadhātu. If a Bhikṣu who possesses it does not fall from it, and if he does not lose it, he will not be able to repeat his birth in Rūpadhātu.[248]

According to another school,[249] the absorption of extinction also belongs to the Fourth Dhyāna and is not subject to falling.

This opinion is not correct. This absorption does not belong to the Fourth Dhyāna, for the Sūtra teaches that one acquires nine absorptions one after the other.[250]

How then do you explain the *vyukrāntaka* absorption (viii.18c) in which the ascetic passes over different stages of absorption?

The rule of the successive production of the absorptions concerns the beginner.[251] He who has acquired mastery passes over the absorptions at will.

***

There are differences between these two absorptions:

1. from the point of view of their spheres: the first is of the Fourth Dhyāna, the second of Bhavāgra (*naivasaṁjñānāsaṁjñāyatana*)

2. from the point of view of their antecedents or preparations (*prayoga*): the first proceeds from the idea of deliverance falsely identified with non-consciousness; the second, from the idea of stillness;

3. from the point of view of the person (*saṁtāna*): the first is produced in a Pṛthagjana; the second, in an Āryan;

4. from the point of view of the nature of their retribution: the first produces birth among the Non-Conscious Ones; the second, birth in Bhavāgra (*Kathavatthu*, xv.10);

5. from the point of view of the characteristic of their retribution. The retribution of the first is necessary, and takes place in the next existence; the retribution of the second is necessary in the case of an Anāgāmin, but not necessary in the case of an Arhat; and when it does take place, it takes place in the next existence or later;

6. from the point of view of its production for the first time. The first is indifferently produced within the two spheres of existence; the second, only among humans.

***

The characteristic common to these two absorptions is the arresting of the mind and its mental states.

Why is the first called "absorption free from ideas" (*asaṁjñisamāpatti*) and the second "absorption of extinction of ideas and sensations" (*saṁjñāveditanirodhasamāpatti*)?

Because the preparation from the first merely opposes ideas,[252] whereas preparation for the second opposes both ideas and sensations. In the same way *paracittajñāna* (vii.5b), "knowledge of the mind of another," bears on the mental states of someone else: it receives this restrictive name because its preparation alludes only to the mind of another.[253]

***

In the two absorptions, the mind is interrupted for a long time.[254] How, upon coming out of this absorption, can a new mind be born from a mind destroyed for a long time?[255]

The Vaibhāṣikas find no difficulty in this: past *dharmas* exist (v.25). Consequently the mind previous to this absorption, the mind-in-absorption (*samāpatticitta*) or "the mind of entry into the absorption" is the similar and immediate cause (*samanantarapratyana*, ii.62) of the mind after the absorption or the "mind-of-leaving" (*vyutthānacitta*; *Vibhāṣā, TD* 27, p. 777b18).

[The Sautrantikas reason as follows:] When a person is born in

Ārūpyadhātu, *rūpa* or matter is cut off for a long period of time (iii.81b): if this person is then reborn in Kāmadhātu or in Rūpadhātu, his new *rūpa* does not proceed from the series of *rūpa* previously interrupted for a long time, but rather, from the mind. In the same way, the mind of leaving the absorption does not have for its cause the mind previous to the absorption: it is born from "a body possessing organs". This is why the Ancient Masters said, "Two *dharmas* are the seed one of the other: these two *dharmas* are a mind and a body possessing organs."

Vasumitra says in the treatise entitled *Paripṛcchā*:[256] "This difficulty, i.e., 'How is the mind reborn after absorption?', interests those who consider the absorption of extinction as free from mind. But I maintain that this absorption is accompanied by a subtle mind. The difficulty does not exist for me."[257]

The Bhadanta Ghoṣaka regards this opinion as wrong. In fact, if any consciousness (*vijñāna*) resides in this absorption, there would be contact (*sparśa*) through the coming together of the three, consciousness, organ, and object; by reason of contact, there would be sensation (*vedanā*) and ideas (*saṁjñā*) (iii.30b). As the Blessed One teaches, "By reason of the mental organ and the *dharmas*, mental consciousness arises; by the coming together of these three, there is contact; sensation, ideas, and volition arise at the same time."[258] Hence, if one admits that the mind (*vijñāna, citta*) continues to exist in this absorption, sensation and ideas will not be arrested in it. Now this absorption is called the extinction of sensation and ideas (*saṁjñāveditanirodha*).

[Vasumitra answers:] The Sūtra says, "By reason of sensation, there is thirst," and yet, although Arhats experience sensation, thirst does not arise in them. The same here: every contact is not a cause of sensation.

This reasoning is not conclusive. The Sūtra, in fact, specifies, "Thirst arises by reason of sensation born of contact which is accompanied by ignorance" (iii.27).[259] Whereas it says, "Sensation arises by reason of contact." Hence, say the Vaibhāṣikas, the mind is interrupted in the absorption of extinction.

[Vasumitra asks:] If this absorption is completely free of mind, how is it an absorption (*samāpatti*)?

It is called an absorption because it puts the primary elements into a state of equilibrium[260] contrary to the production of the mind; or rather because ascetics penetrate (*samapadyante*) it by the power of their minds: it is for this reason that the Dhyānas, etc., are called *samāpattis*.

***

Should one consider the two absorptions as existing in and of themselves (*dravyatas*)?

Yes, [answer the Sarvāstivādins,] for they thwart the arising of the mind.

No, [answer the Sautrāntikas,] it is not what you term "absorption" that hinders the arising of the mind; rather, it is the "mind in absorption" (*samāpatticitta*), the mind that preceeds the state of absorption: this mind, being opposed to the arising of the mind, causes other minds to not arise for a certain time. The mind of absorption renders the person[261] or series contrary to, and unfitted to the arising of the mind. What is called "absorption" is simply the non-existence of the mind for a certain period of time; not a thing in and of itself (*dravyadharma*), but a "thing of designation" (*prajñaptidharma*).

[The Sarvāstivādins:] How can an absorption be conditioned (*saṁskṛta*) if it is not a thing in and of itself?

This "non-existence of the mind" was not realized before the mind of absorption; it ceases when the ascetic produces anew the mind (*vyutthānacitta*: the mind leaving the absorption). One can then, in a manner of speaking, designate it as being "conditioned," since it begins and ends. Or rather, what we call "absorption" is the condition of the person, a condition that results from the mind of absorption.

The same holds for non-consciousness (*āsaṁjñika*, ii.41b-c). *Āsaṁjñika* is not a thing in and of itself that hinders the arising of the mind; but we designate by this term the state of non-consciousness of the Non-Conscious gods, a state that results from a certain mind.

The Vaibhāṣikas do not agree with this opinion; they maintain that *āsaṁjñika* and the two absorptions are things in and of themselves.[262]

***

What is the vital organ?

45a. *Jīvita* is life (*āyus*).[263]

In fact, the Abhidharma[264] says, "What is the *jīvitendriya*? The *āyus* of the three spheres of existence."

What sort of *dharma* is the *āyus*?

45b. The support of warmth and consciousness.

For the Blessed One said, "When life, warmth and consciousness leave the body, the body lies abandoned, like wood, lacking feeling.[265]

There exists then a distinct *dharma*, a support of warmth and of consciousness, a cause of the duration of the series, named *āyus*.[266]

***

[The Sautrāntikas deny that the vital organ exists in and of itself.]

[1. The Sautrāntikas:] If the *āyus* supports warmth and consciousness, what supports it?

[The Vaibhāṣikas:] It is supported by warmth and consciousness.

[The Sautrāntikas:] If these three *dharmas*,—life, warmth, and consciousness, —mutually support one another and continue to exist by means of this mutual support, how do they come to an end? Which perishes first, the destruction of which entails the destruction of the others? For if one of them does not perish first, then these three *dharmas* will be eternal and will not perish.

[The Vaibhāṣikas:] The *āyus* is supported by means of actions; the *āyus* has been projected through actions and continues to exist as long as the projection of action allows it to do so.

[The Sautrāntikas:] If this is so, why admit that warmth and consciousness are supported by actions? What do we have to do with the *āyus*?

[The Vaibhāṣikas:] That which is supported by action is, in its nature, retribution. If the consciousness were supported by action, all consciousness from the womb to death, would be retribution: and this is false. Hence the necessity of the *āyus*, supported by action, the support of warmth and consciousness.

[The Sautrāntikas:] You say then that action supports warmth and that warmth supports consciousness. Then the *āyus* is useless.

[The Vaibhāṣikas:] The *āyus* is necessary, for warmth is absent in Ārūpyadhātu. What is the support of consciousness in Ārūpyadhātu if the *āyus* does not exist?

[The Sautrāntikas:] In Ārūpyadhātu, consciousness is supported by action.

[The Vaibhāṣikas:] Do you have the right to change your mind? Sometimes you maintain that the consciousness is supported by warmth, and sometimes you maintain that it is supported by actions.[267] But on the other hand, you have admitted that one should avoid the conclusion that all consciousnesses, from the womb to death, are retribution. Consequently the *āyus* exists, and it is the support of warmth and consciousness.

[2. The Sautrāntikas:] We do not deny the existence of the *āyus*. We only say that the *āyus* is not a thing in and of itself.

[The Vaibhāṣikas:] Then what is the *dharma* that you call *āyus*?

[The Sautrāntikas:] It is a certain power that the action of a previous existence places in a being at the moment of its conception, a power through which the *skandhas* renew themsleves for a determined length of time in this homogeneous series that constitutes an existence (*nikāyasabhāga*, ii.41), in the same way a seed places a certain power in the sprout by which the plant develops to maturity. In this same way too a shot arrow has a certain power which causes it to travel for a certain period of time.

[The Vaibhāṣikas believe that] a certain sort of *guṇa* or "quality," called *saṁskāra* or *vega* (impetus) arises in the arrow. By the force of this *guṇa*, the arrow travels without stopping until the moment it falls.[268]

The *saṁskāra* is unique; on the one hand, the arrow does not encounter any obstacle: hence no difference is possible in the speed of the arrow. On the other hand, the arrow will not fall. Would you say the the "wind" creates an obstacle to the *saṁskāra*? The "wind" which creates an obstacle is the same either far or near, and so the arrow would either fall at first, or it will never fall.

The Vaibhāṣikas maintain that the *āyus* is a thing in and of itself.[269]

[ii. How Death takes Place.]

Does death take place solely through the exhaustion of life?

The *Prajñaptiśāstra*[270] says, "It happens that one dies through the exhaustion of life without one dying through the exhaustion of merit. Four alternatives: 1. death through exhaustion of action that ripened in life; 2. death through the exhaustion of actions that ripened in objects of enjoyment;[271] 3. death through the exhaustion of these two types of actions; and 4. death through the fact of not avoiding causes that harm, for example, excess of food."

We must add death due to the abandoning of the *āyuḥsaṁskāra* (ii.10).[272]

When life is exhausted, the exhaustion of actions that ripen in the objects of enjoyment has no efficacy for death; and vice versa. Consequently the third alternative should be understood as "death because the two types of actions are exhausted."

[iii. Death before its proper time (*akālamaraṇa*, iii.85c).]

The *Jñānaprasthāana (TD* 26, p. 997b28) says, "Should one say of the *āyus* that it is 'dependent on the series,' or that 'it lasts once it has arisen?' The *āyus* is of the first category for beings in Kāmadhātu who are not in one of the two absorptions (*asaṁjñisamāpatti* and *nirodhasamāpatti*); but it is of the second category for beings in Kāmadhātu who are in the two absorptions, and for beings in Rūpadhātu and Ārūpyadhātu."

What is the meaning of this passage?

If the *āyus* is killed when the body is killed, then the *āyus* is "bound to the body-series." If the body cannot be damaged, then the *āyus* lasts all the time for which it has been produced, and one says that the *āyus* lasts once it has arisen.[273]

The Masters of Kaśmīr say that the first type of *āyus* is "subject to obstruction," but that the second is not subject to obstruction.

Thus there is premature death.[274]

According to the Sūtra, there are four modes of existence:[275] existence that can be destroyed by oneself and not by another, etc.[276] Four alternatives: 1. existence destroyed by oneself: certain beings in Kāmadhātu, namely the Krīḍāpradūṣika gods and the Manaḥpradūṣika gods[276] destroy their own existence through their excess of joy or anger; we must also add the Buddhas who enter into Nirvāṇa; 2. existences destroyed by others: beings in the womb and in eggs; 3. existences destroyed by oneself and by others: beings in Kāmadhātu in general; we must exclude beings in hell, beings in the intermediate state (iii.12), etc.; 4. existences that are neither destroyed by oneself nor by others: beings in the intermediate state, all beings in Rūpadhātu and Ārūpyadhātu, and a part of the beings in Kāmadhātu: beings in hell (iii.82), the inhabitants of Uttarakuru (iii.78c), persons in the absorption of kindness (vii.29), persons in the non-conscious absorption (ii.42, *Kathāvatthu*, xv.9); the Rājarṣi, that is, the Cakravartin who has left the householders's life; a messenger of the Buddha;[278] persons whom the Buddha prophesized would live a certain length of time:[279] Dharmila, Uttara, Gaṅgila,[280] the son of the merchant Yaśas, Kumāra, Jīvaka, etc.; the Bodhisattva in his last existence; the mother of the Bodhisattva pregnant with the Bodhisattva; the Cakravartin; the mother of the Cakravartin pregnant with the Cakravartin.

[Objection:] The Sūtra tells us of a question by Śāriputra and the Blessed One's answer to it: "'Lord, What are the beings whose existence cannot be destroyed either by themselves, or by others?' 'Śāriputra, beings who are born in Naivasaṁjñānāsaṁjñāyatana . . .'" that is, in the highest sphere of Ārūpyadhātu, Bhavāgra. How can you say, in the light of this passage, that the existence of all beings in Rūpadhātu and Ārūpyadhātu is protected from all destruction, either by themselves or others?

The School (*Vibhāṣā, TD* 27, p. 772a29) explains, "Beings in Rūpadhātu and the first three stages of Ārūpyadhātu can destroy their existence 'by themselves,'" that is, by a course of action within their own realm, and 'by others,' namely by a course of action belonging to the preliminary stages of a higher stage (vi.48, viii.22). But in the last stage of Ārūpyadhātu a course of action belonging to this stage and also of actions of a superior stage are both absent; hence the existence of beings who reside therein cannot be modified either by themselves or by others.

This answer appears weak to us; in fact, one can, in the last stage of Ārūpyadhātu practice a course of action belonging to the immediately lower stage (*akiñcanyāyatana*, viii.20). One must then admit another explanation (*Vibhāṣā*, ibid.). In his response to Śāriputa, the Buddha, by naming the beings of Naivasaṁjñānāsamjñāyatana, intends to designate all beings in Rūpadhātu and Arūpyadhātu, for in naming the last one designates the first. We can demonstrate that such is the usage. Sometimes Scripture names the first term of a list the totality of which is alluded to, for example, "The first *sukhopapatti* (iii.72), namely (*tadyathā*) the Brahmakāyika gods." We should then also understand, "the Brahmakāyikas, the Brahmapurohitas, and the Mahābrahmās." Sometimes Scripture names the last term, "The second *sukhopapatti*, namely the Ābhāsvara gods." We should then understand, "the Parīttābhas, the Apramāṇābhas, and the Ābhāsvaras."

But one can contest this explanation. In the two passages given above the word *tadyathā* is used to introduce an example. We must translate *tadyathā* not as "namely" but as "for example." It is a rule concerning examples that when one names one case one designates all similar cases. And we admit that, in the two above passages on the *sukhopapattis*, the Scripture designated all the terms of the list by naming only the first and the last. However the answer of the Blessed One to Śāriputra does not contain the word *tadyathā*.

We would say that this explanation does not introduce an example, for we find it in Sūtras that give a complete enumeration, "Material beings, diverse of body, diverse of ideas, namely (*tadyathā*) human beings and part of the gods . . ." (iii.6). Thus the word *tadyathā* introduces a definition (*upadarśanārtha*). Hence the Blessed One, in his answer to Śāriputra, designates the beginning by naming the end, that is, he is speaking of the totality of the two higher spheres.[281]

***

What are the characteristics of conditioned *dharmas*?

> 45c-d. Their characteristics are arising, old age, duration, and impermanence.[282]

These four *dharmas*, arising, old age, duration, and impermanance, are the characteristics of conditioned things. A *dharma* in which these characteristics are found is conditioned; a *dharma* in which they are not found is unconditioned.[283]

Arising produces or causes to produce conditioned things; duration stablizes them or causes them to last; old age makes them deteriorate; and impermanence destroys them.

Does not the Sūtra teach the existence of some three "conditioned characteristics" of conditioned things? The Sūtra says, in fact, "There are, oh Bhikṣus, three characteristics of conditioned things, which are themselves conditioned. What are these three? The production or origin of conditioned things is an object of consciousness; its disappearance and also its duration-modification is an object of consciousness."[284]

[The Vaibhāṣikas:] The Sūtra should enumerate four characteristics. The characteristic that it omits is the characteristic of duration or *sthiti*. Truth to tell, it does use *sthiti* in the compound, *sthityanyathātva*, "duration-modification;" but *sthityanyathātva* is an expression that signifies "old age." As the Sūtra says "production" (*utpāda*) in place of "arising" (*jāti*) and "disappearance" (*vyaya*) in place of "impermanence" (*anityatā*), in this same way it also says *sthityanyathātva* in place of "old age" (*jara*).

If the Sūtra specifies only three characteristics, it is because, with a view to rousing disgust among believers, it points out as the characteristics of conditioned things those *dharmas* which cause conditioned things to pass through the three time periods: the power of its arising causes it to pass from the future into the present; old age and impermanence cause it to pass from the present into the past, and, after old age has weakened it, impermanence finishes it. The School gives a comparision (*Vibhāṣā, TD* 27, p. 201b7): Suppose there is a man in a dark forest, and there are three enemies there who wish to kill him. The first causes this man to leave the forest; the second weakens him, and the third destroys his vital principle. Such is the role of the three characteristics with regard to conditioned things.[285] Duration, on the contrary, sustains conditioned things and causes them to last; this is why the Sūtra does not count it among the characteristics. Further, the unconditioned lasts eternally in its own nature: the characteristic of duration is not without resemblance to the persistence of the unconditioned. So in order to avoid any confusion, the Sūtra does not indicate duration as a characteristic of conditioned things.

[The Sautrāntikas think that] the Sūtra does name duration; it names it by associating it with old age: *sthityanyathātva*, that is to say, "*sthiti* and *anyathātva*."

What advantage is there, would you say, in making one single characteristic out of these two characteristics?

Persons are attracted to duration: in order to incite disgust with respect to duration, the Sūtra names it together with old age, like prosperity associated with black ears.[286]

Conclusion: there are four characteristics.

***

The arising, duration, etc., of any sort of *dharma* is also conditioned. They should also arise, last, grow old, and perish; they should then, in their turn, possess four characteristics: arising-of-arising, etc., which will be the secondary characteristics (*anulakṣaṇa*) of the *dharma* under consideration. These secondary characteristics, being conditioned, have in their turn four characteristics, and so we have infinite progression.

There is no infinite progression.

> 46a. They have in their turn characteristics termed arising-of-arising, duration-of-duration, etc.;

Four primary characteristics are as described above.

The four secondary characteristics (*anulakṣaṇa*) are arising-of-arising, duration-of-duration, old age-of-old age, and impermanence-of-impermanence.

All conditioned things are conditioned by these primary characteristics; these, in their turn, are conditioned by the four secondary characteristics.

You say that each of the primary characteristics should have, exactly as the *dharma* that it characterizes, four characteristics, and thus following: you do not understand that these are the activity, the operation (*vṛtti=dharmakāritra=puruṣakāra*, iv.58) of the different characteristics.

> 46b. The primary characteristic refers to eight *dharmas*, the secondary characteristic to one *dharma*.[287]

When a *dharma* arises—which we will term the principle *dharma* or *mūladharma*, a mind or a mental state—nine *dharmas*, including it, arise together: the principal *dharma*, four primary characteristics, and four secondary characteristics. The first primary characteristic, primary arising causes the principle *dharma*, plus three primary characteristics (duration, old age, and impermanence), plus the four secondary characteristics to arise: in all eight *dharmas*. It does not cause itself to be produced: it arises through the secondary characteristic arising-of-arising (*jāti-jāti*). In the same way a hen lays many eggs and each egg causes the birth of only one other chicken (*Vibhāṣā*, *TD* 27, p. 200c19); in the same way primary arising causes eight *dharmas* to arise, whereas arising-of-arising causes only one dharma to arise, namely primary arising.

It is the same for the other primary and secondary characteristics. Duration-of-duration causes primary duration to last, which in turn causes the principal *dharma* to last, as well as the three primary characteristics and the four secondary characteristics comprising duration-of-duration. The same for primary old age and impermanence which causes eight *dharmas* to age and to perish, and which age and perish themselves through the secondary characteristics which correspond to them, old age-of-old age and impermanence-of-impermanence.

Hence the characteristics themselves have characteristics called *anulakṣaṇas*; they are four in number and not sixteen, and there is no infinite progression.

***

The Sautrāntikas say:

i. All this is to analyze emptiness![288] Arising, duration, etc., are not entities, separate things in and of themselves. We know things either through direct perception, through inference, or through the testimony of Scripture: these three means of correct knowledge (*pramāṇa*) are missing with respect to these characteristics.

But, [reply the Sarvāstivādins,] the Sūtra says "The production of conditioned things is an object of consciousness . . ."[289]

Ignorant! You are attached to the words and err with regard to their meaning. The Blessed One however said that it is the meaning, and not the letter, that is the recourse.[290] As for the sense of this Sūtra, it is obvious.

Blinded by ignorance, foolish persons imagine that the series of conditioned phenomena (*saṁskāras*) is a "self" or belongs to a "self," and, as a consequence, they are attached to this series. The Blessed One wanted to put an end to this erroneous imagination and to the attachment which results from it: he wanted to show that the series is conditioned, that is to say, "produced through sucessive causes" (*pratītyasamutpanna*); and he taught the three marks of that which is produced through successive causes, saying that "Three *saṁskṛtalakṣaṇas* of the *saṁskṛta* are the object of consciousness." It is the series that the Blessed One means to designate as conditioned, for, quite clearly, he does not attribute the three marks to each moment of the series, since he says that these marks are the object of consciousness: in fact, the production of the moment, its aging, and its disappearance, are not the objects of consciousness; whatever is not the object of consciousness cannot be a mark.

If the Sūtra uses the word *saṁskṛta* twice, "There are three *saṁskṛtalakṣaṇas* of the *saṁskṛta*," this is in order that one should know that these three marks are not marks showing the presence of the *saṁskṛtas*, as herons indicate the nearness of water; nor are they qualitative signs of the *saṁskṛta*, as the marks of a young girl permit one to say that she is good or bad; no, when these marks are found on a thing, they show that this thing is a *saṁskṛta*. [Hence we would translate this canonical text as "Conditioned things possess three visible marks which show that it is conditioned, that is, produced through successive causes. These marks are its arising, its duration-modification, and its impermanence."]

ii. According to us, what one should understand by production or arising is the fact that the series begins; disappearance or impermanence is the end or cessation of the series; duration is the series continuing from its beginning until its end; evolution or old age is the modification of the continuous series, the difference between its successive states. It is from this point of view—that is, by considering arising, enduring, prolonging itself, and modifying itself—that the Blessed One says to Sundarananda, who is perpetually attentive to his states of mind, "Fine, my man! You know that your sensations arise, last, end, and disappear."[291]

We would then say,[292]

"Arising is the beginning of the series, disappearance is its rupture; duration is the series itself; evolution is the difference between its successive states."

And again,

"Arising is existence following upon non-existence; duration is the series; impermanence is the rupture of the series; and evolution is supposed to be the difference between the successive states of the series."

"Since the *dharmas* are momentary, would you say that the *dharmas* will perish [immediately] if duration is lacking? But [if the *dharmas* are momentary], they perish spontaneously: in vain you attribute duration to a momentary *dharma*."[293]

Consequently it is the series that the Sūtra refers to when it speaks of duration, and the definition of the Abhidharma (*Prakaraṇapāda*, *TD*, p. 694a26) is justified, "What is duration? The *saṁskāras* arisen and not destroyed." The nature of the "moment" (*kṣaṇadharmatā*) cannot be "arisen and not be destroyed."

Yet the *Jñānaprasthāna* (*TD* 26, p. 926b21) says, "Relative to one mind, what is production? It is arising. What is disappearance? It is death. What is evolution? It is old age."

But this passage of the Śāstra does not refer to a moment of the mind, but to the mind of a homogeneous existence (*nikāyasabhāgacitta*). [In a homogeneous existence (ii.41) the minds are multiple, but this multiplicity can be designated as being one mind.]

iii. However, since one cannot consider characteristics as things in and of themselves, one can say that each moment taken separately possesse the four characterisitcs.

In fact, (1) each moment exists after having been non-existent: its existence, following upon its non-existence, is its arising; (2) after having existed, it does not exist anymore: this is its disappearance; (3) the duration of the moment is the concatenation or the process of successive moments: in fact, if the subsequent moment resembles the previous moment, it is then its substitute: the previous moment still exists or still lasts. Thus the subsequent moment can be considered as the duration of the previous moment; (4) the dissimilitude of duration is its transformation.

Would you say that there is no dissimilitude when the successive moments are similar (*sadṛśa*)?

There is dissimilitude, as this results from the difference in time of the slower or faster falling of a *vajra* that is or is not projected, and which is projected with or without force: difference due in each case to a transformation or a difference of the primary elements of the *vajra*. When the *dharmas* succeed themselves in a homogeneous series, the difference is small; that is why, although they differ, they are considered as similar.

[The Sarvāstivādins object:] Your definition of characteristics does not hold for all conditioned *dharmas*. In fact, your definition of duration supposes a subsequent moment: but such a moment does not exist for the last moment of the mind of an Arhat. Hence the last moment of a sound, a flame, or an Arhat, has neither duration nor transformation.

We do not attribute duration to all conditioned *dharmas*! We say rather, that all duration is subject to transformation. The Blessed One teaches three characteristics, because, in certain cases, there are three characteristics. But, for the last moment of a flame, there is only producation and disappearance, and no duration or transformation.

In short, conditioned *dharmas* exist after having existed; after having existed, they no longer exist; the series of *dharmas* is their duration; dissimilarity of the series is their transformation. Such is the teaching that the Blessed One gives in the *Sūtra of the Three Characteristics*. This has nothing to do with things in and of themselves, arising, etc.

[iv. The Vaibhāṣikas object:] According to you, arising is the *dharma* itself in so far as it exists after having been non-existent. The *dharma* which is the "thing characterized" (*lakṣya*), would then be the characteristic (*lakṣaṇa*) also.

What is wrong with that? The marks of a Mahāpuruṣa are not different or distinct from the Mahāpuruṣa himself. The horns, the hump, the fetlock, the hoof, and the tail of a cow, which are its marks, are not different from the cow. The primary elements do not exist apart from their individual characteristics, solidity, etc. (i.12d). In this same way, for the Vaibhāṣikas who affirm the "momentariness" of the *dharmas*, the rising of smoke is none other than the smoke itself[294]

Let us look at this a bit closer. Although I grasp the individual nature of visible things, etc., which are conditioned, yet as long as I do not know the fact that they did not exist previously, that they will not exist later, and that their series transforms itself, then I shall not know their quality of being conditioned. Consequently, the quality of being conditioned does not have for a mark the quality of being conditioned, but rather previous non-existence, etc.[295] And there do not exist characteristics, things in and of themselves, distinct from visible things and other conditioned things.

v. If we admit the reality of characteristics, then since they are given as simultaneous, we would have to admit that one *dharma* arises, lasts, grows old and perishes at one and the same time.

It is in vain that the Sarvāstivādins pretend that the characteristics do not exercise their activity at one and the same time; that arising engenders before being born itself, being still in a future state, and that once it is born it does not engender any longer; that duration, old age, and impermanence exercise their activity when they are present and not in a future state; and that, consequently, the last three characteristics are active in a moment when the first is no longer active, so the four characteristics can be simultaneous without contradiction.

Let us first consider arising which, being future, engenders. One must examine whether a future *dharma*, supposing that it does exist, can be active. If future arising produces the operation of engendering, how can one say that it is future? In fact, according to the Vaibhāṣikas, a future *dharma* is one that does not exercise its activity. You would have to define future. On the other hand, when a *dharma* has arisen, has been engendered, and the operation of arising is past, how can you say that arising is then of the present? You would have to define present.

And either the activity of the other characteristics is exercised simultaneously, or their activity is exercised in succession. In the first hypothesis, whereas duration makes a *dharma* last, old age makes it age and impermanence destroys it: the *dharma* lasts, ages and perishes at the same time. As for the second hypothesis, to admit that the activity of these characteristics is not simultaneous is to admit three moments, and this is to renounce the doctrine of momentariness.[296]

[The Vaibhāṣikas answer:] For us, the *kṣaṇa* or moment is the time during which the characteristics have achieved their operation.[297]

Then explain why, in this hypothesis, duration, arising at the same time as old age and impermanence, accomplishes its operation of "making last that which should last" before old age and impermanence accomplish their operation of making things age and destroying them. If you answer that duration, being stronger, accomplishes its operation first, then we would ask how duration is weakened later in such a manner that, encountering old age and impermanence, it ages and perishes, not alone, but with the *dharma* that it should have made last.

You say perhaps that duration, having achieved its task, cannot perform it again, in the same way that arising, having engendered something, engenders no more. The comparison is not legitimate. The operation of arising consists of attracting the *dharma* that it should engender from the future and causing it to enter into the present; once the *dharma* has entered into the present, arising is incapable of making it enter therein again. But the operation of duration is to make the *dharma* "which should be made to last" last, of hindering the *dharma* which makes old age and perishing last. Duration is capable of making that which lasts last indefinitely. Consequently, duration is capable of repeating its operation.

By reason of what obstacle or from what adverse forces would the activity of duration cease once it has begun? Would these forces be old age and impermanence, old age weakening duration which impermanence then kills? Since, in this hypothesis, old age and impermanence are stronger than duration, it is proper then that they exercise their activity first. Further, according to your conception of duration and its role, it is through the activity of duration that, not only the principal *dharma*, but also old age and impermanence, last. Hence, when the activity of duration ends, the principal *dharma*, as well as old age and impermanence, cease their duration. We ask how, and with regard to what object, old age and impermanence exercise their activity of aging and causing to perish?

We do not see what it is that old age and impermanence have to do. It is through duration that one *dharma*, once it arises, does not perish for *a certain time*, does not perish as soon as it arises. If duration, its task completed, neglects the *dharma*, it will quite certainly not last any longer; that is to say, it perishes in and of itself.

We well understand the duration and impermanence of the *dharma*, "A *dharma*, after having arisen, does not perish," "A *dharma*, after having lasted, perishes." But how can one attribute old age to a *dharma*? Old age is a transformation, a dissimilarity between two states. Now, can one say of a single *dharma* that it becomes different from itself?

"If it remains this, it is not that; if it is transformed, it is no longer this. Hence the transformation of a *dharma* is impossible."

According to another School,[298] it is with the cooperation of external causes of destruction, fire or a hammer, etc., that the characteristics of impermanence causes certain *dharmas* to perish, as wood or a pot.

This is a theory as absurd as a sick person, who, after having taken a medicine, begs the gods to render it efficacious! In the logic of this system, it is the external causes of destruction which destroy, and the characteristic of impermanence serves no function.

The same School admits that the mind and its mental states, like sound or a flame, perish immediately, without any foreign causes intervening, through the chacteristic of impermanence. Impermanence and duration accomplish their operation at one and the same time: a *dharma* lasts and perishes at the same time. This is inadmissable.

We conclude that it is with regard to the series that the Blessed One teaches the characteristics of conditioned things. Thus understood, the Sūtra does not invite criticism, "There are three characteristics that show that the conditioned is conditioned, that it is produced through successive causes . . ."[299]

***

If arising engenders, in a future state, the *dharma* that it should engender, why do not all future *dharmas* arise at one and the same time?[300]

> 46c-d. Arising engenders the *dharma* that it should engender, but not without the cooperation of causes and conditions.[301]

Isolated arising does not have the force of engendering the *dharma* that it should engender independent of the cooperation of causes and conditions.

[1. Objection of the Sautrāntikas:] If this is the case, we rather believe that it is the cause that engenders, and not arising; this characteristic accompanies the *dharma* since the beginning of time and causes the *dharma* to arise when, finally, the cause of this *dharma* encounters another! When the causes are completed, the *dharma* arises; when they are not completed, it does not arise: what efficacy can we attribute to arising?[302]

[2. The Sarvāstivādins answer:] Do you pretend to know all the *dharmas* that exist? The nature of *dharmas* is subtle![303] Even though one sees them, one does not know their nature.

Moreover, in the absence of the characteristic "arising," the idea of "birth" (*jatabuddhi* = *jata iti*) would be absent.[304] And if arising is nothing other than the *dharma* itself exisitng after having been non-existent, the genitive "the arising of warmth" or "the arising of sensation" would not be justified; for this amounts to saying "the warmth of warmth" or "the sensation of sensation." This is the same for duration, old age, and extinction.

[3. Reply of the Sautrāntikas:] This theory leads you very far afield: in order to justify the idea of empty (*śūnya*), or the idea of the impersonal, you would admit the existence of an entity called "emptiness" or the existence of an entity called "non-self." And again, in order to justify the ideas of one and two, large and small, separate, associated and disassociated, this and that, existant, etc., you would admit, in agreement with the Vaiśeṣikas, a long series of entities: number, extension, individuality, conjunction, disjunction, quality of being that, quality of being this, existence, etc. It obliges you to create a "pot-ness" in order to justify the idea of a pot.

As for the genitive, you do not admit that the individual nature of warmth and warmth are different things, and yet you speak of the individual nature of warmth.

Hence you have not proven that "arising" is a thing in and of itself; you have not proven that this is not merely a designation of a *dharma* in so far as it exists after having been non-existent.

When I want to teach someone that a certain *dharma* exists which formerly did not exist, I say to him, "This *dharma* has arisen," and I designate this *dharma* as being born. Many *dharmas*,—warmth, sensation, etc.,—arise, that is to say, "exist after having been non-existent." Hence there are many arisings, that is, many *dharmas* arising. Since arising is multiple, in order to distinguish it from other arisings, so that my questioner knows that it refers to an arising having the name "warmth" and not to an arising having the name "sensation," I will employ the genitive, "the arising of warmth," or "the arising of sensation," although the arising of warmth is only the warmth arising. In the same way one says, in the world, "the odor of sandalwood," although sandalwood is only odor, or "the body of the bust," although a bust is only its body.[305]

[4. The Sarvāstivādins answer:] We hold to the existence of the characteristic "arising," which belongs to conditioned things and does not belong to unconditioned things, and we can easily explain this by virtue of the fact that unconditioned things do not arise. But if conditioned things arise without "arising," why do unconditioned things, space, etc., not arise?

We say that conditioned things arise, for they exist after having been non-existent. But how can unconditioned things arise, since they are eternal? You explain that certain *dharmas*,—the unconditioned *dharmas*,—are devoid of the characteristic "arising," because, you say, such is the nature of things (*dharmatā*): we say, rather, that by virtue of the nature of things, none of the *dharmas* are susceptible of arising. Moreover, according to you, all conditioned things equally possess the characteristic "arising" that you refuse to unconditioned things: yet you admit that certain causes are capable of producing warmth but incapable of producing sensation. In the same way, according to you, since conditioned and unconditioned things are equally devoid of the characteristic of "arising," all causes that produce conditioned things are ineffacacious with regard to unconditioned things.

[5. The Vaibhāṣikas say that] the four characteristics, arising, etc., are things in and of themselves.[306]

Why?[307] Should we abandon the Āgamas[308] for the sole reason that there are persons who object to them? One does not renounce sowing for fear of deer, and one does not renounce eating dainties because of flies.[309] One must refute objections and adhere to the

Doctrine.

***

What is *nāmakāya, padakāya*, and *vyañjanakāya*?

> 47a-b. *Nāmakāya*, etc., are collections of *saṁjñās, vākyas*, and *akṣaras*.[310]

1. *Nāman*, "name" or "word" is understood as "that which causes ideas to arise,"[311] for example the words "warmth," "sound," "odor," etc.

2. *Pada* or "phrase" is understood as *vākya*, a discourse, a phrase allowing the development necessary for a complete sentence,[312] for example the stanza, "Impermanent are the *saṁskāras* . . ." and the rest.[313] Or rather, one should understand *pada* as that which causes one to comprehend the different modalities of activity, quality, and time which concern a certain person: for example, he cooks, he reads, he goes; it is black, yellow, or red;[314] he cooks, he will cook, or he cooked.[315]

3. *Vyañjana* is understood as *akṣara* or phoneme (*varṇa*), vowels and consonents, for example, *a, ā,* [*i, ī,*] etc.

But are not the *akṣaras* the names of the letters?

One does not make or one does not pronounce phonemes with a view to designating, or of giving an idea of the letters; but one makes or one writes the letters with a view to giving an idea of the phonemes, so that, when one does not understand them, one still has an idea of them through writing. Consequently the phonemes are not the names of letters.

4. *Kāya* or "body" means "collection;" *samukti*, in fact, has the sense of *samavāya* according to the *Dhātupāṭha*, iv.114.

Hence we have: *nāmakāya* = color, sound, odor, etc.; *padakāya* = "The *saṁskāras* are impermanent, the *dharmas* are impersonal; Nirvana is tranquil . . ." etc.; and *vyañjanakāya* = *ka, kha, ga, gha* . . .

***

[1. Objection of the Sautrāntikas:] Are not words, phrases, and phonemes (*nāman, pada, vyañjana*) "voice" (*vāc*) by nature, and consequently "sound" (*śabda*)? Hence they form part of the *rūpaskandha*; they are not *saṁskāras* disassociated from the mind as the Sarvāstivādins believe.

[The Sarvāstivādins:] They are not "voice." Voice is "vocal sound," and a vocal sound only; for example, a cry does not cause one to attain to or comprehend an object. But a word (*nāman*) which moreover is a function of vocal sound, illumines, causes one to attain to, or signifies the object.

[The Sautrāntikas:] What I call "voice" is not merely vocal sound, but a vocal sound that causes one to attain to an object, that is, a vocal sound with regard to which persons who are speaking are in agreement as to what a certain thing signifies. It is thus that the Ancients have invested the sound *go* with the power to signify nine things: "The sages have established the sound *go* in nine things, that is, cardinal region, cattle, land, a beam of light, a word, a diamond, an eye, a haven, and water."[316] The philosopher for whom "it is the word (*nāman*) which illumines the object" should admit that the sound *go* has been endowed by convention with these different meanings. Then if a given object is signified to the hearer by a certain word, it is indeed vocal sound and nothing else, that signifies it. What advantage is there in supposing the existence of an entity you call "word?"

[2. The Sautrāntikas continue:] A word is either produced by the voice[317] or revealed[318] by the voice.

a. In the first hypothesis, since voice is vocal sound by nature, any vocal sound whatsoever, even the cry of an animal, would produce a word. If you answer that a word is produced solely through a vocal sound of a certain nature—the articulation of sound, *varṇātmaka*—we would say that this sort of vocal sound which is capable of producing a word would be quite capable of designating an object also.

In the second hypothesis, this same criticism holds by replacing the verb "to produce" with the verb "to manifest."

b. But it is absurd to suppose that the voice produces a word. In fact, sounds do not exist at the same time—one has, for example, *r-ū-p-a*—whereas the word, which you define as a *dharma*, an entity, cannot arise in parts. Then how can the voice, when it produces a word, produce it? You say that the case is analogous to that of *avijñapti* (iv.3d): the last moment of the *vijñapti*, a corporeal or vocal act, creates *avijñapti* by reason of its previous moments. But, we would say, if the last moment of the sound of the voice creates the word, it would suffice to understand the last sound in order to attain or comprehend the object.

It is not an evasion to suppose that voice engenders the phoneme (*vyañjana*), that a phoneme engenders a word, and that a word causes comprehension of objects. In fact, the same objection is present, "The phonemes do not exist at the same time, etc."

For these same reasons, it is absurd to suppose that the voice manifests a word. [Sounds do not exist at the same time, and a *dharma*, one entity, such as a word, cannot be mainfested in parts . . . and following].

c. [The hypothesis that "voice" engenders a phoneme—a hypothesis that we have previously tolerated—calls moreover for some new remarks]. Experts vainly apply their minds but do not discover a phoneme distinct from the voice. Moreover, the voice neither engenders nor manifests the phoneme, for the same reasons that allow that the voice neither engenders nor manifests a word. [Since the "voice" is vocal sound by nature, all vocal sound would engender or manifest phonemes. If you reply that phonemes are only engendered or manifested by the vocal sound of a certain nature . . . as above *ad* 2a2.]

[3. But the Sarvāstivādins may suppose that] a word arises with its object, like the characteristic "arising." The question of knowing whether it is produced or manifested by the voice, disappears.

In this hypothesis, no present word would designate a past or future thing. Moreover, a father, a mother, or other persons arbitrarily fix the word that is the proper name of a son, etc.: how can you admit that the word, like the characteristic "arising," arises simultaneously with the object? Finally, unconditioned things would not have any name, since they do not arise: a consequence that the Sarvāstivādins cannot admit.

[4. But the Sarvāstivādins are warranted by a text.] The Blessed One said, "A stanza (*gāthā*) depends on words, and a poem depends on stanzas."[319]

[The Sautrāntikas answer that] word (*nāman*) is a sound (*śabda*) upon which persons have come to an agreement that it signifies a certain thing.[320] A stanza (*gāthā*) is a certain arrangement of words: it is in this sense that it, according to the Blessed One, depends on words. To admit an entity in and of itself called *pada*, is a very superfluous hypothesis. You might as well maintain that there exists, distinct from ants and minds, things in and of themselves termed "a row of ants" or "a succession of minds."[321] Recognize then that only the phonemes (*akṣaras*), which are sounds, exist in and of themselves.

The Vaibhāṣikas admit *nāmakāya, padakāya*, and *vyañjanakāya*, as *saṁskāras* disassociated from the mind, for, they say, none of these *dharmas* serve as a gate of understanding.[322]

***

We ask: (1) to which sphere of existence do the phonemes, words, and phrases belong? (2) Do they belong to living beings (*sattvākhya*, i.10b)? (3) Are they of retribution, of accumulation or of out-flowing (i.37)? and (4) Are they good, bad, or neutral?

> 47c-d. They exist in Kāmadhātu and Rūpadhātu; they belong to living beings; they are out-flowing; and they are neutral.[323]

The phonemes, etc., belong to two spheres of existence. According to one opinion, they also exist in Ārūpyadhātu, but there they are "unpronounceable."[324]

They belong to living beings, being produced through the efforts of living beings and consisting of articulated sounds (*varṇa*), etc. In fact, they belong to the person who speaks, not to the things that they designate.

They are an out-flowing, being produced through *sabhāgahetu* (ii.52); they are not of retribution, since they proceed from the desire of the person who speaks; they are not of accumulation, since they are not material.

They are non-defiled-neutral (*anivṛtāvyākṛta*, ii.28).[325]

***

We shall briefly explain the characteristics, not as yet mentioned, of the other *dharmas* disassociated from the mind (ii.35).

> 47d-48b. The same for "genre," (*sabhāgatā*) which is also from retribution, and which belongs to the three spheres of existence.

"The same for," that is to say, like phonemes, words, and phrases, *sabhāgatā* is of the first two spheres of existence; it belongs to living beings; it is from out-flowing; and it is non-defiled-neutral.

But *sabhāgatā* is not only from out-flowing: it is also of retribution; it not only belongs to the first two spheres of existence, it also belongs to the third.

> 48b. Possession (*prāpti*) is of two types.[326]

It is of out-flowing and of retribution.

> 48c. Its characteristics also.

Its characteristics, arising, etc., are of two types, like possession.

> 48c-d. The absorptions and non-possession (*aprāpti*) are of out-flowing.

The two absorptions and non-possession are only out-flowings.

As for their spheres, their relationship with living beings, their moral qualifications (good, etc.), the explanations have been given above. The characteristics belong to all conditioned things, hence they belong to living beings and to non-living beings. For the *āsaṁjñika* and the *āyus*, see ii.41d and 45a.

***

We have seen (9ii.47c-d) that arising, in order to engender the *dharma* that it should engender, needs the cooperation of *hetus* or causes, and *pratyayas* or conditions. What are the *hetus*, and what are the *pratyayas*?[327]

> 49. The *hetus* are sixfold: *kāraṇahetu*, *sahabhū*, *sabhāga*, *saṁprayutaka*, *sarvatraga*, and *vipāka*.[328]

Kāraṇahetu is reason for existence; *sahabhūhetu* is coexistent cause; *sabhāgahetu* is parallel cause; *saṁprayuktakahetu* is associated cause; *sarvatragahetu* is universal cause, and *vipākahetu* is retributive cause: such are the six types of causes that the Ābhidhārmikas (*Jñānaprasthāna*, *TD* p. 920c5) recognize.[329]

> 50a. All *dharmas* are *kāraṇahetu* with regard to all, with the exception of themselves.

A *dharma* is not a *kāraṇahetu* of itself.

With this exception, that all of the *dharmas* are *kāraṇahetu* with regard to all other conditioned *dharmas*, because no *dharma* constitutes an obstacle to the arising of the *dharmas* susceptible of arising.

It results from this definition that the *dharmas* that are *sahabhūhetu*, etc., are also *kāraṇahetu*: all other *hetus* are included within *kāraṇahetu*. The *hetu* that does not receive a special name, which is simply *kāraṇa*, "reason for existence," without any other qualification is *kāraṇahetu*: it receives as its particular name the name that suits all the *hetus*. Compare this with the name of the *rūpāyatana* (i.24).

***

Kāraṇahetu calls for the following observations:

1. Vices are produced among the ignorant; once the Truths are known, they are not produced, as the stars are not visible when the sun shines. Hence the consciousness of the Truths, or the sun, causes an obstacle to the vices, or to the stars. Then it is false to say that all conditioned *dharmas* are *kāraṇahetu* because they create no obstacle to arising.

We understand that the consciousness of the Truths and the clarity of the sun create no obstacle to the arising of the *dharma* which is "arising" (*utpadyamāna*), that is to say of the *dharma*, which, its causes being completed,[330] continues to exist.

2. What is called cause or reason for existence, may be what is capable of causing, or of not causing, an obstacle! In fact, when their lord does not oppress them, villagers say, "We are fortunate through the actions of our master."[331] But can one call cause that which, being incapable of causing an obstacle, does not cause an obstacle? Nirvāṇa is incapable of creating any obstacle to the arising of any conditioned thing: such too are future *dharmas* with regard to past *dharmas*, or creatures of hell or animals with regard to beings in Ārūpyadhātu: Nirvāṇa, future *dharmas*, or creatures in hell are as if they did not exist with regard to their being an obstacle to the arising of the conditioned things in question. Can one consider them as causes?

They are causes; for, even when the lord is incapable of harming them, the villagers express themselves as we have said; but not about a non-existent lord.

3. The definition that we have given of *kāraṇahetu* is a general definition and includes that which is *kāraṇahetu par excellence* and that which is simply *kāraṇahetu*. *Kāraṇahetu par excellence* is the generating cause: in this sense, eye and color are the *kāranahetu* of the consciousness of sight; as food is with regard to the body,[332] the seeds, etc., with regard to the sprout, etc. (see ii.56b).

[4. Objection.] If all the *dharmas* are the causes of other *dharmas* because they do not cause any obstacle, why do not all the *dharmas* arise together?[333] Why, when one murder is committed, are not all creatures, like the murderer himself, guilty of the crime of murder?

This objection is useless. In fact, all the *dharmas* receive the name of *kāraṇahetu* because they do not create any obstacle: it is not that they are all agents.

5. According to other masters, all *kāraṇahetus* possess a real efficacy with regard to all *dharmas*. For example Nirvāṇa and the consciousness of sight: a mental consciousness, good or bad, arises having Nirvāṇa as its object (*ālambana*, ii.62c-d); from this mental

consciousness there later arises a consciousness of sight; then Nirvāṇa has efficacy, albeit mediately, with regard to the consciousness of sight.

The same argument applies to future *dharmas*, to beings in hell, etc.

***

> 50c-d. *Sahabhūhetu*, coexistent causes, namely the elements (*bhūta*), the mind and the companions of the mind, characteristics and the thing characterized, are the *dharmas* that are causes one of the other.[334]

11. The *dharmas* that are causes (*puruṣakāraphala*, ii.58) one of the other, are called *sahabhūhetu*.[335]

For example, the primary elements (*mahābhūta*)[336] are, among themselves, *sahabhūhetu*. The same for the mind and its companions (ii.51); the same for the characteristics, arising, etc. (ii.45b), and the *dharmas* that they characterize.

In the category of *sahabhūhetu* are then included all conditioned *dharmas* which are in a mutual relationship of causality.[337]

2. We have reason not to complete the above definition. A *dharma* is a *sahabhūhetu* of its secondary characteristics (*anulakṣaṇa*, ii.45) without being in a mutual relationship of causality with them: for the secondary characteristics are not the *sahabhūhetu* of their *dharma*. This is a case to be added to the definition.[338]

***

What *dharmas* are called "the companions of the mind?"

> 51a-c. The companions of the mind are: the mental states; the two disciplines (*saṁvara*); and the characteristics (*lakṣaṇas*) of the mental states, the two disciplines and the mind.

These are all the *dharmas* associated with the mind (*cittasaṁprayukta*, ii.24), the discipline of absorption and pure discipline (iv.17d), and the characteristics, arising, etc. (ii.45b) of all these, and also of the mind.

[Why are they termed "companions of the mind"?]

> 51d. From the point of view of time, of result, etc., and of goodness, etc.

The companions are associated with the mind:

1. In regard to time: they have the same arising, the same duration, and the same destruction as does the mind; they are of the same time period as the mind.

When we say "the same arising . . . ," we understand the word "same" in the sense of concomitance: the companions arise, last, and perish at the same time as does the mind; but their arising is distinct.

The minds that are not destined to arise do not arise, nor last, nor perish: the same for their companions. This is why the phrase, "The companions are of the same time period as the mind" is added. [The mind which should arise is future until the moment when it arises if it is to arise: its companions are hence future; it is past after the moment when it shall perish if it arose: its companions are then past.][339]

2. In regard to the result, etc. Result means *puruṣakāraphala* (ii.58a-b) and *visaṁyogaphala* (ii.57d); and "et cetera" refers to *vipākaphala* (ii.57) and *niṣyandaphala* (ii.57c).

The companions have the same result, the same *vipāka*, and the same *niṣyanda* as the mind: "same" indicates identity.

3. In regard to goodness, etc. The companions are good, bad, or neutral, like the mind which they accompany.

There are then ten reasons why the companions are termed companions.[340]

***

The mind having the least number of companions[341] is a *sahabhūhetu* of fifty-eight *dharmas*: namely 1) the ten *mahābhūmikas* (ii.23) with the four characteristics of each of them; and 2) the four characteristics and the four secondary characteristics (*anulakṣaṇa*, ii.46).

If, from these fifty-eight *dharmas*, the four secondary characteristics of the mind—which have no effect upon it—are set aside, then we have fifty-four *dharmas* that are *sahabhūhetu* of the same mind.[342]

According to another opinion, only fourteen *dharmas* are *sahabhūhetu* of this mind, namely its four characteristics and the ten *mahābhūmikas*. As the secondary characteristics have no effect on the mind, the characteristics of the *mahābhūmikas* likewise have no effect on the mind.

The Vaibhāṣikas reject this opinion—that the forty characteristics of the *mahābhūmikas* are not *sahabhūhetu* of the mind,—as contradictory to the doctrine of the *Prakaraṇagrantha* according to which "the four characteristics,—arising, duration, old age, and impermanence,—of the belief in self (*satkāyadṛṣṭi*) . . . and in the *dharmas* associated with this belief (comprising the *mahābhūmikas*), are at the same time a result and a cause of the belief in self."[343]

Certain Masters, in their reading of the *Prakaraṇagrantha*, omit the words, "and of the *dharmas* associated with this belief." According to the Vaibhāṣikas of Káśmīr, these words figure in the text; or, if they are missing, the context indicates that one should supply them and that the passage as it stands is incomplete.

***

Any *dharma* that is a *sahabhūhetu* cause is a *sahabhū* or a coexistant item. But there are some coexistant items that are not *sahabhūhetu*:

1. the secondary characteristics of the principal *dharma* (*mūladharma*) are not a *sahabhūhetu* regarding this *dharma* (ii.46a-b);

2. these same are not *sahabhūhetu* among themselves;

3. the secondary characteristics of the companions of the mind are not a *sahabhūhetu* regarding the mind;

4. these same are not a *sahabhūhetu* among themselves;

5. derived matter, blue, etc., susceptible of resistance and which has also arisen together, are not a *sahabhūhetu* among themselves;

6. a part of derived matter not susceptible to resistance and also arisen together with them, is not a *sahabhūhetu*; with the exception of the two disciplines (see I.136);

7. no derived matter, even though arisen with the elements, is a *sahabhūhetu* with the elements;

8. possession (*prāpti*), even when it arises with the *dharma* to which it is related, is not a *sahabhūhetu* to it.

The *dharmas* of these eight categories are coexistant (*sahabhū*), but are not *sahabhūhetu*, because their results, *vipāka* or *niṣyanda*, are not identical (see p. 259). As for possession, it does not always accompany the *dharma*: it arises either before the *dharma*, or after it, or at the same time as it (ii.37-38).

***

[The Sautrāntikas criticize the doctrine of coexistant causes.]

All this may be right, that is, "what is a *sahabhūhetu* cause, a mutually coexistant cause, is a coexistant item," and the rest. Nevertheless, in the world, the relationship of cause to effect is well proven in certain cases: the cause is previous to the effect. It is in this way that a seed is the cause of the sprout, the sprout of the stalk, etc. But one does not prove a similar relationship between simultaneous things. You should then demonstrate that *dharmas* arisen together can be in a cause and effect relationship.

[The Sarvāstivādins supply two examples.] The lamp arises with its light; the sprout, growing in the light, arises with its shadow. Now a lamp is the cause of its light and a sprout is the cause of its shadow. Thus cause and effect can be simultaneous.

[The Sautrāntikas:] These examples are not proven. We must examine whether a lamp is the cause of its light, or if, as we think, a lamp with its light are both the effect of a complex of previous causes and conditions, oil, wick, etc. In the same way, a complex of previous causes (seed, light) is the cause of the sprout and its shadow, of the sprout with its shadow.

[The Sarvāstivādins:] The relationship of cause and effect is proven by the existence and the non-existence of what is called effect, similar to the existence and the non-existence of what is called cause. The definition of the Logicians (*hetukas*) is very good: "When A is or is not, and when B is or is not, then A is considered as cause, and B is considered as effect." Granted this, if we examine the *dharmas* that we have defined as mutually coexistent and *sahabhūhetu*, we see that they all exist when one of them exists, and that none exist when one of them is absent.[344] They are then in a relationship of mutual cause and effect.

[The Sautrāntikas:] Admitting that among the simultaneous *dharmas*, one *dharma* can be the cause of another *dharma*, then the organ of sight is the cause of visual consciousness.[345] But how many simultaneous *dharmas* are the cause and effect of one another?

[The Sarvāstivādins:] Mutual causality is proven by the definition that we have given of causality. When the mind exists, its mental states exist, and vice versa.

[The Sautrāntikas:] Very well, but then the Sarvāstivādins should revise their system. In fact, they have denied mutual causality to derived matter (physical matter, taste, etc.) although physical matter never exists without taste (ii.22); they have denied mutual causality to derived matter and to the primary elements, and mutual causality to secondary characteristics and the mind.

[The Sarvāstivādins:] In the same way that three staffs stand up supported one on the other, the causal relationship of simultaneous things, the mind and its mental states, etc., is proven.

[The Sautrāntikas:] This new example should be examined. We ask whether the three staffs stand up together through the force that the three staffs possess through arising together, or rather, if the force of the complex of previous causes which caused them to arise together does not now also cause them to arise supported one on the other. Further, there are things here other than the mutual force of support: there is a rope and a hook, and there is the ground.

But, [reply the Sarvāstivādins,] mutually coexistant items have causes other than the *sahabhūhetu*, namely *sabhāgahetu, sarvatragahetu*, and *vipākahetu*, which have a role analogous to that of the cord, etc. *Sahabhūhetu* is then proven.

***

52a. Similar *dharmas* are *sabhāgahetu* or similar causes.[346]

Similars (*sabhāga*) are *sabhāgahetu* of similars.

1. The five good *skandhas* are *sabhāgahetu* of the five good *skandhas*. When they are defiled, that is to say, bad, and defiled-neutral, they are *sabhāgahetu* of defiled ones. Neutral, that is, undefiled-neutral, they are *sabhāgahetu* of neutral ones.

Nevertheless, different masters are not in agreement on this last point. According to some, neutral *rūpa* is *sabhāgahetu* of the five neutral *skandhas*, but the four *skandhas*,—sensation, etc.—are not *sabhāgahetu* of *rūpa*.[347]

According to others, four *skandhas* are *sabhāghetu* of the five; but *rūpa* is not *sabhāgahetu* of the four.

And according to others, *rūpa* is not *sabhāgahetu* of the four, and vice versa.

2. From the point of view of one existence, the first embryonic state is the similar cause of ten states: these are the five embryonic states, *kalala, arbuda, peśin, ghana*, and *praśākhā*; and the five post-embryonic states, *bāla, kumāra, yuvan, madhya* and *vṛddha*. The second embryonic state is the *sabhāgahetu* of nine states (*arbuda* to *vārddha*), and thus following. A previous moment of each state is the similar cause of the later moments of that same state (compare iv.53).

From the point of view of the states of existence followed by the same species, each of the states of the previous existence is the similar cause of the ten states.

The same holds for external things, corn, rice, etc., that is, the quality of *sabhāgahetu* remains confined in each series: corn is a similar cause of corn, not of rice.

[3. The Dārṣṭāntikas deny that] physical matter (*rūpa*) is a similar cause of matter; but this contradicts the Book (*Jñānaprasthāna, TD* 26, p. 985b14), which says, "Past primary elements are the *hetu* and the *adhipati* of future primary elements." *Adhipati* means *adhipati-pratyaya* (predominating conditions, ii.62d); and *hetu* means *sabhāgahetu*, for the *hetus* are here evidently apart from cause.

***

Are all similar *dharmas* similar causes of similar *dharmas*? No. Similar causes are the similar *dharmas* which

> 52b. Belong to the same category (*nikāya*) and the same stage (*bhū*).

This means that the *dharmas* belonging to a certain category and to a certain stage (*bhūmi*) are a similar cause of *dharmas* of the same category and the same stage.

The *dharmas* are classed into five categories accordingly as they are susceptible of being abandoned through Seeing each of the Four Truths, or through Meditation (i.40).

The *dharmas* belong to nine stages: they are either in Kāmadhātu, or in one of the Four Dhyānas, or in one of the Four Ārūpyas.

A *dharma* susceptible of being abandoned through Seeing the Truth of Suffering is a similar cause of another *dharma* susceptible of being abandoned through Seeing the Truth of Suffering, and not of the *dharmas* belonging to the other four categories; and thus following.

***

Sabhāgahetu has not yet been exactly defined. In fact, only those *dharmas* are similar causes which have

> 52b. Arisen previously.

An arisen *dharma*, that is to say, any previously past or present *dharma* is a similar cause of a later similar *dharma*, arisen or not arisen. A future *dharma* cannot be a similar cause.[348]

1. On what authority does this definition rest?

It rests on the Mūlaśāstra, for the *Jñānaprasthāna* (*TD* 26, p.

920c15) says, "What is similar cause (*sabhāgahetu*)? The root of good, arisen and previous, is a cause in the quality of a similar cause with regard to the later root of good and of the *dharmas* associated with it, of the same category and stage. In that way, the roots of good of the past are a similar cause with regard to past and present roots of good; past and present roots of good are similar causes with regard to future roots of good."

2. [Objection:] A future *dharma* is a similar cause, for we read in this same *Jñānaprasthāna*, "[Question:] Is there a period when the *dharma* which is the cause of a certain *dharma* is not a cause? [Answer:] There is never a time when this *dharma* is not a cause."

[The Vaibhāṣikas:] This text does not contradict the first; for the *Jñānaprasthāna* does not refer to that which is a cause in the quality of a similar cause (*sabhāgahetu*), but rather that which is a cause in the qualities of *sahabhūhetu, saṁprayuktakahetu*, or *vipākahetu.*

According to another opinion, that of the "followers of the last place" (*paramāvasthāvādin*), the answer of the *Jñānaprasthāna*, "There is never a time when this *dharma* is not a cause" refers to *sabhāgahetu*, and they justify themselves as follows: A future *dharma*, in an arising state, is certainly *sabhāgahetu.* Hence, taking into account a future *dharma* in its last place, the *Jñānaprasthāna* can say that there is never a time when the *dharma* is not a cause, that it is always a cause, since, at a certain moment in the future, it is a cause.

This explanation does not resolve the difficulty. In fact, if a future *dharma*, after not having been a cause becomes a cause by arriving at a state of arising, then it has not always been a cause: but now the *Jñānaprasthāna* says absolutely that there is never a time when it is not a cause.

Furthermore, this explanation cannot be reconciled with the answer that the *Jñānaprasthāna* (p. 1026b19; *Vibhāṣā, TD* 27, p. 87a2) gives to another question, "Is there a period in which the *dharma* that is an immediately antecedent condition (*samanantara*, ii.62a-b) of a certain *dharma* is not *samanantara*? Yes, when it has not yet arisen." Now the case of *samanantara* is analogous to that of *sabhāgahetu*: future *samanantara*, arriving at a state of arising, is *samanantara.*

Hence if the interpretation of the answer, "There is never a time when this *dharma* is not a cause," in the sense of "In the future, in an arising state, it is *sabhāgahetu*" is correct, then the *Jñānaprasthāna*, dealing with *samanantara*, should answer as for *sabhāgahetu*, "This *dharma* is never *samanantara*." Now the *Jñānaprasthāna* answers, "It is not *samanantara* when it has not arisen." Hence the word "cause" in the first answer should not be understood as *sabhāgahetu*.

The "followers of the last place" say that the *Jñānaprasthāna* answers the first question by saying, "There is never a time when it is not a cause," and the second by saying, "It is not a cause when it has not arisen," in order to show that one can answer in these two ways in order to express the same sense. One can answer the first question as the second, and the second as the first.

What a singular process of explanation! The author of the Śāstra would then be totally useless! Hence the first explanation proposed is the best explanation.

3. If a future *dharma* is not a similar cause (*sabhāgahetu*), why does the *Prakaraṇapāda* teach that future *satkāyadṛṣṭi* has *satkāyadṛṣṭi* as its cause, and is in turn the cause of *satkāyadṛṣṭi*? We read, in fact (in the text quoted in note 342, para. B1(b)), "with the exception of future *satkāyadṛṣṭi* and the Truth of Suffering which is associated with it" (*anāgatāṁ satkāyadṛṣṭi tatsaṁprayuktaṁ ca duḥkhasatyaṁ sthapayitvā.*)[349]

This reading, [answer the Vaibhāṣikas,] is corrupted. It should read, "with the exception of the Truth of Suffering associated with future *satkāyadṛṣṭi* (*anāgatasatkāyadṛṣṭisaṁprayuktaṁ*). If we were to suppose that your reading is authentic, we must, because of the sense that the text expresses, consider it as without authority (*na tantram*), and as having been determined by the context of discourse (that is, through imitation of the preceeding phrase).

4. If a future *dharma* is not *sabhāgahetu*, how do you explain the following *bhāṣyam* of the *Prajñapti*?[350] This Treatise says in fact, "All the *dharmas* are determined from a fourfold point of view: cause, result, support (*āśraya*), and object (*ālambana*)."[351]

[The Vaibhāṣikas answer:] When it says, "This *dharma* is never the cause of that *dharma*," the Treatise does not mean to speak of all types of causes. By cause, we must understand *saṁprayuktakahetu* and *sahabhūhetu*; by result, *adhipatiphala* and *puruṣakāraphala* (ii.58);[352] by support, the six organs (organ of sight, etc.); and by object, the six spheres (*viṣaya*), visible things, etc.

5. If a future *dharma* is not *sabhāgahetu*, then *sabhāgahetu* did not exist at first, but then does exist.

But this is precisely what the Vaibhāṣikas affirm! The condition (*avasthā*) of *sabhāgahetu* of the *sabhāgahetu* is new, that is, it exists after having been non-existent; but the thing itself, the *dravya* which is a certain *sabhāgahetu*, is not new. A future *dharma* is not *sabhāgahetu*, but once it has arisen, it becomes *sabhāgahetu*. In fact, the result of the complex of causes, is the condition of a thing and not the thing itself (*dravya*), the *dharma*. (A future *dharma* exists as a thing, *dravyatas*; the complex of causes causes it to pass from the future into the present, endows it with the condition of the present, and endows it, by this fact, with the quality of *sabhāgahetu*; see v.25.)

6. What harm do you see in this future *dharma* being a similar cause (*sabhāgahetu*) in the same way that it is a retributive cause (*vipākahetu*, ii.54)?

It it were *sabhāgahetu*, it would be mentioned as such in the *Jñānaprasthāna* (see above p. 263 line 27); now the *Jñṣnaprasthāna*, answering the question, "What is *sabhāgahetu*?" does not say that future roots of good are *sabhāgahetu* of future roots of good.

We do not think that the omission of future *dharma* from this text creates an argument against us. This text, in fact mentions only the *sabhāgahetus* that are capable of "grasping" and of "giving forth" a result (*phaladānagrahaṇasamartha*, ii.59).

No, for the result of *sabhāgahetu* is an "out-flowing result of out-flowing," a result similar to its cause (*niṣyandaphala*, ii.57c), and this type of result does not suit a future *dharma*, because, in the future, there is no anteriority and posteriority. One cannot, on the other hand, admit that a past or present *dharma* already arisen is an out-flowing of a future *dharma*, in the same way that a past *dharma* is not an out-flowing of a present *dharma*, for a result is not anterior to its cause.

Hence a future *dharma* is not a similar cause.

7. If this is the case, then a future *dharma* would no longer be a *vipākahetu*, a retributive cause (ii.54c), for 1) a retributive result (*vipākaphala*, ii.56a) cannot be either simultaneous or anterior to its cause; and 2) because future *dharmas* have no earlier or later periods of time.

[The Vaibhāṣikas answer that] the cause is not the same. A similar cause (*sabhāgahetu*) and its out-flowing (*niṣyanda*) result are similar *dharmas*. Now this is to suppose that they exist in the future, that they lack anteriority and posteriority, and that they are the mutual cause of one another, and as a consequences the results of one another: now it is not admissable that two *dharmas* are an out-flowing of one another. On the contrary, a retributive cause and a retributive result are dissimilar. Even if the anteriority and the posteriority were absent, a cause remains only a cause, and a result remains only a result. The quality of *sabhāgahetu* results from a condition or state (*avasthā*): a future *dharma* is not *sabhāgahetu*; but when it enters into a present or a past condition, it becomes *sabhāgahetu*. Its quality of retributive cause results from the nature of the *dharma* itself.

***

We have said that a *dharma* is a similar cause (*sabhāgahetu*) of only those *dharmas* that belong to its stage. Does this restriction apply to all the *dharmas*?

It applies only to impure *dharmas*, not to pure *dharmas*:

> 52c-d. But the Path is *sabhāgahetu* to the Path, without distinguishing the nine stages.

The Path is of nine stages or spheres—the *anāgamya*, the *dhyānāntara*, the Four primary (*mūla*) Dhyānas, and the three inferior, primary Ārūpyas (vi.20c)—in the sense that an ascetic, abiding in these nine states of absorption, can cultivate the Path.

The *dharmas* that constitute the Path are similar causes of the *dharmas* that constitute the Path, from stage to stage. In fact, the Path resides in the different stages as a visitor, without forming part of the spheres of existence to which these stages belong: the desire of Kāmadhātu, of Rūpadhātu, of Arūpyadhātu, are not on the Path. The Path, whatever be the stage upon which the ascetic relies in order to cultivate it, stays of the same nature; the Path is hence a similar cause of the Path.

Nevertheless, the complete Path is not a similar cause of the complete Path. One does not have to take into account the stage in which it is cultivated, but rather the characteristics proper to the Path itself.

52d. The Path is *sabhāgahetu* to an equal or superior Path.

Not of an inferior Path, because the Path is always acquired through effort.

Let us define the terms, "inferior," "equal," and "superior Path."

1. When past or present *duḥkhe dharmajñānakṣānti* (the first moment of the Path of Seeing, *darśanamārga*, vi.25d) is a similar cause of this same *kṣānti* of the future, the caused Path is equal to the causing Path.

When this *kṣānti* is a similar cause of *duḥkhe dharmajñāna* (the second moment of the Path of Seeing, *darśanamārga*, vi.26a) the caused Path is superior to the causing Path.

And thus following up to *anutpādajñāna* (vi.50) which, not having a superior, can only be the similar cause of an equal Path, namely a future *anutpādajñāna*.

To state it more precisely, the Path of Seeing (*darśanamārga*) is a similar cause of the Path of Seeing, the Path of Meditation (*bhāvanā-mārga*), and the Path of the Aśaikṣas (*aśaikṣamārga*); the Path of Meditation is a similar cause of the Path of Meditation and the Path of the Aśaikṣa; and the Path of the Aśaikṣa is a similar cause of an equal or superior Path of the Aśaikṣa.

3. Any Path can be cultivated by an ascetic of weak faculties or active faculties: a Path of weak faculties is the similar cause of the same Path of weak faculties and of active faculties; a Path of active faculties is the similar cause of the same Path of active faculties. Consequently

the Paths of *śraddhānusārin* (vi.29), *śraddhādhimukta* (vi.31) and *samayavimukta* (vi.56-7) are, respectively, the similar causes of six, four, and two Paths; the Paths of *dharmānusārin* (vi.29), *dṛṣṭiprāpti* (vi.31) and *asamayavimukta* (vi56-7) are, respectively, the similar causes of three, two, and one Path.

When a Path cultivated in a higher stage is the similar cause of a Path cultivated in a lower stage, how can it be the cause of an equal or higher Path?

The Path cultivated in a lower stage can be equal or higher 1) from the point of view of the faculties (*indriyas*) which can be weak or active in any stage, or 2) from the point of view of the accumulation of causes.[354]

It does not follow that the same person successively grasps *śraddhānusārin* and *dharmānusārin* Paths; yet the first, in the past or present, is a similar cause of the second, the later one.[355]

***

Does the rule of equal or higher results apply only to the pure *dharmas*, that is, to the *dharmas* that form part of the Path?

> 53a. The *dharmas* acquired through cultivation are *sabhāgahetu* of the same two classes, the equal and the higher.

Worldly *dharmas* acquired through effort or exercise are similar causes of equal or higher *dharmas*, but not of inferior *dharmas*.

What are the *dharmas* acquired through effort?

> 53b. Those which arise through hearing, through reflection, etc.

The *dharmas* "acquired through effort" are the opposite of the "innate" *dharmas*. These former *dharmas* are qualities (*guṇa*) proceeding from hearing (*śruta*), that is, from the Word of the Buddha, from reflection (*cintā*), and from meditation (*bhāvanā*).

Since they are acquired through effort, they are the similar cause of greater or of equal, but not of lesser, good.

The *dharmas* of hearing in Kāmadhātu are similar causes of the *dharmas* of hearing and reflection in Kāmadhātu; but not of the *dharmas* of meditation, because these *dharmas* do not exist in Kāmadhātu, and because a *dharma* is a similar cause of *dharmas* of the same sphere of existence.

The *dharmas* of hearing in Rūpadhātu are similar causes of the *dharmas* of hearing and meditation in Rūpadhātu; but not of the *dharmas* of reflection, because these *dharmas* do not exist in this sphere of existence: in Rūpadhātu, as soon as one begins to reflect, one immediately enters into absorption (*samādhi*).

The *dharmas* of meditation in Rūpadhātu are similar causes of the *dharmas* of meditation in Rūpadhātu, but not of the *dharmas* of hearing in Rūpadhātu, because these are less good.

The *dharmas* of meditation in Ārūpyadhātu are the similar causes of the *dharmas* of meditation in Ārūpyadhātu. The *dharmas* of hearing and of reflection do not exist in this sphere of existence.

Furthermore, one must consider that the *dharmas* acquired through effort are of nine classes: weak-weak, medium-weak, etc. The weak-weak are the similar causes of *dharmas* of nine classes; the medium-weak, of *dharmas* of eight classes, with the exception of the weak-weak; and thus following.

The nine classes of the "innate" good *dharmas* are similar cause of one another. The same holds for the defiled *dharmas*.

The undefiled-neutral *dharmas* are of four categories (ii.72), the following being "better" than the preceding: *dharmas* arisen from retribution (*vipākaja*, i.37); *dharmas* relative to lying down, to sitting attitudes, etc.; *dharmas* relative to professional work; and the mind that can create fictive beings (*nirmāṇacitta*, vii.48). These four categories are, respectively, the similar cause of four, three, two, and one category.

Furthermore, as a mind capable of creating fictive beings of the sphere of Kāmadhātu can be the result of each of the Four Dhyānas (*Vibhāṣā, TD* 27, p. 89a12), there is reason to establish here the same distinctions: the minds capable of creating fictive beings constitute four classes, and are, according to their class, similar causes of four, three, two, or one mind capable of creating fictive beings. In fact, since it is a result of a higher Dhyāna, the mind capable of creating fictive beings is not the similar cause of a mind capable of creating fictive beings which is the result of a lower Dhyāna: from one similar cause (a mind capable of creating fictive beings) realized with the greatest effort, there cannot proceed a *dharma* less good, realized with less effort.

***

Once these principles have been established, the following questions are stated and resolved:[356]

1. Is there a pure *dharma*, already arisen, which is not the cause of a pure *dharma* not destined to arise?

Yes. *Duḥkhe dharmajñāna* already arisen is a cause of *duḥkhe dharmajñānakṣāntis* not destined to arise. Furthermore, a better good is not the cause of lesser good.

2. Is there, in a series, a pure *dharma*, previously acquired (of which one has first obtained the *prāpti*), which is not the cause of a pure *dharma* arisen later?

Yes. Future *duḥkhe dharmajñānakṣānti* [whose possession (*prāpti*) has been obtained in the first moment of the Path] are not the cause of *duḥkhe dharmajñāna* already arisen. This is because a result cannot be anterior to its cause, and because a future *dharma* is not a similar cause.

3. Is there a pure *dharma*, arisen previously, which is not the cause of a pure *dharma* arisen later?

Yes. The best is not the cause of less good. For example, when one realizes an inferior result after having fallen from a superior result, the superior result was not the cause of this inferior result. Furthermore, possession of *duḥkhe dharmajñāna* which has previously arisen is not a cause of the possession of the *dharmajñānakṣānti* which will arise in the following moments (*duḥkhe'nvayajñānakṣāntikṣaṇe*, etc.), because these new possessions are less good.

***

53c-d. The mind and its mental states are only *saṁprayuktakahetu*, causes through association.[357]

Mind and mental states are *saṁprayuktakahetu*.

Is this to say that minds and mental states, arisen at different moments and in different series, are among themselves *saṁprayuktakahetu*?

No.

Would you then say that the mind and mental states of the same aspect, that is, having the same aspect of blue, etc., and of the same object (*ekālambana*), that is, having for their object the same blue, etc., are *saṁprayuktakahetu*?

No. This definition gives rise to the same criticism: minds and mental states of different time periods and of different series can have the same aspect and the same object.

Would you say that the mind and mental states of the same aspect and the same object, can be, furthermore, of the same time period?

This still does not suffice: for many persons can see a new moon at one and the same time.

Consequently, the author adds

53d. Which has the same support.

The mind and mental states which have the same support are, among themselves, *saṁprayuktakahetu*.

"Same" signifies single or undivided.[358]

For example, a given moment (*kṣaṇa*) of the organ of sight is the support 1) of a visual consciousness, and 2) of the sensation (*vedanā*) and the other mental states which are associated with this consciousness. And the same for the other organs until *manas*: a certain moment of the mental organ (*manas*) is the support of a mental consciousness and of the mental states associated with this consciousness.

Whatever is *saṁprayuktakahetu* is also *sahabhūhetu*. What is the difference between these two causes?[359]

Some *dharmas* are called *sahabhūhetu* because they are mutually the results of one another. As companions in a caravan travel thanks to the support that they give one another, in this same way the mind is the result of mental states, and the mental states are the result of the mind.

Some *dharmas* are called *saṁprayuktakahetu*, mutual cause through association, because they function identically, that is, because there is among them the five similarities or identities defined above ii.34. The travel of the companions in a caravan is assured by the mutual support that they give one another; furthermore, they use the same food, the same drinks, etc. In this same way, the mind and its mental states use the same support, have the same aspect, etc.: if one of these five identities is missing, they no longer function in the same way and are not associated.

***

> 54a-b. Former universals are *sarvatragahetu* or universal causes of the defiled *dharmas* of their own stage.

Universals, which we shall study in the Chapter on the Defilements (v.12), arisen previously, that is, of the past or present, and belonging to a certain stage (*bhūmi*), are the universal cause of later defiled *dharmas*, of the same stage, which are defiled by nature, either through association or through their origin (iv.9c).

Universals are only the cause of defiled *dharmas*; they are the cause of defiled *dharmas* in their own category and in other categories (*nikāya*, ii.52b): it is through their power that there arises, with their following, defilements belonging to categories different from them.[360] They then constitute a cause different from *sabhāgahetu*.[361]

Then would the defiled *dharmas* of an Āryan (*rāga* or lust, etc.) have the universals for their cause? Yet the Āryan has abandoned all universals, for these are abandoned by Seeing the Truths.

The Vaibhāṣikas of Kaśmīr admit that all defiled *dharmas* have the *dharmas* abandoned through Seeing the Truths for their cause. For the *Prakaraṇapāda*[362] expresses itself in these terms: "What *dharmas* have for a cause the *dharmas* abandoned through Seeing the Truths? Defiled *dharmas*[363] and the retribution of the *dharmas* abandoned through

Seeing the Truths.

"What *dharmas* have for a cause neutral (*avyākṛta*) [*dharmas*]? Neutral conditioned *dharmas*[364] and bad *dharmas*.

"Is there a *duḥkhasatya* which has for its cause a belief in self (*satkāyadṛṣṭi*) and which is not in turn the cause of a belief in self? . . ." and the rest to: "with the exception of the arising-old age-duration-impermanence of the belief in a future self[365] and its following, and of all other defiled *duḥkhasatya*."

[Objection:] If some bad *dharmas* have for their causes not only some bad *dharmas* but some neutral *dharmas* as well, how should one explain this *bhāṣyam* of the *Prajñapti*,[366] "Is there a bad *dharma* which has only a bad *dharma* for its cause? Yes; the first defiled volition (*cetanā*) that an Āryan produces upon falling from detachment."[367]

[Answer:] The neutral *dharmas*, which are abandoned through Seeing the Truths, are the cause (i.e., *sarvatragahetu*) of this bad volition. If the *Prajñapti* does not mention it, it is because it intends to name only the causes that have not been abandoned.

***

> 54c-d. Bad *dharmas* and impure good *dharmas* are retributive causes.[368]

1. Bad *dharmas*—which are all impure—and impure good *dharmas* are only retributive causes, because their nature is to ripen.

Neutral *dharmas* are not retributive causes, because they are weak: as rotten seeds, even though moistened, do not grow.

Pure *dharmas* are not retributive causes because they are not moistened[369] through desire (*tṛṣṇā*): as intact seeds, not moistened, do not grow.

Furthermore, pure *dharmas* are not bound to any sphere of existence: thus to which sphere could the result of retribution that they would produce belong?

The *dharmas* that are neither neutral nor pure possess the two qualities necessary for retribution, the proper force, and the moistening of thirst, the same as intact and moistened seeds.

2. [Objection:] What is the meaning of the expression *vipākahetu*? You have a choice between two interpretations of this compound: *vipākahetu* signifies either "cause of *vipāka*" or "cause which is *vipāka*."

In the first case, the suffix *a (ghan)* marks the state (*bhāva*): the *vipāka* (=*vipakti*) is the result of the operation indicated by the root *vi-pac*.

In the second case, the suffix *a* marks the operation (*karman*): the *vipāka* is that which become ripe (*vipacyate*), that is to say, the action arrives at the moment when it gives forth a result.

To which of these two interpretations do you hold? If you accept the first, how would you justify the text (*Jñānaprasthāna, TD* 26, p. 974a26), "The eye arises from *vipāka*?" If you accept the second, how would you justify the expression, "*vipāka* of action?"

[Answer:] We have shown (i.37) that both explanations of the word *vipāka* are correct. When one examines results, one must understand the word *vipāka* according to the first explanation; the meaning is result of retribution. The text, "The eye arises from *vipāka*" should be understood as "The eye arises from the cause of *vipāka*."

3. What is the meaning of the compound *vi-pāka*?

The prefix *vi* indicates difference. *Vipāka* is a *pāka* or result dissimilar from its cause.[370]

How is that?

In Kāmadhātu, 1) a retributive cause (*vipākahetu*) consisting of only one *skandha* can produce a single result: possession (*prāpti*, ii.36b) with its characteristics (*lakṣaṇas*, ii.45c); 2) a retributive cause consisting of two *skandhas* can produce a single result: bodily and vocal action with its characteristics; 3) a retributive cause consisting of four *skandhas* can produce a single result: the mind and its mental states, good and bad, with their *lakṣaṇas*.

In Rūpadhātu, 1) a retributive cause consisting of a single *skandha* can produce a single result: possession with its characteristics, that is, *asaṁjñisamāpatti* (ii.42a) with its characteristics; 2) a retributive cause consisting of two *skandhas* can produce a single result: *vijñapti* (iv.2) of the First Dhyāna with its characteristics; 3) a retributive cause consisting of four *skandhas* can produce a single result: a good mind, not of absorption (for the mind of absorption always consists of *rūpa* and discipline, iv.13, and is thus five *skandhas*), with its characteristics; 4) a retributive cause consisting of five *skandhas* can produce a single result: the mind of absorption with its characteristics.

In Ārūpyadhātu, 1) a retributive cause consisting of a single *skandha* can produce a single result: possession, *nirodhasamāpatti* (ii.43), with their respective characteristics; 2) a retributive cause consisting of four *skandhas* can produce a single result: the mind and its mental states with their characteristics.

4. There is action the retribution of which is included in a single *āyatana*, in a single *dharmāyatana* (i.15): action that has for its retribution the vital organ (*jīvitendriya*, ii.45a).[371]

In fact, action that has the vital organ for its retribution necessarily has the vital organ and its characteristics (ii.45c) for its retribution; both form part of the *dharmāyatana*.

Action that has the mental organ (*manas*) for its retribution necessarily has two *āyatanas* for its retribution, namely the *mana-āyatana* (i.16b) and the *dharmāyatana* (which embraces sensations, etc., and the characteristics which necessarily accompany the mental organ).

Action that has tangible things (*spraṣṭavyāyatana*, i.10d) for its retribution necessarily has two *āyatanas* for its retribution, namely the tangible things and the *dharmāyatana* (which includes the characteristics of tangible things).

Action that has the organ of touch (*kāyāyatana*, i.9a) for its retribution necessarily has three *āyatanas* for its retribution, the organ of touch, tangibles (namely the four primary elements that support the organ of touch), and the *dharmāyatana* (which includes its characteristics).

In the same way, action which has either physical matter (*rūpāyatana*), odors (*gandhāyatana*), or taste (*rasāyatana*) for its retribution, necessarily has three *āyatanas* for its retribution: tangible things and the *dharmāyatana* as above, plus, according to the cause, the *āyatana* of physical matter, odor, or taste.

Action which has either the eye, the ear, the nose, or the tongue for its retribution, necessarily has four *āyatanas* for its retribution: 1) one of the four organs, 2) the organ of touch, 3) tangible things, and 4) the *dharmāyatana*.

An action can have five, six, seven, eight, nine, ten, or eleven *āyatanas* for its retribution.[372]

Action, in fact, is of two types: of varied result and of non-varied result. The same holds for seeds: lotus, pomegranate, fig, millet, corn, etc.

5. The retribution of an action can belong to a single time period or to three time periods;[373] but the reverse is not true,[374] for a result cannot be inferior to its cause. The retribution from an action lasting an instant can last numerous instants; but the reverse is not true, for the same reason (*Vibhāṣā, TD* 27, p. 98a7).

Retribution is not simultaneous to the action which produces it, for a retributive result is not experienced at the moment when the action is accomplished. Retribution does not immediately follow an action, for it is the immediately antecedent condition (*samanantarapratyaya*, ii.63b) that attracts the moment that immediately follows the action: in fact, the retributive cause depends on the development of the series for the realization of its result.

***

To which time period should a *dharma* belong in order that it might be each of these six causes? We have implicitely stated this rule, but we have not yet taught it in the Kārikā:

> 55a-b. *Sarvatragahetu* and *sabhāgahetu* are of two time periods; three causes are of three time periods.[375]

A past and present *dharma* can be *sarvatraga* and *sabhāgahetu* (ii.52b). Past, present, and future *dharmas* can be *saṁprayuktaka, sahabhū*, and *vipākahetu*. The Kārikā does not speak of *kāraṇahetu* (ii.50a)): the conditioned *dharmas* of the three time periods are *kāraṇahetu*; the unconditioned *dharmas* are outside of time.

***

Which causes correspond to which results? By reason of which results are they recognized as causes?

55c-d. Conditioned things and disconnection are results.[376]

The Mūlaśāstra says, "What *dharmas* are results? Conditioned things and *pratisaṁkhyānirodha*."[377]

[Objection:] If the unconditioned is a result, it should have a cause, from which cause one could say that it is the result. Furthermore, since you maintain that it is a cause (*kāraṇahetu*, ii.50a), it should have a result, from which result one could say that it is a cause.

Only conditioned things, [the Sarvāstivādins answer,] have cause and result.

55d. The unconditioned has neither cause nor result.[378]

For we cannot attribute to it any of the six causes, nor any of the five results.

i. 1. Why not admit that the part of the Path which is called *ānantaryamārga*[379] is the *kāraṇahetu* of the result of disconnection (*visaṁyogaphala*, ii.57d)?

We have seen that *kāraṇahetu* is a cause that does not create any obstacles to arising; but disconnection, being unconditioned, does not arise. Thus one cannot attribute a *kāraṇṇahetu* to it.

2. Then how is disconnection a result? Of what is it the result?

It is the result of the Path, for it is obtained due to the force of the Path (vi.51): in other words, it is through the Path that an ascetic obtains possession (*prāpti*, ii.36c-d) of disconnection.

3. Hence it is the obtaining or the possession of disconnection which is the result of the Path, and not disconnection itself: for the Path is efficacious with regard to the obtaining of disconnection, but not with regard to disconnection.

Wrong! The efficacy of the Path possesses diversity with regard to both obtaining and disconnection.

The Path produces obtaining; the Path causes one to obtain disconnection. Hence, although the Path is not the cause of disconnection (=*prastisaṁkhyānirodha*), one can say that it is the result of the Path.[380]

4. Since no unconditioned thing has *adhipatiphala* (ii.58d), how can one define it as *kāraṇahetu*?

Any unconditioned thing is *kāraṇahetu*, for it does not create an obstacle to the arising of any *dharma*; but it does not have any result, for, being outside of time, it can neither project nor produce a result (ii.59a-b).

[5. The Sautrāntikas deny that] an unconditioned thing is a cause. In fact, the Sūtra does not say that a cause can be unconditioned; it says that a cause is only conditioned, "All the *hetus*, all the *pratyayas* which have for a result the production of physical matter . . . of the consciousiness, are also impermanent.[381] Produced by impermanent *hetus* and *pratyayas*, how can physical matter . . . and consciousness be permanent?"

[The Sarvāstivādins answer:] If a permanent thing, that is, an unconditioned thing is not a cause, it will not be "an object as condition" (*ālambanapratyaya*, ii.63) of the conciousness that it refers to.

[The Sautrāntikas:] The Sūtra declares that the *hetus* and the *pratyayas* which are capable of producing are impermanent. It does not say that all conditions (*pratyayas*) of the consciousness are impermanent. An unconditioned thing could then be "an object as condition" of the consciousness; for "an object as condition" is not itself productive.

[The Sarvāstivādins:] The Sūtra says that productive causes are impermanent: hence the Sūtra does not deny that an unconditioned thing is *kāraṇahetu*, that is, "a cause that does not create an obstacle."

[The Sautrāntikas:] The Sūtra admits the existence of "an object as a condition" (ii.61c); but it does not speak of a *kāraṇahetu*, "a cause that does not create an obstacle." It is not proven that an unconditioned thing is a cause.

[The Sarvāstivādins:] In fact, the Sūtra does not say that that which does not create an obstacle is a cause; but it does not contradict this. Many Sūtras have disappeared. How can you be sure that some Sūtra does not attribute the quality of *kāraṇahetu* to unconditioned things?

***

[ii. The Sautrāntikas:] What is the *dharma* that is called *visaṁyoga* or disconnection?

[The Sarvāstivadins: The Mūlaśāstra (*Jñānaprasthāna, TD* 26, p. 923b6) says that] disconnection is *pratisaṁkhyānirodha* (ii.57d).

[The Sautrantikas:] When I asked you (i.6) what *pratisaṁkhyā-nirodha* is, you answered, "It is disconnection;" I asked you what disconnection is, and you answered, "It is *pratisaṁkhyānirodha*!" The two answers are circular and do not explain the nature of the *dharma*, the unconditioned, to which they refer. You owe us another explanation.

[The Sarvāstivādins:] This *dharma*, in its nature, is real, but indescribable; only the Āryans "realize" it internally, each for himself. It is only possible to indicate its general characteristics, by saying that there is a real entity (*dravya*), distinct from others, which is good and eternal, and which receives the name of *pratisaṁkhyānirodha*, and which is also called disconnection or *visaṁyoga*.

***

iii. The Sautrāntikas affirm that the three types of unconditioned things (i.5b) are not real. The three *dharmas* that it refers to are not distinct and real entities like color, sensation, etc.[382]

1. What is called "space" (*ākāśa*) is solely the absence of any tangible thing, that is, the absence of a resistant body. Persons say, in their obscurity, that there is space when they do not encounter any obstacle.

2. What is called *pratisaṁkhyānirodha* or Nirvāṇa is—when both the defilements already produced and the existence already produced

are destroyed—the absence of any other defilements or any other existence, and that by reason of the force of the consciousness (*pratisaṁkhyā=prajñā*).[383]

3. When, independent of the force of consciousness (*pratisaṁkhyā*) and by reason of the mere absence of causes there is an absence of arising *dharmas,* this is what is called *apratisaṁkhyānirodha.* For example, when premature death interrupts existence (*nikāyasabhāga*, ii.10, 14), there is *apratisaṁkhyānirodha* of the *dharmas* which would have arisen in the course of this existence if it had continued.

4. According to another school,[384] *pratisaṁkhyānirodha* is the future non-arising of the defilements by reason of consciousness (*prajñā*); *apratisaṁkhyānirodha* is the future non-arising of suffering, that is, of existence, by reason of the disappearance of the defilements, and not directly by reason of consciousness. (The first would then be *sopadhiśeṣa nirvāṇadhātu*, and the second would be *nirupadhiśeṣa nirvāaṇadhātu*).

But, [the Sautrāntikas remark,] the future non-arising of suffering supposes consciousness (*pratisaṁkhyā*); it is then included within *pratisaṁkhyānirodha.*

***

5. Another School[385] defines *apratisaṁkhyānirodha* as "later non-existence of the *dharmas* which have arisen" by virtue of their spontaneous destruction.[386]

In this hypothesis, *apratisaṁkhyānirodha* would not be eternal, since it is non-existent as long as the *dharma* as cause (i.e., the defilement) has not perished.

But does not *pratisaṁkhyānirodha* have a certain consciousness, the *pratisaṁkhya*, for its antecedent? Consequently it too would not be eternal, for, if its antecedent were absent, its consequence would also be absent.

You cannot say that *pratisaṁkhyānirodha* is not eternal because its antecedent is *pratisaṁkhyā*: in fact, it does not have *pratisaṁkhyā* for its antecedent. One cannot say that *pratisaṁkhyā* is earlier, or that the "non-arising of the non-arisen *dharmas*" is later. Let us explain. Non-arising always exists in and of itself. If *pratisaṁkhyā* is absent, the *dharmas* would arise; but if *pratisaṁkhyā* arises, the *dharmas* would absolutely not arise. The efficacy of *pratisaṁkhyā* with regard to their non-arising consists in this: 1) that before *pratisaṁkhyā*, there is no obstacle to their arising; 2) but given *pratisaṁkhyā*, the *dharmas*, the arising of which has not been previously hindered, do not arise.

***

[iv. The Sarvāstivādins refute the Sautrāntikas.] If Nirvāṇa is simply non-arising (*anutpāda*), how does one explain the Sūtra (*Saṁyuktagama, TD* 2, p. 182b15) which says, "The cultivation of the five faculties,—faith, etc.,—has for its result the abandoning of past, present, and future suffering"? [387] In fact, this abandoning is nothing other than Nirvāṇa, and there can only be non-arising of a future *dharma*, not of a past or present *dharma*.

[1. The Sautrāntikas:] This Sūtra does not contradict our definition of Nirvāṇa. In fact, "the abandoning of past and present suffering" means the abandoning of the defilements bearing past and present suffering. Our interpretation is justified by another text (*Saṁyukta, TD* 2, p.19a8?) which says, "Abandon desire (*chandarāga*[388]) relative to *rūpa*, to sensation . . . and to consciousness. When desire is abandoned, *rūpa*, . . . and consciousness will be abandoned and comprehended by you." [389] It is in this manner that we should understand "the abandoning of past and present suffering" of which the Sūtra speaks when it speaks of the faculties.

If one adopts another reading of this Sūtra on the faculties, to wit, "The cultivation of the faculties . . . has for its result the abandoning of past, present, and future defilements," the explanation is the same.

Or rather, past defilement is the defilement of a previous existence; present defilement is the defilement of the present existence; these do not refer to the defilement of a given past or present moment. The same for the eighteen *tṛṣṇāvicaritas* (*Anguttara*, ii.212) or "modes of thirst": the modes (*vicaritas*) that are related to a past existence are called past modes, those that are related to a present existence are called present modes, and those that are related to a future existence are called future modes.

Past defilements and present defilements place in the present series seeds that bring forth the arising of future defilement: when these seeds are abandoned, past and present defilement is abandoned: in the same way as one says that an action is exhausted when its retribution is exhausted.

The "abandoning" of future suffering and future defilement is the fact that they absolutely do not arise, given the absence of seeds.

How does one otherwise understand the abandoning of past or present suffering? There is no good reason to make an effort to destroy that which has perished or that which is perishing.

[2. The Sarvāstivādins:] If unconditioned things do not exist, how can the Sutra say "Detachment (*virāga*) is the best of all conditioned and unconditioned *dharmas*?" How can a *dharma* which does not exist be the best among the *dharmas* which do not exist? [390]

[The Sautrāntikas:] We do not say that unconditioned things do not exist. They exist in fact in the manner in which we say that they exist. Let us explain. Before sound is produced, we say "There is non-existence (of sound) prior to the sound;" after the sound has perished, we say "There is non-existence (of sound) after the sound," and yet it had not been proven that non-existence exists: [391] the same holds for unconditioned things.

Although it is non-existent, one unconditioned thing merits being praised, namely detachement (*virāga*), the absolute future non-existence of any wrong. This non-existent thing is the most distinguished of all non-existent things. The Sūtra praises it by saying that it is the best, so that believers shall conceive joy and affection with regard to it.

[3. The Sarvāstivādins:] If *pratisaṁkhyānirodha* or Nirvāṇa is non-existent, how can it be one of the Truths. How can it be the Third Noble Truth?

What should we understand by "Noble Truth" or *ārayasatya*? Without doubt the sense of *satya* (Truth) is "not incorrect." The

Āryans see that which exists and that which does not exist in a not incorrect manner: in that which is suffering, they see only suffering, and in the non-existence of suffering, they see the non-existence of suffering. What contradiction do you find between the non-existence of suffering and *pratisaṁkhyānirodha* being a Truth?

And this non-existence is the Third Truth, because the Āryans see it and proclaim it immediately after the Second Truth.

[4. The Sarvāstivādins:] But if unconditioned things are non-existent, the consciousness that has space and the two extinctions for its object would have a non-thing for its object.

We do not see any inconvenience in this, as we shall explain in the discussion on the past and future (v.25).

[5. The Sarvāstivādins:] What harm do you see in maintaining that unconditioned things really exist? What advantage do you see in this?

This advantage that the Vaibhāṣika doctrine is found to be safegarded.

May the gods be charged with defending this doctrine, if they judge that it is possible! But to maintain the existence of unconditioned things in and of themselves is to affirm a non-existent thing to be real. In fact, unconditioned things are not known through direct perception (*pratyakṣa*), as is the case for physical matter, sensation, etc.; and they are not known through inference (*anumāna*), by reason of their activity, as is the case for the sense organs.

6. Furthermore, if *nirodha* or extinction is a thing in and of itself, how do you justify the genitive, *duḥkhasya nirodhaḥ*, "the extinction of suffering," as the extinction of the defilement, or the extinction of the object of defilement? In our system, the extinction of a thing is simply the non-existence of this thing. "Extinction of suffering" means that "suffering will not exist any more." But we cannot conceive of any cause and effect relationship, of any effect and cause relationship, of a relationship of the whole to the part, etc., between the things, that is to say, the defilements, and its extinction conceived of as an entity in itself, which would justify the genitive.

We affirm, [answer the Sarvāstivādins,] that extinction is a thing in and of itself. Yet we can specify extinction as being in a relationship with such things (extinction of lust, etc.), for one takes possession (*prāpti*, ii.37b) of extinction at the moment when one cuts off the possession of a certain thing.

But, we would answer, what is it that determines or specifies the taking of possession of extinction?[392]

[7. The Sarvastivadins:] The Sutra speaks of the Bhikṣu who has obtained Nirvāṇa in this life.[393] If Nirvana is non-existence, how could he obtain it?

[The Sautrāntikas:] The Bhikṣu, through the possession of the adverse force of the antidote, that is, through the possession of the Path, has obtained a personality (*āśraya*) contrary to the defilements, and contrary to a new existence. This is why the Sūtra says that he has obtained Nirvāṇa.

8. Moreover we have a text that shows that Nirvāṇa is pure non-existence. The Sūtra (*Saṁyukta*, TD 2, p. 88a7)[394] says, "The complete abandoning, the purification, the exhausting, the detachment, the extinction, the abatement, the definitive passing away of this suffering; and the non-rebirth, the non-grasping, the non-appearance of another suffering—this is calm, this is excellent, namely the rejection of all *upadhi*, the exhausting of thirst, detachment, extinction, Nirvāṇa."

[The Sarvāstivādins:] When the Sūtra says that Nirvāṇa is the non-appearance of a new suffering, the Sūtra means that there is no appearance of suffering in Nirvāṇa.[395]

[The Sautrāntikas:] I do not see that the locative "in Nirvāṇa" has any force to establish that Nirvāṇa is a thing. In what sense do you understand the locative *asmin*? If this means *asmin sati*, "if Nirvāṇa exists, there is no appearance of suffering," then suffering would never appear, since Nirvāṇa is eternal. If this means *asmin prāpta*, "if Nirvāṇa has been obtained," you would have to admit that future suffering will not appear while the Path—by virtue of which you suppose that Nirvāṇa is obtained—either is, or rather has been obtained.[396]

9. Consequently the comparison of the Sūtra is excellent, "The deliverance of his mind is like the Nirvāṇa of a flame."[397] That is to

say, as the extinction of a flame is only the "passing away" of the flame and not a certain thing in and of itself, so too is the deliverance of the mind of the Blessed One.

[10. The Sautrāntikas] are still warranted by the authority of the Abhidharma wherein we read, "What are the *avastuka dharmas*? They are the unconditioned things."[398] The term *avastuka* signifies "unreal," "without self-nature."

[The Vaibhāṣikas do not accept this interpretation.] The term *vastu*, in fact, is used in five different meanings: 1. *vastu* in the sense of a thing in and of itself, for example, "When one has obtained this *vastu* (*aśubhā*, vi.11), one is in possession of the *vastu*" (*Jñānaprasthāna, TD* 26, p. 1026cll; *Vibhāṣā, TD* 27, p. 985a22); 2. *vastu* in the sense of any object of consciousness, for example "All the *dharmas* are known through different knowledges, each knowing its own object" (*Prakaraṇa, TD* 26, p. 713c20); 3. *vastu* in the sense of "bond of attachment," for example, "Is the person who is bound to a *vastu* through the bond of affection, bound to this same *vastu* through the bond of hostility?" (*Vibhāṣā, TD* 27, p. 298b-c); 4. *vastu* in the sense of cause, for example, "What are the *dharmas* possessing a cause? The conditioned *dharmas*" (*Prakaraṇa, TD* 26, p. 716a4);[399] 5. *vastu* in the sense of "act of appropriating to oneself", for example, "*vastu* of fields, *vastu* of a house, *vastu* of a shop, *vastu* of riches: abandoning the act of appropriating these to himself, he renounces them" (*Vibhāṣā, TD* 27, p. 288b5).[400]

The Vaibhāṣikas conclude: In the passage that concerns us, *vastu* has the meaning of cause; *avastuka* signifies "that which has no cause." Unconditioned things, although real, always lack activity, have no cause which produces them, and produce no effects.

***

We must explain what type of result proceeds from each type of cause.

56a. Retribution is the result of the last cause.[401]

The last cause is the retributive cause, *vipākahetu*, because the retributive cause is named last in this list. The first result, *vipākaphala* (iii.57), is the result of this cause.

56b. The predominating result is the result of the first.[402]

The first cause is *kāraṇahetu* or reason for being; the last result proceeds from it.

This result is called *adhipaja*, arisen from predominence, or *adhipata*, belonging to predominance, because it is the result of the predominating cause (*adhipatiphala*, ii.58c-d). The *kāraṇahetu* is considered as playing the role of a master (*adhipati*).

But, we say, the quality of not creating an obstacle (*anāvaraṇa-bhāvamātrāvasthāna*, ii.50a) suffices to constitute *kāraṇahetu*. How can one regard it as a "predominating cause?"

Kāranahetu is either a "non-efficacious cause" and one then regards it as predominant because it creates no obstacle; or an "efficacious cause," and one then regards it as predominant because it possesses mastery, a predominating and generating activity. For example, the ten *āyatanas* (form and the organ of sight, etc.) are predominant with regard to the five sense consciousnesses; the collective action of living beings is predominant with regard to the physical world.[403] The organ of hearing exercises an indirect predominence (*ādhipatya*) with regard to the visual consciousness, for, after having understood, a person experiences the desire to see. And thus following. (See ii.50a).

56c-d. Outflowing is the result of the similar cause and the universal cause.

An outflowing result (*niṣyandaphala*) proceeds from *sabhāgahetu* (ii.52) and from *sarvatragahetu* (ii.54): for the result of these two causes is similar to its causes (ii.57c; iv.85).

56d. The *pauruṣa* or virile result, is the result of two causes.

The result of *sabhāgahetu* (ii.59) and *saṁprayuktakahetu* (ii.53c) is called *prauruṣa* or virile, that is, the result of *puruṣakāra* or virile activity.

Puruṣakāra or virile activity is not distinct from the person himself, for action is not distinct from him who accomplished the action. The result of virile activity (*puruṣakāraphala*) can thus be termed the virile (*pauruṣa*) result.

What do we understand by "virile activity?"

The activity of a *dharma* is termed its virile activity (*puruṣakāra*), because it is similar to the activity of a person (*puruṣakāra*). In the same way, in the world, a certain plant is called *kākajaṅghā*, because it resembles the foot of a crow; heros are called *mattahastin*, because they resemble an enraged elephant.

Are *saṁprayuktahetu* and *sahabhūhetu* the only causes that result in virile activity?

According to one opinion, all other causes have this type of result, with the exception of retributive causes (*vipākahetu*). This result is, in fact, either simultaneous to, or immediately following its cause; but such is not the case with a retributive result.

According to other Masters,[404] a retributive cause also distantly results in virile activity, for example the fruits reaped by a laborer.

(Hence a *dharma* is 1) *niṣyandaphala*, because it arises similar to its cause, 2) *puruṣakāraphala*, because it arises through the force of its cause, and 3) *adhipatiphala*, because it arises by reason of the "non-obstacle" of its cause.)

***

What are the characteristics of the different results?

57a. Retribution is a neutral *dharma*.

Retribution (*vipāka*) is an undefiled, neutral (*anivṛtāvyākṛta*) *dharma*.

Among the undefiled, neutral *dharmas*, some belong to living beings, while others do not belong to living beings. Consequently the author specifies

57b. Belonging to living beings.

that is, they arise in the series of living beings.

Some of those *dharmas* belonging to living beings are said to be of accumulation (*aupacayika*, having come from food, etc., i.37) and some are said to be of an outflowing (*naiṣyandika*, coming from a cause which is similar to them, i.37, ii.57c). Consequently the author specifies

57c. They arise later than a non-neutral *dharma*.

A non-neutral action is called this because it produces retribution; non-neutral actions are bad actions and good-impure (*kuśalasāsrava*, ii.54c-d) actions. From actions of this nature there arises later,—not at the same time, and not immediately afterwards,—the result that one terms "retributive result" or "matured result" (*vipākaphala*).

Why not consider the *dharmas* that do not form part of living beings,—mountains, rivers, etc.,—as retributive results? Do they not arise from good or bad actions?

The *dharmas* that do not form part of living beings are, by nature, common in that everyone may partake of them. Now retributive results, by definition, are unique: another person never experiences the retributive results of actions that I accomplish. Action produces a "predominating result" (*adhipatiphala*) in addition to a retributive result: all beings experience this result in common, because the collectivity of their actions cooperate in their creation (see above, note 403).

57d. A result that resembles its cause is called outflowing.[405]

A *dharma* resembling its cause is an outflowing result (*niṣyanda-phala*). Two causes, the similar cause and the universal cause (*sabhāgahetu*, ii.52, and *sarvatragahetu*, ii.54a-b) produce an outflowing result.

If the result of the universal cause is an outflowing result, a result similar to its cause, why not give the universal cause the name of similar cause?

A result of a universal cause is always similar to its cause 1) from the point of view of the stage: like it, it belongs to Kāmadhātu, etc.; and 2) from the point of view of its moral character: like it, it is defiled.

But it can belong to a different category than the category of its cause. "Category" means the method of abandoning: it is susceptible of being abandoned by Seeing the Truth of Suffering, etc. (ii.52b). When there is a similarity between a cause and its result from this last point of view, the universal cause is at one and the same time a similar cause.

Four alternative cases present themselves:

1. A similar cause which is not a universal cause: for example, a non-universal defilement (*rāga*, etc.) related to the defilements of their own category;

2. A universal cause which is not a similar cause: the universal defilements related to a defilement of another category;

3. A universal cause which is also a similar cause: the universal defilements related to a defilement of their own category;

4. All other *dharmas* are neither similar causes nor universal causes.[406]

> 57e. Extinction through intelligence is disconnection.

Disconnection (*visaṁyoga*) or *visaṁyogaphala*, "result that consists of disconnection" is extinction (*kṣaya*=*nirodha*) obtained by the speculative consciousness (*dhī*=*prajñā*). *Visaṁyogaphala* is hence *pratisaṁkhyānirodha*. (See above p. 280).

> 58a-b. A *dharma* is the result of the virile activity of the *dharma* through the force by which it arises.

This refers to a conditioned *dharma*.

Examples: the absorption of the First Dhyāna is the result of the virile activity of a mind in Kāmadhātu which instigates it or prepares it; the absorption of the Second Dhyāna is the result of the virile activity of a mind in the First Dhyāna.

A pure *dharma* can be the result of the virile activity of an impure *dharma* (the *laukikāgradharmas* have *duḥkhe dharmajñānakṣānti* for their result, vi.25c-d).

A mind that can create fictive beings (*nirmāṇacitta*) is the result of the virile activity of a mind in a Dhyāna (vii.48). And thus following.[407]

Pratisaṁkhyānirodha or Nirvāṇa is considered to be a "result of virile activity;" now the definition given in Kārikā 58a-b does not apply to *nirodha* which, being eternal, does not arise. We say then that it is the result of the virile activity of the *dharma* by the force of which one obtains possession of it.

> 58c-d. Any conditioned *dharma* is the predominating result (*adhipatiphala*) of conditioned *dharmas*, with the exception of the *dharmas* that are later than it.[408]

What difference is there between the result of virile activity and a predominating result?

The first refers to the agent; the second refers to both the agent and the non-agent. For example, a created thing is the result of the virile activity and the predominating result of the artisan who created it; it is only the predominating result of what is not the artisan.

***

In what condition (*avasthā*)—the past, present, or future—is each of the causes (*hetu*) found when they grasp and when they produce their result?

> [59. Five causes grasp their results in the present; two produce it in the present; two produce it in both past and present; and one produces it in the past.[409]

What is understood by "grasping a result" and "producing a result?"[410]

A *dharma* grasps a result when it become its seed.[411]

A *dharma* produces a result at the moment when it gives this result the power of arising, that is, at the moment when, the future result being turned towards arising or is ready to arise, this *dharma* gives it the power that causes it to enter into the present.]

59a-b. Five causes grasp their result in the present.

Five causes grasp their results only when they are in the present: in the past, they have already grasped their results; in the future, they have no activity (v.25).

The same holds for *kāraṇahetu*; but the stanza does not mention it, because *kāraṇahetu* does not necessarily have a result.

59b. Two produce their result in the present.

The mutually coexistent cause (*sahabhū*) and the associated cause (*saṁprayuktaka*) produce their results only when they are in the present: these two causes in fact grasp and produce their results at the same time.

59c. Two produce their results in both the past and the present.

The similar cause (*sabhāga*) and the universal cause (*sarvatraga*) produce their results both when they are in the present and when they are in the past.

How can they produce their outflowing results (*niṣyanda*, ii.56c) when they are in the present? We have seen (ii.52b, 54a) that they are earlier than their results.

One says that they produce their results in the present, because they produce them immediately. When their result has arisen, they are past: they have already produced it; they do not produce the same result twice.[412]

***

i. It happens that, at a given moment, a good similar cause (*sabhāgahetu*) grasps a result but does not produce a result. Four alternatives: to grasp, to produce, to grasp and to produce, and to neither grasp nor to produce.[413]

1. The possession of the roots of good that the person who has cut off the roots of good (iv.80a) abandons at the last moment, grasps a result, but does not produce a result.[414]

2. The possession of the roots of good that the person who again takes up the roots of good (iv.80c) acquires in the first moment, produces a result, but does not grasp a result.

We must say:[415] This same possession,—the possession abandoned at the last moment by the person who has cut off the roots of good,—produces its result, but does not grasp it at the moment when this person again takes up the roots of good.

3. The possession of the person whose roots of good are not cut off—with the exception of the two proceeding cases: that of the person who has achieved cutting them off, and that of the person who again takes up the roots of good—both grasp and produce.

4. In all other cases, possession neither grasps nor produces: for example, the possession of the roots of good of a person whose roots of good are cut off; the possession of the roots of good of a superior stage by a person who has fallen from this stage: these possessions have already grasped their result, and hence do not grasp it any more; they do not produce it, since the person cannot have possession of these roots at the present time.

ii. The *Vibhāṣā* establishes the same alternatives with respect to bad similar causes:

1. The possession of the bad *dharmas* that a person who obtains detachment from desire abandons at the last moment.

2. The possession that a person who fell from detachment acquires in the first moment.

We must say: These same possessions, when a person falls from detachment.

3. The possession of a person who is not detached, with the exception of the two preceding cases.

4. Possession in all other cases: for example the possession of a person detached and not subject to falling.

iii. There are also four alternatives regarding defiled-neutral similar causes:

1. The last possession of defiled-neutral *dharmas* that the saint who becomes an Arhat abandons.

2. The first possession that a fallen Arhat acquires.

Or better: the aforementioned possession of an Arhat who has fallen.

3. The possession of a non-detached person in Bhavāgra, the two preceding cases being excluded.

4. Possession in all other cases: the possession of an Arhat.

iv. When an undefiled-neutral similar cause produces its result, it grasps it (for the undefiled-neutral lasts until Nirvāṇa), but it can grasp its result without producing it: for example, in the case of the last *skandhas* of an Arhat which have no outflowing (*niṣyanda*).

v. We have up to now considered the *dharmas* that are not "subject to consciousness" (*sālambana*). If we consider the mind and its mental states in their sucessive moments, we can establish the four following alternatives for good similar causes:

1. It grasps but does not produce. When a good mind is immediately followed by a defiled or undefiled-neutral mind, this good mind, as a similar cause, grasps, that is, projects an outflowing result, namely a good future mind, which is or is not destined to arise; it does not produce an outflowing result, since the mind that follows it, defiled or undefiled-neutral, is not the outflowing of a good mind.

2. It produces but does not grasp. When a good mind immediately follows a defiled or undefiled-neutral mind, a good earlier mind produces an outflowing result, namely the good mind that we have just considered; this earlier mind does not grasp a result, since it grasped it formerly.

3. It grasps and it produces. Two good minds follow one another, the first grasping and producing an outflowing result, which is the second mind.

4. It neither grasps nor produces. When defiled or undefiled-neutral minds succeed one another, the earlier good mind, as a similar cause, formerly grasped its result and shall later produce its result; but for an instant it neither grasps nor produces.

We can in like manner establish the alternatives regarding bad similar causes.

59d. One cause produces its result in the past.

The retributive cause produces its result when it is in the past, for this result is not simultaneous to, nor immediately following its cause.

***

Some other Masters, [the scholars of the West (*Vibhāṣā, TD* 27, p. 630b15)] say that there are four results different from the five results that we have just mentioned. These four are:

1. *pratiṣṭhāphala*, a base result: a circle of water is the result of the circle of wind (iii.45) and thus following to plants, which are the result of earth;

2. *prayogaphala*, a result of preparatory exercise: *anutpādajñāna*, etc. (vi.50) is the result of *śubhā*, etc. (vi.11);

3. *sāmagrīphala*, a result of a complex: the visual consciousness is the result of the organ of sight, of a visible thing, of light and of an act of attention (*Madhyamakavṛtti*, 454);

4. *bhāvanāphala*, a result of meditation: a mind capable of creating fictive beings (vii.48) is the result of a Dhyāna.

[According to the Sarvāstivādins,] the first of these four results is included in the category of the predominent result; the other three are included in the category of virile result.

***

We have explained causes and results. We must now examine how many causes produce the different *dharmas*.

From this point of view, the *dharmas* are ranged into four categories: 1. defiled *dharmas*, that is, the defilements, the *dharmas* associated with a defilement, and the *dharmas* having their origins in a defilement (iv.8); 2. retributive *dharmas* or *dharmas* arisen from a retributive cause (*vipākahetu*, ii.54c); 3. the first pure *dharmas*, that is, *duḥkhe dharmajñānakṣānti* (i.38b, vi.27) and the *dharmas* coexistent with this *kṣānti*; and 4. the other *dharmas*, that is, the neutral *dharmas*, with the exception of the *dharmas* of retribution, and the good *dharmas*, with the exception of the first pure *dharmas*.

60-61b. The mind and its mental states are: 1) defiled; 2) arisen from a retributive cause; 3) others; and 4) pure for the first time, arising from causes that remain when one excludes, in this order, 1) the retributive cause, 2) the universal cause, 3) these two causes, 4) these two causes plus the similar cause. The associated cause is further excluded with respect to the *dharmas* that are not mind or mental states.[416]

The mind and its mental states, 1) when they are defiled, arise from five causes excluding the retributive cause; 2) when they are retributive, they arise from five causes with the exclusion of the universal cause; 3) when they are different from these two categories and from the fourth, they arise from four causes, with the exclusion of the retributive cause and the universal cause; 4) when they are pure for the first time, they arise from three causes, with the exclusion of the aforementioned two causes and the similar cause.

The *dharmas* that are not mind or mental states, namely the material *dharmas* and the *saṁskāras* not associated with the mind (ii.35), accordingly as they fall into one of four categories, arising from causes proper to this category with the exclusion of the associated causes are: defiled and retributive, four causes; different, three causes; pure for the first time (*anāsravasaṁvara*, iv.13), two causes.

These is no *dharma* that comes from a single cause: the reason for being and the mutually coexistant cause are never absent.

***

We have explained causes (*hetu*). What are conditions (*pratyaya*)?

61c. The *pratyayas* are said to be four.[417]

Where is this said?

In the Sūtra, it says "There are four conditions (*pratyayas*), namely causes as a condition (*hetupratyayatā*), an equal and immediately antecedent condition (*samanantarapratyayatā*), an object as condition (*ālambanapratyayatā*), and a predominating influence as condition (*adhipatipratyayatā*)."

Pratyayatā means "a type of *pratyaya*."[418]

***

What is "cause as a condition"?

61d. The *pratyaya* that bears the name of *hetu* is five *hetus*.

Excepting *kāraṇahetu*, the five remaining *hetus* constitute *hetupratyayatā*, causes as condition.

***

What is "an equal and immediately antecedent condition"?

> 62a-b. The mind and its mental states that have arisen, with the exception of the last ones, are an equal and immediately antecedent condition.

If one excepts the last mind and the last mental states of the Arhat at the moment of Nirvāṇa, all minds and mental states which have arisen are an equal and immediately antecedent condition.

i. Only mind and mental states are equal and immediately antecedent conditions. Of what *dharmas* are they the equal and immediately antecedent conditions?

1. This type of condition is called *samanantara* (equal and immediately antecedent) because it produces equal (*sama*) and immediate (*anantara*) *dharmas*. The prefix *sam* is understood in the sense of equality.

Consequently[419] only minds and their mental states are equal and immediately antecedent conditions, for there is no equality between a cause and its result with respect to the other *dharmas*, for example the material *dharmas*. In fact, after a *rūpa* of the sphere of Kāmadhātu, there can arise at the same time two *rūpas*, one of Kāmadhātu, the other from Rūpadhātu[420] , or two *rūpas*, one from Kāmadhātu, the other pure;[421] whereas one mind in Kāmadhātu and one mind in Rūpadhātu can never arise at the same time after a mind in

Kāmadhātu. The appearance of the *rūpas* is confused: now an equal and immediately antecedent condition does not produce confused results; hence material *dharmas* are not equal and immediately antecedent conditions.

Vasumitra says: A second *rūpa* of accumulation can arise in the same body, without which the series of a *rūpa* of accumulation would be broken; hence *rūpa* is not an equal and immediately antecedent condition.[422]

The Bhadanta[423] says: A *rūpa dharma* is immediately followed by more or by less. Hence it is not an equal and immediately antecedent condition. Less arises from more: as when a great mass of straw, burned, becomes ash. More arises from less: as when a small seed produces the roots of a fig tree, its trunk, its branches, and its leaves.

2. [Objection:] When minds immediately succeed one another, do they always admit the same number of types of associated mental states? No. The earlier mind admits of a larger number of types of mental states, and the following mind, a lesser number; and vice versa. Minds, good, bad, or neutral, succeed one another; but they do not admit of the same number of associated mental states (ii.28-30); the absorptions, which succeed one another, admit of or do not admit of *vitarka* and *vicāra* (viii.7). Hence there is no equality for the mental states as well as for the material *dharmas* (*Vibhāṣā, TD* 27, p. 52a21).

That is true: there is a succession from less to more, and vice versa (second opinion of the *Vibhāṣā*); but only by the accumulation or the diminution of the number of types of mental states (*Vibhāṣā, TD* 27, p. 50c5). There is never any inequality with respect to a determined type: more numerous sensations never arise after less numerous sensations, nor vice versa; this means that a mind accompanied by a single sensation is never followed by a mind associated with two or three sensations. The same for ideas (*saṁjñā*) and the other mental states.

Thus is it only in relation to its own type that an earlier mental state is an equal and immediately antecedent condition of a later mental state? Is sensation then the equal and immediately antecedent condition of a single sensation?

No. In a general way the earlier mental states are equal and immediately antecedent conditions of the mental states that follow, and only of the mental states of their type. But there is no succession from less to more with respect to one type, and vice versa: this justifies the expression *samanantara*, "*equal* and immediate."

3. The Ābhidhārmikas who take the name of Sāṁtānasabhāgikas (*Vibhāṣā, TD* 27, p. 50c5) maintain on the contrary that a *dharma* of a certain type is only an equal and immediately antecedent condition of a *dharma* of that same type: mind arises from mind, sensation arises from sensation, etc.

[Objection:] In this hypothesis, when a defiled (*kliṣṭa=akuśala* or *nivṛtāvyākṛta*) *dharma* arises after an undefiled *dharma*, this defiled *dharma* does not proceed from an equal and immediately antecedent condition.

It is a previously destroyed defilement that is the equal and immediately antecedent condition of the defilement that defiles this second *dharma*. The previous defilement is considered as immediately preceeding the later defilement, even though it is separated by an undefiled *dharma*, separation by a *dharma* of a different nature does not constitute separation, as the leaving-mind of the absorption of extinction (*nirodhasamāpatti*, ii43a) has for its equal and immediately antecedent condition the mind-of-entry-into-absorption which was previously destroyed: absorption does not constitute a separation.

We think that the theory of the Sāṁtānasabhāgikas is inadmissible, for, in this theory, a pure mind produced for the first time (i.38b) would not have any equal and immediately antecedent condition.

4. The *saṁskāras* dissociated from the mind (*viprayukta*, ii.35),[424] like the material *dharmas*, are produced disparately: hence they are not equal and immediately antecedent conditions. In fact after possession in the sphere of Kāmadhātu, possession relative to the *dharmas* of the three spheres of existence and to pure *dharmas* etc., can be produced at the same time.

ii. Why deny that the future *dharmas* are equal and immediately antecedent conditions?

Future *dharmas* are disparate: there is not, among them, any early and later (see p. 266).[425]

A. Then how does the Blessed One know that such and such a future *dharma* will arise first, and that such and such a *dharma* will arise later? He knows the order of the arising of all that arises until the end of time.

1. First answer.[426] His consciousness results from an inference (*anumāna*) drawn from the past and the present. He sees the past:[427] "From such a type of action such a retributive result arises; such a *dharma* proceeds from such a *dharma*;" and he sees the present: "Here is such a type of action: such a retributive result shall arise in the future from this action; here is such a *dharma*: such a *dharma* shall proceed from this *dharma*."

However the consciousness of the Blessed One is called *praṇidhijñāna* (vii.37), and is not a consciousness from inference. By means of inferences drawn from the past and from the present, the Blessed One immediately sees the *dharma* that resides, disparately, in the future, and he produces the consciousness, "This man, having accomplished such an action, shall certainly receive such a future retribution."[428]

To believe you, if the Blessed One does not consider the past, then he does not know the future. Hence he is not omniscient.

2. According to other Masters,[429] there is in the series of beings a certain *dharma* which is the indication of the results which will arise in the future, namely a certain *saṁskāra* disassociated from the mind. The Blessed One contemplates it,[430] and he knows future results without his having cultivated the Dhyānas and the Abhijñas (vii.42; *cyutyupapādajñāna*) for it.

The Sautrāntikas: If this is the case, then the Blessed One would be an interpreter of signs;[431] he would not be a "seer."

3. Consequently the Blessed One knows immediately and at his will all things, not be inference, and not by divination. This is the opinion of the Sautrāntikas, justified by the word of the Blessed One (*Ekottara, TD* 2, p.640a4; comp. *Dīgha*, i.31), "The qualities of the Buddhas, the spheres of the Buddhas, are incomprehensible."

B. If the future does not have any earlier or later division of time, how can one say, "Only *duḥkhe dharmajñānakṣānti* arises immediately after the *laukika agradharmas*, and not any other *dharma*" (vi.27) and thus following until "*Kṣayajñāna* arises immediately after *vajropamasamādhi* (vi.46c)?"

[The Vaibhāṣikas (*Vibhāṣā, TD* 27, p. 51bl) answer:] If the arising of this *dharma* is bound to that *dharma*, then immediately after that, this arises, as a bud arises after the seed without any equal and immediately antecedent condition intervening.

iii. Why are the last mind and the last mental states of the Arhat equal and immediately antecedent conditions (*Vibhāṣā, TD* 27, 50a22)?

Because no mind or mental states arise after them.

But you have said (i.17) that the *manas* is the mind that is disappearing and which serves as the support of the following mind. Since no mind follows the last mind of an Arhat, this last mind should not receive either the name of *manas*, or the name of equal and immediately antecedent condition; and yet you consider it as being *manas*.

The case is not the same. That which constitutes the *manas* is not its activity, the fact of supporting the susequent mind; rather, it is the quality of being a support (*āśraya*) for this mind; whether his (latter mind) arises or does not arise is of little importance. The last mind of an Arhat is "support:" if a subsequent mind, which would be supported by this support, does not arise, it is through the lack of other causes necessary to its arising. On the contrary, what constitutes an equal and immediately antecedent condition is its activity. Once this condition has grasped or projected a result, nothing in the world can hinder this result from arising. Hence the last mind of an Arhat is justly called *manas*, but not an equal and immediately antecedent condition.

iv. Does a *dharma* which is *cittasamanantara*, that is, which has a certain mind (*cittanirantara*) for its equal and immediate antecedent condition, immediately follow this mind?[432]

There are four alternatives:

1. The mind and the mental states of leaving of the two absorptions free from mind (ii.41), and all the moments of these two absorptions with the exception of the first, have the mind entering into absorption for their equal and immediately antecedent condition,

but they do not immediately follow this mind (ii.64b).

2. The characteristics (*lakṣaṇas*, ii.45c) 1) of the first moment of the two absorptions, and 2) of all minds and all mental states of a conscious state, immediately follow a mind, but do not have any equal and immediately antecedent condition.

3. The first moment of the two absorptions, and all minds and mental states of a conscious state, have the mind that they immediately follow for their equal and immediately antecedent condition.

4. The characteristics 1) of all the moments of the two absorptions with the exception of the first, and 2) of the mind and the mental states of leaving these two absorptions, have no equal and immediately antecedent condition, for they are *dharmas* disassociated from the mind (*viprayukta*, ii.35); and they do not immediately follow a mind.

***

What is an object as condition?

62c. All *dharmas* are the objects of consciousness.

All the *dharmas*, conditioned as well as unconditioned, are "objects of consciousness" of the mind and its mental states, but not indiscriminately so. For example, the visual consciousness and the mental states, sensation, etc., which are associated with it, have all visible things for their object; the hearing consciousness, sounds; the smelling consciousness, odors; and the touch consciousness, tangible things. The mental consciousness and the mental states that are associated with it have all the *dharmas* for their objects. (Kārikā 62c is then understood literally with respect to the *manas*).

When a *dharma* is the object of a mind, it is not possible that this *dharma*, at any moment, is not the object of this mind. This means that even if a visible object is not grasped as an object by the visual consciousness, it is an object, for, whether it is grasped or not grasped as an object, its nature remains the same, as fuel is combustible, even when it is not on fire.

We can establish a threefold determination in considering the problem from the point of view of the mind that grasps a *dharma* as its object. The mind is determined 1) with regard to its *āyatana*: for example, a visual consciousness is supported only on a visible thing (*rūpa-āyatana*); 2) with regard to the *dravya* or substantial thing: a certain visual consciousness, the consciousness of blue, of red, etc., is supported by blue, red, etc. (see i.10); and 3) with regard to a moment (*kṣaṇa*): a certain visual consciousness is supported in a certain moment of blue.

Is the mind determined in the same way with regard to its support (*āśraya*), that is, its organ, the organ of sight, etc.?

The response is affirmative.[433] However, in the present, the mind is bound to its support; but in the past and the future, it is separated from it.

According to others, it is bound to its support in both the past and the present.[434]

***

What is a predominating condition?

62d. The cause termed *kāraṇa* is called *adhipati*, predominant.

Adhipatipratyayatā or predominating condition is *kāraṇahetu*, the "reason for being" cause (ii.50a), for *kāraṇahetu* is a "predominating condition" (*adhipatipratyaya*).

This name is justified from two points of view. The predominating condition is that which belongs to the greatest number of *dharmas*, and which is exercised with respect to the greatest number of *dharmas*.

1. All the *dharmas* are "an object as condition" of the mental consciousness. However the *dharmas* coexisting with a certain mind are not the object of this mind, whereas they are *kāraṇahetu* of it. Thus the *dharmas*, without exception, are "predominating conditions" as *kāraṇahetu*, not as "an object as condition."

2. Every *dharma* has all *dharmas* for its *kāraṇahetu*, with the exception of itself.

No *dharma* of any type is a condition of itself. And a conditioned *dharma* is not a condition of an unconditioned *dharma*, and vice versa.

***

In what state (*avasthā*), past, present, or future, are the *dharmas* found with regard to which the diverse conditions exercise their activity?

Let us first examine cause as condition, that is, as five causes, with the exclusion of *kāraṇahetu*.

> 63a-b. Two causes exercise their activity with regard to a perishing *dharma*.[435]

"Perishing" means "of the present." A present *dharma* is called "perishing," "in the act of perishing," because, having arisen, it is turned towards its destruction.

Sahabhūhetu (ii.50b) and *saṁprayuktakahetu* (53c) operate with regard to a present *dharma*, because they operate with regard to a *dharma* that arises at the same time as they do.[436]

> 63b-c. Three, with regard to an arising *dharma*.

"An arising *dharma*" means a future *dharma*, because a future *dharma*, not having arisen, is turned towards arising.

The three causes in question are *sabhāgahetu* (ii.52a), *sarvatragahetu* (54a), and *vipākahetu* (54c).

Concerning the other conditions:

> 63c-d. Two other conditions, in reverse order.

First in the list of conditions there comes the equal and immediately antecedent condition: it exercises it activity as do the three causes, namely with regard to an arising *dharma*, for the minds and mental states of a given moment cede their place to the mind and mental states which are arising.

Next in the list there comes an object as condition: it exercises its activity as do the two causes, namely with regard to a perishing *dharma*: this perishing *dharma* is mind and mental states, the "subjects of the consciousness" (*ālambaka*), which, perishing,—that is, of the present,—grasp a present object.

The activity of predominent influence as a condition only consists in not creating any obstacle either to a past, present, or future *dharma.*

***

The different types of *dharmas* arise by reason of how many conditions?

> 64a. The mind and its mental states arise by reason of four conditions.[437]

1. Causes as conditions: the five causes; 2. equal and immediately antecedent condition: the earlier mind and mental states, which have arisen not separated by other minds or mental states; 3. an object as condition: the five objects of which physical matter is the first, or, in the case of the mental consciousness, all the *dharmas*; and 4. a predominating influence as condition: all the *dharmas*, except the mind and its mental states whose arising is under consideration.

> 64b. The two absorptions, by reason of three.

One must exclude the object as condition, because the absorption of non-consciousness (ii.42) and the absorption of extinction (ii.43) do not grasp an object. We have: 1. causes as conditions: two causes, *sahabhūhetu* (the *lakṣaṇas*, arising, etc. ii.45c, of the absorption), and *sabhāgahetu* (the good former *dharmas*, already arisen, belonging to the stage of absorption, that is, to the Fourth Dhyāna or to Bhavāgra, according to the case); 2. an equal and immediately antecedent condition, the mind of entry into the absorption and the mental states that are associated with this mind; the mind of entry is not separated by any mind of any of the moments of the absorption; and 3. the predominating influence as condition, as above.

These two absorptions arise from an application, from an inflection of the mind: they then have the mind as an equal and immediately antecedent condition. They hinder the arising of the mind: thus they are not equal and immediately antecedent conditions of the mind leaving the absorption, even though they are immediately contigous to it (*nirantara*, see p. 301).

64c. The other *dharmas*, by reason of two.

The other *dharmas*, namely the other *saṁskāras* disassociated form the mind and the material *dharmas*, arise by reason of the causes as conditions and the predominating influence as condition (*Vibhāṣā, TD* 27, p. 702b21).

***

All the *dharmas* that arise arise by reason of the five causes and the four conditions that we have just explained. The world does not proceed from a single cause that is called God, or Puruṣa, or Pradhāna, or any other name.[438]

How do you prove this thesis?

If you think that the thesis is proven through arguments, you betray your doctrine that the world arises from a single cause.

64d. Not from God or from any other cause, since there is a succession, etc.[439]

That things are produced by a single cause, by God, Mahadeva, or Vāsudeva, is inadmissable for many reasons.

1. If things were produced by a single cause, they would arise all at the same time: now each of us knows that they arise successively.

[The Theist:] They arise successively by virtue of the desires of God, who says, "May this arise now! May this perish now! May this arise and perish later!"

If this were the case, then things do not arise from a single cause, since the desires (of God) are multiple. Moreover these multiple desires would have to be simultaneous, since God, the cause of these desires, is not multiple, and things would all arise at the same time.

a. [The Theist:] The desires of God are not simultaneous, because God, in order to produce his desires, takes into account other causes.

If this were so, then God is not the single unique cause of all things. And the causes that God takes into account are produced successively: they depend then on causes which are themselves dependent on other causes: an infinite regression.

[The Theist:] It is admitted that the series of causes has no beginning.

This would admit that *saṁsāra* does not have an origin. You then abandon the doctrine of a single cause and return to the Buddhist theory of causes (*hetus*) and conditions (*pratyaya*).

b. [The Theist:] The desires of God are simultaneous, but things do not arise at the same time because they arise as God wishes them to arise, that is, in succession.

This is inadmissible. The desires of God remain what they are. Let us explain. Suppose that God desires "May this arise now! May that arise later!" We do not see why the second desire, at first non-efficacious, will be efficacious later; why, if it is efficacious later, it will not be so initially.

What advantage does God obtain from this great effort by which he produces the world?

[The Theist:] God produces the world for his own satisfaction (*prīti*).

He is then not God, the Sovereign (*īśvara*), in what concerns his own satisfaction, since he cannot realize it without a means (*upāya*). And if he is not sovereign with regard to his own satisfaction, how can he be sovereign with regard to the world? Further, do you say that God finds satisfaction in seeing the creatures that he has created in the prey of all the sufferings of existence, including the tortures of the hells? Homage to this God! Well said, in truth, is the popular stanza, "He is called Rudra because he burns, because he is excited, ferocious, terrible, an eater of flesh, blood, and marrow."[440]

3. The followers of God, the single cause of the world, deny visible causes,—causes and conditions,—the efficacy of the seed with regard to the sprout, etc. If, modifying their position, they admit the existence of these causes, and pretend that these causes serve God as auxiliaries, this then is no more that a pious affirmation, for we do not maintain

any activity of a cause besides the activity of the so-called secondary causes. Furthermore, God would not be sovereign with regard to auxiliary causes, since these cooperate in the production of the effect through their own efficacy. Perhaps, in order to avoid the negation of causes, which are visible, and in order to avoid the affirmation of present action by God, which is not visible, the Theist would say that the work of God is creation: but creation, dependent only on God, would never have a beginning, like God himself, and this is a consequence that the Theist rejects.

We would refute the doctrine of Puruṣa, of Pradhāna, etc., as we have refuted the theist doctrine, *mutatis mutandis*. Thus, no *dharma* arises from a single cause.

Alas, persons are unclear! Like the birds and the animals, truly worth of pity, they go from existence to existence, accomplishing diverse actions; they experience the results of these actions[441] and falsely believe that God is the cause of these results.[442] (We must explain the Truth in order to put an end to this false conception.)

***

We have seen (ii.64c) that the material *dharmas* arise by reason of two conditions, causes as conditions and predominating influences as conditions. We must specify and see how the primary elements (*bhūtas* or *mahābhūtas*), and the *dharmas* of derived matter (*upādāyarūpa* or *bhautikas*), are causes as conditions, either among themselves, or one from the other.

> 65a. The primary elements are the cause of the derived elements in two ways.[443]

The four primary elements of earth, etc., are causes of the four primary elements in the quality of similar causes (*sabhāgahetu*), and of mutually coexistant causes (*sahabhūhetu*).

> 65b. And of the derived elements, in five ways.

The four primary elements are causes of the derived elements—

color, taste, etc.—in five ways, in the quality of *janana, niśraya, pratiṣṭhā, upastambha*, and *upabṛṁhaṇahetu.*[444]

Jananahetu or generating cause, because the derived elements arise from them, like a child from his parents.[445]

Niśrayahetu or tutelage cause, because the *bhautikas*, once arisen, submerge their influence, as a monk is under the tutelage of his Ācārya and his Upādhyāya.

Pratiṣṭhāhetu or supporting cause, because the derived elements are supported by them, as a picture is supported by a wall.[446]

Upastambhahetu or maintaining cause, because the primary elements are the cause of the non-interruption of the derived elements.

Upabṛṁhaṇahetu or growth cause, because the primary elements are the cause of the development of the derived elements.

This means that the primary elements (*bhūtas*) are, with regard to the derived elements (*bhautikas*), the cause of arising (*janmahetu*), the cause of transformation (*vikārahetu*), the supporting cause (*ādhāra-hetu*), the cause of duration (*sthitihetu*), and the cause of development (*vṛddhihetu*).

> 65c. Derived elements are the cause of the derived elements in three ways.

In the qualtiy of *sahabhū, sabhāga* and *vipākahetu.* We do not mention *kāraṇahetu*, for any *dharma* is a *kāraṇahetu* of any other *dharma.*

1. The actions of the body and voice of the category described in ii.51a (i.e., the two disciplines), which are derived elements, are *sahabhūhetu.*

2. All the derived elements which have arisen, are, with regard to similar (*sabhāga*) derived elements, *sabhāgahetu.*

3. The actions of the body and voice are *vipākahetu*: the eye is produced through retribution of action, etc.

> 65d. And the cause of the primary elements, in one way.

The actions of the body and voice produce the primary elements as a retributive result: they are then *vipākahetu.*

***

We have seen that antecedent minds and mental states are the equal and immediately antecent condition of subsequent minds and mental states. But we have not explained how many types of mind arise immediately after each type of mind.

In order to define its role, we must first establish a classification of the mind.

First, we must distinguish twelve categories.

> 66a. Good, bad, defiled-neutral, undefiled-neutral minds in Kāmadhātu.[447]

Four types of minds belong to Kāmadhātu: good, bad, defiled-neutral, and undefiled-neutral.

> 66b. Good defiled-neutral, undefiled-neutral minds in Rūpadhātu and in Ārūpyadhātu.

Three types of minds are in the two higher spheres: all of the above, excluding the bad mind.

> 66c. And two pure minds.

The two pure minds are those of the Śaikṣa and the Arhat or Aśaikṣa. In all, these constitute twelve minds.

[These twelve minds do not indiscriminately arise one after the other:]

> 67a. Nine types of minds can arise after a good mind in Kāmadhātu.[448]

1. Immediately after a good mind in Kāmadhātu there can arise nine minds, namely: (1-4) the four minds in Kāmadhātu; (5-6) two minds in Rūpadhātu: good, when a ascetic enters into absorption, and defiled-neutral, when a person who dies in Kāmadhātu with a good mind passes into the intermediate existence of Rūpadhātu (iii.38); (7) a mind in Ārūpyadhātu, a defiled-neutral mind, when one dying in Kāmadhātu is reborn in Ārūpyadhātu; not good, for, since Ārūpya-

dhātu is estranged from Kāmadhātu by four estrangements,[449] one cannot pass directly from Kāmadhātu into an absorption of Ārūpyadhātu; (8-9) the two pure minds, of Śaikṣa or of Aśaikṣa, at entry into the Understanding of the Truths (vi.27).

67b. Such a [good] mind can arise after eight types of minds.

2. A good mind can arise immediately after eight minds, namely: (1-4) the four minds in Kāmadhātu, (5-6) two minds in Rūpadhātu, good and defiled-neutral minds, upon leaving an absorption. It happens in fact that an ascetic, bothered by a defiled (*kliṣṭa*) absorption, leaves this absorption: after the defiled (*kliṣṭa=nivṛta*) mind, which is this absorption, he produces a good mind of a lower stage (viii.14); and (7-8) two pure minds, of Śaikṣa or Aśaikṣa, upon leaving the Understanding of the Truths.

67c. A bad mind can arise after ten types of minds.

3. A *kliṣṭa* mind, that is to say, a bad and a defiled-neutral mind can arise after ten minds—excluding the two pure minds, for a mind of rebirth into Kāmadhātu is defiled (ii.14, iii.38) and can follow any kind of mind belonging to the three spheres of existence.

67d. Four types of minds can arise after such a (= bad) mind.

4. Four minds can arise after a *kliṣṭa* mind, namely the four minds of Kāmadhātu.

67e. The same for a defiled-neutral mind.

5. An undefiled-neutral mind can arise after five minds.

68a. An undefiled-neutral mind can arise after five types of mind.

Namely the four minds in Kāmadhātu, plus a good mind in Rūpadhātu: for a mind capable of creating fictive beings (*nirmāṇacitta*) in Kāmadhātu, a mind that has for its object the creation of an object of Kāmadhātu, follows a good mind in Rūpadhātu.

> 68b. Seven types of mind can arise after an undefiled-neutral mind.

6. After an undefiled-neutral mind there can arise seven minds, namely: (1-4) the four minds in Kāmadhātu, (5-6) two minds in Rūpadhātu, good minds, for, after the aforementioned mind of creation, a good mind reappears in Rūpadhātu, and a defiled-neutral mind, when a person, dying with this mind, is reborn in Rūpadhātu the first mind of which is necessarily a defiled-neutral mind (iii.38); (7) a mind of Ārūpyadhātu, a defiled-neutral mind, when a person, dying with this mind, is reborn in Ārūpyadhātu.

> 68c. In Rūpadhātu eleven types of minds can arise after a good mind.

1. Eleven minds, excluding an undefiled-neutral mind in Rūpadhātu, can arise immediately after a good mind in Rūpadhātu.

> 68d. A good mind can arise after nine types of minds.

2. A good mind can arise after nine minds, excluding the two defiled minds in Kāmadhātu (bad and defiled-neutral) and an undefiled-neutral mind in Ārūpyadhātu.

> 69a. A defiled-neutral mind can arise after eight types of minds.

3. A defiled-neutral mind can arise after eight minds, excluding the two defiled minds in Kāmadhātu and the two pure minds.

> 69b. Six types of minds can arise after a defiled-neutral mind.

4. Six minds can arise after a defiled-neutral mind, namely the three minds in Rūpadhātu, and the good, bad, and defiled-neutral minds in Kāmadhātu.

> 69c. An undefiled-neutral mind can arise after three types of mind.

5. An undefiled-neutral mind can arise after the three minds in Rūpadhātu.

69d. Six types of mind can arise after such a (defiled-neutral) mind.

6. Six minds can arise after an undefiled-neutral mind, namely: (1-3) the three minds in Rūpadhātu, (4-5) the two defiled minds in Kāmadhātu (bad and defiled-neutral), and (6) the defiled mind in Arupyadhatu (defiled-neutral).

69e. As above, so too in Ārūpyadhātu, for these (undefiled-neutral minds).

1. An undefiled-neutral mind in Ārūpyadhātu can arise after the three minds of this sphere.
2. Six minds can arise after an undefiled-neutral mind in Ārūpyadhātu, namely: (1-3) the three minds of this sphere, and (4-6) the defiled minds in Kāmadhātu (two) and Rūpadhātu (one).

70a. Nine types of minds can arise after a good mind.

3. Nine minds can arise after a good mind, with the exception of a good mind in Kāmadhātu and an undefiled-neutral mind in Kāmadhātu and Rūpadhātu.

70b. Such a (good mind) can arise after six types of mind.

4. A good mind can arise after six minds, namely (1-3) the three minds in Ārūpyadhātu, (4) a good mind in Rūpadhātu, and (5-6) the two pure minds.

70c. Seven types of minds can arise after a defiled-neutral mind.

5. Seven minds can arise after a defiled-neutral mind, namely (1-3) the three minds in Ārūpyadhātu, (4) a good mind in Rūpadhātu, (5-6) two defiled minds in Kāmadhātu, and (7) a defiled mind in Rūpadhātu.

70d. And the same for it.

6. A defiled-neutal mind can arise after seven minds, with the exception of the two defiled minds in Kāmādhatu, a defiled mind in Rūpadhātu and the two pure minds.

> 70e. A Śaikṣa mind can arise after four types of minds.

A Śaikṣa mind, the mind belonging to the saint who is not an Arhat, can arise after four minds, namely a Śaikṣa mind and a good mind in each of the three spheres.

> 70f. But five types of minds can arise after such (a Śaikṣa mind).

Five minds can arise after a Śaikṣa mind, namely the four that have just been named and an Aśaikṣa mind.

> 70g. An Aśaikṣa mind can arise after five types of minds.

An Aśaikṣa mind can arise after five minds, namely after a Śaikṣa mind, an Aśaikṣa mind, and a good mind of each of the three spheres.

> 71a. Four types of minds can arise after such (an Aśaikṣa mind).

Four minds can arise after an Aśaikṣa mind, namely an Aśaikṣa mind and a good mind of each of three spheres.

The twelve types of mind succeed one another in conformity with these rules.

And again,

> 71b. The twelve types of mind make twenty.

How is this?

> 71c. By dividing the good mind of the three Dhātus into two, the acquired and the innate minds.

1. A good mind of each of the three spheres is divided into two categories, 1.) that acquired through effort,[450] and 2.) that acquired by birth.[451] [We then have six types of good mind corresponding to three types of the first list.]

> 72a. By dividing an undefiled-neutral mind in Kāmadhātu into four: the retributive mind, the mind of attitude, the mind of application, and a mind that can create fictive beings.

An undefiled-neutral mind of Kāmadhātu is divided into four categories: a.) arisen from a retributive cause (*vipākaja*, ii.57); b.) relative to attitudes (*airyāpathika*), walking, standing, sitting, lying down; c.) relative to the arts (*śailpasthānika*);[452] and c.) relative to fictive creations: the mind by which a possessor of supernatural power creates visible things, etc., is called the result of *abhijñā (abhijñāphala*, vii.49) (see above p. 270).

> 72b. By excluding the undefiled-neutral mind of application in Rūpadhātu.

An undefiled-neutral mind in Rūpadhātu is divided into only three categories, for *śailpasthānika* does not exist in this sphere.

[There is no reason to divide the undefiled-neutral mind of Ārūpyadhātu, for it is exclusively arisen from a retributive cause.]

We then have seven types of undefiled-neutral minds corresponding to the two undefiled-neutral minds of the first list. By taking into account the good minds, we obtain a total of twenty.

Three undefiled-neutral minds, the *airyāpathika* mind and following, have visible things, odors, taste, and tangible things for their object.[453] The *śailpasthānika* mind, furthermore, has sound for its object.[454]

These three undefiled-neutral minds are solely mental consciousnesses. However the five sense consciousnesses preceed and prepare the *airyāpathika* and *śailpasthānika* minds.[455]

According to another opinion,[456] there is a mental consciousness produced by the *airyāpathika* mind,[457] which has the twelves *āyatanas*, from the organ of sight to the *dharmāyatana*, for its object.

2. Twenty minds arise one after another, in conformity with the following rules:

i. Kāmadhātu: eight types of mind of the sphere of Kāmadhātu, namely two good minds, two *kliṣṭa* (bad, defiled-neutral) minds, and four undefiled-neutral minds.

1. Good Acquired through Effort.

Followed by ten: (1-7) seven minds of the same sphere, with the exception of *abhijñāphala (nirmāṇacitta*); (8) a mind of Rūpadhātu acquired through effort; and (9-10) a Śaikṣa mind and an Aśaikṣa mind.

It follows seven: (1-4) four minds of the same sphere, the two good minds and the two *kliṣṭa* minds; (5-6) a mind acquired through effort and an undefiled mind of Rūpadhātu; (7-8) a Śaikṣa mind and an Aśaikṣa mind.

2. Good Acquired through Birth.

Followed by ten: (1-7) seven minds of the same sphere, with the exception of *abhijñāphala*; (8-9) undefiled-neutral minds of Rūpadhātu and Arūpyadhātu.

It follows eleven: (1-7) seven minds of the same sphere, with the exception of *abhijñāphala*; (8-9) a mind acquired through effort and an undefiled-neutral mind of Rūpadhātu; (10-11) a Śaikṣa mind and an Aśaikṣa mind.

3-4. Bad and defiled-neutral.

Followed by seven minds of the same sphere, with the exception of *abhijñāphala*.

They follow fourteen: ((1-7) seven minds of the same sphere, with the exception of *abhijñāphala*; (8-11) four minds of Rūpadhātu, with the exception of a mind acquired through effort and *abhijñāphala*; (12-14) three minds of Arūpyadhātu, with the exception of a mind acquired through effort.

5-6. *Vipākaja* and *airyāpathika*.

Followed by eight: (1-6) six minds of the same sphere, with the exeption of a mind acquired through effort and *abhijñāphala*; (7-8) an undefiled-neutral mind of Rūpadhātu and of Arūpyadhātu.

They follow seven minds of the same sphere follow, with the exception of *abhijñāphala*.

7. *Śailpasthānika*.

Followed by six minds of the same sphere, with the exception of a mind acquired through effort and *abhijñāphala*.

They follow seven minds of the same sphere, with the exception of *abhijñaphala*.

8. *Abhijñāphala*.

Followed by two minds, *abhijñāphala* of the same sphere and a mind acquired through effort in Rūpadhātu.

It follows two: the same.

***

ii. Rūpadhātu: six types of mind of the sphere of Rūpadhātu, namely two good minds, one *kliṣṭa* (defiled-neutral) mind, and three undefiled-neutral minds.

1. Good Acquired through Effort.

Followed by twelve: (1-6) six of the same sphere, (7-9) three of Kāmadhātu: good acquired through effort, good acquired through birth; and *abhijñāphala*; 10) a mind of Arūpyadhātu acquired through effort; and (11-12) a Śaikṣa mind and an Aśaikṣa mind.

If follows ten: (1-4) four of the same sphere, excepting *airyāpathika* and *vipākaja*, (5-6) two of Kāmadhātu, acquired through effort and *abhijñāphala*; (7-8) two of Arūpyadhātu, acquired through effort and defiled-neutral; and (9-10) a Śaikṣa mind and an Aśaikṣa mind.

2. Good Acquired through Birth.

Followed by eight: (1-5) five of the same sphere, except *abhijñāphala*; (6-7) two of Kāmadhātu, bad and defiled-neutral;[458] and (8) a defiled-neutral mind of Arūpyadhātu.

It follows five of the same sphere, except *abhijñāphala*.

3. Defiled-neutral minds.

Followed by nine minds: (1-5) five minds of the same sphere, with the exception of an *abhijñāphala* mind; (6-9) four minds of Kāmadhātu, two good minds and two *kliṣṭa* minds.

They follow eleven minds: (1-5) five minds of the same sphere, with the exception of an *abhijñāphala* mind; (6-8) three minds of Kāmadhātu, an mind acquired through birth, an *airyāpathika* mind, and a *vipākaja* mind; (9-11) three minds of Arūpyadhātu, with the exception of a mind acquired though effort.

4-5. *Vipākaja* and *airyāpathika* minds.

Followed by seven minds: (1-4) four minds of the same sphere, with the exception of a mind acquired through effort and an *abhijñāphala* mind; (5-6) two minds of Kāmadhātu, a bad mind and a defiled-neutral mind; (7) one mind of Ārūpyadhātu, a defiled-neutral mind.

They follow five minds of the same sphere, with the exception of an *abhijñāphala* mind.

6. *Abhijñāphala.*

Followed by two minds of the same sphere, a mind acquired through effort and an *abhijñāphala* mind.

It follows two minds: the same.

***

iii. Ārūpyadhātu: four types of mind of the sphere of Ārūpyadhātu, namely two good minds, a defiled-neutral mind and a *vipākaja* mind.

1. Good Acquired through Effort.

Followed by seven mind: (1-4) four minds of the same sphere; (5) a mind of Rūpadhātu acquired through effort; and (6-7) a Śaikṣa mind and an Aśaikṣa mind.

2. Good Acquired through Birth.

Followed by seven minds: (1-4) four minds of the same sphere; (5) a defiled-neutral mind of Rūpadhātu; (6-7) a bad mind and a defiled-neutral mind of Kāmadhātu.

It follows four minds of the same sphere.

3. Defiled-neutral.

Followed by eight minds: (1-4) four minds of the same sphere; (5-6) a mind acquired through effort and a defiled-neutral mind of Rūpadhātu; (7-8) a bad mind and a defiled-neutral mind of Kāmadhātu.

It follows ten minds: (1-4) four minds of the same sphere; (5-10) a mind acquired through birth, an *airyāpathika* mind, and an *vipākaja* mind of Rūpadhātu and Kāmadhātu.

4. *Vipākaja.*

Followed by six minds: (1-3) three minds of the same sphere, with the exception of a mind acquired through effort; (4) a defiled-neutral mind of Rūpadhātu; (5-6) a bad mind and a defiled-neutral mind of Kāmadhātu. Four minds follow, of this same sphere.

***

v. The two pure minds:

1. Śaikṣa.

Followed by six minds: (1-3) a mind acquired through effort of the three spheres; (4) an mind acquired through effort of Kāmadhātu; and (5-6) a Śaikṣa mind and an Aśaikṣa mind.

It follows four minds: (1-3) a mind acquired through effort of the three spheres; (4) a Śaikṣa mind.

2. Aśaikṣa.

Followed by five minds: the six minds which follow Śaikṣa with the exception of the Śaikṣa mind.

It follows five minds: (1-3) a mind acquired through effort of the three spheres, (4-5) a Śaikṣa mind and an Aśaikṣa mind.

***

3. Remarks.

a. *Vipākaja, airyāpathika* and *śailpasthānika* minds arise immediately after a mind in Kāmadhātu acquired through effort. For what reason is this not reciprocally true?

A *vipākaja* mind is not favorable to a mind acquired through effort, because it is weak, and because it develops spontaneously.

Airyāpathika and *śailpasthānika* minds are not favorable to a mind acquired through effort because their reason for being is the creation of an attitude or a created thing.

Contrarily, the *niṣkramaṇacitta* or the mind of leaving,—that is, any mind, a *vipākaja* mind, etc., by which a Yogin leaves the series of minds acquired through effort, such as reading, philosophical reflection, etc.—develops spontaneously. The mind of leaving can then immediately follow a mind acquired through effort.

b. Objection: If a mind acquired through effort does not arise immediately after the *vipākaja*, etc., because these are not favorable to it, still less will it arise after a defiled (*kliṣṭa*) mind which is contrary to it.

A defiled mind is contrary to a mind acquired through effort. Yet, when an ascetic is exhausted from the activity of the defilements, a mind acquired through effort arises from the fact that the ascetic lays hold of a perfect consciousness (*parijñāna*) of this activity.

c. The innate good mind of Kāmadhātu is sharp; hence it can arise after the two pure minds and also after a mind in Rūpadhātu acquired through effort, but, as it develops spontaneously, it is not followed by these same minds.

An innate good mind of Kāmadhātu, being sharp, can arise after a defiled mind of Rūpadhātu; but an innate good mind of Rūpadhātu, not being sharp, cannot arise after a defiled mind of Arūpyadhātu.

[4. The minds arise immediately one after another, and they arise by reason of an act of attention. We must then study the act of attention.]

i. We can distinguish three acts of attention:

1. *Svalakṣaṇamanaskāra*, an act of attention to specific characteristics, for example the judgements "*Rūpa* has *rūpaṇa* for its characteristic . . . *vijñāna* has *prativijñapti* for its characteristic" (i.13, 16).

2. *Sāmānyalakṣaṇmanaskāra*, an act of attention to common or general characteristics, to the sixteen aspects of the Truths, impermanence, etc., and "The conditioned *dharmas* are impermanent" (see vii.10).

3. *Adhimuktimanaskāra*: this act of attention is not, like the first two, directed to that which exists; rather, it proceeds from *adhimukti*, that is, from constructive imagination (*adhimuktyā . . . manaskāraḥ*, see p. 190); it presides over the contemplations of *aśubhā* (vi.9),[459] the *apramāṇas* (viii.29), the *vimokṣas* (viii.32) the *abhibhvāyatanas* (viii.34) the *kṛtsnāyatanas* (viii.35), etc.

[c. The innate good mind of Kāmadhātu is sharp; hence it can arise after the two pure minds and also after a mind of Rūpadhātu acquired through effort, but, as it develops spontaneously, it is not followed by these same minds.

An innate good mind of Kāmadhātu, being sharp, can arise after a defiled mind of Rūpadhātu; but an innate good mind of Rūpadhātu, not being sharp, cannot arise after a defiled mind of Ārūpyadhātu.]

[According to the first Master quoted by the *Vibhāṣā, TD* 27, p. 53a19) one can realize the Path after these three acts of attention, and, inversely, one can produce these three acts of attention immediately after the Path. This opinion is supported by the text, "He produces the part of Bodhi called memory in company with (that is, after) the contemplation of repulsive things (*aśubhā*)."[460]

[According to the third Master quoted in the *Vibhāṣā*) it is solely after an act of attention to general characteristics that one can realize the Path; after the Path, one can produce the three acts of attention. As for the text quoted by the first Master, it should be understood in the sense that, after having subdued his mind by means of the contemplation of repulsive things, an ascetic is capable of producing an act of attention to general characteristics, after which he realizes the Path. The text refers to this indirect action of the contemplation of repulsive things and so says, "*aśubhāsahagatam* . . ."

[According to the fourth Master of the *Vibhāṣā*,) it is only after an act of attention to general characteristics that an ascetic can realize the Path; furthermore, after the Path, he can only produce acts of attention to general characteristics.

The author refutes the third Master: Certainly, we indeed see that an ascetic who has entered into *samyaktvaniyāma*, onto the Path (see iv.27) by relying on one of the three lower stages (i.e., *anāgamya*, First Dhyāna, *dhyānāntara*), can produce, upon coming out of the Path, an act of attention to general characteristics in Kāmadhātu and can be established in hearing or in reflection, because the stages in question are near; but, when an ascetic has entered *samyaktvaniyāma* by relying on the Second, Third, or Fourth Dhyāna, to which stage could the act of attention to general characteristics belong that he produces upon coming out of the Path?

He will produce an act of attention to general characteristics in Kāmadhātu, because Kāmadhātu is too estranged from the higher Dhyānas. He will not produce an act of attention to general characteristics of the sphere of one of the three higher Dhyānas, because he has not previously obtained conscious acts of attention, except in the course of the practice of the *nirvedhabhāgīyas* (vi.17: contemplations preliminary to entry onto the Path): now an Āryan cannot again realize the *nirvedhabhāgīyas*, for we cannot admit that he would for a second time realize the preparatory path, since he already possesses its result.

But, we would say, there exists other acts of attention to general characteristics (*sāmānyamanaskāras*) which have been cultivated at the same time as the *nirvedhabhāgīyas* (as they refer to the Truths, but which differ by not refering to all their sixteen aspects): for example, seeing that "all *saṁskāras* are impermanent," "all *dharmas* are impersonal," "Nirvāṇa is tranquil" (a general or *sāmānya* judgement, since it refers to any Nirvāṇa). It is this other type of *sāmānyamanaskāra* that an ascetic brings forth upon leaving the Path.

The Vaibhāṣikas do not accept this opinion, because it is illogical. [In fact, the cultivation of the *manaskāras* of this type is bound to the *nirvedhabhāgīyas*]. (*Vibhāṣā, TD* 27, p. 53b3).

(The correct doctrine is that the Path can be followed by the three categories of the act of attention.) When one obtains the result of Arhat based on Anāgāmya (*Vibhāṣā, TD* 27, p. 53b25), the mind leaving the absorption is either of this stage (Anāgāmya) or of the sphere of Kāmadhātu. When one obtains the same result based on Ākiñcanya, the mind of leaving is either of this same stage (Ākiñcanya), or of *naivasaṁjnānāsaṁjñāyatana* (Bhavāgra). When one obtains the same result by relying on any other stage, the mind of leaving is solely of this other stage.

ii. There are four types of acts of attention: 1.) an innate or natural act of attention, *upapatipratilambhika*, 2.) attention produced from the teaching, *śrutamaya*, 3.) from reflection, *cintāmaya*, and 4.) from meditation, *bhāvanāmaya*. Three are possible in Kāmadhātu, the first, the second, and the third, for meditation is not of Kāmadhātu. Three are possible in Rūpadhātu, the first, the second, and the fourth, for, in this sphere, as soon as one meditates or reflects (*cintā*), one enters into absorption. Two are possible in Ārūpyadhātu, the first and the fourth. There are then eight acts of attention, three, three and two (*Vibhāṣā, TD* 27, p. 53b14).

The Path is never produced after an act of innate attention, to whichever sphere it may belong, for the Path requires effort. The Path is hence produced after five acts of attention, two of Kāmadhātu, two of Rūpadhātu, and one of Ārūpyadhātu. But, after the Path, an act of innate attention of Kāmadhātu can arise, because it is sharp.

***

How many minds are acquired when one manifests each of the twelve types of minds?

> 73a-b. With the defiled mind of each of the three spheres, there is obtaining of six, of six, and of two minds respectively.

"Obtaining" means taking possession of what one did not previously possess.

i. Obtaining the six minds with a defiled mind of Kāmadhātu.

a. One obtains a good mind of Kāmadhātu (1) when one again takes up the roots of good with a mind of doubt, which is defiled (iv.80c); or (2) when one returns to Kāmadhātu by falling from the higher spheres. The mind of conception is necessarily defiled (iii.38); with this mind one takes possession of a good mind of Kāmadhātu, for one did not previously possess it.[461]

b-c. One obtains a bad mind and defiled-neutral mind of Kāmadhātu (1) when one returns to Kāmadhātu by falling from the higher spheres: for then one takes possession of whichever of these two minds manifests itself; or (2) when one falls from the detachment of Kāmadhātu.

d. One obtains a defiled-neutral mind of Rūpadhātu when one falls from Ārūpyadhātu into Kāmadhātu. One in fact takes possession of a defiled-neutral mind of Rūpadhātu with a defiled mind of conception in Kāmadhātu.

e-f. One obtains a defiled-neutral mind of Ārūpyadhātu and a Śaikṣa mind when one falls from the quality of an Arhat through the mind of Kāmadhātu.

ii. Obtaining the six minds with a defiled mind of Rūpadhātu.

One obtains one undefiled-neutral mind of Kāmadhātu (the mind capable of creating fictive beings, *nirmāṇacitata*) and the three minds of Rūpadhātu when one falls from Ārūpyadhātu into Rūpadhātu.

One obtains a defiled-neutral mind of Ārūpyadhātu and a Śaikṣa mind when one falls from the quality of an Arhat through a mind of Rūpadhātu.

iii. One obtains a defiled-neutral mind of Ārūpyadhātu and a Śaikṣa mind with the defiled mind of Arūpyadhātu when one falls from the quality of Arhat through a mind of Arūpyadhātu.

> 73b-c. There is the obtaining of three with a good mind of Rūpadhātu.

One obtains three minds with a good mind of Rūpadhātu: this mind itself, and the undefiled-neutral minds of Kāmadhātu and Rūpadhātu, that is, the minds capable of creating fictive beings relative to these two spheres.

> 73c-d. There is an obtaining of four with a Śaikṣa mind.

When one realizes the first Śaikṣa mind, namely *duḥkhe dharmajñānakṣānti* (vi.25d), one obtains four minds: (1) the Śaikṣa mind itself, (2-3) two undefiled-neutral minds, one of Kāmadhātu and one of Rūpadhātu (the mind capable of creating fictive beings), and (4) a good mind of Ārūpyadhātu: there is, by virtue of the Path, entry into the Path (*niyāmāvakrānti*, vi.26a) and detachment from Kāmadhātu and Ārūpyadhātu.

> 73d. One obtains these same minds with the other minds.

One obtains the minds not specified above only when they manifest themselves.

According to another opinion, without making any distinction among the spheres, it is said that "The wise say that, with a defiled mind, one obtains nine minds; with a good mind one obtains six; and with a neutral mind one obtains a neutral mind."[462]

Concerning the good mind, one should correct this passage so that it reads "one obtains seven." When a person again takes up the roots of good by means of Right View (*samyagdṛṣṭi*, iv.80), he obtains a good mind of Kāmadhātu; when he detaches himself from Kāmadhātu, he obtains the minds capable of creating fictive beings of Kāmadhātu and Rūpadhātu, which are two undefiled-neutral minds; when he takes up the absorptions of Rūpadhātu and Ārūpyadhātu, he obtains the good minds of these two spheres; upon entry onto the Path, he obtains a Śaikṣa mind; upon his entry into the result of Arhatship, he obtains an Aśaikṣa mind.

For the two other minds, the reckoning of the minds obtained is established according to the explanation that we have given. Here is a stanza which serves as a memory-aide:

> "At conception, in absorption, in detachment, in falling, and in the taking up again of the roots of good, one obtains minds that one did not possess."

1. Below *ad* ii.2a, *ādhipatya* = *adhikaprabhutva*, sovereignty or predominating power. See *Siddhāntakaumudī* quoted in Dict. de Saint-Petersbourg; Garbe, *Sāṁkhya-Philosophie*, 257. Compare the explanation of the *indriyas* in the *Atthasālinī*, 304, etc.

2. *Kārikā* ii.1, in the *Samayapradīpikā*, omits the word *kila* by which Vasubandhu indicates that he does not share this doctrine of the School. *Kārikās* ii.2-4, where Vasubandhu presents the teaching of the Sautrāntikas, are omitted in the *Samayapradīpikā*.

3. Buddhaghosa explains in *Atthasālinī* (641) that boys' games are not the same as girls' games.

4. According to the *Vyākhyā*, Ancient Masters (*pūrvācārya*).

5. *Saṁyutta*, i.39. Asanga (*Sūtrālaṁkāra*, xviii.83, p. 151 ed. Levi) demonstrates the predominance of the mind over the *saṁskāras: cittenāyaṁ loko nīyāte cittena parikṛṣyate cittasyotpannasya vaśe vartate. (Aṅguttara*, ii.177).

6. Hsüan-tsang: "for all the pure *dharmas* arise and develop following them."

7. "The mind of one who experiences agreeable sensation is recollected." An extract from the *Sūtra on the Vimuktyāyananas*, quoted in *Vyākhyā*, p. 56 *ad* i.27; *Mahāvyutpatti*, 81.

8. "Faith arises from suffering," *Saṁyutta*, ii.31. For this sense of the word *upaniṣad*, "cause," see below ii.49 (note on *hetu* and *pratyaya*), *Aṅguttara*, iv.351 = *Suttanipāta (Dvayatānupassanasutta)* (. . . *kā upanisā savanāya), Sūtrālaṁkāra*, xi.9 (*yogopaniṣad* = having effort for its cause). In the sense of "comparision," "to being together," *Pāṇini* i.4.79, *Vajracchedikā*, 35.10, 42.7 and Hoernle, *Manuscript Remains*, i. p. 192 (*upaniśāṁ na kṣamate), Sukhāvatīvyūha*, 31.9, *Mahāvyutpatti*, 223.15 (where the Tibetan has *rgyu*). In the sense of *upāṁśu*, "secret," Yaśomitra (*ad* ii.49) mentions *Dīgha*, ii.259 (*sūryopaniṣado devāḥ* = *suriyassūpanissā devā*)*: upaniṣacchabdas tu kadācid upāṁśau kadācit prāmukhye tadyathā sūryopaniṣado devā ity upāṁśuprayoga upaniṣatprayoga iti*. (E. Leumann, *ZDMG*, 62, p. 101 supposes *upaniśrā* = *upanissā* = *Grundlage, Nahe,* from whence the adjective *upanissa*). See Minaev, *Zapiski*, ii.3, 277); Wogihara, *ZDMG*, 58, 454 (*dānopaniṣadā śīlopaniṣadā . . . prajñayā*) and Asanga's *Bodhisattvabhūmi*, p. 21; S. Lévi, *Sūtrālaṁkāra, ad* xi.9.

9. The Sūtra says: *cakṣurvijñeyāni rūpāṇi pratītyotpadyate saumanasyaṁ naiṣkramyāśritam / . . . manaḥ pratītya dharmāṁś cotpadyate saumanasyam / . . . daurmanasyam . . . upekṣā.*

Naiṣkramya = "pure or impure path," or rather "departure (*niṣkramaṇa*) or detachement from one sphere of existence (*dhātu*) or from *saṁsāra*." See also iv.77b-c.

Aśrita = "having for its object," or rather "favorable to."

We have then: "There is, by reason of visible things, etc., six sensations of satisfaction, six sensations of dissatisfaction, and six sensations of equanimity, favorable to *naiṣkramya*."

Compare *Majjhima*, iii.218, *Saṁyutta*, iv.232, *Majjhima*, iii.217, *Milinda*, 45 (*nekkhammasita*).

10. Vasubandhu says: "Some other masters . . ."

11. Compare *Dhammasaṅgaṇi*, 633, and *Atthasālinī*, 641.

12. The Japanese editor, Kyokuga Saeki, refers to the *Madhyamāgama TD* 1, p. 458a24. Compare *Saṁyutta*, iv.208: *yo sukhāya vedanāya rāgānusayo so anuseti.*

13. Sensation-of-pleasure (*sukhā*) also means sensation-of-satisfaction (*saumanasya*); see ii.7.
Compare v.23 and 54; also *Yogasūtra*, ii.7-8: *sukhānuśayi rāgaḥ /duḥkhānuśayī dveṣaḥ.*

14. In the worldly (*laukika*) path faith and the other moral faculties disturb the defilements; in the *nirvedhabhāgīyas* (vi.45c), they "lead to" the Path; pure, they constitute *anājñātamājñāsyāmi*, etc. (ii.9b, vi.68).

15. Paramārtha and Hsüan-tsang translate the first line: "By reason of their predominence with respect to the acquisition of higher and higher paths, of Nirvāṇa, etc."
Dhammasaṅgaṇi, 286, 505, 553; *Nettipakaraṇa* 15, 60; *Compendium*, p. 177.

16. *Ājñātāvīndriya* is confused with the quality of Arhat; it includes *kṣayajñāna* and *anutpādajñāna*: knowledge that the defilements are destroyed and will no more arise, etc. (vi.45, *Nettipakaraṇa*, p. 15); he is "delivered" (*vimukta*) through deliverence from the defilements (*kleśavimukti*) and through deliverence from existence (*saṁtānavimukti*): it is thus predominant in relation to *parinirvāṇa* or *nirupadhiśeṣanirvāṇa*.

17. Objection of the Sāṁkhyas. *Sāṁkhyakārikā*, 34.

18. This *kārikā* becomes *kārikā* 2 in the *Samayapradīpikā*.

19. We encounter this expression i.35 (see also note 20). The six supports of the organs (*indriyādhiṣṭhāna*), that is to say the visible eye, etc., and the six consciousnesses (*ṣaḍ vijñānakāyaḥ*) are also *sattvadravya*, constituents of the living being, but not primary (*maula*) constituents, for they depend on the predominating quality of the six organs.

20. *Ṣaḍāyatana* is essentially the living being who is said to transmigrate: it is thus the support of transmigration.

21. Only two *āyatanas, kāya* and *manas*, exist from conception (ii.14).

22. The newborn infant can see, but cannot speak. Words are action (*karman*) of the tongue which is the support (*adhiṣṭhāna*) of the organ of taste (*jihvendriya*). For the Sāṁkhyas, the organs of action (*karmendriya*) are, like the organs of consciousness, suprasensible substances (*atīndriya*). "Voice" is the power to speak, "hand" is the power to grasp, etc.

23. You affirm that snakes possess subtle (*sūkṣma*) hands and feet, but you must prove it.

24. *Upastha* is conceived as distinct from the male or female organ, which is one part, one place, of the organ of touch (*kāyendriyaikadeśastripuruṣendriyavyatiriktakalpita*).
"Pleasure" (*ānanda*) is *kliṣṭa saukhya*.

25. Compare the definitions of the *Vibhaṅga*, p. 123.

26. The body is the organ of sight and the four other organs of sense consciousness: these organs, in fact, are collections (*kāya*) or accumulations (*saṁcaya*) of atoms. Sensation which is produced in a "body," or which accompanies a "body" upon which they are supported, is called bodily. (See ii.25, or bodily *praśrabdhi*).

27. *Sukha* is *sāta*, the agreeable, that which does good (*sātatvād hi sukham ucyate*); in addition, satisfaction supposes joy (*prīti*).
This problem is taken up again viii.9b.

28. One should make an exception of agreeable mental sensation which proceeds from absorption (*samādhi*) or which is the result of retribution (*vipākaphala*) (ii.57).

29. It is solely *vipākaphala* and *naiṣyandikī* (ii.57c).

30. In fact, the group (*kalāpa*) which is made up of the three pure *indriyas* includes only seven *indriyas*, for the three sensations never coexist. When an ascetic, in order to cultivate the Path, abides in the first two Dhyānas, he possesses a single sensation of satisfaction (*saumanasyendriya*); he possesses a single sensation of pleasure (*sukhendriya*) when he cultivates the Path in the third Dhyāna; and he possesses a single sensation of indifference (*upekṣendriya*) when he cultivates the Path in the other stages (*anāgamya, dhyānāntara*, Fourth Dhyāna, first three *Ārūpyas*). See ii.16c-17b.

31. *Darśanamārga* includes the first fifteen moments of the comprehension of the Truths (*abhisamaya*), moments in the course of which one sees that which one has not previously seen (vi.28c-d). It is exclusively pure, *anāsrava*, vi.1.

32. In the Abhidhamma, we have *anaññātaññassāmītindriya* (*Vibhaṅga*, p. 124).

33. The term *bhāvanā* has many meanings. In the expression *bhāvanāmaya*, it is synonymous with *samādhi* or absorption. Some other meanings are studied vii.27 (compare ii.25.2). In the expression *bhāvanāmārga*, "Path of Meditation," *bhāvanā* signifies "repeated view, meditation."

There are two *bhāvanāmārgas*:

a. Pure (*anāsrava*) or supermundane (*lokottara*) *bhāvanāmārga*, which is under consideration here: this is a meditation on the Truths which have already been seen in *darśanamārga*. This path begins with the sixteenth moment of the comprehension of the Truths (vi.28c-d) and terminates with the acquisition of the quality of Arhat.

b. Impure (*sāsrava*) or worldly (*laukika*) *bhāvanāmārga*; it does not have the Truths for its object (vi.49); it disturbs (*viṣkambh*) the defilements without uprooting them; it can precede and follow *darśanamārga*.

34. *Dhātupāṭha*, i.631.

35. Paramārtha differs from Hsüan-tsang.

36. The Japanese editor quotes on this subject Harivarman's *Ch'eng-shih lun, TD* 32, p. 282a18.

37. According to the Japanese editor, the Mahīśāsakas; the Hetuvādins and the Mahiṁsāsakas in *Kathāvatthu*, xix,8. Compare *ibid.* iii.6.

38. *Saṁyutta*, vi.204: *yassa kho bhikkhave imāni pañcindriyāṇi sabbena sabbaṁ sabbathā sabbaṁ natthi taṁ ahaṁ bāhiro puthujjanapakkhe ṭhito ti vadāmi.* See ii.40b-c.

39. This text is quoted in the *Vijñānakāya, TD* 26, p. 535b29 and foll. with some elaboration.

40. Compare *Sumaṅgalavilāsinī*, p. 59, on the two types of *pṛthagjana*, the *andha* and the *kalyāṇa*.

41. *Dīgha*, ii.38, *Majjhima*, i.169. The *Kathāvatthu* quotes *Dīgha*, ii.38 (. . . *tikkhindriya mudindriye* . . .).

42. *Saṁyuktāgama, TD* 2, p. 183al. Compare *Saṁyutta*, v.193 and following. *Vibhāṣā, TD* 27, p. 8a14.

43. Compare *Vibhaṅga*, p. 125; *Vibhāṣā, TD* 27, p. 741b19.

44. On life and death, see ii.45.

45. Commentary: *tad āyuḥ praṇidhāya cetasikṛtvā. Vibhāṣā,TD* 27, p. 656b17-c3.

46. *Vyākhyā*: The Buddha for the good of others, the Śrāvaka for the duration of the Law. See Lévi and Chavannes, "Les seize Arhats protecteurs de la Loi," J.As. 1916, ii.9 and following.

47. One should understand *roga, gaṇḍa*, and *śalya*, corresponding to the three sufferings, vi.3.

48. Literally: "his series is not supported by the defilements." These are the *kleśas* which support and make the series last. A *samayavimukta* Arhat is free from the defilements, but does not have mastery of absorption; a *dṛṣṭiprāpta* Arhat possesses this mastery, but he is not free from the defilements (vi.56).

49. Compare *Divyāvadāna*, 203; *atha Bhagavāṁs tadrūpaṁ samādhiṁ samāpanno yathā samāhite citte jīvitasaṁskārān adhiṣṭhāya āyuḥsaṁskārāna utsraṣṭum ārabdhaḥ*. We have the singular in the *Mahāvastu*, i.125.19.

Dīgha, ii.99: *yan nūnāhaṁ imaṁ ābādham viriyena paṭippaṇāmetvā jīvitasaṁkhāram adhiṭṭhāya vihareyyam*; ii.106 . . . *āyusaṁkhāram ossaji*. (Compare *Saṁyutta*, v.152, *Aṅguttara*, iv.311, *Udāna*, vi.1). Burnouf, *Lotus*, 291.

50. The Pali has the plural in other contexts, *Majjhima*, i.295 (*aññe āyusaṁkhārā aññe vedaniyā dhammā), Jātaka*, iv.215 (*āyusaṁkhārā khīyanti*).

51. *Vibhāṣā, TD* 27, p. 657c10 and foll., enumerates fourteen opinions on this point.

52. Eleventh opinion in the *Vibhāṣā*.

53. Sixth opinion in the *Vibhāṣā*.

54. Doctrine of the Sāṁmitīyas, according to the Japanese editor.

55. Opinion of the Sautrāntikas.

56. According to the Japanese editor, this is the opinion of the author.

57. *Vibhāṣā, TD* 27, p. 657c5, the fifth of the six opinions.

58. According to the very clear version of Paramārtha, "a *kalpa* or more than a *kalpa*," but customarily translated as "a *kalpa* or the rest of the *kalpa*" (Windisch, Rhys Davids, 0. Franke). *Dīgha*, ii.103, iii.77; *Divya*, 201. *Kathāvatthu*, xi.5.

59. They adopt the sixth opinion of the *Vibhāṣā*.

60. *Dharmasaṁgraha*, lxxx; *Mahāvastu*, iii.273, 281; *Śikṣāsamuccaya*, 198.10; *Madhyamakavṛtti*, 49 n. 4, xxii, 10; *Bodhicaryāvatāra*, ix.36 (The Blessed One is a *jina* because he has conqured the four Māras); *Yü-chia chih-ti lun*, xxix, translated by S. Lévi, *Seize Arhats*, p. 7 (*J.As*.. 1916, ii). In inconography (Foucher, *École des Hautes Études*, XIII, ii.19), the Buddha is flanked by four Māras, blue, yellow, red and green. The list of the four Māras in word-lists, Zachariae, *Gel. Gott. Anz*. 1888, p. 853. See also the lists of Childers (five Māras with the addition of *abhisaṁskāramāra*). The *Nettippakaraṇa* distinguishes *kilesamāra* and *sattamāra (=devaputra)*.

61. The sensation of suffering (*duḥkhendriya*) is never *airyāpathika*, etc.

62. *Ekottarāgama, TD* 2, p. 602b13. The Tipiṭaka speaks of *sukhavedanīya karman*, "which is retributed in pleasure" (*Aṅguttara* iv.382, etc.) (see iv.45); *sukhavedanīya, daurmanasyavedanīya sparśa (Saṁyutta*, v.211, etc.). See iv.57d.

63. According to the etymology of the author, *saumanasyavedanīya* signifies "action allowing satisfaction to be experienced by right of retribution (*saumanasyaṁ vipākatvena vedanīyam asya*). According to the Vaibhāṣikas, "action in which satisfaction should be experienced" (*saumanasyaṁ vedanīyam asmin*): this is *saṁprayogavedanīyatā* (iv.49).

64. According to the Sūtra, those "non-detached" have two thorns, physical suffering (*kāyika duḥkha*) and mental suffering (*caitasika daurmanasya*); those "detached" are free from mental suffering.

65. Thus persons who are detached do not possess all the *indriyas* which are retribution.

66. Omitted by Hsüan-tsang.

67. The quality of an androgyne, that is the possession (*pratilambha*) of the two organs, is a *dharma* disassociated (*viprayukta*) from the mind, ii.35.

68. This is to implicitely say that the first eight *indriyas*, as well as the last three, are always without retribution. Hsüan-tsang completes the *kārikā* in order to explicitely fix this point.

The *kārikā* has *tat tv ekaṁ savipākam: tu* in the sense of *eva*, and out of place; the meaning would appear to call for: *tad ekaṁ savipākam eva* = only dissatisfaction exclusively "possesses retribution."

69. Hsüan-tsang: The last eight are solely good; dissatisfaction is good or evil; the mind and the other sensations are of three types; the first eight are solely neutral.
Compare *Vibhaṅga*, p. 125.

70. See the definition of the Tathāgatabalas in *Vibhaṅga*, p. 336: *aṭṭhānam etaṁ anavakāso yaṁ itthi sakkattaṁ kāreyya mārattaṁ kāreyya brahmattaṁ kāreyya n'etaṁ ṭhānaṁ vijjati.*

71. *Dīgha*, iii.262, *Aṅguttara*, iv.408, v.150.

72. Compare i.40; *Vibhaṅga*, p. 133.

73. Compare *Kathāvatthu*, xiv.2, *Abhidhammasaṁgaha (Compendium*, p. 165).

74. Which we should understand as, "because the *rūpas* are luminous (*accha* = *bhāsvara*) there," or rather "because the *rūpas*, not the *kāmaguṅas*, are important there." See i.22a-b, no. 4, a different doctrine.

75. Compare *Saṁyutta*, ii.123.

76. Compare *Abhidhammasaṅgaha, Compendium*, p. 166.

77. On the psychological state at death, see iii.42-43b. In what part of the body the mental consciousness is destroyed, iii.43c-44a. How the vital parts perish, iii.44b.

78. *Indriyaprakaraṇe*. Some understand: "in the exposition that we give here of the *indriyas*;" other understand: "in the *Indriyaskandhaka*," the sixth book of the *Jñānaprasthāṇa* (Takakusu, *Abhidharma Literature*, p. 93).

79. For, at the moment when he obtains the fruit of Srotaāpanna, the ascetic is always in the state of *anāgamya* absorption (vi.48), which includes the sensation of indifference.

80. The fruit of Srotaāpanna is obtained in the sixteenth moment of the comprehension of the Truths; the first fifteen are *ājñāsyāmi*, the sixteenth *ājña*.

81. The first moment is *ānantaryamārga*; the second, *vimuktimārga*; and thus following. But one can consider all the moments which preceed the sixteenth moment as *ānantaryamārga* in relationship to this moment.

82. *Ānantaryamārga* destroys the defilements and leads to the possession of disjunction from defilement: it drives out the thief. *Vimuktimārga* closes the door. The Japanese editor here quotes the *Vibhāṣā TD* 27, p. 465c9, where the masters of the West, followers of a non-Kaśmīrean doctrine, are quoted.

83. The fruit of Arhat is obtained at the moment of *vajropamasamādhi* (vi.44c-d), or *ānantaryamārga*, which is *ājñedriya*. Thus *ājñendriya* is actually present. *Kṣayajñāna*, or *vimuktimārga*, which is *ājñātāvīndriya*, is in the process of arising (*utpādābhimukha*). Sensation of satisfaction, etc. according to the nature of the absorption in which the ascetic realizes *vajropamasamādhi*.

84. This doctrine of the wordly path is condemned in the *Kathāvatthu*, i.5 and xviii.5. Buddhaghosa attributes it to the Saṁmitiyas.

85. Only the *ānupūrvaka* changes from absorption, not the *vītarāga*. This later, in fact, if he begins the comprehension of the Truths (*satyābhisamaya*) in the absorption of *anāgamya*, will not pass to the sixteenth moment in the First Dhyāna. What interests him is the comprehension of the

Truths, not the Dhyāna with which he is familiar. On the contrary, the *ānupūrvaka* is interested in *dhyāna* which is new to him.

86. The Anāgāmin who falls from the detachment of the higher spheres, up to and including the Second Dhyāna, will not fall because of this from the result of Anāgāmin: he remains an Anāgāmin when he falls from the detachement of the First Dhyāna: having thus fallen, he cannot reobtain the result by the *indriya* of pleasure, for this *indriya* is of the Third Dhyāna, and the Third Dhyāna is beyond his scope.

Would one say that he can reobtain this result through the *indriya* of satisfaction? He would be able to if, setting out again to obtain this result in the absorption of *anāgamya*, he would be capable of passing, in the last moment, into the First Dhyāna. But he does not lose it: only an ascetic whose mental faculties are active can carry out this passage, and the ascetic that is under consideration here is of weak mental faculties, since he has fallen. Only ascetics of weak faculties fall from a result.

Would one say that, having fallen, an ascetic can carry out the transformation of his faculties (*indriyasaṁnicāra*, vi.41c-61b) and make them active? Without doubt, and he will obtain the result with eight or nine *indriyas* accordingly as his path is worldly or pure, as we have said, for, in no case will he reobtain this result with the *indriya* of pleasure.

87. The Āryan possesses the "pure" organ of pleasure, for he does not lose this organ by changing his sphere (see note 93).

88. Omitted by Hsüan-tsang. See viii.12a-b.

89. There is, in Kāmadhātu, an organ of pleasure in relation to the five sense consciousnesses; in the First Dhyāna, an organ of pleasure in relation to three sense consciousnesses (smell and taste being excluded, i.306); in the Second Dhyāna, there is no organ of pleasure (viii.12); and in the Third Dhyāna, there is an organ of pleasure related to the mental consciousness (ii.7c-d). Thus a being born in the heaven of the Second Dhyāna, if he does not practice the absorption of the Third Dhyāna, he will not possess the organ of pleasure, for, by being reborn in the Second Dhyāna, he has lost the organ of pleasure in the lower spheres. Response: according to the Vaibhāṣika doctrine (*siddhānta*) every being born in a lower sphere possesses the defiled (*kliṣṭa*) organ of the higher spheres if he has not abandoned it.

90. See iv.80a which quotes the *Jñānaprasthāna, TD* 26, p. 997a16 and 1000c3. *Ad* iv.79d, the number of the organs in the first Dvīpas.

91. How is a possessor of *ājñendriya*,—which means a Śaikṣa,—necessarily in possession of the organs of pleasure and satisfaction? He can in fact be found in the heaven of the Fourth Dhyāna or in Ārūpyadhātu.

An Āryan necessarily obtains the organ of satisfaction when he is detached from Kāmadhātu; he necessarily obtains the organ of pleasure when he is detached from the Second Dhyāna; even when he transmigrates (*bhūmisaṁcāra*), he does not lose the good (*śubha*) that he has obtained (according to iv.40); he loses the good obtained (iv.40), but this is in order to obtain the same type of good of a superior quality.

92. But can he be without sex? This is a difficulty, for we have seen (p. 154) that beings without sex cannot obtain either the discipline, nor a result, nor detachment.

According to one opinion, the person who has obtained the discipline can obtain a result; now this person preserves the discipline even though he loses his sex, for the Abhidharma specifies that he loses the discipline by becoming an androgyne (iv.38c) and it does not specify that he loses it by losing his sex. One can again envision gradual death: a person who has practiced the *nirvedhabhāgīyas* (vi.17) could, after the loss of the sexual organ, see the Truths at the moment of his death.

Second opinion. The possessor of *ājñāsyāmīndriya* is never without sex. But he does not possess the female organ when he is a male, and she does not possess the male organ when she is a female. Thus one cannot say that one necessarily possesses the one or the other.

93. See i.48c.

94. On the meaning of this term, see below page 187.

95. According to Saṁghabhadra (*TD* 29, p. 799a24-29): Among the *rūpas* "susceptible of resistance" (*sapratigha*), the most subtle part, which is not susceptible of being divided again, is called *paramāṇu*; that is to say: the *paramāṇu* is not susceptible of being divided into many parts by another *rūpa*, or by the mind. This is what is called the smallest *rūpa*; as it has no parts, it is called the "smallest." In the same way a *kṣaṇa* is called the smallest amount of time and cannot be divided in half-*kṣaṇas* (iii.86).

An agglomeration of these *aṇu*, which is not susceptible of disaggregation, is called *saṁghātāṇu*.

In Kāmadhātu, a minimum of eight things (*dravya*) arise together in order to constitute a *saṁghātāṇu* which is not sound, nor an organ. What are these things? Four *mahabhūtas* and four *upādāyas*, namely, *rūpa, rasa, gandha*, and *spraṣṭavya*.

96. The molecules into which the organ of touch, the organ of sight, etc., enter, are not the "atoms" which are mentioned i.44a-b.

97. Vasubandhu follows Dharmottara, *Abhidharmahṛdaya, TD* 28, p. 811b5, Upaśānta, *Abhidharmahṛdaya, TD* 28, p. 837c15, and Dharmatrāta, *Abhidharmahṛdaya, TD* 28, p. 882b4: "The atoms which reside in four organs are of ten types; in the organ of touch, of nine types; elsewhere, of eight types, when there is smell (that is to say: in Kāmadhātu)." Upaśānta: " . . . external, of eight types: in a stage where there is smell."

An analogous doctrine is the Abhidhamma of Buddhaghosa (*Atthasālinī*, 634) and the *Compendium* (p. 164). See below i.13, 43c and Th. Stcherbatiski, *The Soul Theory of the Buddhists*, p. 953.

98. One molecule of sound produced by the hands is made up of the four primary elements, the four derived matters, sound, and the organ of touch: or of ten substances; produced by the tongue, eleven substances, with the addition of the organ of taste whose invisible atoms are arranged over the tongue (Note of de La Vallée Poussin).

99. See J. Bloch, *Formation de la langue marathe*, p. 42: *siṅka (śikya)*, "a cord to suspend objects."

100. Elemental water (*abdhātu*) exists in wood (*dāru*): it is elemental water which holds things together (*saṁgraha*) and which prevents them from dispersing. Elemental fire (*tejas*) matures (*pakti*) and rots wood. And it is by elemental wind that wood moves (*vyūhana, prasarpana*). Elemental earth exists within water, since water supports (*dhṛti*) ships, etc. See i.12c-d, *Vyākhyā*, p. 34.

101. Fire creates by reason of its heat, and so contains elemental water; water becomes solid by cold, and so contains elemental earth; solid bodies, rubbed one against the other, become hot; thus they contain elemental fire, etc.

102. One the meaning of *dhātu*, i.20.

103. A presence which results from the definition, "The molucule includes eight substances."

104. See also i.13c-d.

105. Blue is a *dravya*.

106. *Rūpa* possesses the characteristic of "resistance" (*rūpyate*) which is common to color and shape, to blue, etc.

107. We have seen (i.13) that an atom or monad never exists in an isolated state. The Japanese editor quotes on this point the six chapter *Commentary* of Hui-hui. Pelliot discovered this quotation in T'ao 83.5, for. 414 (=vol. 83, p. 414 *recto* b of the *Zoku zōkyō*), where it is accompanied by a gloss that justifies the number of 1,379 atoms in one molecule of a visible thing, etc.

Here, barring error, is the meaning of this gloss:

An atom never exists in an isloated state. We have, at a minimum, groups—or molecules—of seven atoms: four faces, top and bottom: six sides; plus the center; thus seven. A molecule of derived matter (*mahābhūtāny upādāya rūpam, bhautikaṁ rūpam*, for example a molecule of "visible matter" (*rūpa*) or of smell (*gandha*), consists of seven atoms of visible matter and of smell.

Each of these seven atoms is supported by complexes of seven atoms, seven atoms having for their natures the four primary elements, seven atoms where the four great elements are present.

Each of these seven atoms included four atoms, atoms of earth, water, fire, and wind: the atoms of earth includes seven atoms of earth, etc.

Thus we have (1) seven atoms of earth, water, fire, and wind,—in all twenty-eight atoms,—which constitute an atom of four-primary-elements.

(2) An atom of four-primary-elements does not exist in an isolated state: seven are grouped together (7 x 28 = 196 atoms) in order to support one atom of derived matter.

(3) The atoms of derived matter, with its supports, atoms of four-primary-elements (1 x 197 = 197 atoms), form a group with six other similar atoms: each atom of derived matter is thus made up of 1,379 atoms (7 x 197).

(But all derived matter possesses visiblity, smell, taste, and tangibility. Thus this number should be multiplied by four in order to obtain the smallest part of matter existing in an isolated state.)

108. *Citta* = *manas* = *vijñāna; caitta* = *caitasa* = *caitasika* = *cittasaṁprayukta.*

109. A. Theory of *caittas* according to Vasubandhu, and according to the Sautrāntikas.

B. *Prakaraṇapāda* and *Dhātukāya.*

C. The Abhidhamma.

A. The commentary of the *Vijñaptimātraśāstra* says that the Sautrāntikas have two systems. One, the Dārṣṭāntikas, maintain that only the mind exists, that mental states do not exist, in agreement with Buddhadeva (see i.35 note); others admit the existence of mental states and are divided into many opinions: that there are three mental states: *vedanā, saṁjñā, cetanā*; that there are four (with the addition of *sparśa*), ten (the ten *mahābhūmikas*), fourteen (with the addition of *lobha, dveṣa, moha, māna*); furthermore certain Sautrāntikas admit all the mental states of the Sarvāstivādins. (The references of Wassilief, p. 309, differ; read "the Bhadanta Sautrāntika" instead of Bhaṭṭopama).

See ii.26c-d; iii.32a-b.

Vasubandhu presents his doctrine of the mental states in his *Pañcaskandhaprakaraṇa, TD* 31, p. 848c3-9: "What are the *caittas*? The *dharmas* associated (*saṁprayukta*) with the mind, namely (1) five universals (*sarvaga*): *sparśa, manaskāra, vedanā, saṁjñā*, and *cetanā*; (2) five particulars (*pratiniyataviṣaya*): *chandra, adhimukti, smṛti, samādhi*, and *prajñā*; (3) eleven good: *śraddhā, hrī, apatrāpya, alobha kuśalamūla, adveṣa kuśalamūla, amoha kuśalamūla, vīrya, praśrabdhi, apramāda, upekṣā*, and *ahiṁsā*; (4) six defilements (*kleśa*): *rāga, pratigha, māna, avidyā, dṛṣṭi*, and *vicikitsā*; (5) the others (*śeṣa*) are *upakleśa: krodha, upanāha, mrakṣa, pradāsa, īrṣyā, mātsarya, māyā, śāṭhya, mada, vihiṁsā, āhrīkya, anapatrāpya, styāna, auddhatya, āśraddhya, kausīdya, apramāda, muṣitasmṛtitā, vikṣepa*, and *asamprajanya*; (6) four, of unstable character (*gzhan du yaṅ'gyur ba*): *kaukṛtya, middha, vitarka*, and *vicāra*."

B. According to the *Prakaraṇapāda (TD* 26, p. 692b20):

There are five *dharmas*: 1. *rūpa*, 2. *citta*, 3. *caittadharma*, 4. *cittaviprayuktasaṁskāra*, 5. *asaṁskṛta* . . . What is *citta*? *Citta* is *manas, vijñāna*, that is to say the six categories of *vijñāna*, consciousness of sight, etc. What are the *caittas*? All the *dharmas* associated with the mind. What are these *dharmas*? They are *vedanā, saṁjñā, cetanā, sparśa, manasikāra, chanda, adhimukti, smṛti, samādhi, prajñā, śraddhā, vīrya, vitarka, vicāra, pramāda, apramāda, kuśalamūla, akuśalamūla, avyakṛtamūla*, all the *saṁyojanas, anuśayas, upakleśas, paryavasthānas* (v.47), all knowledge (*jñāna*, vii.1), all opinion (*dṛṣṭi*), all comprehension (*abhisamaya*, vi.27); furthermore all *dharmas* of this type, associated with the mind, are *caitta*.

Later on (p. 698b28; see also *Dhātukāya, TD* 26, p. 614b10): "There are 18 *dhātus*, 12 *āyatanas*, 5 *skandhas*, 5 *upādānaskandhas*, 6 *dhātus*, 10 *mahābhūmikas*, 10 *kuśalamahābhūmikas*, 10 *kleśmahābhūmikas*, 10 *parīttakleśabhūmikas*, 5 *kleśas*, 5 *saṁsparśas*, 5 *dṛṣṭis*, 5 *indriyas*, 5 *dharmas*, 6 *vijñānakāyas*, 6 *sparśakāyas*, 6 *vedanākāyas*, 6 *saṁjñākāyas*, 6 *cetanākāyas*, 6 *tṛṣṇākāyas*, What are the 18 *dhātus*? . . . What are the six *dhātus*? The primary element of earth . . . (*Kośa*, i.28). What are the ten *mahābhūmikas*? *Vedanā* . . . *prajñā*. What are the ten *kuśalamahābhūmikas*? *Śraddhā, vīrya, hrī, apatrapā, alobha, adveṣa, praśrabdhi, upekṣā, apramāda, ahiṁsā*. What are the ten *kleśamahābhūmikas*? *Aśrāddhya* . . . *pramāda* (list quoted above ii.26a-c). What are the ten *parīttakleśabhūmikas*? *Krodha, upanāha, mrakṣa, pradāsa, īrṣyā, mātsarya, śāṭhya, māyā, mada, vihiṁsā*. What are the five *kleśas*? *Kāmarāga, rūparāga, ārūpyarāga, pratigha, vicikitsā* (v.1). What are the five *dṛṣṭis*? *Satkāyadṛṣṭi, antagrāhadṛṣṭi, mithyādṛṣṭi, dṛṣṭiparāmarśa, śīlavrataparāmarśa* (v.3)What are the five *saṁsparśas*? *Pratighasaṁsparśa, adhivacanasaṁsparśa, vidyāsaṁsparśa, avidyāsaṁparśa, naivavidyānāvidyasaṁparśa* (iii.30c-31a). What are the five *indriyas*? *Sukhendriya, duḥkhendriya, saumanasyendriya, daurmanasyendriya, upekṣendriya* (ii.7). What are the five *dharmas*? *Vitarka, vicāra, vijñāna, āhrīkya, anapatrāpya*. (In the *Kośa*, ii.27, *vitarka* and *vicāra* are classified as *aniyata*; ii.26d, *āhrīkya* and *anapatrāpya* are classified as *akuśalamahābhūmika*, a category conceived later, see iii.32a-b; the *vijñāna* refered to here in the *Prakaraṇa* and the *Dhātukāya*, without doubt refers to the six *vijñānakāyas*.)What are the six *vijñānakāyas*? *Cakṣurvijñāna* . . . *manovijñāna*. What are the six *saṁparśakāyas*? *Cakṣuḥsaṁsparśa* . . . *manaḥsaṁsparśa* (iii.30b). What are the six *vedanākāyas*? *Cakṣuḥsaṁsparśajavedanā* . . . (iii.32a). What are the six *saṁjñākāyas*? *Cakṣuḥsaṁsparśajasaṁjñā* . . . What are the six *cetanākāyas*? *Cakṣuḥsaṁsparśajacetanā* . . . What are the six *tṛṣṇākāyas*? *Cakṣuḥsaṁsparśajatṛṣṇā* . . . The *Dhātukāya* proceeds by explaining the *mahābhūmikas*: "What is *vedanā*?" (See ii.24, note lllB).

C. *Kathāvatthu*, vii.2-3, the Rājagirikas and the Siddhatthikas deny the *saṁprayoga* of the *dharmas*, and deny the existences of the *caitasikas*; ix.8, the Uttarāpathakas make a *mahābhūmika* of *vitarka* (the technical term is missing). *Visuddhimagga*, xiv. *Abhidhammasaṁgaha*, ii. In *Compendium*, p. 237, S. Z. Aung and C. A. F. Rhys Davids have some interesting observations on the development of the doctrine of the *cetasikas*.

110. According to the *Vibhāṣā TD* 27, p. 80b8, quoted by the Japanese editor: What is the meaning of the expression *mahābhūmikadharma*?

a. The mind is great; these ten *dharmas* are its *bhūmi*, the locus of the origin of the mind; being the *bhumi* of the "great," they are called *mahābhūmi*. Being *mahābhūmi* and *dharmas*, they are *mahābhūmikadharmas*.

b. Some say: The mind is great, due to the superiority of its nature and its activity; it is great and it is *bhūmi*, and it is called *mahābhūmi*, because it is the locus which serves as the support of the *caittas*. Because one encounters the ten *dharmas, vedanā*, etc., throughout the *mahābhūmi*, they are called the *mahābhūmikadharmas*.

c. Some say: The ten *dharmas, vedanā*, etc., are found everywhere with the mind, and so are called "great;" the mind, being their *bhūmi*, is called *mahābhūmi; vedanā*, etc., being inherent in the *mahābhūmi*, are called *mahābhūmikadharmas*.

Vasubandhu reproduces the third etymology.

We shall see (iii.32a-b) that Śrīlābha does not admit this definition of the term *mahābhūmika*.

111. A. Hsuan-tsang corrects: *Vedanā, saṁjñā, cetanā, sparśa, chandra, prajñā, smṛti, manaskāra, adhimukti*, and *samādhi*.

The order of the Abhidharma (*Prakaraṇapāda, Dhātukāya*) is: *adhimukti, smṛti, samādhi*, and *prajñā*. Vasubandhu (*Pañcaskandhaka*) distinguishes five universals (*sarvaga*): *sparśa, manaskāra, vedanā, saṁjñā*, and *cetanā*, and five particulars (*pratiniyataviṣaya*): *chandra, adhimukti, smṛti, samādhi*, and *prajñā*.

The order of *Mahāvyutpatti* 104 (which reads *adhimokṣa*) differs from other sources.

B. The *Dhātukāya* (*TD* 26, p. 614c22) gives some definitions which are completely in the style of the Abhidharmma. For example, *samādhi* is defined: "The *sthiti* of the mind, *saṁsthiti* (*teng-chu* 等住), *abhiṣṭhiti* (*hsien-chu* 現住), *upasthiti* (*chin-chu* 近住), *avikṣepa* (*pu-luan* 不亂), *aghaṭṭana* (*pu-san* 不散), *Mahāvyutpatti*, 245.226) *saṁdhāraṇa* (*?she-ch'ih* 攝持), *śamatha, samādhi*, and *cittasyaikāgratā*, is what is called *samādhi*." (*Vibhaṅga*, p. 217, *Dhammasaṁgaṇi*, 11).

In the same way *vedanā* is *vedanā, saṁvedanā, pratisaṁvedanā, vedita*, that which feels, that which is included within *vedanā*. *Smṛti* is *smṛti, anusmṛti, pratismṛti, smaraṇa, asaṁpramoṣatā . . . cetaso'bhilāpa*.

112. The word *kila* shows that the author is presenting the opinion of the School. He explains his own doctrine in the *Pañcaskandhaka* (*Vyākhyā*).

113. Compare *Atthasālinī*, 329: *kattukamyatā*. According to the *Pañcaskandhaka: abhiprete vastuny abhilāṣaḥ*. (See ii.55c-d, iii.1, where *chanda* is defined as *anāgate prārthanā*).

114. *Pañcaskandhaka: upaparīkṣye vastuni pravicayo yogāyogavihito'nyathā ca*.

115. *Pañcaskandhaka: saṁstute vastuny asaṁpramoṣaḥ / cetaso' bhilapanatā*. See i.33.

116. On *ābhoga*, S. Lévi *ad Sūtrālaṁkāra*, i.16, and *Muséon*, 1914.

117. This term presents a difficulty. *Vyākhyā: adhimuktis tadālambanasya guṇato'vadhāraṇāda (-ṇam?) rucir iti anye / yathāniścayaṁ dhāraneti yogācāracittāḥ*: "*Adhimukti* is the consideration of the object from the point of view of its qualities; according to others, complaisance; according to the Ascetics (the Yogācārins), the contemplation of the object in conformity with the decision taken." (This last point is explained *ad* ii.72, *adhimuktimanaskāra*).

According to the the *Pañcaskandhaka, adhimokṣa* is *niścite vastuny avadhāraṇam*.

See the *Prakaraṇapāda, TD* 26, p. 693a17.

Paramārtha translates: "*Adhimukti* (*hsiang liao* 相了) is a *dharma* which makes the mind lively (*ming liao* 明了 , *paṭu*) with respect to the characteristic of the object." This is a gloss, not a translation.

Hsüan-tsang translates: "*Adhimukti*, that is *neng yü ching yin-k'o* 能於境印可 ." We can translate: "that which makes a sign of approbation with respect to the object." The expression *yin (=mudrā) k'o* (possible) is mentioned by Rosenberg in many word lists. A. Waley, who has consulted the Japanese glosses, translates: "the sign of approval given to a disciple who has understood what has been taught him." We would thus have *k'o* = *k'o-i* = "this is allowable"(A. Debesse). *Adhimukti* is the approbation of the object, the *dharma* by reason of which one grasps the object under consideration; it marks the first stage of the act of attention. See the note of Shwe Zan Aung, *Compendium*, p. 17 and 241, on *adhimokkha*: " . . . the settled state of a mind . . . ; it is deciding to attend to this, not that irrespective of more complicated prodedure as to what 'this' or 'that' appears to be."

Saṁghabhadra (*TD* 29, p. 384b9): Approbation (*yin-k'o*) with respect to an object is called *adhimukti*. According to other masters, *adhi* signifies "superiority, sovereignty;" *mukti* siginifies *vimokṣa*. *Adhimukti* is a *dharma* by virtue of which the mind exercises its sovereignty over an object without any obstacle; like *adhiśīla*. *Adhimukti* is a separate object, for the Sūtra says: "The mind, by reason of *adhimukti*, approves of (*yin-k'o*) the object." When the mental states arise, all approve (*yin*) the object:; as a consequence *adhimukti* is a *mahābhūmika*. Nevertheless the Sthavira says: "It is not proven that *adhimukti* is a separate thing, for we see that its characteristic is not distinguished from that of knowledge (*jñāna*): the characteristic of *adhimukti* is that the mind is determined (*niścita*) with respect to its object. But this is not different from the characteristic of knowledge (*jñāna*). Consequently *adhimukti* is not a separate thing." This is not correct, for approbation (*yin-k'o*) brings about determination.

Some say: "*Adhimukti* is determination (*avadhāraṇa, niścaya*)." This is to give the cause of determination (namely *adhimukti*) the name of its effect. If this is the case, then *adhimukti* and determination would not be simultaneous. No: for these two mutually condition one another: by reason of discernment (*pratisaṁkhyā*) there arise approbation, and by reason of approbation there arises determination (*niścaya*). There is no contradition: thus there is no obstacle to their being simultaneous. If all thought include these two, then all the categories of mind will be approbation and determination. This objection is worthless, for it happens that their activity is damaged when they are dominated by *dharmas*: even if there is approbation (*yin*) and determination, they are small and recognized only with difficulty.

118. *Pañcaskandhaka: upaparīkṣye vastuni cittasyaikāgratā.*

119. According to the *Vibhāṣā, TD* 27, p. 220b2, and the *Prakaraṇa: śraddhā, vīrya, hrī, apatrapā, alobha, adveṣa, praśrabdhi, upekṣā, apramāda, avihiṁsā.* The *Mahāvyutpatti* (104) lists the third root (*amoha*) and places *vīrya* after the roots. The *Pañcaskandhaka* also lists the third root and has the same order as the *Mahāvyutpatti* with the exception that it places *apramāda* before *upekṣā*.

120. In other words, *śraddhā* is the *dharma* by which (*yadyogāt*) the mind, troubled by the *kleśas* and the *upakleśas*, becomes clear, as troubled water becomes clear by the presence of a gem which purifies water (*udakaprasādakamaṇi*). Same example in *Atthasālinī*, 304.

121. Explanation adopted by Vasubandhu in the *Pañcaskandhaka*.

122. *Bhāvanā* signifies "taking possession," "frequentation" (*pratilambha, niṣevaṇa*) according to vii.27.

123. The Mahāsāṁghikas. Diligence holds the mind safe from the *dharmas* of defilement (*sāṁkleśika*).

124. The Abhidhamma distinguishes *passaddhi* and *lahutā* (*Dhammasaṁgaṇi*, 40-43) which the Abhidharma appears to identify. *Praśrabdhi* in the *dhyānas* is analyzed viii.9.

125. According to the Japanese editor. *Pañcaskandhaka: "Praśrabdhi* is an attitude of the mind and body, a *dharma* opposed to *dauṣṭhulya*" (S. Lévi, *Sūtrālaṁkāra*, vi.2, Wogihara, p. 29).

126. *Praśrabdhisambodhyaṅga* is twofold, *cittapraśrabdhi* and *kāyapraśrabdhi* (*Prakaraṇapāda, TD* 26, p. 700a16). *Saṁyuktāgama, TD* 2, p. 191c5: . . . *tatra yāpi kāyapraśrabdhis tad api praśrabdhisaṁbodhyaṅgam abhijñāyai saṁbodhaye nirvāṇāya saṁvartate / yāpi cittapraśrabdhis tad api saṁbodhyaṅgam* . . . A shorter recension in *Saṁyutta*, v.111. In the presence of this text, say the Sautrāntikas, how can you define *praśrabdhi* as solely "an attitude of the mind?"

127. Compare *Saṁyutta*, v.108.

128. The Blessed One said that the nine *āghātavastus* (*Aṅguttara*, iv.408) are *vyāpādanīvaraṇa*.

129. When the Path is made up of three elements, *śīlaskandha, samādhiskandha,* and *prajñāskandha*, resolution and effort are placed within the *prajñāskandha* with Seeing which, alone, is *prajñā* by its nature. We read in the *Prajñāskandhanirdeśa: prajñāskandhaḥ katamaḥ / samyagdṛṣṭiḥ samyaksaṁkalpaḥ samyagvyāyāmaḥ.*

130. This *saṁskāropekṣa* is to be distinguished from *vedanopekṣa* (i.14, ii.8c-d) and from *apramāṇopekṣa* (viii.29). The *Atthasālinī* (397) lists ten *upekṣas*: here we have a definition of *jhānupekkhā: majjhattalakkhaṇṇṇā anābhogarasā avyāpārapaccupaṭṭhānā* . . . (p. 174.2).

131. Literally: There are some things difficult to know that one can know. But it is quite difficult to know (or to admit) that there is no contradiction (opposition, impossibility of coexistence) between contradictory *dharmas: asti hi nāma durjñānam api jñāyate / idaṁ tu khalu atidurjñānaṁ yad virodho'py avirodhaḥ.*

132. According to Hsüan-tsang and the glosses of the Japenese editor:

The Vaibhāṣikas. What contradiction is there in that attention is flexion of the mind, and that indifference is non-flexion of the mind? In fact, we consider attention and indifference to be distinct *dharmas*.

The Sautrāntikas. Then attention and indifference will not have the same object; or rather one should admit that all mental states (greed, hatred, etc.) are associated.

We encounter other *dharmas (vitarka, vicāra)* which present the same characteristics of opposition . . .

133. The *Pañcaskandhaka* places *amoha* among the *kuśalamahābhūmikas* (by the fact that *prajñā* can be "erroneous"). *Alobha* is the opposite of *lobha, udvega* and *an-upādāna* (?). *Adveṣa* is the opposite of *dveṣa*, namely goodwill (*maitrī*, viii.29). *Amoha* is the opposite of *moha, samyaksaṁkalpa* (vi.69).

134. *Pañcaskandhaka: "Avihiṁsā* is compassion (*karuṇā*, viii.29), the opposite of *vihiṁsā*."

135. Endurance is good action (*kuśalakriyā*); for endurence in evil action is not *vīrya*, but *kausīdya*. The Blessed One said: "The *vīrya* of persons foreign to this religion (*itobāhyaka*) is *kausīdya*" (ii.26a). *Pañcaskandhaka: "Vīrya* is the endurance of the mind in good, the opposite of *kausīdya*."

136. According to the gloss of the Japanese editor, the Path of Seeing expells *avidyā*, the Path of Mediation expells *ajñāna*, and the Path of Aśaikṣa expells non-clearness.

137. Compare *Dhammasaṅgaṇi*, 429.

138. See above note 109.

139. *Ko'yaṁ devānāṁpriyo nāma / ṛjukajātīyo devānāṁpriya ity eke vyācakṣate /aśaṭho hi devānāṁ priyo bhavati /mūrkho devānāṁpriya ity apare /yo hīśvarāṇām iṣṭaḥ sa na tāḍanena śikṣata iti mūrkho bhavati (Vyākhyā)*. The Japanese editor quotes numerous glosses.

140. *Pāṭhaprāmāṇyamātreṇa daśa kleśamahābhūmikāḥ prāptā ity etām eva prāptiṁ jānīte (Vyākhyā).*

Vasubandhu reproduces the formula of the *Mahābhāṣya ad* ii.4.56 (the story of the Grammarian and the Cow-herder).

See S. Lévi, *J.As.* 1891, ii.549 ("Notes de chronologie indienne. Devānāṁpriya, Açoka et Kātyāyana"). According to Kern, *Manual*, 133, the meaning of "idiot" derives from the sense of "harmless, pious": this appears to be somewhat possible. See de La Vallée Poussin's note in the *Bulletin de l'Academie de Bruxelles*, 1923.

141. *Vyākhyā: ābhidhārmikāḥ.*

Perhaps by the plural (*āhuḥ*) Vasubandhu is designating Dharmatrāta, the author of

Saṁyukta-Abhidharmahṛdaya, TD 28, number 1551, and his followers. This appears to result from the passages which follow (*TD* 28, p. 881b17):

". . . The *kleśamahābhūmikas* are: *mithyādhimokṣa, asaṁprahanya, ayoniśomanaskāra, aśrāddhya, kausīdya, vikṣepa, avidyā, auddhatya,* and *pramāda.*

"*Mithyādhimokṣa* consists of the ten *kleśamahābhūmikas* which are found in all defiled minds. *Ahrī* and *atrapā* are called *akuśalamahābhūmikas.*

"The ten *kleśamahābhūmikas* are found in all defiled minds. The ten *dharmas* the first of which is *mithyādhimokṣa,* accompany all defiled minds, sense consciousnesses or mental consciousnesses, of Kāmadhātu, Rūpadhātu, and Ārūpyadhātu. They are thus *kleśamahābhūmikas.* Question: *Styāna* is found in all defiled minds; why is it not counted among the *kleśamahābhūmikas?* Answer: Because it is favorable to *samādhi.* This is why *styāna* is not counted in the list. Is a *dharma* which is a *mahābhūmika* also a *kleśamahābhūmika?* Four alternatives: 1. *mahābhūmikas* without being *kleśamahābhūmikas . . .*"

142. The author does not admit this opinion. Torpor (*styāna, laya*) and dissipation, which are defiled *dharmas,* are opposed to the "white" *dharmas,* like *samādhi.*

143. According to the *Vibhāṣā, TD* 27, p. 220b4, there are five *akuśalamahābhūmikas: avidyā, styāna, auddhatya, ahrī,* and *anapatrapya.* See iii.32a-b and above note 102.

144. Hsüan-tsang translates: " . . . the *dharmas* of this nature (=*iti*) are termed *parīttakleśabhūmikas.*"

Saṁghabhadra: The text says "the *dharmas* of this nature," in order to include *akṣānti, arati āghāta,* etc. (*TD* 29, p. 392a6).

145. Dharmatrāta: Because they are abandoned through Meditation and not through the Seeing of the Truths, because they are associated with the mental consciousness and not with the five other consciousnesses, and because they do not arise with all minds and exist separately, they are *parīttakleśabhūmika.*

146. According to the Chinese. The Japanese editor explains the final *et cetera* by *rāga (v.2), pratigha, māna* (v.10), and *vicikitsā.*

The *Vyākhyā* reads: "*kaukṛtya, middha,* etc." and explains "etc." by *arati, vijṛmbhitā, tendrī, bhakte'samatā,* etc. It continues: The *kleśas, rāga,* etc., are also indeterminate, for they are not classified in any of the five categories: they are not *mahābhūmikas,* because they are not found in any minds; they are not *kuśalamahābhūmikas,* because they are repugnant to the good; they are not *kleśamahābhūmikas,* because they are not found in any defiled mind: for there is no *rāga* or lust in a mind full of hatred (*sapratigha*).

The Ācārya Vasumitra has written a summary, mnemonic *śloka*: "The tradition (*smṛta*) is that there are eight *aniyatas,* namely *vitarka, vicāra, kaukṛtya, middha, pratigha, śakti (=rāga), māna,* and *vicikitsā*". But we do not admit this number of eight. Why are the *dṛṣṭis* (v.3a) not *aniyata?* There is no *mithyādṛṣṭi* in a mind full of hatred or scepticism.

147. Compare *Kathāvatthu,* xiv.8.

148. *Dhammasaṅgaṇi,* 1161, *Atthasālinī,* 784-787.

149. Compare i.37.

150. *Āveṇika* = *rāgādipṛthagbhūta.*

151. All *dṛṣṭi* is *saṁtīrikā prajñā* (i.41c-d, vii.1).

152. The mind of the First Dhyāna, when it is good, contains twenty-two mental states; defiled-neutral, it contains eighteen mental states whether it is independent of, or associated with *dṛṣṭi,* nineteen when it is associated with *rāga, māna* or *vicikitsā . . .*

153. Literally: The word "also" (*api*) shows that in addition to *vicāra*, one should exclude *śāṭhya* and *māyā*.

154. According to the Japanese editor, the *Saddharmasmṛti upasthāna sūtra*, *TD* 17, p. 193b16. *Vibhāṣā*, *TD* 27, p. 670b24.

155. By adding: "I am the great Brahmā", he distinguishes himself from the other Brahmas.

156. Compare *Dīgha*, i.219, and below iv.8a, v.53a-b.

157. *Jñānaprasthāna*, i. Para. 5 (according to Takakusu, p. 87). See *TD* 26, p. 924c26 and following.

158. *Pratīśa* = *guru*, because *śiṣyaṁ pratīṣṭaḥ*.

159. Compare the definition of *adhiśīla: . . . aṇumātreṣv apy avadyeṣu bhayadarśī . . .*

160. These masters observes that the two roots *hrī* and *trap* (*Dhātupāta*, iii.3 and i.399) are synonyms and signify shame (*lajjā*): from whence one cannot see how *ahrī* would be disrespect and *atrapā* the absence of fear in the commission of transgressions.

161. Vasubandhu, in the *Pañcaskandhaka*, adopts this definition.

162. *Jñānaprasthāna*, i. Para. 4 (according to Takakusu, p. 87). See *TD* 26, p. 923a13 and following.

163. *Vibhāṣā*, *TD* 27, p. 151a15.

164. For one cannot have respect for impure (*sāsrava*) *dharmas*. (Note of the Japanese editor).

165. This definition comes from a Sūtra which is not designated in our sources. See i.33.

166. Seventh opinion of the *Vibhāṣā*, *TD* 27, p. 219b3.

167. Argument presented in the *Vibhāṣā*, *TD* 27, p. 269b10, and attributed to the Dārṣṭāntikas.

168. That is, "it makes the voice surge forth," *vāksamutthāpaka*.

169. Compare *Majjhima* i.301, *Saṁyutta* ov.293: *pubbe kho . . . vitakketvā vicāretvā pacchā vācaṁ bhindati*. On the other hand, *Vibhaṅga*, 135: *vācīsaṁcetanā* = *vācīsaṁkhāro*.

170. Samghabhadra says that *vitarka* and *vicāra* are associated with each thought; but these two *dharmas* do not enter into activity, do not reveal themselves by their action (*udbhūtavṛtti*) at one and the same time: the mind and mental states are grosser when *vitarka*, which is always present, enters into activity . . . In the same way *rāga* and *moha* are coexistent: but a person is termed *rāgacarita*, acting though *rāga*, when *rāga* manifests itself . . .

171. *Vitarka* and *vicāra* do not exist simultaneously, but successively (*paryāyeṇa*). What is the difference between *vitarka* and *vicāra*? The ancient masters (*pūrvācārya*) say: "What is *vitarka*? A mental conversation (*manojalpa*) of inquiry (*paryeṣaka*), which has for its support volition (*cetanā*) or the speculative consciousness (*prajñā*) depending on whether it does or does not contain deduction (*abhyūha*). This is the grosser state of mind. What is *vicāra*? A mental conversation of appreciation, of judgment (*pratyavekṣaka*), which has for its support volition . . ." According to this theory, *vitarka* and *vicāra* constitute almost two identical psychological complexes: they differ in that the first includes "inquiry" and the second "judgment." Some give an example: Someone feels numerous pots in order to know which one is well baked, and which one is soft: this inquiry (*ūha*) is *vitarka*; finally, this person arrives at the conclusion, "There are such a number of each category:" this is *vicāra*.

The *Vyākhyā*, *ad* i.37, quotes Vasubandhu's *Pañcaskandhaka* which is very close to the opinion of some ancient masters: *vitarkaḥ katamaḥ /paryeṣako manojalpaś cetanāprajñāviśeṣaḥ / yā cittasyaudārikatā // vicāraḥ katamaḥ / pratyavekṣako manojalpaś cetanāprajñāviśeṣaḥ / yā cittasya sūkṣmatā. //* The *Vyākhyā* adds: *anabhyūhāvasthāyāṁ cetanā abhyūhāvasthāyāṁ prajñeti vyavasthāpyate.*

See *Dhammasaṅgaṇi*, 7-8, *Compendium*, p. 10-11, *Milinda*, 62-63. *Atthasālinī*, 296-297 defines *vitarka* as *ūhana* and gives it as *olarika*, whereas *vicāra* is *sukhuma*. Vyāsa *ad Yogasūtra*, i.17: *vitarkaś cittasyālambana sthūla ābhogaḥ / sūkṣmo vicāraḥ*; i.42-44.

172. *Paryādīyate* = *saṁnirudhyate*; see *Śikṣāsamuccaya*, 177.15, *Divya*, *Sūtrālaṁkāra*, i.12.

Saṁghabhadra's definition: *yaḥ svadharmeṣv eva raktasya darpaś cetasaḥ paryādānam kuśalānyakriyābhyupapattisaṁhāro madaḥ.*

173. *Mada* is sensation, "defiled satisfaction" (*kliṣṭa saumanasya*). The Vaibhāṣikas do not admit this explanation: in fact, satisfaction does not exist beyond the Second Dhyāna: but, according to v.53c, *mada* exists in the three spheres of existence.

174. Compare *Dīgha*, i.21, *Saṁyutta*, ii.94.

175. Its meaning is that it accumulates good and evil (*Vyākhyā*). Tibetan: *'byed pas*: because it distinguishes. *Atthasālinī*, 293: *ālambanaṁ cintetīti cittam.*

176. *Dhātupāṭha*, 4.67.

177. The *Vyākhyā* adds: *bhāvanāsaṁniveśayogena sautrāntikamatena yogācāramatena vā.*

Paramārtha reads: *citaṁ śubhāśubhair dhātubhis tān vā cinotīti cittam.* The Tibetan translates in the same way: "because it is charged (*bsags-pas*) with good and evil *dhātus*."

178. The consciousness (*vijñāna*) discerns a blue object, etc.; sensation feels it as agreeable, etc.; ideas grasp its characteristics, etc. Or rather: consciousness perceives the object, in a general manner, as a perceptible (*upalabhyatārūpaṁ gṛhṇāti*); the mental states perceive its specific characteristics (*viśeṣarūpeṇa*): sensation is susceptible of being agreeably experienced (*anubhavanīyatārūpam*); ideas are susceptible of being defined (*paricchedyatārūpam*), etc. (i.16a).

179. That is to say *saha vistaraprabhedābhyām* or *aha vistaraprabhedena.*

180. The *iti* indicates that one should add other *viprayuktas* like *saṁghabheda* (iv.99), etc. to this list. The *Prakaraṇa* says: *ye'py evaṁjātīyakāḥ*: "The *dharmas* which are of this type are also *cittaviprayukta*." Same formula in the *Skandhapañcaka.*

According to the *Prakaraṇa*, the *saṁskāras* disassociated from the mind are: *prāpti, asaṁjñisamāpatti, nirodhasamāpatti, āsaṁjñika, jīvitendriya, nikāyasabhāga, āśrayaprāpti, dravyaprāpti (?), āyatanaprāpti, jāti, jarā, sthiti, anityatā nāmakāya*, and *vyañjanakāya* and all the other *dharmas* of this type disassociated from the mind.

Prāpti is defined as *dharmāṇāṁ prāptiḥ; āśrayaprāpti* is *āśrayāyatanaprāpti; dravyaprāpti* (?) is *skandhānāṁ prāptiḥ; āyatanaprāpti* is *ādhyātmikabāhyāyatanaprāpti* (*TD* 26, p. 694a19).

Prakaraṇapāda (p. 694a14): What is *prāpti? Prāpti* of the *dharmas*. What is *asaṁjñisamāpatti?* The cessation of the mind and mental states having for its antecedent the idea of departure attached to the abandoning of the defilement of the Śubhakṛtsanas but not to the abandoning of higher defilements. What is *nirodhasamāpatti?* The cessation of the mind and mental states having for its antecedent the idea of calm attached to the abandoning of the defilement of *ākiṁcanyāyatana*. What is *āsaṁjñika?* The cessation of the mind and mental states of those who are born among the Asaṁjñisattva gods. What is *jīvitendriya? Āyus* of the Three Dhātus. What is *nikāyasabhāga?* The resemblance of beings.

181. See i.38c-d, ii.59b.

The terms *lābha* and *samanvāgama* do not have the same meanings in the Abhidharma and in the *Kathāvatthu*, ix.12. For the Theravādins, *lābha* signifies "possession," for example the power that the Saints posses to realize at their will any given absorption; *samanvāgama* is understood as the actual realization. Elsewhere (iv.4) *paṭilābhasamannāgama* and *samaṅgibhāvasamannāgama*, possessor of power (*samanvāgama* of the Abhidharma) versus its actual possession (*saṁmukhībhāva* of the Abhidharma) are distinguished. See also xix.4.

182. There is in me *prāpti* or *aprāpti* relative to my defilement, to my action . . ., that is to say, I possess or do not possess my future or past defilement . . . But there is no relation of possession or of non-possession between me and the defilement of another.

183. Hairs should be regarded as "belonging to a living being," for they are bound (*saṁbaddha*) to the material organs.

184. A person "bound with all the bonds" (*sakalabandhana*) is one who has not obtained, by the worldly (*laukika*) path, the abandoning (=*pratisaṁkhyānirodha*) of any of the nine categories of defilements of Kāmadhātu. An Āryan, at the first moment(*ādikṣaṇa* = *duḥkhe dharmajñānakṣānti*) has not yet obtained the abandoning of the defilements abandoned through the Path (vi.77). A person who has obtained the abandoning of one category of defilement is called *ekaprakāropalikhita* (vi.30a).

185. *Dravyadharmaḥ* = *dravyato dharmaḥ*, or rather *dravyaṁ ca tad dharmaś ca sa dravyadharmaḥ*, that is to say *vidyamānasvalakṣaṇo dharmaḥ* See below p. 211-212.

186. These ten *dharmas* are the eight parts of the Path, plus *samyagvimukti* and *samyagjñāna* (*Aṅguttara*, v.222); the five abandoned items are not the group of *satkāyadṛṣṭi, śīlavrataparāmarśa, vicikitsā, kāmacchanda*, and *vyāpāda*, for this group has been abandoned with the acquisition of the result of Anāgāmin; rather, it is a group relative to the higher spheres, *rūparāga, ārūpyarāga, auddhatya, māna*, and *avidyā*.

187. *Dīgha*, iii.59: *Dalhanemi . . . sattaratanasamannāgato*.

188. According to Scripture, things (*vastu*) are either *dravyasat* or *prajñaptisat*, "really existant," or "existing as designation."

189. The cause of arising of a thought of greed is the "possession" of this future thought of greed.

190. The pure *dharmas*, *duḥkhe dharmajñānakṣānti*, etc.

191. The undefiled and defiled *dharmas* of Kāmadhātu respectively.

192. These definitions answer the questions of the Vaibhāṣikas: "Is the seed a thing (*dravya*) different from the mind, or not different from the mind?," "Is this series a permanent (*anasthita*) thing within which different *dharmas* successively arise?," "Should *pariṇāma* be included as is the *pariṇāma* of the Sāṁkhyas?"

See ii.54c-d. The doctrine of the evolution of the series is presented again iv.3c.

193. Tibetan and Paramārtha. Hsüan-tsang: "The two paths (the doctrine of the Sautrāntikas and the doctrine of the Vaibhāṣikas) are good. How is this? The first is not in contradiction with reason; and the second is our system."

Pañcaskandha: prāptiḥ katamā? pratilambhaḥ samanvāgamaḥ / . . . bījaṁ vaśitvaṁ saṁmukhībhāvo yathāyogam. (According to the Tibetan).

194. The *prāpti* of past *dharmas* is (1) either past, that is: "which has arisen and which has perished:" it was either earlier (*agraja*), or later (*paścātkālaja*), or simultaneous (*sahaja*) to these *dharmas*; (2) or it is future, that is: "that which has not arisen:" it will be later than these *dharmas*; (3) or present, that is: "that which has arisen and which has not perished:" it is later than these *dharmas*. And thus following.

No *dharma* is susceptible of this threefold *prāpti*. For example, the *prāpti* of the *dharmas* "of retribution" is solely simultaneous to these *dharmas* (ii.38c). One does not "possess" these *dharmas* before they have arisen, nor after they have perished.

195. The impure *dharmas* belong to the planes of existence, *dhātvāpta, dhātupatita.*

196. These are the *apariyāpannas* of the Abhidhamma.

197. *Pratisaṁkhyānirodha* or "disjunction of defilement" (*visaṁyoga*, i.6a-b, ii.57d) can be obtained by a Pṛthagjana or by an Āryan. In the first case, the *prāpti* is of Rūpadhātu or Ārūpyadhātu depending on whether the *nirodha* is obtained by a (worldly) path of Rūpadhātu or Ārūpyadhātu. In the second case, it is of Rūpadhātu and pure, when the *nirodha* is obtained by a Rūpadhātu (or worldly) path; of Ārūpyadhātu and pure, when the *nirodha* is obtained by a path of Ārūpyadhātu; and pure, when the *nirodha* is obtained by the pure Path (according to the principle formulated vi.46).

198. The *Śaikṣa dharmas* are the pure *dharmas* of the Śaikṣa, of the saint who is not an Arhat; the *dharmas* of an Aśaikṣa are the pure *dharmas* of the Arhat.

199. Paramārtha: "The same way as the *prāpti*, obtained by a non-Āryan, of *apratisaṁkhyānirodha* and *pratisaṁkhyānirodha*." Hsüan-tsang: ". . . the *prāpti* of *pratisaṁkhyānirodha* obtained through a non-Āryan path."

200. One case is not envisioned: the *prāpti* of *pratisaṁkhyānirodha*, by means of a worldly path, by an Āryan. This *prāpti* is at one an the same time pure and impure, as we shall see vi.46.

201. *Durbalatvāt: anabhisaṁskāravattvāt*, because it is not the result of an effort.

202. *Vyākhyā*: The Vaibhāṣikas. For example, Viśvakarman, the heavenly artisan, possessess past, present, and future *śailpasthānikas*; the Sthavira Aśvajit possesses the *airyāpathikas*.

203. The non-possession of the defilements is not defiled, for, in this hypothesis, it would be lacking in a person liberated from the defilements: but it is not good, for it is lacking in the person who has cut off the roots of good (*Vibhāṣā, TD* 27, p. 799a21).

204. If an *aprāpti* can be pure, this would be the *aprāpti* of the pure *dharmas*; now the definition of a Pṛthagjana proves that the *aprāpti* of the pure *dharmas* is not pure.
On the *pṛthagjana*, see i.40, 41a, ii.9b-d, iii.41c-d, 95a, vi.26a, 28d, 45b.

205. Second masters of the *Vibhāṣā*.

206. Compare *Kathāvatthu*, iv.4.

207. *Aprāpti* or *alābha* belongs to the sphere of existence (*dhātu*) to which the person belongs who is endowed with it (ii.40a). Thus a being in Kāmadhātu is solely endowed with the quality of Pṛthagjana (which is *aprāpti*, ii.40b-c) of the sphere of Kāmadhātu. Thus one cannot say that, by the acquisition of the Path, this being loses the quality of Pṛthagjana of the sphere of the three realms of existence. Nevertheless, by the acquisition of the Path, any quality of Pṛthagjana, of whatever sphere, becomes impossible. One can thus say that this quality, under its triple form (of Kāmadhātu, etc.), is abandoned, even though a given being is endowed with it under but one form.
Two aspects of its abandoning are distinguished, *vihāni* and *prahāṇa*.

208. A Pṛthagjana, detaching himself from Kāmadhātu, passes into the First Dhyāna: he loses the quality of Pṛthagjana of the sphere of Kāmadhātu, but he does not become, by this fact, an Āryan: for another quality of Pṛthagjana, of the sphere of the First Dhyāna, appears. The same way for the other stages, whether one ascends or descends.

209. By taking possession of the good *dharmas* of hearing and reflection of Kāmadhātu, one loses the *aprāpti* of these *dharmas*; by taking possession of the innate good *dharmas* (ii.71b), one loses the *aprāpti* of the roots of good which have been cut off (*samucchinnakuśala*). When, dying in Kāmadhātu, one is reborn in the First Dhyāna, one loses the *aprāpti* of the *dharmas* of the First Dhyāna . . . This theory raises some delicate problems which the *Vyākhyā* summarily examines.

210. Compare ii.45c-d: the play of birth (*jāti*) and the arising of birth (*jātijāti*).

211. The case of the neutral (*avyākṛta*) *dharma* is not examined here, because this *dharma* is possessed solely at the moment when it exists (*tasya sahajaiva prāptiḥ*): the numbers differ.

212. The Japanese editor observes that one should add four *lakṣaṇas* and four *anulakṣaṇas* (ii.45c-d) for each of these three *dharmas*; we thus have twenty-seven *dharmas* of the first moment.

213. At the fourth moment one possesses twenty-seven *prāptis*, namely the *prāptis* of the *dharmas* produced at the three preceeding moments, three, six, and eighteen, plus twenty-seven *anuprāptis*, or forty-four *dharmas*. At the fifth moment, eighty-one *prāptis* and as many *anuprāptis*.

214. *Prakaraṇa, TD* 26, p. 694a23:"What is *nikāyasabhāga*? The commoness of nature (*t'ung-lei hsing*) of living beings."

215. Each living being possesses his own *sattvasabhāgatā*. Nevertheless *sattvasabhāgatā* is said to be general because it is not differenciated. To conceive of it as unique and eternal is an error of the Vaibhāṣikas.

216. By *et cetera* one should understand: *upāsikā, bhikṣuṇī, the naivaśaikṣanāśaikṣa*, etc.

217. "It is by reason of their *dharmasabhāgatā* that the *dhātus* are of Kāmadhātu . . ."

218. Compare *Aṅguttara*, iv.247, etc. The *Daśabhūmaka* replaces the formula *sa ced* . . . with *atha cet punar manuṣyeṣūpapadyate*.

Divya, 194.30: *manuṣyāṇāṁ sabhāgatāyaṁ upapanna iti* (*Mahāvyutpatti*, 245.54); 122.16: *brahmalokasabhāgatāyāṁ copapanno mahābrahamā saṁvṛttaḥ*. *Śikṣāsamucacaya*, 176.9: *sarva nikāyasabhāge devamanuṣyāṇāṁ priyo bhavati*.

219. Hsüan-tsang translates: "This is not admissible, for it is in contradiction with our system;" he omits the formula "The Vaibhāṣikas say" (The Vaibhāṣikas say: "This is not admissible . . ."

220. *Prakaraṇa, TD* 26, p. 694a19. *Dīgha*, iii.263: *sant'āvuso sattā asaññino appatisaṁvedino seyyathāpi devā asaññasattā*. i.28, iii.33 . . . *saññuppādā ca pana te devā tamhā kāyā cavanti*. One of the nine *sattvāvāsas*, *Aṅguttara*, iv.401; *Kośa*, iii.6c.

221. *Vibhāṣā, TD* 27, p. 615a5, five opinions.

222. But the foreigners pretend that there are nine divisions in the heaven of the Fourth Dhyāna. On the Vṛhatphalas (Vehapphalas), see Burnouf, Introduction, p. 614.

223. Opinion of the Andhakas, condemned in the *Kathāvatthu*, iii.14.

224. On the meaning of the word *samāpatti*, see p. 232.

225. The complete name is *saṁjñāveditanairodhasamāpatti*, see p. 230.

Prakaraṇa, TD 26, p. 694a19: *Asaṁjñisamāpatti* is an arresting of the mind and mental states which has for its antecedents the idea of deliverence (*niḥsaraṇamanasikārapūrvaka*) and which is obtained by a person free from defilements of the Śubhakṛtsnas, but not from higher defilements. *Nirodhasamāpatti* is an arresting of the mind and mental states which has for its antecedents the idea of calmness, and which is obtained by a person free from the defilements of *ākiñcanyāyatana*. Vasubandhu, in his *Pañcaskandhaka*, draws his inspiration from these definitions.

226. One obtains *apratisaṁkhyānirodha* or the definitive disappearance of bad realms of rebirth, *āsaṁjñika*, birth among the Mahābrahmas and the Kurus, and an eighth rebirth by entry into *niyāma*.

227. Whoever enters into the Fourth Dhyāna obtains in the same body the *prāpti* of all the four Dhyānas which he has cultivated or will cultivate in the course of his transmigration.

228. The future good mind is the object of a former *prāpti*.

229. On *nirodhasamāpatti, saṁjñāveditanirodhasamāpatti* (see below p. 230, see vi.43c-d, viii.33a (*vimokṣa), Kathāvatthu*, vi.5, xv.7. In the *Vibhāṣā, TD* 27, p. 777a14 numerous opinions on this absorption: for some, it is only one thing (*dravya*), *nirodhasākṣātkāra*; for others, eleven things: the ten *mahābhūmikas* and *cittanirodha*; for others, twenty-one things: the *mahābhūmikas*, the *kuśalamahābhūmikas* and *cittanirodha* . . .

230. *Vihāra* = *samādhiviśeṣa*.

231. It is "retributed later:" when an existence in Rūpadhātu in interposed between an existence in Kāmadhātu in the course of which one produces it, and an existence in Bhavāgra which is its result.

232. This absorption takes place in Bhavāgra, from whence matter (*rūpa*) is absent. Pṛthagjanas fear that the arresting of the mind and mental states is, under these conditions, annihilation. They do not have the same fear with respect to *asaṁjñisamāpatti*, which takes place in the Fourth Dhyāna, where matter persists. By this fact, there remains, within *nirodhasamāpatti, nikāyasabhāga, jīvitendriya* and other *saṁskāras* disassociated from the mind; but Pṛthagjanas do not see them.

233. According to one varient, followed by the Chinese translaters, *dṛṣṭadharmanirvāṇasya* . . . That is, "The Āryan hopes to obtain, aims to obtain Nirvāṇa-at-death by means of this absorption, within this absorption."

234. The *Vyākhyā* quotes a stanza of the Stotrakāra, i.e., Mātṛceṭa (*Varṇanārhavarṇana*, 118: F. W. Thomas, *Indian Antiquary*, 1905, p. 159): *na te prāyogikaṁ kiṁcit kuśalaṁ kuśalānuga* /

235. The Japanese editor quotes different opinions of old commentaries on the *Kośa*: the Westerners are the Sarvāstivādins of Gandhāra, or the Sautrāntikas, or the masters of the land of Indhu. They are called "Westeners"because they are to the west of Kásmīr, and "foreigners" (*bahirdeśaka*) because they are outside of Kasmir. See below note 237.

236. See iv.24c-d. Compare *Kathāvatthu*, i.5, xviii.5.

237. The Masters of the land of Indhu, of the same opinion as the Westerners.

238. *Vyutthānāśaya* = *vyutthānābhiprāya*: "having a resolution susceptible of giving up, of surrending." According to another interpretation, *āśaya* = *kuśala* = *kuśalamūla*; thus: "having roots of good susceptible of giving up, of being interrupted." Now the roots of good of the Bodhisattvas are such that, once they have begun to be actualized, they do not cease before Bodhi is obtained.

Vyutthāna also signifies "departure from absorption" (*Saṁyutta*, iii.265, etc.).

239. See *Vibhāṣā TD* 27, p. 204b3-c4: All the attitudes are good. Why does the Bodhisattva take up the sitting attitude? . . .

240. Hsüan-tsang adds: "The first doctrine is the best, because it is our system."

241. *Vibhāṣā, TD* 27, p. 773bll. Three opinions: solely in Kāmadhātu; also in the three lower Dhyānas; and also in the Fourth Dhyāna.

According to the *Vibhāṣā, nirodhasamāpatti* cannot be prolonged beyond seven days-and-nights.

242. The *Jñānaprasthāna, TD* 26, p. 1024a8, posits a fourfold question: Is there an existence in Rūpadhātu which does not include the five *skandhas*? Is there an existence including the five *skandhas* and which is not Rūpadhātu? Is there an existence in Rūpadhātu which includes the five *skandhas*? Is there an existence which is neither in Rūpadhātu and which does not include the five *skandhas*?

243. The *Jñānaprasthāna* and the *Kośa* do not emply the word *skandha* but a synonym, a word that the MSS of the *Vyākhyā* transcribe as both *vyavahāra* and *vyavacāra*. Hsüan-tsang translates this is *hsing* 行 , the equivalent of *saṁskāra, viharaṇa*, etc.; Paramārtha translates this as *p'an* 判 , the equivalent of *nīti, naya*, "to judge," "to decide." The reading *vyavakāra* appears certain according to Pali sources.

a. Pali sources. *Vokāra* = *khandha* (Childers); *Vibhaṅga*, 137: *saññābhavo asaññābhavo nevasaññānāsaññābhavo ekāvokārabhavo catuvokārabhavo pañcavokārabhavo; Yamaka*, according to *Kathāvatthu*, trans. p. 38; *Kathāvatthu*, iii.11: if non-conscious beings possess an existence including *vokāra* or five *vokāras*. (Buddhaghosa explains: *vividhena visuṁ visuṁ karīyati*).

b. *Vyākhyā. Vyavakāra* is the name that the Buddha Kasyapa gives to the *skandhas. Vyavakāra (viśeṣeṇāvakāra)* signifies *savyavakāra* according to Panini, v.27.127; thus, "that which deceives, that which contradicts (*visaṁvādanī*) by its impermanence," a definition which applies to the *skandhas* according to the stanza "*Rūpa* is like foam . . ." (*Saṁyutta*, iii.142).

c. *Vibhāṣā, TD* 27, p. 959bll. The former Tathāgatas Samyaksaṁbuddhas called the *skandhas vyavakāras*; but the Tathāgata Samyaksambuddha Śākyamuni calls the *vyavakāras skandhas*. The former Buddhas spoke of five *vyavakāras*, Śākyamuni speaks of five *upādānaskandhas*. Here, in the Abhidharma, one speaks of existence "having five *vyavakāras*," (*pañca*-) in order to show that the five *skandhas* of which Śākyamuni speaks are the five *vyavakāras* of which the former Buddhas spoke. Why did the former Buddhas use the term *vyavakāra*, whereas the present Buddha uses the word *skandha*? Because the Buddhas see that this is suitable to say to their followers . . . Why this expression *vyavakāra*? By reason of *pravṛtti* (*saṁcāra?, liu-ch'uan* 流轉 the *skandhas* which have formerly arisen develop by reason of the later *skandhas*, or rather the *skandhas* which have arisen later develop by reason of former *skandhas* . . .

244. When these beings, conscious by nature, become non-conscious in one of the two absorption, they are *visabhāgacitte sthita*, "placed in a mind contrary to their nature."

245. This Sūtra was preached by Śāriputra: it bears the name of Udāyin, because the adversary of Śāriputra is Udayin. The Sanskrit redaction is very close to the Pāḷi text. *Madhyamāgama TD* 1, p. 449c7 and *Aṅguttara*, iii.192. *śrāvastyāṁ nidānam / tatrāyuṣmān śāriputro bhikṣūn āmantrayate sma / ihāyuṣmanto bhikṣuḥ śīlasaṁpannaś ca bhavati samādhisaṁpannaś ca prajñāsaṁpannaś ca / so'bhikṣṇaṁ saṁjñāveditanirodhaṁ samāpadyate ca vyuttiṣṭhate ca / asti caitat sthānam iti yathābhūtaṁ prajānāmi / sa nehaiva dṛṣṭa eva dharme pratipattyaivājñām ārāgayati nāpi maraṇasamaye bhedāc ca kāyasyātikramya devān kavaḍīkārabhakṣān anyatamasmin divye manomaya kāya upapadyate / sa tatropanno . . .*

Vyākhyā: pratipattyaiva = pūrvam eva.

This Sūtra is discussed viii.3c (the thesis of the existence of *rūpa* in Ārūpyadhātu). Compare *Dīgha*, i.195.

246. *Ājñām ārāgayati*, as in *Mahāvastu*, iii.53.9. Paramārtha: "He does not obtain *ājñatāvīndriya*." Hsüan-tsang: "He does not apply himself in the manner to obtain the quality of Arhat . . . "

247. It is termed *manomaya* or mental, because it arises independently of the elements of generation; but this does not mean that it is a body created from ideas, *saṁjñāmaya (Dīgha*, i.195), and belonging to Ārūpyadhātu, as Udāyin thinks.

On the "mental bodies" of the Bodhisattva in the *Mahāvastu*, see *Opinions sur l'histoire de la dogmatique*, p. 258.

248. Note of the Japanese editor: i. The mental body gods of which the Sūtra speaks are (a) of Rūpadhātu, for the Sarvāstivādins (same opinion, *Dīgha*, i.195); (b) of Rūpadhātu and Ārūpyadhātu, for the Sautrāntikas; or (c) the Asaṁjñisattvas, for Udāyin. ii. According to the Sarvāstivādins there is falling from the absorption of extinction; but there is no falling, according to the Sautrāntikas and Udāyin.

But, according to the *Vyākhyā*, the Sautrāntikas admit a falling from absorption; they nevertheless deny that a Saint falls out of Āryamārga (*contra* the Sarvāstivādins), from whence the difficulties that the *Vyākhyā* resolves.

249. The Mahāsāṁghikas, etc., according to P'u-kuang, *TD* 41, p. 99c15.

250. *Dīrgha, TD* 1, p. 110a24; *Dīgha*, iii.266; *Mahāvyutpatti*, 68.7: *navānupūrvasamāpattayas*: the four *dhyānas*, the four *ārūpyas* and the absorption of extinction.

251. *Prāthamakalpikaḥ* = *āditaḥ samāpattividhāyakaḥ*.

252. One prepares himself for *asaṁjñisamāpatti* by thinking: "*Saṁjñā* is a sickness, a thorn, an abscess; the cessation of *saṁjñā* is tranquil, excellent."

253. The preparation includes the resolution "I shall know the mind of another."

254. The philosphical systems (*siddhānta*) are in disagreement. The Vaibhāṣikas, etc., hold that the absorptions and *asaṁjñika* are lacking mind (*acittakāny eva* . . .): the Sthavira Vasumitra, etc., hold that they are endowed with mind (*sacittakāni*) from the fact of a non-manifested mental conciousness (*aparisphuṭamanovijñāna*); and the Yogācārins hold that they have mind from the fact of the *ālayavijñāna* (*Vyākhyā*).

255. This question is posed by the Sautrāntikas. For them, the mind which has just perished, and the mind which perished a long time ago, are equally non-existent: however the mind which has just perished is the cause of the mind which immediately follows it: compare the movement of the beam of a balance (*tulādaṇḍonnāmāvanāmavat*, comp. *Śālistamba* in the *Bodhicaryāvatāra*, 483.3).

256. The author indicates the name of the treatise because Vasumitra (called either the Sthavira or Bhadanta) wrote other books, the *Pañcavastuka*, etc. (*Vyākhyā*). There is a commentary on the *Pañcavastuka* by Dharmatrāta, *TD* 28, number 1555.

The Japanese editor remarks that this does not refer to the Vasumitra of the *Vibhāṣā*, but to a Sautrāntika. (See P'u-kuang, *TD* 41, p. 100b12.)

257. *Vibhāṣā, TD* 27, p. 774a14: "The Dārṣṭāntikas and the Vibhajyavādins maintain that there is a subtle mind which is not interrupted in the absorption of extinction. They say, 'There are no beings who are at one and the same time without mind and without *rūpa*; there is no absorption which is without mind. If an absorption were without mind, then the vital organ would be cut off; one would not term this established in absorption, but rather "dead."'"

258. *Saṁyuktāgama, TD* 2, p. 74b20 and following; compare *Saṁyutta*, ii.72 and sources quoted *as Kośa*, iii.30b.

259. *Saṁyuktāgama, TD* 2, p. 83a2; *Saṁyutta*, iii.96.

260. This formula occurs in the *Mahāvyutpatti*, 68.9.

Vibhāṣā, TD 27, p. 782a22: One who is in *nirodhasamāpatti* cannot be burned by fire, drowned by water, wounded by the sword, or killed by another (Compare the legends of Saṁjīva, Khāṇu-Koṇḍañña, in the *Visuddhi*, xii. *JTPS*, 1891, 112). Why does he possess this quality? Vasumitra says because this *samāpatti* cannot be damaged; thus he who is in it cannot be damaged. Moreover *samāpatti* produces equality of the mind. Here, there is not mind, so how can one speak of *samāpatti*? *Samāpatti* is of two types: that which produces equality of mind, and that which produces equaltiy of the primary elements. Even though the two *samāpattis* cut off the equality of the mind since they interrupt the mind, they bring about the equality of the primary elements.

261. *Āśraya* has been defined ii.5-6; see also p. 209.

262. Hsüan-tsang translates: "This theory is not good, for it is in contradiction with our system." Let us add: "So say the Vaibhasikas." See above note 218.

263. Buddhaghosa attributes to the Pubbaseliyas and to the Sammitiyas the Abhidharma doctrine that the *jīvitendriya* is a *cittacippayutta arūpadhamma*. See *Kathāvatthu*, viii.10, *Compendium*, p. 156; *Vibhaṅga*, p. 123, *Dhammasaṅgaṇi*, 19, 635, *Atthasālinī*, 644.

264. *Jñānaprasthāna, TD* 26, p. 991b25 (*Indriyaskandhaka*, 1), *Prakaraṇa, TD* 26, p. 694a23.

265. *Saṁyukta, TD* 2, p. 150b9, *Madhyama, TD* 1, p. 789al, *Saṁyutta*, iii.143 (varients); compare *Majjhima*, i.296. Quoted below ad iv.73a-b.

266. *Vibhāṣā, TD* 27, p. 771a7: This Sūtra is quoted by the Vibhajyavādins in order to prove that these three *dharmas*,—life, heat, and consciousness,—are always united and not separated. But Vasumitra observes that the Sūtra refers to the series of a certain *āśraya* . . . Life (*āyus*) forms part of the *saṁskāraskandha*, the *dharmadhātu*, and the *dharmāyatana*; heat, of the *rūpaskandha* and the *spraṣṭavyāyatana*; and consciousness, of the *vijñānaskandha*, the seven *dhātus* and the *manāyatana*: thus one should not take the Sūtra literally. Furthermore, if these three *dharmas* always go together, there would be heat in Ārūpyadhātu, life and consciousness among non-living beings, and consciousness in the non-conscious absorption.

267. Hsüan-tsang: "In addition to that we have said. What have you said? In order to avoid this consequence . . ."

268. *Vaiśeṣikadarśana*, v.1.16; H. Ui, *Vaiśeṣika philosophy*, p. 163. The example of the arrow has no real value for the Vaiśeṣikas who hold that *vega* is a thing in and of itself. Thus the author here refutes the theory of the Vaiśeṣikas.

269. Hsüan-tsang: "There is a thing in and of itself, the support of heat and consciousness, called *āyus*: this is the best doctrine." Note of the Japanese editor: The author adopts the opinion of the Sarvāstivādins. But we may suppose that Hsüan-tsang has omited the words "The Vaibhasikas say:. . . ," for in his *Pañcaskandhaka*, Vasubandhu adopts the Sautrāntika thesis.

270. *Karmaprajñāptiśāstra*, Chap. xi (Mdo 72, fol. 240b).

271. On the different results of action, iv.85 and following. On *bhoga, Yogasūtra*, ii.13.

272. Missing in Paramārtha. See above, p. 167. *Vibhāṣā, TD* 27, p. 103b3.

273. This is an explanation of the Foreigners (Bahirdeśaka). The explanation of the Kaśmīreans differs only in its words. Or rather these latter understand that the *āyus* of the first category is "bound to its own series (*svasaṁtatyupanibaddha*), but susceptible of being hindered."

274. According to *Kathāvatthu*, xvii.2, the Rajagirikas and the Siddhatthikas deny the premature death of an Arhat (*Kośa*, ii.10). According to Rockhill (*Life of Buddha*, p. 189) and Wassilieff, p.

244, the Prajñaptivādins deny premature death. The *Bodhicaryāvatāra* (ii.55) admits a "natural" (*kāla*) death and one hundered premature deaths, due to each of the humors (*vāta, pitta, śleṣman*) and to the humors joined together, for a total of four hundred and four deaths.

Further (1) *samucchedamaraṇa*, the death of an Arhat; (2) *khaṇikamaraṇa*, the constant disappearance of the *dharmas* eaten up by impermanence; (3) *sammutimaraṇa*, the death that one attributes to a tree, etc. The Abhidhamma distinguishes (1) *kālamaraṇa* (natural death) (a) by exhaustion of merit (*puñña*), (b) by exhaustion of the span of life (*āyu*), and (c) by exhaustion of the two; (2) *akālamaraṁa* (premature death) by reason of an action which cuts off existence (*upacchedakakammaṇā*), in the case of Dūsī Māra, Kalabhū, etc., and in the case of persons assassinated in retribution of a previous action (*Visuddhimagga*, viii. *apud* Warren, p. 252; *Commentary on the Anguttara*, P.T.S., p. 111; *Nettipakaraṇa*, p. 29; *Milinda*, p. 301. *Abhidhammasaṅgaha, Compendium*, p. 149.

Jain doctrine, Umāsvāti, *Tattvārthādhigamasūtra*, ii.52: *dvividhāny āyuṁsi* . . .

275. Literally: taking possession of existence, *ātmabhāvapratilambha*. *Majjhima*, iii.53 distinguishes two types, *savyāpajjha* and *avyāpajjha*.

276. *Dīgha*, iii.231, *Aṅguttara*, ii.159: *atth'āvuso attabhāvapaṭilābho yasmiṁ attabhāvapaṭilābhe attasaṁcetanā yeva kamati no parasaṁcetanā* . . . See *Kośa*, vi.56. *Vyākhyā*: *ātmasaṁcetanā* = *ātmanā māraṇam; parasaṁcetanā* = *pareṇa māraṇam*.

277. *Dīgha*, i.19, iii.31. *Vibhāṣā, TD* 27, p. 997b9. There is no agreement as to whether this refers to the Four Kings and the heaven of the Thirty-three Gods, or to other categories of gods in Kāmadhātu.

278. For example a certain Śuka was sent by the Blessed One to Āmrapālī; the Licchavis were engaged in military exercises (*yogya*), and seeing him they covered him with a rain of arrows. But the messanger of the Buddha cannot be killed before he has completed his mission.

279. Perhaps we should understand: "the persons to whom the Buddha gives an order know that they will live yet that much more time." The notes of J. Przyluski on Yaśas and Jīvaka make this version plausible enough:

"In *Mahāvagga*, i.7, Para. 4 is almost incomprehensible. Yaśas cries out 'What a danger!' and we do not know to what danger he is alluding. In the corresponding passage of the *Vinaya* of the Sarvāstivādins everything is explained: 'Then Yaśas, having passed beyond the gate of the village, arrived at the river of Vārāṇasī. Then the Blessed One was walking on the bank of this river. Yaśas, seeing the water, gave forth a cry as he had formerly done. The Buddha, hearing this cry, said to the young man: 'This place has nothing to cause fear. Cross the current and come'" (Tōk. xvii., 3.26a).

"The wife of Subhadra (comp. *Divyāvadāna*, 262-270) died before having given birth; the body was cremated but the infant was not burned. The Buddha told Jīvaka to go and take the infant from out of the midst of the flames: Jīvaka obeyed and returned without having had any ill effect (xvii.1.6a)."

280. Tibetan: *gaṅ ga len*. The Chinese transcriptions give Gañjila; see the unsuccessful suicide attempts of Gaṅgika, *Avadānaśataka*, 98.

281. The fact that the word *tadyathā* is lacking in the response of the Blessed One does not prove that this response should be understood literally.

282. Paramārtha: "Further, there are the *lakṣaṇas* of the *saṁskṛtas* . . ."

Hsüan-tsang: "The *lakṣaṇas*, are namely the arising, duration, change, and destruction of the *saṁskṛtas*."

Vibhāṣā, TD 27, p. 198a8 and following; Dharmottara's *Abhidharmahṛdaya, TD* 28, p.

811b17.

A provisional definition of *saṁskṛta* has been given i.7a-b.

283. But cannot one say that duration is a characteristic of an unconditioned thing? No. Characteristics are things in and of themselves (*dravyāntararūpa*) distinct from the *dharmas* characterized, which causes arising, duration, decline and the perishing of this same *dharma*. An unconditioned thing lasts but does not possess the characteristic "duration," see below p. 239 line 11.

284. This is *Trilakṣaṇasūtra* (see below p. 242 line 9). *Saṁyuktāgama, TD* 2, p. 85b10; *Aṅguttara*, i.152: *tīṇ'imāni bhikkhave saṁkhatassa samkhatalakkhaṇāni / katamāni tīṇi / uppādo paññāyati vayo paññāyati ṭhitassa aññāthattaṁ paññāyati.* The Sanskrit redaction has: *sthityanyathātva* (*Madhyamakavṛtti*, p. 145); *Kathāvatthu*, trans. p. 55: *ṭhitānaṁ aññāthatta.*

On *anyathābhāva, Saṁyutta*, ii.274. The Abhidhamma only admits three characteristics: certain masters omit even *sthiti* (*Kathāvatthu*, trans., note p. 374).

The four *lakṣaṇas* of the Vijñānavāda, *Bodhisattvabhūmi*, I, xvii. Para. 15. (*Madhyamakavṛtti*, p. 546).

285. The same comparison, with a different moral, *Atthasālinī*, 655.

286. Compare Burnouf, Introduction, p. 255.

287. The theory of the *lakṣaṇas* and *anulakṣaṇas* is refuted by Nāgārjuna, *Madhyamaka*, vii.1 and following. See *Madhyamakavṛtti*, p. 148, on the theory of the Sāṁmītiyas who admit seven *lakṣaṇas* and seven *anulakṣaṇas: utpāda, utpādotpāda*, etc.

288. Space is a pure negative, a pure absence of any matter susceptible of resistance. It cannot be analyzed (*vipaṭyate, vibhidyate*).

289. See note 293.

290. See the sources quoted in *Madhyamakavṛtti*, 268, 598.

291. *Saṁyukta, TD* 2, p. 73b23. *pravāhagatā hi vedanās tasya viditā evotpadyante / viditā avatiṣṭhante / viditā astaṁ parikṣayaṁ paryādānaṁ gacchanti / na kṣaṇagatāḥ kṣaṇasya duravadhāratvāt* (*Vyākhyā*).

Tibetan: The *kulaputra* Nanda (Comp. *Aṅguttara*, iv.166).

Compare *Saṁyutta*, vi.180; *Majjhima*, iii.25 (where the Blessed One says to Śāriputra what he says here to Nanda): *dhammā viditā uppajjanti viditā upaṭṭhahanti viditā abbhatthaṁ gacchanti.*

292. *Majjhima*, iii.25 contains the formula *evam kila me dhammā ahutvā sambhonti* which becomes the thesis of the Sautrantikas: *abhūtvā bhāva utpādaḥ* (p. 243 line 17), which we read in *Milinda*, p. 51: *ahutvā sambhoti*, and which is contradicted by the Sarvāstivādins and by *Milinda*, p. 52: *natthi keci saṁkhārā ye abhavantā jāyanti.* Nāgasena is a Vibhajyavādin, p. 50.

293. If one says, "It is by reason of its duration (*sthitisadbhāvāt*) that a *dharma*, once arisen, does not perish for a moment; lacking duration, even this moment itself would not exist," such is not the case, for the moment exists by reason of the cause which produces it.

If one says, "It is duration which causes, which embraces (*upagṛhṇāti*) a *dharma* engendered by causes," we would ask, "If duration does not accomplish this task, what will happen?" "The *dharma* would not exist (*ātmasattā dharmasya na bhavet*)." "Then say that duration engenders, not that it cause something to endure."

If one says, "Duration causes the series to continue (*avasthāpayati*)," then the name of duration should be reserved for its causes.

294. Smoke is momentary; when it "reproduces itself" in a place higher than that which it first

occupied, persons say that it rises (*ūrdhvagamanākhyāṁ labhate*) and they conceive of the rising (*ūrdhvagamanatvam*) as distinct from the smoke (see iv.2b).

295. If, grasping the unique self nature of a visible thing, I were to grasp it as being conditioned (*saṁskṛtam iti*) before knowing of its former non-existence, one could say that "conditioned" is a mark of a conditioned thing, that a conditioned thing is characterized by a conditioned thing (*tenaive tal lakṣitaṁ syāt*). But such is not the case.

296. The Vaibhāṣikas are "followers of momentariness" (*kṣaṇikavādin*): *dharmas* last only a moment and perish of themselves. See iv.2b; Wassilief, p. 325. But the difficulty is: what does *kṣaṇa* mean?

297. Some other definitions, iii.86a.

298. The Saṁmitīyas (see iv.2c).

299. In the Introduction we have studied the different theories relative to impermanence (*anityatva*) and momentariness (*kṣaṇikatva*).

300. See above p. 245. A conditioned *dharma* is engenderd by its characteristic "arising." "Arising" arises at the same time as the *dharma* which it engenders; being "future" it engenders it before arising itself.

301. Causes (*hetu*) and conditions (*pratyaya*) are defined ii.49, 61c.

302. The *Vyākhyā* quotes the response made by the Bhadanta Anantavarman to this objection: "The eye does not produce the visible consciousness without the coming together of clearness, etc.; it is no less a cause of the visual consciousness." Response: "We state that the blind do not see, that the non-blind do see: thus we state the efficacy of the eye. The same does not hold for arising."

Anantavarman is quoted in the *Vyākhyā ad* ii.71b-72, iii.35d and vii.32.

303. The nature of the mental states, *sparśa*, etc. is subtle and difficult to distinguish. Without doubt, reply the Sautrāntikas, but the Blessed One explained the efficacy of *sparśa*, etc.: "All that which is *vedanā*, *saṁjñā*, and *saṁskāras*, exists by reason of *sparśa* . . . ;" but he did not explain the efficacy of "arising."

304. The idea of "color" has for its object specific characteristics (*svalakṣaṇa*) of the "color." But the idea of "arisen," as "the color has arisen," does not bear on the color, since I have the same idea of arising when it refers to sensation: "sensation has arisen." Thus the idea of "arisen" bears on the action produced by a certain *dharma*, independent of its color, its sensation, and its "arising."

305. The Buddhists (*baudhasiddhānta*) believe that sandalwood is only a certain collection of odors, etc. (*gandhādisamūha*). The Vaibhāṣikas believe that sandalwood exists in and of itself; this is why the author gives the example of the bust, an example admitted by the Vaibhāṣikas. See *Madhyamakavṛtti*, p. 66; *Sāṁkhyapravacanabhāṣya*, p. 84, 148, etc.

306. *Vibhāṣā, TD* 27, p. 198a15: Some maintain that the *saṁskṛtalakṣaṇas* are not real things, namely the Dārṣṭāntikas who say: "The *saṁskṛtalakṣaṇas* are included within the *viprayuktasaṁskāraskandha*; the *viprayuktasaṁskāraskandha* is not real; thus the *saṁskṛtalakṣaṇas* are not real." In order to refute their opinion . . .

307. Hsüan-tsang: "This theory is best. Why?"

308. Namely the Abhidharmaśāstras.

309. We have four proverbs which have the same meaning, that is, one should not renounce a

thing in and of itself because of the defects that it presents, or because of the risks that it entails.

a. *Na hi bhikṣukāḥ santīti sthālyo nādhiśrīyante.*

b. *Na ca mṛgāḥ santīti yavā* (var. *śālayo*) *nopyante.*

These two proverbs, which often go together, have been studies by Col. Jacob, in his *Second Handful of Popular Maxims* (Bombay, Nirnayasagar, 1909, p. 42, index *sub voc. na hi bhikṣikāḥ*), with the references which follow: *Mahābhāṣya*, i.99, ii.194, iii.23 (Kielhorn), in the same context (*na hi doṣāḥ santīti praibhāṣā na kartavyā lakṣaṇaṁ vā na praṇeyam / na hi bhikṣukāḥ . . .*); *Vācasapatimiśra, Nyāyavārtikatātparyaṭīkā*, pp. 62, 441; Bhāmatī, p. 54; *Sarvadarśanasaṁgraha*, p. 3 of Cowell's translation. We should add the *Kāmasūtra* (see Cat. Oxford, 216b), where the two proverbs are attributed to Vātsyāyana (mentioned by Weber, *Indische Studien*, XIII, p. 326).

c. *Ato'jīrṇabhayān nāhāraparityāgo bhikṣukabhayān na sthālyā anadhiśrayaṇam doṣeṣu prativdhātavyam iti nyāyah.*

Col. Jacob quotes, for this third proverb, *Pañcapādikā*, p. 63 (of which the final *doṣeṣu prativdhātavyam* is found in Vasubandhu), *Jīvanmuktiviveka*, p. 8 (which attributes the proverb to Anandabodhācārya), and *Hitopadeśa*, ii.50, *doṣabhīter anārambhaḥ* . . .

d. *Na makṣikāḥ patantīti modakā na bhakṣyante.*

A proverb for which we do not have any other references than Vasubandhu. It appears that the Buddhists, being *bhikṣus*, have substituted mendicant (*bhikṣuka*) and *sthālī* in the proverb, making it a proverb less biting than one containing flies and cakes.

310. Surendranath Dasgupta, in his *Study of Patañjali* (Calcutta, 1920), give in brief (p. 192-201) the various theories concerning *sphoṭa*.

311. The word *Saṁjñākaraṇa* belongs to popular language (*lokabhāṣā*); it is the equivalent of *nāmadheya*, name or appellation, for one says "'Devadatta' is a *saṁjñākaraṇa* sound." But here it means "That which makes an idea arise." In fact *saṁjñā* is a mental *dharma*, "idea," "notion," or "concept" (i.14c-d); *nāman* is what "creates" or engenders this *dharma*.

312. This does not refer to *pada* as a declined or conjugated form (Pāṇini, i.4.14).

313. One should consider the entire stanza as a *pada*:

anityā vata saṁskārā utpādavyayadharmiṇaḥ /
utpadya hi nirudhyante teṣāṁ vyupaśamaḥ sukhaḥ //

that can be explained in different ways:

a. Thesis (*pratijñā*): "The *saṁskāras* are impermanent." Argument (*hetu*): "because their nature is to arise and to perish." Example (*dṛṣṭānta*): "those things which, born, then die, are impermanent."

b. The argument: "Their nature is to arise and to perish," is proven by the remark: "In fact, being born, they die."

c. "The *saṁskāras* are impermanent, in other words, their nature is to be born and to perish;" "because, being born, they perish"' "being impermanent, they are suffering, thus the arresting of them is happiness:" this is what the Buddha intended to teach to his followers.

This is the stanza that Śakra uttered at the death of the Blessed One, *Dīgha*, *TD* 1, p.26c21; *Saṁyutta*, i.158; *Dialogues*, ii.176; *Jātaka*, 94; *Madhyamakavṛtti*, p. 39; Manuscript Dutreuil de Rhins, *J. As.* 1898, ii.300 (quoted in part, p. 108); *Udānavarga*, i.1; Mdo, 26, *Anityatāsūtra*; J. Przyluski, *Funerailles*, p. 9.

314. A type of "nominal phrase."

315. *Nāman* manifests (*dyotaka*) unique self characteristics (*svalakṣaṇa*); *pada* manifests the diverse relationships in which the thing whose self characteristic is known is to be found.

316. Compare Amarasiṁha, iii. *Nānārthavarga*, 25.

317. That is to say: "given a voice, a word—a *dharma* disassociated from the mind—arises" (*vāci*

satyāṁ sa cittaviprayukta utpadyate).

318. This means that "a word—a *dharma* disassociated from the mind—arises with its vocal sound in the process of arising: the vocal sound manifests it with a view to designating an object" (*ghoṣeṇotpadyamānena sa cittaviprayukto dharma utpadyate / sa taṁ prakāśayaty arthadyotanāya*).

319. *Saṁyuktāgama, TD* 2, p. 266b9. *Saṁyutta*, i.38: *nāmasaṁniśritā gāthā. Gāthā* is a "phrase" (*vākya*); it depends on words, since it exists when sounds have arisen. Consequently, word and phrase exist in and of themselves.

320. *Mahāvyutpatti*, 245.319, has the word *kṛtāvadhi.*

321. *Paṅktivat*, "like a line of ants;" but the different ants which form the line exist at the same time; we shall give a new example, *cittānupūrvyavat*, "like a succession of thoughts."

322. The *dharmas* which are of the sphere of consciousness of the Tathāgatas (*tathāgatajñānagocarapatita*) are *tarkagamya.*

323. *Vibhāṣā, TD* 27, p. 71c25-72a29.

324. Phonemes, etc. are not "voice" by their nature. Nothing prevents their existing in Ārūpyadhātu, but, as the voice is missing in this sphere of existence, they cannot be pronounced there. The Vaibhāṣikas: But how can you say that they exist where they are not pronounced?

325. The words that designate good *dharmas* are not themselves good, for when a person who has cut off the roots of good speaks of the good *dharmas*, he then possesses (*prāpti*) the words which designate these *dharmas.*

326. Hsüan-tsang corrects: The *prāptis* are of three types, *kṣaṇika* (i.38), outflowing, and retribution.

327. The *Vyākhyā* makes the following remarks: a. There is no difference between *hetu* and *pratyaya*, for the Blessed One said: *dvau hetū dvau pratyayau samyagdṛṣṭer utpādāya / katamau dvau / parataś ca ghoṣo'dhyātamaṁ ca yoniśo manasikāraḥ.* (*Aṅguttara*, i.87: *dve'me bhikkhave paccayā sammādiṭṭhiya uppādāya . . . parato ca ghoso yoniso ca manasikāro*).

b. *Hetu, pratyaya, nidāna, kāraṇa, nimitta, liṅga*, and *upaniṣad* are synonyms.

c. Why is a separate exposition of the *hetus* and the *pratyayas* given? Because the exposition of the *hetus* includes an examination of its cause as "non-obstructing cause," "mutual cause," "parallel cause," etc. (ii.49); an exposition of the *pratyayas* includes an examination of its cause as *hetu*, immediately antecedent cause, etc. (ii.62).

328. See *Abhidharmahṛdaya, TD* 28, p. 811c17.

329. In what Sūtra are the six types of *hetu* taught? In fact the Abhidharma only explains, appreciates, and comments on the Sūtra (*sarvo hy abhidharmaḥ sūtrārthaḥ sūtranikasaḥ sūtravyākhyānam*).

The Vaibhāṣikas say that the Sūtra which treats of this point has disappeared (*antarhita*). The *Ekottarāgama* enumerates the *dharmas* up to the categories of one hundred *dharmas*; it does not contain any more than ten categories up to ten (*ādaśakāt*) (See *Introduction*).

But there are some Sūtras which characterize each type of *hetu*, and the *Vyākhyā* furnishes some examples borrowed, it would appear, from Saṁghabhadra (*TD*, 29, p. 79b16).

(a) *kāraṇahetu*: "The visual consciousness arises by reason of the organ of the eye and visible things" (*Saṁyutta*, iv.87, etc.).

(b) *sahabhūhetu*: "These three parts of the path accompany (*anuvart*) Right Views." "Contact is the coming together of the three; then there arises together sensation, ideas, and volition."

(c) *sabhāgahetu*: "This person (*pudgala*) is endowed with good *dharmas*, and with bad *dharmas*; his good *dharmas* may perish, his bad *dharmas* may develop, but an *anusahagata* root of good is not cut off (*asti cāsyānusahagataṁ kuśalamūlam asamucchinnam*), from whence there arises another root of good: this person, in the future, will become pure" (*visuddhidharmā bhaviṣyati*, cp. *Aṅguttara*, iii.315).

In a similar context, *Saṁyutta*, iii.131 (compare *Kathāvatthu*, p. 215) has *anusahagata* which Saṁghabhadra here translates exactly (*sui chü hsing* 隨俱行); this refers to a strong root of good, indentified (Saṁghabhadra, TD 29, p. 99b19) with the *purāṇa-anu-dhātu* (?) (*chiu sui chieh* 久隨界) of the school of the Sthaviras.

But the MSS of the *Vyākhyā* have *anusahagata* and we see that, in the *Bhāṣyam* of iv.79d, the Chinese translation of the *Jñānaprasthāna* gives the exact equivalent: *wei chü hsing* 微俱行 . In this passage *anusahagata* is the equivalent of *mṛdu-mṛdu*: "What are the roots of good termed *anusahagata*? Those which are abandoned last of all when the roots of good have been broken; those through the absence of which the roots of good are said to hav.e been broken. (We have seen above, p. 210, that, properly speaking, the roots of good are never broken off.)

(d) *saṁprayuktakahetu*: "Faith (*śraddhā*) has Seeing (*darśana*) for its root, and is associated with *avetyajñāna* (vi.74): what this person knows (*vijānāti*), he penetrates to through *prajñā* (*prajānāti*)."

(e) *sarvatragahetu*: "The bodily actions, the vocal actions, the volition, the resolution, and the *saṁskāras* which follow the actions of a person who has false views (*mithyādṛṣṭi*, v.7), etc.,—all these *dharmas* have for their consequence unhappiness and hideousness. Why? Because he has a transgressed (*pāpikā*) view, namely false views." (*Aṅguttara*, v.212).

(f) *vipākahetu*: "He shall savor the retribution of action done here . . ."

330. Since the consciousness of the Truths has taken place, the causes of the defilements are not completed, because the *prāpti* of the defilements is cut off by this consciousness.

331. Montaigne, iii.9: The princes give me much, if they show me nothing; and it is good enough for me if they do not do me ill.

332. According to the text: *āhārasamudayāt kāyasya samudayaḥ*. Compare *Saṁyutta*, iii.62.

333. All cause should be an effect: *kāraṇe sati kāryeṇa bhavitavyam*.

334. The suffix *vat* in the sense of *tadyathā*.

335. One does not say that all the coexistent (*sahabhū*) *dharmas* are *sahabhūhetu*. For example, derived (*bhautika*) *rūpa*, blue, etc., coexist with the primary elements: but it is not *sahabhūhetu* with them. (See p. 259-260).

336. See i.24, ii.22, 65.

337. A conditioned *dharma* and its characteristics are *sahabhūhetu* among themselves; a *dharma* is not *sahabhūhetu* with the characteristics of another *dharma*.

338. *Vyākhyā: Upasaṁkhyānakaraṇaṁ ca mahāśāstratāpradarśanārthaṁ sopasaṁkhyānaṁ hi vyākaraṇādi mahāśāstram dṛśyate.*

339. The first part of this paragraph is based on the *Vyākhyā*.

340. The ten reasons are not always joined together. For example, in the case of the neutral mind not destined to arise, its companions are companions for four reasons: (1)same time period, (2) same result (*puruṣakāra*), (3) same *niṣyanda*, and (4) same quality of being neutral.

341. Namely the undefiled-neutral (*anivṛtāvyākṛta*) mind after the second *dhyāna; vitarka, vicāra*, the *kuśalamahābhūmikas* are missing from it.

342. The mind reigns (*rājayate*) over its *anulakṣaṇas*: these have no action (*vyāpāra*) over the mind, as we have seen ii.46.

343. The Japanese editor refers to the *Prakaraṇa, TD* 26, p. 745a25. See below p. 265 and p. 273 where the same text is refered to.

The *Prakaraṇa* examines the relationship between the Four Truths and the belief in a self (*satkāyadṛṣṭi*). The *Vyākhyā* gives the following extract:

A. There are Four Truths. Among the Truths, how many have *satkāyadṛṣṭi* for their cause without being a cause of *satkāyadṛṣṭi*; how many are a cause of *satkāyadṛṣṭi* without having *satkāyadṛṣṭi* for their cause; how many have *satkāyadṛṣṭi* for their cause and are at the same time are a cause of *satkāyadṛṣṭi*; and how many do not have *satkāyadṛṣṭi* for their cause and are not a cause of *satkāyadṛṣṭi*? Answer: Two Truths do not have *satkāyadṛṣṭi* for their cause and are not a cause of *satkayādṛṣṭi*, namely the Truth of Extinction and the Truth of the Path; one must distinguish the two other Truths.

B. The Truth of Suffering can (1) have *satkāyadṛṣṭi* for its cause without in turn being a cause of *satkāyadṛṣṭi*; (2) have *satkāyadṛṣṭi* for its cause and not be a cause of *satkāyadṛṣṭi*; and (3) not have *satkāyadṛṣṭi* for its cause and not be a cause of *satkāyadṛṣṭi*: there are only three alternatives; the second (to be a cause of *satkāyadṛṣṭi* without having *satkāyadṛṣṭti* for its cause) is missing.

1. To have *satkāyadṛṣṭi* for its cause without being a cause of *satkāyadṛṣṭi* are all the Truths of defiled Suffering (that is to say, all the *dharmas* which are suffering and which are *kliṣṭa*) with the exception of (a) the past and present defilements (*anuśaya*) which can be abandoned by the Seeing of Suffering, and by the Truth of Suffering associated with these defilements (for example the sensation associated with *satkāyadṛṣṭi* which is abandoned by the Seeing of Suffering); (b) the future Truths of Suffering which are associated with *satkāyadṛṣṭi* (see p. 265 line 22); and (c) the arising-old age-duration-impermanence of *satkāyadṛṣṭi* and of the *dharmas* associated with this belief (*tatsaṁprayuktānāāṁ ca dharmāṇāṁ*: these last words are omitted in certain recensions).

2. The Truth of Suffering which has been excluded in the preceeding paragraph has *satkāyadṛṣṭi* for its cause and is a cause of *satkāyadṛṣṭi*.

3. The Truth of undefiled Suffering, (that is, the *dharmas* which are suffering but which are good) do not have *satkāyadṛṣṭi* for their cause and are not a cause of *satkāyadṛṣṭi*.

The Chinese versions, *TD* 26, number 1541 (p. 673b20) and *TD* 26, number 1542 (p. 745a), correspond to the preceeding texts. Some omissions (the phrases: "To this question, it answers," *iti praśne visarjanaṁ karoti*, and "There are only three alternatives; the second is missing," *trikoṭikam, dvitīyā koṭir nāsti* are missing). There are some sensible enough variations in the definition of the *dharmas* which have *satkāyadṛṣṭi* for their cause and which are a cause of *satkāyadṛṣṭi*: (a) past and present defilements which can be abandoned by the Seeing of Suffering, and the Truth of the Suffering associated with these defilements (*TD* 26, number 1542: and the Truth of Suffering associated, coexistent, etc., with these defilements), (b) past and present universal (*sarvatraga*) defilements which can be abandoned by the Seeing of Arising, and the Truth of Suffering which is associated with it (*TD* 27, number 1542: associated causes, mutually coexistent causes, etc.), and (c) future Truth of Suffering which is associated with *satkāyadṛṣṭi* and of the *dharmas* associated with it.

344. Where a *mahābhūta* is found, the other *mahābhūtas* are found also, etc.

245. I understand: "One moment (*kṣaṇa*) of the *cakṣurindriya* is a cause of simultaneous visual consciousness."

346. See ii.59.

347. According to the *samaviśiṣṭayoḥ* rule, ii.52d. The four non-material *skandhas* are "best" or *viśiṣṭa*, whereas *rūpa* is "less good," *nyūna*.

348. According Paramārtha. Missing in Hsüan-tsang.

349. According to the opponent of the Vaibhāṣikas, the *Prakaraṇa* teaches that future *satkāyadṛṣṭi* and the *dharmas* which are associated with it are at one and the same time the effect and the cause of *satkāyadṛṣṭi*. Now future *satkāyadṛṣṭi* is neither a mutually coexistent cause (*sahabhū*), nor an associated cause (*saṁprayuktaka*), nor retribution (*vipāka*); the rest, excluding *kāraṇahetu*, are similar (*sabhāga*) and universal (*sarvaga*) causes.

For the Vaibhāṣikas, the *Prakaraṇa* speaks here, not of future *satkāyadṛṣṭi*, but of the *dharmas* (sensation, etc.) associated with this *satkāyadṛṣṭi* as coexistent and associated cause, and the effect of *satkāyadṛṣṭi* is considered as coexistent and associated causes.

We have three readings; in addition to the two readings quoted here, there is also the text: *anāgataṁ ca satkāyadṛṣṭisaṁprayuktaṁ duḥkhasatyaṁ sthāpayitvā*: "with the exception, furthermore, of the Truth of future Suffering and which is associated with *satkāyadṛṣṭi*." (See note 343, section B.1.b).

350. See below note 365.

351. This means: "The *dharma* which is the cause of a certain *dharma* is never the non-cause of this same *dharma*; the *dharma* which is the result of a certain *dharma* . . . ; the *dharma* (organ of sight, etc.) which is the support of a certain *dharma* (visual consciousness, etc.) . . . ; the *dharma* (color, etc.) which is the object of a certain *dharma* (visual consciousness) is never the non-object of this same *dharma*.

352. According to Hsuan-tsang: "Cause refers to *kāraṇa, sahabhū, saṁprayuktaka* and *vipākahetus*; result, the *adhipati, puruṣakāra* and *vipākaphalas*." Paramārtha: "Cause refers to the *saṁprayuktakahetu*; result, the *adhipati* and *puruṣakāraphalas*.

353. The paths of *śraddhānusārin, śraddhādhimukta* and *samayavimukta* are the paths of *darśana, bhāvanā* (=*Śaikṣa*) and *Aśaikṣa* of the ascetics of weak faculties; the paths of *dharmānusārin, dṛṣṭiprāpta* and *asamayavimukta* are respectively the same path of the ascetics of strong faculties.

354. The second of the first fifteen moments (*darśanamārga*, vi.27), produced in a lower stage, is superior to the first moment in a higher stage, because it has for its causes (1) the cause of the first moment, and (2) its own cause, and thus following; *bhāvanāmārga* has for its causes (1) the causes of *darśanamārga*, and (2) its own causes; and the *aśaikṣamārga* has for its cause (1) the causes of *darśana* and *bhāvanāmārga*, and (2) it own causes.

Furthermore, in *bhāvanāmārga* and *aśaikṣamārga*, the path destroys nine categories of defilements, strong-strong, strong-mediocre, etc.; it is successively weak-weak, weak-mediocre, weak-strong, mediocre-weak, etc. Now the weak-mediocre path has for its causes (1) the cause of the weak-weak path, and (2) its own causes.

355. One can say that the path of *śraddhānusārin* is the *sabhāgahetu* of six paths. This thesis gives rise to a discussion in which the master Vasumitra wrongly maintains that a *śraddhānusārin* is capable of making his faculties strong. (*Vyākhyā*).

356. Paramārtha: The masters say. *Vibhāṣā, TD* 27, p. 89b5.

357. *Vyākhyā: tuśabdo'vadhāraṇe bhinnakramaś ca.*
Vibhāṣā, TD 27, p. 80b22. *Kathāvatthu*, vii.2 on the *saṁpayuttas*.

358. *Sama* can be understood as *tulya*, parallel; this is why the author states it precisely.

359. *Vibhāṣā, TD* 27, p. 81b9, mentions six opinions on this point.

360. The defilements susceptible of being abandoned by the Seeing of Arising, Extinction and the

Path, and by Meditation, proceed from the universal causes suceptible of being abandoned by the Seeing of Suffering. The defilements susceptible of being abandoned by the Seeing of Suffering, Extinction and the Path, and by Meditation, proceed from the universal causes susceptible of being abandoned by the Seeing of Arising.

361. They are called "universals" (*sarvaga*), because they go towards (*gacchanti*), "occupy" (*bhajante*), and have for their object (*ālambante*) all categories of defilement; or because they are the cause (*hetubhāvaṁ gacchanti*) of all categories of defilement.

362. See above p. 259.

363. Since the text has "the defiled *dharmas*," without specifying otherwise, this refers to the defiled *dharmas* of the Pṛthagjanas and the Āryans.

364. This refers to the neutral *saṁskṛtas*, *nivṛtāvyakṛta* and *anivṛtāvyākṛta*, not to the two neutral *asaṁskṛtas*, space and *apratisaṁkhyānirodha*.

365. The word "future" is missing in Paramartha. See above p. 259.

366. Hsüan-tsang translates: "How should one explain the *Prajñaptipādaśāstra*," for "this *Bhāṣya* of the *Prajñapti*" signifies "this explanation that one reads in the *Prajñapti*." See the Tibetan version of the *Karmaprajñapti*, Chap. ix. (Mdo. 63, fol. 229b-236a): Para. 1. Does there exist a past volition which arises from a past cause, but not from a future cause, nor from a present cause? . . . Para.2: Do there exists good *dharmas* which arise from good causes? . . . Do there exist neutral *dharmas* which arise from bad causes? Yes: (1) the *dharmas* which are the retribution of bad action; (2) the *dharmas* of Kāmadhātu associated with *satkāyadṛṣṭi* and *antagrāhadṛṣṭi*. Para. 3. Do there exist good *dharmas* which arise solely from good causes? Yes: the volition associated with the parts of Bodhi . . . Do there exist bad *dharmas* which arise solely from bad causes? . . ."

We know through J. Takakusu (*JPTS*. 1905, p. 77) that the *Karmaprajñapti* no longer exists in Chinese. *TD* 26, number 1538 is the *Kāraṇaprajñapti*; *TD* 32, number 1644 is a treatise analogous to the *Lokaprajñapti*: one will find a summary of these two *Prajñaptis* in *Cosmologie bouddhique*, p. 295-350.

367. "At the moment when he falls from detachement, the bad volition of the Āryan has solely bad *dharmas* for its cause, causes in the quality of *sahabhū* and *saṁprayuktakahetu*; it does not have neutral *dharmas* for its cause since the Āryan has abandoned *satkāyadṛṣṭi* and *antagrāhadṛṣṭi*:" such is the interpretation of the objector.

368. Self power (*svaśakti*) is lacking in neutral *dharmas*, and a co-factor (*sahakārikāraṇa*) is lacking in pure *dharmas*. See iii.36b.

369. *Mahāvyutpatti*, 245.181.

370. Here Hsüan-tsang has some remarks missing in Paramārtha:

According to the Vaibhāṣikas, the prefix *vi* indicates difference: *vipāka* signifies "a different *pāka*" (*Mahāvyutpatti*, 245.182). That is to say only the *vipākahetu* gives forth a *pāka* or result not similar to itself. *Sahabhū*, *saṁprayuktaka*, *sabhāga*, and *sarvatragahetus* give forth results similar to themselves (good, bad, neutral); *kāraṇahetu* gives forth a dissimilar result: *vipākahetu* is never neutral but its result is always neutral.

(According to the Sautrantikas,) a result receives the name of *vipāka* under two conditions: it should be produced by the last state of the evolution of a series (*saṁtānapariṇāmaviśeṣa*; see above p. 211); and it should more or less last a long time by reason of the more or less great force of its cause. Now, the results that have issued from *sahabhū* and *saṁprayuktakahetu* do not present the first characteristic, for these causes project and realize their result at the same time as they (ii.59); and the results that have issued from the three causes, *kāraṇa, sabhāga,* and *sarvatragahetu,* do not present the second characteristic; for there is no limit to the arising repeated by these results during the length of their transmigration. Consequently the sole explanation of *vipāka* is "transformation (*vipariṇāma?*) and maturation."

371. *Vibhāṣā, TD* 27, p. 97c7. (Hsüan-tsang: "the action which produces the vital organ, etc." *Et cetera* refers to either *nikāyasabhāga* or its characteristics).

The Ācārya Vasumitra does not admit this proposition. The vital organ of life (*jīvitendriya*) is the result of an action which projects an existence (*ākṣepakakarman,* iv.95). If the retribution which constitutes this organ matures (*vipacayate*) in Kāmadhātu, one necessarily has *kāya-indriya* and *jīvita-indriya* in the first stages of his embryonic life; in the last stages five other organs (*indriya*) are added. If the vital organ matures in Rūpadhātu, one has seven *āyatanas*; in Ārūpyadhātu, one has *manāyatana* and *dharmāyatana.* Yaśomitra discusses these remarks and quotes Saṃghabhadra. The propositions combatted by Vasumitra refers to Ārūpyadhātu: at a certain moment, there is no mind (*manaāyatana*) which is retribution for a being born in this sphere.

372. Never twelve, for the *śabdāyatana* is never retribution (i.37b-c).

373. The retribution of a former action can have begun, can continue in the present moment, and can prolong itself in the future.

374. The Japanese editor gives the heroic career of the Bodhisattva as an example of a prolonged action.

375. Compare ii.59.

376. Disconnection (*visaṁyoga*) or *visaṁyogaphala* (ii.57d, vi.46), is *pratisaṁkhyānirodha* or Nirvāṇa (i.6), one of the unconditioned things (*asaṁskṛrta*). It does not have a cause, and it is not a result; but it is a cause (*kāraṇahetu,* ii.50a) and it is a result (ii.57d).

377. *Prakaraṇa, TD* 26, p. 716b9, which can be reconstructed: *phaladharmāḥ katame / sarve saṁskṛtāḥ pratisaṁkhyānirodhaś ca / na phaladharmāḥ katame / ākāśam apratisaṁkhyāniro-dhaḥ / saphaladharmāḥ katame / sarve saṁskṛtāḥ / aphaladharmāḥ katame / sarve 'saṁskṛtāḥ:* "What *dharmas* are result? All conditioned things and *pratisaṁkhyānirodha.* What *dharmas* are not result? Space and *apratisaṁkhyānirodha.* What *dharmas* have a result? All conditioned things. What *dharmas* do not have a result? All unconditioned things." See also *Jñānaprasthān, TD* 26, p. 941bll.

378. *Milinda,* 268-271.

379. *Ānantaryamārga* cuts off defilements and is followed by *vimuktimārga,* "the path in which the defilement is already cut off," within which the ascetic takes possession (*prāpti*) of disconnection, vi.28.

380. Certain masters maintain that there are five types of causes: (1) *kāraka,* efficient cause, the seed of the bud; (2) *jñāpaka,* indicating cause, the smoke of the fire; (3) *vyañjaka,* revealing cause, the lamp on the pot; (4) *dhvaṁsaka,* destructive cause, the hammer on the pot; and (5) *prāpaka,* the adducent cause.

381. *Saṁyukta, TD* 2, p. 2a22: *ye hetavo ye pratyayā . . . vijñānasyotpādāya te py anityāḥ.*

382. In the pages which follow, Vasubandhu does not do full justice to the arguments of the Sarvāstivādins-Vaibhāṣikas; he does not mention the texts, for example *Udāna,* viii.3 (*Itivuttaka,* 43, *Udānavarga,* xxvi.21), which at least renders the reality of Nirvāṇa likely. Saṁghabhadra refutes Vasubandhu and the other masters who deny unconditioned things (*Nyāyānusāra, TD* 29,

p. 431b17-c2). His exposition is too long to include here: we have given a partial translation of it in the *Introduction.*

383. a. The extinction of *anuśaya* is the Extinction of the Arising of Suffering (*samudayasatyanirodha*, Extinction of what is, in truth, the Arising of Suffering): *sopadhiśeṣanirvāṇa.*

The Extinction of Arising or existence (*janman*) is the Extinction of Suffering (*duḥkhasatyanirodha*, Extinction of what is, in truth, Suffering): *nirupadhiśeṣanirvāṇa.*

b. *Anuśaya* means the traces (*vāsanā*) of the ninety-eight *anuśayas* described in Chapter V.

384. According to the Japanese editor, the Sthaviras.

385. According to the Japanese editor, the Mahāsāṁghikas.

386. *Svarasanirodhāt*, not by the force of *prajñā*, as is the case for *pratisaṁkhyānirodha.*

387. Compare *Kathāvatthu*, xix.1.

388. That is, *chanda* (future desire: *anāgate prārthanā*) and *rāga* (attachment to what one possesses: *prāpte'rthe'dhyavasānam*)

389. The *prahāṇa* of *rūpa* is to be understood as *ānantaryamārga*, and *parijñā* is to be understood as *vimuktimārga* (vi.30). (Gloss of the Japanese editor).

Compare *Saṁyutta*, iii.8 (for its doctrine).

390. *Saṁyukta, TD* 2, p. 222c4: *ye kecid bhikṣavo dharmāḥ saṁskṛtā vā asaṁskṛtā vā virāgas teṣāṁ agra ākhyāyate* (quoted in *Vyākhyā*, iv.127) *Aṅguttara*, iii.34, *Itivuttaka*, Para. 90: *yāvatā Cundi dhammā saṅkhatā vā asaṅkhatā vā virāgo tesaṁ aggam akkhāyati.*

"Detachement" or *virāga* is *rāgakṣaya, pratisaṁkhyānirodha, nirvāṇa.* Nirvāṇa is better than *apratisaṁkhyānirodha* and space (iv.127d).

391. Hsüan-tsang differs: One can not say from its non-existence that it exists. The value of the verb "to be" is thus proven (:this verb does not signify "to exist"). It is thus that Scripture states that they are unconditioned things.

392. *Vyākhyā: tasya virodhasya yo'yaṁ prāpter niyamaḥ / asyaiva nirodhasya prāptir nānyasyeti // tasmin prāptiniyame ko hetuḥ//na hi nirodhasya praptyā sārdhaṁ kaścit saṁbandho'sti hetuphalādibhāvāsambhavāt.*

393. *Dṛṣṭadharmanirvāṇaprāpta*, that is "which is to be found in Nirvāṇa with residue" (*sopadhiśeṣanirvāṇastha*).

394. A varient of the end of *Mahāvastu*, ii.285: *etaṁ śāntam etaṁ praṇītam yathāvas etam aviparītam yam idaṁ sarvopadhipratiniḥsargo sarvasaṁskāraśamatho dharmopacchedo tṛṣṇākṣayo virāgo nirodho nirvāṇam.*

We have *Aṅguttara* i.100: *parikkhaya pahāṇa khaya vaya virāga nirodha cāga paṭinissagga*; v.421: *asesavirāga nirodha cāga paṭinissagga mutti anālaya; Saṁyutta*, i.136: *sabbasaṁkhārasamatha . . . ; Itivuttaka*, 51: *upadhippaṭinissagga.* See also the Sanskrit versions of *Majjhima*, i.497 in Pischel, *Fragments of Indikutsari*, p. 8 (*vyantibhāva*) and *Avadānaśataka*, ii.187 (*vāntībhāva).*

395. In other words, *aprādurbhava* = *nāsmin prādurbhāvaḥ.* This is an *adhikaraṇasādhana* etymology. The Sautrāntikas understand *aprādurbhāva* as *aprādurbhūti* (an *abhāvasādhana* etymology).

The explanation of the Sarvāstivādins is reproduced in *Madhyamakavṛtti*, p. 525, and attributed to the philosophy which considers Nirvāṇa as a *bhāva*, a *padārtha* similar to a dike which arrests the process of the defilements, action and arising.

396. In fact the Path destroys the Arising of Suffering, *duḥkhasamudaya.* Who could imagine a thing in and of itself called *nirodha* with respect to the Path?

397. *Dīgha*, ii.157; *Saṁyutta*, i.159; *Theragāthā*, 906:

pajjotasseva nibbānaṁ vimokho cetaso ahū.

The Sanskrit redaction (*Avadānaśataka*, 99, *Madhyamakavṛtti*, 520, *Dulva*, Nanjio, 118, *apud* J. Przyluski, *J.As.* 1918, ii.490, 509):

pradyotasyeva nirvāṇaṁ vimokṣas tasya cetasaḥ.

This happens at the moment of Nirvāṇa-without-residue. The definition *bhavanirodha nibbānam*, *Aṅguttara*, v.9, *Saṁyutta*, ii.116, etc.

398. See *Vibhāṣā*, *TD* 27, p. 161a10. We read in *Prakaraṇa*, *TD* 26, p. 716a3, a definition that can be reconstructed: *avastukā apratyayā dharmāḥ katame? asaṁskṛtā dharmāḥ* (see i.7).

399. This is the text quoted *ad* i.7.

400. The *Vyākhyā ad* i.7 (Petrograd edition, p. 22) reproduces all these explanations.

401. The Japanese editor quotes the *Vibhāṣā*, *TD* 27, p. 629c4.

There are five types of results: 1. *niṣyandaphala*, 2. *vipākaphala*, 3. *visaṁyogaphala*, 4. *puruṣakāraphala*, 5. *adhipatiphala*.

a. *niṣyandaphala*: good produced by good, bad produced by bad, and neutral produced by neutral.

b. *vipākaphala: vipāka* is produced by bad or good-impure *dharmas*; if the cause is good or bad, the result is always neutral. As this result is different from its cause and has "matured" (*pāka*), it is called *vipāka* (*visadṛśa pāka*).

c. *visaṁyogaphala*: The *ānantaryamārgas* cut off the defilements; they have the cutting off of the defilements for their *visaṁyogaphala* and *puruṣakāraphala;* they have the *vimuktimārga* for their *niṣyandaphala* and *puruṣakāraphala*; and they have all the former paths, equal or higher than their types, for their *niṣyandaphala*.

See also the *Abhidharmāvatāraśāstra* (*TD* 28, p. 988b12) ii.14, where the names of the results are explained.

402. iv.85a-b, 110a.

403. The "receptacle" or physical world (*bhājanaloka*, iii.45, iv.1) is produced by the good and bad actions of the totality of living beings: it is neutral; however it is not retribution *vipāka*), because retribution is a *dharma* "belonging to living beings" (p. 289); consequently, it is the *adhipatiphala* of actions considered as *kāraṇahetu*.

404. Missing in Paramārtha.

405. The prefix *ud* in *udbhava* signifies "later" (*uttarakāla*). Absorption (*samādhi*) produces an increase of the primary elements of the body: these primary elements are called "of increase" (*aupacayika*) because they arise either at the same time as the absorption, or immediately after; they are not retribution. In this way a mind that can create fictive beings (*nirmāṇacitta*, i.37, vii.48) is neutral, belonging to a living being, created by a definite action (i.e., an absorption); but, arising immediately after the absorption, it is not retribution. Furthermore, the result of retribution always belongs to the same stage as the action from whence it proceeds.

406. Good *dharmas* are not the *sabhāgahetu* of defiled dharmas, etc.

407. The mind at death (*maraṇacitta*) of a being who dies in Kāmadhātu can have for its virile result the first moment of an intermediary being of Rūpadhātu. These examples show the difference between the *puruṣakāraphala* and the outflowing result (*niṣyandaphala*). Four cases: 1. *puruṣakāraphala* which is not *niṣyandaphala*: examples as above; 2. *niṣandaphala*, the result of *sabhāga* and *sarvatraga* causes which do not immediately follow; 3. *niṣyanda* and *puruṣakāraphala*, parallel result, of the same stage, but immediate; 4. neither of the two: fruit of retribution.

408. See ii.56b and iv.85.

409. Compare ii.55a-b.

410. These definitions are given later (vi.22a7) in the original. De La Vallée Poussin placed them here for the convenience of the reader.

411. The *dharma* always exists, whether it is in the past, the present or the future. We say that it takes or projects a result at the moment when, becoming present, it becomes the cause or seed of a result. The *Vyākhyā* observes that the comparison of the seed is a Sautrāntika theory. Also "this reading does not exist in certain manuscripts" (*kvacit pustake nāsty eṣa pāṭhaḥ*). Moreover the *Vyākhyā* explains: *pratigṛhṇantīty ākṣipanti hetubhāvenopatiṣṭhanta ity arthaḥ*.

412. On this subtle point, see Saṁghabhadra, *Nyāyāvatāra, TD* 29, 98a3.

413. According to the *Vibhāṣā, TD* 27, p. 89b13.

414. The last *prāptis* of good that one cuts off, namely the *prāptis* of the roots of good which are weak-weak (*mṛdumṛdu*) project their result (*phalaparigrahaṁ kurvanti*), but they do not give forth their result (*niṣyandaphala*), since the "good" moment in which they should give forth or engender (*janya*) it is lacking.

415. Vasubhandhu criticizes the doctrines of the Vaibhāṣikas. In fact, this paragraph is poorly worded (*sāvadya*): when a person again takes up the roots of good, he acquires, tri-temporally, the *prāptis* of the roots of good: the past *prāptis* acquired at this moment give forth their result, but they do not grasp it: for they have already grasped it; but how can one say that present *prāptis* do not grasp their result? Thus the proposed definition is lacking precision. Saṁghabhadra defends the reading of the *Vibhāṣā*.

416. Compare *Abhidharmahṛdaya*, ii.12-15.

417. *Vibhāṣā, TD* 27, p. 79a26: "It is true that these six causes (*hetu*) are not mentioned in the Sūtras; the Sūtra only says that there are four *pratyayatās*."

The Japanese editor quotes Mahāyāna sources, *TD* 16 number 716 (trans. by Dharmagupta), the *Ghanavyūha, TD* 16 number 717 (trans. by Hsüan-tsang), and the *Madhyamaka-kārikā* (see *Madhyamakavṛtti*, p. 76).

With respect to the relation of the *hetus* and the *pratyayas*, the first master of the *Vibhāṣā* says that (1) the *hetupratyaya* includes five *hetus*, with the exception of *kāraṇahetu*, and (2) *kāraṇahetu* includes the other three *pratyayas*. The second master of the *Vibhāṣā* says that (1) *hetupratyaya* includes five *hetus*, and (2) *kāraṇahetu* is only *adhipatipratyaya*: this is the system adopted by Vasubandhu. In the Mahāyāna, *sabhāgahetu* is at one and the same time *hetupratyaya* and *adhipatipratyaya*, whereas the other five *hetus* are *adhiptipratyaya*.

The *Prakaraṇa, TD* 26, p. 712b12, enumerates four *pratyayas*. The *Vijñānakāya, TD* 26, p. 547b22, defines them as functions of the *vijñānas*: "What is the *hetupratyaya* of a visual consciousness? The coexistent (*sahabhū*) and associated (*saṁprayukta*) *dharmas*. What is its *samanantarapratyaya*? The mind and its mental states to which it is equal and immediate, the visual consciousness arisen and arising. What is its *ālambanapratyaya*? Visible things. What is its *adhipatipratyaya*? All the *dharmas*, with the exception of itself . . . Of what is the visual consciousness the *hetupratyaya*? Of the coexistent and associated *dharmas*. Of what is it the *samanantarapratyaya*? Of the minds and mental states, arisen or arising, equal and immediate to this visual consciousness. Of what is it the *ālambanapratyaya*? Of the minds and mental states which grasp it for an object. Of what is it the *adhipatipratyaya*? Of all the *dharmas* with the exception of itself."

The four *pratyayas* are defined in the *Abhidharmahṛdaya*, ii.16, as in our book: the *hetupratyaya* includes the five *hetus*; and *adhipatipratyaya* corresponds to *kāraṇahetu*.

For the *paccayas* of the Abhidhamma, the *Dukapaṭṭhāna* appears to be the capital authority. Its points of contact with the Abhidharma are numerous, but the nomenclature differs; for example, the *sahajātādhipatipaccaya* is our *sahabhūhetu*. See also *Kathāvatthu*, xv.1-2.

418. Namely *pratyayaprakāra*, as one says *gotā*, a type of cow (*Vyākhyā*).

419. *Vibhāṣā*, *TD* 27, p. 52a8 and following, the second masters.

420. This refers to *avijñaptirūpa*. When, after having undertaken the Prātimokṣasaṁvara (an *avijñaptirūpa* in Kāmadhātu), a person enters into impure (*sāsrava*) *dhyāna*, he produces the *saṁvara* of *dhyāna* (an *avijñaptirūpa* in Rūpadhātu), whereas the *avijñaptirūpa* in Kāmadhātu continues to reproduce itself (see iv.17b-c).

421. In the case where, having undertaken the Prātimokṣasaṁvara, a person enters into pure *dhyāna*.

422. This is the second opinion presented in the *Vibhāṣā*. When, after having eaten, a person falls asleep or enters into absorption, there arises at the same time a *rūpa* of increase produced by sleep or absorption (see i.37).

423. On the Bhadanta, the Sautrāntika Sthavira (*Vyākhyā*), see note 93. Fourth opinion of the *Vibhāṣā*.

424. *Vibhāṣā*, *TD* 27, p. 52a21, gives two opinions. Vasubandhu presents the second.

425. Simultaneous *dharmas*, presenting neither anteriority nor posteriority, cannot be in and of themselves *samanantarapratyaya*.

426. The first masters of the *Vibhāṣā*, *TD* 27, p. 51b15. Hsüan-tsang: "He infers from the past and from the present, but sees in a direct manner."

427. *Vibhāṣā*, *ibid.* and p. 897b9.

428. Hsüan-tsang: The Blessed One sees that such a result arises from such a past action: such a *dharma* immediately arises from such a *dharma*; that, from such a past action, there arises such a result: from such a *dharma* there immediately arises such a *dharma*. Having seen in this manner, he is capable of knowing, with regard to future confused *dharmas* that such a *dharma* will immediately arise after such a *dharma*. Although he knows in this manner, this is not a knowledge from induction, for the Blessed One, infering according to the sequence of the arising of the causes and effects of the past and the present, knows then by a direct seeing the confused *dharmas* of the future and says, "In the future, such a being will accomplish such an action, and shall receive such a retribution." This is *praṇidhijñāna*, not *anumānajñāna*.

429. Second opinion of the *Vibhāṣā*, *TD* 27, p. 897b26; the third opinion presented in the *Nyāyāvatāra*, *TD* 29, p. 444b23.

Paramārtha (*TD* 29, p. 194b10) differs: "There is, in the series of beings, a certain conditioned *dharma* associated with the mind which is an indication of the future result."

Nyāyāvatāra: "There is presently, within beings, an indication of the causes and results of the future, similar to a prognostic sign (*yin-hsiang* 印相, *chāyā nimitta*), or rather a *rūpa*, or a *saṁskāra* disassociated from the mind."

Paramārtha and the *Nyāyāvarāra*: *hsien-hsiang* 先相; Hsüan-tsang: *hsien-chao* 先兆, presage or omen.

430. Japanese editor: by means of the *lokadhātusaṁvṛtijñāna* (vii.3).

431. Hsüan-tsang: If it were thus, the Buddha would know the future by reason of indications (*chan-hsiang* 占相) . . .

432. According to *Vibhāṣā, TD* 27, p. 52c12; compare *Prakaraṇa, TD* 26, p. 764a28 and following.

433. *Vibhāṣā, TD* 27, p. 983b13.

434. The first two opinions of the *Vibhāṣā, TD* 27, p. 57a14. Third opinion: the mind is bound to its support in the past, the present, and the future.

435. According to *Vibhāṣā, TD* 27, p.,703a3 and following.

436. Hsüan-tsang: "because they cause a result arisen at the same time as they have to possess operation."

437. Compare *Abhidharmahṛdaya, TD* 28, p. 812a27.

438. *Vyākhyā*: Īśvara, Puruṣa, Pradhāna, time (*kāla*), unique or self nature (*svabhāva*), atoms, etc.

439. Compare *Bodhicaryāvatāra*, ix. 119; *Ṣaḍdarśanasaṁgraha*, p. 11; the *Suhṛllekha (JPTS*, 1886), 50, etc.

440. Śloka of Vyāsa in the *Śatarudrīya (Vyākhyā), Mahābhārata*, vii.203, 140, xiii, 161.7: *yan nirdahati yat tīkṣṇo yad ugro yat pratāpavān / māṁsaśoṇitamajjādo yat tato rudra ucyate.* Burnouf, *Introduction*, p. 568, has mentioned this quotation.

441. *Vipāka* and *puruṣakāraphala*.

442. Addition of Hsüan-tsang.

443. On the *bhūtas*, i.12, ii.22.

444. Hsüan-tsang adds that these five causes are all varities of *kāraṇahetu*.
See *Vyākhyā*, i.11, where the causal relationship between the *bhūtas* which form part of the person (*āśraya*), and that type of *bhautika* which is *avijñapti*, is explained.

445. These definitions according to *Vibhāṣā, TD* 27, p. 663a28. Saṁghabhadra, *TD* 29, p. 452a19 and following, presents other explanations, and gives other examples.

446. See above *ad* 59d. First *pratiṣṭhāphala*.

447. The doctrine of the twelve minds is presented in *Vijñānakāya TD* 26, p. 593b7 and in the work of Dharmatrāta, *TD* 28, p. 954b12 and following: "In Kāmadhātu, four; in Rūpadhātu and Ārūpyadhātu, three each, also Śaikṣa and Aśaikṣa engender nine and it is produced by eight . . . "There follows (*kārikās* 35-46) the doctrine of twenty minds (*Kośa*, ii.71b-72) which includes the exposition, in *kārikās*, of the rules of succession of the minds. Vasubandhu contents himself, as we shall see, with giving a *bhāṣyam*; but Yaśomitra, under the name of *saṁgrahaślokas*, furnishes us with a versified redaction of them which perhaps preserves for us a fragment of the original text of Dharmatrāta.

448. Compare *Kathāvatthu*, xiv.1. where the Theravādins maintain, against the Mahāsāṁghikas, that good is not followed by bad, etc.

449. The four estrangements are *āśraya, ākāra, ālambana*, and *pratipakṣadūratā*:
a. Persons (*āśraya*) of Ārūpyadhātu cannot "manifest" (*saṁmukhīkar*), or assimilate to themselves, any dharma of Kāmadhātu, whereas beings in Rūpadhātu manifest, or assimilate to themselves a mind capable of creating fictive beings (*nirmāṇcitta*) of Kāmadhātu (ii.53b).
b. The mind of the sphere of Ārūpyadhātu does not apply to Kāmadhātu the categories (*ākāra*) of "grosser," etc. (vi.49) as does a mind of the sphere of Rūpadhātu.
c. And in the same way, it does not grasp Kāmadhātu as an object (*ālambana*).
d. And in the same way it does not oppose the defilements of Kāmadhātu as do the Dhyānas.
On four other estrangements, vi.62.

450. That is to say 1. *śrutamaya*, 2. *cintāmaya*, 3. *bhāvanāmaya*, produced by hearing or study, by reflection, and by absorption. One and two exist in Kamadhatu, one and three in Rupadhatu, and three in Arupyadhatu, as we have seen above p. 269-270 and following; compare p. 322.

451. This is the *kuśala* of which a being, who is reborn in Kāmadhātu or Rūpadhātu, obtains possession (*prāpti*) at the moment of the arising of *antarābhava* (*antarābhavaprastisaṁdhikṣaṇe*); at the moment of arising for a being who is reborn in Ārūpyadhātu.

452. A list of the *śilpathānakarmasthānas* (*Mahāvyutpatti*, 76.5) is quoted in the *Divyāvadāna*, p. 58, 100: the art of riding on the head of an elephant, on the back of a horse, the art of archery, etc.

453. The visible things, etc. (1) of the bed and the body, etc. (2) of instruments (bow, arrow, etc.), and (3) of the thing that one wants to create.

454. Because one learns the arts by listening to instruction. *Vipākaja* is not mentioned here; thus it has the five *bhautikas*, visible things, etc., for its object.

455. In fact the mind relative to walking, etc., takes place after one has seen, felt, etc. Hsüan-tsang corrects the *Bhāṣya*: "Four or five sense consciousnesses are preparatory to *airyāpathika* and to *śailpasthānika* respectively." One should understand that the auditory consciousness is lacking for *airyāpathika*.

456. *Vibhāṣā, TD* 27, p. 661a16. The Bhadanta Anantavarman (*Vyākhyā ad* ii.46c-d), in his *Explanation of the Vibhāṣā* (*Vibhāṣāvyākhyāna*), presents the opinion according to which one should admit the *anivṛtāvyākṛtas* not included within the four abovementioned *avyākṛtas*, namely the *anivṛtāvyākṛtas* defined vii.51.

457. Hsüan-tsang: "through *airyāpathika* and *śailpasthānika*."

458. First mind of the intermediary existence (*antarābhava*) of Rūpadhātu.

459. By an effort of imagination, by virtue of a decision, the ascetic sees the body as the body really is not, namely as being made up only of rotten bones, etc.: this is the meditation on the repulsive, *aśubha*. In the same way, in the *ṛddhis* (vii.48), the ascetic imagines that the earth element is small, and that the water element is great (compare *Dīgha*, ii.108).

460. *Saṁyuktāgama, TD* 2, p. 197b3: *aśubhāsahagataṁ smṛtisaṁbodhyaṅgaṁ bhāvayati.* "Mindfulness" forms part of the Path; *sahagata* signifies "immediately following."

461. The *Vibhāṣā* discusses whether the *kuśala* mind of which one thus takes possession is solely *upapattiprātilambhika* (acquired through birth), or also *prāyogika* (acquired through effort).

462. This is a *kārikā* from the hand of Dharmatrāta, *TD* 28, p. 944bll-12: "If one obtains nine types of *dharmas*, he should know that this is with a *kliṣṭa* mind; the *kuśala* mind obtains six types; the *avyākṛta* mind, *avyākṛta*" (Trans. of Saṁghavarman). Paramārtha: "When the *kliṣṭa* mind is produced, one obtains, it is said, nine types of mind; with the *kuśala* mind . . ." (*TD* 28, p. 198a6).